19KS

AMERICA'S LEGISLATIVE PROCESSES:

Congress and the States

Fred R. Harris
Paul L. Hain

University of New Mexico

Scott, Foresman and Company

Glenview, Illinois Dallas, Tex. Oakland, N.J.

Palo Alto, Cal. Tucker, Ga. London, England

Credit lines for copyrighted materials appearing in this work are included in the Acknowledgments section beginning on p. 485. This section is to be considered an extension of the copyright page.

Library of Congress Cataloging in Publication Data

Harris, Fred R., 1930–
  America's legislative processes.

  Includes bibliographical references and index.
  1. United States. Congress. 2. Legislative bodies—
United States—States. 3. Legislators—United States.
I. Hain, Paul L., 1939–   . II. Title.
JK1061.H27 1983   328.73   82-25018
ISBN 0-673-15357-6

To Marg and Sue

Preface

As we write in the Epilogue of this book, Bismarck was reputed to have said that those who would retain their respect for law and sausages should never see either being made. Yet, there is no way to understand democracy without understanding legislatures. And to understand legislatures, it is not enough, for example, to know *how* a bill goes through a legislative body. One must also know *why* it does—or does not. We have worked hard to address such issues in *America's Legislative Processes: Congress and the States.*

In four parts, we examine the legislative process in the United States: how legislatures fit into the American political system; the connections between legislators and their constituents; the organization and procedures of legislatures; and the role of legislatures in our governmental system. There is also a kind of latest-word, overview Epilogue at the end.

We have brought our experiences in the practical world of politics as well as our academic backgrounds to the writing of this book. Reading about America's legislative processes can be dull enough to make the eyes glaze over. But the dynamics that, for example, cause a person to campaign to be a legislator or that cause a legislator, once elected, to vote one way or another on a particular issue can be fascinating. While being careful to cover well the basics of America's legislative processes, we have also tried hard to present them in the engaging and readable manner they deserve.

The text has been carefully documented and footnoted, so that it will be equally useful as a reference work and as a textbook. In each chapter, discussions of the U.S. Congress and of state legislatures are clearly separated. We have done this to help students understand the similarities and differences without confusing generalities. We have included a considerable amount of comparative, cross-national material, so that students can clearly see how legislative bodies in the United States, and their practices, differ from those in other nations. This can give students a sharper focus on and a quicker understanding of the way things work legislatively in the United States.

Other distinguishing features of the book are: an emphasis on the importance of citizen participation and its effect on legislative processes; a chapter stressing the role of the news media in the legislative process, a focus that is unusual among similar texts; a strong chapter on legislative staff, much stronger on *state* legislative staff than is usually found in similar texts; and inserts that provide concrete examples tying down theoretical discussions or that give "insider" perspectives.

We have had, of course, a great deal of help in the preparation and production of this text. Bruce Borland and Bob Johnson of Scott, Foresman and Company played important roles in the conception and organization of the book. Christine Silvestri, head of political science acquisitions, and Paula Fitzpatrick, our first-rate editor, were very helpful, as was Meredith Hellestrae in Marketing.

We also wish to thank our colleagues in the political science department at the University of New Mexico for their encouragement, especially our departmental chair during most of our work on this book, Professor Robert Sickels. Our wives, Margaret Elliston and Sue Hain, gave helpful insights and viewpoints and cheered us on.

Our aim from the very first conception of this book has been to make learning about America's legislative processes as interesting as possible. We have also entertained the hope that those who read and study this book may better understand how they, as citizens and perhaps as legislators, could have greater impact on American legislatures and thus on government policies that affect all our lives.

Fred R. Harris
Paul L. Hain
Albuquerque, New Mexico

Contents

AMERICA'S LEGISLATIVE PROCESSES:
Congress and the States

PART I

Legislatures in the American Political System

chapter *1*

The Evolution of Legislative Bodies in the United States

Preview

In both the Old World and the New, legislatures have evolved to meet the needs and demands of society. In America, the structure of colonial government was affected both by the British model and by circumstances in the colonies. Over many generations, legislatures developed substantial authority in colonial affairs and great support among the people. Following the close of the Seven Years War in 1763, Britain challenged the power of the colonial legislatures by directly levying taxes on the colonists—leading ultimately to the Revolutionary War. After the revolution, these legislatures reasserted their strength and in fact pressed their powers far. The framers of the Constitution, fearful of an injudicious use of authority, by either the legislature or the executive, decided on a separation-of-powers, checks-and-balances type of government with a strong national legislature at the center and an equally strong and separate executive and judiciary. In the ensuing years, at both state and national levels, the three branches of government have struggled for influence over ultimate policy decisions.

HISTORY OF LEGISLATIVE BODIES

Of the three branches of American government—executive, judicial, and legislative—the legislative branch is the most recently evolved. Executive and judicial functions of government have existed since earliest recorded history, although they have often been combined into a single office. Independent representative legislatures are of more recent origins. The roots of modern legislatures can be traced back some 700 years, to the Middle Ages. Institutions similar to representative bodies existed prior to that time, but they were not representative institutions in today's sense; in any event, there seems to be no historic linkage between the Greek and Roman assemblies and the modern legislature.[1]

The modern legislature's beginnings can be traced to the need of medieval monarchs to obtain the cooperation of the various estates and classes within the monarch's realm. Power in medieval society was diffuse (at least at the upper levels), and monarchs ignored at their own peril the interests and desires of the estates of the realm (nobility, clergy, landed gentry, and, eventually, burgesses of the towns).

In the interests of "the conservation of the peace, the administration of lucrative justice, and the replenishment of their royal treasuries," monarchs typically called to their castles representatives of communities and estates to give counsel and to grant the monarchs money.[2]

In the nations of continental Europe, the seventeenth century saw the end of diffuse authority among the medieval estates and the centralization of authority in the monarchs. Toward the end of the eighteenth century, socioeconomic developments led some monarchs to enlarge their circle of advisors or to appoint new advisory bodies capable of coping with the changes that were occurring in society. New and emerging social groups eventually began to demand more formal representation in the government also, and, at different times in different nations, parliaments began to develop.[3]

The first "modern" legislative institution was the British Parliament. As early as 1689, Parliament had constitutional powers (and a severely restricted franchise). Its powers had expanded substantially by the time the European continent's first governing parliament was established in France in 1792. Some of the European parliaments established in the late eighteenth century and early nineteenth century were consciously modeled after the British Parliament, while others were less directly influenced by British practice.[4] The structure of government in the American colonies, of course, was also greatly influenced by British ideas and practice.

In Great Britain, the Parliament originally was thought of as representing components of the realm, while the monarch represented the whole. Members of Parliament (MPs) negotiated both individually and collectively with the monarch's ministers. As the British Parliament's strength grew, the representative body began to assert the power to limit the monarch's choice of ministers. Eventually the Parliament came to view itself—and to be viewed by others—as being not just a congregation of delegates sent to London to speak for their respective local interests, but, collectively, as being representative of the nation just as much as the monarch was. As this fundamental change in political philosophy became more accepted, the Parliament succeeded in limiting the monarch's choice of advisors and ministers, first to persons acceptable to the Parliament and, eventually, to the leaders of the majority faction of the Parliament. Rather than undercutting the authority of the executive branch of government, then, the Parliament gradually placed its own leaders in charge of the executive branch.[5]

AMERICAN LEGISLATURES: THE PREREVOLUTIONARY EXPERIENCE

Legislative bodies have been part of American government since 1619, when twenty-two elected members of a representative assembly (two from each of eleven communities) met with the governor of colonial Virginia and his appointed council in Jamestown. The twenty-two elected colonists served as the lower house of the legislative body, while the appointed governor's council served as the upper house. Following the practice in England, the governor's council also served as the supreme court of the colony.[6]

Each of the other British colonies in North America also came to have a legislative body to represent local interests. Since this was the part of government that the colonists controlled, it is not surprising that they soon strongly favored the idea that the right to enact laws belongs to a representative assembly.[7]

The American experience differed from that of Great Britain. The British Parliament, with its evolving constitutional status, could exercise its power by limiting the king's choice of ministers and thus capture the power of the executive. The colonial legislatures had no such constitutional status. Many of the colonial legislatures *were* able to gain a measure of control over lesser colonial executive officers, but they were unable to control the choice of colonial governors. They, therefore, worked instead to limit the formal power of the colonial executive, while enlarging their own authority.[8]

A leading student of American colonial legislatures argues that, while the specific dates and developments differed from colony to colony, each popularly elected branch of the various colonial legislatures passed through three phases of development:

> During most of the 17th century the lower houses were still in a position of subordination, slowly groping for the power to tax and the right to sit separately from the council and to initiate laws. Sometime during the early 18th century most of them advanced to a second stage at which they could battle on equal terms with the governors and councils and challenge even the powers in London if necessary. . . . By the end of the Seven Years War (1756–1763, in America often called the French and Indian War) . . . or earlier, the lower houses had reached the third and final phase of political dominance.[9]

In this third phase the lower house in each colony held greater power than the governor and his (appointed) council. By 1763, the popularly elected lower houses in the American colonies all had some control over their own affairs, although not complete control. They had obtained freedom of debate and freedom from arrest, the right to expel members, control over internal procedures, and the right to elect a presiding officer. Most, however, were less successful in their efforts to gain control over the clerk of the lower chamber, the creation of constituencies, the setting of qualifications for members or voters, or the frequency of legislative elections or sessions.[10]

The popularly elected representative bodies in the colonies had gained extensive authority over taxing and spending. The lower houses in Connecticut and Rhode Island held virtually complete authority over these matters, and those of Pennsylvania and Massachusetts were also very powerful. The Pennsylvania lower chamber had achieved substantial authority by 1701 and by the 1740s held almost complete dominance over colonial affairs. In 1691, the Massachusetts House of Representatives had been accorded a voice in the selection of the council. By 1730, the Massachusetts House had control of the colony's finances, including salaries of executive officers.[11]

In 1708 the New Jersey lower house successfully insisted on the right to confirm the treasurer of the province. In that same year, the revenue bill set the salary for each provincial officer.[12] But the popularly elected New Jersey assembly encountered determined opposition from the colonial governors, and its power grew more slowly than some of the other colonial legislatures.[13]

The New York House of Assembly began to demand a greater voice in colonial affairs in the early 1700s, in part because of the governor's mismanagement. By 1739, the assembly listed the salaries for public officials by name and amount in the Appropriations Act. This practice enabled the assembly to gain some influence over appointments to executive offices by refusing to appropriate salaries for individuals they found unacceptable. About this time, too, the New York assembly began making annual rather than long-term appropriations. Such a practice, of course, meant that the assembly had to convene each year to appropriate further monies, and this, too, increased its authority.[14]

The lower houses of Georgia, North and South Carolina, and Virginia also increased their respective scopes of authority greatly during the first half of the eighteenth century, although the Georgia Commons held less power than the others at the end of the Seven Years War. By 1763, all four of these popularly elected colonial legislative bodies had gained firm control of colonial finances, including some powers to audit expenditures by public officials. They used these financial powers to gain a measure of control over many activities which traditionally had been considered to be within the executive's authority alone. Public works often were built by commissioners employed by the lower house, for example, rather than by the executive. The lower houses of North Carolina, South Carolina, and Virginia gained the right to appoint the public treasurer.[15]

AMERICAN LEGISLATURES: THE REVOLUTIONARY EXPERIENCE

After 1763, in an effort to find the money to pay for the French and Indian War, the British Crown and the British Parliament began to deliver a series of challenges to the authority of the colonial legislatures. The most important challenge to their power was

> the question of Parliamentary taxation, the heart of the lower houses' controversies with Great Britain after 1764. Between 1764 and 1766 Parliament's attempts to tax the colonists for revenue directly challenged the colonial legislatures' exclusive power to tax, the foundation of legislative authority in America. Upon that power the lower houses had built their political fortunes. . . . The realization that Parliamentary taxation was a direct challenge to their political power and might eventually even lead to the abolition of colonial lawmaking bodies forced (the colonial legislatures) to resist.[16]

As the struggle against the British developed, the colonists were forced to be explicit about their views of the constitutional status of the colonial legislatures within the British Empire. These colonial views were at great variance with official British understanding, and they led to increased British efforts to bring the colonies to heel. The need to keep informed of events in other colonies and to coordinate colonial activities led the colonial legislatures to establish Committees of Correspondence which kept such lines of communication open. Later, in 1774, the legislatures sent delegates to a Continental Congress.[17]

The First Continental Congress convened with delegates representing twelve of the thirteen colonies. After extended debate, the delegates agreed that each colony would have equal voting power in Congress, an equality which was retained in the Second Continental Congress.[18]

Conservatives in the Congress wanted to seek a more democratic structure of colonial governance within the British Empire, but the plan presented to accomplish that end was tabled and never really debated. Rather, the Congress petitioned the king for a repeal of various oppressive laws enacted since 1863; approved the radical Suffolk Resolves, which called for withholding tax revenues from the crown; and approved defensive action against British soldiers if necessary. Congress also approved a boycott of British trade.[19]

The Second Continental Congress (1775–81) convened in May 1775, soon after the battles of Lexington and Concord. That Congress declared the need for the colonists to defend themselves against the British and appointed George Washington to command the colonial army. But there were still so many colonists who hoped to find an accommodation with the British within the empire that radical leaders in Congress did not immediately declare independence. Thomas Paine and other pamphleteers, however, agitated for such a declaration, and subsequent events closed the door to reconciliation with the British. Finally, on July 2, 1776, Congress appointed a committee to draft the Declaration of Independence. That document was designed to justify the revolution which already was well under way. The Second Continental Congress had had little choice but to assume the leadership of that revolution, despite its weak authority and its dependence on the thirteen colonies for sustenance.[20]

The Declaration of Independence no longer discussed the rights of colonists as British citizens. Rather, it stressed their inalienable rights as human beings, and, in addition, their right to elect their own government officials and to hold them accountable, voting them out of office if they chose. A major battle cry of the colonists was "no taxation without representation." That position had developed as a result of the taxes imposed directly on the colonists by the British Parliament after the French and Indian War, even though no colonists sat in Parliament. The colonists' insistence on representation in whatever body was levying taxes on them, as noted above, was a major factor in the dynamics which led to the revolution.

THE EMERGENCE OF A STRONG NATIONAL LEGISLATURE

While the war was still in progress, the Continental Congress drafted the Articles of Confederation. Under the Articles, the Congress was the center of a national government which had no separate executive or judicial branches. The first Congress of the Confederation met in March 1781. Each state sent two to seven delegates to Congress, selected according to the desire of each state's legislature. Each state's delegation was allowed to cast only one vote. Nine votes (of the thirteen total) were required for a measure to pass. Since ultimate authority remained with the individual states, however, the central government under the Articles had very limited powers.

The weakness of this government was a major factor in the movement which eventually led to the drafting of the U.S. Constitution in 1787. A growing lack of economic and political order engendered by the inability of the Congress to pass legislation binding on the states led those influential in the newly independent country to hold a Constitutional Convention in 1787 for the purpose of revising the Articles of Confederation.[21] The leading framers of what was to become a new Constitution had become alarmed by the powers asserted by many of the state legislatures following the revolution.[22] These state legislative bodies had, in some cases, overturned court decisions against debtors, refused to fully recognize property and creditor rights, and sometimes even asserted their right to amend state constitutions. Mindful of their experience under British rule, however, the framers were equally concerned about the possibility of executive tyranny and decided to divide governmental powers into three branches—executive, legislative, and judicial—providing each branch with "checks" over the power of the other branches.[23] The Congress created by the U.S. Constitution, however, was granted wide powers and made the center of government. It was then, and remains, one of the strongest—probably the very strongest—national legislatures in existence.

PARLIAMENTARY GOVERNMENT VS. SEPARATION OF POWERS

The American decision to form national and state governments with clearly separated executive, judicial, and legislative branches (often referred to as a "separation-of-powers" system of government), instead of adopting parliamentary forms of government, obviously affected the nature of American legislatures and the individual legislator's role and function. Both systems have their strengths and weaknesses.[24] The parliamentary system—where the majority party in the parliament elects the head of the executive branch, the "government," from its own number and its own party—often provides for more unified government policy that is more responsive to a mandate from the voters. But this is not nearly so true when no single party has a majority in the parliament (the situation in most parliamentary systems today). When this is the case, a party may have to make compromises or concessions in order to secure enough votes from another party, or parties, to form a coalition majority and establish a government.

The fact that the leaders of the majority party in the British House of Commons are also the ministers in charge of the government (and in charge of drafting proposed laws) means that the committees of the House of Commons have much less influence and independence than the committees of the U.S. Congress, which routinely make extensive revisions in legislation drafted by the administration.[25] Sometimes Congressional committees refuse to pass administration-proposed legislation at all, whether or not the President is of the majority party in Congress.

The type of contribution permitted experienced legislators also differs in the two types of systems. In the parliamentary system, the leaders of the government are chosen from among the members of the parliament. Persons seeking to take charge of executing as well as initiating government policy must first become members of Parliament. British members of Parliament who have specialized for years in health policy or defense programs, for example, are likely to become executive ministers in such fields. In the American separation-of-powers system, in contrast, legislators are forbidden to serve simultaneously in the executive branch. Subject-matter experts in a legislature thus must content themselves with shaping legislation in their fields of expertise; if they are elected or appointed to serve in the executive branch, they must resign from the legislature. Most remain in Congress, where they develop subject-matter expertise which adds greatly to the authority of Congress and its committees.

In a parliamentary system, a citizen's vote in parliamentary elections determines which political party or coalition of parties will control the executive branch of the government. It is the only vote a citizen casts concerning the composition of the government. In the American separation-of-powers system, in contrast, the citizen's vote for a legislative candidate is separate from his or her vote for which party will control the executive branch of government. Thus, a citizen can vote for a U.S. representative or senator without affecting who will be in charge of national defense or the treasury. Partly as a result, many Americans "split their ticket" on election day.

As most sports aficionados are aware, the rules under which the game is played make a great deal of difference in the outcome. As in sports, the rules governing the political—and legislative—game affect the relative advantages of different actors and thus significantly affect outcomes. Subsequent chapters will note additional differences between the parliamentary and the separation-of-powers governments—differences which substantially affect the political processes and the decisions made in the two political systems.

STATE LEGISLATURES IN THE UNITED STATES

As discussed earlier, the American colonial legislatures had developed substantial independent power by the end of the Seven Years War in 1763. After the Revolutionary War the distrust of the executive carried over into the constitutions of the newly independent states. Power was granted liberally to their legislatures, while their executives, by and large, were held in check. In all but four states the state legislature chose the governor, and in most of the states, the governor's chief decisions were subject to approval by a council which was chosen by the legislature.

The New York and Massachusetts structures of government were the exceptions which provided for a relatively strong executive, elected directly by the people in both states and armed with the power to veto legislation. The New York Constitution was written as the British were invading the state so the framers of that state constitution saw the need for a strong executive.[26]

Except for New York, the legislatures dominated the new state governments, although each state constitution did provide for separate executive and judicial branches. In all the states except New York, the executive was expected to implement policies developed by the legislature and not to be a forceful independent political actor. Several decades passed before the executive and judicial branches of most of the state governments began to accrue authority comparable to that held by the state legislatures.

That the states would adopt the separation-of-powers structure, rather than the parliamentary structure of government, was fairly evident from the beginnings of independence, but any of them could have adopted a parliamentary structure of state government. Indeed, other former British colonies like Australia and Canada have developed dynamic federal systems within a framework of parliamentary government at the provincial (state) and national levels.[27]

The American executive branches of state governments slowly moved out of the legislature's shadow in all the states, as the people developed greater faith in their executives, partially based on their observations of the presidency and the governorship of New York. The change, over time, to direct election of the various state governors reduced their dependence on the legislatures, but the separate election of numerous executive officers in each state kept any governor from holding too much power. Such a "plural executive," and short terms for state governors, resulted in weak governors. State legislatures thus maintained positions of substantial power in the various states, particularly until after the Civil War.

In the latter part of the nineteenth century, as the national economy became more industrialized and the railroads were expanded throughout the nation, corruption was rampant as many state legislatures became dominated by railroad and corporate interests. Much financial irresponsibility on the part of the state legislatures during the late 1800s also resulted in a growing lack of public confidence in state governments generally—and especially in state legislatures. Numerous state constitutional amendments were passed and numerous constitutional conventions were held to reform state government and especially the state legislatures.

While state legislatures were demonstrating weaknesses, American society was also changing, becoming more complex. For instance, the increased reliance of farmers on the railroads, and the repeated demonstration that the railroads required regulation, resulted in the realization that the executive branch of state government would have to assume more and more responsibilities. Thus, slowly, state constitutions were changed to increase the power and independence of the state governors. Typically, however, state executive offices are still fragmented in most states, because their occupants are independently and directly elected by the voters.

It should not be assumed that state legislatures are less powerful in any absolute sense than they used to be. In fact, the role of government generally has greatly increased, and thus in *absolute* terms the powers of state legislatures have increased. The change in the power of the legislature over the last two centuries has been a *relative* one. Relative to the power of the executive branch, the power of state legislatures has declined in the American states since the era immediately following the revolution against the British.[28]

SUMMARY

The modern Western legislature has developed gradually over the past 700 years, as various groups in society have been recognized as having a legitimate right to a voice in the rules by which the society is governed. The oldest governing national legislative body in the world is the British Parliament, which has been in continuous existence for almost three centuries. The British parliamentary system has served as the model for many other legislative bodies.

Legislative bodies in America have existed since 1619, when the governor of Virginia met with elected representatives from the various towns. The colonial legislatures developed great powers over colonial government, through their successful assertion that they alone had the power to tax and the power to appropriate money. Those powers, of course, developed very slowly. The American colonial legislatures' assertions of their powers was a major factor in the political struggle which culminated in the revolution against the British in 1776.

Although the colonists' experience with colonial executives had not been a happy one, the newly independent states did not adopt the parliamentary form of government. In part reflecting the tendency not to change things too much, and in part because of a fear of concentrating power in one place, the newly independent states chose to erect a government based on separation of powers and checks and balances, rather than adopting the parliamentary system of government. The U.S. Congress, created in 1787, was—and is—one of the strongest national legislatures in the world.

Except for New York, however, the governments established in the various states left the preponderance of power with the legislative branch of government. Only after several decades of experience did the executive officers of the various states begin to gain authority comparable to that held by the legislatures. After the Civil War, because of the rampant corruption in the various state legislative bodies and because of an increasingly complex society which was thought to require an invigorated executive, the constitutions of the various states were amended or rewritten to give the executive greater power in state government. The state legislatures today are still bodies of substantial power, but they operate in an environment which includes a strong state executive.

Notes

1. Charles A. Beard and John D. Lewis, "Representative Government in Evolution," in *Legislative Behavior: A Reader in Theory and Research,* ed. John C. Wahlke and Heinz Eulau (Glencoe, Ill.: Free Press, 1959), p. 24; originally published in *American Political Science Review* 26 (April 1932): 223–40.

2. Ibid. See also their footnotes 14–17.

3. Peter Gerlich, "The Institutionalization of European Parliaments," in *Legislatures in Comparative Perspective,* ed. Allan Kornberg (New York: David McKay, 1973), pp. 95–97; Samuel P. Huntington, *Political Order in Changing Societies* (New Haven, Conn.: Yale University Press, 1968), pp. 98–102.

4. Gerlich, "The Institutionalization of European Parliaments," pp. 100–101.

5. Gerhard Lowenberg and Samuel C. Patterson, *Comparing Legislatures* (Boston: Little, Brown, 1979), pp. 10–11.

6. A. Berriedale Keith, *Constitutional History of the First British Empire* (Oxford: Clarendon Press, 1930), pp. 22–25.

7. George S. Blair, *American Legislatures: Structure and Process* (New York: Harper and Row, 1968), p. 4.

8. Lowenberg and Patterson, *Comparing Legislatures,* p. 12.

9. Jack P. Greene, *The Quest for Power: The Lower Houses of Assembly in the Southern Royal Colonies, 1689–1776* (Chapel Hill, N.C.: University of North Carolina Press, 1963), p. 4.

10. Ibid., pp. 359–60.

11. Ibid., pp. 4–5. Details, of course, vary with each colony, since their historical and constitutional backgrounds differed considerably. For such details, see Greene; see also Keith, *Constitutional History of the First British Empire.*

12. John E. Pomfret, *Colonial New Jersey* (New York: Charles Scribner's Sons, 1973), p. 129.

13. Greene, *The Quest for Power,* p. 6.

14. Michael Kammen, *Colonial New York: A History* (New York: Charles Scribner's Sons, 1975), p. 212.

15. Greene, *The Quest for Power,* pp. 363–64.

16. Ibid.

17. Ibid., Chapters 19–22; see also Keith, *Constitutional History of the First British Empire,* Chapter 16.

18. Edmund Cody Burnett, *The Continental Congress* (New York: Macmillan, 1941), Chapters 3–9.

19. John C. Miller, *Origins of the American Revolution* (Boston: Little, Brown, 1943), pp. 381–84.

20. Ibid., Chapters 19 and 20.

21. For more extensive information, see Merrill Jensen, *The New Nation: A History of the United States During the Confederation, 1781–1789* (New York: Alfred A. Knopf, 1950); and Burnett, *The Continental Congress.*

22. See generally Charles Warren, *The Making of the Constitution* (Boston: Little, Brown, 1928); and Alfred deGrazia, *Public and Republic: Political Representation in America* (New York: Alfred A. Knopf, 1951).

23. Richard E. Neustadt argues that the U.S. Constitution created a government of separated institutions sharing powers, rather than a government of separated powers. See his *Presidential Powers: The Politics of Leadership* (New York: John Wiley, 1960), p. 33.

24. See generally David M. Olson, *The Legislative Process: A Comparative Approach* (New York: Harper and Row, 1980); John E. Schwartz and L. Earl Shaw, *The United States Congress in Comparative Perspective* (Hinsdale, Ill.: Dryden Press, 1976); and Harold W. Chase, Robert T. Holt, and John E. Turner, *American Government in Comparative Perspective* (New York: New Viewpoints, 1979).

25. Kenneth Bradshaw and David Pring, *Parliament and Congress* (Austin, Texas: University of Texas Press, 1972), Chapter 5.

26. Louis Koenig, *The Chief Executive* (New York: Harcourt, Brace and World, 1968), pp. 14–16.

27. "Federalism in Australia: Current Trends," in a special issue of *Publius: The Journal of Federalism* 7 (Summer 1977); and David V. Smiley, "The Canadian Federation and the Challenge of Quebec Independence," *Publius: The Journal of Federalism* 3 (Winter 1973): 199–224.

28. Wilder Crane, Jr., and Meredith W. Watts, Jr., *State Legislative Systems* (Englewood Cliffs, N.J.: Prentice-Hall, 1968), pp. 3–6.

chapter 2

Democratic Theory: Representation and Participation

Preview

This chapter discusses theoretical perspectives on representation and on participation by the average citizen in the selection of the government, especially the legislature. There are four distinct dimensions of representation: formal representation, involving how the representative is selected; descriptive representation, involving who the representative is and whether he or she is like us; symbolic representation, involving whether we can believe in the representative because he or she is on our side; and substantive representation, involving the question of what the representative is doing, and is it in our interest? This last dimension confronts the question of whether our legislator is to be a mere delegate, blindly voting the constituents' will, or a trustee, exercising independent judgment. The citizen's role in the selection of the government can be a participatory one, through voting. If, as Jefferson stated, democratic government reflects the popular will, there should be greater efforts to encourage citizen participation in elections from all sectors of the population.

Our governmental system and its legislative bodies exist within a framework of political and governmental principles. These principles are embodied in such familiar terms as *democracy, representative democracy,* and *a republican form of government.* As familiar as they are, these terms are not simple, easily explained concepts. They importantly affect how modern legislators and legislative bodies act—and how we expect them to act.

Democracy means, literally, "rule of the people." Some early American leaders—Roger Williams, John Wise, and Patrick Henry, for example—used the word *democracy* freely. Most early American leaders, however, shied away from the term because of its connotation of "mob rule." They preferred the word *republic.* [1]

The characteristics of a republican form of government were described by Thomas Jefferson, who had been largely responsible for the wording of the Declaration of Independence in 1776. In this fundamental American document, he wrote that governments derive their "just powers from the consent of the governed"—words which Jefferson, a student of the English philosopher John Locke (1632–1704), declared to be the "common sense" of colonial America of the time. [2] To Jefferson, democracy—or, as he would have called it, republicanism—was understood to involve both a particular process and a particular result. In stating the principle of democratic *process,* Jefferson wrote, "For let it be agreed that a government is republican in proportion as every member composing it has an equal voice in the direction of its concerns (not indeed in person, which would be impracticable beyond the limits of a city, or small township, but,) by representatives chosen by himself, and responsible to him at short periods."[3] Jefferson emphasized the importance of democratic *results* by stating that "governments are republican only in proportion as they embody the will of their people, and execute it."[4] America's democracy, then, according to the ideals set forth by Jefferson, is a system in which the people elect representatives who establish governmental policy which is in accord with the popular will.

REPRESENTATION

Obviously, *representation* is a key concept in our system of government, but what does it mean; how does it happen; how does it work? In the literal or dictionary sense, *representation* means making present what, in fact, is not present—one person standing for another, for example. How is it possible to make present what is not, in fact, present? In carrying out the functions of representation, when can it be said that legislators or legislative bodies are truly representative—that is, that they truly "stand for" the people? Hanna F. Pitkin has divided the consideration of the concept of representation into four major aspects: formal, descriptive, symbolic, and substantive.[5]

Formal Representation

Formal representation has to do with the process by which the consent of the governed is given or withheld. It may be thought of in terms of either "authorization" or "accountability." The writings of English political philosopher Thomas Hobbes are cited as the basis for the authorization view of formal representation. In *Leviathan* (1615), Hobbes maintained that governments are based upon a social contract among the people which authorizes someone to act in their behalf. By that means, he said, the multitude becomes one person.[6] The authorization view of formal representation emphasizes the delegation or granting of authority in advance of representation. The accountability view of formal representation emphasizes that a representative is held to account at the end of his or her representation. Whether formal representation is seen from the beginning or the end, from the authorization or accountability standpoint, it is clear that the focus of formal representation is on elections. They must be regular, free, and fair. Thus, it can be said that the U.S. Senate became a more formally representative body with the 1913 ratification of the Seventeenth Amendment, which provided for the direct election of U.S. senators, in place of the earlier system of selection by state legislatures.

Questions of formal representation involve the rules governing legislative districting or apportionment, a subject that will be discussed at length in Chapter 5. It is difficult to argue that, collectively, a legislature represents the population when residents of some areas have a much greater voice in the selection of legislators than residents of other areas do. Legislative refusal to recognize adequately the great rural-urban migration of the preceding century had resulted by 1960 in major inequalities between the populations of most state's legislative districts and between the populations of Congressional (U.S. House of Representative) districts in many states. Normally, urban legislative districts had many more citizens per legislator than did rural districts, meaning urban residents were badly underrepresented in the legislature. In half of the forty-two states with two or more Congressional districts, the largest district had twice the population of the smallest district.[7] Even greater malapportionment existed in most state senates. In Maryland, for example, three fourths of the 1960 population resided in the city of Baltimore or in one of the state's four largest counties, but Baltimore and these four counties were represented in the Maryland Senate by only one third of the members of that chamber.[8] In the face of continued legislative resistance to fair legislative apportionment, the U.S. Supreme Court ruled in 1962 (in the Tennessee case, *Baker* v. *Carr*[9]) that malapportionment violated the Equal Protection Clause of the Fourteenth Amendment to the U.S. Constitution and that courts could accept jurisdiction over the matter. The series of judicial decisions which followed *Baker* v. *Carr* brought approximate equality of populations to the districts of the nation's state legislatures and, within each state, to Congressional districts. Formal representation in American legislatures thus was greatly enhanced.

There is, then, a formal aspect to the concept of representation. Whether on the basis of formal authorization of representation, or on the basis of making representation accountable to the people, or both, formal representation requires institutionalized, regular elections which are free and fair. Thus, formal representation deals with the question, "How was the representative selected?" But there is more to the concept of representation than this process-oriented aspect.

Descriptive Representation

Must representatives "look like" their constituents? That is the question raised by the descriptive aspect of the concept of representation. Clearly, no single representative can completely mirror his or her constituents' characteristics—sex, race, socioeconomic status, age, and occupation. But should the total representative body mirror the characteristics of the total group being represented? From the viewpoint of descriptive representation, the answer is "yes."

The early American leader John Adams felt that "a representative legislature should be an exact portrait, in miniature, of the people at large, as it should think, feel, reason and act like them."[10] This view of representation was based upon the realization that it was not possible for the entire citizenry of a state or nation to assemble and legislate directly; therefore, those who "substitute" for them should be "typical" of them. How is typicality determined?

In "functional" representation, various groupings and interest groups and segments of the society would choose the legislative representatives. In "proportional" representation—which is used in some European countries—seats in a legislative body are allocated to each party in direct proportion to the percentage of the total votes received by the party's legislative candidates. Neither functional nor proportional representation has gained much support in the United States. Our legislators are typically chosen from single-member districts in winner-take-all elections. The rules governing the political process (including the legislative process) are *not* neutral; they affect outcomes. Often the impact is not foreseen. In this instance, the dominant method for accomplishing formal representation—the use of single-member legislative districts—greatly reduces the chance that our legislative bodies will be descriptively representative.

Perhaps the only way that a legislative body could be made wholly "descriptive" would be for its members to be chosen by the kind of random sampling used in scientific polling. Nobody responsible has suggested that our legislators be chosen in this way, rather than by election, and nobody knows just what such a legislature might *do,* although it is assumed that if a legislature were made up of people typical of the whole population, it would act in very much the same way the whole population would act if they were assembled together and had the same information.

Advocates of descriptive representation tend to think of legislative bodies more as forums for the expression of viewpoints of the people and as watchdogs over the government, rather than as policymakers. And one criticism of the descriptive idea of representation is that if every group and every interest were mirrored in a legislative body, it would be extremely difficult to put together a majority in the body for *action.*

Another criticism of the idea of descriptive representation was voiced by Alexander Hamilton in the *Federalist.* He declared that elections will always produce representatives who are not "typical" of the total population; but does a legislative body have to be a mirror image of us in order to represent us? Hamilton thought not:

> It is said to be necessary that all classes should have some of their own number in the representative body, in order that their feelings and interests may be the better understood and attended to. But we have seen that this will never happen under any arrangement that leaves the votes of the people free. Where this is the case, the representative body, with too few exceptions to have any influence on the spirit of the government will be composed of landholders, merchants, and men of the learned professions. But where is the danger that the interests and feelings of the different classes of people will not be understood or attended to by these three descriptions of men?[11]

When President Richard Nixon nominated Clement Haynesworth to serve as a member of the U.S. Supreme Court, then-U.S. Senator Roman Hruska of Nebraska, a supporter of the nomination, made an offhand, later-regretted remark, which alluded to the charge that Haynesworth's judicial and legal record was a mediocre one. Senator Hruska said that even mediocre people are entitled to be represented on the U.S. Supreme Court. Most people would say that this reasoning takes descriptive representation too far. For no one would suggest that "lunatics" are entitled to have some of their number sitting for them in legislative bodies, nor that, "while we might wish to complain that there are not enough representative members of the working class among Parliamentary representatives, we would not want to complain that the large class of stupid or maleficent people have too few representatives in Parliament: rather the contrary."[12]

Legislative bodies in the United States are clearly not descriptively representative. This will be discussed at length in Chapter 4. Women are little over half of the population of the United States, yet in 1981 there were only 2 women in the U.S. Senate and only 19 women in the U.S. House of Representatives. Out of 535 members of the combined U.S. House and Senate, there were only 17 blacks (all in the House), 5 Asian-Americans, and 5 Hispanic-Americans.[13] Women and racial minorities are also badly underrepresented in the state legislatures, U.S. House and U.S. Senate members, as well as state legislators, tend to come from "high-status" occupations, with lawyers predominating. There are also a large number of members whose backgrounds are in business and banking. Well over 90 percent of the members of Congress have attended college, as compared with only 31 percent of the general adult population in the country. Congress and American state legislatures are made up of people who are mostly white, mostly male, and mostly from middle- and upper-income levels. One authority, Samuel Krislov, emphasizing the lack of descriptive representation in American legislatures, has written that "youth, left-handers, atomic physicists, and even classicists are more commonly found in the dusty halls of executive office buildings than in the debating halls of legislatures."[14] Krislov's point was that unelected bureaucracies are more descriptively representative than elected legislatures.

Descriptive representation asks, "Who is the representative, and is he or she like us?" Legislative bodies in the United States cannot be said to be mirror images of the people they represent. It is true that one need not be a steelworker in order to speak for the interests of steelworkers. Nevertheless, many Americans would feel more "represented" if legislators were more typical of the general population—particularly in regard to race and sex.

Symbolic Representation

Symbolic representation might be said to deal with the question, "Can we believe in the representative because he or she is on our side?" Just as the American flag can be said to symbolize the United States of America, a representative may be said to "stand for," symbolically, his or her constituents, if the constituents *believe* in the representative.[15]

A member of Congress usually spends a considerable amount of time and effort to develop and reinforce the belief of his or her constituents in the member's symbolic representativeness. To do so, they may engage in symbolic acts, particularly legislative symbolism and, as Richard F. Fenno, Jr., has put it, "homestyle" symbolism.[16]

A member of a legislative body may introduce a bill for several reasons. One may be an actual legislative purpose, of course, with the member intending and expecting that the sponsored bill or amendment will be adopted. Another reason may be for informational purposes, allowing the member to use the introduction of a legislative measure to focus public opinion and discussion on an issue. Third, a member may introduce a bill or amendment with a symbolic purpose in mind, to demonstrate to his or her constituents that they share similar views on an issue. Thus, a member might introduce a proposed constitutional amendment to require that the federal budget be kept in balance, while knowing that there is little or no chance that such a proposal will actually receive the necessary two-thirds vote in both houses of Congress.

Homestyle symbolism may be furthered in a number of ways, all of which are intended to convey the "on-our-side" image by showing that "I'm easily accessible to you" and "I know your problems." Many legislators believe that this symbolic image is fundamentally important. As one member of Congress put it, "The people back home don't know what's going on. Issues are not most important so far as the average voter is concerned. The image of the candidate plays a much greater role."[17]

A representative may use a number of homestyle techniques to develop and reinforce the desired image. Typically, the representative will go back home a great deal and will hold regular and publicly announced open-office hours, when anyone who wants to can come and see the representative about any subject. Many legislators—particularly members of the U.S. House of Representatives—regularly mail out questionnaires on issues to a wide number of their constituents, largely for symbolic effect. Members appear at civic meetings and other kinds of public gatherings, even funerals, and conduct handshaking tours on streets and in business establishments. U.S. Senator Lawton Chiles of Florida originated the idea of a candidate for office walking across his or her state, and this example has been widely copied by a large number of other candidates throughout the country. U.S. Senator William Proxmire of Wisconsin has developed another popular homestyle technique; from time to time, he has worked for a day in some typical back-home job—as a garbage collector or supermarket/grocery sacker. Richard F. Fenno, Jr., again, has said that all of this is an essential part of the two-way communication involved in representation:

> Although the congressman can engage in this kind of communication with only some of his supportive constituents, he can give many more the assurance that two-way communication is possible. That is exactly the kind of assurance that most members try to give their supportive constituents by going home as much as they do, by presenting themselves in the great variety of contexts they do, by identifying with as many of their constituents as they can, and even, as we have said, by some of their advertising. Above all, perhaps, they stress accessibility. Access to some carries the assurance of two-way communication. The more accessible they are, House members believe, the more will their constituents be encouraged to feel that they can communicate with the congressman when and if they wish. As we have said frequently, however, this kind of assurance is not obtained by one-shot offers. It is created over a long time and underwritten by trust. Access and assurance of access, communication and the assurance of communication—these are irreducible underpinnings of representation."[18]

To be sure, homestyle symbolism may also have a great deal to do with increasing citizen participation in the political process and in influencing the substantive actions of legislators. But it may also have another effect, as has been pointed out by Murray Edelman.[19] It is possible for acts of symbolic representation to be used to satisfy the great mass of people *psychologically* while the representative or representative body satisfies the *actual* economic and other wants of special interests. And that brings us to the fourth aspect of the concept of representation: substantive representation.

Substantive Representation

We have considered three aspects of the concept of representation: formal, involving how the representative was chosen; descriptive, involving who the representative is and whether he or she is like us; and symbolic, involving the question of whether we can believe in the representative because he or she is on our side. But there is still more to representation than these three aspects. Even after all of the questions inherent in them have been answered, there is still the question, "What is the representative doing, and is it in our interest?" This is the focus of substantive representation.

Substantive representation "means acting in the interests of the represented, in a manner responsive to them."[20] But how responsive? Should a representative be a "rubber stamp" for his or her constituents? It has been argued that a mere word-for-word translation is not representation; it is reproduction.[21] Similarly, if political decisions can be made as a result of a kind of scientific or mathematical process, no representative would be needed; popular decisions could be made by using computers and other electronic means.[22] Thus, by definition, representation includes some discretion on the part of the representative. Indeed, in the Federal Republic of Germany (West Germany) in 1958, an attempt to organize a popular referendum on atomic armaments was held to be unconstitutional because it would illegally pressure the parliament, instead of allowing it to decide public policy freely and independently. In France in 1960, President Charles DeGaulle rejected an appeal for a special session of the parliament because he said there would be too much pressure on the deputies from farmers' organizations, in violation of the constitutional obligation of the deputies to act independently.[23]

In the United States, the roles of the representative and the represented, are not so clearly separated. And this creates conflicts. Former U.S. Representative Emanuel Celler of New York has said, "The 'good' representative is he who effectively accommodates opposing interests within his constituency; who successfully relates the needs of his constituents to those of the people as a whole; and who harmonizes his responses to the demands made upon him with the dictates of his conscience."[24] A representative must decide which of conflicting positions to take on a particular issue. Thus (assuming there is no clearly discernible majority view among a representative's constituents on a particular issue), the representative must decide which position to support among the conflicting views in the home district. But, suppose there *is* a clearly discernible majority view among the representative's constituents on a particular issue. Then, Celler has pointed out, the representative may have to decide whether to follow the majority view in his or her district or to support the national interest, if the two conflict. Similarly, the representative may have to decide whether to follow his or her own conscience on the issue, if it conflicts with the majority view in the home interest.

Concrete examples of these problems were seen in the U.S. Senate in 1979, during consideration of the Panama Canal Treaty. It was clear to both U.S. Senator Edward Zorinsky of Nebraska and U.S. Senator Dennis DeConcini of Arizona that at the time of the final vote on the treaty a majority of the people in each of their home states was opposed to ratification. Both senators came to the conclusion—as their consciences told them and as they announced—that the national interest would best be served by ratification of the treaty. Yet, Senator Zorinsky voted *against* ratification, and Senator DeConcini, in opposition to the majority view in his home state, voted *for* it. Senator Zorinsky said that he felt that he had been elected to represent the majority view in his home state, no matter what his own view. Senator DeConcini said that, in this case at least, he had to do what he felt was right, even though a majority in his home state wanted him to do the opposite. The Zorinsky-DeConcini examples illustrate vividly two basic theories about substantive representation: the *delegate* theory and the *trustee* theory.

Delegate When Senator Zorinsky voted against the Panama Canal Treaty, in spite of his own conscience and what he felt was the national interest, he was doing so because he saw himself as the "delegate" of his constituents, with a mandate to serve as their agent, to do just what they wanted done, regardless of his own wishes. This theory of a representative's duty was expressed quite succinctly by Hilaire Belloc and G. K. Chesterton, when they wrote:

> Either the representative must vote as his constituents would vote if consulted, or he must vote in the opposite sense. In the latter case, he is not a representative at all, but merely an oligarch; for it is surely ridiculous to say that a man represents Bethnel Green if he is in the habit of saying 'Aye' when the people of Bethnel Green would say "No."[25]

A modern-day member of the U.S. House of Representatives made the same point by saying, "I'm here to represent my district. This is part of my actual belief as to the function of a congressman. What is good for the majority of my district is good for the country. What snarls up the system is these so-called statesmen-congressmen who vote for what they think is the country's best interest."[26]

Trustee When Senator DeConcini voted for the ratification of the Panama Canal Treaty, despite what he knew to be the wishes of a majority of his constituents, he was acting as a trustee; in this instance, at least, he conceived his representative role as that of a free agent, with independence to exercise his own judgment. Eighteenth-century conservative British writer and parliamentarian Edmund Burke stated this view quite plainly. He said that a representative should give great weight to the wishes and opinions of constituents and should "sacrifice his repose, his pleasure, his satisfaction, to theirs—and above all, ever, and in all cases, to prefer their interests to his own," but that "his unbiased opinion, his mature judgment, his enlightened conscience he ought not sacrifice to you, to any man, or any set of men living. . . . Your representative owes you, not his industry alone, but his judgment; and he betrays, instead of serving you, if he sacrifices it to your opinion."[27]

Delegate, Trustee, or Both?   Most representatives are probably what have been called "politicos"—that is, they are sometimes (most often) delegates and sometimes (less often) trustees. But there are two main problems with the delegate theory of representation. First, the representative may not clearly understand the wishes of his or her constituents. This is an important consideration because, as some authorities have stated:

> The representative must feel obligated to respond to district preferences *and* the constituency must provide a consistent cue so that the representative can act in accordance with constituency opinion. In the absence of either or both of these conditions, the delegate theory breaks down. Only when both of these conditions are fulfilled simultaneously can we expect the theory to operate fully.[28]

A representative may not get a clear and consistent cue from constituents for a number of reasons. There may not be a majority opinion on issues not seen by the voters to be salient, or important, to them. Members of Congress may vote as many as 2,000 times a year; not every one of these measures is felt by their constituents (if they think about the measures at all) to be important enough for a majority to form an opinion about them. Some issues may be very complicated or may involve classified information—for example, the Strategic Arms Limitation Treaty II; concerning these, at least in the early discussions, a majority of the people may not be sufficiently informed to form an opinion. Even when there is a majority opinion on an issue, members of Congress may not gauge it accurately. They cannot depend upon the mail on public issues because it is often unrepresentative.[29] Further, representatives tend to talk with community leaders, rather than a broad cross section of their constituents, and these community leaders may not be well-informed about general community opinion.[30] It is not surprising then that members of Congress frequently are unable to state accurately what majority opinion among their constituents actually is on a particular issue.[31]

The more visible an issue is—and, thus, the greater likelihood that a representative's constituents will be informed and have an opinion about it—the more likely that a representative will act on that issue as a delegate. "While most congressmen in 1958 could be classified as trustees on the issue of foreign involvement, the increased visibility of this issue area brought about by the war in Indochina suggests that most legislators in the early 1970s were acting in terms of the delegate role in this area."[32]

> Whether legislators from marginal (competitive) districts are more or less likely to be delegates than those from safe districts is a matter of some controversy.[33] Some observers argue that the legislator from a competitive district must stay closely attuned to the constituency to insure reelection, since any defections at the polls could be disastrous. Others note, however, that "public opinion" in a competitive district is harder to discover than in a safe district. Fiorina, for in-

stance, argues that legislators from safe districts are likely to be representative of modal constituency opinion, seeking out consensus policy positions, while in competitive districts, winning electoral coalitions are likely to be formed of ideologues on one side or the other. "The representatives from these (competitive) districts represent their part of the constituency and the devil take the other."[34]

A second problem with the delegate theory of representation is that the constituent-representative relationship is not just a one-way relationship, and the representative may sometimes properly be expected to lead. This results from the duty of democratic government both to govern and to represent. As one writer has put it, "A democratic government is charged with the two often conflicting responsibilities of representing the citizens and exercising authority over them. As a government, it must be able to lead, concomitantly binding the electorate to its actions; as a democratic government, it must respond to the issues of the electorate."[35] Because of this responsibility of the government to lead—and thus to *act*—one authority has said that "the government cannot postpone actions and decisions until vague images and myths eventually coalesce into opinion. In the present world of politics, action must at all times be the forerunner of opinion. Even where public opinion is already formed, it can be disastrous to follow it."[36]

Often, there may not be a majority public opinion on an issue—because of the lack of visibility of the issue, the lack of widespread information concerning it, or the lack of an inclination to consider it carefully—until the representative or public official has first taken a position concerning it. Similarly, majority opinion may be changed when a public official takes a position on an issue—supplying the visibility, information, and sense of importance concerning the issue which the majority of people may need to form a strong opinion about it. The more a representative sees the principle involved in an issue as being fundamental, the more likely it is the representative will act as a trustee. During the Vietnam War, for example, U.S. Senator George McGovern of South Dakota, the late U.S. Senator Robert F. Kennedy of New York, and former U.S. Senator Eugene McCarthy of Minnesota began to speak out against America's involvement in the war, long before they were supported by majority opinion. But majority opinion changed, and these officials helped to change it. There are those who say that the majority of Americans would never have come around to a position in opposition to the war unless such representatives had first spoken out against it when they were still in the minority. Similarly, when President Jimmy Carter first proposed that the U.S. Senate ratify the Panama Canal Treaty, polls showed that a majority of Americans opposed the treaty; but, following all the debate and discussion, and before the matter was finally voted on in the U.S. Senate, majority opinion changed to support the treaty. It is also interesting that, while legislators from competitive, marginal districts are likely to act as delegates where majority opinion is clear, they are also more willing to try new ideas, and thus to be policy innovators, perhaps seeking to gain additional support in upcoming, close elections by their leadership in these areas.[37]

Clearly then, if the second requirement of the classic definition of Jeffersonian democracy (that public policy should reflect the will of the majority) is to be met, no concept of representation is complete unless it includes the aspect of substantive representation. Yet, as Hanna F. Pitkin has said, "There need not be a constant activity of responding, but there must be a constant condition of responsiveness, of potential readiness to respond."[38] One of the drafters of the U.S. Constitution, James Wilson, explained substantive representation in terms of a chain of communication between the represented and the representative.[39] Similarly, it has been observed

19

more recently that, so long as this chain of communication, or interaction, "consists in a sharing of *reasons,* regardless of who gets the idea first, neither the autonomy of the representative nor the autonomy of the principal is threatened."[40]

Thus, the representative need not necessarily reflect the popular will on a day-to-day basis. But, at least, "he must not be found persistently at odds with the wishes of the represented without good reason in terms of their interest, without good explanation of why their wishes are not in accord with their interest."[41]

POLITICAL PARTICIPATION

A troublesome matter in the modern American system of representation is our relatively low rate of popular participation—our low voter-turnout rate. Many observers argue that low rates of participation in elections lessen the legitimacy of the elected government, even if few formal barriers are placed in the way of participation. Low electoral participation rates are especially troublesome when one realizes that as participation levels decline, citizens of lower socioeconomic status (SES) are much more likely to cease voting than their better-educated, better-paid fellow citizens and that the younger citizens and members of racial minorities are the least likely to vote.[42] Thus it is a matter of substantial concern that voter turnout in the 1980 national election was only 53.9 percent and that some of those voters cast votes only for President, not for Congress. The 1980 national election was the fifth consecutive one in which voter turnout declined.[43] American voter turnout is not only low in an absolute sense, it is also low compared to other Western democracies. There is some danger in assuming that the party which wins the election has won a mandate when that majority translates into active indication of support from less than a third of the nation's adults. That is especially the case when one knows that the participants in the election are not descriptively representative of the entire population and probably are not representative of the entire population in policy preferences.

Citizen Nonparticipation

The factors which lead citizens to participate or not cause a middle-class bias in the actual electorate when it is compared to the total adult population. Those citizens whose childhood and adult political socialization are least likely to lead to feelings of political efficacy and political competence or to include emphasis on political activism as a citizen's duty are those who attended schools in working-class communities, who are racial minorities, and who are low-income earners.[44] The net effect, which creates the theoretical difficulty, is that the 54 percent or so of the citizenry which goes to the polls and elects the government is not itself statistically a representative sample of the populace. A bias exists (self-selected, but the result of powerful socialization factors) against working-class and lower-income or racial-minority Americans in terms of voter turnout in the United States. The resulting government thus is much more representative of middle- and upper-income white Americans than of poor and minority Americans.

Not only is there a descriptive bias among the voters, it appears there is also an attitudinal difference between voters and nonvoters. Many nonvoters do not vote because they think it will not make any difference.[45] Nonvoters have a greater sense of helplessness and indifference. For instance, in 1976, 60 percent of them (as compared to only 40 percent of the voters) agreed with the statement, "The country needs more radical change than is possible through the ballot box."[46] Nonvoters, then, apparently are *dissatisfied* with the outputs of the political system, but do not feel that they can improve things by voting. And their nonparticipation should not necessarily be interpreted as an endorsement of politics as usual.

Greater citizen participation in American elections is possible, although not all political interests would be equally benefited by increased electoral participation.[47] Among the steps suggested for improving voter participation would be more complete and public competition in American politics—to engage the involvement of citizens and give them a clearer choice.[48] Included here would be more party and candidate clarity on issues and requirements for greater openness in public meetings and decision-making.

Greater electoral participation would also be encouraged by removing the procedural barriers which are only a minor inconvenience to middle-class citizens but loom large to lower-status citizens. Voting on the basis of identification only, without prior registration, as President Jimmy Carter suggested, would be one such step. Reductions in wealth and income disparities—through tax reform, guaranteed jobs, welfare reforms, and the like—might also improve participation rates.[49] If Daniel Webster was correct in his assertion that "A great equality of condition is the true basis, most certainly, of popular government," then achieving truly popular government may be difficult in a nation in which the wealthiest 1 percent of the people own eight times as much as the entire bottom half, and in which the top 20 percent of the population earns 41.4 percent of the income while the lowest 20 percent makes do with only 5.4 percent.[50]

A more equal *exercise* of power could be brought about by reducing the political power of money—particularly through campaign-financing reform and the provision of public financing for congressional and other campaigns, the same as is now provided for presidential campaigns. Increased public financing of campaigns would also tend to increase public competition—by giving challengers a better chance against incumbents, who now enjoy a great advantage in raising money.

Pluralism vs. Elitism

But even if greater citizen political participation could be achieved, is it desirable? One theory which seeks to explain how democracy works in America, even though a large percentage of Americans do not participate politically, is *pluralism*.[51] Pluralist theorists maintain that political power is divided among various and competing groups and organizations, and that government referees and eventually legitimizes the compromises which have been worked out by these groups. Other theorists disagree. They argue that most people do not look to organizations for realization of their political goals and that only one out of three people in America belongs to any organization which seeks to exert political influence. Low-income people, particularly, are less well represented by groups or organizations.[52] Second, it is said that organizations tend to be dominated by elites, or leaders,[53] and that, indeed, "division into elite and mass is universal,"[54] and "government is always government by the few."[55] Some scholars argue we have a "unified" elite society in which the elites are in basic agreement on most matters.[56] Others argue that there is competition within the ruling elites which permits the masses some influence.[57] In any event, contemporary elite-mass democratic theorists fall into two broad schools of thought concerning the value of participation in a democracy.

One of these schools gives great weight to stability in democracy. It relies on studies which indicate that, while people in lower socioeconomic levels tend to be liberal on economic issues, they are not liberal on issues involving civil liberties, civil rights, and democratic values.[58] This perspective suggests that the continuation of democracy depends on the "upper activist stratum" of elites who believe in, and should be trained to believe in, the "technical rules of the game by which the system operates."[59] They tend to fear that greater participation by the masses of Americans could mean a decline in the consensus or agreement on democratic ideals which they feel are necessary to democracy. Giovanni Sartori has argued that "what we have to fear . . . is that democracy—as in the myth of Saturn—may destroy its own leaders, thereby creating the conditions for their replacement by undemocratic counter-elites," or demagogues.[60] More recently, Samuel P. Huntington has argued that the "challenge to democracy" which is posed by greater participation and greater demands by citizens is potentially as serious a threat to democracy as "aristocratic cliques, fascist movements, and communist parties."[61] There is also a tendency for some scholars to redefine democracy in terms of process, thereby accepting only one aspect of Jefferson's definition, leaving out the second half, which requires that government policy reflect the will of the majority.[62]

Other democratic theorists take a normative approach to the elite-mass issue—frankly stating desirable standards for democracy. They say that there is value in the ideal of democracy, pressing America toward achievement of it, even though it has not been fully realized.[63] They maintain that theorists who argue that the stability of democratic government is founded on civil-libertarian liberalism, rather than economic liberalism, are normative too. Thus, if one assumes that democracy depends on economic liberalism—rather than on civil-libertarian elites—the conclusion would have had to be drawn that it is greater participation by the elites, not by the masses, which threatens democratic stability.[64]

These theorists also state that there is value, both for the individual and for society, in political participation. There is the "instrumental," or self-protective effect of participation, by which a participant seeks to influence public policy in his or her own self-interest.[65] Thus, if more people were more politically participant, government policy would be more likely to reflect their wishes, and government would be better informed about popular wants and desires.[66] As a result, people would more likely be allegiant to the political system, making it more stable.

Past the instrumental effect of participation, one can also cite the "developmental" effect. That is, people who participate politically gain a greater sense of "self-rule" and "self-realization," becoming fuller and more rounded human beings.[67] As J. Roland Pennock has put it, "The objective of equality (of power) is not merely the recognition of a certain dignity of the human being as such, but it is also to provide him with the opportunity—equal to that guaranteed to others—for perfecting and advancing his interests and developing his powers and personality.[68]

In short, one can argue that both society and the individuals involved would be better off as a result of greater political participation. They would agree with New York's Governor Al Smith who declared that the cures for the ills of democracy are more democracy, and with Alexis de Tocqueville, who wrote, "When I am told that the laws are weak and the population is wild, that passions are excited and virtue is paralyzed, and that in this situation it would be madness to think of increasing the rights of people, I reply that it is for these very reasons that they should be increased."

Some scholars also question the methodology and findings of those who maintain that the great mass of Americans are illiberal on civil-libertarian issues, civil-rights issues, and democratic principles. Indeed, there is good evidence that working-class Americans are as loyal to such principles as are middle-class Americans.[69] One can also argue that it is "blaming the victim" to accuse the voters of being "uninformed" when it is the elites—mainly the candidates and public officials—who often try to prevent the people from knowing what their stands on issues are.[70] It is also "blaming the victim" to say that the masses can't be trusted to support democratic regimes, when the regimes have failed to act on the serious economic problems faced by a majority of the citizens.[71]

The late Kalman H. Silvert declared that lower voter turnout in the United States signals dissatisfaction, not satisfaction, with the way government is performing and that more people would participate if they felt that it would make a difference in government performance and policy.[72] He and like-minded democratic theorists maintain that government would be more stable and more responsive to citizen desires if more people participated, and that the citizens themselves would become "better" people as a result of their political participation.

SUMMARY

It is important to understand *representation* in all of its various aspects: formal representation (Is the consent of the governed given or withheld?); descriptive representation (Does the legislature mirror the characteristics of the population?); symbolic representation (Is our legislator on "our side?"); and substantive representation (Is the representative acting in our interest on the various issues the legislature decides and should a legislator be a delegate or a trustee?). Much of what follows in subsequent chapters relates to these various dimensions of representation. If it is to be said in America that "the people" elect public officials and that government policy reflects the will of the people, then it is necessary to place a greater emphasis on widespread citizen political participation. Otherwise the effective electorate will continue to be biased in favor of middle- and upper-class citizens.

Notes

1. See, generally, Saul K. Padover, *The Meaning of Democracy* (New York: Praeger, 1963).

2. Carl L. Becker, *The Declaration of Independence* (New York: Vintage Books, 1958), p. 25.

3. Jefferson to Samuel Kercheval, January 12, 1816, in Saul K. Padover, *The Complete Jefferson* (New York: Duell, Sloan, and Pierce, 1943), p. 288.

4. Ibid.

5. See, generally, Hanna F. Pitkin, *The Concept of Representation* (Berkeley: University of California Press, 1967), pp. 38–59. In regard to the representational functions of Congress, see David J. Vogler, *The Politics of Congress,* 2nd ed. (Boston: Allyn and Bacon, 1977), pp. 6–13.

6. Thomas Hobbes, *Leviathan* (New York: Collier Books, 1962), p. 127.

7. Andrew Hacker, *Congressional Districting: The Issue of Representation* (Washington, D.C.: Brookings Institution, 1963), p. 2.

8. Daniel P. Grant and H. C. Nixon, *State and Local Government in America,* 3rd ed. (Boston: Allyn and Bacon, 1975), p. 250.

9. 369 U.S. 186 (1962).

10. Quoted in Pitkin, *The Concept of Representation,* p. 60.

11. *The Federalist,* Number 35, ed. E. M. Earle (New York: Modern Library, 1937), p. 214.

12. A. Phillips Griffiths and Richard Wollheim, "How Can One Person Represent Another?" Aristotelian Society, supplementary vol. 34 (1960), p. 190.

13. *Congressional Quarterly Weekly Report,* November 8, 1980, p. 3303; and January 24, 1981, pp. 198–200. The nonvoting delegate from the District of Columbia is also black.

14. Samuel Krislov, *Representative Bureaucracy* (Englewood Cliffs, N.J.: Prentice-Hall, 1974), p. 130.

15. Pitkin, *The Concept of Representation,* pp. 92–111.

16. Richard F. Fenno, Jr., *Homestyle: House Members in Their Districts* (Boston: Little, Brown, 1978), Chapter 3.

17. Quoted in Charles L. Clapp, *The Congressman: His Work as He Sees It* (Washington, D.C.: Brookings Institution, 1963), p. 421.

18. Fenno, *Homestyle;* pp. 239–40.

19. Murray Edelman, *The Symbolic Uses of Politics* (Champaign-Urbana: University of Illinois Press, 1967).

20. Pitkin, *The Concept of Representation,* p. 209.

21. Hanna F. Pitkin, "Commentary: The Paradox of Representation," in *Representation,* ed. J. Roland Pennock and John W. Chapman (New York: Atherton Press, 1968), p. 46.

22. Pitkin, *The Concept of Representation,* pp. 211–212.

23. See Mareck Sobolewski, "Electors and Representatives: A Contribution to the Theory of Representation," in Pennock and Chapman, *Representation,* p. 96.

24. Emanuel Cellar, "Pressure Groups in Congress," *Annals of the American Academy of Political and Social Sciences* 319 (1958): 1.

25. Hilaire Belloc and G. K. Chesterson, *The Party System* (London: S. Swift, 1911), p. 17.

26. Quoted in Lewis Anthony Dexter, "The Representative and His District," in *New Perspectives on the House of Representatives,* ed. Robert Peabody and Nelson W. Polsby (Chicago: Rand McNally, 1969), p. 6.

27. Ross J. S. Hoffman and Paul Levack, eds., *Burke's Politics: Selected Writings and Speeches of Edmund Burke on Reform, Revolution and War* (New York: Alfred A. Knopf, 1969), p. 6.

28. Donald J. McCrone and James H. Kuklinski, "The Delegate Theory of Representation," *American Journal of Political Science* 23, no. 2 (May 1979):282.

29. See Philip E. Converse, "The Nature of Belief Systems in Mass Publics," in *Ideology and Discontent,* ed. David Apter (New York: Free Press, 1964); and Sidney Verba and Richard A. Brody, "Participation, Policy Preferences and the War in Vietnam," *Public Opinion Quarterly* 18 (1965): 325–32.

30. Roberta Sigel and H. Paul Frisema, "Urban Community Leader's Knowledge of Public Opinion," *Western Politics Quarterly* 18 (1965): 881–95.

31. Warren Miller and Donald Stokes, "Constituency Influence in Congress," *American Political Science Review* 57 (1963): 45–46.

32. Vogler, *The Politics of Congress,* p. 85.

33. See, for example, Robert V. Bartlett, "The Marginality Hypothesis: Electoral Insecurity, Self-Interest, and Voting Behavior," *American Politics Quarterly* 7 (October 1979): 498–507; Robert S. Erikson and Gerald C. Wright, Jr., "Electoral Marginality and Congressional Representation," (Paper delivered at the Annual Meeting of the American Political Science Association, New York, 1978); and Walter J. Stone, "The Dynamics of Constituency: Electoral Control in the House," *American Politics Quarterly* 8 (October 1980): 399–424.

34. Morris P. Fiorina, "Electoral Margins, Constituency Influence, and Policy Moderation: A Critical Assessment," *American Politics Quarterly* 1 (October 1973): 478–98.

35. Eric A. Nordlinger, "Representation, Governmental Stability, and Decisional Effectiveness," in Pennock and Chapman, *Representation,* p. 110.

36. Jacques Ellul, *Propaganda* (New York: Alfred A. Knopf, 1965), p. 124.

37. Vogler, *The Politics of Congress,* pp. 88–92.

38. Pitkin, *The Concept of Representation,* p. 233.

39. James Wilson, *Works,* ed. James Andrews (Chicago: Collaghan and Company, 1896), 1: 389.

40. B. J. Diggs, "Practical Representation," in Pennock and Chapman, *Representation,* p. 37.

41. Pitkin, *The Concept of Representation,* pp. 209–10.

42. Sidney Verba and Norman H. Nie, *Participation in America: Political Democracy and Social Equality* (New York: Harper and Row, 1972).

43. *Congressional Quarterly Weekly Report,* April 25, 1981, p. 716.

44. See Angus Campbell, Phillip E. Converse, Warren E. Miller, and Donald E. Stokes, *The American Voter* (New York: John Wiley, 1960); Norman H. Nie, Sidney Verba, and John R. Petrocik, *The Changing American Voter* (Cambridge, Mass.: Harvard University Press, 1976); Warren E. Miller and Theresa E. Levitan, *Leadership and Change* (Cambridge, Mass.: Winthrop, 1976); and Edgar Litt, "Civic Education, Community Norms, and Political Indoctrination," *American Sociological Review* 28 (1963): 69–75.

45. James D. Wright, "Alienation and Political Negativism: New Evidence From National Survey," *Sociology and Social Research* 60, no. 2 (January 1976): III.

46. *New York Times*/CBS News Poll, November 16, 1976.

47. See Peter Bachrach, *The Theory of Democratic Elitism: A Critique* (Boston: Little, Brown, 1967); Carol Pateman, *Participation and Democratic Theory* (London: Cambridge University Press, 1970); and Robert A. Dahl, "On Removing Certain Impediments to Democracy in the United States," *Political Science Quarterly* 92, no. 12 (Spring 1977): 1–8.

48. E. E. Schattschneider, *The Semisovereign People* (New York: Holt, Rinehart, and Winston, 1960), pp. 141–42; Richard F. Hamilton, *Class and Politics in the U.S.* (New York: John Wiley, 1972), pp. 59–60.

49. Regarding the value of the democratic ideal in moving America toward equality in terms of both access to power and exercise of power, see J. Roland Pennock, "Democracy and Leadership," in *Democracy Today,* ed. William Chambers and Robert Salisbury (New York: Collier Books, 1962), p. 127.

50. Robert Lekachman, *Economists at Bay* (New York: McGraw-Hill, 1976), p. 57; and U.S. Bureau of the Census, *Current Population Reports,* Series P-60, no. 105 (Washington, D.C.: U.S. Government Printing Office, 1976), p. 406.

51. See David B. Truman, *The Governmental Process* (New York: Alfred A. Knopf, 1951); and Robert Dahl, *Who Governs?* (New Haven, Conn.: Yale University Press, 1961).

52. Hamilton, *Class and Politics in the United States,* pp. 34–36; and Schattschneider, *The Semisovereign People,* p. 35.

53. E. H. Carr, *New Society* (Boston: Beacon Press, 1951), p. 72; Robert Michels, *Political Parties* (1913: reprint ed., Glencoe, Ill.: Free Press, 1949) refers to the regular domination of organizations by elites as "the iron law of oligarchy."

54. Harold Lasswell and Abraham Kaplan, *Power and Society* (New Haven, Conn.: Yale University Press, 1960), p. 219.

55. Harold Lasswell and Daniel Lerner et al., *The Comparative Study of Elites* (Stanford, Calif.: Stanford University Press, 1959), p. 7.

56. C. Wright Mills, *The Power Elite* (New York: Oxford University Press, 1956): and G. William Domhof, *Who Rules America?* (Englewood Cliffs, N.J.: Prentice-Hall, 1967).

57. Raymond Aron, "Social Structure and the Ruling Class," *The British Journal of Sociology* 1 (March 1950): 10; Robert A. Dahl, *Pluralist Democracy in the United States* (Chicago: Rand McNally, 1967); and Dahl, *Who Governs?*

58. Seymour M. Lipset, *Political Man* (Garden City, N.Y.: Doubleday, Anchor Books, 1963), p. 92.

59. V. O. Key, Jr., *Public Opinion and Democracy* (New York: Alfred A. Knopf, 1961), p. 155; and Robert Dahl, *A Preface to Democratic Theory* (Chicago: University of Chicago Press, 1967), p. 77.

60. Giovanni Sartori, *Democratic Theory* (Detroit, Mich.: Wayne State University Press, 1969), p. 119.

61. Michael J. Crozier, Samuel P. Huntington, and Joji Watanuki, *The Crisis of Democracy: Report on the Governability of Democracies to the Trilateral Commission* (New York: New York University Press, 1975), pp. 59–60.

62. Joseph Schumpeter, *Capitalism, Socialism, and Democracy* (New York: Harper and Brothers, 1960), p. 269; Austin Ranney and Wilmore E. Kendall, "Basic Principles for a Model of Democracy," in *Empirical Democratic Theory,* ed. Charles F. Cnudde and Deane E. Neubauer (Chicago: Markham, 1969), pp. 41–63.

63. Bachrach, *The Theory of Democratic Elitism,* pp. 6, 86–87.

64. Bachrach, *The Theory of Democratic Elitism,* pp. 93–94. See, also, Pateman, *Participation and Democratic Theory,* pp. 15–16; and Jack L. Walker, "A Critique of the Elitist Theory of

Democracy," in *Political Elites in a Democracy,* ed. Peter Bachrach (New York: Atherton Press, 1971), p. 71.

65. Bachrach, *The Theory of Democratic Elitism,* pp. 94, 98–99; and J. Roland Pennock, in *Participation in Politics,* ed. J. Roland Pennock and J. W. Chapman (New York: Leiber-Atherton, 1975), p. 71.

66. Geraint Parry, ed., *Participation in Politics* (Manchester, England: Manchester University Press, 1979), pp. 19–20.

67 Geraint Parry, "The Idea of Participation," in Parry, *Participation in Politics,* pp. 26–38.

68. J. Roland Pennock, "Democracy and Leadership," in Chambers and Salisbury, *Democracy Today,* pp. 126–27.

69. Richard F. Hamilton, *Class and Politics in the United States,* pp. 135, 456–57.

70. Ibid., pp. 59–60.

71. See Max Lerner, *It Is Later Than You Think* (New York: Viking Press, 1943); Alan Bullock, *Hitler: A Study in Tyranny* (London: Harper and Row, 1954), pp. 253–55; and Carl Becker, *Modern Democracy* (New Haven, Conn.: Yale University Press, 1941), p. 67.

72. Kalman H. Silvert, *The Reason for Democracy* (New York: Viking Press, 1977), p. 44.

chapter 3

Legislative Structures and Powers

Preview

Both American national government and the fifty state governments are organized according to the "separation-of-powers" principle, with separate executive, judicial, and legislative branches each having its own stipulated powers. Except for Nebraska, the legislatures are all bicameral and organized by political parties. The vice-president presides over the U.S. Senate, and in most states the lieutenant governor presides over the state senate. With those exceptions, American legislators choose their own leaders from among their membership and normally do so along party lines. All American legislatures make extensive use of committees to perform their work, and some types of committees are much more important than others. All American legislatures are also sites of substantial independent power within the government, in large part because of the legislatures' control over taxation and spending policies. There are many similarities, then, among the fifty state legislatures and between the state legislatures and Congress. But there are many differences as well, both between the Congressional pattern and the states and among the various state legislatures. Those differences often are not as obvious as the similarities, but they are every bit as important.

American legislative structures and powers have their origins in the history of legislative bodies, though they have changed and developed over time. Structural factors—the terms of members, leadership roles and responsibilities, internal organization, committees, and staff—and the overall powers and restraints on powers of state and national legislatures are basic considerations in understanding the importance and functions of American legislatures.

CONGRESS

The U.S. Congress is a *bicameral* legislative body. That is, it consists of two legislative chambers, the House of Representatives and the Senate. The bicameral nature of the national legislature was, in part, the result of colonial experience, which caused the founding fathers to distrust concentrations of power. It was also partly the result of a compromise between the large and small states. Of course, the bicameral legislatures in the various American states and in the British Parliament furnished a readily adaptable pattern, too.

The Articles of Confederation had provided for a Congress in which each of the states had equal voting power, regardless of population. The small-state delegates to the Constitutional Convention wanted to continue that equality of the states in the national legislature. They feared that the new government would be dominated by the more heavily populated states. Delegates from the larger states, on the other hand, wanted a national legislature in which the large states would have a greater voice than the smaller states. After extensive debate and negotiations on this issue, the Convention agreed to a *bicameral* legislature in which one chamber would represent the states on the basis of their population and the other would represent the states on an equal basis no matter what their population. This plan was called the *Connecticut Compromise* because of the strong support the Connecticut delegates gave it. The Connecticut Compromise also provided that each slave be counted as three fifths of a free person for purposes of determining representation in the U.S. House of Representatives—a fundamental concession to the southern states.[1]

Every state, regardless of population, has two U.S. senators. Originally, senators were elected by the state legislatures. The Seventeenth Amendment to the Constitution, passed in 1913, changed that, providing for direct election of senators by the people. When the legislature of each state chose its U.S. senators, the Senate was removed one step from the people. This made it clear that senators represented their states, not the people directly.[2]

From the first, U.S. representatives have been elected directly by the people—with citizens who are eligible to vote for the lower house of their own state legislature also eligible to vote for U.S. representatives. Article I, Section 2, of the U.S. Constitution guarantees each state at least one seat in the U.S. House of Representatives, with additional seats apportioned on the basis of population. In the 1970s, for example, Alaska, Delaware, Nevada, North Dakota, Vermont, and Wyoming each had only one U.S. representative—but, of course, two U.S. senators. California, on the other hand, had forty-three representatives, New York had thirty-nine, Pennsylvania had twenty-five, and Illinois and Texas had twenty-four each. Each of the more populous states, however, had the same number of U.S. senators as the sparsely populated states—two. The Constitution requires redistribution of House seats every ten years, following the census. The 1980 census resulted in more House seats for California, Florida, Texas, and some other "Sunbelt" and western states, but fewer seats for Illinois, New York, Ohio, Pennsylvania, and some other "Frostbelt" states.[3]

The U.S. House of Representatives

Members of the U.S. House of Representatives must be at least twenty-five years old and must have been U.S. citizens for at least seven years. U.S. representatives are normally referred to as *congressmen* or *congresswomen,* terms which technically include all members of Congress, representatives and senators alike. However, U.S. Senators, of course, prefer to be called *senators.*

The first House of Representatives, meeting in 1789, contained 65 members. As America's growing population moved West, Congress, by statute, periodically increased the membership of the House to aid the eastern states which otherwise would have lost representatives after each census. The process of increasing total House membership to aid certain states continued until 1913, when the House reached its present size. Congress then fixed the size of the House at 435 members, with the understanding that, with future shifts in population, some states would lose representatives. A temporary increase to 437 representatives was made in the late 1950s, when Alaska and Hawaii became states, but in 1960 the House returned to 435 members.[4]

Term of Office   U.S. representatives serve two-year terms. All 435 members of the House must seek reelection in November of every even-numbered year. In forty-five states, state and county officials are elected at the same election as are members of the U.S. House. The President is elected at every other Congressional election. A representative from one of the half dozen least populous states must run statewide, since those states have only one seat each in the House. Representatives from states entitled to two or more seats in the House are elected from Congressional districts. Each Congressional district elects one U.S. representative and, since *Wesberry* v. *Sanders* (1964) was decided by the U.S. Supreme Court, each district in a state must contain approximately the same number of people.[5]

The writers of our Constitution purposely kept the term of office for U.S. representatives relatively short, in order to keep the House in touch with popular opinion. James Madison argued for a three-year term, to give representatives time to learn about the needs and interests of other states. Elbridge Gerry and many other delegates to the Constitutional Convention, on the other hand, wanted annual elections (which were common at the time for state legislators) as a defense against tyranny. It was said that a short term would "force the representatives to return home and mix with the people" and would keep them accountable.[6] Constitutional framers eventually compromised on two-year terms.

In recent years, proposals have been made to lengthen the House term to four years—a change that would require a constitutional amendment (thus requiring concurrence by the U.S. Senate as well as three-fourths of the states). The U.S. Senate is unlikely to approve the four-year representative term for a number of reasons, one being that U.S. senators may not want to make it easier for ambitious House members in their states to run against them.[7] Presently, a House member who runs for the Senate must give up his or her House seat, since both offices come up for election at the same time. If a representative had a four-year term, on the other hand, he or she would have the opportunity to run for the U.S. Senate in the middle of the House term. This could increase the number of representatives willing to seek promotion to the Senate, increasing the electoral vulnerability of incumbent senators.

A more serious reason for objecting to longer House terms is, of course, one voiced by the framers of the Constitution—a desire to keep the House sensitive to the opinions of ordinary people. Another objection to a four-year term for House members is that Congress would not necessarily continue to be independent of the President. Most proposals for a four-year House term would require that the entire House be elected at the same time as the President. If that were done, some "coattail" effect of a presidential campaign might always be present when the House was elected.[8]

Presently, there is little agitation in the House for a four-year term, partly because few feel such a proposal has a chance of passage.[9] The lack of agitation for a longer term is also the result of the fact that most U.S. representatives today are from "safe" districts: they regularly win reelection by 55 percent or more of the vote.[10]

Still, the two-year House term does cause many representatives to feel that they are almost constantly campaigning. Some observers argue that this causes representatives to be less interested in legislation and more interested in constituency relationships and "casework"—helping constituents, people in the home district, resolve problems with federal agencies, such as the Veterans Administration or the Social Security Administration.[11]

Because the entire House of Representatives must be elected every two years, each Congress lasts two years. The First Congress met in 1789 and 1790. The Second Congress, elected in the fall of 1790, met in 1791 and 1792. The Ninety-eighth Congress, elected in 1982, convened in January 1983, to serve until the Ninety-ninth Congress convenes in January 1985. Each Congress is divided into a first and second session, with a break in between at Christmas. A bill must pass during the Congress in which it was introduced, or it dies. Sponsors may, of course, introduce the bill again during the following Congress. Thus, because of the many probable points of delay in the route a bill must travel on the way to becoming law, it usually has a better chance of passage if it is introduced early in the first session of a Congress.

House Leaders   The U.S. House of Representatives, like the U.S. Senate and forty-nine of the fifty state legislatures, is elected and organized on a partisan basis. The Speaker of the House, elected by the entire chamber, presides over the House and is its most important member. The Speaker is also the majority party's top leader. Party discipline on the vote for Speaker insures that the nominee of the majority party is elected Speaker. The majority party also selects a majority leader (who is second in the party hierarchy) and a majority whip. The minority party's top leader is the minority leader, assisted by the minority whip. The leaders are chosen by their respective party caucuses. Each party also has a chairperson of its caucus (or conference, as the Republicans call their caucus), a policy committee, and/or a committee on committees.[12] These positions and committees will be considered in greater detail in subsequent chapters.

The United States Senate

The United States Senate consists of one hundred senators, two from each state. A senator's term of office is six years—with thirty-three or thirty-four Senate terms expiring every two years. Americans who are at least thirty years old and who have been citizens for at least nine years may serve in the U.S. Senate. While some senators represent less than half a million citizens, others represent over twenty-five million citizens.

The States as Equals   The Senate is the decision-making site of the federal government where the thinly populated states have their strongest voice, since each state's Senate delegation is the same size. The importance of the U.S. Senate in looking out for the interests of the small states is pointed up, for example, by the fact that federal revenue sharing, by which federal funds are distributed to the states, was set up in such a way as to give greater monies to the small states than they would have received had the distribution been based upon state population alone.[13]

Senate Leaders   The Senate has no single office with powers analogous to those of the Speaker of the House. Article I, Section 3, of the U.S. Constitution makes the vice-president of the United States the president of the Senate. But the vice-president does not normally preside over Senate proceedings. The vice-president has no Senate vote, except to break a tie. In the absence of the vice-president, the Senate president pro tempore (usually called the president pro tem) has the right to preside, but, usually, a junior senator is called upon to serve as temporary presiding officer, as a boring, almost "pledge" chore. The most senior member of the majority party is, by custom, elected president pro tem. Neither the office of president of the Senate nor that of president pro tem provides its incumbent with much power in the Senate, although the president pro tem may individually be a powerful senator.

The most powerful single Senate leader ordinarily is the majority leader, who is chosen by the majority party caucus.[14] The majority leader looks out for his party's interests in the Senate and dominates the scheduling of the Senate's floor business, in consultation with the minority leader. As will be discussed in Chapter 13, the majority leader's control of the scheduling of Senate business can result in substantial dominance of policy decisions.

The majority party also elects a majority whip, who assists the majority leader. As is the case in the House, the main responsibility of the whip and the assistant whips is to find out which senators support or oppose the party leadership on the more important bills and to keep the majority leader apprised of such information. The whip organization is also responsible for insuring the attendance of supporting senators for key votes on the floor of the Senate.

The minority-party caucus (or conference, as the Senate Republicans call their caucus) elects a minority leader and a minority whip. The minority leader represents the party's interests, marshals support for the party's position on each issue, and insures that the minority party's criticism of majority-party performance is put on record. The minority leader also speaks for the President, if a member of the President's party. The minority whip's duties are similar to those of the majority whip.

The majority leader and minority leader are the dominant figures within their respective Senate parties, although the leaders of the standing committees of the Senate have substantial power as well. Each party has an organized caucus or conference and party committees to determine party policy positions and to decide which senators will be assigned to which committees.

Congressional Committees

The American national government has become extremely complex. One consequence of the government's growth and complexity is that thousands of bills and resolutions are introduced in each Congress. Most fail to be enacted into law. But Congress could not possibly consider in detail all measures introduced, without some way of dividing up the work. Subsequent chapters will show how the mechanisms for dividing the workload affect the decisions of Congress. It should be noted here, however, that when a bill or resolution is introduced in Congress, it is referred to a committee for detailed examination. Most bills never even emerge from committee. Those which are reported out of committee are usually amended (changed). Once out of committee, the bill must win the approval of the entire chamber (in a floor vote), win approval of the appropriate committee in the other chamber, and then win approval on the floor of the other chamber. Furthermore, each bill must pass both chambers in exactly the same language. So, even if the House and Senate are in general agreement on a subject, a relatively minor difference of opinion between the two chambers may delay the passage of a bill, or even defeat a low-priority bill.

There are four types of Congressional committees: standing committees, select committees, joint committees, and conference committees (all of which will be discussed at length in Chapter 10). In the Ninety-seventh Congress, in 1982, the Senate had fifteen standing committees and the House had twenty-two. In addition, the

Senate and the House each had five select committees. There were four joint committees.

The standing committees of each chamber are the most important, although some are much more important than others. These are permanent committees which exist in every Congress and have clearly defined subject-matter jurisdictions. These are the committees which consider most of the business of Congress and submit legislation to the floor of the chamber. Each standing committee has several subcommittees. The chairs of the standing committees are figures of substantial power and prestige in Congress.

Select committees sometimes last through several Congresses but, technically, are not permanent committees. They are created to study a particular problem or a set of related problems which are not being addressed satisfactorily by the standing committees. Select committees sometimes develop proposals which result in legislation, but frequently do not have the authority to submit legislation to the floor of the chamber, and, instead, must have their legislative proposals considered by appropriate standing committees.

Joint committees, in contrast to select and standing committees, include *both* representatives and senators as members. Joint committees make recommendations to both chambers but do not report legislation to the floor of either chamber. They have very little power, when compared to the standing committees of each house.

Congressional Compensation

In 1980, each U.S. representative and senator received a salary of $60,662 per year, plus a stationary allowance, free mailing privileges for official business (the "frank"), ample allowances for long-distance telephone calls, office space in the home district and in Washington, numerous paid trips home annually to stay in touch with constituents, and fringe benefits including recreation facilities, life and medical insurance, and a retirement plan. To the average American, such a compensation package looks very attractive. Many members of Congress, however (especially those without outside income), find it difficult to meet their expenses of maintaining two homes, entertaining, and supporting their families at the level they feel they should.[15] Some leave Congress because they feel they cannot afford to stay.

Privileges and Immunities of Members of Congress

It is generally considered to be in the public interest for Congressional debate to be full and robust, rather than timid and limited to safe subjects. If members of Congress had to fear a slander or libel lawsuit every time they inquired into or discussed a subject, many fundamental and serious questions might not be asked and much-needed legislation might not be enacted. For that reason, Article I, Section 6, of the Constitution provides "for any Speech or Debate in either House, they shall not be questioned in any other Place." There are no legal limits, then, on what a senator or representative may say on the floor or in committee sessions. Informal norms of Congressional behavior do, in fact, ordinarily provide certain restraints of propriety on Congressional remarks, but "Congressional immunity" gives members of Congress important freedom in the exercise of their powers.

Less important today, but still worthy of note, is another provision of this same constitutional section: "They shall in all Cases, except Treason, Felony and Breach of the Peace, be privileged from Arrest during their Attendance at the Session of their respective Houses, and in going to and returning from the same." Our national legislators thus may criticize the executive without fear of being suddenly jailed for such criticism.

Members of Congress also suffer a restriction in regard to their possible appointment to federal office. Again, Article I, Section 6, of the Constitution provides that:

> No Senator or Representative shall, during the Time for which he was elected, be appointed to any Civil Office under Authority of the United States, which shall have been created, or the Emoluments whereof shall have been increased during such time; no Person holding any Office under the United States, shall be a Member of either House during his Continuance in Office.

Members of Congress, then, who accept cabinet appointments must resign from Congress. Thus, Melvin Laird of Wisconsin was required to vacate his House seat in order to accept President Nixon's appointment as secretary of defense in 1969. Some senators have refused cabinet appointments because they did not want to have to resign from the Senate.[16] Edmund Muskie of Maine did do so, however, when he was named by President Carter to the position of secretary of state in 1980. In the prohibition against simultaneous legislative and executive service, the U.S. political system differs dramatically from parliamentary systems (such as Britain and Canada); in those political systems, an aspirant for the post of minister of defense must first get *into* the national legislature.

POWERS OF CONGRESS

The U.S. Congress is unusual among national, bicameral legislative bodies in that the upper and lower chambers of the legislature have substantially equal power, although each chamber has some special power not shared by the other. As noted earlier, all legislation passed by Congress must be approved, in exactly the same language, by both chambers before it becomes law. In contrast, the British House of Lords has only the seldom-exercised power to delay for up to thirteen months the effective date of legislation passed in two successive sessions by the House of Commons, and does not have even that power over "money bills" (for taxation and appropriation).[17] The Bundesrat, the upper chamber in the Federal Republic of Germany (West Germany), more closely approaches the U.S. Senate in its legislative role. In contrast to the popularly elected Bundestag (lower chamber), the forty-five members of the Bundesrat are selected by the various state (länder) governments, three to five per state, depending on population. The Bundesrat's major purpose is to protect the states in the federal system, and the Bundesrat may reject proposals passed by the Bundestag. Such rejections are final on proposed legislation concerning the powers of state government. Bundesrat rejections of other legislation may be overridden by the Bundestag, but a two-thirds vote of the Bundestag is required if two thirds of the Bundesrat objects to the proposed legislation. Often, the Joint Mediation Committee, composed of members from both chambers, is able to arrive at a version of proposed legislation that is satisfactory to both chambers. This happens both on bills for which the Bundesrat's rejection is final and on bills where the Bundesrat's veto can be overridden.[18]

The U.S. government is a government of delegated powers—powers delegated by the states to the national government, through the U.S. Constitution. The Constitution divides the powers of the national government among the legislative, executive, and judicial branches—with some sharing of powers and with the various branches of the government each able to check the others. The American structure of government embodies a separation of institutions and a sharing of powers, rather than a clear-cut separation of powers.

For a law passed by Congress to be held constitutional, there must be more than a demonstration that the U.S. Constitution does not *forbid* the enactment of such a law; since Congress is the legislature of a government of delegated powers, there must also be a demonstration that Congress is *authorized* to enact such a law.[19] Article I, Section 8, of the U.S. Constitution provides two types of such authority: a set of *express,* or stated or enumerated, powers; and less clearly specified, *implied* powers. The first seventeen clauses of Article I, Section 8, contain express delegations of authority to Congress. These express powers include the power to levy taxes; to borrow and spend money; to regulate commerce with foreign nations, among the states, and with the Indian tribes (the commerce clause); to coin money; to establish a post office and post roads; to declare war; to maintain the armed services; and to establish federal courts inferior to the U.S. Supreme Court. Each of the express powers has, of course, been clarified over time, through executive and Congressional action and by court decisions. Especially important in this respect is the commerce clause, which has been the constitutional basis for much of the domestic-policy legislation of the past half century.

The eighteenth clause of Article I Section 8 (often called the "necessary-and-proper" clause), is the source of the *implied powers* of Congress. This clause gives Congress the power to:

> make all laws which shall be necessary and proper for carrying into execution the foregoing powers, and all other Powers vested by this Constitution in the Government of the United States, or in any Department or Officer thereof.

The relationship of the necessary-and-proper clause to the seventeen clauses preceding it (the express powers) has been a continuing source of controversy between advocates of an activist national government and those who want a more restricted national government. The controversy was of major importance in the First Congress, where the debate on the issue was focused on Alexander Hamilton's plan to create a national bank. The Constitutional Convention had discussed giving the new national government the power to create corporations but had rejected the idea. Nor did the Constitution contain express authorization for Congress to create a bank. After much debate, a bill creating a national bank was passed by the First Congress and sent to the President.

President Washington invited Thomas Jefferson, who was opposed to the creation of a national bank, to submit arguments why the President should veto the bill. Jefferson stressed the "necessary" of the necessary-and-proper clause, pointing out that all of the express powers of the national government could be accomplished without the creation of a national bank. Therefore, argued Jefferson, the national government was not authorized to create a national bank.

Alexander Hamilton was invited to submit arguments in support of the bank bill. He maintained that the constitutional grant of power to Congress gave Congress the right to employ "all the means requisite and fairly applicable to the attainment of the ends of such power," within the constraints of morality and unless the means were specifically forbidden by the Constitution. Hamilton's arguments in favor of a broad interpretation of Congressional power carried the day, and President Washington signed the bank bill into law.[20]

Hamilton's broad interpretation of the necessary-and-proper clause, generally called the doctrine of implied power, was adopted by the U.S. Supreme Court in 1819 in the case of *McCulloch* v. *Maryland* and is accepted constitutional doctrine today, giving Congress great power to legislate in the area of domestic affairs. *Mc-*

Culloch v. *Maryland* centered on the questions of whether the national government did, indeed, have the power to establish a bank and whether Maryland could tax a branch of that bank. The Supreme Court ruled in support of the implied power of the government to charter a bank. The ruling went against the state of Maryland since the bank as a federal instrument was protected from state interference in the form of a tax.

Lawmaking Power

Article I, Section 1, of the U.S. Constitution states that "All legislative Powers herein granted shall be vested in a Congress of the United States, which shall consist of a Senate and House of Representatives." Congress exercises this legislative, or lawmaking, power to establish overall national policy. By passing laws, Congress may, for example, decide whether the United States will have a military draft, whether a high or low priority will be placed on further space exploration, or whether much of Alaska's wilderness will remain untouched or opened to development. Of course, the executive and judicial branches also make policy, but the framers of the Constitution expected, and most Americans today expect, that the fundamental policy decisions of the national government will be made, or at least legitimized, by the Congress.

The constitutional allocation of powers to the legislative, executive, and judicial branches of the national government should not be interpreted as having eliminated any disputes among them concerning their respective spheres of authority. Rather, the Constitution provides a framework within which the various branches of government struggle over the extent to which each should influence or dominate the making of fundamental national policy. The legislature and the executive have each been dominant in different periods of American history. Although there were degrees of differences, the executive generally dominated Congress from the first administration of President Franklin D. Roosevelt, during which the nation grappled with the Great Depression, on through the administrations of Presidents Lyndon B. Johnson and Richard M. Nixon. Even when FDR was President, however, Congress repeatedly frustrated administration attempts to pass fundamental social legislation, especially after Roosevelt's first reelection.

Congressional and public reaction to the handling of the Vietnam War by Presidents Johnson and Nixon and to the Watergate scandal, which eventually caused President Nixon to resign, led to greater Congressional aggressiveness in asserting its policymaking authority. Because the executive authority at the national level is concentrated, while authority in the Congress is fragmented, and because the executive department often has better access to information, can command greater national attention, and has a national, rather than a parochial focus, the executive branch is likely to continue to overshadow Congress. Still, as President Carter discovered, Congress can demonstrate great independence and authority, and can successfully challenge the executive. That became especially evident during President Nixon's second term.

The grant of all lawmaking power, along with the express or enumerated powers delegated to Congress, makes the Congress a formidable center of power within the national government. Most of the powers of Congress are exercised through the enactment of legislation—including legislation that establishes public policy (such as the Price-Anderson Act, which limits the liability of utility companies, if a nuclear-power-plant accident occurs), that appropriates money, and that levies taxes.

Fiscal Powers

The national government can spend money only after Congress has authorized the expenditure of the money for a particular purpose and has appropriated money, subsequent to the authorization. That fact means that Congress can control the "purse strings" of the national government. However, following the Great Depression and World War II, as the complexity of our government grew, Congress began to rely more heavily on the executive branch to pull together the budget requests of the various federal agencies and to evaluate the relative merits of those budget requests.[21] Congress then adjusted the numbers up or down a bit, but the focus of discussion was the President's budget recommendations prepared by his budgetmakers in the Office of Management and Budget (OMB). In essence, then, Congress had abdicated to the executive branch much of its power over the priorities and actions of the national government, since for the most part the priorities expressed in the executive budget tended to survive marginal adjustments made in Congress. That has not been true in all policy areas all of the time, of course. The appropriations committees of Congress are very powerful. On specific policy issues where the committee has disagreed strongly with the executive branch, such as on foreign-aid funding levels, presidents have found their powers of office inadequate. The committees often prevail.[22] Control of the budget is not just a technical matter. Control of the budget carries with it control over what kind of policies the government will pursue and how vigorously various goals will be pursued. Control of the budget is very nearly control of the government.

The *fiscal policy* adopted by Congress can dramatically affect the nation's economy. In times when consumer or investor spending is low and unemployment is, because of a lack of consumer demand, high, Congress may authorize greater government spending, or reduced taxes, or both, to stimulate spending for consumer goods and investment purposes. In times when consumer and investor spending is high, especially when too much consumer money is chasing too few goods, producing what is called "demand-pull" inflation, Congress can reduce government spending, or raise taxes, or both, to take more money out of the economy, reducing demand. In seeking to hold down the rate of inflation, Congress could also authorize the President to administer wage and price controls as a tool of economic management. *Monetary power* is exercised for the most part by the largely independent Federal Reserve Bank. The "Fed" operates under a broad grant of authority from the Congress. Its chairperson and board members are appointed by the President, subject to confirmation by the U.S. Senate. The Fed controls the size and growth rate of the nation's money supply, and, thus, interest rates also. The Fed usually goes along with the economic policies of the President, although it does not have to. It affects the money supply by buying or selling bonds out of its own portfolio—soaking money up out of private bank accounts when it sells, freeing more private money when it buys. It can also raise or lower the discount rate which member banks must pay when they borrow from the Fed, pledging notes the member banks hold—making loans easier or harder to get, thereby expanding or contracting the money supply. The Fed may also affect the money supply by the reserve requirements it sets for member banks, which determines the percentage of a bank's holdings the member banks may loan to customers. Congress could, itself, legislate more specifically about the size and growth rate of the nation's money supply, but it has largely chosen not to do so.

Spending power. Decisions by Congress in regard to spending can have three important effects. The *fiscal effect* can influence the rate of unemployment and inflation, as noted earlier. The *regulatory effect* can influence the behavior of individuals and corporations—as through cash-loan subsidies to farmers or local or regional airlines. The *distributional effect* can take money from one group and give it to another.

Article II, Section 3, of the Constitution directs the President to "take Care that the Laws be faithfully executed." An appropriations act is a law, and the executive branch is required to faithfully execute an appropriations act. Nobody wants to waste money, of course, so if a program to build a new highway should actually cost several hundreds of thousands of dollars less than anticipated in the appropriations act, the President is expected to be fiscally prudent and "impound" the left over money—achieving the objective of providing the authorized kind of highway for less than was appropriated. After his reelection in 1972, President Nixon was not as successful in controlling the federal budget and priorities for spending as he desired. (Congress made more changes in the proposed executive budget than the President liked.) He branded Congress "fiscally irresponsible" and announced he was unilaterally impounding $9 billion in clean-water funds and that he was terminating certain other programs. Congress perceived the President's action as an assault upon the institutional integrity and constitutional authority of Congress.[23]

Congressional frustration with executive dominance of the budgetary process and the frustrations of members resulting from their attempts to grapple with taxation and appropriations in bits and pieces, rather than comprehensively, coupled with Congressional anger at President Nixon's assault on the fiscal authority of Congress, led to the passage of the Budget and Impoundment Control Act of 1974.[24] That act created a Budget Committee in each chamber, and created the Congressional Budget Office, a joint professional staff intended to give Congress a coordinated approach to the budget to parallel that of the executive branch's Office of Management and Budget (OMB).

The Budget and Impoundment Control Act of 1974 requires that Congress adopt a tentative budget in May of each year, by a vote in both houses, and a final budget in September of each year, also by a vote in both houses. Tax measures and appropriation bills must conform with this final budget.

Under this act, restrictions on the power of a president to impound funds were also enacted. If the President delays spending funds that have been appropriated by Congress, either house of Congress may, by a simple resolution, force the immediate expenditure of the funds. The President can no longer indiscriminately impound appropriated funds unless both houses of Congress approve the impoundment within forty-five days after it occurred.

Borrowing Power   Control over the national debt and the national government's authority to borrow is, as noted earlier, an express power granted to Congress by Article I, Section 8, of the Constitution. The national debt limit is set by act of Congress. Congress periodically raises the limit because, otherwise, the federal government would not be able to pay its bills which had previously been authorized and appropriated for by Congress.

The Power to Tax   Only Congress can levy new taxes for the national government or change existing tax laws. Such decisions are made with advice from the executive, but *Congress* decides. Taxes are necessary to raise money to pay for the operation of the national government. But Congressional control over tax policy also means both the power to reward friends and punish enemies and the power to affect the behavior of individuals and corporations. Few major policy innovations are enacted which consist merely of a stated policy goal, instructions for attaining the goal, and an appropriation. Most also include changes in tax policy. Programs to encourage preservation of historic buildings, for instance, include special tax incentives and disincentives, and the tax provisions may be the most important components of the program in terms of persuading Americans to preserve historic buildings.[25]

Control over tax policy provides Congress with substantial authority over the society, not just over government agencies, and that power is jealously guarded both by Congress as an institution, and, within Congress, by the committees (the House Ways and Means Committee and the Senate Finance Committee) that have authority over tax legislation. Congressional decisions concerning the degree of progressivity of the federal income tax, and what types of income will be taxed lightly or not at all, affect the degree of economic equality or inequality of Americans and have important consequences for the type of society we live in. Tax policy may be as important a tool for encouraging economic equality or inequality as are the various explicit programs for coping with poverty and inequality.

Power of Investigation

If Congress is to legislate intelligently and effectively, it must have information. From the broad legislative powers of Congress come that body's investigative powers.[26] But the power of Congress to investigate goes beyond mere fact-finding relevant to pending legislation. Investigations may be conducted as part of the watchdog, or oversight, function of Congress to oversee the executive department. Many such activities—which have substantial impact on executive agency behavior—are hardly noticed by the public. Congress may also investigate the actions of one of its members. Other investigations are conducted primarily to inform or educate the public and, perhaps, other political leaders. Congress also conducts investigations concerning presidential appointees and proposed treaties.

The Congressional power of investigation has sometimes been used to badger witnesses and expose them to public ridicule and disapproval. The late Senator Joseph McCarthy of Wisconsin was especially well known for his rough treatment of witnesses in a series of hearings by the Senate Permanent Investigating Subcommittee between 1950 and 1954 on the question of Communist infiltration of the federal government. Senator McCarthy was finally censured by the Senate in 1954, but the difficult question of rights of witnesses before Congressional committees versus the legitimate needs of Congress remains. Equally well publicized were the more meritorious Senate committee hearings on Watergate-related offenses (chaired by Senator Sam Ervin in 1973). Information obtained in those hearings contributed greatly to the full airing of the scandal and to President Nixon's loss of support and eventual resignation. Few investigations achieve anything like the attention given to the McCarthy or the Watergate hearings.

The U.S. Supreme Court has held in a number of recent cases that the investigative power of Congress is very broad. In one decision, the Court declared that, "So long as Congress acts in pursuance of its constitutional power, the judiciary lacks authority to intervene on the basis of the motives which spurred the exercise of that power."[27] But since the early 1960s, the Supreme Court has reversed "almost every contempt conviction that came before it,"[28] although it did so each time on narrow legal grounds that did not challenge the scope of the investigatory power of Congress or inquire into the motives of the Congressional investigators.

Impeachment Power

The seldom used, but immensely important, impeachment power is placed in the hands of Congress by Article I, Sections 2 and 3, of the Constitution. Impeachment, the bringing of charges against any officer of the federal government, requires a majority vote in the House of Representatives. When the House votes for impeachment, the trial is then conducted in the U.S. Senate, where it takes precedence over all other nonemergency business. A two-thirds vote of senators present and voting is required for conviction. When the President or vice-president is on trial in the Senate, the chief justice presides. Punishment for conviction is removal from office, and, in the words of Article I, Section 3, "disqualification to hold and enjoy any Office of Honor, Trust, or Profit under the United States." The Senate verdict, one way or another, does not prevent separate prosecution in court for a crime.

A federal officer may be impeached for treason, bribery, or "other high crimes and misdemeanors." While there is some difference of opinion among authorities concerning just what constitutes an impeachable offense, it is clear that a crime need not be charged or proved. Counsel for the accused, however, characteristically insist that the phrase "other high crimes and misdemeanors" refers only to an indictable offense.[29] But Alexander Hamilton, in *Federalist Paper* No. 65, argued that the offense intended is mainly *political* in nature and "relates chiefly to injuries done to the society itself." Discussing the attempt to impeach Justice William O. Douglas in 1970, then House Minority Leader Gerald Ford argued that "an impeachable offense is whatever a majority of the House of Representatives considers it to be at a given moment in history. . . ."[30]

The House of Representatives has impeached thirteen federal officers. Ten were federal district judges, one was a Supreme Court justice, one was secretary of state, and one was President Andrew Johnson. Four of the thirteen impeached officials were convicted by the Senate. All were federal district judges.[31] President Johnson was acquitted when the Senate vote fell one short of two thirds of the senators present and voting. In 1974, the House Judiciary Committee recommended impeachment charges against President Richard Nixon for his wrongdoing in connection with the Watergate scandal and other matters. Before these charges could come before the full House of Representatives, President Nixon resigned. His resignation would not have prevented the House from voting on the impeachment charges or the Senate from conducting a trial on them—but both Houses decided to proceed no further. Just as conviction or acquittal on impeachment charges would have been no bar to separate prosecution in court for alleged crimes, President Nixon's resignation did not prevent his separate criminal prosecution, either. But prosecution was barred when President Gerald Ford, succeeding to the presidency, issued a blanket pardon for President Nixon for any crimes he may have committed during his term of office.

Foreign Affairs

Congress has substantial influence over the conduct of foreign affairs, although the President is designated by the Constitution to receive ambassadors, be commander in chief of the military, and (with the advice and consent of the Senate) appoint ambassadors and enter into treaties with foreign powers. Explicit Congressional authority over foreign affairs is based upon certain express constitutional requirements: that major presidential appointments, including the secretary of state, the secretary of defense, and ambassadors, must be confirmed by the Senate; that treaties be approved by a two-thirds vote of the Senate; and that only Congress may declare war. Other Congressional power over the conduct of foreign affairs comes from Congressional control over spending and taxes.

In matters of war and peace, as with some other matters, the powers of the Congress overlap with those of the President. Of course, no treaty negotiated by a President is binding until it has been ratified by a two-thirds vote in the Senate. But all presidents have claimed the power to make "executive agreements," and have asserted that such agreements need not be sent to the Senate for ratification. In regard to war, President Harry Truman sent troops to Korea in what was termed a "police action," without any declaration of war by Congress. This was full-scale war without the name, and President Truman justified his action on the basis that, technically, these troops were fighting under the auspices of the United Nations, of which the United States is a member by reason of a treaty. Similarly, President Lyndon Johnson sent troops to a full-scale war in Vietnam, and President Nixon kept them there, without any declaration of war by Congress. This action was justified on the grounds, among others, that Congress had passed a simple resolution, the "Tonkin Gulf Resolution," authorizing President Johnson to take whatever steps were necessary to protect American interests in that area.

At any time during administrations in which Congress felt the President was exercising inordinate power in regard to war or peace, circumventing its constitutional powers, Congress could have acted to halt such presidential actions, by cutting off funds, for example. It did not choose to do this, but, by the 1970s, members of Congress did begin to feel that presidents had overstepped constitutional bounds in the field of foreign affairs. The U.S. Senate passed a nonbinding resolution putting presidents and foreign countries on notice that they would no longer be automatically bound by executive agreements. Congress passed the binding Case Act which requires that the President immediately notify Congress of the details of any executive agreement which may be entered into. In 1973, over the veto of President Nixon, the Congress also passed a War Powers Act.[32] This act limits the President's power to involve America in military hostilities for longer than sixty days without formal approval by both the House and the Senate. A more extensive discussion of the relationship between Congress and the President may be found in Chapter 14.

Constitutional Amendments

Article V of the Constitution provides two procedures for proposing an amendment to the U.S. Constitution. Both involve Congress. The procedure which has *not* been used is for amendments to be proposed by a national constitutional convention, called by Congress, upon the application of two thirds of the state legislatures. The procedure which has been used for the existing twenty-six amendments to the Constitution provides that amendments may be proposed by a two-thirds vote (of the members present and voting) in both the House and Senate. A number of groups have from time to time in recent years attempted to secure sufficient support in the states to petition Congress to call a constitutional convention. These groups have included those who desire to have the Constitution amended to allow so-called "voluntary" prayer in the public schools, those who seek to overturn a ruling of the U.S. Supreme Court in favor of the right of a woman to have an abortion during the first three months of pregnancy, and those seeking a constitutional amendment to require a balanced federal budget. So far, no such effort has been successful in securing the support of two thirds of the states. No constitutional convention has been called nationally (although there have been a number of state constitutional conventions) since the original Constitutional Convention of 1787.

Ratification of amendments—no matter how proposed—requires approval by three fourths of the states—either by the state legislatures or by state conventions called for that purpose. All but the Twenty-first Amendment have been ratified by action of the state legislatures. Congress has the power to decide whether to submit a proposed amendment to the state legislatures or to state ratifying conventions. The President has no formal role to play in the amending process; a joint resolution proposing an amendment does not go to the President for approval or disapproval.

Powers of Each Chamber

The House and Senate each have powers which can be exercised independently of any action by the other. Under various statutory "legislative veto" provisions, for instance, one chamber's objection is enough to block presidential reorganization of the executive branch. Each chamber also has certain constitutional prerogatives such as being solely responsible for judging the qualifications of its members, establishing its own rules of procedure, electing its own officers, and disciplining its own members. The House must originate "all bills for raising Revenue," although the Senate can amend such bills as it can other legislation.

The Senate, as we mentioned earlier, has the *confirmation power.* That power is not shared with the House. The President does not actually appoint members of his cabinet, members of the federal judiciary, or ambassadors; he *nominates* them. The Senate then accepts or rejects the President's nominations. Individual senators—when they are of the same political party as the President—have used this institutional power of the Senate to gain great personal influence over the appointment of federal district judges, U.S. attorneys, and U.S. marshals in their home states.

The Senate must also approve all treaties entered into by the United States, and must do so by a two-thirds vote (of those present and voting). The House has no authority over treaties. Senate ratification is sometimes withheld and debates over major treaties have occasionally become major issues in national elections. The most famous such confrontation was the Senate's rejection of President Wilson's Treaty of Versailles, in 1920, ending World War 1 and establishing the League of Nations.

President Carter was successful in securing Senate ratification of the treaty he had negotiated with Panama concerning the Panama Canal. At first, he lacked support of a sufficient number of senators to secure ratification of this treaty—and public opinion was against the treaty, too, at least as it was expressed by those who had an opinion on the matter. President Carter made a vigorous campaign in favor of the Panama Canal Treaty, holding numerous conferences and meetings and sending speakers throughout the country. He held numerous individual meetings with members of the Senate. A combination of these and other efforts changed public opinion and the situation in the Senate. The Senate ratified the treaty—at a time when public opinion had swung around in its favor. President Carter was not so fortunate with the Strategic Arms Limitation II, a treaty which he had negotiated with the Soviet Union to slow the arms race. After this treaty was barely voted out of the Senate Foreign Relations Committee and there was a buildup of opposition to the Soviet Union among the American public, primarily because of a Soviet invasion of Afghanistan, the treaty ran into so much opposition in the U.S. Senate, that, with President Carter's agreement, it was sent back to the Senate Foreign Relations Committee without having been formally considered on the Senate floor.

The House and Senate play separate roles in selecting the President and vice-president, if no candidate receives a majority electoral vote. In that situation, the House is charged with selecting a President from among the three candidates with the highest number of electoral votes. Each state delegation in the House has one vote in electing the President under these circumstances, and a majority of the states (twenty-six votes) is required for election. The Senate chooses the vice-president, considering only the two vice-presidential candidates with the highest number of electoral votes. Each senator casts one vote, and a majority of all the senators (fifty-one votes) is required to elect the vice-president in this manner.

Restraints on Congressional Power

Congress is a powerful institution, but there are external restraints on the exercise of that power. First among them, as noted earlier, is the principle of separation of powers. One consequence of the separation-of-powers arrangement is that Congress may not delegate its powers to any other official or agency without establishing clear standards for the exercise of such delegated power. Another restriction on the legislative power of Congress is, of course, the presidential veto. The President may either sign a bill or veto it; he must send a vetoed bill back to the House in which it originated, with a written statement of his objections. At that point, in order to become law, the bill must then receive a two-thirds vote (of those present and voting) in both the House and Senate.

The Constitution makes certain topics "off limits" for Congressional action. Article I, Section 9, prohibits the passage of bills of attainder and ex post facto legislation. A *bill of attainder* is a legislative act which punishes an individual without a judicial trial. (*Attainder* is the forfeiture of all property and civil rights.) Such acts were common practice in medieval England and often applied to the children of a condemned person, as well. An *ex post facto law* makes illegal a particular act, or increases the punishment for an illegal act, retroactively. Congress is also forbidden by the Constitution to grant titles of nobility.

A major controversy during the campaign to ratify the Constitution was its lack of specific provisions to protect the people from the government. One reason the framers of the Constitution had not included such provisions was that each of the states had its own bill of rights. Alexander Hamilton also argued that, since the new federal government was to be one of limited powers, it would be dangerous to specifically prohibit it from transgressing certain rights because this might encourage the government to transgress rights which were not expressly mentioned. He also said that because the proposed Constitution already contained prohibitions against ex post facto laws, bills of attainder, and titles of nobility, as well as protection of the right of habeus corpus (a safeguard against illegal detention), other provisions were not necessary. Virginian George Mason was among those who, on the other hand, opposed ratification of the new Constitution on the ground, among others, that it contained no specific protections of individual rights. Thomas Jefferson also thought the Constitution was deficient in this regard, but not sufficiently enough to require rejection of it. But during the campaign for and against ratification throughout the states, a general understanding developed that ratification would be contingent upon the Constitution's being amended immediately after its adoption to add protections of individual liberties. Thus, when the first Congress met in New York in 1789, James Madison, who had been elected to the House of Representatives from Virginia, came prepared. He proposed fourteen amendments for this purpose. Ten eventually made their way through the proposal and ratification process, and they are today known as the Bill of Rights. They limit actions of all three branches of the national government, including Congress. Among other restrictions, Congress is forbidden to enact legislation restricting the freedom of the press, speech, or religion. Congress cannot establish a religion; there can be no "official" church in the United States and, unlike England, tax revenues cannot be used to support a particular church.

THE STATE LEGISLATURES

The fifty American state legislatures all exist within state-level separation-of-power systems. None of the states has a parliamentary government. Like the national government, each state has a legislative branch of government, an executive branch, in which the principal officers are elected independently of the legislature, and an independent judicial branch, although the legislature does elect the judges in some states. Nebraska is the only state with a unicameral legislature, elected on nonpartisan ballots. The other forty-nine states have partisan bicameral legislatures in which the upper chamber is called the senate and the lower chamber is usually called the House of Representatives.

In each state, the upper chamber has fewer members than the lower chamber, but upper chamber size varies dramatically from a low of twenty members in Alaska and Nevada to a high of sixty-seven members in Minnesota. The lower state chambers also vary widely in size, from forty representatives in the Alaska and Nevada lower chambers to four hundred in New Hampshire.[33] Despite the varying numbers, though, it should be noted that state legislatures are considerably smaller than the national Congress. This can be important, because the size of a legislative body may affect how well legislators know each other and the manner in which legislative business is conducted.

The term of office of an American state legislator is either two or four years, with two years being most common for representatives (forty-five states) and four years being the norm for senators (thirty-eight states). Only Alabama, Louisiana, Maryland, and Mississippi provide a four-year term for their representatives. State senators serve two-year terms in twelve states. Where the senate term of office is four years, many states elect a part of the senate membership every two years. To keep the state senate elections staggered, some state senate terms are for only two years following each reapportionment.

Amateur or Professional Legislators

Some states have paid, full-time legislators, with expense accounts, staff assistance, and office facilities. State legislators in those states are generally called "professionals." Other states continue to have "citizen" or "amateur" legislators, who meet for only two or three months each year (or less), have limited or no staff assistance, receive little or no pay, and depend on private occupations for their livelihood. The more heavily populated states tend to have the professional full-time legislators; less populated, less industrialized states tend to have amateur legislators.

Comparing the compensation of state legislators is difficult because of the different ways in which they are compensated. Louisiana state legislators, for example, are each paid $50 per day in salary for up to eighty-five calendar days of legislative business per year. But they can also receive $50 per day salary for up to thirty days of special-session activity and committee business per year, between legislative sessions. Further, in addition to the $50 per day salary for days worked, they may also receive unvouchered expense money, for which no receipts are necessary, in addition to vouchered expense money for rent, utilities, and other outlays for the home-district office.[34]

The Council of State Governments estimates annual state legislative "compensation" (salary plus unvouchered expense monies) for each state. This compensation varies from a salary of $100 per year (and severely limited expenses), in New Hampshire, to $30,800 per year (including unvouchered expenses, but not including vouchered expenses and transportation allowances), in California. As of 1978, twenty-three states paid their legislators $12,000 per year or more in salaries and unvouchered expense monies. The top four (California, New York, Michigan, and Illinois) paid their legislators over $23,000 in annual salary and unvouchered expense monies, plus certain vouchered expenses. The bottom four states in legislative compensation (New Hampshire, Rhode Island, Utah, and New Mexico) paid their legislators $1,800 per year or less in salary and expense monies.[35] Legislative leaders receive additional compensation in most states, usually either a modest salary increment or extra expense monies.

Level of compensation is one of the standards for describing a state's legislators as professional or amateur, because the higher the legislative compensation, the lower the turnover in the legislature.[36] In poorly compensated amateur or citizen legislatures, there are higher percentages of inexperienced, first-term members.

Does it matter whether a state has a professional or an amateur legislature? Apparently, it does. A professional state legislature appears to be more responsive to popular desires, producing decisions more liberal and more favorable to people in lower economic levels, than an amateur legislature.[37] In this case and in others, rules make a difference on outcomes, and that impact is not always immediately obvious.

Organization of State Legislatures

State legislatures, in the main, are similar to Congress in their formal organizational structure. There are numerous important variations, however, both in organizational structure and—more importantly—in the way things are done. Further, an unwary observer, familiar with Congress or with one state legislature, may make the mistake of assuming that officials with similar titles have the same powers in different state legislative chambers. That is often not the case. The office of president pro tempore in many state senates, for example, is a post of much greater power than the position of the same name in the U.S. Senate. It should also be noted that there are usually exceptions to any generalizations concerning state legislatures, in part because the various states periodically change their rules or amend their constitutions.

State Senates   The presiding officer of most American state senates is the lieutenant governor, just as the vice-president of the United States is the president of the U.S. Senate. In three fifths of the states, this is a result of a provision in the state constitution, providing for a popularly elected lieutenant governor. These lieutenant governors actually preside over most state senate sessions (unlike the vice-president, who seldom presides over the U.S. Senate) and may be more involved in state senate business than the vice-president is in U.S. Senate business. In some states, the state senate elects its own presiding officer (called the president of the senate, or the speaker of the senate), and that official sometimes is next in line of succession to the governor and may also carry the title of lieutenant governor.

Where a popularly elected lieutenant governor is imposed on a state senate as presiding officer by the state constitution, senate rules usually give this official only limited authority in senate affairs, with most of the chamber's authority actually exercised by a committee of senate leaders, the majority leader, or the president pro tem, who is chosen from among the senators and presides in the absence of the lieutenant governor. A major reason for limiting a lieutenant governor's power within the state senate seems to be that a popularly elected lieutenant governor might well not be a member of the senate's majority party. In a few states (mainly one-party states), though, the popularly elected lieutenant governor has substantial power under the senate rules, including the power to appoint senators to committees.

Where the presiding officer of a state senate is elected by the senators from among their number, the rules of the senate usually give this official greater authority within

44

the chamber, usually as the leader of the majority party, with powers similar to those of the speaker in most state lower chambers.[38] It should be kept in mind, however, that as with other organizations and institutions, the official formally in authority in a particular state legislative chamber may or may not be an independent decisionmaker and may or may not have decisive influence over other legislators. It is not unusual in some states for a strong governor actually to be making many of the legislative decisions.

Like the U.S. Senate, the forty-nine partisan state senates are organized along party lines, and even Nebraska's nonpartisan senate is organized around caucuses which look suspiciously like Republican and Democratic gatherings. Each state senate has a majority and a minority caucus, and each elects a leader and a whip. The majority party caucus normally makes the actual selection of the president pro tem, who, technically, is elected by the entire senate. Similarly, in those senates which elect a speaker or president (states where the lieutenant governor does not preside over the senate), the majority party caucus determines the selection of that official.

In some states, the majority leader has the most authority in the upper chamber. In other states, most of the authority is exercised by the president pro tem. In either case, the majority leader is usually responsible for scheduling the flow of legislation (often in consultation with others) and for representing party interests in the senate. Frequently, the majority leader serves as the governor's spokesperson on the senate floor.

The minority leader heads the minority party in the senate and represents its interests. In a few states, the senate minority leader decides which minority-party members will serve on which committees, and in other states has a formal voice in the committee assignment process, often as a member of the committee on committees.[39] The minority leader normally speaks for the governor, when a member of the same party as the governor.

The party whips perform functions similar to the officials of the same name in the U.S. Congress, although in small state senates, there is little need for formal head counts, and not all state senates have such an office. A senate whip often assists the floor leader and acts in the floor leader's absence.

State Lower Chambers   The forty-nine state lower chambers are similar to the U.S. House of Representatives in that each elects its own presiding officer, the speaker, from among its members. The speaker is normally a figure of great authority in the legislature and in state politics generally, often considered one of the two or three most powerful people in a state's government.

The speaker ordinarily is the leader of the majority party in the House or of the dominant faction in one-party states. Although the position is filled by vote of the entire chamber, party discipline normally insures that the nominee of the majority party wins. Once in a great while, a cross-party coalition will form between majority-party dissidents and the minority party to deny the majority party's dominant faction control over the selection of the speaker. In 1979 such coalitions appeared in both the New Mexico and the Vermont Houses of Representatives; this was unusual.[40] Sometimes, in practice, the governor picks the speaker.[41] That practice appears to be on the decline, but governors still intercede occasionally in many states, especially when the governor's fellow partisans in the lower chamber cannot agree on a leader.

The speakers of the state lower chambers have more control over internal chamber organization and proceedings than the Speaker of the U.S. House of Representatives has within the U.S. House. This is partly because the seniority system is very strong in the U.S. House of Representatives and there is generally more continuity in committee membership and chairs. In over three fourths of the states, the speaker appoints members to lower-chamber committees and names the chairperson of each committee. In the remaining states, the speaker has a strong voice in committee assignments. A speaker usually has a fairly good idea of what issues will be before the legislature in the coming two years, and those who appoint committees or influence their make-up can often structure committees in such a way as to assure that they will pass, kill, or amend bills—in accordance with the speaker's wishes.

Skill at coalition building and distribution of rewards—among interest groups, ambitious fellow legislators, other government officials, and party factions—is normally a prerequisite for becoming speaker. Speakers are influential figures because of this skill and their powers of office: control over referral of bills to house committees; scheduling of legislation for floor action (usually in cooperation with the majority leader); recognition of members to speak; rulings on procedural questions; appointment of house members to conference committees; and superior information as the center of the party whip's communications network. The post is frequently used as a springboard to the governor's office or another statewide elective office, or to a seat in Congress. Occasionally, a speaker prefers to remain at the center of state legislative power and holds the position for a decade or longer.

The majority leader (or majority floor leader) normally is the majority party's leader on the floor of the house and is second in his or her legislative party's hierarchy. The majority leader is usually elected by the majority caucus, but may actually be chosen by the speaker, or, less often, by the governor. The majority leader looks out for the party's interests in the house, coordinates the party's legislative program, plays a major role in the scheduling and conduct of debate, and serves generally as a traffic manager for the conduct of business in the house. If a member of the governor's party, the majority leader often acts a spokesperson for the governor.

Like the senate minority leader, the house minority leader (or minority floor leader) is the head of the minority party in the lower chamber. This official and the minority whip look out for the minority party's interests in house procedure and debate, plan party strategy, seek to build a party record and to make political capital of the actions or inactions of the majority party, and seek to form majority coalitions on certain issues with dissident members of the majority party. In a few states, the house minority leader controls minority-member committee assignments; in some others, he or she serves on the house committee which makes committee assignments. In most states, the minority leader is limited to making committee assignment recommendations to the speaker, although a strong norm has developed in some of these states that the speaker should honor such recommendations unless he has compelling reasons to do otherwise.[42]

Committees in the State Legislatures

Like Congress, the various state legislatures divide their workloads by assigning to committees the details of obtaining information and considering legislation. State legislatures—like Congress—have standing committees, select committees, joint committees, and conference committees. Some state legislatures make extensive use of joint committees to consider legislation, something Congress does not do. Among the state legislatures which are constitutionally restricted to relatively short annual or biennial sessions, most have "interim committees," which meet in the interim between legislative sessions to study problems and make recommendations to the legislature for enactment of legislation during the next session. Often, the members of each interim committee serve on a standing committee with jurisdiction over the subject matter of interest.

The standing committees of the state legislatures are the workhorses of the state legislative process. The number of standing committees varies from state to state, in part because of political idiosyncracies, different-sized legislative bodies, and socioeconomic differences between the states. Two states (Connecticut and Maine) rely entirely on joint committees, and several other states make extensive use of such committees. Excluding those states which make the greatest use of joint committees, and thus have the fewest committees in each chamber, the number of standing committees in each lower chamber ranges from six to forty-five. Most state lower chambers had between ten and twenty standing committees in 1978. The state senates, on average, had fewer committees, generally between nine and eighteen standing committees each. The number of standing committees in state legislative chambers has been declining over the past two decades.[43]

CONSTITUTIONAL STATUS OF STATE LEGISLATURES

American state governments, including their legislatures, must organize themselves and conduct their business under the terms set forth in their respective state constitutions. The state constitutions prescribe the structure of the state governments, stipulate the terms of office and the powers granted to the various state officials, and include the manner of amending the state constitution. Every state constitution includes a bill of rights, and each also contains other specific limitations on the powers of the legislature. All laws passed by the state legislature, of course, must conform to the state constitution. The state constitutions and state statutes also must be consistent with the U.S. Constitution, in so far as the latter document applies to state action. It was the U.S. Supreme Court's interpretation of the Equal Protection Clause in the Fourteenth Amendment to the U.S. Constitution, for example, which led to the extensive reapportionment of American state legislatures in the latter half of the 1960s. The judiciary may hold a particular act of the state legislature to be in violation of the state constitution, or the federal constitution, or both.

As noted earlier, a law passed by Congress is constitutional only if, first, the U.S. Constitution does not forbid Congress to act, and second, the U.S. Constitution authorizes Congress to enact such a law. The state legislatures are on a bit more solid constitutional ground. State legislatures have *residual* powers. That is, the authority of the state legislature includes all powers not given to some other agency of state government or not forbidden to the state legislature by the state or national constitution. Specific grants of authority need not be found to uphold a law passed by a state legislature.

Powers of the State Legislatures

State legislatures are important centers of policymaking in their respective states, and they have substantial power. But extensive provisions in the state constitution often limit the exercise of legislative powers over powerful economic interest groups. In some states, the legislature is restricted, for example, in its regulation of utilities; elsewhere special tax loopholes are written into the state constitution. Reformers, who seek vigorous state action to solve various social problems, have succeeded in removing such constitutional restrictions on state legislatures in some states and are seeking to do so in others.

47

In every state, amendments to the state constitution may be initiated by a vote of both houses of the legislature on a resolution proposing the change. Most require extraordinary majorities in each legislative chamber. Except in Delaware, the proposed amendment must be ratified by a vote of the people. In about a third of the states, the legislature does not have exclusive control over constitutional amendments, because the people can use the initiative petition to force a popular vote on a constitutional amendment. State legislatures are the bodies which normally ratify (or refuse to ratify) proposed amendments to the U.S. Constitution, approval by three fourths of the states being necessary for adoption. (Congress could require ratification by state conventions, but has done so only once.)

State legislatures levy such taxes as the state government collects. They enact legislation concerning domestic relations (such as marriage, divorce, and adoption), the state criminal code, tax policy, state environmental policy, traffic laws, public-employee salary structures, and a host of other state matters. As is true in the national government, the state government can spend only such money as has been appropriated by the legislature. The state legislature decides how much money to appropriate for the various state services, programs, and agencies. Thus, state legislatures are the center of basic policymaking in the state, and their decisions determine most of the fundamental policies pursued by state government agencies. The legislatures can conduct investigations, and they have the power of oversight over state agencies and the tools needed to modify the behavior of those agencies.

State legislatures also have some authority in the selection of state officials. In some states, the legislature, sitting in a joint session of both houses, elects state judges. In some other states, judges are appointed by the governor with the consent of the state senate. And in most states, important gubernatorial appointments to state boards and commissions and to certain executive positions in state government require confirmation by the state senate. Some state legislatures actually appoint certain state executive officers, including the insurance commissioner in South Carolina, the state treasurer in New Hampshire, and, in a number of states, the state auditor.

In all states except Oregon, legislatures are given the power to remove state officials through impeachment. In all but two of those forty-nine states, the procedure is very similar to that used at the national level except that some states suspend impeached officials pending the outcome of the senate trial.[44] Oregon, and twelve of the states which also provide for legislative impeachment power, provide for removal of state officials by *recall*—a system in which a requisite number of voters must sign a petition requesting a special election to vote on the official's removal from office.

For much the same reason that members of Congress have certain privileges and immunities, members of the state legislatures are also generally exempt from arrest while attending the legislature (except for treason, breach of the peace, or commission of a felony). Nor can they be held accountable in court for statements made or votes cast in the legislature. As at the national level, these protections are intended to encourage full and robust debate on public issues.

Each state legislative chamber has the authority to settle election contests concerning its membership. Normally a hearing is held, and the decision is by vote of the members of the chamber whose election was not challenged.

Each state legislative chamber also has the authority to discipline its own members. Expulsion from the legislature, which seldom occurs, normally requires approval by an extraordinary majority of the members of the legislative chamber in which the accused member serves. A lesser number of votes is required for other types of member punishment. The late V. O. Key, Jr., reported concerning the Mississippi Senate's effort, in 1910, to expel Theodore Bilbo from that chamber. Senator

Bilbo escaped expulsion by one vote, but the Mississippi Senate then passed the following resolution:

> Resolved, in view of the unexplained inconsistencies and inherent improbabilities in the testimony of Senator Bilbo, his established bad character and lack of credibility, that the Senate of Mississippi does hereby condemn his entire bribery charge, and the statement of the role he played as detective and decoy, as a trumped-up falsehood, utterly unworthy of belief; resolved further, that as a result of the conduct of Theodore G. Bilbo in this matter, and the testimony produced in this investigation, the Senate pronounces Bilbo as unfit to sit with honest, upright men in a respectable legislative body, and he is hereby asked to resign.[45]

To the dismay of many Mississippi state senators, not only did Bilbo *not* resign, he was later elected lieutenant governor of the state, in 1911, and governor, in 1915, and he served as U.S. Senator from Mississippi from 1934 until his death in 1947, where, apparently Bilbo not having changed his ways, a Senate committee found that "Senator Bilbo improperly used his high office as U.S. Senator for his personal gain in his dealings with war contractors."[46]

Restrictions on State Legislatures

The early state constitutions were embodiments of the faith that the people placed in their legislatures as defenders of democracy. The constitutions gave the legislatures broad grants of power. But public confidence in legislators and legislatures began to wane in the middle of the nineteenth century, as scandals were reported in many states, and constitutional restrictions began to be placed on the legislatures. These scandals usually involved the bribery and corruption of legislators to secure passage of special-interest legislation. As William J. Keefe points out, however, corruption in the state legislatures was only one factor which led to constitutional restrictions on them. Another was that wealthy people began to feel that the legislatures were overly democratic—too responsive to the desires of ordinary people. The economic elite feared a combination of democracy and corruption, and they led the fight to restrict the powers of the state legislatures.[47]

Constitutional restrictions placed on the state legislatures included: provisions which spelled out certain required legislative procedures (such as requiring that each bill concern only one topic, or that a bill not be passed the same day it was introduced); explicit limitations protecting individual rights against the power of the legislature; limits on the legislature's control over taxation (by establishing maximum tax rates, earmarking certain taxes, or listing tax exemptions, for example); limits on the legislature's authority to incur debts on behalf of the state; prohibitions against the passage of special legislation to exempt specific individuals or corporations from the application of general laws; restrictions on the length of legislative sessions; and detailed legislative provisions of narrow concern which most constitutional scholars believe should be in the state statutes (passed by and repealable by the legislature), rather than in the constitution.[48] These legislative or "statutory" provisions in some state constitutions limit the authority of the legislature to make public policy in certain aspects of taxation policy, labor and contract law, regulation of corporations and utilities, education policy, environmental policy, and regulation of professions and occupations.

Constitutional grants of authority to various independently elected state executive officials or commissions sometimes restrict a state legislature's authority, by removing certain policy areas from their effective legislative control. Some state courts, in addition, have held that there are implied limitations on their state legislatures, despite the theory of residual powers, as a result of the fact that some powers of the legislature are specifically enumerated in the state constitution.

In the ordinary course of legislative activity, the most important restriction on the state legislature is the governor's veto power. That power enables the governor to block legislation, even though a majority of each legislative chamber has approved it. Only the governor of North Carolina lacks the veto power, but some states permit the governor's veto to be overridden by a simple majority of each chamber, on reconsideration. Most states require an extraordinary majority vote (usually 60 percent or two-thirds) in the legislature to override a veto. Governors in about eighty percent of the states have an *item* veto on appropriations bills, meaning they can delete particular items from an appropriations act and accept the rest. That is a very useful power. It is not available on ordinary legislation, so the legislature often combines the bitter with the sweet in these measures, giving the governor items he or she wants along with some the governor would veto if the items were not all presented in the same piece of legislation.

The governor's budgetary authority and his or her control over information from the bureaucracy also limit the legislature's ability to dominate public policy in the state. Many state legislatures have begun to develop a budgetary competence within the permanent legislative staff, to avoid being so dependent on the executive branch, but the governor remains the single most influential figure in the legislative process of most states. Legislative-executive relationships will be discussed at length in Chapter 14.

Initiative and Referendum

In addition to the above restrictions on legislative authority, many state legislatures also share their legislative authority directly with the people, who can use the process of the *initiative* to enact legislation directly or, in some states, to amend the state constitution. The initiative became popular at the end of the nineteenth century, especially among Americans who were dissatisfied with their state legislatures. Many people felt that the legislatures were dominated by big business and other special interests. This dissatisfaction led to the adoption in a number of states of constitutional provisions allowing for the right of initiative or referendum or both.[49]

Twenty-one states allow for the statutory initiative, which permits the enactment of statutes (ordinary laws such as legislatures enact) directly by vote of the people. Seventeen states, most of them the same ones, allow the initiative procedure to be used to amend the state constitution.[50] Supporters of the proposed statute or state constitutional amendment draft the proposal and then obtain a required minimum number of signatures of registered voters on petitions. The states typically require that an initiative petition be signed by from somewhere between five and ten percent of the voters who voted in the state's last general election.

There are two kinds of statutory initiatives. Four of the twenty-one states which allow for the statutory initiative have a system of *indirect initiative*.[51] This means that the voters in those states may, by petition, propose a new law for the consideration, first, of the state legislature and then, only if the legislature fails to act, have the proposed measure voted upon by the people directly. Most of the statutory initiative states provide for a *direct initiative*. By this means, the voters may petition to have a legislative proposal voted on directly by the people without the intervening step of having it considered by the legislature. If a majority of the voters vote "yes," the measure becomes law. Through statutory initiatives of one kind or another, in 1978, for example, the voters of Florida required public disclosure of finances by public officials, the voters of Michigan and Maine enacted returnable-bottle laws, and the people of Arizona legislated a new system for selecting judges. Best known, probably, is California's "Proposition 13" to cut state taxes.

A *referendum* is a vote of the people on a measure concerning, or as a result of, prior action by a state legislature (or city governing body). All the statutory initiative states, and sixteen more, allow for a state referendum.[52] There are three types. A *compulsory referendum* is one which involves a measure that *must* be referred by the legislature for a vote of the people before the measure can go into effect. These are usually measures which involve proposed constitutional amendments. A *voluntary referendum* is one which involves measures that a state legislature *may,* voluntarily, refer to the people for their vote, before the measures can go into effect. These usually are controversial proposals which the legislature does not want to decide by itself. A *protest referendum* is one in which the people may, by petition, prevent a legislative measure passed by a state legislature from going into effect until there can be a statewide vote of approval or disapproval.[53] An example of recent referendum actions in the states was when the New Jersey legislature, in 1978, referred a question concerning legalized gambling on jai alai games to the people—a measure which the people of New Jersey rejected.

Like most other features of government, permitting the people to legislate directly has both advocates and detractors.[54] Some argue that direct popular legislation is bad because it impairs the sense of responsibility of a legislative body, that it impairs the essential workings of representative government, that it gives too much power to those minorities or special interests with sufficient resources to get a question on the ballot, and that it confuses the public by putting too many questions to them for a vote.

On the other hand, those in favor of direct popular legislation argue that it is an important way of controlling special interests, that it strengthens popular sovereignty by giving the people a means of circumventing legislative bodies which may not be popularly responsive, that it improves legislative performance because of the threat of a popular vote, and that it improves possibilities for voter education and voter participation in decision-making.

The above arguments are all applied, as well, to the question of amending the U.S. Constitution to provide for the initiative at the *national* level, something not now permitted. Initiative America is an organization which proposes that, upon the petition of 3 percent of those who voted in the last U.S. presidential election, Americans be allowed to initiate and vote on national legislation directly. At its highwater mark, in 1978, the national initiative idea had gained thirty-five Congressional sponsors and had been endorsed by one hundred U.S. representatives who were up for reelection. A poll that year showed some three fourths of Americans who had an opinion on the matter favored it.[55] Whatever the arguments for and against, there is, today, no national right of initiative and referendum, although such procedures are available in a number of America's states. Lawmaking in America is still, then, largely a matter of "representation" and of "representative democracy."

SUMMARY

Congress and the American state legislatures all function within a separation-of-powers structure of government. Except for the Nebraska legislature, all are bicameral and are organized along partisan political lines. Each lower chamber elects its own presiding officer, who normally is the most powerful member in the chamber. The upper chambers have less focused leadership. Even in those states where the state senate elects its own presiding officer, the concentration of authority in the office of the senate president tends to be less extensive than is found in the office of the speaker of the state house. All American legislatures are institutions of substantial authority and independence. All have the basic lawmaking power, which permits them to create or (if they choose) eliminate most executive agencies of government. Some states permit direct lawmaking participation by citizens, through the use of the processes of the initiative and/or the referendum. Most laws, however, are written by the legislature. Congress and the fifty state legislatures have extensive powers to tax and spend, and must exercise those powers if the executive branch of government is to function. All have the power to investigate, and all but one have the power to impeach and remove from office officials of the other branches of government. Though they are organized in similar ways, each legislative chamber has important unique characteristics, and one must take care not to overemphasize either their similarities or their differences.

Notes

1. Additional information on the Constitutional Convention is available from Charles Beard, *An Economic Interpretation of the Constitution of the United States* (New York: Free Press, 1965); originally published in 1913; Max Farrand, *The Framing of the Constitution of the United States* (New Haven: Yale University Press, 1913); and Clinton Rossiter, *1787: The Grand Convention* (New York: Macmillan, 1966).

2. George H. Haynes, *The Senate of the United States* (Boston: Houghton Mifflin, 1938), Chapter 20.

3. *Congressional Quarterly Weekly Report,* January 10, 1981, p. 71.

4. George B. Galloway, *History of the House of Representatives* (New York: Thomas Y. Crowell, 1961), pp. 22–23.

5. C. Herman Pritchett, *The Federal System in Constitutional Law* (Englewood Cliffs, N.J.: Prentice-Hall, 1978), Chapter 10.

6. Charles Warren, *The Making of the Constitution* (Boston: Little, Brown, 1928), pp. 241–42.

7. See, David W. Rohde, "Risk-Bearing and Progressive Ambition: The Case of Members of the United States House of Representatives," *American Journal of Political Science* 23 (February 1979); Martin D. Levine and Mark S. Hyde, "Incumbency and the Theory of Political Ambition: A Rational Choice Model," *Journal of Politics* 39 (1977); Joseph A. Schlesinger, *Ambition and Politics* (Chicago: Rand McNally, 1966), p. 17, and Chapter 6.

8. Charles Press, "Presidential Coattails and Party Cohesion," *Midwest Journal of Political Science* 7 (November 1963); George C. Edwards, III, "The Impact of Presidential Coattails on Outcomes of Congressional Elections," *American Politics Quarterly* 7 (January 1979): 94–107; Herbert M. Kritzer and Robert B. Eubank, "Presidential Coattails Revisited: Partisanship and Incumbency Effects," *American Journal of Political Science* 23 (August 1979): 614–25; Samuel Kernell, "Presidential Popularity and Negative Voting: An Alternative Explanation of the Midterm Congressional Decline of the President's Party," *American Political Science Review* 71 (March 1977): 44–66; and James Piereson, "Presidential Popularity and Midterm Voting at Different Electoral Levels," *American Journal of Political Science* 19 (November 1975): 686–94.

9. Charles L. Clapp, *The Congressman: His Work as He Sees It* (Washington, D.C.: Brookings Institution, 1963).

10. David R. Mayhew, "Congressional Elections: The Case of the Vanishing Marginals," *Polity* 6 (Spring 1974). Eighty-two percent of all 1980 House elections were won by "safe margins," and among incumbents seeking reelection, the vote was higher. See *Congressional Quarterly Weekly Report,* April 25, 1981, pp. 717–25.

11. Charles O. Jones, *Every Second Year: Congressional Behavior and the Two-Year Term* (Washington, D.C.: Brookings Institution, 1967); and John D. Cranor, "Congressional District Response to the Housing and Community Development Act of 1974: An Exploration of Casework as a Basis for Policy Evaluation and Adjustment" (Paper delivered at the 1979 Annual Meeting of the Southern Political Science Association, Gatlinburg, Tennessee).

12. Randall B. Ripley, *Party Leaders in the House of Representatives* (Washington, D.C.: Brookings Institution, 1967), especially Chapter 3.

13. Herbert Jacob and Kenneth N. Vines, *Politics in the American States,* 3rd ed. (New York: Little, Brown, 1976), pp. 30–34.

14. Robert L. Peabody, *Leadership in Congress: Stability, Succession, and Change* (Boston: Little, Brown, 1976), especially Chapter 11.

15. See *Wall Street Journal,* May 11, 1977, pp. 1, 27.

16. *New York Times,* December 10, 1968, p. 38.

17. Kenneth Bradshaw and David Pring, *Parliament and Congress* (Austin, Tex.: University of Texas Press, 1972), Chapter 4.

18. Gerhard Loewenberg, *Parliament in the German Political System* (Ithaca, New York: Cornell University Press, 1967), pp. 265–67.

19. Pritchett, *The Federal System in Constitutional Law,* p. 202.

20. Ibid., p. 203.

21. The agency that coordinates the executive budget is the Office of Management and Budget (OMB), which began in 1921 as the Bureau of the Budget in the Treasury Department. President Roosevelt moved the Bureau of the Budget to the Executive Office of the President in 1939 to oversee all executive-branch budget requests. The organization has since received expanded responsibilities and has been renamed the Office of Management and Budget. See Joel Havermann, *Congress and the Budget* (Bloomington: Indiana University Press, 1978).

22. Richard F. Fenno, Jr., *The Power of the Purse: Appropriations Politics in Congress* (Boston: Little, Brown, 1966) pp. 145–46.

23. John W. Ellwood and James A. Thurber, "The New Congressional Budget Process: The Hows and Whys of Senate Differences," in Lawrence C. Dodd and Bruce I. Oppenheimer, *Congress Reconsidered* (New York: Praeger, 1977), pp. 163–70; James A. Thurber, "New Powers of the Purse: An Assessment of Congressional Budget Reform," in Leroy N. Rieselbach, *Legislative Reform* (Lexington, Mass.: Lexington Books, 1978).

24. For a concise and authoritative treatment of the Budget and Impoundment Control Act, see *Powers of Congress* (Washington, D.C.: Congressional Quarterly, 1976), pp. 32–43. This source also provides authoritative summations of Congress' other powers.

25. Historic preservation tax incentives are provided in the 1976 Tax Reform Act (PL94-455).

26. James Hamilton, *The Power to Probe: A Study of Congressional Investigations* (New York: Random House, 1976).

27. *Barenblatt* v. *United States,* 360 U.S. 109 (1959). See also, *Wilkinson* v. *United States,* 365 U.S. 399 (1961); and *Braden* v. *United States,* 365 U.S. 431 (1961).

28. Pritchett, *The Federal System in Constitutional Law,* p. 254.

29. Louis Fisher, *The Constitution Between Friends* (New York: St. Martin's Press, 1978), p. 152.

30. *Ibid.,* p. 151, quoted from the 1970 *Congressional Record.*

31. Raoul Berger, *Impeachment: The Constitutional Problem* (Cambridge: Harvard University Press, 1974).

32. Thomas M. Franck, "After the Fall: The New Procedural Framework for Congressional Control Over the War Power," *American Journal of International Law* 71 (July/October, 1977): 611–14; Harvey G. Zeidenstein, "The Reassertion of Congressional Power: New Curbs on the President," *Political Science Quarterly* 93 (Fall 1978): 393–409.

33. Information on the number of legislators in each state, their compensation, and their term of office is from *Book of the States, 1978–79* (Lexington, Kentucky: Council of State Governments, 1978). Compensation estimates assume no special session is held and include no days of committee work between sessions.

34. *Book of the States, 1978–79,* p. 29.

35. Ibid.

36. Alan Rosenthal, "Turnover in State Legislatures," *American Journal of Political Science* 18 (August 1974): 609–16.

37. John G. Grumm, "The Effects of Legislative Structure on Legislative Performance," in *State and Urban Politics,* ed. Richard I. Hofferbert and Ira Sharkansky (Boston: Little, Brown, 1971), pp. 298–322; Lance T. LeLoup, "Reassessing the Mediating Impact of Legislative

Capability," *American Political Science Review* 72 (June 1978): 616–21; Edward G. Carmines, "The Mediating Influence of State Legislatures on the Linkage Between Interparty Competition and Welfare Policies," *American Political Science Review* 65 (September 1974): 1118–24.

38. Eugene Declercq, "Inter-House Differences in American State Legislatures," *Journal of Politics* 39 (August 1977): 774–85; and Citizens Conference on State Legislatures, *State Legislatures: An Evaluation of Their Effectiveness* (New York: Praeger, 1971).

39. Citizens Conference on State Legislatures, *State Legislatures: An Evaluation of Their Effectiveness.* This study includes recommendations for improving the various state legislatures. In those states where the minority party of either chamber does not control its members' committee assignments, this study recommends that "Minority party members should be assigned to committees by the minority leader in consultation with the minority caucus."

40. Eleven conservative Democratic New Mexico representatives joined with Republican representatives to elect a conservative Democratic Speaker and to share House chairmanships with the Republicans. Forty-one of 70 New Mexico representatives were Democrats. *Comparative State Politics Newsletter* 1, no. 1 (October, 1979): 17. In Vermont, Republicans won 81 of 150 House seats but the secret ballot for speaker reelected the Democrat who had been speaker in the prior session. *Congressional Quarterly Weekly Report,* August 25, 1979, p. 1746.

41. See V. O. Key, Jr., *Southern Politics* (New York: Alfred A. Knopf, 1949); and Malcolm E. Jewell, *The State Legislature: Politics and Practice* (New York: Random House, 1962), Chapters 4 and 5.

42. Citizens Conference on State Legislatures, *State Legislatures: An Evaluation of Their Effectiveness.*

43. *American State Legislatures: Their Structures and Procedures*, rev. ed. (Lexington, Ky.: Council of State Governments, 1977).

44. When the governor or lieutenant governor is impeached, the chief justice of the state Supreme Court is normally called on to preside over the impeachment trial. In Alaska the state senate impeaches and the state house conducts the trial. In Nebraska the state senate impeaches and the state Supreme Court tries the case.

45. V. O. Key, Jr., *Southern Politics,* p. 239.

46. Ibid., p. 245.

47. William J. Keefe, "The Functions and Powers of the State Legislature," in *State Legislatures in American Politics,* ed. Alexander Heard (Englewood Cliffs, N.J.: Prentice-Hall, 1966).

48. Keefe, "The Functions and Powers of the State Legislature"; and Charles Press and Kenneth VerBurg, *State and Community Governments in the Federal System* (New York: John Wiley, 1979), Chapter 5.

49. Eugene C. Lee, "The Initiative and Referendum: How California Has Fared," *National Civic Review,* February 1979, pp. 69–76, 84.

50. Council of State Governments, *Book of the States, 1978–79* (Lexington, Ky.: Council of State Governments, 1979), pp. 195, 210, 243. Florida and Illinois allow for constitutional initiatives only.

51. Concerning the *indirect initiative* and the *direct initiative,* see Karl E. Lutrin and Allen K. Sattle, "The Public and Ecology: The Role of Initiatives in California Environmental Politics," (Paper delivered at the 1973 Annual Meeting of the American Political Science Association, New Orleans).

52. David R. Berman, *State and Local Politics,* 2nd ed. (Boston: Holbrook Press, 1978), pp. 86–91.

53. See Raymond E. Wolfinger and Fred I. Greenstein, "The Repeal of Fair Housing in California: An Analysis of Referendum Voting," *American Political Science Review* 62 (September 1968): 753–69.

54. For the case for and against direct popular legislation, see Russell W. Maddox and Robert F. Fuquay, *State and Local Government,* 3rd ed. (New York: D. Van Nostrand, 1975), pp. 282–87.

55. See Michael Nelson, "The Federal Initiative Idea," *The Nation,* February 25, 1978, pp. 210–12; and Everett Carll Ladd, Jr., "What The Voters Really Want," *Fortune,* December 18, 1978, p. 48.

PART II

Connections:
Legislators and
Their Constituents

chapter 4

Characteristics and Recruitment of American Legislators

Preview

Congress and the state legislatures are bastions of well-educated white, male, middle-aged, and middle-class America. The brokerage occupations—especially the law—dominate American legislatures, in part because the people engaged in such pursuits have the resources (including flexible work schedules) to pursue and hold legislative office. The winnowing process through which local elites effectively screen the possible candidates leads to the selection (and financial backing) of mostly male legislative candidates who are not only acceptable to those local political and economic elites but also look much like the dominant ethnic and religious group(s) in the legislative district. Although women and racial minority citizens have increased their representation in American state legislatures substantially over the past two decades, they are still substantially underrepresented, descriptively, both there and in Congress, where little change has occurred recently. There is some evidence that legislators who are women or racial minorities perceive some social problems differently from their white, middle-class, male colleagues. Thus, public policy on some issues might well be different if our legislatures more closely approximated being descriptively representative. In addition to its possible impact on policy decisions, the distortion of legislative membership toward white, middle-aged, middle-class male clubs may also affect the extent to which many Americans feel committed to our political process. That consideration alone makes the process of legislative recruitment and membership a subject worthy of study.

More than any other branch of government, the legislature, at both the state and the national level, is supposed to represent the "voice of the people." Yet, as noted in Chapter 2, the membership of the nation's legislatures is not a mirror representation of the population—even the voting-age population. A statistical sampling of the *citizenry* of each state, or of the nation, would include *fewer* older, college-educated, prosperous white males than one finds in our legislatures, and *more* women, racial minorities, blue-collar workers, and people under thirty. This is pretty much true, too, of the legislatures of other democratic nations.[1] It was also noted in Chapter 2 that whether a random sampling of the citizenry (a miniaturized "mirror" of society) would constitute the best legislature is arguable,[2] but we should at least understand the degree to which our legislatures are not "descriptively" representative in a strictly statistical sense and the reasons they are not. Thus, the following sections will examine in greater detail the characteristics of our state and national legislators and then look at the process of "recruitment" to the legislature, or how the legislators get there.

THE STATE LEGISLATORS

American state legislators are generally of higher social status than their constituents, especially in terms of education and occupational achievement. Few earn their livings with their hands in what are usually called "blue-collar" occupations. Most are members of their district's dominant ethnic and religious groups.

Education

American state legislators are much better educated than the average citizen. As Table 4.1 indicates, the American state legislature is made up of mainly college-educated citizens. A substantial number of the legislators hold earned graduate or professional degrees. For instance, in the 1967 Iowa legislature, the 1973 Michigan legislature, and the 1977 California and New Mexico legislatures, over one fourth of the members held advanced degrees.[3]

Occupations

State legislators usually come from relatively high-status occupations, as might be expected from their educational attainments. Almost none are hourly wage earners. Their occupations tend to be those which permit *flexible scheduling* of commitments. Attorneys, independent businesspeople, and insurance and real-estate brokers can plan their work schedules to leave time for political campaigning and legislative service. Further, their incomes are generally high enough so that they can afford to take time off for politics. Adequate personal income is especially important in the one third of the states in which the legislature meets for less than ninety days per year and legislative compensation is not intended as a primary source of income—the states with "citizen" or "amateur" legislators, rather than "professional" ones.

TABLE 4.1
Education Levels of Americans and of American State Legislators

Education Level Attained	U.S. Population Over Age 25 (1979)	State Legislators					
		Calif. (1957)	Iowa (1967)	N.J. (1957)	N.M. (1981)	Ohio (1957)	Tenn. (1957)
High School Diploma or Less	69%	15%	22%	13%	12%	23%	26%
Some College	15	31	33	24	36	19	28
College Graduate	16	54	45	63	53	58	46

Sources: Data from John C. Wahlke, Heinz Eulau, William Buchanan and Leroy C. Ferguson, *The Legislative System* (New York: John Wiley, 1962), p. 489; Samuel C. Patterson, Ronald D. Hedlund and G. Robert Boynton, *Representatives and Represented* (New York: John Wiley, 1975), p. 28; Bureau of the Census, *Statistical Abstract of the United States, 1980* (Washington, D.C.: U.S. Government Printing Office, 1980), p. 149; *Legislative Supplement,* (Santa Fe: New Mexico Rural Electrification Cooperative Association, 1981).

Some states with brief legislative sessions schedule the sessions during January and February, and this makes it easier for farmers to serve in the legislature, although legislative reapportionment and rural-to-urban population migration have reduced the number of farmer-legislators. Farmers had a majority of Tennessee's legislative seats, for example, for the first forty years after Tennessee statehood, and over one third of the seats up until World War I. Today, farmers comprise barely one tenth of Tennessee's legislators. In industrialized Ohio, farmers held eleven percent of the seats in 1949, but only four percent in 1969. Charles S. Hyneman reported that farmers held a little over a fifth of the nation's state legislative seats during the period from 1925 to 1935.[4] Today, the farmer-legislative percentage is less than half that. (See Table 4.2).

TABLE 4.2
Occupations of Legislators in Selected State Legislatures

	Thirteen Lower Chambers and Twelve Senates During 1925–1935		Eight Legislatures of the 1970s	
	Number	*Percent*	*Number*	*Percent*
Farmers	2,722	21.5	103	7.1
Lawyers	3,555	28.0	343	23.7
Teachers (K-12 and Administrators)	—	—	93	6.5
Other Professional	639	5.0	97	6.7
Union Representatives	—	—	18	1.2
Journalism—News Media	369	2.9	21	1.5
Blue Collar & Crafts	205	1.6	48	3.3
Government Employees	—	—	64	4.4
Other White Collar	—	—	38	2.6
Contractors	273	2.2	32	2.2
Manufacturing/Industrial/Management	445	3.5	72	5.0
Insurance/Real Estate	869	6.8	153	10.6
General Sales	525	4.1	101	7.0
Engineers	184	1.5	20	1.4
Banking/Finance	352	2.8	26	1.8
Merchants	1,263	10.0	130	9.0
Not Otherwise Classified	704	5.5	34	2.4[a]
Not Known	584	4.6	52	3.6
Total	12,689	100.0	1,445	100.0

[a]This category for the 1970s includes 1.5 percent homemakers, 0.4 percent students, and 0.5 percent retired. Of the Vermont legislators, 27.5 percent indicated they had retired but their career occupations were classified elsewhere when known.

Sources: Charles Press and Kenneth VerBurg, *State and Community Governments in the Federal System* (New York: John Wiley, 1979), p. 250. Data for 1925–35 from Charles S. Hyneman, "Tenure and Turnover of Legislative Personnel," *Annals of the American Academy of Political and Social Science* (1938), p. 255. Some of Hyneman's classification titles have been modified. Data for the 8 legislatures were taken from the state manuals for the following states; Illinois (1973–1974), Rhode Island (1975–1976), Oregon (1975–1976), Texas (1970–1971), Michigan (1975–1976), Pennsylvania (1972–1973), Indiana (1975–1976), and Vermont (1973–1974).

Brokerage Occupations   The dominant occupations in today's state legislatures are what might be called the "brokerage" occupations (law, real estate, and insurance). As noted earlier, legislators from these occupations are most likely to have flexible schedules which would allow for time to campaign and to take off to attend committee meetings and sessions of the legislature. They are likely, also, to have partners or associates who can look after their professional or business affairs while they are away from their offices. By contrast, physicians, architects, small businesspeople, and salaried employees of large firms are frequently unable to serve in the legislature because, by doing so, they could fall behind in their profession, lose their jobs, miss a promotion, or allow their business to decline badly. It should be noted, too, that people in the "brokerage" professions may be especially attracted to legislative service because it offers an opportunity to enhance their private profession or business. The increased status which may accompany legislative membership, and the recognition and responsibility it implies, may permit an attorney to secure new clients or a more lucrative law business. Similarly, accounts and commissions, formerly out of reach for an insurance or real estate professional, might become available for such a person who serves in the legislature. Campaign publicity and political news coverage can help, too. Some young attorneys, realtors, and insurance brokers may even seek a legislative seat primarily to help them in their private occupations.[5]

Why So Many Attorneys?   Lawyers are perceived as "natural" legislators. That is, there is a convergence between the professional training and attitudes required of a lawyer and the skills needed to be a successful legislator. Lawyers are trained in advocacy, which is a great deal of what a politician does, also. They are trained in the law. Most people are aware that legislators write the laws, and people want an effective advocate for their point of view. Thus, it is not unusual for citizens to want to be represented by a trained advocate who is knowledgeable in the law—a lawyer.[6]

Lawyers are able to stand the risks of politics more readily than members of other professions. As one writer has stated, "In a highly competitive society, where occupational success is the most highly valued goal for the ambitious, who can, with the least danger, leave their jobs for the tremendous risks of a political career? Among the high-prestige occupations it seems to be the lawyers. . . ."[7] Not only can lawyers more easily bear the risks of politics—particularly the risk of defeat, which is ever present, even in a "safe" district, when a person needs some business or profession to fall back on—but, as noted earlier, they may actually enhance their careers through legislative service, through free and legitimate advertising and through increased contacts with prospective clients and important lawyers. They also remain current with the law through their legislative work.

Lawyer-legislators may also gain the additional benefit of becoming acquainted with career bureaucrats whose decisions or attitudes may be crucial for the lawyer-legislator's future legal clients. People in the business world must wend their way through a complex set of state regulations, and many frequently employ attorneys to help them do so. A present or former legislator, who is also an attorney, can sometimes cut through a bureaucratic tangle with a single phone call to the appropriate bureaucrat whom the legislator knows and who trusts him or her. A nonlegislator-lawyer, with no connections afforded by service in the legislature, might spend weeks or months in formal correspondence just trying to define that same problem. Potential conflicts of interest can, of course, arise here, when a present lawyer-legislator makes contacts for a client with a bureaucracy which must get its support and funds from the legislature, or even the committee, of which the lawyer-legislator is a member.

Another reason why there are more lawyers in legislatures than even the other "brokerage" professions of real estate and insurance is that the American political system provides extraordinary opportunities and advantages to lawyers.[8] Any upright citizen can be elected sheriff, a member of the city council, a state legislator, or governor. But only attorneys are allowed to hold certain offices in our system—prosecuting or district attorney and their assistants, attorney general, U.S. district attorney, judge. Numerous appointive positions at the state or local level, such as municipal attorney, are available only to lawyers. The presence of such "lawyers only" positions in the political-opportunity structure in America gives lawyers extra incentive to become active in politics, and they can help cushion electoral defeat. Appointive "lawyers only" posts are especially helpful in getting young lawyers started in their political careers and getting them better known by, and better acquainted with, their prospective constituents. A classic 1957 study of state legislators in four states found, for example, that almost one third of the lawyer-legislators in those states had first held "lawyers only" positions before being elected to the state legislature.[9]

Although law is the most overrepresented occupation in American legislatures, the share of the nation's state legislative seats held by attorneys has declined from 26 percent in 1966 to 20 percent in 1979. The Delaware legislature is unique in that it has had *no* attorneys among its sixty-two members since 1974.[10] In part, the declining percentage of legislator-lawyers may reflect a slip in the profession's prestige as a result of the Watergate scandal and subsequent political scandals involving attorneys. As a spokesperson for the National Conference of State Legislatures observed, voters have a "universal distrust of lawyers after Watergate," leading people to "want someone in office closer to the average person (than an attorney)."[11] Other factors also probably contribute to the declining number of American lawyer-legislators, but it seems unlikely that many other states will match Delaware's record. Legislative service is likely to remain very attractive to lawyers, especially young ones.

In terms of their subsequent political careers, state legislative service for lawyers appears to be much more valuable for them than similar service for nonlawyers. The lawyer-legislators move on to other offices at a much higher rate than their nonlawyer legislative colleagues—and the difference is accounted for by the number of lawyer-legislators who move from the legislative position to a "lawyers only" position.[12] By contrast, Mogens Pedersen noted that in the Danish parliament—the Folketing—only four percent of the seats were held by lawyers. Pedersen suggested that the lack of judicial rewards for lawyer-legislators helps to account for this fact, stating that "the (judicial) selection procedures and the prevailing norms of proper behavior in the Danish judicial system have effectively hampered an interplay of judicial and political careers."[13]

Age and Political Socialization

State legislators are predominantly middle-aged or older. The median age in different state legislative chambers is between the mid-forties and the low fifties, with the upper chamber in most states tending to be a bit older than the lower chamber. Some retirees, including a few people in their eighties, serve in state legislatures, but few members are under age thirty. Even though the minimum age for legislative service is usually twenty-one years, a legislator under age twenty-five is rare and legislatures composed entirely of people over age thirty are common.[14]

Age is more than just an interesting characteristic. It may also affect the perspectives and behavior of legislators. Barely a fourth of the Connecticut legislators classified by James David Barber as "Advertisers" and "Lawmakers" were over forty, for instance, while 67 percent of the "Spectators" and 59 percent of the "Reluctants" were past age forty.[15] More of the younger legislators tend to be in the legislature to make laws or contacts, while many of the oldest members may be there reluctantly or may be just enjoying being active and having a bit of income. To a certain extent, a legislator's age also reflects his or her political socialization. The older state legislators still have vivid memories of the Great Depression, for example, while those under forty-five grew up in a basically prosperous society. Different ambitions and perspectives may affect votes on issues.

Some state legislators first developed an interest in politics as adults, but most acquired an interest in politics at an early age. Most had parents or other close relatives who were actively involved in politics. Many have relatives in public office. Most have middle-class or upper-middle-class family backgrounds. Most began political activities without planning to seek election to the legislature, and about one half began by working in a campaign for a particular candidate or for a political party. The stimulus to candidacy for the legislature is sometimes a particular issue, is sometimes simply being asked to run, and is sometimes related to one's occupation or profession. The occupational stimulus occurs more frequently among men than women.[16]

Legislators who report having been interested in politics before age twenty seem to have needed less external stimulus in deciding to run for the legislature. They appear to be "self-starters." A study of legislators in Massachusetts, North Carolina, Oregon, and Utah found that such legislators were also more likely than others to interact often with lobbyists and to participate actively in the legislative bargaining process.[17] Yet, other research has indicated little if any difference in legislative role orientation between legislators whose political interests were awakened in adolescence and those who became interested and active in politics as adults.[18]

Most legislators are long-time residents of their communities. Many grew up in or near the legislative district represented, and residency in the district or county for thirty years is common. Among legislative candidates, those with lengthy local residency are much more likely to be elected than are relative newcomers.[19] Legislators representing newly developed suburban areas are, of course, the exception.[20]

Prior Political Experience

For many, the state legislature is an "entry" position. That is, the state legislative post is the first public office held. State legislative bodies vary greatly in the percentage of members with prior officeholding experience. For instance, 29 percent of Colorado legislators elected from 1957 to 1966, 30 percent of the 1969 Washington House of Representatives, but 43 percent of the 1972 Michigan legislature had held public office before election to the legislature; for the remainder of the legislators in those states, the legislative office was an "entry" office.[21] Forty-one percent of the 1931 New York legislature had prior government office experience, a proportion which increased to 52 percent in 1951; the legislature was the first public office for the others.[22] The bulk of those prior offices were school board, city council, county commission, assistant district attorney, and similar local posts. Another growing type of prelegislative office experience is pointed out by a study which showed that close to one fifth of the members of the 1978 California General Assembly had served as paid aides to elected officeholders immediately prior to their election to the state legislature.[23]

States, and areas within states, vary in regard to level of interparty competition. They also vary in the extent to which prior office experience is required before one is thought "eligible" to seek election to the legislature, in large part because of the impact of party competition on recruitment patterns. In areas with strong competition between the parties there is ". . . greater emphasis . . . on entry into politics at the local level of government or party organization, and on having had some governmental experience before running for the state legislature."[24] Experience as a party official is sometimes substituted for experience as a public official in demonstrating one's ability and thus becoming "eligible" for the legislative nomination.

The ability of inexperienced aspirants to win election to the state legislature is also affected by the status of legislative office within the state, a factor which affects competition for the office. Where competition for the honor is less keen, a candidate's other attributes (including education, community status, or party office experience) may make up for lack of public-office experience. This is especially the case in states where legislative districts are small and legislative compensation is meager. In small towns in Connecticut, for example, the problem is one of "who is available?" rather than "which of these contestants should we favor?"[25]

Use of the legislature as an "entry" position is more frequent in poorly paid (basically amateur) than in better-paid (basically professional) legislatures. In part, the greater prior office experience found among the better-paid state legislators is the result of constituency size. Legislative districts containing only a few thousand people (such as are found in the more sparsely populated states, which tend to have amateur legislatures) are unlikely to encompass the constituencies of numerous other political posts. Large legislative districts, on the other hand, are likely to encompass numerous municipalities, school districts, and even counties.[26] Large legislative districts are found in the most heavily populated states, the states which also tend to have reasonably well-paid professional legislatures. One fifth of the states have senate districts with over 200,000 people each, and in California, state senate districts are larger than Congressional districts. Even state representative districts in California, New York, and Ohio have over 100,000 people in each.

Race

Most American state legislators are white. Some black, Hispanic, native-American and Asian-American legislators now sit in the state legislatures, but, when the percentage of racial minorities in the general population is compared to their proportion of the state legislative seats, it is clear that minorities are underrepresented.

Blacks   There are twenty-three million black people in America. They are generally underrepresented in state legislatures. In the South, until relatively recently, this was a result of legal and illegal barriers to black voting. For example, as late as 1965, there were only fifty black officeholders in the eleven states of the old Confederacy.[27]

New federal measures—the Twenty-fourth Amendment to the U.S. Constitution, outlawing the poll tax (1966), the Civil Rights Act of 1964, the Voting Rights Act of 1965, and the appointment of federal voter registrars—dramatically increased the number of blacks who were registered to vote. By 1972, there were 1,944 black officeholders in the old South—but this was still only 2.5 percent of all elected officials in that region.[28] The black community is still underrepresented in southern state legislatures, but a study in 1973 showed that blacks were better represented

62

TABLE 4.3
Black Legislative Representation in Selected States, 1971

State	Percent Black Population	Percent Black Legislators	Representativeness Ratio*
Colorado	3.0%	4.0%	1.33
Michigan	11.2	10.3	.92
Ohio	9.1	8.3	.92
Nevada	5.7	5.0	.88
California	7.0	5.8	.83
North Carolina	22.2	1.8	.08
South Carolina	30.5	2.4	.08
Alabama	26.2	1.4	.05
Mississippi	36.8	0.6	.02

*A representativeness ratio of 1.0 is "fair."

Source: Reprinted from Lee Sigelman and Albert K. Karnig, "Black Representation in the American States: A Comparison of Bureaucracies and Legislatures," *American Politics Quarterly*, Vol. 4, No. 2, pp. 241–242, © 1976 Sage Publications, Inc., with permission of the publisher and the author.

in southern legislative positions than they were in any other type of elective office.[29] The overwhelming majority of black state legislators are, however, members of the lower chamber, not the state senate, and in Georgia they all represent urban areas.[30]

Table 4.3 shows the underrepresentation of black citizens in some state legislatures in both the North and South. Underrepresentation can be attributed partly to lower participation rates, and partly to legislative districting. Of thirty-eight states in which more than 1 percent of the population was black in 1971, eighteen had less than half the number of black state legislators that the black population would be entitled to if representation were on an ethnic-population basis. In Alabama, Mississippi, North Carolina, and South Carolina, population figures suggest that there should have been twelve to fifty times as many black legislators as were actually in office in those states in 1971. In that same year, however, blacks actually held more Colorado legislative seats than their share of the state's population.[31]

Hispanics   Whether the nation's twelve million Hispanic Americans are considered to be a racial minority or an ethnic-language minority, or both, Hispanics have suffered from discrimination in the United States and are underrepresented in American state legislatures. Spanish-speaking and Spanish-culture Americans are mainly of Mexican, Cuban, and Puerto Rican extraction, although Hispanics from many other countries also live in the United States. The largest U.S. Hispanic group are the Mexican-Americans, or Chicanos (as many prefer to be called), most of whom live in five southwestern states. Many live in the same communities where their great-grandparents and even more distant ancestors had lived, prior to U.S. occupation of the area. Their concentration in the Southwest has permitted them to make themselves felt politically in recent years. Thus, most of the research on Hispanics in American politics has been focused on the Southwest, even though hundreds of thousands of Hispanics also live in New York, Florida, Illinois, Pennsylvania, and elsewhere.

TABLE 4.4
Hispanic Legislative Representation in Five Southwestern States, 1978

State	Percent Hispanic Population	Percent Hispanic Legislators	Representativeness Ratio
New Mexico	40%	32%	.80
Colorado	13	8	.62
Arizona	18	11	.61
Texas	18	11	.61
California	15	5	.33

Sources: Calculated from F. Chris Garcia and Rudolph O. de la Garza, *The Chicano Political Experience: Three Perspectives* (North Scituate, Mass.: Duxbury Press, 1977), pp. 104–7; Fernando V. Padilla and Antonio Sisneros, "Chicano Politics," unpublished manuscript, 1980, p. 4.

In the five southwestern states, Mexican-Americans constitute 13 to 40 percent of the population, but—as Table 4.4 shows—hold smaller shares of their states' legislative seats.

Few Chicano legislators have been chosen for legislative leadership positions over the years, but in Arizona, Colorado, and (especially) New Mexico, they have increasingly held positions as majority leader of one chamber or the other or as president of the Senate or Speaker of the House.[32]

Except for New Mexico, substantial Chicano representation in state legislatures is a fairly recent development. The first Chicano state senator elected in California in sixty-four years was seated in 1975. Only seventeen Chicanos served in the California legislature during the entire period between 1864 and 1973, a period in which a total of some four thousand individuals served in that body.[33] Similarly, the 1932 and 1952 Texas legislatures each contained only one Hispanic, as did the 1942 and 1952 Arizona legislatures, compared to an average of over twenty Hispanics in the New Mexico Legislature in those years. The Colorado legislature regularly included one or two Hispanics, but more than that have been elected only relatively recently.[34]

Other Minorities   Little research has been done on the American legislative representation for other minorities. One reason is that few native-Americans and Asian-Americans have been elected to the state legislatures. In California, for example, "no person identified as an 'Indian' has ever served in the state legislature."[35] Yet, some 150,000 Californians (under 1 percent of the population) are Indians.

In 1980, native-American state legislators included an Oklahoma state representative, who is chief of the Choctaw Nation and who represents a district with many Choctaw residents; two representatives and a senator in Arizona, all from the northeast area of the state where the Navajo reservation lies; and a representative and a senator in New Mexico, both from the Navajo northwestern part of the state.

Some Eskimos and native Hawaiians serve in the Alaska and Hawaii legislatures, and the latter body also includes more legislators of Asian ancestry than any other state legislature. No more than two or three Asian-Americans serve in any other state legislative body.

Why So Few Minority Legislators?   The explanation for the underrepresentation of racial minorities in American state legislatures (and in Congress, as will be noted later) lies, partly, in the lower voting-participation rates of racial minorities, partly in white prejudice against minority candidates, partly in the electoral system (especially the use of single-member districts, as discussed in Chapter 5), and partly in the interaction of all those factors. Much has to do with elite behavior in the recruitment process and in districting. It is not uncommon for a state to gerrymander a minority community so that it receives less than its fair share of legislative seats. In the 1970 California apportionment, for example:

> . . . the Chicano community in East Los Angeles, where almost a million Chicanos reside, was sliced into nine state assembly districts, seven state senate districts, and six U.S. Congressional districts. None of these is forty percent Chicano.[36]

In Arizona and Texas, the establishment of county-wide, at-large legislative districts has caused the candidates from black and Chicano communities to be overwhelmed by the votes of the larger community. Minority candidates who do manage to win the nomination of the Democratic or Republican party in such districts then tend to lose in the general election, partly because of opposing "bloc voting" by the white majority.[37]

In Illinois, three-member legislative districts, with cumulative voting (used until 1980), appear to have been less unfair than the Arizona and Texas at-large districts, but they still have produced fewer black legislators than would be elected from fairly drawn single-member districts.[38] Similarly, multimember state legislative districts in Indianapolis result in dilution of the votes of blacks in the inner-city areas of Indianapolis.[39] Were large multimember districts combined with a system of proportional representation, the results would probably be dramatically different, as will be seen in the next chapter.

Women Legislators

Most state legislators are men, although the percentage of women state legislators has increased dramatically in the past decade (see Figure 4.1). In 1969, less than 5 percent of the nation's state legislators were women. In 1979, that figure had increased to about 10 percent.[40] Female representation in the legislatures of the various states is not uniform, but all states now regularly have women legislators. Those states with the largest contingents of women legislators have tended to be the less-populous ones.[41] Only one of seven women state legislators serves in an upper chamber. In 1979, women held one fourth of the legislative seats in New Hampshire, a fifth of the seats in Connecticut, and over 10 percent of the seats in fifteen other state legislatures. In sixteen states, however, women held 5 percent or less of the legislative seats. Nine of the eleven southern states are among those with the fewest female legislators.

Progress toward electing more women to legislatures seems to proceed irregularly in each state, although virtually all of the states have more women legislators now than they had a decade ago. In Florida, for example, only five women had ever served in the state legislature before 1960. Following reapportionment in 1963, three women were elected to the Florida House and one (the first ever) won a seat in the Florida Senate. Today, Florida is among the one third of the states where women hold 10 percent or more of the legislative seats.[42] By contrast, the 1957 Tennessee General Assembly included only two women in the house and one in the senate (2.3 percent of all members) and, after two decades of reapportionment, Tennessee still had only two women in the 1977 house and one in the 1977 senate. Irene Diamond found that, from 1971 to 1975, states with relatively high proportions of women

FIGURE 4.1

Percentage of American State Legislators Who Are Women, 1917-1981

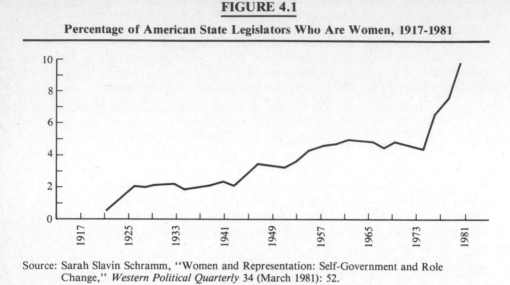

Source: Sarah Slavin Schramm, "Women and Representation: Self-Government and Role
Change," *Western Political Quarterly* 34 (March 1981): 52.

legislators continued to have high proportions, and states with low percentages of
women legislators continued to be relatively low, despite a substantial overall increase in the number of women state legislators.[43]

But a promising early start in regard to the number of women legislators is not
necessarily a guarantee that a state will continue to be a leader in this field. The
California Assembly of 1922, for example, included five women among its eighty
members, although all forty California senators were men. During the ensuing decades, the number of women in the assembly fluctuated between one and five, with
no senators. In 1975, there were two California assemblywomen. The first woman
California senator was elected in 1976, and five women were elected to the assembly.
In the 1978 election, female representation increased again. Nine assemblywomen
and two women senators (9.2 percent of the state's legislators) sat in the 1979 California legislature,[44] a substantial gain in two elections but not enough to put California in the forefront on this dimension of representation.

Characteristics of Women Legislators Like their male colleagues, most women
state legislators are white, middle-class, married, and college educated. Most grew
up in families whose high levels of political participation gave them an early
exposure to, and understanding of, politics.[45] But female legislators seem to have
begun their legislative careers some five or six years later in life than did their male
colleagues, presumably because they were less able to get out of the home earlier.[46]
Some 88 percent of women state legislators serving in 1971 or 1973 had a
post-high-school education, a percentage almost identical to the male legislators
serving at the same time. More of the male legislators had completed college,
however, and more men had post-college educations (especially law school).[47]

Although the proportion in each state varies widely, depending on the nature of
the state, about one fourth of American women state legislators listed their
occupations as homemaker.[48] Occupations of women legislators outside the home

are from a wider range of pursuits than those of male legislators. In general, as Irene Diamond points out, women legislators who work outside the home are more likely to work for someone else and to be less economically independent than men.[49] Many women legislators are in sales, clerical, and service occupations, positions seldom producing male legislators. Law is much less prevalent among women legislators than among their male colleagues. Some 17 percent of women legislators are members of the bar. Very few women legislators are in banking, real estate, or insurance.[50] The brokerage occupations, thus, are much less common among female legislators than among male legislators.

Women legislators are disproportionately concentrated in states with relatively small numbers of citizens in each legislative district—states with amateur legislatures. As the population of the legislative districts increases and the availability of legislative seats constricts—in professional legislator states—there is increased competition, and fewer women legislators are nominated and elected. In a competitive situation, the qualifications for any serious candidate are higher, and female aspirants, of course, must have educational, occupational and background characteristics similar to their male competitors.[51] The educational and occupational characteristics of women legislators more closely resemble those of men legislators in states with professional legislatures and fewer women legislators.[52] Because women state legislators are found mostly in the states with less competition (and less professional legislatures), a comparison of the nation's female state legislators to the nation's male state legislators may make the differences between the two sets appear larger than is probably the case in various individual state legislatures.

Why So Few Female Legislators?   There are fewer women than men in law and other "brokerage" professions, which helps keep their numbers low in state legislatures (and Congress). In addition, a woman who wants to be a legislator must be willing to tolerate the role strain between the conservative image of a woman as wife and mother only and expectations about the personality characteristics which make a good legislator.[53] Women also have been more burdened by domestic responsibilities than men, especially when their children are small. Men, active in politics, often tend to feel that women aspirants must overcome personal weaknesses if they want to succeed, while women politicians feel there is institutionalized sexism in politics and that the political recruitment system is stacked against them.[54] That is, many women political activists feel that the system of winnowing potential legislative candidates automatically favors males—that the local political elites often are sexist. Some evidence suggests that as a region becomes accustomed to the idea of women legislators, more women will be elected. Thus, women now serving, mainly in lower chambers, are thought to be preparing the way for additional women in both legislative chambers.[55] Some observers also suggest that the increased number of women legislators over the past decade is a direct function of the increased number of women candidates, and that this is the result of increased awareness and encouragement of political opportunities.[56] Both observations lead to the expectation that increasing numbers of women will be elected to American legislatures.

Do Race and Gender Matter?

Even though most American legislators are white males, one can argue that each legislator was elected by all members of the constituency, and, thus, all members of society, and that, so long as there is adequate *formal* representation, *descriptive* representation is not necessary. While to some extent that argument is valid, the extreme case demonstrates the weakness of the argument. For a century after the Civil War, blacks were systematically excluded from most state legislatures. Were the white state legislators, collectively, as concerned about the problems of black constituents as they were those of middle-class white voters? Clearly not. Further, we must consider the importance of *symbolic* representation. If we wish people to work within the established political and social system, we must hold out the hope of success to all citizens and must provide each citizen with some evidence that his or her voice is being heard. At least *some* legislators must resemble the citizen and must seem to be on the citizen's side, or the system courts the alienation of those who are excluded. Thus, it would be important for women and racial minorities to be included in legislative membership, even if they had exactly the same political perspectives as white male legislators.

Since they do *not* have identical views, however, their inclusion is even more important—for *substantive* representation. Not all racial minority legislators and not all women agree on all issues, obviously. But the distribution of their opinions on important issues often differs from that of white male legislators, just as their experience differs. Women state legislators, for example, favored the national Equal Rights Amendment (ERA) by a margin of six to one. Were even a third of the nation's state legislators women, the Equal Rights Amendment to the U.S. Constitution would not have been stalled three states short of ratification.[57] Similarly, women in the Florida legislature have proved to be much more supportive than men of legislation enacted to improve the status of women.[58] Women in four New England legislatures, when asked concerning the best means of discouraging riots and disorders, "were more likely to emphasize solving the problems of poverty while men more often stressed using all available force. Women tended to be more generous with regard to the provision of day-care services."[59] The opinion of these New England legislators also differed by sex on the extent to which state labor laws protected the interests of women and whether the state's abortion law should be repealed.

Blacks, Hispanics, and other minority legislators differ from their other colleagues in their outlook on a number of fundamental political issues. At the most basic level, the election of black legislators tends to reduce the ability of racist white legislators to advance openly their segregationist causes.[60] That race is important was demonstrated by the Miller and Stokes 1958 study, "Constituency Influence in Congress," which showed that the policy dimension with the greatest agreement between a representative's voting record and his or her constituents' opinions was "approval of federal action to protect the rights of Negroes."[61] Racial minority legislators differ from their white colleagues, both in their positions on numerous issues and in the intensity with which they support those positions. Voting in support of certain bills is helpful but working hard to push those bills through the legislative process—a matter of intensity of commitment and of priorities—is also important.

Issues on which minority legislators are generally agreed and on which their intensity of commitment tends to be greater than that of most white legislators include: encouraging active government intervention in society against racial discrimination; support for the civil liberties and equality of citizens; and support for social-welfare programs for the poor. Hispanic and native-American legislators are more supportive of bilingual-education programs than are most other legislators. When it comes to garnering support within the legislature for measures which are explicitly for minority people, the ability of the minority legislators to define the issue in such a way that white legislators will consider the measure legitimate becomes a crucial legislative skill.[62]

MEMBERS OF CONGRESS

For much the same reasons as apply to state legislatures, the U.S. Congress is dominated by well-educated white males who are middle-aged or older. Congress draws its members from an even higher strata of society than is true of the state legislatures, partly because the rewards of service are greater and partly because Congressional constituencies are, for the most part, larger than state legislative constituencies.

Education

Members of Congress have even higher levels of education than state legislators. As of 1966, 93 percent of the U.S. representatives and 96 percent of the senators had attended college; 79 percent of the representatives and 83 percent of the senators were college graduates. Furthermore, 60 percent of the representatives and 69 percent of the senators had education beyond the college level, either in law school or in graduate school. Many are members of the national scholastic honorary society, Phi Beta Kappa. The educational level of today's members of Congress is little changed from 1966. A highly educated national legislature is the norm in Western democratic nations; few national legislators have pursued occupations which do not require at least some university training.[63]

Occupations

Almost half of the members of Congress are attorneys, an occupation which accounts for only about one tenth of one percent of the nation's work force. In 1981, 59 of the 100 senators and 194 of the 435 representatives held law degrees. The number of lawyers in the Senate was 65 in the previous Congress, and the number of lawyers in the House continued to decline: from 220 in 1977 to 205 in 1979, when lawyers constituted less than half the House membership for the first time in recent memory.[64] A large proportion of members of Congress have always been from the legal profession. Over half of the members of the Continental Congress, for instance, were lawyers.[65] About a third of the representatives in the first U.S. Congress (1789) were lawyers. The number of lawyers gradually increased until, in 1847, they constituted some 76 percent of the House membership. An irregular, slow decline in the percentage of lawyers has occurred since, especially since the late 1890s.[66] The Senate, too, has long contained many lawyers. About two thirds of the U.S. Senate in the 1930s were lawyers, as were 54 percent of all the senators who served between 1947 and 1957.[67]

Other brokerage occupations are also found in Congress. Business (including insurance and real estate) and banking accounted for 134 representatives and 28 senators in 1981, although some of these self-identified members were also listed as lawyers. Educators, including college professors, numbered 59 representatives and 10 senators, while 52 representatives and 13 senators were primarily from public service or political backgrounds (as were some members listed as lawyers). The only other occupations with a dozen or more members of Congress in 1979 were agriculture (37) and journalism (28).[68]

Although the law is the most overrepresented occupation in the House of Representatives and is the most prevalent single occupation in the Senate, law is no longer the most overrepresented occupation in the U.S. Senate. Only a handful of Americans can claim to be astronauts, but one of them, John Glenn of Ohio, is a senator, as was Harrison Schmitt of New Mexico.

Age

Only Americans age 25 or older may serve in the U.S. House of Representatives. A person must be 30 or older to be a U.S. senator. In practice, only a few members are elected at such early ages. Less than 2 percent of U.S. representatives are in their twenties when they first enter the House, and less than 2 percent of U.S. senators are under age 35 when they first enter the Senate. The most common age for initial election to the U.S. House is between ages 40 and 44, with ages 45–49 and 35–39 close behind. The most common age for first election to the U.S. Senate is the early fifties, with the late forties and the late fifties next most common.[69]

The average age of House members is normally younger than the average age of senators, usually by four or five years. When Congress convened in January 1981, the average U.S. representative was 48.4 years old. Eight representatives (an unusually large number) were under age 30 (seven of them were freshmen); one was 80; twelve were in their seventies; and another eighteen, including the Speaker, were age 65 or older. The number of elderly representatives has decreased somewhat in recent years, and the average age of the House has declined regularly for a decade, from an average of 52.2 years in January 1969. Four of the twenty standing committees of the 1981 House were chaired by members over age 70; three more were chaired by members in their late sixties. Most chairmen were in their fifties, and the three youngest committee chairpeople were in their forties.[70]

In January 1981, the average age of U.S. senators was 52.5 years, the lowest average Senate age in the last fifteen Congresses (30 years). The youngest senator was age 32 and another was 33, both unusually young for Senate membership. Eleven more were age 39 or less. Twelve senators were past age 65, including seven in their seventies.[71] Of the Senate's fifteen standing committees, only three were chaired by senators age 60 or older, a substantial change from the Ninety-sixth Congress. Older Republican senators, long in the minority, seem to have been more willing to retire than their older Democratic colleagues, who were chairmen of committees and subcommittees, and in charge of the legislative process. The new Republican majority in the Senate thus meant five chairmen in their forties and seven in their fifties.

Social Backgrounds

Members of Congress have middle- to upper-class backgrounds. A study of the Senate in the 1950s pointed out that "the senators were sons, with only a handful of exceptions, of men possessing upper and middle class occupations."[72] Only 7 percent of the senators were the children of "low-salaried workers, wage earners, servants and farm laborers" who comprised 66 percent of the work force at the time when those senators were children. Another 7 percent were clearly "patricians"—members of wealthy "old families."[73] William Domhoff found that 15 percent of the senators in the Eighty-ninth Congress (1965–66) were members of "the American upper class," although "a mere handful" of the representatives qualified as upper class.[74]

Perspective on the social status of members of Congress can also be gained by looking at their wealth. As a result of recent reforms, members are now required to file financial disclosure reports, in which they list their assets and liabilities in certain financial categories. It is difficult to determine a particular member's exact wealth, but about twenty senators are millionaires, and another dozen or more may be. Senator John Heinz of Pennsylvania, heir to the pickle-and-ketchup fortune, appears to be the wealthiest member, with unearned income of about half a million dollars in 1978 on assets worth over $16 million. Missouri's Senator John Danforth,

Ralston Purina heir, was worth over $5 million in 1978.[75] At the other end of the scale, some senators have only modest wealth, and a few have announced their departure from the Senate, giving as one reason that they could no longer afford to serve. There is no limit on members' "unearned" income (dividends, rents, etc.) but House members may receive no more in honoraria (from writing and speaking) and earned income each year than 15 percent of their Congressional salary, and senators may receive no more in honoraria and earned income than $25,000 per year.

The House of Representatives has its wealthy members, too, but there is a larger percentage who are merely prosperous and some whose assets are small and whose income consists solely of their Congressional salary. About 25 of the 435 representatives are millionaires, and another half dozen may be. Most member wealth is invested in real estate, banks, agricultural land, and stocks in major businesses.[76]

Casual observation leads one to note that some families produce many members of Congress, as well as other high government officials. The Lodge and Taft families of Massachusetts and Ohio are legendary. U.S. Representative Hamilton Fish of New York is, today, the fifth generation of his family to serve in Congress. The fathers of Senators Harry Byrd, Russell Long, and Alan Simpson were also U.S. senators. Barry Goldwater, Jr., the son of Senator Barry Goldwater of Arizona, is a U.S. representative, although from a different state, California. Senator Howard Baker's father served as a U.S. representative for thirteen years. His father-in-law, the late Everett M. Dirksen of Illinois, was minority leader when Baker was first seated in the Senate. When Edward M. Kennedy (son of an ambassador) first ran for the U.S. Senate from Massachusetts, his Democratic primary opponent was Edward McCormack, the state's attorney general, whose uncle, John McCormack, was then Speaker of the U.S. House of Representatives. Senator Kennedy's brother was President of the United States at the time.

Are we governed, then, by legislators who have "inherited" their posts? Is the nation which perceives itself as the epitome of modernization and meritocracy in fact governed by an elite based on kinship ties, as in a traditional society? We have not gone that far, of course, but family ties can be important, evidencing strong local roots and ties, in winning election to the state legislatures, to Congress, and to other offices. One study showed that the number of U.S. representatives and senators who "were sons, grandsons, nephews, brothers, or first cousins of another member (or members) of Congress" slowly declined from 24.2 percent of the members in 1789 to 5 percent of the members in 1960.[77] On the other hand, responses from 85 of 200 members sampled in 1967 showed that 54.1 percent had close relatives in *some* kind of elective office at the local, state, or national level, including 5.9 percent who had relatives serving in or who had served in Congress.[78]

Members of Congress, like state legislators, are mostly long-time residents of the districts they represent, although they are somewhat less parochial, as a group, than are state legislators. The U.S. Constitution requires that a representative be a resident of the state he or she represents; tradition requires residency in the Congressional district represented. The percentage of newly elected members of Congress who were born outside the state or region they represent in Congress has declined over the past century, mostly because many western members in the late 1800s had originally gone West as children. The frontier era is over, and localism has reasserted itself.[79]

It is frequently said that most members of Congress are rural or small-town products who represent a "simpler" America. That apparently was the case before the reapportionment revolution of the 1960s, but it is no longer true. A study by Donald R. Matthews of U.S. senators serving from 1947 to 1957, for example, found that some two thirds of them had been born in rural areas or small towns.[80] But, today, rural and small-town products are no longer found in disproportionate numbers among members of Congress.[81] Because small towns are still well represented among the leaders of Congress, however, the image of the small-town, parochial member of Congress still lingers on.[82]

Religion

Most members of Congress are Protestants—with Episcopalians, Methodists, and Presbyterians found more frequently than the other Protestant denominations. Over two thirds of the 1981 Senate were Protestants, while seventeen senators were Roman Catholic, six were Jewish, four were Latter Day Saints (Mormons), and two were Greek Orthodox. Among U.S. representatives in 1981, well over half were Protestants, 27 percent were Roman Catholic, 6 percent were Jewish, 2 percent were Mormons, and the remaining few either listed no religion or were the only one or two members of their faith in the Congress.[83] Twenty years ago, Roman Catholics and Jews were underrepresented in Congress, but, today, as best as can be determined from the figures on percentage of the population adhering to the various doctrines, the major American religions are reasonably fairly represented in Congress. If anything, Roman Catholics and Jews are now somewhat overrepresented. A few members of Congress are also members of the clergy, an eventuality which is forbidden in Great Britain, Israel, and Mexico.[84] In 1980, Representative Robert Drinan, a Jesuit priest, withdrew as a candidate for reelection following the issuance of a directive by Pope John Paul II against priests holding elective office.

Racial Minorities in Congress

As is true of state legislators, most members of Congress are white. In 1983, only 20 of the 435 U.S. representatives (4.6 percent) were black. All black members were Democrats. The only black senator elected since Reconstruction, Edward Brooke of Massachusetts (a Republican), was defeated for reelection in 1978. Black representation in the U.S. House has grown substantially in the past quarter century, from 2 black members of Congress in 1953 to 20 in 1983, but the number of black U.S. representatives has grown by just 4 since 1975.[85] Blacks make up a little over 11 percent of the nation's population, and, if they were represented in Congress in proportion to their numbers, there would be close to 50 black representatives and 11 black senators. In the 1970s, blacks constituted 25 percent or more of the constituents in fifty-eight Congressional districts, but of the forty-five districts where they constituted between 25 percent and 49.9 percent of the people, they were able to elect only three members of Congress. The 1980 reapportionment resulted in 3 more black representatives, but one student of the subject sees little likelihood that blacks will achieve much more than 4 to 5 percent of the U.S. House seats in the near future.[86]

The black members of the Ninety-sixth Congress were all college graduates with about a fourth of them trained for the law and another fourth educators. Twenty-nine percent listed themselves as businessmen, with the rest from the clergy or medicine. Almost all had held public office before running for Congress, and most had been leaders in the civil-rights movement or the anti-poverty program.[87]

All black U.S. representatives belong to the Congressional black caucus, formed in 1969 to focus the attention of the people, the Congress, and the President on the concerns of black-Americans and to provide them with symbolic representation in Congress. The black caucus has worked hard for legislation which will help black-Americans and has also used its collective abilities to change racially discriminatory bureaucratic behavior in various government agencies.[88] It has also pushed for legislation which would help all poor people. Thus, it has made great efforts to obtain continued funding for the Office of Economic Opportunity's programs and for the Humphrey-Hawkins Full Employment bill.[89]

The 1983 House of Representatives included nine Hispanic-Americans, eight of whom were Mexican-Americans from the Southwest. The ninth, Robert Garcia of New York, is of Puerto Rican ancestry. All were Democrats, except for Republican Manuel Lujan of New Mexico. The only Hispanic U.S. senators have been from New Mexico.[90] The most recent was the late Joseph M. Montoya, who served in that position for twelve years until his defeat in 1976. Hispanic-Americans comprise some 5 to 6 percent of the total U.S. population. If they held a proportionate number of Congressional seats, some twenty-four Hispanics would be U.S. representatives and five or six would be U.S. senators. In California, where Chicanos make up over 15 percent of the population, only two of the state's 45 U.S. representatives (4.4 percent) are Chicanos. In Texas, where over 18 percent of the people are Chicanos, three of twenty-seven representatives (11.1 percent) are Chicanos.

Native-Americans are more underrepresented in Congressional membership. The nation's million Indians have no member of Congress.[91] Asian-Americans, who make up about 6.7 percent of the population, hold two Senate seats (both from Hawaii) and two House seats.

Women in Congress

Over one half of all Americans are women, but, in 1983, only twenty-three of the 535 members of Congress (4.3 percent) were women. The number of women in the House has increased only by five since Eisenhower was President (see Figure 4.2). The two elected women U.S. senators constitute an all-time high. The American situation is not unusual. Data from various national legislatures in 1968, 1969, or 1970 confirm the male dominance of other national legislatures. Australia had no women legislators. Only 2 percent of France's deputies were women, 5 percent of New Zealand's MPs (Members of Parliament) were women, and 4 percent of Great Britain's MPs were women. On the other hand, some nations do substantially better than the U.S., especially those which elect legislators from large constituencies using proportional representation rules. Although they have few women MPs, Great Britain does have a woman prime minister, Margaret Thatcher. In Israel, where a woman, the late Golda Meir, was recently prime minister, women hold about 6 percent of the seats in the Knesset. Women hold over 15 percent of the seats in the national legislatures of Guinea, Finland, and Sweden.[92]

"Widow's succession" has long been a major mechanism by which women have arrived in Congress, although, today, more incumbent women members of Congress have won election independently than have succeeded their late husbands. As Diane Kincaid has pointed out, the expression, "widow's succession," implies that the widow became a member of Congress almost without effort and in a rather passive manner. While that may be true sometimes, in about 90 percent of the cases, the widow who seeks her late husband's seat in the House has had to compete for the office in either the primary election, or the general election, or both.[93] It is worth noting here that the widow (or husband) of a U.S. senator *can* be temporarily appointed as the deceased spouse's successor, if the survivor can secure the nod from the governor. Vacancies in the U.S. House, on the other hand, are filled by election (either a special election or the next general election)—*never* by appointment—so, the representative's surviving spouse must win the party's nomination and must also

FIGURE 4.2

Percentage of Women in the U.S. House of Representatives, 1917-1981

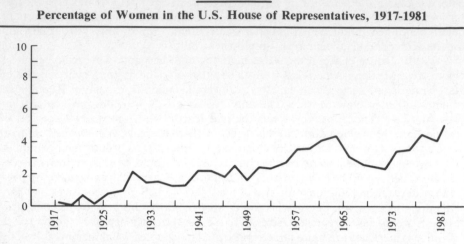

Source: Sarah Slavin Schramm, "Women and Representation: Self-Government and Role
   Change," *Western Political Quarterly* 34 (March 1981): 52.

win a general or special election. That is almost never accomplished without opposition. It certainly is not accomplished without the active participation of the surviving spouse, and many are defeated in the attempt. For the sixty-year period which ended in 1976, less than 3 percent of the senators who died in office were succeeded by their surviving spouses, and less than 9 percent of the representatives were replaced by their surviving spouses.[94]

Prior to 1950, only 27 percent of the "widow-succession" women in Congress sought reelection. Since 1950, 69 percent have sought one or more additional terms. Some "widow-succession" members have served in Congress a long time. Margaret Chase Smith of Maine won her late husband's House seat in 1940, served in the House until 1948, and then served twenty-four years in the U.S. Senate. Leonor Sullivan of Missouri was denied the party's nomination to seek her late husband's House seat in a special election, but, then, the party's candidate lost. At the next election, Sullivan overcame primary and general-election opposition and went on to serve twenty-four years in the House.[95]

Most women members of the 1983 Congress were elected to Congress without Congressional widowhood. That included the two women senators. Senator Paula Hawkins, a Florida Republican, was state Public Service Commission Chair before her election to the Senate. Senator Nancy Landon Kassebaum, a Republican, of Kansas, is the first woman elected to the U.S. Senate without having been first appointed to that office or having been a Congressional widow. Senator Hawkins is the second. Senator Kassebaum, like many of her male colleagues, had a politically prominent father. Alf Landon, a wealthy oilman, was twice elected governor of Kansas and was the Republican presidential nominee against President Franklin Roosevelt in 1936.

Women members of Congress are from both parties, although both women senators are Republicans. Women in Congress take on role orientations similar to those of their male colleagues, but there are some distinctive female perspectives. Like their male colleagues, their voting behavior is affected by district characteristics, political-party affiliation, and their respective positions within the Congressional structure, but from 1961 through 1975, the level of agreement among the voting patterns of women members of Congress increased significantly.[96] They have formed a woman's caucus, although not all women members have joined.

Prior Political Experience

Most people who are elected as a U.S. representative or U.S. senator have already held a local or state office. Of those who have not, the great majority have been active participants in their political party, and many have held party office. An increasing number, however, are relative newcomers to politics. That category includes some, such as Senator William Bradley of New Jersey, who translated his popularity as a professional basketball player into votes for the Senate.

In his study of U.S. senators who served from 1947 through 1957, Donald Matthews found that the "average senator" had "held about three public offices and had devoted about ten years . . . to officeholding before arriving at the upper chamber."[97] Over three fourths of them had been elected to public office before they were forty years old. Of the 180 senators who served in that decade, only 17 had held no public office before election to the Senate.[98] Another study of all 450 senators who were popularly elected to the U.S. Senate up to 1958 found similar patterns over a forty-four year time span; only 8 percent of the senators had held no prior office. Many had served as governor of their state. Others had been U.S. representatives, had held statewide elective office, served in the state legislature, or in a law-enforcement office.[99]

More recently, the increasing impact of television and the lessening control of political-party organizations over nominations are evident in a comparison of the freshmen U.S. senators first elected in 1978 and those first elected to the Senate in 1958. The average freshman senator in 1958 was almost fifty years old. The newcomers in 1978 averaged forty-three years. In 1958, only one of the eighteen new senators had held no prior office, and eleven of them had been U.S. representatives. In 1978, only seven of twenty first-year senators had seen House service, and six had held no prior public office at all.[100]

Members of the U.S. House of Representatives, while not averaging as much prior office experience as U.S. senators, still are more experienced politically than state legislators. Indeed, over one third of them served in a state legislature before winning a seat in Congress. And some 30 percent held a law-enforcement post before election to Congress. On the other hand, one fourth or so of the House members won a Congressional seat as their first public office. Many members of the House (including some who had been law-enforcement officials or state legislators) had also held local offices. A few members had held a statewide elective position before election to Congress, although most such high state officials have usually preferred to seek a seat in the Senate.[101]

RECRUITMENT OF AMERICAN LEGISLATORS

As we have seen, not all Americans are equally likely to become state legislators or members of Congress. Middle-aged, white, middle-class males, who are long-time residents of their communities, especially those in the brokerage occupations, are more likely than other Americans to be elected to legislative positions.

75

One way to think about recruitment to the legislature is to perceive the recruitment process as a series of separate selection phases in which the original pool of potential legislators in each constituency is winnowed down until the eventual single legislator takes his or her seat.[102] The major distinction is between what Lester G. Seligman calls "certification" (the social and political parameters, or boundaries, which define eligibility for consideration) and "selection" (the actual choice of specific candidates).[103] Although many people active in politics seldom give it a thought, the *actual* pool of potential legislators (those who might remotely be considered for the post) is substantially smaller than the *legally defined* pool. Under the laws of the various states, any registered voter over a certain minimum age (usually twenty-one or twenty-five) is eligible to seek election to the state legislature. In fact, however, only those citizens who can afford to serve (or to seek election and lose) and those thought to be most acceptable to the voters in the legislative district are likely to be seriously considered as potential candidates, either in their own minds or in the minds of the *agents* of political recruitment. This is the "certification" phase of political recruitment, resulting, as discussed earlier in this chapter, in consideration, mainly, of long-time male residents of the constituency who are well educated and fairly successful, and who share religious, cultural, and ethnic characteristics with the voters in the district.[104]

The agents of political recruitment include, early in the process, *friends and coworkers* (such as one's law partners), *interest groups* with which one agrees (economic interest groups primarily, but also environmental and "good government" groups), ethnic-group associations, individual leaders in the community, *public officials* already in elected office, and *party leaders.* The party officials become more important as the recruitment process proceeds into the selection phase, but their alternatives normally are restricted by the activities of other agents earlier in the process.[105] The importance of party officials is also affected by a state's laws governing legislative nominations and the extent to which those laws restrict participation in the formal nominating process.[106]

Some observers suggest that the white male dominance of American legislatures stems in large part from the attitudes of elite local political actors who control the candidate-winnowing process. As long as these elite local decision-makers actively discourage minorities and women while actively encouraging white males, then women and minorities will remain underrepresented in American legislative bodies.[107] Thus it may not be entirely coincidental that the number of women state legislators has been increasing—especially in Republican states—during the time period that the national political parties (especially the Republicans) have been actively recruiting attractive candidates for the state legislatures, training them, and assisting them financially in the campaign. The national party's field representatives constitute an intrusion—and a powerful one—on the local political elite's domination of the legislative nominating process.

Competition for a legislative seat obviously varies with the desirability of the post. Congressional seats and seats in the better-paid professional state legislatures are normally sought by more than one aspirant, especially when an incumbent retires. Seats in the poorly paid or unpaid amateur state legislatures, however, are less eagerly sought, and in some constituencies party leaders have to actively recruit somebody to run.[108] Career possibilities to which legislative service may lead are probably as important as the pay and conditions of legislative service in inducing candidacies. If the legislature is widely perceived as the entry position in an opportunity structure, and legislative service is thought likely to lead to a more desirable office, competition for the legislature may be strong, even though the legislative post itself is not very exciting.[109]

Competition for a party's nomination to the legislature varies with the value of the nomination. In a district where no party member has won the election in decades, the party's nomination may go begging. In such districts, the party organization still prefers to field a candidate—a willing sacrificial lamb—for the benefits a full slate of candidates gives to the party's candidate for governor, President, or senator. The reward for entering such a legislative contest may be an appointment by the party's candidate (if successful) for the higher office, a chance to be the candidate later in a more promising race, or the chance to get some free advertising as a young attorney or insurance agent.[110]

The more valuable the legislative office, the greater the competition for the seat and the more likely it is that the successful contender will have proved his or her abilities in a prior public office (usually a local office) and will have met all the expected criteria of education, occupation, long-time district residency, social status in the community, ethnic/racial identification with the constituents, and being male. Thus, Irene Diamond found that for the relatively low-status New Hampshire House seats, women were more easily able to secure the nominations, since few people wanted them. Further, while none of the eighty-six women serving in the Connecticut and New Hampshire legislatures in 1972 were attorneys, all five women first elected to the U.S. House of Representatives in 1972 were lawyers.[111]

Politics in the United States is generally thought of as being less intense than in some other countries, especially in developing nations. It is thus often assumed that anybody can contest for a nomination to the state legislature without running much risk of building up hostilities. That is, it is often assumed that the *risks* of political participation in America are sufficiently low that we need not concern ourselves with this question. But Lester G. Seligman and his colleagues discovered that an urban setting, with its numerous economic opportunities and relatively diffuse economic elite, is much more likely to produce what they call "enthusiastic" candidacies than is a rural district, where political competition "tears apart old friendships and divides the constituency into rivalrous factions. Candidates . . . risk their community standing and reputation when they run."[112] Intense, personal, political conflict is likely to hurt the private career of the small-town attorney or businessperson, while not providing the offsetting advantages so valuable to the urban dweller. After all, in a rural community, the local notable, who is probably the town attorney, realtor, store owner, or banker, is already so well known that the publicity resulting from a rancorous political battle is likely to do more economic harm than good. Further, rural-district office is less likely to lead one on to higher office than is an urban-district office. Thus, most state legislative candidates in rural Oregon were "reluctant" candidates, who had been persuaded to run by others. And "reluctants" were even more frequent in rural two-party districts than in rural one-party districts.[113]

When the rewards of legislative service are relatively low and the costs of seeking election to the legislature (whether or not successfully) are known to be high, few citizens seek election, and incumbents tend to serve until they tire of the legislature. Since this dynamic is present more often in rural districts than in urban ones, it should not be surprising that (despite reapportionment) a disproportionate share of the more senior members of many state legislatures are from rural/small-town districts. Such skewing of legislative experience probably affects the relative power of legislators.

77

POST-LEGISLATIVE AMBITION AND CAREERS

Most state legislators and most members of Congress do not go on to other offices. Sufficient numbers do move on to other offices, however, that post-legislative ambitions and prospects are worthy of a brief examination, especially since where a legislator hopes to go sometimes affects the manner in which he or she handles specific problems in the legislature.[114] As Schlesinger notes, "the constituency to which the (ambitious) legislator is responding is not always the one from which he has been elected, and . . . it is more important to know what he wants to be than how he got to where he now is."[115]

The Ambitions and Prospects of State Legislators

Although most state legislators go no further in public office, service in the state legislature is the most common experience in the backgrounds of our governors, U.S. representatives, and U.S. senators.[116] Many state legislators move on to high appointive posts, serving at the pleasure of the governor; some find mid-level positions within the state or local bureaucracy; and a few are appointed or elected to judgeships. Many more are elected to other offices.[117]

The probabilities of advancement are not equally distributed among legislators. Some are advantaged in seeking promotion by professional qualifications, age, and other personal characteristics (such as family, ethnicity, and sex). Ambitions among the legislators do not fit perfectly with their objective situations, but opportunity is a matter of probabilities, and even the disadvantaged legislators merely have lesser probabilities of success in seeking an alternative office. In a four-state study, for example, 59 percent of 466 legislators in California, New Jersey, Ohio, and Tennessee indicated there was one or more alternative office they would like; 106 of them desired a seat in Congress, the most frequently mentioned alternative post.[118] Only 34 percent of those legislators actually moved to a different public office during the next thirteen years, and only five made it to Congress. The remainder of the 34 percent moved to a wide variety of state and local elected and appointed posts, and a few obtained federal appointive positions (one as a member of the President's cabinet.) Ambition tended not to drop off until about age fifty-five, but the chance of actually achieving another office tended to drop off five years earlier, at age fifty.[119]

Congressional Ambitions and Prospects

Members of Congress normally remain in that institution until retirement, although some tire of the job and leave early.[120] A few are defeated each election, of course. A handful of U.S. representatives abandon the House every two years to seek a U.S. Senate seat, and about a third of them are successful.[121] Increasingly, U.S. representatives seek election to the office of governor of their home state. This route is about one half as popular among representatives as the attempt at a U.S. Senate seat, and about as successful, but in five states it has the added advantage of being risk free: the U.S. representatives in those five states are in the middle of the Congressional term when the gubernatorial election is held, and they do not have to give up their House seat to run.[122] A few big-city U.S. House members run for mayor and, in the past decade, several U.S. representatives have campaigned seriously but unsuccessfully for their party's presidential nomination. Most recently, these include Morris Udall of Arizona in 1976 and John Anderson of Illinois in 1980. Some U.S. representatives also leave the House to accept appointments as ambassadors, federal or state judges, or officials in the executive branch.[123] Most do not leave the House until death, defeat, or retirement.

Fewer U.S. senators are tempted by alternative offices. Some have been appointed to federal judicial posts, but, for most senators, the only attractive alternative to a career in the U.S. Senate is the presidency or, perhaps, the vice-presidency.[124] Occasionally, a defeated U.S. senator will later find contentment in a career in the U.S. House, but such moves are very rare.

SUMMARY

Most American legislators are white males, but the percentage of women and racial minorities in the state legislatures has increased substantially over the past two decades, partly as a result of federal legislation to insure racial and language minorities the right to vote and partly as a result of increased political consciousness among racial minorities and women. As is true of all Western democracies, American legislators are not a cross section of the people living in the state or nation. Instead, legislators are better educated than the general population, engage mainly in middle-class and professional occupations, and are middle-aged or older. Among the professions, lawyers are the most overrepresented. Also found in large numbers, especially in the state legislatures, are the other brokerage professions, especially insurance and real estate. Most American legislators are from middle-class families and have had relatives who were interested and active in politics. Many have close relatives who preceded them in public office.

The bias toward middle-class, middle-aged, male, well-educated, white legislators is in part a result of a recruitment process in which the agents of recruitment seek potential candidates who are like themselves and who seem to have a good chance of being elected. And those who have the best chance are much like the legislators now in office. The pool of citizens who are thought of as possible legislative nominees is thus constricted before conscious thought is given to alternatives. The pool is further restricted by legislative districting which often keeps ethnic and racial groups in the minority in most legislative districts, rather than in the majority in some. These elite-controlled dynamics of the recruitment process contribute greatly to the skewing of American legislatures away from being descriptively representative.

Most state legislators and most members of Congress later hold no public office, but enough do move on to subsequent desirable offices that many legislators aspire to such high-status posts. Among state legislators, a seat in Congress is the most often desired "promotion," although many also desire a state or local office. Many U.S. representatives would rather be U.S. senators, and a few find the governor's office attractive, although most make their careers in the House. Most U.S. senators remain in the Senate, or try to, but, every four years, some seek the presidency. Though the state legislatures and Congress are of primary importance as policymaking institutions, they often are also important training grounds for future high-status political office-holders.

Notes

1. An examination of the membership of twenty-one national legislative bodies in Europe, North and South America, Africa, and Asia in the early 1970s found that "professional, managerial and white-collar" occupations (excluding businessmen and farmers) accounted for from 42 percent of the legislators (Canadian House of Commons) to 87 percent of them (Korean National Assembly). Manual workers were unrepresented in nine of the legislatures and accounted for only 7 percent of the members at best (Swedish Riksdag, French National Assembly, and Finnish Eduskunta). See Gerhard Loewenberg and Samuel C. Patterson, *Comparing Legislatures* (Boston: Little, Brown, 1979), p. 70. On the few women in national

legislatures, see J. Blondel, *Comparative Legislatures* (Englewood Cliffs, N.J.: Prentice-Hall, 1973), pp. 78–79; Walter S. G. Kohn, "Women in the European Parliament" (Paper delivered at the 1980 Annual Meeting of the Midwest Political Science Association, Chicago, Ill.); and Marie Keir, "Women and Political Activism: The Women's Electoral Lobby 1975," in *Politics in New Zealand,* ed. S. Levine (Sidney: George Allen and Unwin, 1978).

2. For a discussion of the question, see Heinz Eulau, "Changing Views of Representation" in *Contemporary Political Science: Toward Empirical Theory,* ed. Ithiel de Sola Pool (New York: McGraw-Hill, 1967), pp. 53–85; and Giovanni Sartori, "Representational Systems," in *International Encyclopedia of the Social Sciences,* ed. D. E. Sills, 17 vols. (New York: Macmillan, 1971), 13: 465–73. See also Hanna F. Pitkin, *The Concept of Representation* (Berkeley: University of California Press, 1967).

3. John H. Culver and John C. Syer, *Power and Politics in California* (New York: John Wiley, 1980), Chapter 5; Samuel C. Patterson, Ronald D. Hedlund, and G. Robert Boynton, *Representatives and Represented* (New York: John Wiley, 1975), pp. 27–28; Gerald H. Stollman, *Michigan: State Legislators and Their Work* (Washington, D.C.: University Press of America, 1979), p. 29; Paul L. Hain, Cal Clark, and Janet Clark, "The Legislature," in *New Mexico Government,* ed. F. Chris Garcia and Paul L. Hain (Albuquerque: University of New Mexico Press, 1981).

4. Charles S. Hyneman, "Who Makes Our Laws?" in *Legislative Behavior,* ed. John C. Wahlke and Heinz Eulau (Glencoe, Ill.: Free Press, 1959), p. 255; originally published in *Political Science Quarterly* 55 (1940); Paul L. Hain, "The Tennessee Legislature: An Historical Perspective" (Paper presented at the 1979 Annual Meeting of the Southern Political Science Association, Gatlinburg, Tennessee); Thomas A. Glinn, "The Ohio General Assembly: A Developmental Analysis," in *State Legislative Innovation,* ed. James A. Robinson, (New York: Praeger, 1973), p. 246.

5. John C. Wahlke, Heinz Eulau, William Buchanan, and LeRoy C. Ferguson, *The Legislative System* (New York: John Wiley, 1962), Chapter 5; Lester G. Seligman, Michael R. King, Chong Lim Kim, and Roland E. Smith, *Patterns of Recruitment: A State Chooses its Lawmakers* (Chicago: Rand McNally, 1974), Chapter 6; Wayne V. McIntosh and John E. Stanga, Jr., "Lawyers and Political Participation," *Journal of Politics* 38 (1976): 434–41. The importance of "reciprocal benefits" as an incentive to legislative service looms even larger when one asks why so few homemakers—with ample time available—seek legislative seats. See Eleanor C. Main and Beth S. Schapiro, "The Recruitment of State Legislators: A Comparison of Male and Female Life Experiences" (Paper presented at the 1979 Annual Meeting of the Southern Political Science Association, Gatlinburg, Tennessee).

6. Heinz Eulau and John D. Sprague, *Lawyers in Politics: A Study in Professional Convergence* (New York: Bobbs-Merrill, 1964), especially Chapter 4. Whether lawyer-legislators are truly policy neutral "intellectual jobbers" is a question which has been addressed with mixed results. See James A. Dyer, "Do Lawyers Vote Differently? A Study of Voting on No-Fault Insurance," *Journal of Politics* 38 (May 1976). Dyer concludes lawyers vote differently and it matters. Other studies conclude lawyers do not tend to bloc vote. See David W. Brady, John Schmidhauser, and Larry L. Berg, "House Lawyers' Support for the Supreme Court," *Journal of Politics* 35 (August 1973): 729; and David R. Derge, "The Lawyer as Decision-Maker in the American State Legislature," *Journal of Politics* 21 (August 1959): 408–33.

7. Donald R. Matthews, *U.S. Senators and Their World* (New York: Vintage Books, 1960), pp. 34–35. Much of the discussion of occupations and politics, especially that concerning attorneys and politics, is based on observations by the German sociologist Max Weber. See his "Politics as a Vocation," in *Essays in Sociology,* ed. and trans. H. Gerth and C. W. Mills (New York: Oxford University Press, 1958).

8. Joseph A. Schlesinger, "Lawyers and American Politics: A Clarified View," *Midwest Journal of Political Science* (May 1957): 26–39.

9. Wahlke, Eulau, Buchanan, and Ferguson, *The Legislative System;* Eulau and Sprague, *Lawyers in Politics: A Study in Professional Convergence,* Table 2.6.

10. "Fewer Attorneys Now Run For State Legislative Posts," *Los Angeles Daily Journal,* January 27, 1981, p. 1; "Delaware's Legislators Make Laws Without Lawyers," *Los Angeles Times,* February 8, 1981, p. 6.

11. "Fewer Attorneys Now Run For State Legislative Posts," p. 1.

12. Paul L. Hain and James E. Peireson, "Lawyers and Politics Revisited: Structural Advantages of Lawyer-Politicians," *American Journal of Political Science* 19 (February 1975): 45; David R. Derge, "The Lawyer in the Indiana General Assembly," *Midwest Journal of Political Science* 10 (February 1966): 484–97. See also Jerry Perkins, Willard Berry, and William Thomas, "Convergence of Legal and Political Careers: A Reconsideration" (Paper delivered at the 1975 Annual Meeting of the Southern Political Science Association, Atlanta, Georgia).

13. Mogens N. Pedersen, "Lawyers in Politics: The Danish Folketing and the United States Legislatures," in *Comparative Legislative Behavior: Frontiers of Research,* ed. Samuel C. Patterson and John C. Wahlke (New York: John Wiley, 1972), p. 63.

14. See, for example, James J. Best, "The Impact of Reapportionment on the Washington House of Representatives," in Robinson, *State Legislative Innovation,* p. 148; and Wahlke, Eulau, Buchanan, and Ferguson, *The Legislative System,* p. 491.

15. James David Barber, *The Lawmakers: Recruitment and Adaptation to Legislative Life* (New Haven, Conn.: Yale University Press, 1965), pp. 27, 72, 121, and 168.

16. Wahlke, Eulau, Buchanan, and Ferguson, *The Legislative System,* pp. 82–85, 489; Patterson, Hedlund, and Boynton, *Representatives and Represented,* pp. 26–27; and Irene Diamond, *Sex Roles in the State House* (New Haven, Conn: Yale University Press, 1977) pp. 34–37.

17. Harmon Zeigler and Michael A. Baer, "The Recruitment of Lobbyists and Legislators," *Midwest Journal of Political Science* 12 (1968): 507.

18. Charles G. Bell and Charles M. Price, "Pre-Legislative Sources of Representational Roles," *Midwest Journal of Political Science* 13 (1969): 260–65; also Kenneth Prewitt, Heinz Eulau, and Betty H. Zisk, "Political Socialization and Political Roles," *Public Opinion Quarterly* 30 (Winter 1966–67): 578.

19. Seligman, King, Kim, and Smith, *Patterns of Recruitment;* Wahlke, Eulau, Buchanan, and Ferguson, *The Legislative System,* p. 488; and Frank Sorauf, *Party and Representation* (New York: Atherton Press, 1963), p. 91.

20. Leonard Ruchelman, *Political Careers: Recruitment Through the Legislature* (Rutherford, N.J.: Fairleigh Dickinson University Press, 1970), pp. 52–55.

21. Best, "The Impact of Reapportionment on the Washington House of Representatives," p. 156; Victor S. Hjelm and Joseph P. Pisciotte, "Profiles and Careers of Colorado State Legislators," *Western Political Quarterly* 21 (1968): 707; and Stollman, *Michigan State Legislators and Their Work,* p. 29.

22. Ruchelman, *Political Careers,* p. 40.

23. Culver and Syer, *Power and Politics in California,* p. 92.

24. Wahlke, Eulau, Buchanan, and Ferguson, *The Legislative System,* p. 98.

25. Barber, *The Lawmakers,* p. 28.

26. For a discussion of the relationships among various office constituencies and the linkages among different offices in the political opportunity structure, see Joseph A. Schlesinger, *Ambition and Politics: Political Careers in the United States* (Chicago: Rand McNally, 1966), especially Chapter 6.

27. Samuel DuBois Cook, "Democracy and Tyranny in America: The Radical Paradox of the Bicentennial and Blacks in the American Political System," *Journal of Politics* 38 (August 1976): 790.

28. Ibid.

29. Charles S. Bullock, III, "The Election of Blacks in the South: Preconditions and Consequences," *American Journal of Political Science* 19 (November 1975): 733, 737.

30. Cook, "Democracy and Tyranny in America," pp. 790–91; and Linda Pryor, "Perceptions of Influence by Black Members of the Georgia General Assembly" (Paper delivered at the 1980 Annual Meeting of the Southern Political Science Association, Atlanta, Ga.).

31. Lee Sigelman and Albert K. Karnig, "Black Representation in the American States: A Comparison of Bureaucracies and Legislatures," *American Politics Quarterly* 4 (April 1976): 240–42.

32. F. Chris Garcia and Rudolph O. de la Garza, *The Chicano Political Experience: Three Perspectives* (North Scituate, Mass.: Duxbury Press, 1977), pp. 104–7. New Mexico has elected three Hispanic governors since statehood (1912), seven Hispanic lieutenant governors,

and has had numerous Hispanic legislative leaders. Overall, Chicanos have fared better politically in Arizona than in Texas. In addition to electing a Mexican-American governor of Arizona in 1974, the 1973 Arizona legislature was 11 percent Hispanic while the 1973 Texas legislature was only 5.5 percent Hispanic.

33. Garcia and de la Garza, *The Chicano Political Experience,* p. 105; and Fernando V. Padilla and Carlos B. Ramirez, "Patterns of Chicano Representation in California, Colorado, and Nuevo Mexico," *Aztlan* 5 (1974): 189–235.

34. Ibid.

35. Jack D. Forbes, "The Native American," *California Journal* 5 (June 1974), cited in Culver and Syer, *Power and Politics in California,* p. 184.

36. California State Advisory Commission on Civil Rights, *Political Participation of Mexican Americans in California,* August 1971, cited in Garcia and de la Garza, *The Chicano Political Experience,* p. 114.

37. Garcia and de la Garza, *The Chicano Political Experience,* pp. 115–17. Most black and Hispanic officeholders (including legislators) are elected from districts which are basically black or Hispanic.

38. Charles W. Dunn, "Black Caucuses and Political Machines in Legislative Bodies," *American Journal of Political Science* 17 (February 1973): 155; *Black Members of State Legislatures,* (Springfield, Ill.: Illinois Legislative Council, 1970).

39. Lucius J. Barker and Jesse J. McCorry, Jr., *Black Americans and the Political System* (Cambridge, Mass.: Winthrop, 1976), pp. 179–80.

40. *Today: The Journal of Political News and Analysis,* February 9, 1979, p. 2; *The Book of the States, 1978–79* (Lexington, Ky: Council of State Governments, 1978), p. 263.

41. Paula J. Dubeck, "Women and Access to Political Office: A Comparison of Female and Male State Legislators," *Sociological Quarterly* 17 (Winter 1976): 43; Emmy Werner, "Women in State Legislatures," *Western Political Quarterly* 21 (March 1968): 42. In 1979, New Hampshire, one of the ten smallest states in population, accounted for over 13 percent of the female state legislators in the U.S.

42. Joan S. Carver, "Women in Florida," *Journal of Politics* 41 (August 1979): 941–55.

43. Diamond, *Sex Roles in the State House,* p. 26.

44. Culver and Syer, *Power and Politics in California,* p. 93.

45. Diamond, *Sex Roles in the State House,* pp. 34–37.

46. Dubeck, "Women and Access to Political Office," p. 47; Susan Gluck Mezey, "Does Sex Make a Difference? A Case Study of Women in Politics," *Western Political Quarterly* 31 (December 1978): 493–95; Diamond, *Sex Roles in the State House,* p. 38. A recent study reports that female state legislators are much less likely than their younger male colleagues to have had children under age ten when they first sought election to the legislature. See Main and Schapiro, "The Recruitment of State Legislators," pp. 19–21. A 1977 survey of women state legislators, however, found fewer women legislators in the over-sixty age group and more women legislators in the under-forty group than did researchers who examined the women serving in the state legislatures in the early 1970s. Thus, it may be that the age difference between the sexes in the legislature is shrinking as a result of changing life-styles. See Roger Handberg and Wanda Lowery, "Women State Legislators and Support for the Equal Rights Amendment," *Social Science Journal* 17 (January 1980).

47. Dubeck, "Women and Access to Political Office," pp. 46–47.

48. Dubeck found, in her study of women legislators in eighteen states in 1971 and 1973, only 5 percent who said they were housewives, although she had no information on 18.8 percent of them. See "Women and Access to Political Office." Diamond found that 46 percent of the women legislators in four New England states in 1971 were housewives, but her sample was not an attempt to portray national patterns, and, as she points out, these legislatures are "amateur" rather than "professional" and have very few people in each district, so the standards for candidacy are less severe. See *Sex Roles in the State House,* p. 37. Main and Schapiro report that 21 percent of their 109 women-legislator subjects were housewives. Their study focused on eleven southern states and five border states. See "The Recruitment of State Legislators," p. 66. Handberg and Lowery report 28.5 percent of their respondents, based on responses from 60 percent of the women legislators in the U.S. in 1977 were housewives. See "Women State Legislators and Support for the Equal Rights Amendment," p. 66.

49. Diamond, *Sex Roles in the State House,* p. 38.

50. Ibid., p. 47.

51. Of the female candidates for the Texas House of Representatives in 1978 (N=26), 80 percent of those elected were college graduates, and half that figure also held an advanced degree. Most of the women who lost were not college graduates, although only one had no college education at all. See Lawrence W. Miller and Lillian Noyes, "The Thrill of Victory and the Agony of Defeat," *Public Service,* September 1979.

52. Diamond, *Sex Roles in the State House,* pp. 1–12, 51–59. Diamond notes that the paucity of female state senators is, in part, a function of the greater prestige of a senate seat, smaller numbers of senate seats, and increased competition. The 1975 New Hampshire House, for instance, had 400 members, 102 of whom were women. The state senate had only 24 members, of whom 2 were women. Similarly, the 150-member Texas House included 11 women in 1981, while the 31-member Texas Senate had only 1 woman member. Janice C. May, "The Texas Legislature," *Comparative State Politics Newsletter* 2 (October 1981): 8.

53. Emily Stoper, "Wife and Politician: Role Strain Among Women in Public Office," in *A Portrait of Marginality,* ed. Marianne Githens and Jewell Prestage (New York: Longman, 1977).

54. Susan Gluck Mezey, "Does Sex Make a Difference," pp. 498–501. See also Wilma Rule, "Why Women Don't Run: The Critical Contextual Factors in Women's Legislative Recruitment," *Western Political Quarterly* 34 (March 1981): 60–77.

55. Diamond, *Sex Roles in the State House,* pp. 9–11.

56. Carver, "Women in Florida," pp. 945–47; Dubeck, "Women and Access to Political Office," pp. 43–51.

57. Handberg and Lowery, "Women State Legislators and Support for the Equal Rights Amendment," p. 67.

58. Carver, "Women in Florida," p. 947.

59. Diamond, *Sex Roles in the State House,* p. 49.

60. For an example of segregationists in charge of a state legislature, see Loren P. Beth and William C. Harvard, "Committee Stacking and Political Power in Florida," *Journal of Politics* 23 (1961): 57–83.

61. Warren E. Miller and Donald E. Stokes, "Constituency Influence in Congress," *American Political Science* Review 57 (March 1963): 45–46.

62. Charles P. Henry, "Legitimizing Race in Congressional Politics," *American Politics Quarterly* 5 (April 1977): 149–76.

63. Charles O. Jones, *Every Second Year* (Washington, D.C.: The Brookings Institution, 1967), p. 49; D. T. Stanley, D. E. Mann, and J. W. Doig, *Men Who Govern* (Washington, D.C.: The Brookings Institution, 1967), p. 18. The large percentage of congressmen with college educations is not a recent phenomenon. Donald R. Matthews reported that 88 percent of the U.S. representatives serving in 1941 had attended college, as had 87 percent of the U.S. senators serving in 1949. *The Social Background of Political Decision-Makers* (New York: Doubleday, 1954).

64. *Congressional Quarterly Weekly Report,* January 10, 1981, p. 93.

65. Eulau and Sprague, *Lawyers in Politics,* p. 11.

66. Roger H. Davidson, *The Role of the Congressman* (Indianapolis: Pegasus, 1969), pp. 37–41.

67. John Brown Mason, "Lawyers in the 71st to 75th Congress: Their Legal Education and Experience," *Rocky Mountain Law Review* 10 (December 1937): 44; cited in Eulau and Sprague, *Lawyers in Politics,* p. 12; Donald R. Matthews, *U.S. Senators and Their World* (New York: Vintage Books, 1960), pp. 30, 282. The U.S. Congress is comparable to other Western national legislatures in the dominance of professionals and businesspeople, but the U.S. Congress has more attorneys than most other legislatures. Colombia's 1970 lower chamber was two-thirds lawyers, but in most nations, lawyers hold a fourth or less of the seats. In Great Britain and Switzerland, the figure is between 15 and 20 percent. In France and West Germany, less than a tenth of the members are attorneys. See Loewenberg and Patterson, *Comparing Legislatures,* p. 71.

68. *Congressional Quarterly Weekly Report,* January 24, 1981, p. 199.

69. Walter Oleszek, "Age and Political Careers," *Public Opinion Quarterly* 33 (Spring 1969): 101; Schlesinger, *Ambition and Politics,* p. 175.

70. *Congressional Quarterly Weekly Report*, January 3, 1981, p. 3; January 10, 1981, pp. 93–102; January 24, 1981, pp. 198–200; *Inside Congress*, 2nd ed. (Washington D.C.: Congressional Quarterly, 1979), p. 23.

71. *Congressional Quarterly Weekly Report*, January 3, 1981, p. 3; January 10, 1981, pp. 93–102; January 24, 1981, pp. 198–200.

72. Matthews, *U.S. Senators and Their World*, p. 19.

73. Ibid., p. 61.

74. G. William Domhoff, *Who Rules America?* (Englewood Cliffs, N.J.: Prentice-Hall, 1967), pp. 111–12.

75. *Inside Congress*, pp. 175–78.

76. Ibid.

77. Alfred B. Clubok, Norman M. Wilensky, and Forrest J. Berghorn, "Family Relationships, Congressional Recruitment, and Political Modernization," *Journal of Politics* 31 (November 1969): 1042–47.

78. Ibid., pp. 1040–47.

79. Michael R. King and Lester G. Seligman, "Critical Elections, Congressional Recruitment and Public Policy," in Heinz Eulau and Moshe M. Czudnowski, *Elite Recruitment in Democratic Politics* (New York: John Wiley, Halsted Press, 1976), pp. 282–85.

80. Matthews, *U.S. Senators and Their World*, pp. 14–18.

81. Leroy N. Rieselbach, "Congressmen as 'Small Town Boys': A Research Note," *Midwest Journal of Political Science* 14 (May 1970): 328–29; and Carl Lee and Leroy N. Rieselbach, "Congressional Parochialism: Another Data Point," *American Journal of Political Science* 24 (November, 1980): 822–824.

82. Representative Carl Albert, Speaker of the House until 1977, was widely known as the most successful resident of Bug Tussle, Oklahoma. Representative Wilbur Mills, long-time chairman of the powerful House Ways and Means Committee until 1974, hailed from Kensett, Arkansas, population 100. Senate majority leader Howard Baker was born in Huntsville, Tennessee, population 500. He grew up, however, as the son of a congressman.

83. *Congressional Quarterly Weekly Report*, January 24, 1981; p. 198; *Inside Congress*, p. 24.

84. Loewenberg and Patterson, *Comparing Legislatures*, p. 79.

85. Barker and McCorry, *Black Americans and the Political System*, pp. 271–73, 285–301; *Congressional Quarterly Weekly Report*, January 24, 1981, p. 200.

86. Henry, "Legitimizing Race in Congressional Politics," pp. 149–69.

87. Robert C. Smith, "The Black Congressional Delegation," *Western Political Quarterly* 34 (June 1981): 209–10.

88. Alex Poinsett, "The Black Caucus: Five Years Later," *Ebony* Magazine, 1973; reprinted in Barker and McCorry, *Black Americans and the Political System*, pp. 288–93.

89. Henry, "Legitimizing Race in Congressional Politics," p. 151.

90. Garcia and de la Garza, *The Chicano Political Experience*, p. 104.

91. By way of comparison to the American procedure, New Zealand has had four special Maori parliamentary seats (out of 87) since 1868. Since 1967, Maoris (indigenous people in New Zealand) have had the choice of voting in a general constituency or in one of the Maori constituencies, and of running for Parliament in either type of constituency. See Alan D. McRobie, "Ethnic Representation: The New Zealand Experience," in *Politics in New Zealand*, ed. Stephen Levine (Sidney: George Allen and Unwin, 1978), pp. 270–83.

92. J. Blondel, *Comparative Legislatures*, pp. 160–61; Keir, "Women and Political Activism," pp. 310–20.

93. Diane D. Kincaid, "Over His Dead Body: A Positive Perspective on Widows in the U.S. Congress," *Western Political Quarterly* 31 (March 1978): 97–99.

94. Ibid., p. 97.

95. Ibid., pp. 98–100.

96. Kathleen A. Frankovic, "Sex and Voting in the U.S. House of Representatives: 1961–1975," *American Politics Quarterly* 5 (July 1977): 315–30; Frieda L. Gehlen, "Legislative Role

Performance of Female Legislators," *Sex Roles* 3, no. 1 (1977): 1–18. A 1975 survey of U.S. representatives found 57 percent of the men approving the CIA's clandestine operations abroad, while only one of twelve women members approved. *Washington Post,* July 1, 1975, p. A-8.

97. Matthews, *U.S. Senators and Their World,* p. 52.

98. Ibid., pp. 50–51.

99. Schlesinger, *Ambition and Politics,* pp. 91–102.

100. Steven V. Roberts, "Senate's New Class Reflects Changing Political Standards," *New York Times,* November 15, 1978, p. A-18.

101. Joseph A. Schlesinger, "Political Careers and Party Leadership," in *Political Leadership in Industrialized Societies,* ed. Lewis J. Edinger (New York: John Wiley, 1967), pp. 278–79.

102. A carefully developed model using such an approach is presented in Seligman, King, Kim, and Smith, *Patterns of Recruitment,* especially Chapter 2. For a succinct outline of the recruitment literature, generally, see Dwaine Marvick, "Continuities in Recruitment Theory and Research: Toward a New Model," in Eulau and Czudnowski, *Elite Recruitment in Democratic Politics,* pp. 29–44.

103. Lester G. Seligman, "Political Recruitment and Party Structure: A Case Study," *American Political Science Review* 77 (1961): 77–86.

104. Frank J. Sorauf, *Party and Representation: Legislative Politics in Pennsylvania* (New York: Atherton, 1963), pp. 88–90. Jeff Fishel suggests that challengers to incumbent U.S. representatives are a bit less white and middle class than incumbent congressmen, but not dramatically so. See his *Party and Opposition* (New York: David McKay, 1973), Chapter 2.

105. Wahlke, Eulau, Buchanan, and Ferguson, *The Legislative System,* Chapter 15.

106. Richard J. Tobin and Edward Keynes, "Institutional Differences in the Recruitment Process: A Four-State Study," *American Journal of Political Science* 19 (November 1975): 667–82.

107. See, for instance, Diamond, *Sex Roles in the State House;* Dubeck, "Women and Access to Political Office"; Mezey, "Does Sex Make a Difference?"; Rule, "Why Women Don't Run"; and Seligman, King, Kim, and Smith, *Patterns of Recruitment.*

108. Barber, *The Lawmakers,* pp. 3–6; Diamond, *Sex Roles in the State House,* pp. 3–7, 59–60.

109. Schlesinger, *Ambition and Politics,* Chapter 3; Joseph A. Schlesinger, "The Structure of Competition for Office in the American States," *Behavioral Science* 5 (1960): 197–210.

110. Schlesinger, *Ambition and Politics,* pp. 129–41; Seligman, King, Kim, and Smith, *Patterns of Recruitment,* pp. 70–73.

111. Diamond, *Sex Roles in the State House,* pp. 7, 28, 70. Similarly, Charles S. Bullock, III, and Patricia Lee Findley Heys found that although status as a recently deceased congressman's widow (with, presumably, some political experience from assisting her husband) sometimes enables a woman to win election to her late husband's seat despite lacking the "normal" qualifications, other women desiring election to Congress are likely to have held prior offices. Only 10 percent of the widow-successors, but 69 percent of the other women elected to Congress had held a prior public office. See "Recruitment of Women for Congress: A Research Note," *Western Political Quarterly* 25 (September 1972): 416–23.

112. Seligman, King, Kim, and Smith, *Patterns of Recruitment,* pp. 69–70.

113. Ibid., pp. 71–78.

114. Diamond, *Sex Roles in the State House,* pp. 102–4; Barber, *The Lawmakers,* Chapter 3; Jack R. Van Der Slik and Samuel J. Pernacciaro, "Office Ambitions and Voting Behavior in the U.S. Senate," *American Politics Quarterly* 7 (April 1979): 198–224; John W. Soule, "Future Political Ambitions and the Behavior of Incumbent State Legislators," *Midwest Journal of Political Science* 13 (August 1969): 439–54.

115. Schlesinger, *Ambitions and Politics,* p. 5.

116. Ibid., pp. 72–75; Schlesinger, "Political Careers and Party Leadership," p. 279.

117. Ruchelman, *Political Careers,* pp. 111–78; Hain and Piereson, "Lawyers and Politics Revisited: Structural Advantages of Lawyer-Politicians," p. 44.

118. Wahlke, Eulau, Buchanan, and Ferguson, *The Legislative System,* p. 129–33.

119. Paul L. Hain, "Age, Ambitions and Political Careers: The Middle-Age Crisis," *Western Political Quarterly* 27 (June 1974): 167–271.

120. H. Douglas Price, "The Congressional Career, Then and Now" in *Congressional Behavior,* ed. Nelson W. Polsby (New York: Random House, 1971), pp. 14–27; Stephen E. Frantzich, "Opting Out: Retirement from the House of Representatives, 1966–1974," *American Politics Quarterly* 6 (July 1978): 251–73.

121. Murray Frost, "Senatorial Ambition and Legislative Behavior" (Ph.D diss. Michigan State University, 1972), pp. 39–41; David W. Rohde, "Risk Bearing and Progressive Ambition: The Case of Members of the U.S. House of Representatives," *American Journal of Political Science* 23 (February 1979): 1.

122. Paul L. Hain and Terry B. Smith, "Congress: New Training Ground for Governors?" *State Government* 67 (Spring 1975): 114–15; "Congressional Challengers for the Office of Governor" (Paper delivered at the 1973 Annual Meeting of the American Political Science Association, New Orleans, La.).

123. Stephen E. Frantzich, "De-Recruitment: The Other Side of the Congressional Equation," *Western Political Quarterly* 31 (March 1978): 113.

124. Robert L. Peabody, Norman J. Ornstein, and David W. Rohde, "The United States Senate as a Presidential Incubator: Many Are Called but Few Are Chosen," *Political Science Quarterly* 91 (Summer 1976): 237–58; Thomas M. Uhlman and Herbert M. Kritzer, "The Presidential Ambition of Democratic Senators: Its Timing and Impact" (Paper delivered at the 1977 Annual Meeting of the Midwest Political Science Association, Chicago, Ill.).

chapter 5

Nomination and Election of American Legislators

Preview

Most American legislators are nominated in primary elections, a process which limits the authority of national political party leaders. The rules governing the nomination and election of American legislators—especially the use of single-member legislative districts—advantage the Democratic and Republican parties over minor parties, and moderate candidates over liberal or conservative ideological extremists. Incumbent legislators have an advantage over challengers, and candidates with more campaign funds do better than those with less. Adequate campaign funding has become of increasing importance as the cost of campaigns has escalated. The worst excesses of malapportionment have been curbed by judicial intervention, but gerrymandering continues to play an important role in predetermining the outcome of legislative elections.

Nomination by a political party and election by popular vote are the formal mechanisms which decide who will serve in the nation's legislatures. Chapter 4 noted that the recruitment process screens out many who might otherwise be legislative candidates. The kind of people who will be nominated or elected to legislative offices—and, thus, the kind of policies they are likely to enact into law—are also greatly affected by the way our political system is structured: the election laws generally, the system of campaign financing, and legislative districting. The rules affect the outcome.

ELECTION LAWS

With the exception of a few requirements of federal law, the laws governing nomination and election to the state legislatures and to Congress are written by the states. Congressional and state legislative elections are administered by state and local officials. Certificates of election to the U.S. House and Senate are issued by the chief state election officer, although election challenges can be brought to the relevant chamber of Congress.

The U.S. Constitution requires that all mentally sound citizens eighteen years or older be allowed to vote in state, local, and national elections and forbids discrimination on the basis of race or sex. Thus, virtually all adult U.S. citizens are eligible to vote, if they register. (In most states advance voter registration is required.) Various structural hurdles, however, such as registration itself, help keep the number of voters lower in the U.S. national elections than in the elections of many other Western democracies.[1]

State Election Laws

Each state decides upon its own detailed rules governing elections. Election laws have an impact on the outcome of elections and some of them skew the electoral system against minor parties and independent candidates. Of some importance in determining election outcomes (as well as in maintaining honest elections) are laws which govern voter registration, the structure of the ballot (can the voter cast a straight party ballot readily?), the nominating process, and access to the ballot. Less important election rules are also established by the states—laws governing the number of registered voters permitted in each precinct, whether to use a voting machine and what kind, the hours the polls are open, who counts the votes, who may serve as a challenger at the polls, and so on. Similar state laws also govern primary elections.

State laws determine which political parties may have their legislative (and other) candidates automatically listed on the ballot in the general election; usually this is on the basis of having received a minimum percentage of the vote (often 15 percent) in the last general election. The Democratic and Republican parties easily meet these requirements, but other parties usually have to circulate petitions to get their candidates on the general-election ballot. Thus, access to the general-election ballot is easier for Democratic and Republican nominees than for minor-party nominees.[2]

Federal Election Laws

The U.S. Constitution (Article I, Section 2) provides that in each state the citizens eligible to vote for members of that state's more numerous branch of the legislature may also vote in that state's Congressional elections. The intent of this provision was to recognize variations in state suffrage requirements 200 years ago and to elect the members of the U.S. House of Representatives by the broadest suffrage acceptable to each state.[3] The provision means that the United States has the same electorate for federal (national) elections as for state elections. In contrast, Australia and Canada, which also have federal systems of government, have national voter-eligibility rules which differ from provincial voter-eligibility rules.[4] In the U.S., national and state electorates are the same, and the national government need not maintain a separate list of eligible voters but can rely on the individual states to maintain such lists and to conduct the national elections.

Despite the importance of state governments in the American electoral process, Article I, Section 4, of the U.S. Constitution gives Congress the power to make or alter regulations concerning Congressional elections, including primaries and preprimaries, and these national regulations supersede any conflicting state laws or regulations. Congress has established the first Tuesday after the first Monday in November of even-numbered years as the date for the federal election; has required the use of Congressional districts in states entitled to more than one U.S. representative; has required the use of the secret ballot; has placed a limit on the expenditures of candidates seeking election to Congress; and has enacted regulations to prevent corruption and fraud in Congressional elections.[5]

PRIMARY ELECTIONS

The primary election as a means of nominating a party's candidates for office is a uniquely American institution. The primary election was designed to reduce the power of unelected, "back-room" party leaders and allow the ordinary citizen a direct voice in determining his or her party's nominees for public office. Primary elections also permit elected officeholders to be more independent of party officials than is possible when nominations are by party convention.

Every state's primary-election law seems to contain some unique provision, but there are certain features common to all of them. Primary elections are administered like general elections. Each voter has the right to cast a secret ballot. Normally, only those parties whose gubernatorial candidates received a minimum percentage of the vote at the last election are eligible to nominate candidates through primary elections. Parties whose candidates received less than the required percentage of the votes at the last general election normally nominate their candidates by convention or by vote of a party committee. Only the Democratic and Republican parties, then, ordinarily use the state-run primary election to select their nominees. Each state sets its primary-election date as it sees fit. Decisions on party nominees for Congress, therefore, are made at different times in different states, even though all general elections for Congress are held on the same day in November of even-numbered years.

There are three basic types of primary elections: the *closed* primary, the *open* primary, and the *blanket* primary. Thirty-nine states use some version of the closed primary, in which only those voters who have either preregistered as members of the party or declared their party affiliation at the time of voting can participate. It is closed to those who are not party members. Eight states use the open primary in which the voter can request both party ballots and, in the privacy of the voting booth, must choose *one* to vote on. Alaska, Louisiana, and Washington have blanket-primary elections in which each voter, again in the privacy of the voting booth, can cross back and forth between the parties for each office, for example, voting in the Republican primary for U.S. senator and in the Democratic primary for U.S. representative.[6]

The characteristics of the people who win elections and serve in the legislature may be affected by the type of primary used. A comparison of Washington State's blanket-primary nominating system to the closed-primary systems used in Connecticut and Pennsylvania suggests that the more closed a nominating system is, "the more likely [state] legislators are to have served in both party and public offices prior to their first election to the [state] legislature."[7]

Most state laws provide that the candidate who receives the most votes (plurality) in a primary election becomes the party nominee, and it is not unheard of for a candidate to win the nomination with as little as a fourth or less of the vote. The run-off primary, used in eleven southern and border states when no candidate wins a majority in the regular primary, makes it unlikely that a candidate who appeals to a minority wing of the party will capture the party nomination and actually hold office.[8]

NOMINATION AND ELECTION TO THE U.S. CONGRESS

There are 435 voting members of the U.S. House of Representatives, and, of course, 100 members of the U.S. Senate. Terms of senators are staggered, so that only one third of the Senate's membership is elected each two years. All 435 seats in the U.S. House of Representatives are up for election every two years. But, before a person may be elected as a senator or a representative, ordinarily he or she must first become the nominee of a party.

Congressional Nominations

Congressional nominations are important decisions for state political parties and citizens—even more so when the nomination is to the Senate. In addition to their legislative duties, U.S. senators and representatives have substantial influence over numerous federal appointments in each state and over the many discretionary decisions made in implementing the federal programs in each state. Seats in Congress are attractive enough to draw the states' top officeholders. Governors and other statewide-elected officials routinely seek election to the U.S. Senate and, in less populated states, sometimes run for the U.S. House of Representatives. Incumbent members of Congress often are major power brokers in political affairs back home.

The politics of a particular state occasionally produces an independent member of Congress, such as Senator Harry F. Byrd, Jr., of Virginia. But over 99 percent of the members of Congress today are always either Democrats or Republicans. Almost all of them will have won their party's nomination through some variant of the primary process, although a few southern Republicans may have been nominated without a primary election. In some states, parties hold endorsing conventions before the primary. Others use the challenge primary, in which the convention-selected nominee can be challenged in the primary election by candidates who win a certain percentage of the convention vote.

In only about 40 percent of the primaries for Congress is there any contest for the nomination, and the percentage is even smaller when an incumbent is seeking reelection and renomination. From 1956 through 1974, for example, only 36.8 percent of incumbent Democratic U.S. representatives and only 20.2 percent of incumbent Republican U.S. representatives faced primary-election opposition (see Table 5.1).[9] Although the number of intraparty challenges has been increasing, especially in competitive districts,[10] incumbents have almost always won such primary-election contests for the past two decades and usually have gone on to win in the general election.[11] By contrast, where no incumbent was seeking reelection during this period and the party was reasonably sure of winning the general election, there were two or more candidates for the party nomination three fourths of the time.[12] Incumbent U.S. senators seldom face primary opposition and usually win.[13] The 1980 primaries were unusual in that four incumbent U.S. senators (and six incumbent U.S. representatives) were defeated. Since 1956, the number of incumbent senators defeated in a primary had been none or one except for 1966, when two were defeated in primary elections, and 1968, when four lost their primaries.

TABLE 5.1
Contested Primary Elections for U.S. House of Representatives, 1956–1974

	Democratic Primary Contests	Republican Primary Contests
Without Incumbent	55.3%	43.9%
With Incumbent	36.8	20.2

Source: Harvey L. Schantz, "Contested and Uncontested Primaries for the U.S. House," *Legislative Studies Quarterly* 5 (November 1980): 548. Copyright the Comparative Legislative Research Center of the University of Iowa.

Nominations to the national legislature, especially the U.S. Senate, are a matter of concern to national party leaders, but they are less able than party leaders in other democratic countries to insure the nomination of legislative candidates they support and to prevent the nomination of candidates they oppose.[14] One reason for this is that in some democratic countries, national parties have the right to veto the choice of candidates of the local parties, though a study of British nominating practices indicates that these formal rules do not represent the whole story.[15] Another reason for the difference is that, in the United States, political parties reflect the fragmentation of federalism and of separation of power. There are state party organizations and national party organizations. The national parties have Congressional wings (represented by the party members in the Congress) and presidential wings (represented by the national committees).

The main reason why there is less national-party control over legislative nominations in the United States than in some other democratic countries is the American primary election. In Britain and other parliamentary countries, national legislative candidates are nominated in caucuses or conventions of loyal party leaders who are likely to have emotional or ideological affinity with national party positions. By contrast, in the United States, a primary election allows candidates to go directly to the members of their party, rather than to the party's leaders, for nomination or renomination.[16] U.S. candidates for Congress frequently run against "the bosses," "the party hacks," or "the politicians." An extreme example of a candidate securing a local nomination for Congress, despite the opposition of the national officials and leaders of his party, is the case where a member of the Ku Klux Klan won the 1980 Democratic nomination to Congress in a southern district in California, even though President Carter and most California Democratic leaders were quick to disassociate themselves from him.[17]

There are other reasons, too, why a member of the British Parliament, say, is less likely to attack or oppose his or her own party leaders than is a member of the U.S. Congress. Members of the U.S. House and Senate have greater individual resources at their command—such as independent campaign contributions and Congressional staff—than members of Parliament, especially "back-bench" members. The seniority system in the U.S. House of Representatives and the U.S. Senate also permits members of Congress considerable leeway to oppose their own party leaders and still retain favored legislative positions. While party discipline in the British Parliament has relaxed substantially in the last decade, advancement in Parliament is still controlled by the party leaders.[18]

Congressional Elections

Incumbent members of Congress are not as difficult to defeat in the general election as they are in their respective parties' primaries, but only because so very few lose their primaries. U.S. senators are much more vulnerable than representatives, even though they need not run for reelection as often. This is apparently because of their greater visibility, the prominence and name recognition of Senate challengers, the greater diversity of senators' larger, statewide constituencies (many House districts are relatively homogeneous politically), and senators' lesser individual contact with their greater number of constituents. They do not win by as large margins as representatives.

In the eight general elections from 1960 through 1974, 84 percent of the 238 U.S. senators who sought reelection were successful. Eleven (4.6 percent) lost primary elections. The rest lost the general election. From 1976 through 1980, however, in-

TABLE 5.2

Incumbency Advantage in Congress: 1960–1980 Elections (in percentages)

Election Year	Successful House Incumbents *	Successful Senate Incumbents *	Senate-House Difference	House Incumbents Winning by More Than 60 Percent **	Senate Incumbents Winning by More Than 60 Percent **	Senate-House Difference
1960	92.1	96.6	+ 4.5	58.9	41.3	−17.6
1962	93.4	82.9	−10.5	63.6	26.4	−37.2
1964	87.5	84.8	− 2.7	58.5	46.8	−11.7
1966	87.7	87.5	− .2	67.7	41.3	−26.4
1968	98.0	71.4	−26.6	72.2	37.5	−34.7
1970	95.2	76.7	−18.5	77.3	31.0	−46.4
1972	93.4	74.1	−19.3	77.8	52.0	−25.8
1974	87.7	85.2	− 2.5	66.4	40.0	−26.4
1976	95.8	64.0	−31.8	69.2	40.0	−29.2
1978	93.7	60.0	−33.7	76.6	31.8	−44.8
1980	90.5	55.2	−35.3	72.4	36.0	−36.4

*Both primary and general election defeats are included in calculations of the percentage of incumbents successful.
**Percentage of incumbents winning by more than 60 percent is based on those who were in the general election.

Sources: Joseph Cooper and William West, "The Congressional Career in the 1970's," in *Congress Reconsidered,* ed. Lawrence C. Dodd and Bruce I. Oppenheimer (Washington, D.C.: Congressional Quarterly Press, 1981), p. 99. Original data are from *Congressional Quarterly Weekly Reports* of March 25, 1978, p. 755; July 7, 1979, p. 1351; and November 8, 1980, pp. 3338–45. Calculations for 1980 are by Harris and Hain.

cumbent senators fared less well.[19] (See Table 5.2.) Only 61 percent were successful at the polls. Five of the seventy-two lost their primary election and twenty more lost the general election. The consequences included a 1981 Senate in which the majority of members were first term, a Republican Senate majority, and a younger and more conservative Senate. Only two incumbents lost in 1982.

In those same eight elections beginning in 1960, 92 percent of the U.S. representatives seeking reelection were successful. The surge in Senate defeats has not appeared in House elections. The three federal elections beginning in 1976 saw an average of 93.3 percent of the incumbents who sought reelection returned to the House, most comfortably.[20] Barely half as many incumbent representatives have been defeated in elections since 1960 as have died or retired during that period. Such a pattern has led one astute observer of Congress to note, only partially in jest, that "seemingly, the primary determinants of change in national policies will soon be individual deaths and retirements [of members of Congress] rather than elections."[21]

From the perspective of the individual members of Congress, however, such figures can be read differently. After all, for them, the future is unclear, and potential challengers lurk in every lesser office in the constituency. Indeed, one authority demonstrated that, for the 435 representatives elected or reelected in 1952, over the next twenty years 42 percent retired, 15 percent died in office, and 13 percent were still in Congress. The remaining 30 percent, however, had been defeated! Thirty-nine of the 435 had lost a primary election, and 95 had lost a general election.[22]

Despite these findings, the House was designed to be the *responsive* branch of Congress and the part of the national government that is supposed to change with the will of the electorate. When the average election sees 93 percent of those House members seeking reelection returned (or, including death and retirements, that the average election sees only 16 percent newcomers in the House), it is not unreasonable to feel that the House is less sensitive to public opinion, at *any given election,* than it should be. Besides, a pessimist might read the data to suggest that two thirds of House members are immune from electoral accountability, even over a period of several elections. (An optimist, of course, is likely to respond that the high reelection rate of U.S. representatives is adequate evidence of their sensitivity to public opinion.)

The Vanishing Marginals   From data on the U.S. House elections of 1956 through 1972, it has been noted that "the number of incumbents running in the marginal zone [was] roughly halved over the 16 year period."[23] The fast sixteen-year drop in the percentage of Congressional incumbents with close reelection fights in the general election was an intensification of a gradual, longer-term trend toward greater electoral security for the Congressional incumbent. The trend is obvious, whether one defines a marginal district as one in which the incumbent lost or was reelected with less than 60 percent of the vote, or whether one defines marginal districts as those in which the incumbent lost or was reelected with less than 55 percent of the vote. Before 1966, some three fifths, or less, of incumbent representatives were *safe—* they won with 60 percent or more of the general-election vote. Forty percent or more regularly won reelection with less than 60 percent of the vote—their districts were *marginal.* Since 1966, at least two thirds of incumbent U.S. representatives seeking reelection have received 60 percent or more of the vote, and, in three of the last eight elections, over three fourths of the incumbents received 60 percent or more of the general-election vote. Thus, the "marginals" now constitute less than a third, and often less than a fourth, of those seeking reelection. No such trend is observed in *open-seat* districts, in which no incumbent seeks reelection.[24] In open-seat election contests, party identification has a greater impact on the outcome.[25]

Why is incumbency so great an advantage to a U.S. representative at a time when many citizens hold Congress in low esteem?[26] Ferejohn and Erikson attribute the increased advantages of incumbency primarily to changes in individual voting behavior, especially a dampened voter response to partisan cues.[27] Fiorina argues that the increased advantages of incumbency are, indeed, related to changes in electoral behavior which have come in response to changed behavior of incumbent members of Congress. That is, as representatives devote more time and effort to constituent service, helping constituents cope with an increasingly important federal government, constituents respond by voting for the incumbent, regardless of party identification. This ombudsman function of the representative cuts across party lines, so in one sense, such voter behavior is quite rational. The party of the member and the party identification of the constituents receiving various benefits are not as important as the fact that the member of Congress can deliver and the constituent wants him or her to do so. And the ability to deliver services, or new VA hospitals, and some help with the government, increases with a member's greater seniority and understanding of how to make the federal agencies respond to the needs of his or her constituents.[28]

One authority has suggested that the increased number of incumbents winning with 60 percent or more of the vote is, since 1966, mainly the result of first-term representatives inducing "voting shifts in their favor by more effectively capitalizing on the opportunities of incumbency"[29] than first-termers had done in the past, rather than the result of public-opinion shifts in favor of all members of Congress. A similar argument is made by another observer, who demonstrates that the added electoral value of one term in the House (the "sophomore surge" in share of the vote) increased from a mean of about two percentage points in extra general-election votes prior to 1966 to a mean of about six percentage points in the elections of 1968 through 1974.[30] Overall, of course, the trend toward greater margins of incumbent electoral safety means that for the minority party to take control of the House away from the majority party will require a very large shift in voter preferences—much larger than in decades past—and may require several successive pro-minority-party elections.[31] The reason is that if the overall vote in Congressional races becomes about 2 percent more Republican, say, than in the prior year, and the range of shift is up to five percentage points in some districts, then only those Democrats who have been winning by less than five percentage points will be endangered. The fewer the number of incumbent Democrats who won last time with less than 55 percent of the district total, the fewer seats the Republicans will win.

Additional insights into the decline of marginal (competitive) Congressional districts for incumbent U.S. representatives can be gained by examining the contrasting electoral experience of incumbent U.S. senators. Not only are they less likely than U.S. representatives to be reelected, those who do win are much less likely to receive 60 percent of the votes. In 1980, for instance, over 90 percent of the 361 incumbent representatives who sought reelection were returned to the House. Over 70 percent of the incumbents received 60 percent or more of the vote in the general election. In contrast, only 55 percent of the twenty-nine incumbent U.S. senators who sought reelection in 1980 won another term, and only nine won 60 percent or more of the general election vote. Why the difference? A major part of the explanation appears to involve name recognition and assessment by voters of the incumbent and, more important, of the challenger.

Some studies have found that only about half of the electorate could recall the name of their district's U.S. representative, although many more were able to recall the name of the incumbent than the challenger. Stokes and Miller, for instance, found only 56 percent of the 1958 electorate could recall the name of their own member of Congress and only 35 percent could recall the name of the challenger.[32] The Gallup and Harris polls found slightly lower levels (46 percent to 53 percent) of ability to recall the member's name in various polls in the 1970s. How can representatives and senators benefit from incumbency when so many of their constituents do not know who they are? The reason is that the voters need not *recall* their representative's name to support him or her. In the voting booth, voters are confronted with a choice, and mere *name recognition* suffices. It turns out that close to 95 percent of the electorate can correctly spot their member's name when presented with a three-name list that includes his or her name.[33] Barely half as many recognize the challenger's name.

Separate analyses of the 1978 National Election Study of the Center for Political Studies agree that voter evaluations of the candidates in their respective Congressional districts (and, for senators, states) are very important in determining their votes. House incumbents fared better than Senate incumbents, in part because the House *challengers* were much less visible than Senate challengers and because House incumbents had been able to interact more intensely with their (smaller) constituencies.[34] Large differences exist between the positive ratings of House incumbents and their less visible challengers. Senate challengers, on the other hand, are more visible, often are major political figures in their own right, and are evaluated by voters almost as highly as incumbent senators. It may be, then, that the major reason incumbent U.S. representatives have had a higher reelection rate, recently, than U.S. senators is because of the difference in the quality of their respective *challengers,* rather than because of differences in the behavior of senators versus representatives or differences in voter perceptions of incumbent representatives and senators.[35]

Although political-party identification is still very important in determining voter choices for Congress, it is less important than it was twenty years ago, especially in contests involving incumbents. While both House and Senate incumbents, in their respective races, gain the lion's share of defections from partisan loyalties, House members are more advantaged by defections than senators. The percentage of voters who defect to the other party's candidate in a House contest has swollen from 9 percent of the voters in 1956 to twice that number in the late 1970s. Most of that growth has been of voters who defect from their self-reported basic partisanship to vote for their incumbent member of Congress.[36]

Incumbents are also helped by their constant publicity throughout the term: canned television and radio programs (produced cheaply at Congressional studios and played as "public-service" programs by many stations), constituent service offices in the district (whose staffs have grown greatly "nonpartisan" in the past couple of decades), frequent "nonpartisan" constituency meetings in different communities in the district throughout the term, letters of congratulations to high-school graduates and parents of new babies, numerous television and radio interviews and "call-in" shows, and frequent newsletters to constituents (postage free, with the "frank").

For all these reasons, incumbency is an increasingly valuable asset in Congressional elections. However, other factors also remain important. The basic Democratic advantage in partisan identification among the electorate helps to "explain" Democratic control of Congress in most years since the Great Depression of the 1930s. And partisan identification and turnout rates also help to explain the well-known decline in the President's party's share of House seats at the midterm election, held two years into each presidential term.

Midterm Elections and Presidential Coattails In the off-year Congressional election which occurs in the middle of the presidential term, the President's party almost always loses seats in the House. The theoretical explanation for the midterm decline is a matter of some debate. That debate essentially is over the extent to which voters behave rationally. Since extensive voter interviewing began in the national elections after World War II, the accepted scholarly explanation of the midterm loss of seats by the President's party has been the "surge-and-decline" thesis, so called after the title of an excellent explication of the argument.[37] The presidential campaign generates great media attention and stimulates voter interest and high voter turnout. The short-run forces generated by the presidential campaign, which lead to above-average voter turnout, also encourage some party identifiers to abandon their standing partisan preference and vote for the opposition party's candidate. Some vote for the other party's candidate for Congress, as well (the "coattails effect"). The degree of crossover voting is higher in presidential elections, because the hoopla of the presidential campaign brings out less intensely committed voters, who have less commitment to their standing partisan identification. In the absence of the stimulation of the presidential campaign, turnout drops at the midterm Congressional election. And, in the absence of the short-term forces of the presidential campaign, the extent of voter crossover drops, swinging marginal districts back to their "normal" party. Hence, the President's party can expect to lose Congressional seats in the midterm elections.

The surge-and-decline thesis has come under criticism as the number of marginal Congressional districts has decreased. The value of presidential coattails is being questioned,[38] and some midterm Congressional elections have resulted in losses for the President's party under circumstances which do not fit comfortably with the surge-and-decline model.[39]

An alternative and attractive explanation of the midterm loss by the President's party is offered by Kernell, who notes that, within the limits established by the underlying partisan loyalties in the various Congressional districts, "levels of presidential popularity and the party distribution of the congressional vote covary in a predictable manner." Kernell's thesis, based on analysis of both aggregate data (election returns) and individual attitudes as revealed in the national surveys of voters each election year, is that midterm Congressional returns are best explained by the public's evaluation of the President's performance. People who disapprove of the President's performance are more likely to vote in the midterm Congressional election than are the President's supporters, and the President's detractors are more likely to vote against the President's party in that election than the President's admirers are to vote in favor of the President's party for Congress. That is, those disenchanted with a President are likely to see the midterm Congressional election as a referendum on the President's performance, while the President's supporters are not. Most presidential supporters, then, if they vote, tend to vote in the midterm election according to criteria unrelated to their positive evaluation of the President's performance. The President's detractors, however, are more likely to vote and to retaliate against Congressional candidates of the President's party. Thus, argues Kernell, partisan identification may work mostly negatively for incumbent members of Congress, and the level of the President's popularity is causally related to his party's success or failure in the midterm Congressional election.[40]

The decline of marginal districts and the importance of single-member districts means, as a matter of electoral structure, that the presidential coattail effect is weakened in presidential years and that an unpopular President does less harm to his party members in Congress than he would if more districts were marginal. A good example is the Nixon landslide over McGovern for President in 1972. Even though President Nixon won over 60 percent of the vote, the Republicans gained only thirteen seats in the House.[41]

The Impact of the Economy   Studying a social phenomenon by different methods often leads to insights not available when only one approach is used. This is the case when one examines the impact of the state of the economy on Congressional elections. Conventional wisdom holds that recession, high unemployment, or excessive inflation hurts Congressional candidates of the President's party, both in presidential-election years (when a poor economy also hurts the President's reelection effort) and in midterm elections. Researchers who examine aggregate data (election returns) find strong relationships between the condition of the economy and Congressional-election outcomes, although, in every such election, local variables also affect outcomes. Those who examine the same question with data based on survey (public-opinion) research have difficulty finding that the *macro* effect (the relationship between the condition of the economy and the election results) is also present at the *micro* level (the level of the individual voter).

Kramer, for instance, linked prevailing economic conditions to aggregate electoral outcomes and explained much of the partisan division of the vote from the 1890s through the 1960s.[42] Kramer's analysis is a persuasive argument that objective economic conditions affect Congressional elections. Tufte supports that argument. He found that popular opinion concerning the President (using the approval rating in the Gallup poll) and changes in real disposable personal income per capita neatly predict the outcome of Congressional elections.[43] Kenski found a relationship between high unemployment and Democratic voting for Congress.[44]

Despite this persuasive scholarly evidence, based on aggregate data, that the state of the economy affects Congressional elections (an assessment with which most politicians agree), survey research has not found the type of individual manifestations which one would expect to find, given the aggregate relationships. For instance, a sophisticated analysis (called path analysis) of responses of voters questioned in the 1974 National Election Study found that voters' economic optimism or pessimism had no direct effect on their votes and only minor indirect effects.[45]

Kinder and Kiewiet may offer much of the explanation for the gap between the strong aggregate-data evidence that the state of the economy affects Congressional elections and the lack of the expected individual responses to survey questions. Their analysis, based on survey research, found that Congressional voting from 1956 through 1976 "was influenced hardly at all by personal economic grievances,"[46] apparently because Americans still do not link their personal economic circumstances to the national government. They tend to blame themselves for losing a job, blame local business conditions, or fix the cause on idiosyncratic circumstances at the plant.

> There remains, nevertheless, the aggregate evidence linking economic conditions and political outcomes. . . . [This] relationship cannot be accounted for at the individual level by voters acting on their personal economic grievances. The link appears to be provided, instead, by voters reaching decisions based partly on their collectively-oriented economic judgements. . . . Candidates of the incumbent party suffer when the economy sputters, not because voters punish them for their private misfortunes. Candidates suffer because voters perceive the party they represent as failing to cope adequately with national economic problems.[47]

Jacobson suggests the link between the condition of the economy and Congressional voting may be even less direct than that.[48] He argues that in Congressional elections the quality of the challenger and the vitality of the challenger's campaign are the crucial variables. Through a process of evaluation and self-selection, elites—including both potential candidates and potential campaign contributors—determine the quality of the individuals who challenge incumbents in any given election and the amount of resources the challenger will have to throw into the campaign. When elites perceive that a bad economy and unpopular President make it a good year to challenge an incumbent of the President's party, or a good economy and a popular President make timely a challenge to a member of Congress not of the President's party, they collectively establish a self-fulfilling prophecy. Furthermore, the best-qualified and best-financed challengers tend to be fielded against the more vulnerable incumbents. Thus, although the individual voter is casting his or her vote primarily on the basis of familiarity with and evaluation of the incumbent and the challenger, those electoral alternatives are not independent of national developments in the economy and in the people's assessment of how good a job the President is doing.

Other Issues   Numerous issues intrude upon Congressional elections besides the economy, the competence of the President, and the voters' comparison of the senator or representative's basic ability with that of the challenger. Indeed, "single-issue" politics has generated substantial press coverage and politician concern. If a major issue, such as abortion, the Vietnam War, gun control, or nuclear-waste disposal causes a substantial constituent vote against a legislator, then members of Congress could face much shorter tenure in office. Obviously, matters have not gotten to that extent yet, or the median seniority in Congress would be much lower. But the possibility of defeat at the hands of a "coalition" of angry single-issue constituents over various "can't-win" issues is enough to cause some members of Congress concern.

Are issues important in Congressional elections? In part, the answer depends on whom one asks. Survey research has led some scholars to conclude that the average voter has insufficient interest and information to reward or punish his or her member of Congress on the basis of issues.[49] Reanalysis of some of the earlier data, however, suggests that issues may have been more important in the late 1950s than early researchers thought.[50] Certainly, the members of Congress interviewed in 1958 thought their voting records (on the issues) were important to their remaining in Congress.[51] The evidence suggests that for extreme conservatives and extreme liberals, at least, such is the case.[52] Members watch other members' primary and general-election returns to determine what issue positions are likely to help or hurt them at the polls. Such observations, reports Mayhew, have affected Congressional behavior concerning school desegregation in general and busing in particular, national health insurance, labor legislation, and the Vietnam War.[53] Fenno notes a degree of electoral anxiety among the members of Congress he observed in their districts, but the members vary in the extent to which they feel issues make or break them.[54]

Hinckley found disappointingly low levels of voter attention to Congressional races in 1972. She suggests there are two kinds of Congressional voters—the attentive and the inattentive. Despite the intense nature of the issues in the 1972 election campaigns, most respondents indicated little awareness of the issue positions of the Congressional candidates. But, although issues were not the major determining factor in voting for Congress in 1972, they did explain 12 percent of the variance among low-attention voters and 27 percent among high-attention voters.[55] The most attentive constituents may well be financial contributors, who are quite aware of candidates' issue positions.[56] Indeed, it may be that much of the difference between low voter knowledge of issue positions and the importance attributed to issue positions by members of Congress lies in the importance of issues to contributors and the importance of contributors to incumbents' campaigns.

Wright's conclusions about the importance of domestic issues in the 1976 Congressional election also support the view that issues are sufficiently important in American Congressional elections that proponents of representative democracy need not fret too much.

> Most House members . . . at some point in their service are within the 5 to 9 percent range where unfavorable issue positions could make the difference in their reelection. And since the candidate's issue stance is one of the few factors relevant to his reelection that is also within his control, (the President's popularity and the condition of the economy are not) the Representative is well advised to bring his issue positions into line with those of his constituency. Not to do so could be the determining factor in electoral defeat. Congressmen, attributing considerable importance to their own records, are apparently aware of this.[57]

Congressional Campaign Finance

Congressional campaigns cost money. Professional campaign consultants; extensive radio and television advertising; printed materials; and computerized lists of voters, contributors, and potential contributors—are all expensive. U.S. Senate contests in large states are, of course, the most expensive. Presidential-election contests are now subject to public funding, and those who accept public funds also accept the expenditure limits which accompany them. No such restrictions exist in regard to spending by Congressional candidates, themselves, however. Nor is there public funding of Congressional campaigns, largely because the present situation is to the advantage of incumbents. Public funding might change that balance in favor of challengers, and incumbents are reluctant to vote for such a fundamental change.

U.S. Senate races are expensive—and getting more so. In 1976, the average Senate winner raised some $638,000; the average major-party loser raised about $583,000.[58] The smallest amount spent by a winner was $700 by incumbent Senator Proxmire of Wisconsin, but this is a rare example indeed. The most spent by a winner was some $3 million by pickle heir John Heinz to win an open seat in Pennsylvania. Over two thirds of the money was his own. The most spent by a loser was the almost $2 million by incumbent John Tunney of California.

In 1978, Senate expenditures went even higher. The average Senate campaign cost just over $928,000. As in the past, incumbents were better financed than challengers, and Republicans outspent Democrats. Four incumbents who spent more than their challengers lost anyhow. All three incumbents who spent less than their challengers were defeated. In 1978, the number of million-dollar Senate campaigns soared. Only four campaigns in 1972 cost over $1 million each. There were seven in 1974, ten in 1976, and fourteen in 1978. Heinz' record $3 million campaign was surpassed in 1978 by Republican Senator Helms' $6.3 million campaign in North Carolina. (See Table 5.3.)

House seats are not cheap, either, but most are less expensive to win than Senate seats, outside the smallest half-dozen states. The obvious reason is that most House districts are in states with two or more representatives. So, except, for the smallest half-dozen states, representatives have half or fewer constituents than senators (who are, of course, elected statewide). Nevertheless, the cost of election to the House, like the cost of Senate races, is also rising.

In 1976, the average incumbent U.S. representative raised just over $91,000 for his or her reelection campaign; the average challenger raised $49,600; and the average contender for an open seat raised $117,310. Overall, the average House campaign cost $73,000 that year. Almost two thirds of the funds raised by House candidates were raised by candidates who wound up winning. Contrary to the normal Senate pattern, Democrats in the House fared a bit better in fundraising than did Republicans, possibly because of the Democratic edge in incumbents (and committee chairs) to whom interest groups are anxious to give campaign contributions. The most expensive House campaign in 1976 was that of a California Democrat, who spent $637,000 in a close but losing effort. The most expensive Republican race was that of a Texas Republican incumbent, whose half-million-dollar campaign was not enough to save him from a challenger who had only half the incumbent's budget.

House campaign expenditures went up in 1978. The average House campaign that year cost $108,000, although some 80 percent of the campaigns cost less. A few, however, were extremely well funded. Forty House campaigns each spent over $300,000. A New York City Democrat spent $1.1 million in a losing effort. Louisi-

TABLE 5.3

The Largest Discrepancies in Spending Between Candidates in United States Senate Races, 1978 (Winners and Losers)

When the Bigger Spender Won	*When the Lower Spender Won*
1. Sen. Ted Stevens (R-Alaska) $297,000 vs. Donald Hobbs (D) $2,000 Winner Spent 14800% of Loser's Total	1. Gordon Humphrey (R-NH) $112,000 vs. Sen. Thomas McIntyre (D) $124,000 Winner Spent 90% of Loser's Total
2. Sen. Sam Nunn, Jr. (D-Ga) $480,000 vs. John Stokes (R) $5,000 Winner Spent 9600% of Loser's Total	2. Roger Jepsen (R-Ia) $521,000 vs. Sen. Dick Clark (D) $738,000 Winner Spent 71% of Loser's Total
3. Gov. David Pryor (D-Ark) $779,000 vs. William Kelly (R) $11,000 Winner Spent 7081% of Loser's Total	3. Rep. Paul Tsongas (D-Mass) $538,000 vs. Sen. Edward Brooke (R) $1,020,000 Winner Spent 53% of Loser's Total
4. Sen. Jesse Helms (R-NC) $6,351,000 vs. John Ingram (D) $217,000 Winner Spent 2927% of Loser's Total	4. Carl Levin (D-Mich) $647,000 vs. Sen. Robert Griffin (R) $1,290,000 Winner Spent 50% of Loser's Total
5. Sen. Mark Hatfield (R-Ore) $179,000 vs. Vern Cook (D) $22,000 Winner Spent 814% of Loser's Total	5. David Durenberger (R-Minn) $811,000 vs. Robert Short (D) $1,810,000 Winner Spent 45% of Loser's Total
6. Sen. James McClure (R-Ind) $369,000 vs. Dwight Jensen (D) $51,000 Winner Spent 724% of Loser's Total	
7. Sen. Pete Domenici (R-NM) $826,000 vs. Toney Anaya (D) $128,000 Winner Spent 645% of Loser's Total	
8. Sen. Walter D. Huddleston (D-Ky) $361,000 vs. Louis Guenthner (R) $65,000 Winner Spent 555% of Loser's Total	
9. Sen. Claiborne Pell (D-RI) $310,000 vs. James Reynolds (R) $69,000 Winner Spent 449% of Loser's Total	
10. Alan Simpson (R-Wy) $330,000 vs. Raymond Whitaker (D) $110,000 Winner Spent 300% of Loser's Total	

Source: From "Nader Study Links Spending and Success in Senate Campaigns" (Washington, D.C.: Congress Watch, November 16, 1978).

ana Democrat Claude Leach spent $771,000 to win. The national Republican party aided challengers in selected districts and helped seven challengers outspend and defeat incumbent Democrats, who had first won election to Congress in 1974 (post Watergate) by defeating incumbent Republicans. As usual, however, the average Congressional incumbent in 1978 was considerably better financed than the average challenger.

A challenger's financial disadvantage is very important, since the amount spent by a challenger seems to have a much greater impact on the outcome of the election than does the amount spent by the incumbent.[59] The incumbent is already well known. The challenger must also become well known to have a chance—and that requires substantial funds.

FEDERAL CAMPAIGN-FINANCE LAWS

Before the mid-1960s, such campaign-finance legislation as was on the books did not restrict anybody very much in what they might want to do.[60] In the 1960s, efforts were begun toward changing the federal laws governing federal campaigns. The Federal Election Act of 1971, and subsequent major amendments, have substantially changed the law concerning Congressional campaigns. The Federal Election Campaign Act, and amendments, established the Federal Election Commission to police Congressional campaigns and to enforce the act, with the help of the clerk of the House and the secretary of the Senate. It requires each political committee and candidate for Congress to report total campaign expenditures and to itemize all expenditures over $200. Copies of these reports must be submitted to the appropriate state official, to make local access more likely. Each political committee and candidate must list the full name, mailing address, occupation, and principal place of business of each contributor to the campaign in reports which are required to be filed periodically, ahead of the election. Legislation passed at the same time provided that persons who contribute to political campaigns may take a tax credit or deduction, as they choose, for political contributions up to $50 per person or $100 per couple. The 1974 amendments limit the amount an individual can contribute to a candidate for federal office to $1,000 for each primary, run-off, and general election—with a maximum annual individual contribution of $25,000 for all federal candidates. Those limits have been upheld by the U.S. Supreme Court as constitutional, but restrictions on how much an individual can spend on his or her own campaign were ruled unconstitutional on the basis of freedom of speech (Buckley v. Valeo).

Political Action Committees

The new campaign laws made it legal for corporations, as well as professional associations, labor unions, trade associations, and ideological groups to create political action committees—PACs. These PACs have had enormous—and growing—impact on Congressional campaigns. In 1978, 1,938 PACs contributed a total of over $35 million to Congressional campaigns—more than three times as much as the combined contributions of the Democratic and Republican parties to those same campaigns.[61] Among the PACs were those organized by the American Medical Association, automobile and truck dealers, realtors, and various corporations and unions. The twenty-three PACs associated with AT & T contributed over $650,000 to political campaigns in 1980.[62] We will consider PACs further in later discussions of interest groups and Congress.

Wealthy Candidates

As noted earlier, the U.S. Supreme Court ruled unconstitutional the provisions of federal laws which would have limited the amount of personal money a candidate could spend on his or her own campaign for Congress. Perhaps coincidentally, recent years have seen an upsurge of candidates who substitute wealth for political experience and contacts. Most "lend" their campaigns money so that they can get at least some of it back if their initial efforts sufficiently stimulate campaign contributions. (Often contributions arrive, belatedly, to help the winner pay off campaign debts.)

Four of the new senators elected in 1978, for example (Bradley, Warner, Simpson, and Kassebaum) all lent substantial personal funds (over $90,000 each) to their campaigns. And Minnesota Representative Donald Fraser was defeated in that state's

Democratic primary for U.S. Senator by Robert Short, who spent $1.2 million of his own money winning the nomination. (Short lost in the general election.) In New York, a Democrat who spent over $600,000 of his own money seeking election to the U.S. House was defeated by a Republican who spent over $400,000 of his own money. Senator Charles Percy of Illinois spent several hundred thousand dollars of his own money for last-minute television advertisements to aid his reelection campaign in 1978. That campaign was close, in part because the challenger also was willing to spend extensively from his own personal fortune.[63] The extent to which the U.S. Congress will become an institution of wealthy individuals, who are able to win elections by hiring consultants and using electronic media, without benefit of prior political experience or political party ties, is yet to be determined. But the trend bears watching.

NOMINATION AND ELECTION OF STATE LEGISLATORS

The federal system of shared sovereignty means that power is fragmented in the United States. It also means that there are a large number of entry points for popular participation in the governmental process and in governmental decisions—either as a citizen or as a candidate and officeholder. Indeed, membership in a state legislative body is often viewed by those interested in public office as an entry-level, or beginning, elective position.

Nominations to State Legislatures

State legislative nominations have not been as thoroughly studied as Congressional nominations, but it is clear that the states provide great diversity in this as in most other political characteristics. Still, there are underlying themes which are worth discussing. As discussed in Chapter 4, an informal, self-appointed screening group of local elites often determines—by encouraging one candidate and discouraging another—who the nominee will be. This informal screening process appears to be much more important in the selection of state legislators than in the selection of members of Congress.

Nominations to the state legislature ordinarily are of primary interest to state and local party officials and interest groups. In 1978 and 1980, however, the national Republican party put on a special drive to recruit attractive nominees to the state legislatures and to elect them, and it contributed $2 million to what was a successful effort. The Republican party made this effort in large part because it wanted Republican legislators to be in the strongest possible positions to affect reapportionment decisions (for Congress and the state legislatures), which the state legislatures would be making following the completion of the 1980 census.[64]

Most state legislators are nominated by primary elections, although many such primaries are uncontested. In the numerous districts in which the weaker party has no chance to win, the real competition occurs in the dominant party's primary; in many cases, that is also the only competition for the seat, because the weaker party often has difficulty finding anybody to be the sacrificial goat.[65] Both primary- and general-election competition is less likely in rural or small-town districts than in urban districts, regardless of party balance in the district. In an urban legislative district, the personal and long-term potential costs to a challenger are not as great. In the rural setting, however, the potential divisiveness and bitterness, even of a general-election campaign, often are enough to deter potential candidates.[66] Rural legislative districts which encompass two or more distinct communities, however, may foster competition between candidates whose main bases of support are in their respective towns or counties. To avoid dominance by one county or town in a district, or to lessen strife, *rotation agreements* occasionally are worked out to be sure each county or town in the district has a chance to send a legislator to the capitol.[67]

The number of legislative districts in which there is a serious contest for the party's nomination varies by state and year, but a fifteen-state study of primary elections from 1972 through 1978 suggests that it is not unusual for 40 percent of a state's districts to have two or more candidates for the Democratic nomination. In the Republican primary, by contrast, it would be unusual to find two candidates in as many as 20 percent of the legislative districts.[68] In part, the lower percentage of contested Republican primaries is caused by the fact that most state legislative districts in the 1970s were Democratic. Only a third or so of each party's primary-election contests for nominations to the state legislature could be considered close. In the remainder, the winner gets over twice as many votes as the loser.

Even though legislative tenure at the state level is much shorter than in Congress, it is not unusual for three fourths or more of a state's legislators to seek reelection. In the fifteen states examined, over 96 percent of the incumbent legislators seeking reelection were nominated.[69] Barely a fourth of the incumbents had opposition in the primary election, although more were challenged in the primary in Oregon and in the southern states than elsewhere. As one would expect, districts with no incumbent running (open seats) had a higher rate of primary-election competition than districts where the incumbent sought another term.[70] In some states, a preprimary party endorsement makes primary-election competition less likely, but endorsements are not always effective in preventing primary competition.[71] In the 1950s and 1960s, incumbent legislators in the South were defeated in their party's primary fairly regularly. A third or more of the incumbents seeking reelection normally lost in Alabama and Louisiana, and substantial numbers were defeated for reelection in the primaries of the other southern states.[72] The high rate of southern primary-election defeats appears to be a regional phenomenon associated with lack of general-election competition. The *only* meaningful election was (and in some sections still is) the Democratic primary.

General Elections for State Legislatures

Many state legislative districts are strongly dominated by one political party, and the real decision on who will represent the district occurs in the dominant party's primary. And in many states, where control shifts back and forth between Democrats and Republicans, the legislative districts are not as competitive as the overall condition might suggest. In some states, that is, there is a fairly close division of the "safe" seats between the parties, and control of the legislature may hinge on the handful of "swing" districts. The citizens in those swing districts determine which party will control the state legislature. The other voters in the state really have little to say about it. On the other hand, the legislators from the swing districts are unlikely ever to gain much experience and power within the legislature. The recruitment of candidates for the swing districts and the attention given the election in those few districts by the governor and the state party may differ substantially from the treatment of the safe districts in the state.

Some states are so strongly dominated by one party that the second party only runs candidates in a fraction of the state's legislative districts. This pattern was common in southern and border states until recently, and is not entirely gone now. The few Republican candidates (and the few Republican state legislators) in those states were from metropolitan areas, except in Kentucky, North Carolina, and Tennessee, where mountain counties which had opposed secession have elected Republicans since the Civil War. More and more districts of the formerly Democratic areas of the southern states are being contested by Republicans, although the spread is uneven. Some southern states today exhibit striking differences from their politics of two decades ago, while others are little changed. South Carolina, for instance, had no Republican state-legislative candidates in 1960, but now regularly experiences Republican contests for a majority of the seats. Republicans normally contested 20 percent or less of Florida's state legislative seats in the 1950s, but now enter candidates in over half the districts. Some states showed a flurry of Republican candidates for a while, but lack of much success caused a fall-off in recent years. In some states, such as Louisiana, Oklahoma, and Texas, the minority party has been able to win the governorship but has not filed candidates in enough legislative districts to really have a chance of converting the governor's popularity into majority legislative status.[73]

There are many unresearched questions concerning why people vote for the state legislative candidate they do. Obviously, *party identification* is a major factor. Many states vote Republican for President, have one or both U.S. senators on the Republican side of the aisle, and elect some Republican U.S. representatives and an occasional Republican governor, but remain steadfast in their election of Democrats to the state legislature. Such patterns appear to be a result of many ticket splitters, who vote by party identification in the contests they know little about, while crossing over, in the more visible contests, to support attractive candidates of the other party.

In two-party states, a very popular or unpopular candidate for governor or U.S. Senate can affect state legislative voting, but the extent to which a popular "top-of-the-ticket" candidate helps his or her party's legislative candidates is influenced by where the legislative contests are located on the ballot, the number of contests on the ballot, and whether the state uses the "office-block" or the "party-column" ballot. The latter, of course, enhances top-of-the-ticket coattails; the former truncates them.[74] The evidence suggests that many attractive gubernatorial candidates have been unable to convert their personal magnetism into votes for their party's legislative candidates. Jewell and Olson found, for example, that forty-three states had had four or more years of divided government since 1946. That is, the governor faced at least one legislative chamber controlled by the other party. Almost two thirds of those lower chambers under opposition control were elected at the same time as the governor. In many of these situations, the governor's share of the vote was much greater than his or her party's share of the legislative vote. To cite the extreme example, the Republican candidate for governor of Rhode Island in 1964 won 61.1 percent of the vote, while the Republican candidates for the state House of Representatives collectively won only 36.8 percent of the statewide vote. Said differently, some 40 percent of those who voted Republican for governor voted Democratic for state representative.[75]

Issue Voting There is issue voting in state legislative contests, but there is apparently much less of it than in Congressional elections. There is impressionistic evidence, for example, that, in some state legislative elections, the candidates' stands on such salient issues as outlawing abortion, passing the Equal Rights Amendment, or tough environmental legislation can determine who wins. But there are equally reliable indications that many voters know little about state legislative contests. Thus, many districts remain staunchly Democratic or Republican, even when the district votes for the other party for President, U.S. Senate, or governor (or all three).

104

The Power of Incumbency Incumbency is an asset, apparently, although its value varies with the legislator's situation as well as by state.[76] In a metropolitan area with one or two dozen state legislators, it is difficult for any individual legislator to gain much visibility. But, even in a metropolitan area, people are more likely to have heard of the incumbent than they are to have heard of the challenger. While not all who recognize a candidate's name will evaluate the candidate positively, voters are not able to evaluate a candidate at all if they have never heard of him or her. In the less densely populated parts of a state, a legislator is likely to represent one or two entire counties, and the local news media (even if only a radio station or a weekly newspaper) consider him or her "good copy." Incumbency is probably a greater asset, then, to small-town and rural legislators (who also tend not to be challenged because of the "costs" involved for rural challengers) than to city legislators. Thus, again, rural legislators have the electoral dynamic in their favor in gaining experience and seniority, when compared to urban legislators. In those states which provide each legislator with a district office, office expenses, and one or more paid assistants, incumbency may well be a greater asset than in states where the legislator loses money each term. In those states where the legislative districts are so small that candidates still campaign by knocking on every door in the district, however, the advantages of incumbency may be more readily overcome.

National Developments State legislative elections are sometimes affected by national developments, but apparently less frequently and less extensively than is the case with Congressional elections. Still, the only time since World War II that Republicans were able to organize either chamber of the New Mexico or Tennessee legislatures, for example, was during President Eisenhower's tenure in the White House, and Republicans did poorly in the state legislative elections after Watergate. Furthermore, one study found that independent voters who had favorable images of President Nixon were more likely to vote for Republican candidates for lower-level state and local offices than were independents with negative views of Mr. Nixon, although the impact of presidential evaluation was negligible on party identifiers.[77]

STATE LEGISLATIVE CAMPAIGN FINANCE

Money is important in state legislative election campaigns, but, in general, it is less important than in Congressional elections.

Costs of State Legislative Campaigns

The importance of adequate financing (and the amount required to run an "adequate" campaign) varies greatly among the states. The major reason for that variation is the range in size of state legislative districts. In lower-chamber districts with 20,000 residents, for example, a door-to-door campaign can be quite effective with expenditures of less than a thousand dollars. A California Senate district, by contrast, is larger in population than a Congressional district, and the expense of an effective election campaign is comparable.

A survey of the cost of running for the state legislature in recent years found, as one would expect, that it is more expensive to get elected to a state senate than to a state lower chamber (senate districts in each state are larger) and that winners, on the average, spend more than losers. (See Tables 5.4 and 5.5.) The median state senate expenditure of winners in 10 states who had overcome opposition (in 1978) ranged from about $8,000 in Kentucky and Nebraska to over $64,000 in California.

TABLE 5.4
Campaign Spending by Candidates for State Lower Chamber
(in thousands of dollars)

State	Year	Average or Median	Average or Median Spending**				
			All Winners	Contested Winners***	Unopposed Winners	Losers	Highest Winner
Calif.	78	M	41.4	43.9	18.0	13.1	162.5
Florida	78	M	—	19.5	1.8	—	102.0
N.J.	77	M	13.7	13.7	none	9.4	44.4
Wash.	78	A	—	12.9	5.7	8.9	35.9
Michigan	78	M	10.2	10.4	6.7	6.8	34.7
Iowa	78	M	3.3	8.4	0.8	2.4	13.9
Penn.	78	M	6.2	6.3	2.1	2.8	32.2
Virginia	73	M	—	4.0	0.3	4.0	28.6
Kentucky	77	M	—	3.6	0.2	—	19.8
Conn.	78	A	3.1	3.1	2.4	2.0	9.3
Kansas	78	M	2.3	—	—	1.3	12.1
N.C.	74	M	—	1.5	0.0	—	15.5
Idaho*	76	A	1.8	—	—	1.4	8.2

*Idaho data include Senate and House races combined.

**Spending figure includes cost of both primary and general election campaigns, except for California, Pennsylvania, and North Carolinia, where costs are reported for general election only.

***Where data are for both primary and general elections, an opponent in either election qualifies legislator for "contested winner" category.

Source: Malcolm E. Jewell, "Survey on State Campaign Financing," *Comparative State Politics Newsletter* 1 (January 1980): 16-17.

Losing candidates had spent, on the average, much less. The most spent by a senate winner in each of the states examined ranged from $15,900 in Nebraska to $346,200 in California.[78] In 1980, the most expensive California state Senate campaign cost $776,000![79] And the cost of seeking a Texas Senate seat has now reached a level ranging from $250,000 to $400,000.[80]

The median 1978 cost of winning election to the state lower chamber, overcoming opposition, ranged from $1,500 in North Carolina to $43,900 in California. Again, losing candidates, on the average, spent less than winners. The most money spent by a 1978 House winner in each of 13 states examined ranged from $8,200 in Idaho to $162,500 in California.[81] The highest costs in each state are normally associated with the cost of campaigning in large urban areas—especially media costs.

The amount of money available to a legislative candidate affects the type of campaign he or she runs. Those able to raise large sums are more likely to hire professional campaign consultants and campaign managers, to commission public-opinion surveys, to hire office workers, instead of relying on volunteers, and to use television and radio extensively. Those without much money are forced to avoid the broadcasting media in favor of newspaper advertisements and outdoor signs and billboards.[82]

The rising cost of campaigns gives legislative leaders an opportunity to bind their legislative followers to them by asking interest groups to contribute to a legislative campaign fund controlled by the leaders. Such a practice is especially well developed in California, but is also used in varying degrees in Connecticut, Kansas, Michigan, Pennsylvania, and Washington.[83]

TABLE 5.5

Campaign Spending by Candidates for State Senate
(in thousands of dollars)

State	Year	Average or Median	All Winners	Contested Winners**	Unopposed Winners	Losers	Highest Winner
				*Average or Median Spending**			
Calif.	78	M	61.8	64.3	7.2	15.7	346.2
Florida	78	M	—	45.4	18.0	—	102.0
Michigan	78	M	32.6	33.2	12.8	21.1	89.8
Penn.	78	M	19.7	19.7	none	8.6	67.5
N.J.	77	M	18.2	18.2	none	12.8	95.4
Wash.	78	A	—	16.4	7.0	15.7	36.1
Iowa	78	M	6.4	13.9	0.8	4.4	20.2
Conn.	78	A	9.6	9.6	none	6.7	23.7
Nebraska	78	M	6.5	8.5	—	3.8	15.9
Kentucky	75+77	M	—	7.4	0.6	—	29.9

*Spending figure includes cost of both primary and general election campaigns, except for California, Pennsylvania, and North Carolina, where costs are reported for general election only.
**Where data are for both primary and general elections, an opponent in either election qualifies legislator for "contested winner" category.

Source: Malcolm E. Jewell, "Survey on State Campaign Financing," *Comparative State Politics Newsletter* 1 (January 1980): 16-17.

State Campaign Finance Laws

Every state but North Dakota requires candidates for state office (including the legislature) to file reports with a state official, disclosing campaign contributions and expenditures. Forty-seven states require both pre- and post-election reports, while Alabama and Wyoming require only post-election disclosure. Details of the laws vary, but most states require that each campaign contributor's name, address, occupation, and principal place of business be reported, along with the date and amount of each contribution. The states have different thresholds above which contributors must be identified. Kansas requires individual identification of every person who contributed $10 or more; Louisiana thinks $1,000 is sufficient.[84]

Half the states place no limit on individual donations to campaigns, and the others vary. Many prohibit direct corporate campaign contributions, and some ban labor-union contributions and contributions by government contractors or heavily regulated industries, such as public utilities, banks, common carriers, or insurance companies. Others merely limit the amount such donors can give. Most states, however, permit the restricted donors to form political action committees to seek voluntary political contributions from employees, stockholders, and members. There is some evidence that not all such donations are completely voluntary, especially among middle- and upper-management personnel.[85]

A few states provide public funding for legislative candidates. Minnesota, for example, has a taxpayer check-off fund, similar to the national program for financing presidential candidates. Seventy percent of the money in the fund is apportioned among candidates for the state legislature, while the rest goes to statewide candidates. Candidates are free to refuse the public funds.[86] Proponents of public funding argue that the law of diminishing returns applies to political campaigns (including legislative campaigns). That is, once a candidate has a sufficient campaign kitty to insure him or her minimal exposure and a fighting chance not to be buried by the opponent's money, then additional campaign money is less crucial and less desperately sought.[87] Thus, the argument runs, a modest state contribution, plus the small "no-strings attached" contributions from ordinary citizens, give candidates substantial independence from the large contributions offered by economic and ideological interest groups (and their PACs), who limit their help to those they can "depend on."

SINGLE-MEMBER DISTRICTS AND PLURALITY ELECTIONS

It would be possible for a state or nation to elect all the members of its legislative body, or bodies, "at large." For example, if there were one hundred members in the state's legislative body, all would have to campaign throughout the entire state, and the voters would each have one hundred votes. This, of course, would be confusing to the voters and, for a number of reasons, would make it less likely that the legislature would be fully representative of the people. Typically, then, states and nations divide themselves into districts for the election of their legislators. In some nations, a number of legislators are elected from the same district on the basis of proportional representation (PR). In these PR systems, each political party is awarded legislative seats from each district in proportion to the party's share of the popular vote in the district. (There are usually "qualifying" rules, too, requiring, for example, that a party get at least enough votes in the district for one seat from the district and that it receive some threshold percentage, such as 5 percent of the total votes cast in all of the districts). This system is intended to give *some* representation to all parties—even small, minor ones—if they have some substantial voter support.

The system of electing legislators by multimember districts on the basis of proportional representation is not the one used in the United States. Here, by statute, all members of Congress and most state legislators are selected by single-member districts in plurality, "winner-take-all" elections. (A plurality occurs when one candidate gets more votes than any other candidate.) These fundamentally important features of the American system for electing legislators—single-member districts and plurality, "winner-take-all" elections—have important consequences and cause some distortions in representation, although there is no evidence the single-member district system was intended, by design, to cause such distortions.

Any formula in use distorts somewhat the translation of the popular vote into legislative seats, tending to give the greatest advantage to the strongest party and the greatest disadvantage to the weakest electoral party. Even proportional representation systems do this, primarily because in some districts the weak party will fail to qualify for even one seat.[88] Such distortions are so common that, after extensive examination of the subject, Douglas Rae concluded:

> Like the Sheriff of Nottingham, electoral systems are apt to steal from the poor
> and give to the rich; strong parties usually obtain more than their proportionate
> share of legislative seats while weak parties receive less than their proportionate
> share of seats. Indeed many legislative majorities are "manufactured" by elec-

toral systems which give more than half the seats to first (strongest) parties which have obtained less than half the votes.[89]

Maximum distortion occurs with single-member legislative districts.[90] Single-member districts press the political system toward two dominant political parties. Thus, single-member legislative districts tend to be found alongside two-party or one-party systems, although strong regional minor parties can survive even in a nation which elects legislators from single-member legislative districts.[91] No national vote "threshold" is required where single-member legislative districts are used.

The use of the single-member legislative district also means that candidates (especially the winners) will generally be located near the public-opinion mode (or the most frequently expressed view) of the people within the legislative district.[92] Thus, many points of view may be screened out early in the process of selecting legislators and legislative views compressed toward the middle portion of political discourse. Not surprisingly, then, most American legislators are philosophically "middle of the road."

There are exceptions to the plurality vote norm in America. Most southern states, as a consequence of a century of Democratic party dominance, require a run-off primary between the two top contenders, if no candidate wins more than 50 percent of the votes cast in the regular election. Similarly, not all American state legislators are elected from single-member districts. Indeed, close to a third of them represent multimember districts. All West Virginia state senators are elected from two-member senate districts, and another dozen states elect some of their state senators from multimember state senate districts.[93] These multimember district elections, though, are not held under proportional representation rules. Rather, each of the contests within the district is a separate election, and a voter has as many votes as there are seats to fill. The effect—on the party system and on the perspectives of legislators—of these multimember state legislative districts is about the same as that of single-member legislative districts. Large multimember state senate districts, however, do tend to make it more difficult for racial-minority candidates to win, because the racial-minority votes tend to be overwhelmed by nonminority votes.[94]

Eight states elect all their state lower-chamber members from multimember districts, usually with two or three legislators per district. Fourteen more states elect some of their lower-chamber members from multimember districts.[95] As with multimember state senate districts, the impact of multimember lower-chamber districts in these states is about the same as single-member districts (except for campaign costs and racial-minority representation), because the seats are contested separately with plurality rules rather than proportional representation. Each legislative contest is separate from the others, and only a candidate or party appealing to the dominant perspective of the multimember district's constituency has a good chance of winning.

The one state which had used a different electoral scheme was Illinois. From 1870 to 1980, it elected its state representatives from three-member districts, using cumulative voting. This plan was designed to overcome a strong upstate-downstate split and to insure that each section of the state elected some Democrats and some Republicans. It was not intended to encourage minor (third) parties and did not. Illinois now elects all its state legislators from single-member districts.[96]

The system in general use for electing American legislators on the basis of single-member districts and plurality vote can, then, produce artificial legislative majorities. In addition, gerrymandering and malapportionment can distort legislative representation.

The Gerrymander

The gerrymander is the act of drawing legislative district boundaries to give advantage to a particular candidate or political party.[97] Advantage may be gained by creating a few legislative districts that are overwhelmingly favorable to the minority party, while creating many districts that are comfortably favorable to the majority party. (See Figure 5.1.)

Americans are very mobile. Each decennial census finds substantial changes in the location of our people, both between states and within each state. As people move from the farm to the city, from the cities to the suburbs, back to rural areas, and from the northern to the southern and southwestern areas of the nation, legislative seats must periodically be reallocated if citizens are to have equal legislative representation.

FIGURE 5.1
Gerrymander

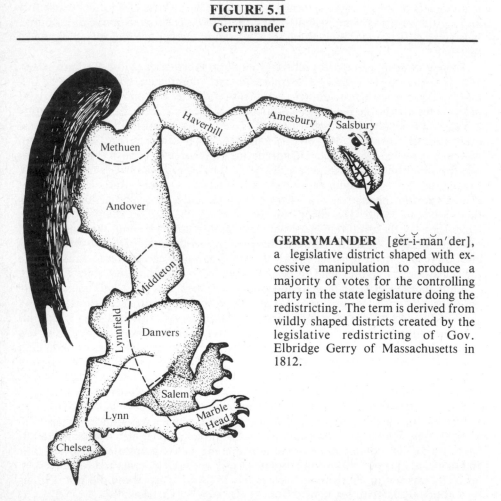

GERRYMANDER [gĕr-ĭ-mănˈder], a legislative district shaped with excessive manipulation to produce a majority of votes for the controlling party in the state legislature doing the redistricting. The term is derived from wildly shaped districts created by the legislative redistricting of Gov. Elbridge Gerry of Massachusetts in 1812.

1812 depiction of the Gerry-mander, fanged and clawed, was titled "a new species of Monster."

Source: *American Government Encyclopedia*, p. 117.

When a state gains or loses members in the U.S. House of Representatives at the beginning of each decade, it must redraw the boundaries of the Congressional districts within the state. Even states that neither gain nor lose representation in Congress may have to redraw Congressional-district boundaries because the population within the state has shifted. Similarly, the boundaries for *state* legislative districts must be changed after each census. Some states have tried (seldom successfully) to avoid purely partisan decisions by assigning legislative redistricting to a commission. Most states restructure their Congressional and state legislative districts every ten years by act of the state legislature.

Every ten years, then, the majority party in the state legislature has the opportunity to manipulate district boundaries for partisan advantage. The opportunity is seldom ignored.[98] Indeed, the Republican National Committee established as a major priority in the 1978 and 1980 elections the winning of the governorship or control of at least one chamber of the state legislature in as many states as possible.[99] The committee simply assumed that gerrymandering would occur in the various states in 1981 (following the 1980 census), and they wanted Republicans to be in a position either to control the gerrymandering or to block Democratic gerrymandering.

When legislative boundaries are drawn to the advantage of one party, it becomes more difficult for the other party (or parties) to dislodge the advantaged party. The gerrymander does not violate the "one person-one vote" requirement of the U.S. Supreme Court, unless racial discrimination is involved.[100] A clever gerrymander, however, can frustrate the will of the electorate and result in the advantaged party's winning a majority of the legislative seats while receiving fewer total legislative votes than the second party in the state. In the 1966 legislative elections in California, for example, the Democrats won a majority of seats, even though they had polled fewer legislative votes statewide than the Republicans, because of the districting plan which had been adopted a year earlier with the support of a Democratic governor and Democratic legislative majorities. Similarly, "for the state legislature in New Jersey, using a mixture of new single-member and multi-member districts, a comfortable but not overwhelming Republican plurality in popular votes in 1967 produced a sweep of two thirds of the seats in each house.[101]

Congressional Apportionment

On the floor of a legislature, each member's vote counts equally, and a majority of members present must vote "yes" if a measure is to pass. Equality within the legislature is consistent with basic democratic values, but whether or not citizens are formally represented in legislative bodies on an equal basis depends in large part on whether the constituencies of the legislators are of equal size. That question of apportionment of the number of citizens to each district—or malapportionment of them—received intense attention in the 1960s and is still a matter of concern today.

Most Americans learn in high school that one of the major compromises of the original U.S. Constitutional Convention was the decision to establish a bicameral national legislature in which representation in the House of Representatives would be based upon population, while all states would have an equal number of members of the Senate. Each state elects at least one U.S. representative, and may be allocated more if it has sufficient population. Each state elects two U.S. senators. During the 1970s, six states had only one representative each. Thirty states elected five or more U.S. representatives each, with California electing the most—forty-three. As a result of the 1980 census, South Dakota lost one of its two representatives in 1983, while Nevada doubled its House delegation to two members. California gained two additional seats, Texas gained three, and Florida four, while New York lost five seats. Other northern states also lost House representation, while western and Sunbelt states gained.[102] (See Figure 5.2.)

The constituencies of U.S. senators vary greatly in size. Since each U.S. senator is elected statewide, a senator from California has more constituents than a senator from any other state—some fifty times as many as a senator from Alaska. Indeed, the fifty-two senators from the twenty-six smallest states represent less than 20 percent of the nation's population. This disparity in the national Senate is well understood and accepted—it is a part of the U.S. Constitution—although similar discrepancies at the state level are not accepted.

Within each state, the Congressional districts (single-member districts from which U.S. representatives are elected) must contain approximately equal population. That has been the rule since the U.S. Supreme Court held, in *Wesberry* v. *Sanders* (1964) that "as nearly as practicable one man's vote in a congressional election is to be worth as much as another's."[103] Because Congressional districts may not cross state lines, and because states with less than three representatives vary greatly in population, substantial variation still exists in the number of people each U.S. representative represents.

The variation today, however, is much less than that which existed prior to *Wesberry* v. *Sanders.* In Illinois in 1940, for example, Congressional-district populations

FIGURE 5.2
U.S. House Districts After 1982

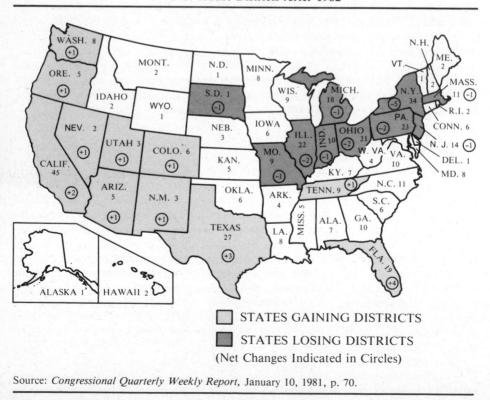

☐ STATES GAINING DISTRICTS

■ STATES LOSING DISTRICTS

(Net Changes Indicated in Circles)

Source: *Congressional Quarterly Weekly Report,* January 10, 1981, p. 70.

ranged from 112,000 people to 914,000. In 1946, in *Colgrove* v. *Green*, the U.S. Supreme Court refused to do anything about malapportionment on the grounds that Congressional districting was a "political question" and that any remedies were a responsibility of the legislative branch.[104] The Court did not want to enter the apportionment "political thicket." That position was reversed eighteen years later by the Warren Court, at a time when urban areas continued to be severely underrepresented in Congress.[105]

How much variation is permitted in Congressional-district populations within a state? Not much. In *Kirkpatrick* v. *Preisler* (1969), the Court held that Missouri's Congressional-districting plan contained too much variation, even though the maximum deviation of any of the districts from the state norm was only 3.1 percent.[106] Such insistence on numerical equality between districts, of course, means that political and geographic boundaries within each state are of much less significance in creating Congressional districts. The possibilities for gerrymandering are thus increased.

State Legislative Apportionment

In forty of the fifty states, apportionment is by legislative act. The other states use apportionment boards or commissions, except for Maryland, where the governor draws the legislative-district boundaries after each census.[107] Because the party which controls the legislature at apportionment time can be expected to draw district lines to benefit itself, the parties make an extra effort to control the state legislature at the beginning of each decade. Failing that, the party seeks at least to control one chamber or the governor's office, so as to block unpalatable state legislative and congressional reapportionment plans.

Today, the districts for both chambers of a state legislature must be of approximately equal population, must be reasonably compact, and the area within each legislative district must be contiguous—that is, one must be able to go from any place in the legislative district to any other place in the district without leaving it. As in Congressional districting, however, great changes have come about in the past two decades. In retrospect, it may look as though one change inevitably led to the next. To the participants at the time, however, that was not the case, and one must consider the great uncertainties involved at the time in order to understand the intensity of emotions of those engaged in the apportionment battles of the 1960s.

The *Colgrove* decision concerning unequal Illinois Congressional apportionment went against those who wanted judicial intervention in legislative districting, but that decision was made by a one-vote majority of the U.S. Supreme Court. The Court hinted at a change in *Gomillon* v. *Lightfoot*,[108] a 1960 decision which declared unconstitutional an Alabama statute which had changed the boundaries of the city of Tuskegee in such a manner as to exclude almost all black residents from the city (and, therefore, from participating in city elections). In order to declare the statute unconstitutional, the Court had to assume jurisdiction and, thus, enter at least the edges of "the political thicket."

The justices decisively entered "the political thicket" in the case of *Baker* v. *Carr*,[109] which arose in Tennessee. There, counties with less than 3,000 people had the same representation in the 1962 Tennessee General Assembly as counties with 25,000 to 33,000 people. Furthermore, the Tennessee General Assembly was required by the state constitution to reapportion itself every ten years, but it had not done so since 1901. Citing *Colgrove*, a three-judge federal district court panel unanimously dismissed the case. Baker, a voter in Nashville (which was grossly underrepresented in the Tennessee General Assembly), appealed to the U.S. Supreme Court, and it agreed to hear the case. The Supreme Court did not try to settle the issues of the case. But it did hold, very importantly, that apportionment problems, generally, are justiciable (the courts can assume jurisdiction) and that "the constitutionality of apportionments were to be adjudicated under the equal protection clause of the Fourteenth Amendment."[110] The Supreme Court, thus, decided that apportionment matters no longer constituted a "political thicket" which the courts could not enter, and then sent the case back to the federal district court for resolution.

Tennessee was not the only state with a malapportioned legislature, and, by the end of 1963, thirty-one reapportionment cases were brought in the federal courts, nineteen in state courts, and eleven in both federal and state courts.[111] By the end of the year, twenty-six states had approved reapportionment plans or adopted state constitutional amendments to reduce population disparities in legislative districts.[112] All this was a result of the Supreme Court's *Baker* decision that apportionment questions were justiciable.

State senate apportionment was then decided by the U.S. Supreme Court. Some states had enshrined in their constitutions "little federal" plans under which each *county* was equally represented in the *state* senate—much like each state was represented in the U.S. Senate. Some states had also assured that each county would have at least one representative in the lower chamber, with additional representatives distributed on the basis of population. A similar result was obtained in other states simply by steadfast legislative refusal to reapportion. As a consequence, some state legislators represented many more citizens than others. There was a definite bias against the growing urban areas.

In June 1964, the U.S. Supreme Court rejected the "federal analogy" under which many state constitutions had given their counties equal representation in the state senate. States had existed prior to the United States, and equality of the states in the U.S. Senate was expressly embodied in the U.S. Constitution when the union was created. Counties are the creatures of the state and have only such powers as the state (through its constitution and its statutes) chooses to give them. Thus, the "federal analogy" is not a valid one, and counties have no constitutional right to equal representation in their state senates. Therefore, said the U.S. Supreme Court in *Reynolds* v. *Sims, both* chambers of state legislatures must be apportioned in accordance with population, not just the lower chamber.[113]

Forcing state senates to be districted according to population brought substantial changes to the politics of many states and removed major inequities in American state legislatures. Prior to *Reynolds,* to cite the most extreme case, the California Senate's largest district had 433 times as many residents as its smallest district. A majority of the California Senate could be elected from districts containing only 10.7 percent of the state's population.[114] Idaho's Constitution provided for one state senator per county, regardless of population. This provision, invalidated by a federal court order in 1965, had produced a state senate in which counties with a bare sixth of the state's population elected a majority of the state's senators.[115] A majority of the Nevada Senate was elected from counties with only 8 percent of the state's population.[116]

How much variation in state legislative districts is permitted? The answer appears to be more than for Congressional districts, but not too much. In *Baker* v. *Carr,* the Supreme Court set no standards for how much population deviation would be permitted. Two years later, however, in *Reynolds* v. *Sims,* the Court ruled that a state must attempt "to construct districts, in both houses of its legislature, as nearly of equal population as is practicable."[117] The *Reynolds* decision suggested, though, that different situations might reasonably lead to some degree of permitted variation.

Following the 1970 and 1980 censuses, the states again reapportioned their legislatures. Litigation over the 1970 apportionments led the Supreme Court to hold that larger variations are permitted for state legislative districts than for Congressional districts. In *Mahan* v. *Howell,* a 1973 Virginia case, the Court accepted a plan in which the smallest district was overrepresented by 6.8 percent and the largest district was underrepresented by 9.6 percent, for a total variation of some 16.4 percent. The Court majority (changed, in the eleven years since *Baker* v. *Carr*) found the use of political-subdivision boundaries in the Virginia districting plan to be a sufficient justification for the differences in the size of the legislative districts,[118] the justification being that precise mathematical equality may not be as important to a citizen as knowing who his or her legislator is.

Factors in Redistricting   When a state legislature or a board or commission begins to redraw a state's Congressional- or legislative-district boundaries, many variables are involved. It is *not* simply a matter of the party in control devising a plan to give itself maximum benefit. Indeed, reapportionment battles can make even apathetic citizens aware of the complexity of America's political system. The party's interests, as perceived by state party leaders, may compete with the individual interests and ambitions of legislators, regional or county preferences, and the wishes of interest groups. For example, a state party chairperson may disagree publicly with the reapportionment plans of the party's legislative leaders. Decisions on how to draw district lines are often intermeshed with current policy issues, and legislators may swap votes—on school-funding formulas or the creation of a new state judgeship, for example—for votes on an apportionment bill. The party's interest is not ignored, but it is not the only consideration for legislators either.

A legislator may resist diluting his or her district's three-to-one partisan advantage, even though the party leaders need some of this partisan turf to make a victory possible in a neighboring district. A lower-chamber member's major concern may be to fashion an upper-chamber district that he or she can win. Some state legislators aspire to Congress and hope to create Congressional districts in which they can win, preferably new districts without incumbents. These and other factors can make calm, rational, disinterested decision-making difficult.[119] A party's greatest advantage in such an environment is the fact that legislatures are organized along party lines, and some consideration must be given to partisan interests by legislators if the party is to emerge from the next election with a legislative majority. Too little attention to partisan interests can, in a competitive state, lock a party into a legislative-minority position for a decade.

The various factors and factions involved are often especially frustrating for members of Congress, whose political careers may well hinge on the redistricting outcome, but who have no vote in the decision-making. Having friends in their home-state legislature may be especially important for U.S. representatives in states which lose House seats.

Consequences of Fair Apportionment   An obvious consequence of the historic reapportionment rulings by the U.S. Supreme Court was that the number of rural legislators decreased. The percentage of legislators earning a substantial share of their incomes from farming and ranching, which had already been on the decline, dropped markedly in the newly reapportioned state legislatures.[120] The number of black and other minority legislators increased sharply.[121] And, in those legislative chambers where malapportionment had been most severe, there was a substantial increase in party-line voting.[122] Further, because the new system was perceived as more fair, urban citizens felt better about the political system, generally. Today, the ethical imperative of equal representation is being met, and that alone is a worthy achievement. But has there been an impact on policy? Yes, a substantial impact. Not as much as reapportionment's most fervent advocates had hoped, perhaps, but much more than skeptics expected.

Many early studies of the subject focused on comparing expenditure patterns in the relatively fairly apportioned states to those in the badly malapportioned states. These studies examined the amounts of money spent by the states for welfare and education, the extent of state participation in education, health, and welfare, and the states' revenue structures. These studies found little reason to expect reapportionment to change state policies much.[123] But a major flaw in the early studies was that important aspects of state regulatory policies—such as vigor of affirmative action for racial minorities, or the extent to which consumer advocates were involved in state utility regulation—were not susceptible to the type of analysis used. Reapportionment has had a substantial impact on such state policies.[124]

In the years since the states were required to apportion both legislative chambers on the basis of population, substantial evidence indicates that fair apportionment has made a difference in public policy. The newly reapportioned Oklahoma legislature, for example, promptly gave the state's municipalities greater freedom of action in various policy areas and the power to levy a one-cent sales tax.[125] The reapportioned New Mexico legislature made substantial changes in the state's formula for distributing state educational funds, primarily benefiting previously underrepresented areas of the state.[126] In Georgia, reapportionment increased the number of urban representatives almost tenfold, the number of urban senators by a factor of twenty, and the number of black legislators substantially. As a result of the dramatically changed balance of power in the Georgia legislature, urban-versus-rural votes became common, and urban interests won much more frequently than before.[127] Similar changes occurred in many other states.[128] The suburbs, it must be noted, gained more in some states than the central cities, which were losing population by the time judicial relief came.

Malcolm E. Jewell predicted (in 1962) that reapportionment of state legislatures would make them more responsive to urban needs in terms of labor and welfare legislation, mass transit, and aid to local schools.[129] Analysis of state expenditures in two of these fields—aid to local education and public welfare—for the years 1953 through 1973 has found Jewell's prediction correct. Statistically significant relationships were found between reapportionment and state expenditures for local education in half of the states and between reapportionment and state expenditures for welfare in forty-two of them.[130]

Practicing politicians have also noticed the impact of reapportionment on policy. Of 145 state senators who had been in office in 1967 and in 1979, a majority thought state policies had become "more liberal" since reapportionment. Few thought policies were "more conservative." Most also felt that urban areas had received more state aid after reapportionment.[131]

SUMMARY

Most American legislators are nominated at primary elections, a process over which party leaders have only limited influence. Incumbents and candidates with ample campaign funds have an advantage over challengers and candidates strapped for cash. Incumbent U.S. senators more often than not win reelection, but their reelection rate is much lower than that of U.S. representatives, for whom incumbency almost always insures reelection. The rise of the importance of incumbency in reelection to Congress has been accompanied by a decline in the importance of party, especially in elections involving House incumbents, but the state of the economy and the popularity of the President also apparently affect Congressional elections as does the issue positions of the member. Still, incumbency and political party usually have a greater impact than the other factors.

The cost of legislative elections has escalated steeply in the past decade, in part because of the high cost of electronic broadcasting, and the million-dollar Congressional campaign has arrived. Wealthy candidates have a special advantage. Campaign finance has become more important, and that importance has been recognized by state and national laws which regulate the size of campaign contributions and require legislative candidates to disclose some or all of their contributor and expenditure records. Campaign contributions go disproportionately to incumbents, especially legislative leaders. Challengers usually have less money to spend, and they usually lose.

The nomination and election of American state and national legislators is a complex process, and the outcome is greatly affected by the rules. The predominant use of single-member legislative districts and election by plurality gives great advantage to the Democratic and Republican nominees and tends to give advantage also to middle-of-the-road candidates over liberal or conservative ideological extremists.

As a result of federal-court decisions, control of legislative bodies is no longer disproportionately in the hands of the nation's rural residents, but the gerrymander is still cleverly used to give advantage to one party or the other. Malapportionment was accepted by the U.S. Supreme Court in the 1960s as a proper subject for judicial consideration, and the federal courts have held that both chambers of state legislative bodies must be apportioned fairly on the basis of one person, one vote. The courts have also required each state to apportion its Congressional districts fairly. These apportionment rulings have had substantial impact on the policy decisions of state legislatures—for example, the distribution of state monies to localities no longer discriminates against urban areas.

Notes

1. William J. Crotty and Gary C. Jacobson, *American Parties in Decline* (Boston: Little, Brown, 1980), pp. 1–25.

2. For a general discussion of ballot forms, voter-registration laws, and other state laws governing elections (and sometimes affecting the outcome of elections) see Frank J. Sorauf, *Party Politics in America* (Boston: Little, Brown, 1980), Chapters 9 and 10.

3. Some states originally had a more restricted suffrage for the state senate than for the state lower chamber. The differences were primarily based on wealth. No such distinctions exist in the U.S. today.

4. Terence H. Qualter, "The Regulation of the National Franchise: A Problem in Federal Politics," *Journal of Commonwealth and Comparative Politics* 13 (March 1975); Joan Rydon, "The Electoral System," in *Australian Politics: A Second Reader,* ed. H. Mayer (Melbourne: Cheshire, 1969).

5. J. W. Peltason, Corwin & Peltason's *Understanding the Constitution,* 8th ed. (New York: Holt, Rinehart, and Winston, 1979), pp. 40–50.

6. Sorauf, *Party Politics in America,* pp. 203–10.

117

7. Edward Keynes, Richard J. Tobin, and Robert Danziger, "Institutional Effects on Elite Recruitment: The Case of State Nominating Systems," *American Politics Quarterly* 7 (July 1979): 285.

8. V. O. Key, Jr., *Southern Politics* (New York: Random House, Vintage Books, 1949); pp. 416–23.

9. Harvey L. Schantz, "Contested and Uncontested Primaries for the U.S. House," *Legislative Studies Quarterly* 5 (November 1980): 548. Looking at 1976 House primaries outside the South, Sorauf found that only 41 percent were contested and barely 20 percent were contested vigorously enough that the winner got less than two thirds of the votes cast. Sorauf, *Party Politics in America,* p. 222.

10. Richard Born, "Changes in the Competitiveness of House Primary Elections, 1956–1976," *American Politics Quarterly* 8 (October 1980): 495–506.

11. Charles O. Jones reports that only 1.6 percent of incumbent U.S. representatives seeking reelection were defeated in primary elections from 1956 through 1974. "Will Reform Change Congress?" in *Congress Reconsidered,* ed. Lawrence C. Dodd and Bruce I. Oppenheimer (New York: Praeger, 1977), p. 254. Counting both primary-election and general-election losses, only 7 percent of all attempts to win reelection to the House resulted in failure from 1954 through 1972. Robert S. Erikson, "Is There Such a Thing as a Safe Seat?" *Polity* 8 (Summer 1976): 623.

12. Schantz, "Contested and Uncontested Primaries for the U.S. House," pp. 553–54.

13. Andrew D. McNitt and Jim Seroka, "Intraparty Challenges of Incumbent Governors and Senators: 1956–1976," *American Politics Quarterly* 9 (July 1981): 321–40.

14. Richard Rose, ed., *Electoral Behavior: A Comparative Handbook* (New York: Free Press, 1974); Austin Ranney, *Pathways to Parliament: Candidate Selection in Britain* (Madison: University of Wisconsin Press 1965). Presidents occasionally intervene, especially in Senate contests, as President Nixon did when he urged Republican Congressman George Bush of Texas to seek the seat of Democratic Senator Ralph Yarborough or as Nixon did in his "purge" of Republican Senator Goodell of New York in favor of Conservative party candidate Buckley, who became a member of the Republican party in the Senate.

15. Ranney suggests it is not so much the national party's right to veto an MP's renomination that leads to loyal party behavior in Commons but the inclination of loyal constituency leaders to refuse renomination to MPs who stray too far from party orthodoxy. Local party leaders in the U.S., in contrast, are likely to side with the errant congressman against the national party leaders. See *Pathways to Parliament.*

16. See, for example, Sandy Maisel, "Congressional Elections in 1978," *American Politics Quarterly* 9 (January 1981): 23–47; David M. Olson, "Congressmen and Their Diverse Congressional District Parties," *Legislative Studies Quarterly* 3 (May 1978): 239–64; and Gerald C. Wright, Jr., "Candidates' Policy Positions and Voting in U.S. Congressional Elections," *Legislative Studies Quarterly* 3 (August 1978): 445–64.

17. *Newsweek,* June 16, 1980, p. 27.

18. John P. Mackintosh, "Reform of the House of Commons: The Case for Specialization," in *Modern Parliaments: Change or Decline?* ed. Gerhard Loewenberg (Chicago: Aldine-Atherton, 1971), p. 39; David R. Mayhew, *Congress: The Electoral Connection* (New Haven: Yale University Press, 1974), pp. 20–23.

19. Calculated from *Congressional Quarterly Weekly Report,* July 7, 1979, p. 1351 and November 8, 1980, pp. 3338–45; and Joseph Cooper and William West, "The Congressional Career in the 1970's," in Dodd and Oppenheimer, *Congress Reconsidered,* p. 99. Appointed senators are excluded.

20. *Congressional Quarterly Weekly Report,* July 7, 1979, p. 1351 and November 8, 1980, pp. 3338–45.

21. Morris P. Fiorina, "The Case of the Vanishing Marginals: The Bureaucracy Did It," *American Political Science Review* 71 (March 1977): p. 177.

22. Erikson, "Is There Such a Thing as a Safe Seat?" pp. 627–28.

23. David R. Mayhew, "Congressional Elections: The Case of the Vanishing Marginals," *Polity* 6 (Spring 1974): 304.

24. *Ibid.,* p. 303.

25. Albert D. Cover, "One Good Term Deserves Another: The Advantage of Incumbency in Congressional Elections," *American Journal of Political Science* 21 (August 1977): 523–42.

26. A majority of the American people regularly rate Congress negatively in various polls conducted by the Harris and Gallup organizations.

27. John A. Ferejohn, "On the Decline of Competition in Congressional Elections," *American Political Science Review* 71 (March 1977): 166–75; Robert S. Erikson, "Malapportionment, Gerrymandering, and Party Fortunes in Congressional Elections," *American Political Science Review* 66 (December 1972): 1240. Yet party identification still counts for a great deal. See Barbara Hinckley, "Issues, Information Costs, and Congressional Elections," *American Politics Quarterly* 4 (April 1976): 149.

28. Fiorina, "The Case of the Vanishing Marginals," pp. 177–81; and Morris P. Fiorina, *Congress: Keystone of the Washington Establishment* (New Haven: Yale University Press, 1977).

29. Richard Born, "Generational Replacement and the Growth of Incumbent Reelection Margins in the U.S. House," *American Political Science Review* 73 (September 1979): 811–17. See also Stephen P. Brown and John F. Hoadley, "Congressional Perquisites and the Vanishing Marginals: The Case of the Class of '74" (Paper delivered at the 1979 Annual Meeting of the American Political Science Association, Washington, D.C.); and Diana E. Yiannakis, "The Grateful Electorate: Casework and Congressional Voting" (Paper delivered at the 1980 Annual Meeting of the Midwest Political Science Association, Chicago, Ill.).

30. Albert D. Cover, "The Advantage of Incumbency in Congressional Elections," (Ph.D. diss., Yale University, 1976) as cited in Albert D. Cover and David R. Mayhew, "Congressional Dynamics and the Decline of Competitive Congressional Elections," in Dodd and Oppenheimer, *Congress Reconsidered,* pp. 59–60.

31. Edward R. Tufte, "The Relationship Between Seats and Votes in Two-Party Systems," *American Political Science Review* 67 (June 1973): 540–54. Mayhew reinforces the point. See *Congress: The Electoral Connection.* As the percentage of marginal (vulnerable) representatives declines, the probability of displacing enough incumbent majority-party members to take control of the House in one election becomes low. Regaining control of the House thus appears to be a long-term project for the "out" party.

32. Donald E. Stokes and Warren E. Miller, "Party Government and the Salience of Congress," in Angus Campbell, et al., eds., *Elections and the Political Order,* (New York: Wiley, 1966), pp. 194–211. Respondents were asked, "Do you happen to know the name of the congressman from your district?"

33. Thomas E. Mann, "Unsafe at Any Margin: Interpreting Congressional Elections," (Washington, D.C.: American Enterprise Institute for Public Policy Research, 1978); Kent L. Tedin and Richard W. Murray, "Public Awareness of Congressional Representatives: Recall v. Recognition," *American Politics Quarterly* 7 (October 1979): 509–17; and Gary C. Jacobson, "Incumbents' Advantages in the 1978 Congressional Elections," *Legislative Studies Quarterly* 6 (May 1981): 183–200.

34. See, for example, Alan I. Abramowitz, "A Comparison of Voting for U.S. Senator and Representative in 1978"; Barbara Hinckley, "The American Voter in Congressional Elections"; and Thomas E. Mann and Raymond E. Wolfinger, "Candidates and Parties in Congressional Elections," all in *American Political Science Review* 74 (September 1980): 617–50.

35. Barbara Hinckley, "House Re-elections and Senate Defeats: The Role of the Challenger," *British Journal of Political Science* 10 (October 1980): 441–60; and Lyn Ragsdale, "Incumbent Popularity, Challenger Invisibility, and Congressional Voters," *Legislative Studies Quarterly* 6 (May 1981): 201–18.

36. Cover, "One Good Term Deserves Another: The Advantage of Incumbency in Congressional Elections," p. 535. Warren Lee Kostroski found, in elections from 1948 through 1970, that the importance of idiosyncratic factors in U.S. Senate elections had increased, along with the importance of incumbency, while the importance of party had declined. See "Party and Incumbency in Postwar Senate Elections: Trends, Patterns, and Models," *American Political Science Review* 67 (December 1973): 1213–34.

37. Angus Campbell, "Surge and Decline: A Study of Electoral Change," in Angus Campbell, et al., *Elections and the Political Order,* p. 41.

38. George C. Edwards III, "The Impact of Presidential Coattails on Outcomes of Congressional Elections," *American Politics Quarterly* 7 (January 1979): 94–108; Herbert M. Kritzer and

Robert B. Eubank, "Presidential Coattails Revisited: Partisanship and Incumbency Effects," *American Journal of Political Science* 24 (August 1979): 615–26.

39. Samuel Kernell, "Presidential Popularity and Negative Voting: An Alternative Explanation of the Midterm Congressional Decline of the President's Party," *American Political Science Review* 71 (March 1977): 44–66.

40. Ibid., p. 50. Stephen D. Shaffer reports that a midterm presidential campaign appearance in a Congressional district tends to cause voters in that district to rely even more on presidential performance. "The Effects of Presidential Campaigning in Midterm Elections" (Paper delivered at the 1980 Annual Meeting of the Midwest Political Science Association, Chicago, Ill.).

41. Gary C. Jacobson, "Presidential Coattails in 1972," *Public Opinion Quarterly* 40 (1976): 194–200.

42. Gerald H. Kramer, "Short-Term Fluctuations in U.S. Voting Behavior, 1896–1964," *American Political Science Review* 65 (March 1971): 131–43.

43. Edward R. Tufte, "Determinants of the Outcomes of Midterm Congressional Elections," *American Political Science Review* 69 (September 1975): 812–26. See also *Political Control of the Economy* (Princeton: Princeton University Press, 1978).

44. Henry C. Kenski, "The Impact of Unemployment on Congressional Elections, 1958–1974," *American Politics Quarterly* 7 (April 1979): 147–54.

45. M. Margaret Conway and Mikel L. Wyckoff, "Voter Choice in the 1974 Congressional Elections," *American Politics Quarterly* 8 (January 1980): 3–14. A study based on disaggregated data similarly found "no linear relationship between changes in the vote for individual Congressional candidates and changes in real income and inflation in the 1972, 1974, and 1976 . . . election." See John R. Owens and Edward C. Olson, "Economic Fluctuations and Congressional Elections," *American Journal of Political Science* 24 (August 1980): 469–93.

46. Donald R. Kinder and D. Roderick Kiewiet, "Economic Discontent and Political Behavior: The Role of Personal Grievances and Collective Economic Judgements in Congressional Voting," *American Journal of Political Science* 23 (August 1979): 521.

47. Ibid., p. 523.

48. Gary C. Jacobson, "The Dynamics of Congressional Elections: Notes Toward a Theory" (Paper delivered at the 1980 Annual Meeting of the Western Political Science Association, San Francisco, Calif.).

49. Donald E. Stokes and Warren E. Miller, "Party Government and the Salience of Congress"; Charles O. Jones, "The Role of the Campaign in Congressional Politics," in *The Electoral Process,* ed. M. K. Jennings and L. H. Zeigler (Englewood Cliffs, N.J.: Prentice-Hall, 1977), pp. 21–41.

50. Robert S. Erikson, "Constituency Opinion and Congressional Behavior: A Re-examination of The Miller-Stokes Representation Data" (Paper delivered at the 1978 Annual Meeting of the Midwest Political Science Association, Chicago, Ill.). For a thoughtful analysis of the extent to which citizens can hope to influence policy by voting in Congressional elections, see Lewis A. Dexter, *The Sociology and Politics of Congress* (Chicago: Rand McNally, 1969), pp. 15–76.

51. Stokes and Miller, "Party Government and the Salience of Congress."

52. Schoenberger found, for instance, that Republican representatives (mostly conservatives) who endorsed Barry Goldwater's candidacy in 1964 lost more frequently than their colleagues, whose campaigns were more distant from Senator Goldwater's. Robert A. Schoenberger, "Campaign Strategy and Party Loyalty: The Electoral Relevance of Candidate Decision-Making in the 1964 Congressional Elections," *American Political Science Review* 63 (June 1969): 515–20. Erikson found that, over a period of several elections, extremely conservative Republicans and, to a lesser extent, extremely liberal Democrats did less well at the polls than their more moderate party colleagues. Robert S. Erikson, "The Electoral Impact of Congressional Roll Call Voting," *American Political Science Review* 65 (December 1971): 1018–32.

53. Mayhew, *Congress: The Electoral Connection,* p. 67.

54. Richard F. Fenno, Jr., *Home Style: House Members in Their Districts* (Boston: Little, Brown, 1978), pp. 80–99.

55. Hinckley, "Issues, Information Costs, and Congressional Elections," pp. 131–52.

56. Lynda W. Powell, "A Study of Financial Contributors in Congressional Elections" (Paper delivered at the 1979 Annual Meeting of the American Political Science Association, Washington, D.C.).

57. Wright, "Candidates' Policy Positions and Voting in U.S. Congressional Elections," p. 459.

58. Campaign-finance information in this section, unless otherwise noted, is from Herbert E. Alexander, *Financing Politics,* 2nd ed. (Washington, D.C.: Congressional Quarterly Press, 1980).

59. Gary C. Jacobson, "The Effects of Campaign Spending in Congressional Elections," *American Political Science Review* 72 (June 1978): 469–91; Gary W. Copeland and Samuel C. Patterson, "Money in Congressional Elections," in *Legislative Reform,* ed. Leroy N. Rieselbach (Lexington, Mass.: D.C. Heath, 1978), pp. 203–6.

60. See Alexander, *Financing Politics,* for a detailed discussion of the history of federal campaign-finance legislation. The details which follow are from Chapter 2.

61. Crotty and Jacobson, *American Parties in Decline,* pp. 108–9.

62. "Pick of the PACs," *Washington Monthly,* June 1981, p. 39.

63. Crotty and Jacobson, *American Parties in Decline,* pp. 105–8.

64. *Congressional Quarterly Weekly Report,* August 25, 1979, p. 1751; and John F. Bibby, "Political Parties and Federalism: The Republican National Committee Involvement in Gubernatorial and Legislative Elections," *Publius* 9 (Winter 1979): 229–36.

65. V. O. Key, Jr., *American State Politics: An Introduction* (New York: Alfred A. Knopf, 1956), pp. 171–73; Malcolm E. Jewell, *Legislative Representation in the Contemporary South* (Durham, N.C.: Duke University Press, 1967), p. 21.

66. Lester G. Seligman, Michael R. King, Chong Lim Kim, and Roland E. Smith, *Patterns of Recruitment: A State Chooses Its Lawmakers* (Chicago: Rand McNally, 1974), pp. 166–70.

67. Edwin L. Cobb, "Representation and the Rotation Agreement: The Case of Tennessee," *Western Political Quarterly* 23 (1970).

68. Craig H. Grau, "Competition in State Legislative Primaries," *Legislative Studies Quarterly* 6 (February 1981): 33–54.

69. Similar findings are reported in a study of legislative elections in 29 states. See Jerry Calvert, "Revolving Doors: Volunteerism in State Legislatures," *State Government* 52 (Autumn 1979): 174–81.

70. Grau, "Competition in State Legislative Primaries." Charles W. Wiggins and Janice Petty found that close to 40 percent of Illinois' primary elections for the state legislature were contested and that districts without an incumbent running had the greater level of intraparty competition. "Cumulative Voting and Electoral Competition," *American Politics Quarterly* 7 (July 1979): 353.

71. Richard J. Tobin and Edward Keynes, "Institutional Differences in the Recruitment Process: A Four State Study," *American Journal of Political Science* 19 (November 1975): 670.

72. Jewell, *Legislative Representation in the Contemporary South,* pp. 30–31.

73. Malcolm E. Jewell and David M. Olson, *American State Political Parties and Elections* (Homewood, Ill.: Dorsey Press, 1980), pp. 90–94.

74. Sorauf, *Party Politics in America,* pp. 228–31.

75. Jewell and Olson, *American State Political Parties and Elections,* pp. 253–62.

76. Craig H. Grau, "The Neglected World of State Legislative Elections" (Paper delivered at the 1981 Annual Meeting of the Midwest Political Science Association, Cincinnati, Ohio).

77. James E. Piereson, "Presidential Popularity and Midterm Voting at Different Electoral Levels," *American Journal of Political Science* 19 (November 1975): 683–702.

78. "Survey on State Campaign Financing," *Comparative State Politics Newsletter* 1, (January 1980).

79. "Financing California Legislative Elections," *Comparative State Politics Newsletter* 2 (May 1981), p. 4.

80. Senator Lloyd Doggett, quoted in *The Texas Observer,* March 13, 1981, p. 11.

81. "Survey on State Campaign Financing."

82. John C. Greenwood, *Legislative Candidates and Campaign Spending in California* (Institute of Governmental Affairs, University of California, Davis, 1974), pp. 55–57.

83. "Survey on State Campaign Financing," pp. 19–20.

84. Alexander, *Financing Politics,* pp. 127–28. The discussion of state campaign-finance laws is from Alexander, Chapter 7, unless a different source is cited.

85. James O'Shea, "Corporate PACs on Increase," *Dallas Times Herald,* November 5, 1980, p. 4G.

86. Alexander, *Financing Politics,* pp. 137–42.

87. W. P. Welch, "The Effectiveness of Expenditures in State Legislative Races," *American Politics Quarterly* 4 (July 1976): 333–55.

88. Douglas W. Rae, *The Political Consequences of Electoral Laws,* rev. ed. (New Haven: Yale University Press, 1971), pp. 70–76.

89. Ibid., p. 86.

90. Ibid., Chapter 5, especially p. 103; see also Tufte, "The Relationship Between Seats and Votes in Two-Party Systems," pp. 540–54. As Tufte points out, even worse distortion occurs when legislators represent significantly different numbers of people and one party dominates most of the small districts while the other party dominates most of the large districts. In many states, prior to the court-ordered reapportionments of the 1960s, it was not uncommon for well over 50 percent of the statewide vote for the state legislature to be Democratic, while well over half of the legislative seats were won by Republicans. The more fair apportionments today make such a gross inversion of the popular will less likely, but, under some circumstances, a clever gerrymander can achieve the same results.

91. Rae, *The Political Consequences of Electoral Laws,* pp. 88–96.

92. Anthony Downs, *An Economic Theory of Democracy* (New York: Harper and Row, 1957), Chapter 8.

93. *American State Legislatures: Their Structures and Procedures* (Lexington, Ky.: Council of State Governments, 1977), p. 4. These multimember state senate districts account for less than a fifth of the nation's state senators.

94. Keith E. Hamm, Robert Harmel, and Robert J. Thompson, "The Impact of Districting on County Delegation Cohesion in Southern State Legislatures: A Comparative Analysis of Texas and South Carolina" (Paper presented at the 1979 Annual Meeting of the Southern Political Science Association, Gatlinburg, Tennessee); Alan Clem and W. O. Farber, "Manipulated Democracy: The Multi-member District," *National Civic Review* 68 (May 1979): 235–43; Stanley Halpin, Jr., and Richard L. Engstrom, "Racial Gerrymandering and Southern State Legislative Redistricting: Attorney General Determinations Under the Voting Rights Act," *Journal of Public Law* 22 (1973): 37; Howard D. Hamilton, "Legislative Constituencies: Single-Member Districts, Multi-Member Districts, and Floterial Districts," *Western Political Quarterly* 20 (June 1967): 321–40; and Timothy G. O'Rourke, "A Comparative Analysis of the Impact of Reapportionment on Six State Legislatures" (Ph.D. diss., Duke University, 1977).

95. *American State Legislatures: Their Structures and Procedures,* p. 5. Some 40 percent or so of the nation's state representatives are from multimember districts.

96. James Kuklinski, "Cumulative and Plurality Voting: An Analysis of Illinois' Unique Electoral System," *Western Political Quarterly* 26 (December 1973): 726–46; Wiggins and Petty, "Cumulative Voting and Electoral Competition: The Illinois House," pp. 345–65; and David H. Everson and Joan A. Parker, "Politics as Usual in Illinois," *Comparative State Politics Newsletter* 2 (March 1981): 9.

97. The gerrymander is named after Elbridge Gerry, an early governor of Massachusetts and early practitioner of drawing legislative districts to his party's advantage. A Congressional district devised in 1812 by Gerry resembled a salamander and was labeled a "gerrymander" in a political cartoon. The name stuck. Additional information on the art of gerrymandering is available in Gordon E. Baker, "Gerrymandering: Privileged Sanctuary or Next Judicial Target?" and Charles Press, "Commentary," both in *Reapportionment in the 1970s,* ed. Nelson W. Polsby (Berkeley, Calif.: University of California Press, 1971), pp. 121–50; and Ernest C. Reock, Jr., "Measuring Compactness as a Requirement of Legislative Apportionment," *Midwest Journal of Political Science* 5 (1961): 70.

98. An ambitious state legislator also has the opportunity to tailor a Congressional district so he or she can win election to Congress. Some legislators' ambitions for promotion and the desire of

others for electoral security as state legislators hamper the party leaders' efforts to maximize the political advantage for the majority party. But some partisan advantage invariably occurs and accrues to the advantage of the party in control of reapportionment decisions.

99. Bibby, "Political Parties and Federalism: The Republican National Committee Involvement in Gubernatorial and Legislative Elections."

100. Barry Miller, "Proof of Racially Discriminatory Purpose Under the Equal Protection Clause: *Washington* v. *Davis, Arlington Heights, Mt. Healthy, and Williamsburgh,*" *Harvard Civil Rights-Civil Liberties Law Review* 12 (Summer 1977): 725–70.

101. Robert G. Dixon, Jr., "The Court, The People, and 'One Man, One Vote,'" in Polsby, *Reapportionment in the 1970s,* pp. 13–14. See also Robert S. Erikson, "The Partisan Impact of State Legislative Reapportionment," *Midwest Journal of Political Science* 15 (February 1971): 55–71.

102. "The Spoils of the Census," *Newsweek,* May 18, 1981, p. 44.

103. *Wesberry* v. *Sanders,* 376 U.S. 1 (1964).

104. *Colgrove* v. *Green,* 328 U.S. 549 (1946); C. Herman Pritchett, *The Federal System in Constitutional Law* (Englewood Cliffs, N.J.: Prentice-Hall, 1978), pp. 182–84.

105. Milton C. Cummings, Jr., "Reapportionment in the 1970s: Its Effects on Congress"; David R. Mayhew, "Congressional Representation: Theory and Practice in Drawing the Districts"; and Charles O. Jones and Allan P. Sindler, "Commentaries," in Polsby, *Reapportionment in the 1970s,* pp. 209–90.

106. *Kirkpatrick* v. *Preisler,* 394 U.S. 526 (1969).

107. *American State Legislatures: Their Structures and Procedures,* pp. 4 and 5. Some of the states which give the legislature the power to draw legislative district boundaries also provide for another state agency to do so in the event the legislature fails to reapportion itself.

108. *Gomillion* v. *Lightfoot,* 364 U.S. 103 (1969).

109. *Baker* v. *Carr,* 369 U.S. 186 (1962).

110. Alexander M. Bickel, "The Supreme Court and Reapportionment," in Polsby, *Reapportionment in the 1970s,* pp. 61–62. Section 1 of the Fourteenth Amendment to the Constitution of the United States reads:

> All persons born or naturalized in the United States, and subject to the jurisdiction thereof, are citizens of the United States and of the State wherein they reside. No State shall make or enforce any law which shall abridge the privileges or immunities of citizens of the United States; nor shall any state deprive any person of life, liberty, or property, without due process of law; nor deny to any person within its jurisdiction the equal protection of the laws.

111. Robert G. Dixon, Jr., *Democratic Representation: Reapportionment in Law and Politics* (New York: Oxford University Press, 1968), p. 139.

112. Ibid., pg. 140.

113. *Reynolds* v. *Sims,* 377 U.S. 533 (1964).

114. John F. Gallagher and Louis F. Weschler, "California," in *Impact of Reapportionment on the Thirteen Western States,* ed. Eleanore Bushnell (Salt Lake City: University of Utah Press, 1970), p. 80.

115. Bernard C. Borning, "Idaho," in Bushnell, *Impact of Reapportionment on the Thirteen Western States,* p. 150. J. T. White and N. C. Thomas note that in 1960 malapportionment gave the rural minority of the population control of both chambers of the state legislature in thirteen states and control of one chamber in six more states. And, in eleven states, where most of the people lived in rural areas, malapportionment was used to even further increase rural area majorities in both chambers. "Urban and Rural Representation and State Legislative Apportionments," *Western Political Quarterly* 17 (1964).

116. Eleanore Bushnell, "Nevada," in Bushnell, *Impact of Reapportionment on the Thirteen Western States.*

117. *Reynolds* v. *Sims,* 377 U.S. 533 (1964).

118. *Mahan* v. *Howell,* 410 U.S. 315 (1973). Later in 1973 the Court also found acceptable a Connecticut apportionment which included a maximum variation of 7.9 percent [*Gaffney* v. *Cummings,* 412 U.S. 735 (1937)] and a Texas apportionment with a maximum variation among state legislative districts of 9.9 percent [*White* v. *Regester,* 412 U.S. 755 (1973)].

123

119. For some of the flavor of redistricting dilemmas, see Mark Gruenberg, "Musical Chairs in Congressional Redistricting: Chicago May Lose One Seat," *Illinois Issues* 5 (February 1979); and Bruce W. Robeck, *Legislators and Party Loyalty: The Impact of Reapportionment in California* (Washington, D.C.: University Press of America, 1978).

120. This is not to say that agricultural interests no longer receive consideration in the state legislatures. Charles R. Adrian notes, "In Michigan, the lobbyist for the American Farm Bureau Federation, after the first session in which the legislature was apportioned in both houses on the basis of population, concluded that farmers had fared well and had gained from several pieces of legislation adopted by the legislature which had been urged for several years by the Farm Bureau. . . . (However) the legislature that year was under Democratic control for the first time in a generation. It is also possible that the . . . legislature . . . made a special effort to allay rural fears." *State and Local Governments* (New York: McGraw-Hill, 1976), p. 319.

121. Ibid., p. 323; Samuel C. Patterson, "American State Legislatures and Public Policy," in *Politics in the American States,* 3rd ed., ed. Herbert Jacob and Kenneth N. Vines, (Boston: Little, Brown, 1976), p. 155.

122. Erikson, "The Partisan Impact of State Legislative Reapportionment," pp. 57–71; Richard Lehne, *Reapportionment of the New York Legislature: Impact and Issues* (New York: National Municipal League, 1972); Bruce W. Robeck, "Legislative Partisanship, Constituency and Malapportionment: The Case of California," *American Political Science Review* 66 (December 1972): pp. 1246–55; and Allan G. Pulsipher and James L. Weatherby, Jr., "Malapportionment, Party Competition and the Functional Distribution of Governmental Expenditures," *American Political Science Review* 62 (December 1968): 1207–19.

123. A summary and critique of this literature is found in William E. Bicker, "The Effects of Malapportionment in the States: A Mistrial," in Polsby, *Reapportionment in the 1970s,* pp. 150–201. See also Herbert Jacob and Michael Lipsky, "Outputs, Structure, and Power: An Assessment of Changes in the Study of State and Local Politics," *Journal of Politics* 30 (May 1968): 510–38. Among the more important such articles are Thomas R. Dye, "Malapportionment and Public Policy in the States," *The Journal of Politics* 27 (August 1965): 586–601; Herbert Jacob, "The Consequences of Malapportionment: A Note of Caution," *Social Forces* 43 (December 1964): 256–61; and Richard Hofferbert, "The Relation Between Public Policy and Some Structural and Environmental Variables in the American States," *American Political Science Review* 60 (1966): 73–82.

124. William R. Cantrall and Stuart S. Nagel, "The Effects of Reapportionment on the Passage of Nonexpenditure Legislation," in *Democratic Representation and Apportionment,* ed. L. Papayanopoulas (New York: New York Academy of Sciences, 1973), pp. 269–79.

125. Samuel A. Kirkpatrick, *The Legislative Process in Oklahoma* (Norman, Okla.: University of Oklahoma Press, 1978), pp. 36–40.

126. Stanley Pogrow and F. Chris Garcia, "The Governance of Public Education," in *New Mexico Government,* ed. F. Chris Garcia and Paul L. Hain (Albuquerque: University of New Mexico Press, 1976).

127. Ira Sharkansky, "Reapportionment and Roll Call Voting: The Case of the Georgia Legislature," *Social Science Quarterly* 51 (June 1970): pp. 129–37.

128. George Frederickson and Yong Hyo Cho, "Legislative Apportionment and Fiscal Policy in the American States," *Western Political Quarterly* 27 (March 1974): 5–37; Roger A. Hanson and Robert E. Crew, "The Policy Impact of Reapportionment," *Law and Society Review* 8 (1973); and Patterson, "American State Legislatures and Public Policy," pp. 139–95.

129. Malcolm E. Jewell, "Political Pattern in Apportionment," in *Politics of Reapportionment,* ed. Malcolm E. Jewell (New York: Atherton, 1962), pp. 1–48.

130. Douglas G. Feig, "Expenditures in the American States: The Impact of Court-Ordered Legislative Reapportionment," *American Politics Quarterly* 6 (July 1978): 309–24.

131. David C. Saffell, "Reapportionment and Public Policy: State Legislators' Perspectives" (Paper delivered at the 1980 Annual Meeting of the Midwest Political Science Association, Chicago, Ill.). At least one senator from each of forty-nine states responded. In only nine states did any respondent perceive policies to have become more conservative. A more extensive study of six states also found legislators of the opinion that more liberal legislation was passed after reapportionment. Timothy O'Rourke, *The Impact of Reapportionment* (New Brunswick, N.J.: Transaction Books, 1980), p. 151.

chapter *6*

Legislators and Their Constituencies

Preview

The relationship between legislators and their constituents is at the heart of representative government. American legislators devote substantial amounts of their time and energies to remaining on good terms with their constituents. Frequent, well-publicized visits to the district, extensive correspondence, and assistance to constituents in their dealings with the bureaucracy all help legislators remain well liked back home even by those critical of the legislature as a body. Legislators' behavior toward different segments of their constituencies and the degree of influence various constituents have on their legislators are affected by the legislators' perceptions of their constituencies. But overall, American legislators seem to represent dominant constituent opinion fairly well.

As noted in Chapter 5, incumbent legislators—especially U.S. representatives—have the advantage over their challengers in seeking reelection. But, even among U.S. representatives, in the long run a third or so are defeated.[1] The knowledge that circumstances—including issues of conscience, the state of the economy, a particularly unattractive candidate on the party's ticket for President or governor, and an especially strong challenger—may cause difficulties in any election makes legislators work at maintaining good relationships with their constituents (the residents of the legislative district).[2] Indeed, their success at promoting and maintaining good relationships with constituents accounts for much of the advantage of incumbency. Concern about future electoral difficulties permeates the relationship of many legislators to their constituents, and this seems to be especially important among the "professional" legislators whose elected position represents a full-time occupation.

A legislator's interactions with constituents, perceptions of the constituency, and image or reputation among the constituents is probably more important to continued officeholding in the United States than in nations with parliamentary systems, or where there are multimember legislative districts in which legislators are nominated on a party list. Either the parliamentary system or the list system changes the importance of the individual legislator's relationship with a district. In the parliamentary system, even with single-member districts, as in Great Britain, the individual voter can vote for his or her party to control the executive branch only by supporting that party's candidate for member of Parliament. Even party members who personally dislike the local MP are likely to support that MP for reelection, if the party members feel strongly enough about national issues or the party's candidate for prime minister. After all, only by having enough partisans in Parliament can a British party leader become prime minister. Conversely, even if one likes the local MP, one may feel constrained to vote against him or her to vote out a national government whose policies one dislikes, or to retaliate against a disliked minister of the government. Either way, the MP's intermediate position between the voter and the choice of a government makes the MP's personal relationship with the constituency less important than it otherwise would be—certainly less important than that of a member of Congress, whose constituents can vote for their preferred presidential candidate and make a separate decision about whom to support for Congress. Not surprisingly, this perspective is accepted by British national party officials but not by the MPs.[3]

The relationship between legislator and constituents may also be less important in electoral systems where numerous legislators are elected from the same district according to party lists. In such situations, a given politician may be able to parlay his or her personal popularity into influence within the party and a place high on the list, where election is almost guaranteed, but the decision normally is made by party officials. Thus, the individual legislator or legislative candidate may seek to develop a strong personal following within the constituency as one of several resources for bargaining with fellow party leaders, but must still deal primarily with party leaders for a preferred place on the list, and subsequent election.

American legislators are much more independent actors than their European counterparts. Elected from single-member legislative districts, for the most part, nominated in primary elections, and elected separately from executive officers, American legislators often are able to make themselves virtually invulnerable to attacks by other leaders of their political party. Such independent electoral strength, of course, is often translated into the ability to affect public policy (by surviving long enough to become a committee chairperson, in Congress, for instance). The relationship with his or her constituency, then, is the fundamental source of the American legislator's independent exercise of political power. And it is that independence which has very significant impact on the degree of party discipline in the legislature.

THE LEGISLATOR'S PERCEIVED CONSTITUENCY

A member of Congress, as Fenno notes, can be thought of as seeing his or her district as a set of concentric circles. The largest of these concentric circles, the entire district, is the *geographical constituency* (or, said differently, the "legal" constituency) which includes all residents of the geographically defined Congressional district—supporters and opponents alike.[4] This perspective is likely to include discussions of ethnicity; types of residences; the rich, poor, or middle-class nature of the district or its sections; and urban-rural-small-town typologies. Discussions of the district at this level also tend to elicit responses from representatives that their districts are either heterogeneous or relatively homogeneous. "The less conflict a congressman perceives among district interests the more likely he is to see his district as homogeneous."[5]

Perhaps more important in how a representative votes and what lengths he or she is willing to go in protecting the district's various interests is the representative's perceived *reelection constituency.*

> As they move about "the district," House members continually draw the distinction between those people who vote for them and those who do not: "I do well here;" "I run poorly here;" "This groups supports me;" . . .⁶

And each member has a fairly clear idea of where he or she can most likely recruit additional support in the general election and where such efforts are hopeless. Do representatives feel secure after winning by 60 percent or more of the vote? No, reports Fenno, because most have had a "testing election" which was won by only a few percentage points and most have a colleague whose apparently impregnable home position was shattered by a particularly able challenger last time out. Thus, most members continue to feel insecure even though they are almost certain of reelection.⁷

Even a member who consistently wins by large margins in the general election must fret about a primary-election loss. Enough members of Congress lose in the primary election that they are intensely aware of their most durable supporters, those Fenno calls the *primary constituency*—whose support the member believes will be there, regardless of who the primary-election opponent might be.⁸ These strong supporters tend to be politically active and are the source of many campaign workers and contributors. A strong primary constituency helps a member protect his or her seat against a primary-election challenge, and it is vital to a member's sense of electoral security.

The smallest circle of supporters is the *personal constituency*—the member's close and intimate friends. Frequently chatting with trusted friends such as these expands the member's net of information concerning how the district feels, what issues are important, and what hidden political developments may erupt, seemingly without warning.⁹ Since the intimates are a biased selection of the constituency, even with the member's interest at heart, they may distort his or her view of what is occurring in the constituency.

Members' perceptions of their constituencies, of course, affect the interests (both organized and unorganized) to which they respond in an official capacity. Members appear to be more responsive to those constituents whose support is more important to their electoral security and less responsive to constituents who are perceived as nonsupportive.¹⁰ Further, it appears that the question of how representatives perceive their various constituencies and whether their districts are seen as homogeneous or heterogeneous affects how members allocate their time among the constituencies' various components and how they present themselves to various types of constituents.¹¹

★ ★ ★ ★

A Legislator's Freedom Is Limited but Real

[Citizens] can make a considerable difference; but this does not mean—even if they are a powerful majority to which there is no strong, manifest opposition—that the Congress is sure to do what they want.

The reciprocal trade and tariff issue was in the 1950s, on the whole, a rather low-priority, low-key one. Sensible and experienced Congressmen realized that few votes were likely to be won or lost from it. They knew, too, that, although their stands and actions on it might affect campaign funds and organized support, they had many other ways of obtaining campaign funds and organized support. So, on the whole, they had on this issue a considerable amount of freedom, so far as constituency and public influences were concerned.

This matter of freedom is worth a moment's attention. Probably a Congressman or Senator who voted against all, or most, of the significant interests and concerns in his constituency would find it difficult to be reelected. If it became very clear that he was voting against all of them, reelection would probably be unlikely. But there are a great many interests and concerns in every constituency; a man would have to be really perverse to vote against all of them. And, indeed, he would have to be lazy or politically indifferent not to work for some of them . . . or at the very least go through the motions of working for them.

For instance: a Congressman may be close to and indebted to various trade-union groups. They may be in favor of protecting some industries against "unfair" foreign competition. But these same groups are in favor of minimum-wage laws; they want federal school funds for their children; they are concerned with some public-works matters in the area, highways or ferries or post offices, or something of the sort. They are interested in safety regulations for workers; their wives are concerned with consumer protection and clean food. And so, if the Congressman picks and chooses among these other issues, and gets some publicity on several of them, he is free enough on the specific matter of foreign imports—free enough in the sense that if, in general, he seems likable and trustworthy, he will not lose any significant number of votes by opposing his labor constituents on reciprocal trade. . . . A Congressman of the sort described above might at most have to declare his rhetorical opposition to unfair foreign competition and try to help specific industries to get anti-dumping or escape-clause protection; but on the major legislative issue, he could be as free as he chose to be. He might, on the other hand, decide to go along with his labor constituents on reciprocal trade, because he considered it more important to break with them on something else. So his freedom is real, but limited.

I do not mean to say that most Congressmen make *calculations* of this sort; but, unarticulated or unconscious, this is the kind of *response* they make to demands and claims upon them. The most frequent response, without any doubt, and the greatest claim for freedom, is of the Congressman or Senator who says: "I have done all these personal service and constituency service matters for you. I have done them competently and well. Now, let me be free on the big legislative issues."

Source: Lewis Anthony Dexter, *The Sociology and Politics of Congress* (Chicago: Rand McNally, 1969), pp. 77–79.

★ ★ ★ ★

KEEPING IN TOUCH

Going Home

One way U.S. representatives and U.S. senators keep in touch with their constituents is by returning home frequently. House and Senate rules encourage such contact by providing ample travel allowances and by scheduling "district work periods" when the member can be in the constituency without fear of being accused of ignoring legislative business.[12] The average U.S. representative, for example, returned to the district thirty-five times in 1973. Less senior members return to the district more frequently than more senior members (both because of differences in perceived electoral security and because of differences in Congressional responsibilities),[13] and members who live nearest Washington, D.C. "spend a good deal more time at home than do the members who live farthest from the Capitol."[14] Members whose families continue to reside in the Congressional district return home more frequently than those whose families move with them to the Washington, D.C. area. Trips home permit both one-on-one conversations with constituents and opportunities to address local breakfast, lunch, and dinner meetings.

★ ★ ★ ★

Keeping in Touch Can Be Difficult

When I returned to my district office there were long and loud complaints that I was spending too much time there and should be in Washington. Then when I didn't make it for several weeks others said, 'Who does that guy think he is? We only see him during elections.' When I came home shortly after being sworn in, driving my old car, they were upset because it looked like something farmers use to haul trash. But, by gosh, when I bought a new one they were sure the lobbyists had gotten to me already. The first time I came home wearing an old suit people said 'Look at him. Just an old bum.' Yet when I bought a new suit, I hear, 'He's gone high-hat with that Ivy League suit of his.' One Sunday I missed church because I was tied up talking with constituents and some people said that being down in Washington had made an atheist of me. Several weeks later, when I was again back home and did get to church, they said, 'Why that pious fraud! He's just trying to dig up votes!'

Source: Representative Silvio Conte of Massachusetts, quoted by Congressman Jim Wright, *You and Your Congressman* (New York: G.P. Putnam's Sons, 1976), p. 202.

★ ★ ★ ★

Communication with the district (or, for senators, state) is made easier for members of Congress by the availability of free long-distance telephone service. In addition, members of Congress do not pay postage; they use "franked" envelopes—with the member's signature in place of a postage stamp. The frank is used to send congratulations to new parents and new graduates and to send constituents a variety of free pamphlets and information made available from various government agencies.

129

The Mail Bag

An important part of keeping in touch with one's constituents is dealing with mail from them. Mail from home includes requests for information and pamphlets—easily dealt with—as well as more serious missives. The mail is so heavy for U.S. representatives—and even heavier for most senators—that the member, alone, could not begin to cope with it. Letters—requesting assistance in obtaining social security or veteran benefits, for example, or in overturning a bureaucracy's ruling—are turned over to "caseworkers," who are staff personnel with detailed knowledge of how particular agencies work. Unless something unusual occurs or the request is from an especially important constituent, the member normally remains uninvolved in the individual cases, but the bureaucracy responds to the inquiry from the member's office.[15] Many federal agencies have explicit rules requiring that each level of the organization respond to inquiries from Congressional offices within only a few working days. In other words, the Congressional inquiry receives priority.

Of course, the bureaucracy will not necessarily overturn its earlier decision, just because a member's staff has inquired about it. But the inquiry is likely to be considered on its merits by a higher official than the one who made the original decision, and, if the decision is one which permits some discretion, the Congressional assistance often pays off. Why the positive bureaucratic response to members of Congress? Congress controls "what bureaucrats value most—higher budgets and new program authorizations."[16] Agencies do not want to get a reputation in Congress as unresponsive, inefficient, or needlessly obstructive; they prefer a positive image. As a result, the federal agencies which are the object of the most casework correspondence with members of Congress have special liaison offices to handle just such matters. Why do the members take casework seriously? Because helping constituents resolve their difficulties with the federal government bureaucracy makes many more friends than enemies. Attention to casework can also help members "buy their freedom" from constituents on policy matters; by serving as ombudsmen, or red-tape cutters, they can often significantly reduce the intensity of opposition of their constituents who disagree with them on policy issues. Many of the casework requests for individual constituent assistance—such as those which the member's staff directs on to the Veterans Administration, the armed forces, and the Social Security Administration—would, if adopted as general policy, not be an agency policy the member would approve.[17]

Letters and postcards also come from constituents who are concerned about basic government policy, although, often, such letters arrive after it is too late for the member to have much impact on the shape of the legislation. The most effective legislative intervention is accomplished when the bill is at the committee stage of the legislative process, when lobbyists often know what is happening, but ordinary citizens do not. By the time the news media begin to give a bill sufficient coverage to call it to the attention of the ordinary citizen, the bill is often so far along that the member can only vote "yes" or "no."

Much policy correspondence, though, is "inspired" by interest groups.

> An experienced mail clerk can spot [inspired mail] quickly. These letters, while not without effect, are heavily discounted as manifestations of public opinion. In some offices, for example, this "pressure mail" is entirely excluded from the mail count. In others, it is counted separately.[18]

Even though most letters to Congress are written by middle-class constituents and are known by members not to be a representative cross-section of constituent opinion, members find the mail bag a convenient way to know what issues are bothering their constituents. Further, each letter received gives the member an opportunity to interact with another constituent and—even if the member must disagree with the constituent—to impress that voter with the member's quick response and courteous consideration of the voter's point of view. Some members find the policy of special courtesy, even to writers of nasty notes and letters, pays off in subsequent letters more subdued in tone and in either positive electoral support or less intense opposition.[19] Occasionally, however, a member will respond in a manner better calculated to improve his or her mental health than to woo votes:

> Once Senator Stephen M. Young (D., Ohio) received a letter asking sarcastically if the correspondent could emulate the wife of the late President Kennedy and have a horse imported to this country without cost. In reply, Young said that he wondered "why you need a horse when there is already one jackass at your address."[20]

Office Visitors

Office visitors provide another opportunity for members of Congress to woo the voters. Representatives and, especially, senators from states close to Washington are almost overrun with home-state constituents, in town to see the sights and, hoping for a moment of the member's time, just to say hello. Visitors from more distant locations, whose members have lighter traffic loads, are more likely to have a chance to chat. Important supporters and significant persons from any constituency usually receive the attention of the member. Others are seen by staff members, who

> urge constituents to sign the guest book (potential additions to the mailing list), furnish them with passes to House sessions, provide them with literature about . . . Washington and a copy of the congressman's current newsletter or questionnaire, and engage them in conversation about their home town. They may even offer to arrange special tours of the White House or the Federal Bureau of Investigation.[21]

Members differ in their desire to personally greet each constituent who visits the office, but all want those constituents to return home with positive memories.

Members have from one to three constituency offices each, depending on how spread out their constituencies are. The constituency office (located within the Congressional district or state) is an important source of contact with constituents.[22] Constituents with problems talk with constituency staff personnel when the member is not back home. When he or she is in the constituency, the member's time is normally scheduled fairly tightly to permit dealing with as many problems and seeing as many people as possible. Problems ordinarily are then turned over to staff members for follow through. Local news personnel also frequently contact the local office to obtain a member's reaction to events in the news.

Constituency offices tend to be equipped with high-speed electronic communication equipment. It is not uncommon for a member with whom a local chamber of commerce affiliate or labor union is on good terms to occasionally permit that organization to use the member's equipment to transmit data to the member's Capitol office, where the organization's Washington office can pick it up. Or the information flow may be in the other direction. When detailed data must be transmitted immediately, and there is no time for mail delivery, such an accommodation can be very important to the local organization and builds substantial goodwill.

Public-Opinion Surveys

Because members of Congress know that their mail gives them a distorted view of constituency opinion, many seek to ascertain public opinion in the constituency by use of survey-research techniques. The most direct such approach (for both incumbents and challengers) is to hire a survey-research firm (usually out of funds other than Congressional monies) to conduct a survey of the constituency. Thus, a member can determine what issues are on the constituents' minds and how they feel about the issues they volunteer are of concern, as well as other issues on which the member seeks to learn constituency opinion.[23]

Another approach used is that of sending a questionnaire to every address in the district (sometimes attached to a newsletter) and asking voters to respond to a set of questions. The self-selection of those who decide to respond biases the results, but a member does gain some feel for what folks back home are thinking. Equally important is the publicity which such a survey generates. Each person who receives the questionnaire is being told that his or her opinion is important to the member, even if that person does not return it. In addition, the member can issue a news release, citing a large number of responses and informing the local people what their overall opinion is on particular issues. Since a member's supporters are much more likely than his or her opponents to mail back the completed questionnaire, the member usually is in a position to announce that public opinion in the district and the member's actions in Congress are in harmony.

Other Public-Relations Techniques

Members of Congress get great mileage out of letters to constituents, speaking engagements to groups in the constituency, attendance at fairs, carnivals, and football games in the constituency, and interactions with local interest-group leaders who then interpret the member's behavior for interest-group members. But representatives and senators must also stay in touch with the constituency generally. To do so, members have staff aides whose primary responsibility is cultivating and maintaining good relationships with the news media.

News releases are one means of communicating a member's position on the bills before Congress and on the emotional social issues of the day. News releases are especially helpful in announcing good news for the district, getting positive press even though the member may have only been indirectly involved in the development. Federal agencies like to allow members of Congress to inform their constituents of good news (such as a new highway, a new post office, or a planned federal recreational facility), because doing so builds good will with members, and their support will be sought for the agency's next program. But news releases, alone, do not insure that a member will remain in the news. Press conferences help, since the mere holding of a press conference can be considered newsworthy by the local media editors.[24] *Doing* something, such as flying with the governor or President to view a disaster area, calling on the Veterans' Administration to investigate problems at the local VA hospital, or chairing a Congressional committee hearing in the home state or district (even if only two or three members appear) gets the representative or senator in the news. As noted earlier, in most states, U.S. senators generally have an easier time keeping their names and activities in the public eye than do U.S. representatives. But senators have a more difficult time of personally staying in touch with the major groups and important individuals throughout the state—because they usually have more people and territory to cover than representatives.

Radio and television talk shows, during which the audience at home can telephone and talk to the member on the air, are quite popular when the member is home. Such shows allow many people with similar questions to obtain direct answers to their questions, and they allow the member to demonstrate a grasp of the issues of the day and a careful consideration of the various perspectives surrounding each major issue. Some members also tape radio and television "public-service" shows for airing by local broadcasters who will use them. Some programs are merely the member's discussion of the issues and his or her views concerning them, while others are discussions between the member and a prominent guest, such as a cabinet member, an agency head, a scientist, or a labor leader. The usefulness of such broadcasts varies with the member's constituency, of course, and not all members feel they are effective.[25]

Members of Congress have a limited amount of patronage,[26] and some "find that filling the few positions available . . . is more trouble than it is worth."[27] In addition to a few jobs in district and state offices, each member of Congress can appoint five cadets, annually, to each of the nation's military academies—where the appointees receive a free education and an expense stipend, if they qualify for admission. Senators who are of the President's party have substantial say in who will be appointed U.S. district attorney and U.S. marshal in their home states, as well as great influence over the appointment of federal district judges. Probably the most valuable "patronage" available to most members of Congress, though, is their ability to assist constituents by intervening on their behalf with federal bureaucracies, discussed earlier.

STATE LEGISLATORS AND THEIR CONSTITUENTS

The need of state legislators to stay in touch with their constituents and to remain visible in the news is as great as that of members of Congress, but the difficulties can be more pronounced. As discussed earlier, state legislators simply are not as good "copy" as members of Congress. That is especially frustrating for legislators from heavily populated states, such as California, where state legislative districts are as large as Congressional districts and present just as many problems of constituency communications. In smaller states—such as Connecticut, New Mexico, or Wyoming—the state legislative constituencies are of manageable-enough size that legislators can become personally acquainted with a large share of constituents and with almost all the district's political-opinion leaders. Patterson and his colleagues found that legislators use the "middlemen" of politics to link up with their constituents. By "middlemen" they mean the local party leaders and politically active constituents, as well as lobbyists, who are of sufficient social stature to interact with state legislators as equals and who are politically active enough both to inform the legislator what the voters are thinking and to serve as "opinion leaders" among the constituents.[28]

State legislators probably view their constituencies in somewhat the same way members of Congress view theirs—as sets of concentric circles of supporters—although the primary constituency in many state legislative districts can be quite small. Sometimes, a few hundred loyal supporters is enough to provide reasonable protection against successful primary-election opposition.

Most state legislators have invested much less time, effort, and money in achieving office than have U.S. representatives and senators. State legislators, as a whole, are probably less concerned than members of Congress about the next election. Certainly the much higher rates of voluntary retirement among state legislators, discussed earlier, suggest as much. Still, state legislators are interested in what their constituents have to say and in communicating their (the legislators') views to their present and (for ambitious legislators) anticipated constituents.

State legislators do not have the staff assistance for constituent correspondence and casework that members of Congress have. Less than half the state legislators have private offices, and fewer than half the states provide their legislators with staff assistance year round. Even during the legislative sessions, half or more of the state legislators either share a typist with several colleagues or utilize the services of a typing pool. Local district offices and staff are provided only in a fourth or so of the states.[29] In most of the states, then, the state legislator reads his or her own mail and acts on it, dictating replies when secretarial service is available, and writing his or her own letters when it is not. Most state legislators, however, receive only a fraction of the mail received by members of Congress. Constituents of state legislators are likely to telephone their concerns, and legislators are normally entitled to use the state telephone system to stay in touch with constituents. New state legislators, indeed, are often surprised how few constituents bother to contact them, even on matters of some importance.

State legislators also serve as red-tape cutters for constituents who are not sure whom in state (or local) government to contact about a problem. They often will personally make a few telephone calls or tell a constituent whom to call or write. In some states, legislators still help supporters find jobs in state government. In the states with more professional legislatures and at least some staff assistance year round, generally those with larger legislative constituencies, the staff helps. In California, for example, many of the routine casework inquiries (how to apply for a "prestige" automobile license plate, obtain a copy of the state constitution, or apply for welfare) are dealt with by staff assistants to the legislators. Inquiries of a more serious nature, or from a more important constituent, however, continue to require the personal attention of California legislators.[30]

State legislators in most states do not conduct public-opinion surveys of their constituents. Most think they have a fairly good idea of what the values of their constituents are, and the rest are either aware that their constituents do not pay close attention, or they are determined to function in the "trustee" role. A good number of Americans are *not* paying attention to their state legislature. A 1965 survey of Minnesota voters taken during the legislative session found that 68 percent had "some interest" or a "great deal of interest" in what the legislature was doing, but a third of the respondents admitted that "they had paid little or no attention to the legislature."[31]

Even though most constituents seem not to be watching very closely, only a third of the state legislators in California, New Jersey, and Ohio stated to interviewers that they were more concerned about the interests of the state as a whole than about the interests of their particular district. The rest either said (43 percent) that they were primarily concerned about their district's interest or said (24 percent) that they were equally concerned about the interests of the state and the district.[32] Those from competitive and semicompetitive districts were more district oriented than were their colleagues from one-party districts. But even those who may want to take constituent views into account simply cannot determine what they are on many issues. To quote the state legislators:

> You can't vote by what you think the constituents' thinking is. You don't know what that thinking is. Even if you receive a hundred letters on a bill, this is a very small proportion in respect to the size of the district.

There isn't much interest in my county. The local newspaper gives me the only indication as to how my constituents feel.

It's hard to tell what the constituency wants. I have a pretty dim view of the constituency. They want economy if it doesn't hurt them; they want lower taxes for themselves, but higher for other groups. All your motives and intentions are suspect and your actions misinterpreted. . . .[33]

Despite the obvious difficulties in obtaining the views of constituents on various issues (discussed in Chapter 2), there is some evidence that state legislators are fairly attuned to those views, at least on the important issues. When asked to predict the outcome in their respective districts of referenda on school busing, school prayer, and a rather vague affirmation of the value of integrated education, for example, nearly all the cooperating members of the Florida House of Representatives were able to correctly predict the district's majority position. As one would expect, their percentage projections were more accurate on the more widely understood school-busing and school-prayer issues.[34] Similarly, a study of Iowa legislators found that most of them correctly predicted their districts' majority opinion on each of four referenda issues on the ballot.[35] When the Texas legislature sent a proposed "liquor-by-the-drink" constitutional amendment to the voters, 85 percent of all legislators voted the same way on the issue as their constituents later voted.[36]

POPULAR SUPPORT FOR AMERICAN LEGISLATURES

Congress

If Congress is to remain an equal branch of the national government, checking both the executive and judicial branches and being the decision-making site in which major policy alternatives are publicly explored, then it must retain some minimal level of citizen confidence and support. If one examined only the high success rate of members of Congress who stand for reelection, one might conclude that Congress as an institution is held in high regard by the citizenry. To the contrary, citizens approve their own individual representatives' performance but not that of Congress as an institution (see Figure 6.1).

The generally lukewarm support for Congress probably reflects the periodic evidence that one or more members of Congress have violated some basic principle of conduct. But, as Richard F. Fenno, Jr., has pointed out, if individual members of Congress viewed the trust of their supportive constituents as working capital, they could use some of it to increase the public's understanding and support of Congress as an institution.[37] Instead, however:

Members run *for* Congress by running *against* Congress. They refurbish their individual reputations as "the best congressman in the United States" by attacking the collective reputation of the Congress of the United States. Small wonder the voters feel so much more warmly disposed and so much less fickle toward the individuals than toward the institution.[38]

Congress' image suffers greatly from its members' attacks, in large part because the

FIGURE 6.1

Congressmen Yes, Congress No

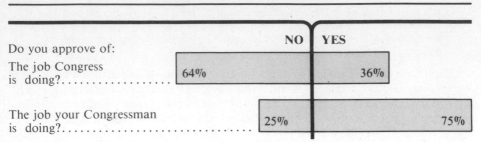

Congress is held in notably low esteem by Americans. Logically, they should welcome any chance to throw out the incompetent rascals, right? Wrong. The people hold their own individual Congressmen in quite high esteem. It is the institution of Congress that is severely faulted for poor performance. The data are from a September, 1978, survey by CBS News/New York Times.

Source: Everett Carll Ladd, Jr., "What the Voters Really Want," *Fortune,* December 18, 1978, p. 48.

average voter knows little about Congress or its complexities but knows a good deal about the local member of Congress, and usually trusts him or her.[39]

Still, the large number of appeals for help which pour into Congressional offices each day suggest that there is a great deal of support for the position of Congress within the national government's structure of authority. Along this line, Ladd argues that American "confidence that government can accomplish those things the people want done has declined . . . to a point lower than at any time in the modern era . . ." but that this pervasive dissatisfaction "has not shaken the public from some fundamental, long-held commitments—and expectations of government."[40] Thus, Ladd suggests the dissatisfaction with Congress (and the rest of government) is the result of unhappiness with the efficiency of our institutions of government, rather than the result of a desire to change those institutions.[41] That implies an *idealized* Congress alongside which the real Congress, warts and all, appears lacking.

Probably the most important reason for Americans' higher evaluation of individual congresspersons than of Congress as an institution, though, is that Americans expect different things from Congress as a whole than they do from their own individual senators and representatives.[42] Congress is expected to solve national problems. Our own members of Congress are expected to perform constituent services and articulate local and individual interests. These expectations can—and often do—come into conflict. Thus, in regard to constituent service, "a zealous member of Congress, pressing a particular constituent's claim, may ask for a generous ruling by a federal agency, such as a liberal definition of disability, which, if it were followed in every case, would result in a different national policy than that laid down by Congress as a whole."[43] Similarly, in articulating the interests of constituents, "a member of Congress may feel that he or she must fight to get a dam built back home or to prevent a military base from closing, even though the legislator—and the legislator's constituents—also favor the idea of cutting back on federal expenditures generally."[44]

★ ★ ★ ★

Sting Ploy May 'Chill' Hill-Public Dealings

Some members of Congress are worried that the FBI's use of hidden tape recorders and video cameras to trap corrupt politicians will have a "chilling effect" on their own dealings with the public.

"It certainly might chill a little our enthusiasm for helping out a businessman who is interested in locating a business in our district," commented one senior House Democrat, who asked not to be named.

In its recent undercover bribery and corruption investigation, FBI agents reportedly posed as representatives of wealthy Arab businessmen in order to lure unsuspecting members into accepting bribes in return for legislative favors or influence peddling. As bait, the agents dangled the possibility they might invest money in the member's district.

Members agreeing to meet with the representatives reportedly were offered a gift of cash. All meetings and other communications between the agents and the members reportedly were recorded or videotaped. No tapes have yet been made public, shown to grand juries or turned over to the House and Senate ethics committees.

"According to the press reports, the members were just asked to help a business get established in their district," the senior Democrat commented. "I am bothered by that. It's as if they cruised around, picked up a congressman and tried to see if he would bite. If he wouldn't, they'd just go after someone else."

"Of course, where it would go over the line would be if the member took money," he acknowledged.

The member's plaint was echoed by a veteran Capitol Hill aide, who said: "It's going to have an effect on the institution. It's going to isolate us from the public."

"The way those guys did it threatens the way we work," the aide said. He said he frequently is called on by the member he works for to meet with businessmen interested in locating a business or investing in the district.

"If a guy calls me up and tells me he wants to invest in a business in my district, I'm going to go talk to him," the aide said. "That's my job. If a problem comes up, I might say, 'Oh, we can take care of that.' Sure, it's loose talk, but people talk that way."

Now, he said, he will no longer agree to meet with potential investors because he might inadvertently say something damaging to an FBI agent who is wired for sound and picture.

"If a guy calls me now, I'm going to tell him to forget it," he said. . . .

Source: *Congressional Quarterly Weekly Report,* February 9, 1980, p. 335.

★ ★ ★ ★

State Legislatures

As indicated in the discussion of the historical development of legislatures in America (Chapter 1), citizen support for the legislative branch of state government has fluctuated greatly, over time. And when the state legislature has not had the confidence of the people, it has declined in importance relative to the governor and the state government executive branch.

Research on citizen attitudes toward, and support for, the state legislature suggests that the legislatures are, on the whole, not well thought of. In a few states, a narrow majority has indicated approval of the job the state legislature has done, but, in most such surveys, the citizens who are supportive of the state legislature are outnumbered by those who disapprove.[45]

Does generalized support for the legislature matter? Yes, if the decisions of the government are to be accepted with minimal governmental coercion; that is, if the political system is to remain democratic. To quote David Easton:

> If the authorities are to be able to make decisions, to get them accepted as binding, and to put them into effect without extensive use of coercion, solidarity must be developed not only around some set of authorities themselves, but around the major aspects of the system within which the authorities operate.[46]

That is, citizens must be supportive enough of the government that they willingly obey the laws.

Despite the relatively unfavorable ratings that ordinary citizens give to their state legislatures, detailed inquiry into the subject in Iowa has persuaded three researchers that they "would expect analyses in other political systems to demonstrate that relative to the appropriate mass public, support for the legislature in Iowa is high. In general, Iowa is a supportive political environment for the legislature."[47] That support becomes even stronger as one moves from the mass public to county party leaders, to attentive constituents (as identified by legislators), to lobbyists, and then to legislators (see Table 6.1).

CONSTITUENCY INFLUENCE ON LEGISLATOR VOTING

As discussed in Chapter 2, some legislators see themselves as "trustees" (free agents who should study all aspects of a problem and then make a decision based on their perception of the public good), others as "delegates" (voting according to what they believe the wishes of the majority of their constituents to be), and still others as both, depending upon the issues involved.

Do American legislators reflect constituent opinion in their voting behavior? To a great extent, yes, and more so on the salient issues on which constituent opinion

TABLE 6.1

Legislative Support for the Iowa Legislative by the Mass Public and by Political Elites (in percentages)

Legislative Support (Principal Component)	Mass Public	Party Leaders	Attentive Constituents	Lobbyists	Legislators
High	15.2	39.6	49.8	45.5	63.5
Medium	32.0	31.9	29.8	38.4	23.8
Low	52.8	28.6	20.5	16.2	12.7
Total	100.0	100.1	100.1	100.1	100.0
No. of cases	1,001	90	484	99	181

Source: Samuel C. Patterson, Ronald D. Hedlund, and G. Robert Boynton, *Representatives and Represented: Bases of Public Support for the American Legislatures* (New York: John Wiley, 1975), p. 117.

is most strongly expressed.[48] Indeed, when one considers the recruitment, nominating, and electoral processes which lead to seats in the American state legislatures and in Congress, it would be odd if the legislator did not vote on most questions in a manner consistent with modal opinion (that most frequently expressed) among the politically active residents of the constituency—even though service as a legislator obviously changes an individual's level of understanding of, and attitudes toward, various social problems. After all, as established in earlier chapters, the people who have the best chance to win election to an American legislature are those with appropriate personal characteristics (race, education, religion, gender, length of time residing in the district, occupation, etc.) and with social and political perspectives compatible with the dominant points of view in the district, including those of the most powerful interest groups. With that kind of filtering process, it very well may not matter whether an individual legislator considers himself or herself a "delegate" or a "trustee." Even the trustee is likely to vote the dominant constituency opinion most of the time—and to do so even if he or she does not hear from a single constituent on the particular issue. There is some evidence, however, that U.S. representatives are more likely to act as delegates on distributive issues, while behaving as trustees on issues of social morality, defense, and foreign affairs.[49]

Additional difficulties confront those who seek empirically to determine whether American legislators' voting records are consistent with constituent opinion. One difficulty, as Fenno notes, is that legislators see several constituencies: the geographical constituency, the reelection constituency, the primary constituency, and the personal constituency. Which constituency should the researcher study when seeking to relate legislative voting to constituent opinion?[50] There are also questions of perception. On which issues does a legislator perceive the constituents feel strongly? Might the legislator misconstrue both the intensity and the distribution of opinion?[51] Unless we are content to let the recruitment/election-filtering process carry the entire load of representation, we must inquire into the legislator's perception of the intensity and distribution of constituency opinion (depending, of course, on the constituency of relevance to the legislator). Furthermore, there are conceptual and methodological difficulties in seeking to assess the degree of policy agreement between legislators and constituents. "Constituents may be asked general questions about their views on policy; legislators must make choices among very specific legislative options. An apparently high correlation between the issue positions of legislators and constituents may be deceptive, unless the two scales have substantively identical end points."[52] And studies which are satisfied merely to relate constituency opinion to roll-call voting miss many of the indicators of a legislator's intensity of commitment on an issue.[53]

Despite the conceptual and methodological difficulties involved in examining questions of constituency influence on legislative voting behavior, it seems fair to conclude that, between constituencies and their respective American legislators at both the state and national levels, legislators do substantively represent dominant constituent opinion reasonably well. Further, there is substantial evidence, again at both the state and national levels, that, collectively, American legislators represent the distribution of public opinion fairly well (although the extremes of opinion suffer a bit). As one researcher concluded:

> . . . however it happened—by recruitment, campaigning, election, adjustment of opinions because of representational role commitments, or whatever—Congress was reasonably representative of the nationwide public on major issues, a finding that might surprise the cynics who assert that our political system does not reflect the will of the people.[54]

Indeed, as Weissberg notes:

> [C]ollective representation will never be worse than dyadic representation. If individual legislators are free to deviate from district opinion it is likely that deviations will approach normality and the institution as a whole will be more representative of national opinion than the average legislator is representative of district opinion.[55]

Does the conclusion that our legislators are reasonably representative of constituent opinion mean that interest-group influence, then, is benign? Not at all. Legislators basically are responsive to interest groups within the substantial latitude their constituents give them. That responsiveness springs from the belief by most legislators that the government ought to be helpful when it can, rather than obstructive, and from politicians' desires to help people and to be liked. Even without bribes and unethical behavior, it is difficult for legislators not to begin to feel personally involved with the lobbyists with whom they interact frequently. And they often find that the needs of the special-interest-group lobbyist are not in conflict with constituency opinion as the members perceive it. A good example is the member of Congress from a hawkish constituency; that member is being quite consistent with constituency opinion when he or she seeks to increase the defense budget or to help a particular contractor (especially one whose plant is in the constituency) nail down a contract for a particular weapons system. In addition, interest groups work at shaping public opinion. Further, as noted earlier, the legislative process confronts each legislator with choices between options and with a sequence of choices which, for the most part, the legislator is not in a position to change. He or she must choose. And it is often possible to choose an option which meets the basic needs of a given interest group while leaving oneself ample opportunity to argue, for example, that by voting for a small program, a larger program was avoided and that voting for no program at all would have been a wasted vote.

SUMMARY

The careers of American legislators are intimately tied to their relationships with their constituents. That is so to a greater degree than in parliamentary political systems or in systems in which legislators seek election in multimember legislative districts that use party-prioritized lists of nominees. American legislators seem to envision their constituencies as consisting of sets of concentric circles, with the personal constituency the most intimate and close, the primary constituency the core of a member's strength, even in a primary-election contest against a challenger from within the party, and the reelection constituency the basis of one's strength in the general election. Much of the legal or geographic constituency is known not to belong to these constituency sets. To the extent legislators are responsive to their constituents, then, they are probably differentially responsive to the sets of different constituencies they see.

American legislators are not always responsive to their constituents. They have a fair amount of freedom in the policy positions they take. But they do desire reelection, are usually aware of the issues on which their constituents feel strongly, and normally support their constituents on such issues. This pattern is probably partially the result of a feeling that they ought to reflect constituent opinion on issues on which their constituents feel strongly, partly a desire for reelection, and partly the logical consequence of the recruitment and election process in the United States. The recruitment and election process tends to filter out those who disagree with the dominant opinion of the constituency on the major issues of the day.

Members of Congress have greater resources than state legislators for keeping in touch with constituents and performing "casework" for them. But most members of Congress are geographically much further away from their constituents than most state legislators. Both state and national legislators seek to answer mail promptly and to assist constituents when they can. State legislators are more personally involved in the constituent-service function than members of Congress, but probably no more concerned about it. The difference seems to be the consequence of the smaller constituencies represented by most state legislators and their smaller staffs and office support.

Public support for Congress and the state legislatures is lukewarm or negative in various public-opinion surveys, but it seems likely that the attitude being tapped by the survey researchers is the frustration or disappointment of the respondents with recent legislative actions, rather than the citizens' degree of support for a political system in which the legislative branch of government plays a fundamental role. Basic support for the legislature, as a legitimate component of the government, would appear to be much stronger than the "approve-disapprove" ratings of the various legislatures.

Notes

1. Robert S. Erikson and Gerald C. Wright, Jr., "Electoral Marginality and Congressional Representation" (Paper delivered at the 1978 Annual Meeting of the American Political Science Association, New York, N.Y.), p. 4.

2. David R. Mayhew, *Congress: The Electoral Connection* (New Haven: Conn.: Yale University Press, 1974), Chapter 1.

3. Austin Ranney, *Pathways to Parliament* (London: Macmillan, 1965).

4. Richard F. Fenno, Jr., *Home Style: House Members in Their Districts* (Boston: Little, Brown, 1978), pp. 1–2.

5. Ibid., p. 6.

6. Ibid., p. 8.

7. Ibid., pp. 12–15. John W. Kingdom found similar electoral insecurity. See his *Candidates for Office: Beliefs and Strategies* (New York: Random House, 1968), pp. 86–89.

8. Fenno, *Home Style,* pp. 18–24.

9. Ibid., pp. 24–27.

10. Richard F. Fenno, Jr., "U.S. House Members in Their Constituencies: An Exploration," *American Political Science Review* 71 (September 1977): 915.

11. Ibid., pp. 898–917.

12. Glenn R. Parker, "Cycles in Congressional District Attention," *Journal of Politics* 42 (May 1980): 540–48.

13. See Burdett Loomis, "The Congressional Office as a Small(?) Business: New Members Set Up Shop," *Publius* 9, no. 3 (Summer 1979): 44, 45.

14. Fenno, "U.S. House Members in Their Constituencies," p. 893.

15. Donald G. Tacheron and Morris K. Udall provide extensive information on how members of Congress handle their mail. See *The Job of the Congressman* (Indianapolis: Bobbs-Merrill, 1966), pp. 63–84. See also John R. Johannes, "Congressional Caseworkers: Attitudes, Orientations, and Operations" (Paper delivered at the 1978 Annual Meeting of the Midwest Political Science Association, Chicago, Ill.); and John D. Macartney, "Congressional District Offices: Their Staffs and Functions" (Paper delivered at the 1979 Annual Meeting of the American Political Science Association, Washington, D.C.).

16. Morris P. Fiorina, "The Case of the Vanishing Marginals: The Bureaucracy Did It," *American Political Science Review* 71 (March 1977): 179.

17. Morris P. Fiorina, *Congress: Keystone of the Washington Establishment* (New Haven, Conn.: Yale University Press, 1977).

18. Donald R. Matthews, *U.S. Senators and Their World* (New York: Random House, Vintage Books, 1960), p. 222.

19. Charles L. Clapp, *The Congressman: His Work as He Sees It* (Washington, D.C.: Brookings Institution, 1963), pp. 71–72.

20. Daniel M. Berman, *In Congress Assembled* (New York: Macmillan, 1964), p. 58.

21. Clapp, *The Congressman,* p. 65.

22. Joseph Westphal and John Cranor, "Congressional District Offices, Federal Programs, and Electoral Benefits: Some Observations on the Passing of the Marginal Representative, 1974–1976" (Paper delivered at the 1978 Annual Meeting of the Midwest Political Science Association, Chicago, Ill.).

23. Eugene J. Alpert, "Sources of Information for Congressional Candidates, 1958 and 1978" (Paper delivered at the 1979 Southwestern Political Science Association Annual Meeting, Denver, Colo.).

24. A member may find the local press tires of running inconsequential news releases. What to do? The wire services ". . . are especially useful as vehicles for laundering press releases into news your local papers will run. . . . Rep. Max Baucus . . . now telecopies his releases to the AP bureau in Helena, which (sometimes) rewrites the lead and always sends the rest of it out verbatim. With the AP imprimatur, the local papers feel less guilty about running Baucus' releases." What if nobody is attending your press conferences? "Sen. Richard Schweiker . . . has friends on the *Philadelphia Bulletin* who will request wire coverage of the Schweiker press conference after Schweiker requests that they request coverage. It's not something the people at the *Bulletin* like to talk about particularly, but they haven't let Schweiker down yet." Joseph Nocera, "How to Make the Front Page," *Washington Monthly,* October 1978, p. 16.

25. Clapp, *The Congressman,* pp. 92–93.

26. Indeed, the patronage available to a U.S. representative is so slight compared to that of many city and county positions that Leo M. Snowiss found that many Chicago politicians prefer local posts to a seat in Congress. See "Congressional Recruitment and Representation," *American Political Science Review* 60 (September 1966): 627–39.

27. Tacheron and Udall, *The Job of the Congressman,* p. 85.

28. Samuel C. Patterson, Ronald D. Hedlund, and G. Robert Boynton, *Representatives and Represented: Bases of Public Support for the American Legislatures* (New York: John Wiley, 1975), Chapter 4.

29. "American State Legislatures: Their Structures and Procedures," (Lexington, Ky.: Council of State Governments, 1977), pp. 23, 43.

30. Alan J. Wyner, "Legislative Reform and Politics in California: What Happened, Why, and So What?" in *State Legislative Innovation,* ed. James A. Robinson (New York: Praeger, 1973), pp. 89–90.

31. *Minneapolis Tribune,* July 11, 1965; and *Des Moines Register and Tribune,* May 1, 1974. Both polls are reported by Samuel C. Patterson, "American State Legislatures and Public Policy," in *Politics in the American States: A Comparative Analysis,* 3rd ed., ed. Herbert Jacob and Kenneth N. Vines (Boston: Little, Brown, 1976), p. 163.

32. John C. Wahlke, Heinz Eulau, William Buchanan, and LeRoy C. Ferguson, *The Legislative System* (New York: John Wiley, 1962), pp. 289–94.

33. Quoted in ibid., pp. 296–97.

34. Robert S. Erikson, Norman R. Luttbeg, and William V. Holloway, "Knowing One's District: How Legislators Predict Referendum Voting," *American Journal of Political Science* 19 (May 1975): 231–46.

35. Ronald D. Hedlund and H. Paul Friesema, "Representatives' Perceptions of Constituency Opinion," *Journal of Politics* 34 (August 1972): 730–52.

36. William C. Adams and Paul H. Ferber, "Measuring Legislator-Constituency Congruence: Liquor, Legislators, and Linkage," *Journal of Politics* 42 (February 1980): 202–8.

37. Fenno, *Home Style,* p. 246.

38. Richard F. Fenno, Jr., "If, as Ralph Nader Says, Congress Is 'the Broken Branch,' How Come We Love Our Congressmen So Much?" in *Congress in Change: Evolution and Reform,* ed. Norman J. Ornstein (New York: Praeger, 1975), p. 280.

39. Glenn R. Parker, "A Note on the Impact and Saliency of Congress," *American Politics Quarterly* 4 (October 1976): 413–21.

40. Everett Carll Ladd, Jr., "What the Voters Really Want," *Fortune,* December 18, 1978, p. 41.

41. Ibid., pp. 40–48.

42. David J. Vogler, *The Politics of Congress,* 3rd ed. (Boston: Allyn and Bacon, 1980), pp. 1–48.

43. Fred R. Harris, *America's Democracy: The Ideal and the Reality* (Glenview, Ill.: Scott, Foresman, 1980), p. 351.

44. Ibid.

45. Samuel C. Patterson, "American State Legislatures and Public Policy," in *Politics in the American States,* ed. Herbert Jacob and Kenneth N. Vines (Boston: Little, Brown, 1976) p. 164.

46. David Easton, *A Systems Analysis of Political Life* (New York: John Wiley, 1965), p. 157.

47. Patterson, Hedlund, and Boynton, *Representatives and Represented,* p. 49.

48. Warren E. Miller and Donald E. Stokes, "Constituency Influence in Congress," *American Political Science Review* 57 (March 1963): 45–56; Robert S. Erikson, "Constituency Opinion and Congressional Behavior: A Reexamination of the Miller-Stokes Representation Data," *American Journal of Political Science* 22 (August 1978): 511–35; Robert S. Erikson, "Public Opinion and Congressional Representation: Evidence from the 1978 CPS Election" (Paper delivered at the 1980 Annual Meeting of the Western Political Science Association, San Francisco, Calif.); and Donald J. McCrone and James H. Kuklinski, "The Delegate Theory of Representation," *American Journal of Political Science* 23 (May 1979): 278–300.

49. Thomas E. Cavanagh, "Role Orientations of House Members: The Process of Representation" (Paper delivered at the 1979 Annual Meeting of the American Political Science Association, Washington, D.C.).

50. Fenno, *Home Style,* p. 28.

51. James H. Kuklinski and Donald J. McCrone, "Policy Salience and the Causal Structure of Representation," *American Politics Quarterly* 8 (April 1980): 139–64; Eugene J. Alpert, "A Reconceptualization of Representative Role Theory," *Legislative Studies Quarterly* 4 (November 1979): 487–603.

52. Robert Weissberg, "Assessing Legislator-Constituency Policy Agreement," *Legislative Studies Quarterly* 4 (November 1979): 605. See also Walter J. Stone, "Measuring Constituency-Representative Linkages: Problems and Prospects," *Legislative Studies Quarterly* 4 (November 1977): 623–39.

53. Donald A. Gross, "Measuring Legislators' Policy Positions: Roll Call Votes and Preferences Among Pieces of Legislation," *American Politics Quarterly* 7 (October 1979): 417–37.

54. Charles H. Backstrom, "Congress and the Public: How Representative is the One of the Other?" *American Politics Quarterly* 5 (October 1977): 432. See also F. Chris Garcia, "Comparative Opinions of New Mexico Voters and State Senators," University of New Mexico, *Division of Government Research Review,* December 1978.

55. Robert Weissberg, "Collective vs. Dyadic Representation in Congress," *American Political Science Review* 72 (June 1978): 547.

chapter 7

Interest Groups and the News Media in the Legislative Process

Preview

Interest groups and the news media play important roles in the legislative process. Both are critical links in the communications process by which legislators learn of the impact which proposed legislation will have. Both also help legislators to know and interpret what is happening in the legislature. The news media, furthermore, interprets legislative activity to the public and can affect that activity by the issues it chooses to stress. The interest-group system is biased in favor of society's dominant economic interests, as the legislative process itself is biased in favor of the status quo. Public-interest groups and environmentalists have gained influence recently but narrow special-interest groups have an advantage—in terms of getting what they want—in that they are usually concerned about limited or technical policy decisions which few others understand or care about. Old-fashioned bribery appears to be rare, but the importance of campaign contributions in gaining access and a sympathetic hearing raises troublesome questions.

Legislators do not serve in a vacuum. The decisions or nondecisions of the legislature affect the entire society. When elected, few legislators are familiar with more than a fraction of the industries, cultures, or areas of the state or nation for which they must legislate. Yet, the legislator's decisions will affect people far beyond the home constituency. The process of learning about the needs of the various sectors of society and balancing the demands of various groups against the general good is time-consuming, hard work. A major component of the legislator's information-gathering process involves interest groups and their lobbyists. The interpretation to the citizenry of what the various groups want and what the legislature decides is the responsibility of the news media, although individual correspondence by legislators and newsletters and announcements by interest groups also play a role in the communications process. The activities of both lobbyists and news-media personnel are important to the network of communications which is an integral component of the legislative process.

INTEREST GROUPS AND LOBBYISTS

The First Amendment to the U.S. Constitution assures Americans the right "to petition the Government for a redress of grievances." One way to seek such redress is to write your senator. More commonly, you may join an organization which will seek to persuade the government of your particular point of view. Such an organization is an *interest group,* sometimes referred to as a *pressure group* because it puts pressure on public officials. More precisely, for our purposes, an interest group is an organization whose members share attitudes or goals and which consciously seeks to influence government public policy in accordance with those attitudes or goals. Thus, an interest group is not just a categorical grouping, such as all left-handed people, although left-handed people could join together to seek government policies to make their lives more pleasant in a right-handed society. Interest-group members may not agree on all issues, but they do agree on the issue or issues on which the organization is based, and they want the organization to achieve its goals through government action.[1] The number of members, the extent to which the members agree on their goals, and the intensity with which the members support the organization greatly influence the interest group's effectiveness.

Interest groups perform some of the same functions as political parties, but they are not the same as political parties. First, the major political parties in the United States differ from interest groups in the range and scope of their concerns. American political parties seek to aggregate and articulate the interests of numerous interest groups, and often manage to appeal to interest groups with conflicting goals. U.S. political parties are umbrella organizations under which interest groups may seek shelter, although many interest groups maintain ties with both the Democratic and the Republican parties. Second, political parties seek to elect party members to office under the party label. Interest groups may seek to have interest-group members elected under the party label, but they do not seek to elect members under the interest-group label. The political party seeks to govern in its own name; the interest group seeks to assist a party in capturing power and then, after the party is in power, to have influence or control over those government policies which most directly affect the interest group.

American observers sometimes refer to a member of Congress as an "oil congressman" or a "coal senator" or to a state legislator as an "inside lobbyist" for the insurance or real-estate industry, the banks, or teachers. Many American legislators were first encouraged to run for office by friendly interest groups and were supported by them for reelection, but the involvement of interest groups in the selection of American legislators has not reached the European level. Loewenberg and Patterson, for example, note that the German process of selecting nominees to the Bundestag (the West German national legislature's lower house) "is responsive to the interest groups which are informally affiliated with each of the parties."[2]

> The major interest groups within each party have claimed a fairly fixed share of winnable places on the list of candidates over a period of time, and have filled these places themselves, so that party lists have in effect become combinations of interest-group sublists.[3]

The consequence is that about a third of the members of the German Bundestag are interest-group representatives who "focus primarily on the groups to which they belong."[4]

Similarly, some British members of Parliament serve as spokespersons for particular interest groups. "In some cases, this direct representation of interest groups involves the payment of a fee or retainer to 'their' legislator."[5] One study found over 30 percent of the members of the British House of Commons were "associated with one or another of the interest groups," ranging from major business and trade-union groups, to religious groups, to local-government or social-cause groups.[6] Yet, despite the obvious legislative influence of major interest groups in Britain and West Germany, observers report that it is not thought proper for a legislator to act solely on the basis of what his or her sponsoring interest group wants. The interest-group leaders, of course, take pains to instruct "their" legislators not to create the appearance of being mere interest-group minions. The BDI (Federation of German Industry), for instance, "makes it clear to the deputies that they must not be tagged as tools of industry. . . ."[7]

While American legislators often are overly sympathetic to one or another private interest, Americans normally use the word *lobbyist* to refer to a hired agent—not a legislator—who seeks to influence public decisions. For our purposes, the lobbyist seeks to influence legislative decisions (although they also seek to influence executive decisions). Indeed, the term *lobbyist* derives from the early practice of special pleaders who would wait in the public lobby of the capitol for passing legislators and then approach them with requests for special consideration. Legislators originally had no offices, just desks or seats in the legislative chamber (where access was restricted), so the pleading was done in the public lobby. Hence the terms *lobbying* and *lobbyist*.

Types of Interest Groups

Interest groups can and have been classified in many different ways. A popular distinction today is between *special-interest* groups and *public-interest* groups. Special-interest groups offer membership only to persons or corporations with special characteristics, such as veterans, physicians, or manufacturers of work gloves. Membership in public-interest groups is open to anyone who wants to join, although limited to those with the modest membership fee. Common Cause, for instance, accepts anybody who is willing to pay the $15 membership fee. Some observers feel it would be better to call consumer and citizen organizations *citizens' lobbies* rather than public-interest groups, in part because doing so would avoid confusion between private special-interest groups and government ("public") agencies which often behave like special-interest groups in their legislative lobbying activities.[8] Agencies of government, such as the Tennessee Valley Authority or the Navy, for example, often lobby Congress in a manner much like that of private special-interest groups, such as the American Medical Association, the Work Glove Manufacturers Association, or the American Petroleum Institute. Still, it is generally understood that a public-interest group attempts to represent the interests of the general public, rather than a special economic, professional, or other narrow interest. While the activities of both types of interest groups are legal (or can be), and most legislators accept lobbyists as legitimate (and, perhaps, desirable) participants in the legislative process, the average citizen often views the activities of special-interest groups with suspicion.

The distinction between special-interest groups and public-interest groups is not completely satisfactory. An increasing number of interest groups, for instance, are "cause" or "ideological" organizations, often referred to as "single-issue" groups. While they resemble special-interest groups in the narrowness of their concerns, they resemble public-interest groups in that they often are fighting for their vision of what is good for society and in that theirs is not an economic interest (such as the oil industry or steel industry) but, rather, a policy issue (such as abortion, women's rights, or gun control). Their membership rosters are usually open to anybody who shares the organization's ideological commitment and has the modest membership fee. Such organizations usually make it quite clear to all concerned that they do not care what a legislator's overall record is; they will judge each legislator only on the basis of the single issue of concern to them.

Different types of interest groups have different types of resources. Public-interest groups have limited financing. The organization staff must work at maintaining a large membership of people who pay nominal dues. Further, organizations which hope to receive tax-deductible contributions from donors must be very careful that lobbying is not their principal activity, or, under federal law and regulations, they could lose their income-tax exemption. Most public-interest groups pay low salaries and experience fairly high turnover of paid personnel, most of whom are young. The major resources of public-interest groups are a large membership, which can be called upon to communicate with legislators, and their standing in the eyes of most ordinary citizens as honest interpreters of public policy. Their major weakness is that it is difficult to sustain intense membership interest in issues over a long period of time, and their opponents often merely delay the decision until the public-interest group can no longer win. Often, of course, the legislative battle is fought between competing special-interest groups, as when the railroads vigorously supported imposition of waterway user fees which barge operators just as fiercely resisted.[9]

Special-interest groups have a variety of resources. Some, such as veterans' organizations and the political arms of organized labor, have large memberships, along with moderate funds. An organization has power in proportion to how actively the members support its political goals. The major professional organizations have ample financial resources, as well as members who are leading citizens in their respective legislative districts, the latter providing *access* to legislators. Often, of course, that access is maintained through campaign donations. Other special-interest groups, especially those representing an industry, primarily rely on their financial resources. They are able to hire the experts necessary to structure information so as to persuade legislators to their point of view. They also can hire enough lobbyists to keep themselves aware of any measures which might affect them in time to take effective action. And, increasingly, they are forming political action committees (PACs) to raise money to help elect or reelect their friends to the legislature. Sometimes, having a large plant or local affiliate in a key legislator's district makes a substantial difference.

Influencing Legislation

Much of the time, interest groups and lobbyists are concerned more about actions or proposed actions by an executive agency than about any legislation that may be wending its way through the legislature. But executive-agency decisions are made by political figures or bureaucrats who need support, and annual appropriations, from the legislature. Many owe their jobs to a particular legislator. Although key legislators vary with the agency of concern, one way that legislators can help remain friends with special-interest groups is by intervening (often privately, by telephone) to ask an agency executive to "consider" the interest group's needs and point of view when making a policy decision. But major, basic policy is set forth in legislation, and the interest-group lobbyists have to know their way around the legislative corridors.

The legislative process is very complex. Major decisions must be ratified repeatedly at different stages of the process of passing a bill into law. Lobbyists with friends in the legislature can be extremely effective in shaping legislation, especially the kind

147

of legislation which is very important to many business and industry special-interest groups but means little to the ordinary citizen. A change in accounting practices for tax purposes, for example, may be very important to certain business firms, and they may be able to get the desired legislation enacted as a minor and almost unnoticed amendment to some obscure bill. The legislative process gives the advantage to groups with very narrow interests and to status-quo groups, those who are basically satisfied with the structure and laws of the society. On the other hand, those who wish to change the status quo must keep struggling to win at every decision point; their opponents need only block them at any one such point in the legislative process. The key victory against a bill may be in a subcommittee, a committee, on the floor, or in conference committee.

Public-interest groups are spread thin. They seek to prevent the enactment of special legislation which they see as granting unfair advantage to various narrow interests in the society. Thus, public-interest groups must attempt to remain abreast of developments in most of the committees of the legislature and seek to influence the decisions of many of those committees. Even without limited funds, the self-appointed task of public-interest groups would be very difficult. Special-interest groups, by contrast, normally focus only on the committees which consider their particular type of legislation, whether that is labor legislation, agricultural law, water law, or subsidies to shipbuilders. The greater financial resources of special-interest groups and the narrower range of issues with which they must be intensely involved give these groups an important advantage.

The expertise and narrowness of mission of special-interest groups have led to what some observers refer to as *subgovernments* in certain areas of policymaking. "Subgovernments are small groups of political actors, both governmental and nongovernmental, that specialize in specific issue areas. . . . They are . . . most prevalent and influential in the least visible policy areas. . . . A typical subgovernment is composed of members of the House and/or Senate, members of congressional staffs, a few bureaucrats, and representatives of private groups and organizations interested in the policy area."[10] Usually, the members of Congress in a particular subgovernment are the few most senior members of the committees or subcommittees with principal or exclusive jurisdiction over the policy area dominated by the subgovernment. Most policy made by such subgovernments appears to be "routine," although that does not mean that no benefits are passed on to the participants. While outsiders in Congress and the executive branch can, and occasionally do, intrude on the relative autonomy of subgovernments, outsiders usually have no incentive to expend their resources by interfering. Thus many so-called routine government decisions are made with the full participation of select interest groups, as well as with great concern for their well being.

Not all interest groups, however, have the governmental access participants in subgovernments have, and not all are fortunate enough to be able to achieve their objectives by means of the subgovernment route. Those interest groups which are not intimate members of a subgovernment find that the techniques for influence available to them depend in large part on their resources. Those with large numbers of dedicated (not apathetic) members, for example, can seek their help in persuading each member's own legislator of the wisdom of supporting the interest group's position. Interest groups with substantial financial resources and an issue position likely to appeal to the public can mount a public relations and advertising campaign that is intended to influence public opinion and, in turn, affect the behavior of legislators. Sometimes, neither the public nor many news reporters may realize that they are receiving biased information. "For example, the Business Roundtable, which was formed by 157 business corporations and organizations, hired the North American Precis Syndicate in 1977 to prepare and mail out 'canned' editorials and cartoons opposing the creation of a new consumer protection agency. The 3800 newspapers that received these prepared materials—and their readers—had no way of knowing that the source was highly biased. The materials appeared approximately 2,000 times throughout the country."[11]

Some interests, primarily those of less advantaged citizens, are often either unrepresented, poorly represented, or ignored.[12] Those citizens must make do with symbolic (rather than economic) payoffs from the legislative process or, frequently, none at all. Farm workers, for instance, are seldom represented in the subgovernments which decide federal policy concerning what constitutes safe pesticide use in the fields, but they bear the brunt of any physical misfortunes (disease, miscarriages, deformed babies, even death) which result from the improper use of such pesticides. Nor are agricultural laborers and sharecroppers likely to overwhelm the alliance of farmowners associations and chemical/pesticide manufacturers in Congressional lobbying.

Functions of Interest Groups

Although many citizens perceive interest groups to be a basic force for corrupting the body politic, most legislators find them sometimes helpful, even if, at other times, they are frustrating. Lobbyists and other defenders of the role of interest groups in the political process note that interest groups perform certain positive functions. First, say their defenders, they serve as links between the people and the policymakers. Legislators find that serving in the legislature is a very educational experience. Many problems they did not know existed are brought up, and, in the process of deciding how to vote on various matters, the legislator is informed by interest-group representatives. Often, lobbyists from both sides will attempt to sway the legislator, each casting the information in a different light or providing new information. The interest groups, accordingly, are "transmission belts" which help the government identify opinions and needs it should respond to.[13]

Second, interest groups supplement formal or official representation, at least for those whose interests are represented by organized groups. Many people who are unable to elect a sympathetic legislator from their single-member legislative district can, nonetheless, join an interest group, which will present their views and represent their interests forcefully in the legislative arena, as well as in judicial and executive settings.

Third, their advocates argue that interest groups may increase political participation by informing their members of recent or pending governmental decisions and suggesting courses of action. Many interest groups hold workshops to train their members in political skills. These skills—and experience—lead to increased feelings of efficacy and competence and to increased political activity, not all of which may be related to the interest group.

Finally, it is said that interest groups assist in the resolution of conflict in the society. Much policymaking results from finding a compromise solution which meets the needs of various elements of the society, even if imperfectly. Often, the legislature lacks sufficient expertise to know the details of how a change in rules in a technical area of the law will affect the various participants, but feels that circumstances re-

149

quire a change. In such a situation, the legislature is likely to turn to the relevant interest groups (usually special-interest groups) and seek the help of the lobbyists for the organizations in finding a solution which everyone can live with. The difficulty here, of course, is that although the resulting solution may be politically satisfactory, it may actually result in substantial costs to the uninvolved, unconsulted, and uninformed general public. This is the situation which public-interest groups seek to ameliorate.

Criticism of Interest Groups

The major criticism of interest groups is nicely summarized by Schattschneider, who argues, "The flaw in the pluralist heaven is that the heavenly chorus sings with a strong upper-class accent. Probably about 90 percent of the people cannot get into the pressure system."[14] The people who are best represented by special-interest groups in the United States are the better educated and the more affluent.[15]

In addition to the bias in interest-group representation, interest groups are usually not internally democratic. Michels' "Iron Law of Oligarchy" applies: each group tends to be dominated by an active minority which makes the major decisions for the organization and often places the interests of the executive director and the staff ahead of the interests of the membership.[16] Even public-interest groups tend to be dominated by their headquarters staffs; individual members are busy earning a living.[17] Thus, although interest groups may provide an alternative channel of representation, it is not as clearly responsive a channel as representation through elected officials who must return for a fresh mandate every two to six years.

Pluralist theorists and other supporters of the interest-group system argue that policies which result from interest-group conflict are as close to the public interest as one can hope to get. But critics note that decisions based primarily on special-interest pressures tend to ignore some important public interests, in part because the diffuse general interest is often not represented in the negotiations.[18] Legislators and other elected officials, of course, are supposed to represent that diffuse general interest, and often do, but that is frequently in spite of, not because of, the activities of special-interest groups. Further, it is likely that interests represented by sophisticated organizations and lobbyists will obtain tangible economic benefits, while the less well-represented citizens will have to be content with symbolic rewards.[19]

★ ★ ★ ★

The Importance of Access

An ambitious young Washington lawyer who represents an association of chemical companies is having lunch with a former classmate who now works in the Environmental Protection Agency (EPA). "My people are getting awfully jumpy about what kind of regulations are going to be issued under the new pesticide legislation," the lawyer says to the EPA staff member.

"I can imagine," she responds. "We're coming out with the final regs next Thursday. There's no secret about it, but we haven't broadcast it because the director doesn't want to be bothered with having everybody on his neck. I can tell you, though, that the regs are going to be pretty tough on pesticides. Of the three plans, the director is going to go for the toughest one."

"Who has the final say?"

"The director's handling this one himself."

After lunch, the young lawyer catches a cab up to the New Senate Office Building on Capitol Hill. "What greedy scheme have you come to lobby me about, now?" the senator asks jokingly as the young lawyer is shown into his office. "You've bought my secretary by bringing her chocolates nearly every time you come up here. You've got my administrative assistant addicted to those fine Cuban cigars you dole out to him one by one, and because of the one-thousand-dollar contribution you made to my last campaign, you think you own me." The senator says all this with mock outrage. He and the lawyer know each other well. They have an easy, friendly relationship.

"What I need, senator, is a call from you down to the director of EPA to ask him to go for the less harsh Plan One regulations on pesticides, instead of the unreasonable Plan Three regulations. He's going to come out with the regulations next Thursday, and they're going to kill the chemical industry unless we can do something."

"I wish you'd come in here sometime with something I could help you on," the senator says. "You know damned well that my environmentalist convictions won't let me help you on this one."

"Well, at least you gave me some of your time," the young lawyer says amicably. "One of these days, you're bound to do something good for me. Anyway, I'll file a report with my people about our conversation, telling them that you can't help us, of course, and I'll get a good fee just for having access to Mr. Environment himself."

Next, the young lawyer goes over to the Old Senate Office Building. When he finds that the senator he wanted to see there is too busy to see him immediately, he speaks with the senator's administrative assistant instead. "All right, I'll make a call down there in the senator's name, and I'll have him sign a letter to the EPA director," the assistant says. "As you know, the senator is a farmer himself, and he's got little use for these red-hot environmentalists who want to save every grasshopper."

Back at his office, the young lawyer places two long-distance calls. One is to the president of his association, who heads a chemical company that manufactures pesticides. "This would be a good time for you to call your friend on the White House staff," he tells the official. "Tough regs are about to come out unless the EPA director gets a stern call from higher up." The other call is to a chemical plant manager in the home state of the senator who is known as "Mr. Environment." The young lawyer tells the plant manager, "The senator and I get along awfully well, but he's gone haywire again. I know he likes you, and I know he wants to protect those jobs in his home state. A call from you right now and also from the business agent of your plant's union, if you can swing that, might push him over the line and get him to help us quietly on this one."

Source: Fred R. Harris, *America's Democracy: The Ideal and the Reality* (Glenview, Ill.: Scott, Foresman, 1980), pp. 220–21.

★ ★ ★ ★

LOBBYING CONGRESS

An estimated *15,000* lobbyists now seek to influence Congressional decisions each session.[20] Less than a fifth of these lobbyists are registered with Congress under the terms of the Federal Regulation of Lobbying Act of 1946. That law contains a number of loopholes, including the definition of what constitutes lobbying. Individuals and organizations that spend their own funds in an effort to influence legislation are not, under various court interpretations of the language of the act, covered by the act unless they also solicit, collect, or receive money for the purpose of lobbying. In addition, some very active lobbies have argued that, since influencing Congress is not their "principal purpose" (part of the law's definition), they are not covered by the law, no matter what they do in the way of lobbying. Only five federal court prosecutions had been brought under the act through late 1979 (none since 1956). Only one of those cases, involving an oil company and two lobbyists, resulted in convictions (of failure to register to lobby), and the punishments ordered were fines and one-year, suspended sentences.[21] Congress has been wrestling seriously with lobbyist disclosure legislation for the past several sessions, and it may enact new legislation concerning lobbying. Penalties prescribed under any new act, however, will probably be civil penalties (fines) rather than criminal (involving possible prison terms).

The most recent lobbying scandal (dubbed "Koreagate") involved violations of numerous statutes concerning bribery, conspiracy, and violation of the Foreign Agents Registration Act, first passed in 1938 and amended in 1966. That law, originally enacted out of fear of Nazi propaganda efforts prior to World War II, requires that a person "who becomes an agent of a foreign principal shall, within ten days thereafter, file with the Attorney General" the details of his agency. A follow-up status report must be filed every six months. The Koreagate scandal, widely reported in the press, involved a South Korean rice dealer who was close to the South Korean government. Indictments in the case included assertions that a key subcommittee chairman had received over $200,000 in illegal payments from the dealer. (The representative was acquitted by a home-state federal jury.) Campaign contributions were given to many other members of Congress. The House reprimanded three of its members for behavior related to the Koreagate scandal.[22]

Such corruption as was found in the Koreagate scandal is the exception, not the norm, although interest groups do assist their friends with campaign funds and (less frequently and occasionally furtively) help challengers of their incumbent opponents, if they think the challenger can win. Many interest groups give campaign contributions to maintain access, the ability to obtain the time and attention of a senator or representative—or that of a key staff member—when necessary, to be sure the member knows how a particular proposal will affect the interest group, although lobbyists try not to wear out their welcome.

Access does not insure that a member will vote the way the lobbyist wants, but, over time, it can make a great deal of difference, since whom one listens to affects what one accepts as "reality." Modern society is extremely complex, and the results of many legislative acts are uncertain. It is very difficult, for example, for the average member of Congress to know just how a change in unemployment-compensation law will affect different sectors of the economy. If a member owns a small business back home and first entered politics with the assistance of the local chamber of commerce, he or she is likely to accept the statement of the chamber of commerce concerning the "real" impact of the bill. Conversely, if the member entered politics through or with the encouragement of organized labor, he or she is likely to accept organized labor's assessment of the impact of a bill as being correct.

★ ★ ★ ★

Lobbies and Campaign Contributions

This town works on personal relationships. Anytime there's an opportunity to develop those relationships, it's a plus. The most anybody figures they can get in this business is access. You can't buy a vote. What you can do is say, "Listen, I've helped you."
—Leslie Israel, professional fundraiser

I know it is true in most cases when members say they can accept money from a PAC and turn around and vote against them. But I think there's still sort of an unspoken *quid pro quo* of some kind. Whether it's lending an ear, or more than lending an ear, I don't know.
—U.S. Representative Don J. Pease (D., Ohio)

Source: "Fund-Raising in Washington," *Congressional Quarterly Weekly Report*, May 17, 1980, pp. 1335, 1346.

★ ★ ★ ★

Access is so important to a lobbyist's image that some lobbyists cultivate it, even apparently to the exclusion of seeking concrete legislative assistance. They do so to impress clients and potential clients, since it is very difficult for the client (or interest-group members) to know whether or not the lobbyist has accomplished anything on their behalf. Even if a decision were "wired" by a lobbyist, the decision-maker would not admit it; rather, the vote or administrative intervention will be defended by the legislator as looking out for the public interest as he or she sees it, or as an attempt at "fair play." If an interest has been successful in getting what it wanted, was it because of the lobbyist or because the legislator or legislators leading the interest group's fight really believed in the cause? If an interest group has not been successful in getting what it wanted, would it have been worse without the lobbyist? Those are difficult questions to answer, and they can result in lobbyists (and organization executive directors) exaggerating a particular threat and then trumpeting their success in defeating that overstated threat.[23]

Access to members of Congress is especially important to interest groups that have to deal with an unfriendly executive branch. Interest groups which fear that a change in partisan control of the presidency will give them an unfriendly executive agency (such as organized labor faces during most periods of Republican dominance of the Labor Department and the National Labor Relations Board) must maintain close relationships with the Congressional membership, especially members of the committees which control legislation of concern to them. Other groups *never* have powerful friends in the executive branch and must depend on friends in Congress to protect them. An example provided by Dexter is the situation of chiropractors. Chiropractic associations want equality of treatment in government health programs, the Department of Defense, and in money for educational grants and for colleges of chiropractic medicine. But they face rigid hostility from the physicians in command of the various relevant executive agencies. Numerous members of Congress, however, feel they have personally benefited from chiropractic adjustments, and others find substantial constituent support for chiropractors. The chiropractic organizations seek help from members of Congress to force "some bureaucrats to take note of the powerful feeling behind the cause. They could also, on some specific

153

matters, require by legislation that grants and aids and opportunities be extended on an equal basis with medical doctors."[24]

Rather than fighting their battles on the floor of Congress, most lobbyists prefer to work out satisfactory terms of accommodation at the committee or subcommittee level, where compromise on wording and amounts can be accomplished with greater ease. Sometimes, important victories are won by quiet negotiation with key committee staff members or by being able to keep a topic off the agenda entirely. Battles are fought in public only when the relevant interest group has no other choice; it has lost in the back rooms and is unable to obtain what it wants from the executive branch, so it has no alternative but to "go public" with its case. Sometimes, of course, an interest group prefers to accept a loss and try again at another time rather than make a public fight.

The strongest lobbies on Capitol Hill are those representing large concentrations of economic power. They mostly seek to maintain the status quo, with the exception of requesting an occasional minor legislative change or a change in the tax code. Such powerful "status quo" groups (called "confident" interest groups by some observers"[25]) include agribusiness, the oil and natural-gas industry, and the defense industry. They seldom fight pitched floor battles. They are supported by the dominant Congressional ideology, as well as by the Congressional rules which favor the status quo. When they do face a major battle, they present their self-interest as that of the nation—noting the importance to the country of a strong defense posture, of being energy independent, or of continuing to be the breadbasket of the world. Whether the weapons program being pushed, or the energy program being supported, is, indeed, in the best interests of the nation is often lost in the rhetoric about the national interest.

Lobbying Techniques

A number of techniques are available to lobbyists who seek to influence members of Congress. As noted earlier, one of the most useful techniques is to provide information to members of the relevant committees and work quietly with interest-group friends in Congress to insure that the interest group's perspective on an issue prevails. Confident interest groups—those whose interests coincide with the dominant ideology of the legislators—are most likely to use such methods and use them effectively. Such techniques are less likely to be useful for those interest groups (such as welfare-rights activists) whose demands run against the grain of most members of Congress. Groups which have few political resources may have to rely on demonstrations, sit-ins, and other disruptive techniques to get the attention of the members, as well as to create pressure with which to bargain.[26]

The lobbying techniques used by the various interest groups are determined, first, by the resources available to each group (financial resources, membership size, membership solidarity, members' social status, and so on); second, by the type of issue which is of concern to the group; and, third, by the Congressional structure for considering the issue or issues of concern to the group. Groups with large numbers of committed members, for example, such as Right to Life or the National Rifle Association, can stimulate large numbers of letters to members of Congress at the appropriate time. Interest groups whose members are local elites, such as television broadcasters or new-car dealers, occasionally ask their members to telephone their respective legislators about a given issue. Each interest group is limited by its resource base in the range of lobbying techniques from which to choose, and its choice depends upon the circumstances.

Relatively noncontroversial issues, such as most public works projects or most subsidies for particular industries (merchant marine or local airports), usually lead to committee-related lobbying that stresses information and persuasion, and the interest groups seek to develop close relationships with the relevant committees, members, and their staffs. Even lobbying for somewhat controversial issues of importance to specific groups (such as postal pay or bank or savings-and-loan regulation) is centered primarily on the relevant Congressional committees, along with the relevant executive branch bureaucracy.[27] The major political issues of the day, such as those discussed in presidential campaigns, are likely to give rise to mass letter-writing campaigns and to more lobbyist concern with floor activity. Even on these issues, however, lobbyists report that their focus is a bit more on the Congressional committees with bill jurisdiction than it is on the floor, although, once the bill leaves the committee, the lobbyists, of course, become more concerned with the general chamber membership.[28]

Political Action Committees

If the members of Congress are basically predisposed to view social issues and legislation from the same ideological perspective as a particular interest group, that group has a great advantage in the legislative process. Conversely, if most members are antithetical toward a group's perspective, that group is unlikely to succeed in lobbying Congress, regardless of the lobbying techniques it employs. No wonder interest groups are concerned about who sits in Congress and about the rules regulating contributions to Congressional campaigns. The rules concerning Congressional campaign financing have been changed substantially in the past decade to give a stronger role in Congressional campaign financing to business and professional associations.

The Federal Election Campaign Act of 1971, and subsequent amendments, requires detailed disclosure of Congressional financing, limits individual contributions to a candidate to $1000 per contributor per election, and limits political party and political action committee (PAC) contributions to each candidate. Limitations on large individual campaign contributions (mainly from business and industry) led businesses and professional associations to create PACs in large numbers, outdoing organized labor's efforts in that field.[29] Indeed, the passage of the legislation—primarily at organized labor's urging—could be used as recent evidence for the old proposition that political actors do not always know their own interests in complex circumstances.

In 1978, political action committees provided almost a quarter of the campaign funds for U.S. House candidates and 13.5 percent of the funds for U.S. Senate candidates—up from comparable figures of 15.9 percent and 11.6 percent, respectively, in 1972 (see Table 7.1).[30] Fred Wertheimer of Common Cause, in testimony before the House Administration Committee in 1979, asserted that the large contributions of PACs were corrupting the political process:

> Fred Radewagen of the U.S. Chamber of Commerce (is quoted) as saying the prevailing attitude today is that "PAC money should be used to facilitate access to incumbents." Justin Dart, the Chairman of Dart Industries, was probably franker than that when he said dialogue with politicians "is a fine thing, but with a little money they hear you better." Dart Industries' PAC was the second leading corporate PAC giver in 1978.[31]

According to Common Cause, "four of the five Senators on the Senate Banking Subcommittee on Financial Institutions received $181,583 in their last campaigns

155

TABLE 7.1

PAC Contributions to House and Senate Candidates, 1972–1978

	1972	1974	1976	1978
House Candidate Receipts (Millions)	$38.5	$45.7	$65.7	$92.2
Percent from PACs	15.9	18.4	22.4	24.8
Senate Candidate Receipts (Millions)	$23.18	$28.2	$39.1	$66.0
Percent from PACs	11.6	11.3	14.8	13.5

Sources: Roland D. McDevitt, "Interest Groups and Political Parties: Their New Roles in Congressional Campaign Finance" (Paper delivered at the 1979 Annual Meeting of the American Political Science Association, Washington, D.C.). Data for 1972 from Robert A. Diamond, ed., *Dollar Politics: The Issue of Campaign Spending,* vol. 2 (Washington, D.C.: Congressional Quarterly Press, 1973); for 1974 from Common Cause, *1974 Congressional Campaign Finances* (Washington, D.C.: Common Cause, 1976); for 1976 from Federal Election Commission, *FEC Disclosure Series,* no. 4 (Washington, D.C., 1977) and Federal Election Commission, *FEC Disclosure Series,* no. 9 (Washington D.C., 1977); for 1978 from Federal Election Commission, *FEC Reports on Financial Activity, 1977–78 . . . U.S. Senate and House Campaigns* (Washington, D.C., 1979).

from individuals and groups associated with banks, savings and loans, and other financial institutions."[32]

A recent study by two political scientists supports the Common Cause position. Ginsburg and Green found that campaign contributions are associated with shifts in Congressional support toward positions more favorable to the contributor, and, the larger the contribution, the greater the favorable shift in roll-call voting.[33]

Who Are the Washington Lobbyists?

What kind of people are the Washington lobbyists? To answer that question briefly, Congressional lobbyists are from about the same middle-class and upper-middle-class social backgrounds as are members of Congress, although a few blue-collar workers have moved up through the ranks of organized labor to become legislative lobbyists, learning the requisite skills along the way.[34] When choosing a spokesperson, a group feels that it will be to its advantage to select someone with whom legislators will feel comfortable and are likely to get along without difficulty. Having a lobbyist with a background similar to the legislators' helps insure such easy relationships and improves access. Not surprisingly, British and French interest-group lobbyists are similarly like their respective national legislators in social background.[35]

One study of 114 Washington lobbyists found that all but 12 had attended college, and well over half were educated beyond the BA degree. Forty percent held law degrees.[36] Only a handful had begun their careers as lobbyists; most had wandered into a career decision in which the next logical step was to become a legislative lobbyist, or in which they were the logical individuals to become legislative lobbyists to advocate their organizations' beliefs. Most had no prior experience on Capitol Hill before becoming lobbyists there. Only three had been members of Congress.[37] Quite a few of the lobbyists were businesspeople, active in their business or trade associations, prior to going to Washington as association executive director or legislative representative.[38] Those few former Congressional staff members who appeared in the sample worked primarily for large trade associations as legislative representatives, not as executive directors. Numerous former *executive branch* employees turned up in the sample of lobbyists. They were mainly persons with detailed knowledge of a narrow area of government regulations.[39]

In addition to their knowledge of technical details relevant to the interest group's needs—which are very helpful in evaluating proposed legislation—former members of the executive branch are also in a better position than former Congressional staff members to be aware of how wording of a bill, or the floor debate creating legislative history, will affect interpretations by bureaucrats and judges. Several lobbyists volunteered to Dexter, for instance, that former members of Congress would make poor lobbyists, mainly because they would not realize that they had a lot to learn about lobbying and because they would not foresee how the bureaus might interpret different kinds of wording.[40] Still, in 1980, more than sixty former members of Congress were actively lobbying Congress.[41]

Although lobbying is obviously a political activity, Washington lobbyists are less active in partisan politics than one might expect. About half the lobbyists interviewed by Milbrath had been active in partisan political activities, but only a fourth of them had continued their partisan activities while serving as lobbyists. Most had made modest personal political contributions in recent years, however. Less than 10 percent had ever run for elective public office, and even fewer had held public offices. Almost a fourth of them, however, had held appointive public office, mostly at the national level.[42]

The Power of the Lobbies

> There is a threat now that the oil lobby will focus its attention on the Senate. I think it's almost a sure thing and unless the American people speak out because of one reason or another claimed by some of the members of the Senate, we will see the windfall profits tax robbed. . . . I think I cannot prevail alone here in Washington with an oil lobby working quietly unless the American people let their voice be heard.[43]

Do well-heeled lobbies dominate Congress? Just as it is difficult for a client or an interest-group member to know the extent to which a lobbyist is actually effective, so it is difficult to "prove" that lobbies do or do not dominate the decision-making process in Congress. The answer probably depends on how important and visible the issue involved is. The less visible and the more "routine" the policy question to be decided, the more likely it is that interest groups in the relevant subgovernment will dominate the decision-making process.

Some observers of Congress argue that lobbyists are not nearly as powerful as former President Carter and certain columnists say they are. Milbrath, for example, found that the members of Congress and the lobbyists he interviewed rated the impact of lobbyists on Congressional decision-making as low, although the lobbyists rated the American Medical Association and the oil and gas lobbies as quite powerful. The lobbyists also tended to list large membership organizations, such as farm groups, veteran groups, and labor organizations, as powerful.[44] Milbrath argues that about all a lobbyist can do is seek access to a member and make the most effective possible presentation in the time and manner permitted by the member (a presentation which seeks to cut through the perceptual screen of the listener and which also subtly communicates the power base of the interest group represented).[45]

Analysis based on interviews of various actors also led Bauer, Pool, and Dexter to conclude that Washington lobbyists are frequently overworked, understaffed, and less influential than is popularly believed.[46] Yet, as Vogler notes, there are good reasons why members of Congress tend not to perceive major lobbying efforts as highly influential. He points out that members of Congress tend to think of lobbying as a situation in which interest-group representatives try to persuade a member to change his or her position on an issue, while lobbyists prefer to work through friends in the legislature, in part, to take advantage of the Congressional "cue network" by which members tend to go along with the subject-matter experts within the legislative body. Quiet lobbying of an interest group's Congressional friends among those experts can, thus, result in votes from other members who, quite correctly, do not recall ever having been lobbied on the issue.[47]

Clausen argues that, because most members of Congress are in relatively safe seats, they are less vulnerable to interest-group pressure than they would be if from competitive districts. Their reelection depends primarily on their own personal political organizations back home. Those personal organizations include certain interest groups on which the member is somewhat dependent, but upon which he or she becomes less dependent as seniority increases and the support base broadens. Because members are reluctant to change basic policy positions without good reasons (the electoral consequences of doing so are hard to foresee), it is unlikely that a member will fall out with his or her basic supporting groups over policy positions. Interest groups which are not part of the member's basic electoral coalition, however, "must *go to* the congressman and win his favor to the point of getting a hearing."[48] The member need not fear them.

Some observers note that the question of influence depends a great deal on the interest group and its goals. Some interest groups (confident groups) are correctly confident that the political "system's bias is such that their demands will be processed with a high probability of favorable outcome,"[49] while other interest groups perceive the system to be neutral or even negative toward their goals. "Confident groups are most likely to use persuasion, whereas neutral and alienated groups are most likely to resort to inducements and constraints, respectively."[50]

The chances of success of various interest groups depend, at least in part, on the type of policy which is of greatest concern to the interest group. Those interested in *distributive* policies, such as getting a new post office or other construction project in their area, subsidies for a particular sector of the economy, or a specific loophole in the tax code, are more likely to meet with success than are interest groups concerned with *regulatory* policies (such as environmental protection or campaign-finance regulation) or interest groups concerned mainly with *redistributive* policy decisions (poverty programs, civil-rights legislation, or school busing, for instance).[51]

The chances of interest-group success also depend, in part, on how many Congressional committees have a piece of the particular policy pie the interest group is concerned with and how many other interest groups are concerned about what each committee decides. "If numerous interest groups fall within a committee's policy domain, the committee and its leaders often have the upper hand; each interest group knows that it needs the committee more than the committee needs it. . . . By contrast, if a committee or subcommittee deals with legislation affecting only a small range of interest groups, the members of the committees are limited in the number of groups they can help and from whom they can receive electoral support. If, simultaneously, the interest groups have numerous other subcommittees or committees to whom they can turn, any one subcommittee tends to become more dependent on one interest group than that group is on the committee or subcommittee.[52]

The process of effective lobbying is subtle, and its results are difficult to measure directly. But it is clear that some interests (mainly those confident groups whose goals accord with the dominant ideology prevalent among members of Congress and the Rotary Club) are more successful than others. Presumably, there is some reason why educated and worldly individuals and corporate executives spend large sums of money to hire lobbyists to represent them on Capitol Hill. The growth in numbers of Washington lobbyists appears to be unabated. Part of that growth, of course, is the result of the increased importance of government in so many aspects of our lives. Another part may be the result of the fear of groups and individuals (even state and local governments) that others will get more than their fair share if "they" are represented by a lobbyist while "we" are not. But it is unlikely that wholesale fraud upon the clients of lobbyists is taking place; lobbyists probably are not receiving high fees for delivering nothing at all. Vogler is probably correct in his assessment of the impact of Congressional lobbying. After noting that lobbyists usually work with and through their friends in Congress, who often fail to perceive such attitudinal reinforcement as lobbying, Vogler concludes:

> Organized economic interests are able to get tangible rewards from the legislature, not by bribing legislators, but rather by using the advantages that the political system gives them. By providing information that reinforces the position of their supporters, by relying on inside lobbyists, by invoking legislative norms and political values that strengthen their position, and by working in conjunction with other political elites for shared benefits, these groups are able to benefit from policies coming out of particular subsystems.[53]

--------------------★ ★ ★ ★--------------------

Lobbies in the Texas Legislature

REPORTER: Who runs the [Texas] legislature in terms of policy; what kind of place is it politically?

SENATOR DOGGETT: I think the legislature is heavily dominated by those organizations that can afford to form a political action committee and hire a full-time lobbyist in Austin. Often on basic pieces of legislation the major players are not the elected officials, but rather the lobbyists who represent those trade organizations who've made the political contributions. . . .

REPORTER: Is legislation bought? Is that the import? I don't mean bribed. . . .

SENATOR DOGGETT: Well, I think we have very little if any of the kind of under-the-table contributions people in general are concerned about, but that's not necessary so long as the cost of elections is as high as it currently is and as that money is provided by a smaller and smaller group of people in the form of political action committees. They can exert influence far beyond their numbers through their political contributions.

Source: Interview by Ronnie Dugger with Texas State Senator Lloyd Doggett, February 23, 1981, reported in the *Texas Observer,* March 13, 1981, p. 11.

--------------------★ ★ ★ ★--------------------

INTEREST GROUPS AND STATE LEGISLATURES

In the past couple of decades, many states have seen the rise of concerned consumer- and ecology-oriented citizens' groups, which have not necessarily opposed the fundamental needs of the basic economic interests in the state but which have reduced the ability of those dominant economic groups to be as freewheeling in their behavior as they once were. Still, many states appear to be dominated by key economic-interest groups, and many state policy decisions are made by interest-group-dominated subgovernments. In general, but with notable exceptions, states characterized by weak legislative parties, a low per capita income in the state, low percentage of urban population, and a small proportion of the work force engaged in industrial occupations tend to have strong pressure-group systems, while states with more urban, industrialized economies and more competitive political party systems tend to have moderate or weak pressure-group systems. Strong pressure group systems are found in all the southern states, for example.[54]

Some pressure-group-dominated states are under the spell of a single interest group. Mining interests, especially the Anaconda Company, dominate Montana politics; oil and natural-gas interests ride astride the Texas political establishment; and the Du Pont Company regularly gets its way in Delaware.[55] "In Oregon, the lumber and ancillary wood products industry is the major source of employment, and its representatives speak often and with authority in state legislative politics,"[56] although the lumber industry has lost some major battles recently over environmental legislation. Other states, such as Maine, are dominated by an alliance of major economic-interest groups whose needs are mutually compatible.[57] In other states, politics is centered around the conflict between two major interests. In Michigan, for instance, that conflict is mostly between labor and management in the state's major industry—the automobile industry.[58] Some of the most powerful interest groups in the various states occasionally find it prudent not to press their self-interest too strongly when they are faced with organized opposition from consumer or environmental groups. But the fundamental concerns of such powerful interest groups are usually already protected by existing law, and they need only block changes in the laws that are important to them in order to protect their fundamental interest. Such negative influence normally can be conducted with a relatively low profile, consistent with a public relations campaign of being a "good neighbor."

Lobbying the State Legislatures

Lobbying in the full-time, professional state legislatures, such as those in California and New York, probably more resembles lobbying in Congress than it resembles lobbying in the part-time, amateur legislatures of states such as New Hampshire or Rhode Island. The number of members to be swayed is much smaller in every state legislature than in Congress but, as we have seen, much of the lobbying in Congress is committee or subcommittee lobbying, involving relatively few legislators. While the evidence is scattered, the importance of floor lobbying—being concerned about the issue positions of all members of the chamber as individuals—appears to be more important in the state legislatures than in Congress. In part, that is because the greater turnover in even the professional state legislatures results in less legislative institutionalization than is found in Congress—including weaker networks of cue givers and somewhat less committee authority. This is even more true in the amateur legislatures, of course. Getting a bill out of committee—or stopping it there—is still the most important chore for a state legislative lobbyist, but, in the state legislatures, unlike Congress, it seems likely that a lobbyist must spend substantial time on members of the chamber who are not on the committee.

Lobby Regulation

States vary in the degree to which they regulate legislative lobbying. Almost all have some sort of law, even if fairly weak. All forbid bribery. Some, such as Iowa, require that lobbyists register not just their presence, but each bill in which they have an interest and their position on each bill.[59] After a 1972 scandal over legislative influence peddling and banking legislation, Texas also passed a fairly rigorous lobby-registration measure. "Anyone who directly communicates with a member or employee of the legislative or executive branch is required to register as a lobbyist, if they either (1) spend $200 per quarter (except for their own personal expenses) or (2) do so for someone else for compensation or as part of their regular employment duties."[60] Texas lobbyists must identify each piece of legislation on which the lobbyist communicates directly with a legislator or a member of the executive branch. New York requires registration only by "those who are specifically hired to influence legislation,"[61] permitting many lobbyists to avoid registering. Other states model their laws after the federal act, complete with loopholes. Some states require reporting of the amount of money spent lobbying, although the states vary in what types of expenses they require information about. Common Cause estimated that in 1976, interest-group expenditures for legislative lobbying were over $3 million in New York, about $1.4 million in Maryland, and over $250,000 in Idaho.[62]

The number of lobbyists dealing with each state legislature varies greatly, and precise comparisons are difficult because of the differences in the various state lobbying laws. Over 3000 people registered as lobbyists for the 1977 session of the Texas legislature,[63] compared to 361 who registered that year in Kansas.[64] Only 112 lobbyists registered with the Oklahoma House in 1974.[65]

The difficulties inherent in evaluating interest-group activity and influence in state legislatures are made obvious in the following excerpt from a study by a political scientist with over a decade of experience as a staff employee and a member of the state legislature (New York) on which he was reporting:

> Campaign contributions can be an important link between politicians and certain lobby groups—although relatively few groups do contribute very substantially. Whether through a direct contribution or the purchase of a table at a legislator's fund raising dinner, or by subscription to an advertisement in a fund raising ad journal, the gift builds a tie between the legislator and the giver, with at least a slight hint at reciprocity implied. Since such contributions are legal, crude direct bribery is unnecessary and probably rarely resorted to. There is, of course, no way to determine the extent of the incidence of direct bribery, but people normally do not take unnecessary risks. Why should a legislator who, for instance, is an attorney get involved in a direct and naked payoff when he can simply and legally accept a retainer from the interested lobby group for his law firm?. . . [With respect to] the question of whether there are some legislators who are beholden to specific interest groups to the extent they act under the influence of personal lucre, the answer must be in the affirmative. Fortunately, the practice is probably not as widespread as the man in the street believes.[66]

And from California treasurer and former House Speaker Jesse Unruh:

> If you can't take their money, drink their booze, screw their women, and look them in the eye and vote against them, you don't belong here.[67]

The Competing Interests

As at the national level, the lobbyists attending the sessions of the state legislatures do not represent all sectors of society equally, and not all interests formally represented at the legislative session are perceived by the legislators to be equally powerful. Indeed, some of the most powerful interest groups are not mentioned by some legislators when researchers ask the legislators to list the most powerful interest groups in their state. State legislators in Oregon, for instance, failed to rank the lumber industry among the ten most powerful interest groups.[68] Michigan legislators similarly neglected to volunteer the importance of the automobile companies in Michigan, although they did volunteer the importance of the United Auto Workers Union, along with that of the farm lobby and the teachers' lobby. When specifically asked about it, the Michigan legislators agreed that the automobile-industry lobby "was, indeed, very influential, but that the lobby preferred to maintain a low profile."[69]

One reason legislators may not think of a business or industry group when asked to list pressure groups is that most state legislators are favorable toward those groups and tend not to perceive "pressure" from groups with whom they agree on the issues. In a study of educational-association lobbying of four state legislatures, for example, Zeigler and Baer found that those legislators who supported the educators' legislative goals were much less likely to feel "pressured" by the education lobbyists than those who opposed the education lobby's goals.[70]

Another explanation of why legislators do not volunteer the importance of a particular powerful lobby may be that it is so powerful that it can achieve its goals quietly, working only with the legislative leadership. An example of this phenomenon occurred some years ago in the amateur Vermont legislature.

> During the session the Associated Industries of Vermont (AIV) . . . and the CIO came to an agreement on a bill. They reached the agreement off the floor and the legislature then passed the bill.
>
> After the session Oliver Garceau and Corinne Silverman interviewed the legislators. One-third had never heard of the AIV and only a few less "had any notion that the labor interests in Vermont were organized." Two-thirds were unable to identify the lobbyists for either group. But the speaker of the House and the president pro tempore of the Senate were directors of AIV, even members of its executive committee. Several chairpersons of standing committees were members. Clearly the AIV lobbyists bypassed many of the amateur members of the legislature.[71]

Overall, lobbying of American state legislatures is weighted toward business and professional groups.

> . . . [R]oughly 58 percent of the registered lobbyists in the American states represent business, acting for either single corporations or trade associations. Additionally, . . . such lobbyists were far and away the most likely to be identified as powerful by legislators.[72]

Despite that skewing, however, observers of interest-group activity and public opinion in Iowa found that "interest group lobbying [of the Iowa legislature] tends to reflect and be supportive of public opinion in society as opposed to being distortive and contrary to it."[73] And a study of Iowa and Texas lobbying found that, as in Congressional decision-making, the influence of interest groups in state legislative deliberations varies with the type of policy.[74] A New Mexico study found that the distribution of opinion on the major issues facing the New Mexico legislature was about the same among state senators as among citizens, but the citizens believed the special interests had too much influence over the legislature.[75]

The dominance of business and professional groups in the lobbies pressuring state legislatures may be declining a bit, however. One observer of state politics suggests:

> The widening of pressure group activity to include interests other than established economic groups may be the most significant development in the 1970s in the states concerning the input agencies of state politics.[76]

The dominance of the lobbies representing narrow business and economic interests is being challenged by citizens' and environmental lobbies. Increasingly, too, cities, counties, local school districts, and other local government entities are lobbying the state legislatures.[77]

But interest groups are important. When state legislators prepare to vote on the many issues before them, interest groups are one of their three most important reference points. Analysis of responses from 1,256 state legislators in fifty states found that fellow legislators were the first choice of state legislators for obtaining voting cues, followed by interest groups and legislative party leaders. The governor and constituents were ranked far behind the above three referents.[78]

Lobbying Techniques

Lobbying techniques in the state legislatures are similar to those in Congress, although state legislative lobbyists do more entertaining than their Washington counterparts—possibly because members of Congress have so many invitations for dinners and parties that they lose much of their appeal.[79] The basic techniques of lobbying used in the state legislatures are set forth in Table 7.2, taken from a four-state analysis of state legislative lobbying. Three facts stand out from the table. First, whatever the technique, lobbyists tend to regard their activities as more effective than do legislators. Second, the various forms of direct personal communication seem to be the most effective. Third, bribery appears to be little used. Hacker, however, found that substantial campaign contributions by the Pennsylvania Motor Truck Association were quite effective in winning votes to increase the weight limitations on trucks, more so than the figures in Table 7.2 would imply.[80] More recently, campaign contributions were found to be a major factor in influencing the votes of Illinois legislators on ratification of the Equal Rights Amendment to the U.S. Constitution.[81]

Legislator Perceptions of Lobbyists

No matter what the lobbying technique, of course, much depends on the attitudes of the legislator toward lobbyists in general. A landmark study of state legislators developed a typology of state legislators as facilitators, resisters, or neutrals toward lobbyists.

> Facilitators: Have a friendly attitude toward interest-group activity *and* relatively much knowledge about it.

> Resisters: Have a hostile attitude toward interest-group activity and relatively much knowledge about it.

> Neutrals: Have no strong attitude of favor or disfavor with respect to interest-group activity (regardless of their knowledge of it), or, have very little knowledge about it (regardless of their friendliness or hostility toward it.)[82]

Some 36 percent of the legislators interviewed were facilitators, almost as many were neutrals, and 28 percent were resisters.

Not surprisingly, 63 percent of the facilitators thought interest groups were indispensable to the legislative process, compared to 39 percent of the neutrals and 14

TABLE 7.2

Effectiveness of Lobbying Techniques, as Perceived by Legislators and Lobbyists, in Four States

Method	Degree of Effectiveness*							
	Massachusetts		N. Carolina		Oregon		Utah	
	Legislators	Lobbyists	Legislators	Lobbyists	Legislators	Lobbyists	Legislators	Lobbyists
Direct, Personal Communication								
Personal presentation of arguments	5.8	6.6	4.7	6.7	6.7	6.9	5.3	6.4
Presenting research results	6.0	5.8	5.4	5.4	6.8	6.0	6.3	5.5
Testifying at hearings	5.2	5.6	4.8	5.3	6.1	5.7	5.1	5.0
Communication Through an Intermediary								
Contact by constituent	2.5	3.2	3.0	5.4	2.7	4.3	3.6	5.0
Contact by friend	2.0	2.5	3.0	4.2	2.4	3.7	3.4	4.0
Contact by other lobbyists	2.4	4.3	2.5	4.2	3.2	4.5	3.0	4.8
Indirect, Impersonal Communication								
Letter-writing campaign	2.0	3.4	1.7	4.0	1.6	4.0	2.8	4.0
Publication of voting records	2.0	2.2	1.3	1.4	1.5	2.0	2.0	2.4
Public relations campaign	3.5	3.7	3.5	4.6	3.5	4.0	4.1	4.6
Keeping Communication Channels Open								
Entertaining legislators	1.0	1.3	2.0	2.5	1.7	2.2	2.8	3.0
Giving a party	1.0	1.0	2.0	1.8	1.4	1.6	2.4	2.3
Campaign contributions	1.0	2.0	1.6	2.4	1.5	2.5	2.1	3.3
Withholding campaign contributions	0.3	0.1	0.3	0.4	0.1	0.1	1.0	1.0
Bribery	0.2	0.1	0.1	1.2	0.03	0.2	0.2	0.3
Mean for all Techniques	2.5	3.0	2.6	3.5	2.8	3.5	3.2	3.7

*Ratings of effectiveness on a scale from 0 (ineffective) to 8 (effective).

Source: Harmon Zeigler and Michael Baer, *Lobbying: Interaction and Influence in American State Legislatures* (Belmont, Calif.: Wadsworth, 1969), p. 176.

percent of the resisters, although even 60 percent of the resisters were fairly tolerant of interest-group activity and recognized some positive aspects of it. Facilitators tended to think of interest groups in specific terms, naming specific organizations or lobbyists in their comments. Resisters tended to refer to "broad interest aggregations" such as "labor" or "farmers."[83] Facilitators also placed greater importance on the views of interest groups and were more likely than their colleagues to report they had worked with interest groups in lining up support for their bills.[84]

Who Are the State Legislative Lobbyists?

Lobbyists are chosen for their posts in large part because of their ability to blend in with legislators and get along easily with them. As one would expect, then, the characteristics of state legislative lobbyists are a bit different from those of Congressional lobbyists. Over half are college graduates, most are men,[85] most are middle-aged. The groups the lobbyists represent, of course, include many citizens with different personal characteristics, including the elderly, children, women, the poor, and so on. Fewer state lobbyists are lawyers than is true in Washington, D.C., although in Virginia and North Carolina, the percentage of lawyers among the legislative lobbyists is comparable to the 40 percent Milbrath found among the Washington lobbyists. Reports from Massachusetts, Michigan, Oklahoma, Oregon, and Utah, however, set the percentage of lawyers among state legislative lobbyists at between 10 and 20 percent.[86] More common is the college-educated executive director or employee of an association whose position is being presented to the legislators.[87] The lobbyists for local governments tend to be the local elected officials or local government employees, although some local governments hire lobbyists.

Relatively few state legislative lobbyists are ex-legislators, but "quite a few have had some form of governmental or political experience,"[88] primarily appointive office, rather than elective, and at the state level more often than the local or national level.[89] But, in 1977, at least twenty-four lobbyists at the Michigan legislature were former legislators. Some of them had substantial lobbying firms with large numbers of clients.[90] Similarly, Sonis reports that "numerous ex-legislators in West Virginia have become valuable [legislative] advocates for coal, banking, and other special interests following their terms of office."[91]

THE NEWS MEDIA

The word *media,* much to the dismay of linguistic purists, has become the standard shorthand phrase for referring to the multifaceted communications media, including both printed and electronic means of communication. Both forms of communication are important to citizen awareness of what the legislature is doing and, in many cases, to the ability of legislators to determine how others are interpreting and reacting to legislative developments.

The news media, or certain members of the fraternity, are sometimes involved in the legislative process as ordinary interest-group participants, such as when lobbying a state legislature concerning a "shield law" to protect journalists' sources, asking Congress to amend parts of the federal law regulating the electronic-communications industry, obtaining special exemption to the federal antitrust act so as to permit the noncompetitive pricing of newspaper advertising in communities with two major daily newspapers, or insuring that a state legislature provides a sales-tax exemption for newspapers.[92] That the media often have a direct interest in legislation and in the success or failure of individual legislators' plans is nothing to ignore. Indeed, the alert citizen should remain aware that the newspaper, or its conglomerate owner, may not choose to proclaim self-interest in its stories (or lack thereof) concerning a particular issue.[93] But the relationship between the news media and the legislature goes beyond the media as a self-interested, economic-interest group.

The news media report what the legislature is doing (and is not doing) and often interpret the significance of that action or inaction. How well or poorly the news personnel do their jobs affects how open or closed the legislative process becomes, how much freedom from outside interference various subgovernments have, and what issues are dealt with seriously by the legislature. News personnel can provide a communications network which supplements or supplants the official one, and the mere existence of such an alternative network can affect public policy decisions.[94] An issue which is widely reported by the media is more likely to receive careful legislative attention than one which is raised only by senior bureaucrats and is endorsed by the appropriate legislative committee. Indeed, media attention can sometimes break open a subgovernment to outside influence and can tip the balance in favor of a bill, especially if the public interest clearly conflicts with a powerful lobby's preferences on an obscure measure.[95]

The various actors in the legislative process—legislators, executive officials, bureaucrats, lobbyists, and legislative staff—seek to use the news media for their own ends, including swaying public opinion concerning policy, testing ideas, and promoting their own careers. Media personnel seek friendly and knowledgeable insiders as sources of information. But much of the information sought by reporters is what the insiders would prefer to keep suppressed. So, although they need each other, the relationship between the media personnel and the other participants in the legislative process is an uneasy one. News personnel sometimes develop symbiotic relationships with key legislators or staff, giving up their independence and right to criticize the patronizing officials in return for "inside dope." And lazy reporters sometimes pass on the self-serving press releases of legislators as though they were reporting "professionally collected, written, and edited news."[96] But each legislator remains vulnerable to criticism by the news media, and each feels the need, to some degree, to compete for favorable media attention. Each legislator works especially hard at currying favor with hometown news personnel.

Congress and the Media

The importance of the media to members of Congress is most evident at election time, when large portions of each campaign budget are devoted to newspaper advertisements and radio and television commercials, and when the incumbent and challenger each structure their respective schedules to optimize chances of getting extensive coverage in local newspapers and on the local television news programs. Some observers even argue that the central role of the political party is being displaced by television-centered campaigns for public office, especially in statewide races, such as U.S. Senate campaigns.[97] In addition to this media interaction with *individual* members of Congress, there is also an *institutional* relationship between Congress and the media which requires attention.

The Impact of Television: House vs. Senate Michael J. Robinson argues persuasively that the development of the television industry has had different effects on the House and Senate. For example, television is less useful in many House campaigns than in most Senate campaigns, because of the lack of "fit" between TV broadcast areas and House districts, while the chance of an adequate "fit" between a TV station's broadcast area and the entire state (a senator's constituency) is fairly good. For similar reasons, the local TV news departments are inclined to slight their U.S. representatives while covering their U.S. senators. After all, the representative may only represent a tenth or fewer of the station's viewers, while the senator is likely to represent a majority of the viewers.[98]

The network news shows also slight the House in favor of the Senate. When seeking a conservative Republican, a Southerner, a Midwesterner, or any other "brand" of Congressional member to set forth a particular point of view on a policy issue, the networks tend to interview senators. Presumably this reflects the fact that senators, as individuals, are seen to "outrank" representatives, that each senator represents an entire state, and that each shares his or her chamber's decision-making with only 99 colleagues rather than 434. Television exposure of senators has increased the number of them who felt they could make a successful run for President. Further, Robinson argues that the more TV coverage an institution and its members receive, the more important the average citizen perceives them to be. Even the Speaker of the House has difficulty competing with senators for television coverage, even though he is normally the most powerful single member of the entire Congress. Thus, relative to the House, television has increased the perceived importance of the Senate and, consequently, has led to increased jealousy between the two chambers.[99] The fact that House sessions are now taped for television and clips from the tapes may be used on news programs is increasing the television exposure of House members somewhat.

Compared to the President, of course, even individual senators are not especially good copy. Thus, the White House generates many more network news stories than does Congress. The President's point of view is duly reported, but that of his opponents in Congress is usually merely commented on, at best. The representatives—and even senators—who oppose the President's policy proposals appear on TV to rebut presidential statements less often than the President appears. Thus, Congress, as an institution, is at a disadvantage relative to the executive in the dynamics of television news.[100]

Media Access to Congressional Activity Congress has not seemed especially anxious to offset the President's advantage in television exposure. With very rare exceptions, Congressional floor activity has always been open to the public and to reporters with pencils and note pads, but radio and television coverage has been more restricted.

Many local newspapers rely on the Associated Press and United Press International for their reports about Congress, although the major newspapers have Congressional correspondents, and some lesser newspapers have Washington correspondents who write about Congress as well as other national-government subjects. The national newsmagazines and broadcasting networks, of course, also keep a close eye on Congressional activity. Specialized trade magazines and newsletters also cover Congress for their narrow audiences, focusing on limited topics such as aviation or chemicals. All told, including photographers, some 2,700 reporters are accredited to the House and Senate press galleries. Most are print-media representatives and must file stories regularly, making it easier for members of Congress and their staffs to "use" reporters, although many of the resulting stories receive little notice. The large number of reporters also means that most committee proceedings and most Congressional developments are, indeed, reported,[101] but they seldom make the evening news on television.

On certain occasions, the respective chambers of Congress have invited radio and television to cover floor proceedings live, but regularly permitting such outside broadcast coverage has been another matter. Radio coverage of committee hearings has long been allowed, as has television coverage of Senate committee hearings. The Legislative Reorganization Act of 1970 opened House committee hearings to TV cameras by permitting (not requiring) committees to allow broadcasting of any hearing open to the public. Thus, both chambers of Congress now permit their committees to have radio and television coverage, if the committee so chooses.

Proceedings of the entire House or the entire Senate ("floor proceedings"), however, are a different matter.

The Senate normally permits neither radio nor television broadcasts of floor debate, although some senators have taken advantage of a loophole in the rules to broadcast their speeches on home-state radio stations. Basically, the technique takes advantage of the electronic speaker in each senator's office, by which senators and their staffs keep abreast of floor debate while remaining in their offices. By hooking into that speaker's connecting wires, the senator's office can transmit an acceptable signal to radio stations back home, using telephone lines.[102] The use of this loophole is apparently accepted by Senate leaders.

The U.S. House of Representatives began to make a live audio "feed" of its proceedings available to radio broadcasters in June 1978. And, in March 1979, the House also began to provide a live color-television "feed" to networks, cable television systems, and individual television stations which want the "feed." The cable systems use the "feed" more than the others. House employees operate House-purchased color cameras to record the floor proceedings; the broadcasters cannot control what appears on camera. In part because of the lack of control by network crews, the commercial network news programs seldom broadcast House floor proceedings live, although some PBS stations and cable TV systems do,[103] but there is some network news use of clips. Control of the cameras was an important point in the discussion about whether to permit TV in the House chamber. Many members wanted to avoid unflattering shots, perhaps showing a sleeping representative or a nearly empty chamber (much of the House's business is routine, and many members are absent during much of it). Others wanted to avoid biases they perceived in commercial news. Explaining why he supported House control of the cameras, for example, Ron Dellums, a black representative from California, noted:

> I want the right to speak out. I am also left of center. I make no bones about that. My politics are progressive politics; but I have stood with many other progressives on the floor of this Congress. . . . Pick up the newspaper. You never see one word about that, and we wonder why. Why are we not invited to speak on *Face the Nation* and *Meet the Press?*[104]

Some observers felt that the televising of House business, especially the right of members to purchase tapes of their own performances, might lead to much posturing, might affect the conduct of House business, and might be one more aid to the survival of incumbent members. In the first two months the system was in operation, only seven members ordered tapes. The one member who had distributed a tape of a floor speech to hometown TV stations found the criticism of abuse of the system more than offset the advantage of being on television.[105] But it is expected that the use of such tapes will increase. House rules prohibit incumbents from using tapes of proceedings in campaign commercials but, in a rare instance in which the rules advantage a challenger, nothing prohibits a challenger from purchasing a tape of an incumbent's poor performance on the floor and showing excerpts of that tape in the challenger's campaign commercials.[106] Few challengers have done so, however.

Does live television coverage matter? As one would expect, the introduction of television does make a difference and creates the potential for even more change. A survey of House members conducted by the House Administration Committee, after a year of televised floor proceedings, found that substantial numbers of members felt TV coverage had led to more floor amendments, more votes on the floor, a more partisan tone to debate, and to less compromise on amendments. Some 15 percent of the members thought broadcast coverage had made floor debate "more substantive and issue-oriented." Most members thought their colleagues were using "special orders" to reach their constituents directly on topics of particular interest at home. A "special order" is a one-minute speech on a topic of the member's choosing. A member is entitled to give such a speech at the beginning or end of each House session. Republican members annoyed the House Democratic leaders by using the "special order" in an organized way to criticize the Democratic majority.[107]

The reluctance of the Senate to admit television to its floor debates—and the opposition TV faces from House Speakers—is based on institutional considerations. For one thing, it is possible that the admission of television to the chamber could create fundamental changes in the relative power of members, once the potential audience increases in size. As Robinson points out, admitting television to floor proceedings

> might make telegenic profile or glibness the key to congressional importance. . . . Television could, if admitted into [Congress's] inner sanctums, produce for congressmen a new source of power *within* the institution, power not drawn from seniority or tradition or party loyalty but from television *savoir faire.*[108]

Further, the refusal of the Senate to permit broadcast media coverage of Senate floor debates and the insistence of the House on controlling House TV cameras has meant that most television coverage of Congress has been coverage of committee meetings. But what is more interesting to the television audience, arcane and detailed discussion of fundamental policies by a Congressional committee seeking to assist the average American meet everyday responsibilities, or an investigation of corruption in high places? The networks prefer covering investigative hearings. This leads to a public perception of "Congress—An Investigative Agency."[109] Because of the limitations of the media or the preference of industry executives, then, television has contributed to a somewhat skewed public perception of Congress. If asked, most Americans would probably say that they know that Congress passes laws. But many people are probably much more aware of the investigatory and impeachment powers of Congress than of its responsibility to write fundamental government policy.

News Coverage of State Legislatures

National news media occasionally find state legislative developments noteworthy, especially in the largest states, or when an amendment to the U.S. Constitution nears passage, but, for the most part, state legislatures are of interest mainly to the newspapers and radio and TV stations in the state. Quality of coverage varies. Legislatures which meet in state capitols that are located in small towns, for example, tend to receive less coverage than legislatures which meet in the state's largest urban center. Associated Press and United Press International have capitol bureaus in every state. These provide legislative news to newspapers and radio and television stations around the state, and they can furnish information also to out-of-state news outlets that want it. Independent capitol observers sometimes publish specialized newsletters, syndicated columns for state newspapers, or daily radio tapes for local, state radio stations. The major television stations and newspapers in a state normally send their own reporters to the legislature. The 1977 Kansas legislative session seemed typical. Twenty reporters covered the session. Seven were with the wire services, five from television or radio stations, and the remainder were from a local wire service and the daily newspapers of Kansas City, Topeka, and Wichita.[110] California, Illinois, New York, Texas and some other states have magazines which devote substantial space to state politics, including legislative politics.

Most state legislatures appear to be more accessible to the electronic media than

169

is Congress. A 1978 Council of State Governments survey found that at least thirty-two states provide special facilities for radio and television reporters. Many states provide television lighting and audio-feed lines in committee-meeting rooms and in the House and Senate chambers, and some states also provide special media rooms. Most states provide free space for the news media—electronic and print—but at least four states charge the media for space or for janitorial or utility expenses. A few states with centrex switchboards permit free use of these state telephone lines by the news personnel.[111]

In a majority of states, news media are given access to legislative chambers during sessions but are usually restricted to one particular area of the chambers.[112] Some newer state legislative buildings include special press booths from which television cameras can tape floor action or report it live.

State legislators have many of the same media frustrations that bother U.S. representatives. The radio and TV news programs and, to a lesser extent, newspapers, can report only a finite amount of news. Only the most dramatic legislative developments capture the attention of the radio and television news personnel, and much hard and important work by rank-and-file legislators is ignored by the news media in general. Even legislative leaders often find difficulty gaining adequate access to the news media to present their positions. The legislature as an institution is thus at a disadvantage in competing with the governor or state attorney general for public attention. Individual legislators are often frustrated by their lack of opportunity to explain their individual points of view to the citizens. Such restricted opportunities to communicate their views make it difficult for state legislators to receive feedback from constituents.

As Kirkpatrick points out, part of the frustration of legislators with the press results from the fact that "what is news to a legislator may not be news to a representative of the media."[113] Kirkpatrick points out that those legislators who manage to view the news from the perspective of the newsperson can avoid at least some of the frustrations of their colleagues by tailoring information and timing its release so that it fits the criteria of the news personnel for reporting. Included among Kirkpatrick's pointers are that the item should have readily understandable consequences, have something odd or unusual about it, be current—today's development, not yesterday's, relate to the reporter's particular audience, include a bit of suspense, be related to an issue concerning somebody or something that is prominent, involve some conflict, and/or have emotional content.[114] Not every news item a legislator wishes to "plant" in the news can be structured around all eight of those propositions and need not be. But the legislator who keeps the news reporter's perspective in mind is more likely than other legislators to succeed in public relations. That is especially true if the legislator's interactions with the press are based on positive and open attitudes. A legislator who is thought to be honest, cooperative, on time in meetings with reporters, and fair to all reporters is, Kirkpatrick argues, more likely to succeed in getting his or her point of view across in the news media.[115]

NEWS MEDIA POWER

How powerful is the news media? Very powerful, especially if one is talking about the power to place issues on the public agenda and to press the legislature to consider those issues. While executive officials have an advantage over legislators in the newsworthiness of what they say and do and in their ability to focus public attention on particular issues, editors, news directors, and reporters can also focus public attention on issues of their choosing. Indeed, a comparison of New Hampshire and

Vermont budgetary policies (decided by their legislatures) reports what may be the extreme case of a single newspaper's influence over the state legislature.

> While income elasticity of the two revenue systems may account for Vermont's acceleration of expenditures in the mid-1950's, the actions of the *Manchester Union Leader,* purchased in 1946 by the conservative William Loeb, have dampened efforts to change and reform New Hampshire's expenditure and tax programs, and therefore the rate of revenue rise.
> . . . [T]he editorial staff and sentiments of the *Leader* have been virtually unchanged over the last three decades. What has developed is a responsive and ideologically sophisticated claque at the public, legislative, and executive levels. . . . There is a well-known group of legislators who espouse the *Leader's* line in their public pronouncements and speeches on the floor. In a sense they are *Leader* vigilantes, ever watchful for possible transgressions on taxing, spending, education, equal rights, and human rights. In turn, they regularly deliver the *Leader's* messages in floor speeches. House and Senate floor action, even over a few days, clearly showed the steady clarification, elaboration, and hardening of the line advocated by the *Leader* in the speeches of the members. This consolidation of views had its parallel in the pages of the *Leader.* A reciprocal reinforcing process seemed to be at work. A common stand on current political issues has worked out in tandem—on the legislative floors and in the pages of the *Leader.* [116]

The news media are also very effective when lobbying in their own behalf, as is evident from their successful opposition, in Congress, to the FTC's planned regula-

---

★ ★ ★ ★

The Influence of Broadcast Lobbyists

Broadcasters act surprised when told about their lobby's influence in Washington.

"The broadcasters have a good story to tell in Washington, but they tell it poorly," network lobbyist Eugene Cowan commented in an interview. . . .

A broadcaster, Cowan said, "is no different than any other constituent. What can a broadcaster do to a congressman? Nothing. And he won't try to do anything either. It just comes down to the congressman not wanting to get many prominent residents of his district mad at him."

Are broadcasters, then, no more powerful than any other prominent constituent?

"Gene Cowan knows better than that," commented House Communications Subcommittee Chairman Lionel Van Deerlin, D-Calif., "It's not true and no one knows it better than Gene Cowan."

As lobbies go, the broadcast industry's is neither the largest nor the smallest, the most powerful nor the least.

"They're rich and have a lot of clout, obviously," [former President] Ford adviser Seidman commented. "But they're nowhere as good as the oil boys or the specialty steel industry."

Source: "The Broadcast Lobby: Resistant to Change," in *The Washington Lobby,* 3rd ed. (Washington, D.C.: Congressional Quarterly, 1979), pp. 205–6.

★ ★ ★ ★

tion of television advertising aimed at children. Or, listen to the then chairman of the Senate Commerce Subcommittee on Communications, Senator Ernest F. Hollings (D., South Carolina): "They are awfully powerful. . . . The average senator . . . [would] vote anything that the local broadcasters want. . . . He's very interested in satisfying that local broadcaster because it's instrumental in his reelection."[117] Seldom, of course, is extensive news analysis devoted to the news media's lobbying efforts on its own behalf, such as its efforts in the late 1970s to enact legislation substantially deregulating itself, and on its own terms. Fortunately, the interests of the various components of the news media often conflict.[118] In addition to print versus electronic media conflicts, the Independent Local Newspaper Association resists takeovers of family-owned newspapers by newspaper chains and has worked to revise inheritance laws for newspaper owners; the interests of radio and television broadcasters are not always identical; local stations and networks often disagree; and cable television is frequently at odds with the rest of the television industry. Still, even though not always unified, the news media are major actors in the legislative process.

SUMMARY

As is true in other democratic societies, the interest-group system surrounding Congress and the state legislatures is biased in favor of the dominant corporate and economic interests. Public-interest groups and environmentally concerned lobbies have become forces to reckon with at both state and national levels, but the special-interest groups, representing, primarily, the professions and specific economic interests, remain the most powerful lobbies in the American legislative process. Much of the power of the special-interest lobbies lies in the fact that they are usually involved with policy decisions about which few others are concerned and are able to get the decisions they want through "subgovernments"—interactions among the relevant members and chairs of legislative committees and subcommittees, high-level bureaucrats, and top interest-group lobbyists. The public-interest groups have difficulty responding to every such decision, and most are won by special-interest groups by default.

Interest groups do help inform legislators and help them ascertain who will be helped or hurt by specific bills being voted on. And interest groups provide citizens with an alternative channel of representation. But interest groups represent the prosperous more than the less prosperous, and few interest groups are internally democratic. Business and professional organizations comprise most of the interest groups represented before American legislatures. Such groups are also advantaged by the dominant ideology found among legislators and by the fact that they often win merely by killing a bill.

Both the national government and the states have rules regulating lobbying, and all forbid bribery. Most of the rules governing lobbying, however, have loopholes which some interests are able to use to their advantage. The favored technique for lobbying is to personally present arguments and data to legislators and committees, but grassroots letter-writing campaigns and telephone calls from important constituents are also used. Interest groups and corporations are increasingly forming political action committees (PACs) to help finance the reelection campaigns of friendly members of Congress. Single-interest groups are increasingly using their resources to oppose legislators who vote against their single issue, a tactic which other interest groups tend to shy away from.

Lobbyists at both the national and state levels tend to be college-educated, middle-aged men. The percentage of lawyers is greater among Congressional lobbyists; the percentage of amateurs is greater among state legislative lobbyists. Both the techniques and the effects of good lobbying are subtle, but lobbying does make a difference.

The news media also affect the operations of the national and state legislatures, both in their agenda-setting role and by keeping the legislative process open to public view. Legislators and reporters seek to use each other, and legislators are quite sensitive to the kind of press coverage they receive. State legislatures are more open to television news coverage than is Congress, although the U.S. House now provides a "feed" from House-controlled TV cameras. Television has long covered Congressional-committee hearings, but tends to cover the investigatory rather than the duller legislative hearings, thus giving the public a somewhat biased view of Congress as an investigatory agency.

Notes

1. More extensive definitions and discussions of interest groups in American politics are available in L. Harmon Zeigler and G. Wayne Peak, *Interest Groups in American Society,* 2nd ed. (Englewood Cliffs, N.J.: Prentice-Hall, 1972); G. David Garson, *Group Theories of Politics* (Beverly Hills, Calif.: Sage Publications, 1978); and Graham Wooten, *Interest Groups* (Englewood Cliffs, N.J.: Prentice-Hall, 1970).

2. Gerhard Loewenberg and Samuel C. Patterson, *Comparing Legislatures* (Boston: Little, Brown, 1979), p. 93.

3. Ibid., p. 94.

4. Gerhard Loewenberg, *Parliament in the German Political System* (Ithaca, N.Y.: Cornell University Press, 1967), p. 126, cited in Loewenberg and Patterson, *Comparing Legislatures,* p. 177.

5. Anthony Barker and Michael Rush, *The Member of Parliament and His Information* (London: George Allen and Unwin, 1970), pp. 265–78, cited in Loewenberg and Patterson, *Comparing Legislatures,* p. 177.

6. Andrew Roth, *The Business Background of MPs* (Old Working, Surrey: The Gresham Press, 1972), cited in John E. Schwartz and L. Earl Shaw, *The United States Congress in Comparative Perspective* (Hinsdale, Ill.: Dryden Press), p. 327.

7. Gerhard Braunthal, *The Federation of German Industry in Politics* (Ithaca, N.Y.: Cornell University Press, 1965), pp. 160–61, cited in Schwartz and Shaw, *The United States Congress in Comparative Perspective,* p. 327.

8. Peter H. Schuck, "Public Interest Groups and the Policy Process," *Public Administration Review* 37 (March 1977): 132–40.

9. T. R. Reid, *Congressional Odyssey: The Saga of a Senate Bill* (San Francisco: W. H. Freeman, 1980), pp. 26–29.

10. Randall B. Ripley and Grace A. Franklin, *Congress, the Bureaucracy, and Public Policy,* rev. ed. (Homewood, Ill.: Dorsey Press, 1980), pp. 7, 8.

11. Fred R. Harris, *America's Democracy: The Ideal and the Reality* (Glenview, Ill.: Scott, Foresman, 1980), pp. 232–33. Harris' account is based on Mark Green, "Why the Consumer Bill Went Down," *The Nation,* February 25, 1978, pp. 198–201.

12. See, for example, Murray Edelman, "Symbols and Political Quiescence," *American Political Science Review* 56 (September 1960): 695–704; William A. Gamson, "Stable Unrepresentation in American Society," *American Behavioral Scientist* 12 (November 1968): 15–21, reprinted in E. S. Malecki and H. R. Mahood, *Group Politics* (New York: Charles Scribner's Sons, 1972); and Theodore R. Marmor, *The Politics of Medicare* (Chicago: Aldine, 1973).

13. L. Harmon Zeigler and Michael A. Baer, *Lobbying: Interaction and Influence in American State Legislatures* (Belmont, Calif.: Wadsworth, 1969), pp. 2–3.

14. E. E. Schattschneider, *The Semi-Sovereign People* (New York: Holt, Rinehart and Winston, 1960), p. 35.

15. Zeigler and Peak, *Interest Groups in American Society,* pp. 40–41.

16. Robert Michels, *Political Parties: A Sociological Study of the Oligarchical Tendencies of Modern Democracy* (New York: Free Press, 1966).

17. Theodore Jacqueney, "Common Cause," *National Journal Reports,* September 1, 1973, pp. 1294–1304.

18. Theodore Lowi, "Interest Groups and the Consent to Govern: Getting the People Out, for What?" *Annals of the American Academy of Political and Social Science* 413 (May 1974): 86–100; and Garson, *Group Theories of Politics,* Chapter 5.

19. Murray Edelman, *The Symbolic Uses of Politics* (Urbana, IL: University of Illinois Press, 1964), pp. 179–80.

20. "The Swarming Lobbyists," *Time,* August 7, 1978.

21. *The Washington Lobby,* 3rd ed. (Washington, D.C.: Congressional Quarterly, 1979), pp. 4, 23.

22. *The Washington Lobby,* pp. 153–64. See also a series of articles in *The Washington Post* beginning October 24, 1976.

23. Lewis Anthony Dexter, *How Organizations Are Represented in Washington* (Indianapolis: Bobbs-Merrill, 1969). Dexter reports the example of a former benefactor from Texas who approached then Majority Leader Sam Rayburn, who asked how he could help. "Just this—let me be seen with you! Let me walk with you from your office to the floor or over to dinner. That's all." "That's All?" commented the Congressman. "You ask a lot less than most!" "Yes," replied the man, "If I am seen enough with you people will think I am somebody" (pp. 114–15).

24. Ibid., pp. 72–73.

25. Zeigler and Peak, *Interest Groups in American Society,* Chapter 9.

26. Michael Lipsky, "Protest as a Political Resource," *American Political Science Review* 62 (December 1968): 1144–58.

27. John M. Bacheller, "Lobbyists and the Legislative Process: The Impact of Environmental Constraints," *American Political Science Review* 71 (March 1977): 252–63.

28. Ibid., p. 257. These issues are often the same types as Lowi and others refer to as *redistributive* issues, which are debated in ideological terms. "Interest Groups and the Consent to Govern."

29. Edwin M. Epstein, "The Emergence of Political Action Committees," in *Political Finance,* ed. Herbert A. Alexander, Sage Electoral Studies Yearbook, vol. 5 (Beverly Hills, Calif.: Sage Publications, 1979). The number of corporate PACs grew from 89 in 1975 to almost 1,200 in 1980, in addition to 608 trade-association PACs, 305 labor PACs, and 377 unaffiliated PACs. *Dallas Times-Herald,* November 5, 1980, p. 4–G.

30. Roland D. McDevitt, "Interest Groups and Political Parties: Their New Roles in Congressional Campaign Finance" (Paper delivered at the 1979 Annual Meeting of the American Political Science Association, Washington, D.C.), p. 7.

31. Quoted in ibid., p. 6.

32. Common Cause, "How Money Talks in Congress: A Common Cause Study of the Impact of Money on Congressional Decision-Making," (Washington, D.C.: Common Cause, 1979), cited in ibid., p. 4.

33. Benjamin Ginsberg and John Green, "The Best Congress Money Can Buy: Campaign Contributions and Congressional Behavior" (Paper delivered at the 1979 Annual Meeting of the American Political Science Association, Washington, D.C.).

34. Lester W. Milbrath, *The Washington Lobbyists* (Chicago: Rand McNally, 1963), Chapter 5.

35. Harry Eckstein, *Pressure Group Politics: The Case of the British Medical Association* (Stanford, Calif.: Stanford University Press, 1960); and Bernard E. Brown, "Pressure Politics in the Fifth Republic," *Journal of Politics* 25 (August 1963): 525.

36. Milbrath, *The Washington Lobbyists,* p. 95.

37. Ibid., p. 69.

38. Ibid., pp. 70–75.

39. Ibid., pp. 69–70.

40. Dexter, *How Organizations Are Represented in Congress,* pp. 78–79.

41. *Congressional Quarterly Weekly Report,* December 27, 1980, p. 3643.

42. Milbrath, *The Washington Lobbyists,* pp. 76–82.

43. Former President Jimmy Carter in a news conference, July 25, 1979. Quoted in Richard A. Smith, "Lobbying Influence in Congress" (Paper delivered at the 1979 Annual Meeting of the American Political Science Association).

44. Ibid., pp. 348–49.

45. Lester W. Milbrath, "Lobbying as a Communications Process," *Public Opinion Quarterly* 24 (Spring 1960).

46. Raymond A. Bauer, Ithiel de Sola Pool, and Lewis A. Dexter, *American Business and Public Policy,* 2nd ed. (Chicago: Aldine-Atherton, 1972).

47. David J. Vogler, *The Politics of Congress* 2nd ed. (Boston: Allyn and Bacon, 1977), pp. 271–74. Richard A. Smith makes a similar argument. See his "Lobbying Influence in Congress."

48. Aage R. Clausen, *How Congressmen Decide: A Policy Focus* (New York: St. Martin's Press, 1973), p. 153 (emphasis in the original).

49. Zeigler and Peak, *Interest Groups in American Society,* p. 215.

50. Ibid., p. 111.

51. Theodore Lowi, "Four Systems of Policy, Politics and Choice," *Public Administration Review* 32 (July/August 1972): 298–310; Ripley and Franklin, *Congress, the Bureaucracy, and Public Policy,* pp. 20–26; and Vogler, *The Politics of Congress,* pp. 264–67.

52. Lawrence C. Dodd and Richard L. Schott, *Congress and the Administrative State* (New York: John Wiley, 1979), pp. 181–82.

53. Vogler, *The Politics of Congress,* p. 282.

54. L. Harmon Zeigler and Hendrik van Dalen, "Interest Groups in State Politics," in *Politics in the American States,* 3rd ed., ed. Herbert Jacob and Kenneth N. Vines (Boston: Little, Brown, 1976), pp. 94–97.

55. Ibid., pp. 98–101.

56. Ibid., pp. 111–12.

57. Ibid., pp. 96–98; and Duane Lockard, *New England State Politics* (Princeton, N.J.: Princeton University Press, 1959), p. 79.

58. Zeigler and van Dalen, "Interest Groups in State Politics," pp. 103–5.

59. Norman R. Luttbeg and Charles W. Wiggins, "Public Opinion Versus Interest Group Opinion: The Case of Iowa" (Paper delivered at the 1980 Annual Meeting of the Midwest Political Science Association, Chicago, Ill.). The authors report that the year after the new rules went into effect a lobbyist was formally brought before the Ethics Committee; the rule is now complied with.

60. Ernest Crain, Charles Deaton, and William E. Maxwell, *The Challenge of Texas Politics: Text with Readings* (St. Paul, Minn.: West Publishing Co., 1980), pp. 144–45.

61. Alan G. Hevesi, *Legislative Politics in New York State* (New York: Praeger, 1975), p. 182.

62. *Common Cause Michigan,* Fall 1977, reported in Charles Press and Kenneth Verburg, *State and Community Governments in the Federal System* (New York: John Wiley, 1979), p. 485.

63. Keith E. Hamm and Charles W. Wiggins, "Interest Groups in State Legislative Politics: A Comparative Analysis" (Paper delivered at the 1980 Annual Meeting of the Midwest Political Science Association, Chicago, Ill.). The Texas statute exempts many state and local officials from the registration requirement.

64. Marvin A. Harder and Raymond G. Davis, *The Legislature as an Organization: A Study of the Kansas Legislature* (Lawrence: Regents Press of Kansas, 1979), p. 24.

65. Samuel A. Kirkpatrick, *The Legislative Process in Oklahoma* (Norman: University of Oklahoma Press, 1978), p. 217.

66. Hevesi, *Legislative Politics in New York State,* p. 189.

67. Lou Cannon, *Ronnie and Jesse: A Political Odyssey* (Garden City, N.Y.: Doubleday, 1969), p. 101.

68. Zeigler and Baer, *Lobbying*, p. 34.

69. Gerald H. Stollman, *Michigan: State Legislators and Their Work* (Washington, D.C.: University Press of America, 1979), p. 80.

70. Zeigler and Baer, *Lobbying*, p. 118.

71. Reported in Press and Verburg, *State and Community Governments in the Federal System*, p. 481, from Oliver Garceau and Corinne Silverman, "A Pressure Group and the Pressured: A Case Report," *American Political Science Review* 42 (September 1954): 672–91.

72. Zeigler and van Dalen, *Interest Groups in State Politics*, pp. 110–11.

73. Luttbeg and Wiggins, "Public Opinion Versus Interest Group Opinion," p. 7.

74. Hamm and Wiggins, "Interest Groups in State Legislative Politics," pp. 14–27.

75. F. Chris Garcia, "Comparative Opinions of New Mexico Voters and State Senators," *Division of Government Research Review*, University of New Mexico, December 1978.

76. Kenneth T. Palmer, *State Politics in the United States*, 2nd ed. (New York: St. Martin's Press, 1977), p. 80.

77. Stephen W. Burks and Eugene DeClercq, "Urban Lobbying in State Legislatures: The Role of the State League of Cities" (Paper delivered at the 1977 Annual Meeting of the Midwest Political Science Association, Chicago, Ill.); and Jeffrey M. Berry, *Lobbying for the People: The Political Behavior of Public Interest Groups* (Princeton, N.J.: Princeton University Press, 1977).

78. Eric M. Uslaner and Ronald E. Weber, *Patterns of Decision Making in State Legislatures* (New York: Praeger, 1977), pp. 33–36.

79. Leon Epstein, *Politics in Wisconsin* (Madison: University of Wisconsin Press, 1958), p. 103; William C. Havard and Loren P. Beth, *The Politics of Misrepresentation* (Baton Rouge, La: Louisiana State University Press, 1962), pp. 235–36; Zeigler and Baer, *Lobbying*, p. 169.

80. Andrew Hacker, "Pressure Politics in Pennsylvania: The Truckers vs. the Railroads," in *The Uses of Power*, ed. Alan F. Westin (New York: Harcourt Brace Jovanovich, 1963), p. 333.

81. Judson H. Jones, "The Effect of the Pro- and Anti-ERA Single Interest Groups on Voting Behavior on the Equal Rights Amendment in the Illinois General Assembly" (Paper delivered at the 1980 Annual Meeting of the Midwest Political Science Association, Chicago, Ill.).

82. John C. Wahlke, William Buchanan, Heinz Eulau, and LeRoy C. Ferguson, "American State Legislators' Role Orientations Toward Pressure Groups," *Journal of Politics* 22 (1960): 213–15.

83. Ibid., p. 215.

84. Ibid., p. 216.

85. The fact that most lobbyists are men causes female legislators to interact with lobbyists less frequently than male legislators. In addition to their attitudes toward "give and take," Diamond notes that female legislators have fewer opportunities for informal contact with lobbyists than do male legislators. ". . . a female legislator said it was difficult for her to have lunch or dinner with lobbyists [alone], . . . whereas 'the men don't have a second thought about it.' " Irene Diamond, *Sex Roles in the State House* (New Haven, Conn.: Yale University Press, 1977), p. 108.

86. Zeigler and van Dalen, *Interest Groups in State Politics*, p. 114.

87. Ibid., p. 114.

88. Ibid., p. 115.

89. Zeigler and Baer, *Lobbying*, p. 52.

90. Press and Verburg, *State and Community Governments in the Federal System*, pp. 484–85.

91. Larry Sonis, "O.K., Everybody. Vote Yes: A Day in the Life of a State Legislator," *Washington Monthly*, June 1979, p. 24.

92. See, for example, Robert Sherrill, *Why They Call It Politics*, 3rd ed. (New York: Harcourt Brace Jovanovich, 1977), pp. 273–76; "How News Business Lobbyists Put Their Press on Congress . . . But with Mixed Feelings," *Congressional Quarterly Weekly Report*, August 2, 1980, pp. 2176–84.

93. While conglomerate ownership of newspapers may be leading the U.S. close to the European situation, the U.S. news media are mostly comprised of what Duverger refers to as "l'industrie de presse" (the newspaper business, whose purpose is to sell information) as opposed to "la presse d'industrie" (the press of industry, which is news media institutions "financed by big industrialists, by banks, and other powerful financial interests that seek to influence the public and the government rather than to make money"). See Maurice Duverger, *Party Politics and Pressure Groups* (New York: Thomas Y. Crowell, 1972), p. 113.

94. L. V. Segal, *Reporters and Officials: The Organization and Politics of News-Making* (Lexington, Mass.: D.C. Heath, 1973), p. 186.

95. A bill which seems to have benefited from such attention was the waterway user charge bill sponsored by U.S. Senator Pete V. Domenici (R., N.M.) in the Ninety-fifth Congress (1977–78). Such a bill had been introduced unsuccessfully for years, but the prestigious *Washington Post* followed the bill closely in 1977 and 1978 as a way to explain the inner workings of Congress to *Post* readers. That careful attention may have made the difference between the bill's success in the Ninety-fifth Congress, as opposed to the failure of similar bills in earlier Congresses. The opposition of barge interests was offset, in part, by support generated by the *Post*'s coverage, as well as by the support of the railroad industry. See Reid, *Congressional Odyssey.*

96. John T. Whelan, "Legislative Process Textbooks and the News Media: A Neglected Link," *Teaching Political Science* 6 (October 1978): 99.

97. William J. Crotty and Gary C. Jacobson, *American Parties in Decline* (Boston: Little, Brown, 1980), pp. 65–67. Edie N. Goldenberg and Michael W. Traugott examined 88 U.S. House contests in 1978 and found some 40 percent of the campaign budget, on the average, was devoted to media advertising. About half of the campaigns used no television advertising. (It is "inefficient" in many metropolitan areas and is too expensive for some poorly financed challengers anyhow.) But those which did use television spent much more on broadcasting expenditures than on print media. Nonincumbents, especially those who thought they might be able to win, spent the most on broadcasting. See "Resource Allocations and Broadcast Expenditures in Congressional Campaigns" (Paper delivered at the 1979 Annual Meeting of the American Political Science Association, Washington, D.C.). Robinson reports that in 1970 no money whatever was spent on radio or television in almost a fifth of the contested districts for the U.S. House, but money was spent on television in every 1970 U.S. Senate contest. Michael J. Robinson, "A Twentieth-Century Medium in a Nineteenth-Century Legislature: The Effects of Television on the American Congress," in *Congress in Change,* ed. Norman J. Ornstein (New York: Praeger, 1975), p. 250.

98. Robinson, "A Twentieth-Century Medium in a Nineteenth-Century Legislature," pp. 245–49.

99. Ibid., pp. 252–54.

100. Ibid., pp. 255–58. Recent presidents have even employed media experts to assist in making sure the President's message was received widely and positively. See, for example, Robert Locander, "Carter and the Press: The First Two Years," *Presidential Studies Quarterly* 10 (Winter 1980): 108.

101. Walter J. Oleszek, *Congressional Procedures and the Policy Process* (Washington, D.C.: Congressional Quarterly Press, 1978), pp. 37–38.

102. Irwin B. Arieff, "Senators Can Beam Home Speeches from Senate Floor," *Congressional Quarterly Weekly Report,* May 19, 1979, p. 948.

103. Ann Cooper, "Curtain Rising on House TV Amid Aid to Incumbent Fears," *Congressional Quarterly Weekly Report,* February 10, 1979, pp. 252–54; *Congressional Quarterly Weekly Report,* April 7, 1979, p. 637; Irwin B. Arieff, "House TV Gets Mixed Reviews But Cancellation Isn't Likely," *Congressional Quarterly Weekly Report,* March 15, 1980, pp. 735–37; and "How the House Fares On-Camera," *Newsweek,* June 15, 1981, pp. 16–18.

104. Richard E. Cohen, "Congressional Focus: Taking Matters into Its Own Hands," *National Journal,* June 24, 1978, p. 1023.

105. Irwin B. Arieff, "Few House Tapes Sold: Cost, Political Fears Cited," *Congressional Quarterly Weekly Report,* May 5, 1979, p. 829.

106. Irwin B. Arieff, "Television System in House Viewed as Election Threat by Some House Incumbents," *Congressional Quarterly Weekly Report,* January 19, 1980, p. 144.

107. *Congressional Quarterly Weekly Report,* March 15, 1980, pp. 735–37.

177

108. Robinson, "A Twentieth-Century Medium in a Nineteenth-Century Legislature," p. 243.

109. Edward J. Epstein, *News From Nowhere* (New York: Random House, 1973), pp. 251–52.

110. Marvin A. Harder and Raymond G. Davis, *The Legislature as an Organization: A Study of the Kansas Legislature* (Lawrence: Regents Press of Kansas, 1979), p. 25.

111. "Legislatures Open to Media," *State Government News* 21 (1978): 4.

112. Ibid.

113. Samuel A. Kirkpatrick, *The Legislative Process in Oklahoma: Policy Making, People and Politics* (Norman, Oklahoma: University of Oklahoma Press, 1978), p. 220.

114. Ibid., pp. 221–22.

115. Ibid., p. 223.

116. Richard Winters, "Political Choice and Expenditure Change in New Hampshire and Vermont," *Polity* 7 (Summer 1980): 610, 613–14.

117. "The Broadcast Lobby: Resistant to Change," in *The Washington Lobby,* p. 205.

118. Dick Brown, Susan Antigone, Richard Cowan, Ron Duhl and Jeremy Gaunt, "Media Lobbyists: An Unreported Story," *The Progressive,* July 1979.

PART III

Organization
and
Procedures

chapter 8

Legislative Leaders

Preview

Legislatures are relatively "flat" organizations rather than hierarchical ones, but a degree of central leadership is still necessary for the conduct of business. For the most part, American legislative leaders are legislative *party* leaders, although the presiding officer of each legislative chamber also has institutional responsibilities. The leadership titles in the various state lower chambers are usually identical to those in the U.S. House of Representatives, but the titles mask great differences among the states and between the dominant state practice and that in Congress. It is especially important to realize that the national Speaker has fewer formal powers within the legislative chamber than do most state lower chamber speakers. Most state senates are similar to the U.S. Senate in formal leadership positions, although twenty state senates elect their own presiding officer. Senates which elect their own presiding officer tend to have tighter leadership than senates presided over by the lieutenant governor. The similarity among senates in leadership titles can also be very misleading. The office of president pro tempore, for instance, is relatively powerless in the U.S. Senate and in many state senates, but in some state senates the president pro tem is the most powerful individual member. That usually is not the case, however, in senates which elect their own presiding officer.

All legislators are, of course, elected political leaders in their own right, and, in each chamber, they are of equal authority when voting on a proposed measure. But if the legislature is to accomplish anything, it must organize itself for action, and that requires some degree of centralized authority within the legislature—legislative leadership. Even those state legislative bodies with less than two dozen members find formal leadership positions important for the conduct of their business. For the two houses of Congress, with 100 and 435 voting members, respectively, centralized authority within each chamber is a necessity.

Centralized legislative authority rests, in the end, on the consent of the membership. So, the authority of legislative leaders is constrained by the membership of the legislative chamber. Leadership authority in legislative bodies is also constrained by the limited sanctions which the leaders have. Unlike most organizational leaders, legislative leaders do not control who may become a legislative member; they cannot adjust a member's pay on the basis of performance; and they cannot fire legislators.

The legislative leader's most important authority is control over the flow of legislation, the ability to expedite or stymie it. The legislative leader must truly lead; others will not (as in a hierarchical organization) obey for long, merely out of deference to a formal organizational structure. As Cooper points out, "Congress cannot tolerate highly differential distributions of organizational authority in any general sense, [but] power in the form of influence can be concentrated. Such distributions, however, run counter to individualist and egalitarian aspects of democratic values and are difficult to legitimize and sustain."[1]

Because American legislative leaders (except in Nebraska) are also *party* leaders, one cannot discuss the leaders and their functions without some reference to the political party in the legislature. Nor can the legislative party be understood without a grasp of the formal structure of leadership and authority within the legislature. Hence the discussion of legislative leaders in this chapter will include some discussion of the legislative party, and the extended discussion of the legislative party in the next chapter will include some observations concerning legislative (as well as party) leaders.

CONGRESSIONAL LEADERS

The leaders of the U.S. House and the U.S. Senate are elected by their colleagues in the respective chambers (except for the president of the Senate, a post reserved for the vice-president of the United States). The leaders of each chamber are independent of each other,[2] although Presidents often invite the Congressional leaders from both chambers to joint breakfasts or briefings. Congressional leaders are *party* leaders, and, when the two chambers are controlled by different parties, further differences arise within the Congressional leadership. The leaders in an American legislature, then, lead only half the legislature and, in each chamber, compete with the executive and other outside forces (especially interest groups and the news media) for control over the chamber's agenda and basic policy decisions. Congressional leaders are also limited by the independent power of the committee and subcommittee chairpersons, who gain their committee power mainly by seniority on the committee and thus need not be responsive to the chamber leadership.

Leaders of the U.S. House of Representatives

When people speak of the leadership of the U.S. House of Representatives, they usually mean the Speaker, the majority leader, the minority leader, the majority whip, and the minority whip. Sometimes they also mean to include the chairperson of the Democratic caucus and the chairperson of the Republican conference. The following discussion will include all these, and references to *committee* leadership will be made clear. Figure 8.1 diagrammatically shows the organization of the U.S. House of Representatives.

The Speaker of the House   The presiding officer of the House of Representatives is the Speaker. The office was established by the U.S. Constitution (Article I, Section 2), and it has existed since the first Congress met in 1789. After the vice-president of the United States, the Speaker is next in line to succeed to the presidency (only if the vice-presidency is vacant). That succession position may add to the status of the office, but does little for its power. Still, depending on the incumbent, many

FIGURE 8.1
Organization of U.S. House of Representatives

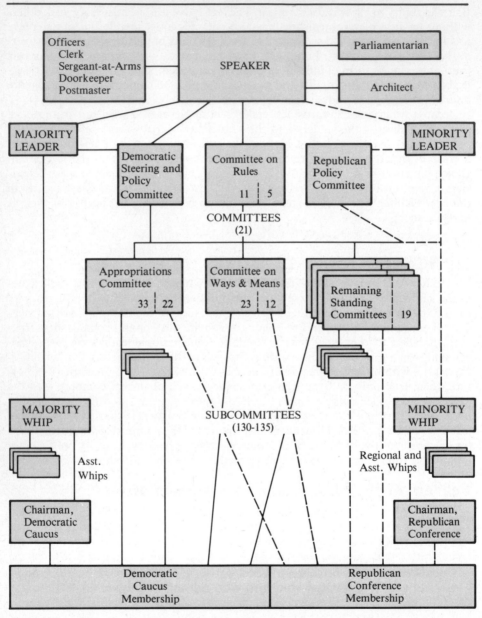

Democratic lines of communication: ——————
Republican lines of communication: ― ― ― ― ―

Source: Adapted from Robert L. Peabody, *Leadership in Congress: Stability, Succession, and Change* (Boston: Little, Brown, 1976), p. 30.

182

observers perceive the Speaker of the House to be the most powerful single member of Congress and perhaps the second most powerful person in the U.S. government. The Speaker is normally perceived to have more power than any single U.S. senator, because no one position in the Senate (as we will see later) combines as many strands of power into one person's hands.

The office of Speaker was originally modeled after the similar office in the British House of Commons, where the title derived from the occupant's duty "to speak before the king" and to convey the desires of the House of Commons to the monarch. Increasingly though, since the middle of the eighteenth century, the British Speaker has been expected to preside over the Commons in an impartial manner and to keep the office separate from party politics.[3]

By contrast, the duties of the Speaker of the U.S. House of Representatives are decidedly partisan. The Speaker is formally elected by the entire House, but, in fact, is chosen by the majority party caucus, all of whose members are expected to vote for the party nominee—thus insuring the election of the majority party's choice. The Speaker's responsibilities are to the chamber as a whole, but they are often subordinated to partisan necessity. To some extent, the partisanship of the American Speaker may be a result of a period of earlier, active partisanship by the British Speaker in the 1770s when American norms were forming, but the duties of the American Speaker also reflect both the present political system and the milieu in which the expectations of the U.S. office formed. The practice in the various state legislatures, in which most members of the first Congress had served, had been to elect a partisan speaker. This was carried over into the U.S. Congress.[4]

There is some evidence that, prior to the Civil War, the speakership was occasionally held by a relatively apolitical member of the House, but the post has been a consistently partisan one since that time.[5] The Speaker is expected both to look out for the interests of the House as an institution and to look after the interests of the Speaker's own party. As Speaker Cannon noted, "I am as fair as I can be, given the exigencies of American politics."[6]

If of the President's party, the Speaker is expected to work with the White House on development of party and presidential programs and to mobilize support for those programs within the House. Yet, the Speaker is primarily responsible to the House, not the President, and must remain conscious of the tension between the role as House leader and the role as spokesperson for the President. Often, the Speaker represents House opinion to the President while a presidential program is being designed, aiding in the tailoring of the program to avoid key opposition in the House.

The combination of powers of presiding officer and leader of party make the Speaker a formidable figure in the national government, if the occupant of the office so desires. As Ripley points out, the individuals who have held the post of Speaker have varied in ability and in hunger for power, and their leadership styles have varied accordingly. To some extent, each Speaker defines the role of the office, although the circumstance of each man's election to the post (only men have held it) has also helped to define his role.[7] During the late 1800s, the powers of the Speaker gradually increased, with substantial increases in the 1890s. The period from 1895 to 1910 marked the apex of the power of the Speaker. Under Speaker Randall (1876–81), the Speaker's power of recognition of those wanting to speak became absolute. Speaker Reed (1889–91 and 1895–99) obtained changes in the House rules which permitted the Speaker to prevent dilatory motions and filibusters in the House. Republican Speaker Joseph Cannon (1903–11) utilized the expanded powers of the office vigorously, especially control over the Rules Committee (which cleared legislation for floor action) and the authority to name anew, each Congress, all members and chairpersons of all House committees.[8] No Speaker since has had such sweeping authority.

> Speaker Cannon did not make changes in the formal rules, but used them to promote his own legislative preferences and to stifle the preferences of progressive Republicans and Democrats. As the progressive movement became larger and aroused more fervor, and as President Theodore Roosevelt became clearly identified with it, the attacks on "Uncle Joe" mounted. Because his position as chairman of the Rules Committee and his power to appoint members to committees were used against them, the progressive Republicans led the demand for rules changes to curb the Speaker's power. Most of the Democrats gleefully joined them, as much for political advantage as from any conviction that rules changes were needed.
>
> Between 1909 and 1911 the House took away much of the Speaker's powers over the rules. . . . These changes limited the Speaker's arbitrary power to control the flow of business. On March 19, 1910, after a fierce floor battle, the Speaker was removed from the Rules Committee, which was enlarged and made elective rather than appointive.[9]

While the 1910 revolt against the Speaker reduced his powers substantially, the office still retained more power than it had had prior to 1890, and the post has gained additional strands of power in the years since.[10] Today, the Speaker presides over the House, decides points of order, refers bills and resolutions to the proper committees of the House, schedules (with the Rules Committee) legislation and resolutions for floor votes, and appoints members to conference committees and joint committees of Congress. The Speaker's power to recognize (or not recognize) members who wish to speak or offer motions allows the Speaker to dominate the course of floor debate. This power is even greater when the House is—by two-thirds vote—expediting business by operating under suspension of its regular procedural rules. Although "suspension of the rules" has traditionally been used mainly for relatively unimportant measures, some major legislation—such as the Emergency Natural Gas Act of 1977—can be passed under suspension of the rules.[11]

By being at the center of the House communications network, the Speaker is in a position to know what various members need and want and to assist them, or hinder them, depending on whether or not they are "team players." Barbara Hinckley argues that in a "large and decentralized organization, in which information is a highly prized political resource, such a position [at the center of the communications network] carries considerable power of its own."[12]

Further, as the highest ranking member of the House, the Speaker is a person whose friendship is desired by other members, enabling him to use psychological preference as a resource. "A smile or nod of the head from the Speaker can bolster a member's ego and lead him to seek further evidences of favor. Being out of favor hurts the individual's pride, and may be noticed by his colleagues."[13]

The power to appoint members to committees was removed from the Speaker in 1910 and was lodged in party committees, where it remains. Each party in the House has a committee which, subject to almost automatic confirmation by the party caucus, decides on committee appointments. As leader of his party, however, the Speaker has had substantial influence over the committee assignments of his party members, especially to the three most important committees: Ways and Means, Appropriations, and Rules.[14] Members of the Speaker's party have continued actively to seek his support of their efforts to gain appointment to desired committees.

The powers of Democratic Speakers were enhanced in the 1970s by changes in the House Democratic party rules. In 1973, the Speaker, majority leader, and caucus chairperson were added to the Democratic Committee on Committees (then consisting, as it had since 1911, of the Democratic members of the House Ways and Means Committee). In 1973, also, the Democratic caucus replaced the inactive Steering Committee with a new Steering and Policy Committee, chaired by the Speaker. Half of the Steering and Policy Committee's twenty-four members are elected by region, but four are appointed by the Speaker, and five others are indebted to the Speaker for appointments to the whip offices, which allow them to serve, ex officio, on the committee.[15]

The 1974 elections brought seventy-five new Democratic members, mostly favoring reform, to the House. With their help and urged on by citizens' lobbies which favored structural changes in Congress, the Democratic Caucus strengthened the powers of Democratic Speakers even further. The Speaker was given the authority to nominate anew (subject to caucus approval) the Democratic members and chairperson of the House Rules Committee, each new Congress. The caucus also transferred the function of the Democratic party Committee on Committees from the Democratic members of the House Ways and Means Committee to the Steering and Policy Committee, which, as noted earlier, is chaired by and dominated by the Speaker.[16] Today's Democratic Speaker does not have the individual authority to appoint members to committees, a power wielded by turn-of-the-century Speakers, but is now the most important single actor in that decision.

Some other fairly recent changes in the rules of the House and the rules of the Democratic caucus have also added to the authority of the Speaker. The Democratic whip system has been strengthened, and this has strengthened the Speaker's hand. The new Congressional budget process (for the adoption of an overall House-approved federal budget to which all taxing and expenditure decisions must conform) has also added to the influence of the Speaker. Just as the Speaker now has increased influence over committee assignments generally, he also has important influence on the assignment of members to the House Budget Committee on which members may serve only four years out of any ten (on leave from their permanent committee assignment), and one of the twenty-five seats on the House Budget Committee is reserved for a member of the leadership of each of the parties. Too, the Speaker, in conjunction with the president pro tempore of the Senate, appoints the director of the Congressional Budget Office.

These gains in the Speaker's power (especially when Democrats are in the majority) are offset by a recent dispersal of committee power to subcommittees, by electronic voting and other new procedural protections for average members (which reduce, somewhat, the Speaker's control over the outcome of close floor votes), and, among Democrats at least, by a resurgent party caucus.[17] There are some—and Speaker Thomas P. O'Neill, Jr., (D., Massachusetts) is one of these—who believe that the power of the Speaker has been so weakened by these recent changes and by the new independence of the younger members of the House that it is difficult to get timely and concerted action in the House for leadership initiatives.[18]

The Majority Leader The position of majority leader (or majority floor leader) in the House has a much briefer history than that of Speaker. Until 1899, the chairperson of the House Ways and Means Committee was normally also considered to be the majority floor leader, "principally because the most important business before the House in most Congresses (the tariff) came from his committee."[19] The Speaker sometimes appointed other members to lead floor activity on specific issues. For twenty years after 1899, the Ways and Means chairperson was also the majority leader, but the two positions were formally separate. Since 1919, the two positions have been held by separate members.[20]

185

The majority leader is almost always the Speaker's chief lieutenant, and, in recent decades (especially in the Democratic party), has ordinarily succeeded to the office of Speaker. The majority leader is the number-two person in the party leadership and, as such, is expected to look out for the legislative party's interests in the House, to mobilize support for party programs and, when of the President's party, to assist in the passage of the President's program. The majority leader assists the Speaker in performing chamber leadership duties and is especially important in the scheduling of legislation and in deciding party strategy on the floor of the House. The authority of this position depends greatly on support from the Speaker, but the majority leader can assist colleagues in scheduling proposed legislation for the floor, is in a central position in the House communications network,[21] is responsible for "maintaining and improving external relations with the White House and the executive branch and with interest groups, the media, and the electorate,"[22] and works to insure the reelection of fellow party members.

When Democrats are the majority party, the majority leader's authority is bolstered a bit by party rules passed in the 1970s. Those rules make the majority leader a member of the party's Steering and Policy Committee, which also serves as the party's Committee on Committees. The Democratic party's floor leader also appoints the party whip, in consultation with the Speaker, when the Democrats are in the majority.[23]

The Minority Leader   The minority party's leader is the minority leader (minority floor leader) who is elected by the minority-party caucus and is the minority party's nominee for Speaker (with no chance of election to the higher office because of the party discipline of the members of the majority party). The minority leader is at the center of the minority party's organization in the House and, thus, at the center of the minority party's communications network. The minority leader is also not far from the center of the House communications network, an asset in maintaining authority within the party. The minority leader usually consults regularly with the Speaker and the majority leader on the House agenda, and the majority-party leaders normally consult with the minority leader on various questions affecting the House as an institution—although former Minority Leader John Rhodes (R., Arizona) complained that, under Speaker O'Neill, this consultation process broke down.[24]

The minority leader, as party leader, has influenced the minority party's choices for House committee assignments ever since those decisions were removed from the power of Speaker in 1910. If Democrats are in the minority, the minority leader's position on the Democratic Steering and Policy Committee would give the minority leader the same authority over committee assignments that the Speaker enjoys when Democrats are in the majority. The formal position of the leader of the House Republicans is not as strong, but this official still can have substantial influence on Republican committee assignments.

The minority leader is expected to defend the minority party's interests in the House, to mobilize support for party positions, and to supervise floor strategy and debate. Minority leaders originally focused on obstructing majority-party legislation, but recent Republican leaders (the minority since 1939, except for four years, 1947–48 and 1953–54) have stressed Republican programs and have sought conservative Democratic votes for their proposals. The minority leader must also, of course, cope with any morale problems which arise from being the minority, not controlling the House agenda or any committee agendas, and often losing on policy issues. Partly as a result of those frustrations, minority leaders have voluntarily left the House much more frequently than have majority leaders.[25] Minority leaders are also more likely than leaders of the majority party to be voted out of the leadership position by their party caucus.[26] The disadvantages of serving as leader of the minority party led Minority Leader John Rhodes to announce, in December 1979, that he would like to be Speaker if the Republicans won enough seats in the 1980 elections to become the majority, but that, if they remained the minority, he would step down as Minority Leader.[27] Despite the increase in House GOP ranks and Republican control of the Senate and the White House, he stepped down, succeeded by Minority Whip Robert H. Michel (R., Illinois).[28]

The minority leader and minority-party members are in a stronger position when their party controls the White House. In such a situation, they can negotiate with the majority party with more forcefulness, sometimes using the threat of a presidential veto, on the one hand, or presidential promises, on the other. Like the Speaker and the majority leader, the minority leader of the President's party speaks for the President's program, maintains liaison with the White House, and mobilizes support (among majority-party members too, if possible) for the President's program.

Party Whips   The party leadership in the House includes, in each party, the party whip. It may be, as one observer suggests, that the "purpose of the party whip system is not so much to lead as to discover whether leadership in any given area is possible or can be effective."[29] The party whip, however, works closely with the minority leader, or the Speaker and the majority leader, and, even the decision not to attempt to assert leadership direction on an issue is a leadership decision. Each party's whip is assisted by a large number of helpers. The Democratic whip for the Ninety-sixth Congress (1979–80), for example, was assisted by a chief deputy whip, three deputy whips, ten at-large whips, and twenty-two zone whips, each of whom was assigned a set of party members to work with from his or her region of the country.[30]

The title *whip* derives from the British fox-hunting term *whipper-in*, used to describe the man responsible for keeping the hounds from leaving the pack. It was first applied to the British Parliament about 1770.[31] The office emerged in the U.S. House just prior to the turn of the century, and the term continues to be appropriate to the office today. Each party's whip organization serves as a communications system to advise the members of the leadership's plans and to communicate member opinion to the leaders—including conducting formal polls on important issues on which the vote is expected to be close, keeping the leadership informed about member-vote intentions, and (when needed) persuading and pressuring enough members to support the leadership to insure victory. Equally important is insuring attendance at the floor vote, which sometimes means arranging special transportation. Effective leadership of a body of 435 successful politicians, each an important person in his or her own right, requires accurate information and an efficient information system. The party whip system is thus very important to the Speaker and the majority and minority floor leaders.[32]

The first Republican whip was appointed by the Speaker in 1897. From 1921 to 1965, the Republican Committee on Committees selected the Republican whip, subject to automatic ratification by the party conference. Beginning in 1965, the House Republican conference (caucus) made the post fully elective again, as it is now.[33]

The first Democratic whip was appointed by the minority leader in 1900, but the office has existed continuously only since 1921. The position has always been appointive, by the Democratic minority leader, or by the Democratic majority leader in consultation with the Speaker. Even the reform-oriented Democratic caucus of the Ninety-fourth Congress declined (by a four-to-one margin) to make the post elective. So, the office is likely to continue to be appointive for the foreseeable future.[34]

Conference or Caucus Chairperson The offices of Republican conference chairperson and Democratic caucus chairperson are not as important in the House leadership hierarchy as the other offices discussed, although the former is more important in the Republican leadership cadre than the latter is in the Democratic framework.[35]

The position of Democratic caucus chairperson was largely honorific until the late 1960s and was rotated every Congress or two "among senior Democrats who had not yet attained the chairmanship of a standing committee."[36] During that era, meetings of the entire Democratic membership of the House were rare and were usually confined to organizational meetings at the beginning of each Congress, at which the party elected a floor leader and, if in the majority, a Speaker, and ratified committee appointments. In the past decade or so, the office of caucus chairperson has developed its own independent identity, as regular caucus meetings began to be held (since 1969), and as the Democratic caucus has come back to life as an instrument through which Democratic members could attempt to assert policy control over the House. This development will be discussed in Chapter 9.

The position of Democratic caucus chairperson could be a stepping-stone to top Democratic House leadership, presumably also serving as a proving ground of an aspirant's abilities. In 1940, for example, Democratic caucus Chairperson John W. McCormack (with White House backing) was elected majority leader to succeed Sam Rayburn, who had just moved up to the speakership.[37] McCormack also later succeeded to the speakership. In 1976, Democratic caucus Chairperson Phillip Burton came within one vote of being elected majority leader, when incumbent Thomas P. "Tip" O'Neill, Jr., was elevated from majority leader to Speaker.[38]

The chairperson of the Republican conference also held a mainly honorific position until Gerald Ford defeated the incumbent for that office in 1963. Unlike that of the Democrats, the Republican post had not rotated. The potential of the office became apparent when conference Chairperson Ford later defeated incumbent Minority Leader Charles Halleck for the higher post, in 1965, and was succeeded as conference chairperson by Melvin Laird, who was later named secretary of defense in 1969. Laird's successor as conference chairman, John Anderson, unsuccessfully sought the Republican presidential nomination in 1980, and then ran for President as an Independent. The House Republican conference chair has substantially increased in importance over the past two decades, and there has been a parallel increase in competition for the office.[39]

Leaders of the U.S. Senate

Leadership in the U.S. Senate, like that in the House, is based on political party, but no single office in the Senate has as much formal authority as that of the Speaker of the House. And, within each party, the norm is for leadership to be more collegial (collective) than in the House. Given the strong egos of individual senators—100 of the nation's leading political figures—and the fact that the Senate is a much smaller body than the House, the Senate has less-rigid rules and, normally, less intense leadership than is found in the House.

President of the Senate The U.S. Constitution (Article I, Section 3) provides that "the Vice President of the United States shall be President of the Senate, but shall have no vote, unless they be equally divided." The vice-president, however, after a few initial appearances early in each term, seldom presides over the Senate. Nor do the senators encourage the vice-president to enter into the deliberations and activities of the Senate. Even former Senate Majority Leader Lyndon Johnson was made to feel uncomfortable when, as vice-president, he sought to enter into Senate activities. That is what one might expect, since the senators do not, themselves, select the vice-president and since the vice-president is often not of the same party as the Senate's majority.

When an important, impending vote appears likely to be close, the vice-president may decide to preside over the Senate, just in case there may be a need to cast a tie-breaking vote (a need which only occasionally occurs). The vice-president can also use the authority of the office as president of the Senate and presiding officer to issue rulings from the chair, subject to an appeal to the entire Senate. The vice-president's opinion can sometimes be very important, as was the case with the effort at the beginning of each Congress in the late 1950s and 1960s to change the Senate's filibuster rule (Rule 22) to allow three fifths of the membership to invoke cloture (shut off debate), rather than two thirds. The way in which the vice-president phrased such a ruling made a substantial difference in the tactical situation of the two sides on the issue.[40] Similarly, when Senate opponents of deregulation of natural-gas prices devised a new technique for delaying legislation (by filing almost 500 amendments to the bill, prior to the cloture vote), Majority Leader Robert Byrd (D., West Virginia) and Vice-President Walter F. Mondale

> devised a new strategy by which the vice president, in his capacity as presiding officer of the Senate, would declare those amendments out of order that he deemed offered for purposes of delay. The vice president ruled he has that power, and his ruling was sustained by a vote of the Senate. This ruling established new authority in the chair, in conjunction with the majority leader, to limit individual members of the Senate. Thereupon the majority leader began calling up the amendments, which were then rapidly and without either debate or appeal ruled out of order by the vice president.[41]

This incident caused a great deal of hard feelings in the Senate, but brought about a tightening of the rules in regard to "dilatory" amendments.

Still, despite the great prestige of the vice-president, a potential for succession to the presidency, and an occasional ability to break a tie vote, the vice-presidency does not qualify as a major center of authority in the U.S. Senate.

President Pro Tempore The office of president pro tempore (president pro tem) of the U.S. Senate is mentioned in Article I, Section 3, of the U.S. Constitution: "The Senate shall chuse their other Officers, and also a President pro tempore, in the absence of the Vice President, or when he shall exercise the Office of President of the United States." Like the office of vice-president, however, that of president pro tem has not developed as an independent source of power in the U.S. Senate, although the office is sometimes held by senators who are, separately and in their individual capacities, very powerful.

The office of president pro tem originally was filled on a truly temporary basis. In some sessions of Congress, more than one senator held the office; in other sessions, nobody was elected to it. A single senator began to serve as president pro tem until "the Senate otherwise ordered" in 1890, and, some twenty years later, the tradition was established of electing to the post the majority party senator with the greatest seniority.[42]

189

Neither the vice-president nor the president pro tem spend much time presiding. Much of the time, Senate floor activity is boring and routine and, therefore, junior senators are drafted by the party leaders to take turns presiding—much like a fraternity pledge chore—when the Senate is idling along. Power in the Senate, to the extent it is centralized, is in the hands of the party floor leaders, the majority leader, and the minority leader, especially the former.

The Senate Floor Leaders Leadership in early Senates was diffuse and changed with the issue. Floor management of bills and resolutions by the relevant committee chairperson or ranking minority member of a committee was common, early on, and only since the period between 1911 and 1913 has the Senate observed "the practice of electing a single majority leader or minority leader who would serve during an entire Congress and presumably would be reelected."[43]

The floor leaders have the right to be recognized first in floor debate—a substantial parliamentary advantage—and they also have some control over who else will be recognized and when. The formal power to schedule legislation resides in the Policy Committee of the majority party, but the majority leader, with the assistance of the majority whip, actually decides when legislation will be scheduled for the floor of the Senate. The majority and minority leaders also have substantial influence over the committee assignments for their parties. Perhaps most important, these leaders are at the center of their Senate party's communications network. Each knows who in the Senate party needs and wants what, and each can, in return for a Senator's support on other issues, be of great assistance to party members. Sometimes, something as simple as insuring a senator that a bill will *not* be considered on the floor while the senator is away on a brief trip is quite important to the senator, and of very little cost to the floor leader.

A description of Lyndon Johnson's development of legislative power from the various strands of authority granted to the majority leader (much less formal authority, for example, than that granted to the Speaker of the House) illustrates the potential of the office:

> The "power of persuasion" may be abetted by some favors Johnson was in a position to perform. He could help a senator move his pet legislation, not only in the Senate but, through his friendship with Speaker Rayburn and other crucially influential leaders, in the House as well. The senator, it should be added, did well to observe a "rule of prudence" and not ask for too much. Because there were always members who would help him on legislation of little interest to themselves, Johnson could muster a respectable vote for a senator's bill or amendment that was bound to lose—a substantial boon to a man who wants his constituents to take him seriously. Johnson had largesse to bestow in the form of assignments to special committees, assistance in getting appropriations for subcommittees, and appointments as representatives of the Senate to participate in international meetings. Because intelligence flowed in to him and he was the center of the legislative party's communication network (in a system which lacks formal, continuous communication among the specialized committees which do the work), a cooperative member could be enormously better informed through the leader's resources than his own. A master of parliamentary technique, Johnson could tell a senator how to do what he wished or untangle the Senate from a procedural snarl, instructing senators what motions to make and bringing them and the chair in on cue.[44]

The majority leader in the Senate is its most powerful officer. In many ways, the office's powers are analogous to those of the Speaker of the House, but far from identical. For example, the majority leader never presides. From the front row seat, next to the aisle separating the political parties in the Senate, the majority leader dominates the flow of Senate business on the floor. The majority leader's formal authority is limited; strands of power must be combined to achieve leadership goals. And some majority leaders (such as Lyndon Johnson) have been much more interested in dominating the Senate than others (such as Mike Mansfield).[45] Further, the authority and independence of the office often depend on whether or not the senator holding it is of the President's party and whether or not the majority leader and the President are in basic agreement on policy matters.[46] But, in any event, it should be noted that while the Senate majority leader performs many of the same functions as the House majority leader, the former is the majority party's leader, not, as with the House Majority Leader, number two.

The Minority Leader is, like the House minority leader, the minority party's leader in the Senate. As in the House, the Senate minority leader represents the party's interest in the chamber and is consulted by the majority leader on matters of concern to the Senate as an institution. If of the President's party, the minority leader speaks for the President's program. If not of the President's party, the minority leader attempts to establish a record both of opposition to the President's program and of alternatives to that program. By working with disaffected members of the majority party, the minority leader can sometimes see that such alternative programs are enacted into law.

Senators have certain expectations of their party leaders. First, they expect them to state the party's positions on at least some legislative matters, although some senators believe that such positions should be stated only when a consensus exists among the party's senators. Senators also expect their party leaders to appeal for party unity and loyalty on important issues, but the members resent coercion. Third, the senators expect their floor leaders "both to distribute and to collect information on scheduling and on substance."[47]

One should not stress the point too much, but it is worth noting that the Democratic party in the Senate concentrates the reins of party leadership in the hands of their floor leader a bit more than the Republicans do. Each party elects a floor leader (majority leader or minority leader, depending on the party balance in the Senate), a whip, or assistant floor leader, and conference secretary. (The conference is the entire party membership in the chamber.) In addition, each party has a Steering Committee, which makes committee assignments for the party's senators, and a Policy Committee, which is concerned with scheduling of legislation and, occasionally, with developing a party position on certain issues. The Democratic party in the Senate elects the same senator to the offices of floor leader, chairperson of the Democratic conference, chairperson of the Steering Committee, and chairperson of the Policy Committee. The Republican party elects four different Senators to these four offices, creating a more collegial leadership structure.

Party Whips   Each party has lesser officers who work with the floor leader. The most important is the party whip, or assistant floor leader, who fills in for the floor leader when that official is not on the floor and assists in daily tasks. In recent years, too, most party whips who were in office when the floor-leader post came open have moved up to the higher position, a prospect which makes the office of party whip attractive, even though it involves much tedious work.[48]

Because the Senate is smaller than the House, the effort required to conduct a poll of members is, of course, much less. Indeed, the floor leader may know pretty well how members will vote on a particular issue, just as a result of frequent interactions with them. But the office of whip in the Senate has nevertheless become more institutionalized in the past twenty years, with appointment of assistant whips by the Democratic floor leader and the appointment of regional whips by the Republican floor leader. Whip notices now alert Senators "to pending floor action, the nature of unanimous consent agreements, and exactly when roll call votes can be expected."[49]

Selection of Congressional Leadership

In theory, each house is free to elect new leaders at the beginning of each Congress. In fact, however, leadership in Congress has become "institutionalized" and fairly stable. The increasing stability (or continuation in office) of Congressional leadership seems in large part to be a consequence of lengthening service and the corresponding desire for stability by members of Congress.

The House of Representatives   The House Democratic whip is appointed by the Democratic floor leader, but the Senate floor leaders and whips, the House Speaker, the House floor leaders, and the House Republican whip are elected by their party colleagues in the chamber. Leadership in the nineteenth century Senate was fluid, as noted earlier. In the nineteenth century, House membership turnover was great and lengthy service was rare,[50] leading to the election of Speakers with only a few years' service in the House. The most dramatic example was the 1811 election of Henry Clay as the seventh Speaker of the House when he was only 34 and had served only eight months in the House. Clay later left the House to negotiate the Treaty of Ghent with Great Britain but, then, returned to the House twice and each time served as Speaker. In those times, the institutional boundaries of the House were not rigid, and "lateral entry" to House leadership was permitted.[51]

Clay was the extreme case but was part of a pattern. Of the thirty-three House Speakers elected prior to 1899, twenty-five had eight years or less of prior House service, and none had more than fourteen years of prior service. Of the fourteen Speakers elected from 1899 on, all had fifteen or more years of prior House service, and twelve had twenty-one or more years of service.[52] Why the difference? Apparently, the internal organizational changes in the House reflected changes in the political party system and in electoral politics. As the national government's importance grew and the possibilities of power inherent in Congress became more obvious, more U.S. representatives sought reelection, but intense partisan politics in most Congressional districts constituted a barrier to long service. The election of 1896, however, resulted in partisan realignment in most Congressional districts, meaning that incumbents could consider making House service a career. The percentage of members who were first-termers began a steady decline, average seniority increased, and the prior service required for election as Speaker increased, as more senior members insisted that their experience and service be recognized (see Figure 8.2).[53]

Today, the route to top leadership positions in the U.S. House of Representatives is long service in the House and service in apprentice leadership posts along the way. Further, once one attains the Speaker's office, one now remains in that office (party majorities permitting) until death or old age requires departure. No longer do Speakers look to the Senate or the presidency. The process of being elected to lesser leadership posts and eventually to the Speakership exposes one to the buffeting of many forces from the larger political world (as interest groups compete to create a friendly leadership atmosphere for their purposes), but the focus of the office has become

192

★ ★ ★ ★

The Congressional Career Then and Now

The structure of the legislative career and the relationship between the two houses on Capitol Hill are largely the result of changes which occurred in the late nineteenth and early twentieth centuries. Throughout most of the nineteenth century service in the House was likely to be a matter of one or, at most, a few terms. . . .

Up until the 1890s only a handful of men had pursued substantial lifetime careers within the House, and they were often the occasion for puzzled comment. Committee chairmen, minority leaders, and even speakers of the House would leap at the chance to leave that body and become freshmen senators (or sometimes governors). . . .

Service in the Senate was highly prized, and after the 1820s it was generally regarded as preferable to *any* position in the House, including the speakership. Henry Clay was only the first speaker to move to the Senate; he was followed by James G. Blaine, John G. Carlisle, Charles F. Crisp, and Frederick H. Gillett. . . .

In the context of the past twenty or thirty years such behavior is unthinkable. Since the 1920s no speaker, majority leader, or minority leader has left the House to seek any other elective office. And the departure of major committee chairmen is almost as rare. . . .

Even before the Civil War a major political career could be carved in the Senate. Thomas Hart Benton's twenty nine and one half years years (1821–1851, defeated in his bid for a sixth term) is only one extreme example. . . . Since the Senate had only one-third of its membership up for election every two years, it operated as a continuing body. Committee selections generally were made as vacancies occurred, and once made they were usually held for as long as a senator served. . . .

The situation in the nineteenth-century House could hardly have been more different. Every two years a member's committee assignment and even his continued service were at the mercy not only of the voters but also of the majority party and the speaker. . . .

If a member was fortunate enough to be renamed by his party, reelected by the voters, and escape a partisan challenge to his right to his seat, he would return to a House where committee assignments and chairmanships were openly bartered for in the process of determining the party leadership. . . .

Such a system provides flexibility, of one sort or another, but virtually rules out making a systematic career of serving in the House. . . .

Source: H. Douglas Price, "The Congressional Career Then and Now," in Nelson W. Polsby, ed., *Congressional Behavior* (New York: Random House, 1971), pp. 16–20.

★ ★ ★ ★

so institutional (inward) that the post, even though more powerful than that of vice-president and next to it in line of succession, is no longer considered a stepping-stone to a serious presidential candidacy. A dramatic change in electoral stability, of course, could alter that situation.

FIGURE 8.2

The Growth of "Seniority" in Membership, Appointment of Chairmen and House Leadership

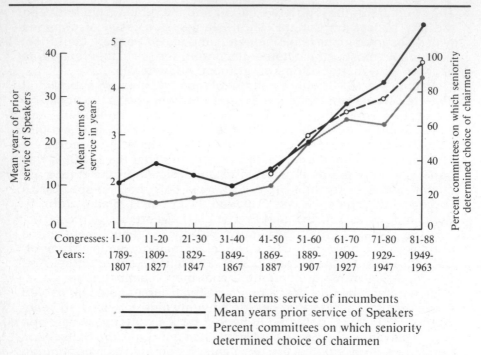

Mean terms service of incumbents
Mean years prior service of Speakers
Percent committees on which seniority
determined choice of chairmen

Sources: Barbara Hinckley, *Stability and Change in Congress,* 2nd ed. (New York: Harper and Row, 1978), p. 74. Data for incumbents and House Speakers from Nelson Polsby, "The Institutionalization of the House of Representatives," *American Political Science Review* (March 1968), pp. 147, 149. Data for seniority in chairmanships from Nelson Polsby, "The Growth of the Seniority System in the U.S. House of Representatives," *American Political Science Review* (September 1967), pp. 792, 793.

Long years of House service (seniority) is not a sufficient condition for selection as a leader but does seem to be a necessary one. While Speakers, floor leaders, and whips are *not* selected on the sole basis of seniority in the House, at least five terms of service (ten years) seems to be a minimum requirement for one to be seriously considered for a House leadership post.[54]

The election of the Speaker is no longer an intense contest. Rather, says Barbara Hinckley,

> the actual selection bears all the marks of a much more automatic procedure. Leaders stay in their posts for a number of congresses. New leaders are recruited from apprenticeship posts. Whip leads to floor leader. Floor leader to Speaker. The clearest case of this recruitment has occurred with the House Democrats.[55]

Further, no House Speaker has failed to be reelected to that post in the twentieth century, except when the Speaker's party lost its majority in the House. Even then, the Speaker remained the party's leader, as minority leader in the next Congress.

The Democratic pattern of promotion from whip (appointed by the majority leader and Speaker) to majority leader and then to Speaker, as the higher offices come open, had, until 1976, gone uninterrupted among Democrats for over thirty years, despite serious challenges for the majority leader position and efforts to have the Democratic whip elected, rather than appointed.[56] Following the 1976 general elections, the Democratic members of the House caucused to elevate Majority Leader O'Neill to the speakership, continuing the automatic-promotion process. But Majority Whip John McFall (D., California) failed to win promotion to the majority leader post, in part because of his conservative views and in part because he was reported to have received contributions to his office account from South Korean lobbyists.[57] Candidates for the Democratic majority leader position included Richard Bolling of Missouri, a leader of the reorganization and internal reform movement in the House; Phillip Burton of California, chairperson of the Democratic caucus; and Jim Wright of Texas. In the third round of balloting, Wright won by one vote. Wright, with twenty-two years of House service, was in line to become chairperson of the House Public Works Committee, a position he relinquished when elected majority leader. He had served four years as one of three deputy whips, following service as an assistant whip for the Texas delegation.[58]

House Republicans have had a much more open recruitment process to the floor leader's job (minority leader in recent years) than the Democrats. For years, the Republican whip had not moved up to higher leadership posts. Indeed, one member served as whip from 1943 through 1974. An observer thus recently concluded, "Unlike the Democratic whip, the Republican whip is not part of the rank structure."[59] Like all other institutions, however, Congress continues to change, and the contest for Republican minority leader for the Ninety-seventh Congress (1981–82) featured a contest between the party whip since 1975, Robert H. Michel, a former chairperson of the Republican Congressional Campaign Committee, and Guy Vander Jogt, the then chairperson of the Campaign Committee. Michel served on the powerful and prestigious House Appropriations Committee, Vander Jogt on the equally powerful and prestigious House Ways and Means Committee. In part because of his performance as whip, Michel won the minority-leader post.[60]

Among the four House Republican (minority) leaders who preceded Michel, Joseph W. Martin of Massachusetts (who also served as Speaker) had served fourteen years in the House and was Republican Congressional Campaign Committee chairperson, as well as an assistant whip, before his election to minority leader. He then served as the leader of the House GOP for twenty years! Charles Halleck of Indiana had served as his party's number-two leader, majority leader, while Martin served as Speaker, in the Eightieth and Eighty-third Congresses respectively. Halleck then defeated Martin for minority leader in the Eighty-sixth Congress, after twenty-four years of service in the House. Six years later, Gerald Ford, with sixteen years of service, defeated Halleck for minority leader, after service as chairperson of the Republican conference and as the ranking Republican on the House Appropriations Committee. Rhodes, a twenty-one year House veteran, was the number-two Republican on the House Appropriations Committee and chairperson of the Republican Policy Committee when he was unanimously elected minority leader after Ford became vice-president.[61]

Recruitment paths to the top House Republican leadership office, then, appear to be more diffuse than is the case among House Democrats, although prior service in some other party leadership office appears to be a prerequisite. By further contrast to House Democrats, House Republicans are willing and able to turn out their leader, as they did in 1959 with Martin and in 1965 with Halleck. The extent to which the greater willingness of House Republicans to displace their top leader is the result of their frustration at being the minority party in the House and their feeling—especially after a particularly severe electoral setback—that they must *do* something is a matter which has been debated at some length.[62] Nelson argues that the difference between the two House parties in their loyalty to incumbent leaders is less a matter of minority or majority status than it is one of party cohesiveness or homogeneity, and is a result of the need of the Democrats to minimize conflict among their "large and heterogeneous mix of contending social groups, regions, and ideologies."[63] An uncontrolled leadership contest in such a legislative party could result in great changes in the party's legislative agenda and substantial changes in the power of individual members or their access to power. The Republicans, Nelson argues, can afford their open recruitment to the top House party-leadership post, because open competition among members of a relatively homogeneous party is unlikely to result in substantial changes in priorities for that legislative party. A further, partial, explanation for the greater leadership stability among House Democrats than among House Republicans may be that the House Democratic membership has been more senior than that of House Republicans. These committee chairpersons and state delegation heads have invested heavily in the existing order and are reluctant to change it.[64]

The Senate Selection of party floor leaders in the Senate during the past thirty years demonstrates much of the same regularity found in the promotion of House Democratic leaders, but there are exceptions in the Senate, too, and, like the House, the exceptions are most significant among the Senate Republicans. Evaluating the succession of whips to floor leader positions from 1913 to 1974, Robert L. Peabody notes:

> Prior to 1947, five incumbent whips (one of them twice) were in a position to succeed to a vacancy in the floor leadership, but only one of these . . . advanced. Since 1947, all three Democrats who had that opportunity . . . did, in fact, become floor leaders. Three of the last four Republican whips with that opportunity . . . made similar advancements. Only Leverett Saltonstall of Massachusetts was passed over. . . . A majority of his Republican colleagues apparently considered him too liberal for the floor leadership position.[65]

Since Peabody's study, another Republican whip has been denied promotion to minority leader, by one vote. In 1977, Howard Baker of Tennessee defeated Republican Whip Robert Griffin for the vacant office of minority leader by a vote of 19 to 18.[66] Senator Baker became majority leader in 1981 when the Republicans took control of the Senate. Since Peabody's study, also, a fourth Democratic whip was routinely promoted, when Senator Robert Byrd of West Virginia was elected majority leader upon the retirement of Senator Mike Mansfield of Montana, who had been in the majority leader post since 1961. Senator Mansfield's sixteen-year tenure as majority leader also indicates the stability of the leadership in the Senate.

At the level of party whip, however, Senate Democrats have had a bit more dissension. Senator Edward Kennedy of Massachusetts defeated Senator Russell Long of Louisiana for Democratic whip in 1969, only himself to lose the post two years later to Senator Robert Byrd, the secretary of the Senate Democratic conference and the nominal number-three Democratic leader in the Senate.[67]

Committee Leaders

So far, our discussion of leadership in Congress has focused on leadership posts which can be considered chamber-leadership posts (or party-leadership posts). The holders of these offices are elected by their party colleagues in the chamber. (The Speaker is formally chosen by all members but, in fact, is selected by the Speaker's party colleagues.) The other set of powerful leaders in Congress are the committee and subcommittee chairpersons and the ranking minority members. Committees and their functions will be discussed in greater detail in Chapters 10 and 11. Here, the means by which a person becomes a committee leader, and the difference between the means of promotion and the procedures leading to the elective posts of Speaker, floor leader, whip, and conference (caucus) chair will be considered.

The fundamental difference is that, with some exceptions and some unwieldy methods for circumventing the automatic nature of the committee and subcommittee chairperson-selection process, committee chairpersons are majority-party members who gain their positions through seniority (years of continuous service) on the committee. Ranking minority members are the most senior minority-party members on the committee and would be committee chairpersons, if their party were in the majority. Subcommittees of the standing committees of Congress are chaired by less senior majority-party members on the committee. Ranking minority members of subcommittees are less senior minority-party members, who would hold subcommittee chairs if their party were the majority party.

★ ★ ★ ★

The Congressional Seniority System

There are two kinds of seniority in Congress: seniority in the chamber and seniority on the committee. With limited exceptions, "the seniority system" usually refers to unbroken service as a Democrat or Republican on the committee or in the chamber. A member's seniority can be reduced by his or her party organization as a punishment, but such action is very rare.

Chamberwide seniority is less important, in terms of independent power, than committee seniority. Chamberwide seniority affects a member's office location and might help in winning an especially desirable committee assignment, but other factors also affect appointment to the best committees.

The power basis of the seniority system developed from the norm (informal rule) of automatically electing as chairperson the majority party member with the longest continuous service on the committee. The rewards of committee seniority do not depend on one's policy positions, so it is not unusual for a Congressional committee chairperson to be in policy disagreement with his or her fellow party members.

The seniority system developed slowly as the length of Congressional service grew, and members sought stability and career rewards. The right to be assigned repeatedly to the same committees is the cornerstone of the seniority system. Members cannot be transferred from one committee to another without their consent.

The power of senior members has been curbed by numerous reforms over the past two decades. Those reforms make it possible to remove committee chairpersons and give greater authority to the majority caucus on committees and to subcommittee chairpersons. But senior members still exercise greater power than junior members, and seniority can still give a member a committee chair despite important policy differences with the party majority in the chamber.

★ ★ ★ ★

As will be discussed in Chapters 9 and 10, recent reforms have weakened the seniority system and have strengthened the authority of the House Democratic caucus over House committee members and chairpersons. Less extensive authority can be readily asserted over their committee members by House Republicans, Senate Democrats, and Senate Republicans. But even among House Democrats, the committee members, and especially chairpersons of standing committees and their subcommittees, have substantial independent power over the decisions which lie within the jurisdiction of their committees. The chamber leaders can influence those decisions and can force matters occasionally, but the chamber leaders have limited power resources. There are differences between the chamber (elected) leaders and the committee (seniority) leaders because of the different methods by which they are selected.

Any member with sufficient committee seniority can become a committee chairperson, regardless of ideological extremity or difficulties in interpersonal relationships with Congressional colleagues.[68] Such characteristics would limit one's chances for an elected party-leadership post, especially the top position in the chamber party. Thus, Representative Phillip Burton of California, chairperson of the House Democratic caucus, appears to have lost the final 1976 run-off vote for majority leader to Representative Jim Wright of Texas (by one vote) at least in part because some Democratic colleagues thought Burton was hard to get along with.[69] And, as mentioned earlier, Senator Saltonstall of Massachusetts was denied his party's floor leader position in part because he was too liberal to suit most of his Republican Senate colleagues.

David B. Truman, in a classic study of Congress, made the case well:

> Given the depth and persistence of the cleavages in both (congressional) parties . . . one would expect that a Leader who accepted any degree of responsibility for the substantive actions of the party would almost certainly be a middleman, not only in the sense of a negotiator but also in a literal structural sense. One would not expect that he could attract the support necessary for election unless his voting record placed him somewhere near the center in an evenly divided party, and one would not expect him to be effective in his role unless he continued to avoid identification with one of the extreme groups within his nominal following.[70]

Testing that hypothesis in the Eighty-first Congress, Truman found that Senate Majority Leader Lucas was, indeed, a "middleman," but Senate Minority Leader Wherry was substantially outside the ideological middle of his party. Truman's analysis of five other Senate floor leaders and whips and of three House floor leaders, however, substantiated his expectation that the leaders would tend to be middlemen.[71] Truman's observation is supported by later research, although Sullivan notes that not all middlemen leaders were ideological centrists before their selection as leaders. Those noncentrists, however, moved toward their party's ideological center after their selection as leaders.[72] And "the center" still leaves substantial room for ideological differences between successive leaders, as the difference between conservative Everett Dirksen of Illinois and moderate Hugh Scott of Pennsylvania (successive Senate minority leaders) emphasizes.

Are the chairpersons of the standing committees of Congress (the seniority leaders) middlemen in their party? Congressional committee chairpersons are senior members, or they would not be chairpersons. They entered Congress much earlier than the average member of their Congressional party, and they usually represent safe districts. (Even in an era of declining numbers of members from marginal districts, some members are still not "safe.") There is no reason to expect the committee chairpersons to be middlemen ideologically. And they are not. Committee chairpersons have been disproportionately conservative and from the South, where Democrats have been in the majority for most of the time since World War II, although, in recent years, that imbalance has begun to be rectified, as senior Southerners have died or retired.[73] Barbara Hinckley's analysis, based on opposition to "conservative coalition" roll-call votes, found that, from 1959 to 1966, committee leaders from both parties (chairpersons and ranking minority members) for the most part have been policy conservatives, while party chamber (elected) leaders have tended to be policy moderates.[74]

As noted earlier, seniority on a committee is the most important consideration for selection of the committee's leaders, while election to a chamber-leadership position can be achieved with only middling seniority. Lyndon Johnson became Senate majority leader, for example, (with help from the Old Guard of the Senate) while still a junior member. Analysis of the seniority of chamber leaders and committee leaders from 1947 to 1966 reveals, however, that, in each of the four Congressional parties, the chamber leaders were of equal or greater seniority, on the average, than the committee leaders and were in about the same age group. That is, both types of Congressional leadership posts seem to draw on the senior strata of members (see Table 8.1).

Some of those who became chamber leaders could have been committee leaders instead, but those who became chamber leaders had usually changed committee assignments more frequently than those who became committee leaders. With each change of committee assignment, of course, a member begins again at the bottom of seniority on the new committee. Thus, many of the members who became chamber leaders were some years away from being able to claim a committee-leadership post.[75] The cause and effect relationship here, as in most social analysis, is not completely clear, but it is doubtful that members became chamber leaders *because* they

TABLE 8.1
Party Leaders and Committee Leaders During 1947–1966 Compared on Some Points of "Seniority"*

	Median Age of Leadership (during terms of service)		Median No. Years to Gain Leadership		Median No. Years in Leadership Position	
	Party Leaders	CC's/ RMM's	Party Leaders	CC's/ RMM's	Party Leaders	CC's/** RMM's
Democrats						
Senate	60	66.0	10	10	6	8
House	62	65.5	21	16	16	6
Republicans						
Senate	64	63.5	11.5	7	3	4
House	62	62.5	16	12	8	6

*Party leaders are taken to include House Speakers, majority and minority leaders, and the two chief party whips; Senate majority and minority leaders and the two whips. All leaders serving during the 1947–1966 period are included.

**CC's are committee chairs; RMM's are ranking minority members.

Source: Barbara Hinckley, *The Seniority System in Congress* (Bloomington: Indiana University Press, 1971), p. 96.

had changed committee assignments too many times. Rather, it is likely that they changed committees more often than other members for the same reason they became chamber leaders: they had wide-ranging policy interests, and they preferred not to let their policy concerns be channeled too severely by the committee structure of the House or Senate. Because of the nature of the committee systems in the two chambers (discussed in detail in Chapter 10), the problem is more serious for the policy-oriented representative than for the similarly concerned senator, since senators can hold more than one desirable committee assignment at the same time.

These differences between chamber (elected) leaders and committee (seniority) leaders should not be overemphasized. After all, the two sets of leaders are of about the same age and seniority. "They have 'grown up together' in Congress and despite the awkwardness engendered by different ideological or policy views, they have been having lunch together for the last 30 years."[76] And both groups, especially the chamber leaders and the leaders of the most important committees, are committed to Congress and to operating in a "responsible" manner in Congress.

LEADERS OF THE STATE LEGISLATURES

Leadership structures in the state legislatures are in many ways similar to, but in some ways different from, those in Congress. In general, leadership structures in the state legislatures are less institutionalized and more subject to raw political change. But the leadership offices in the state legislatures carry titles deceptively similar to those in Congress. Some have similar functions; some are greatly different. The unwary observer, for example, is likely to err in many states by assuming that, like the similarly titled office in the U.S. Senate, the state senate office of president pro tem has few powers. In numerous states, that office has substantial powers; in others, it is a figurehead post. Each state legislative chamber is different in some ways from any other. Because of limitations of space, limitations in the extant literature, and a preference to avoid extensive lists of details, however, the following discussion is largely a general one.

The State Lower Chambers

As discussed in Chapter 3, forty-nine of the fifty states have bicameral legislatures. Nebraska has only one chamber. Its members are called senators, it is presided over by the lieutenant governor, and its leaders will be discussed along with those of the other forty-nine senates. Like the chamber leaders in Congress, then, the chamber leaders in the state legislatures of forty-nine states lead only half the legislature.

The Speaker of the House   Each lower chamber elects a speaker from among its members. The speaker occasionally is a figurehead, selected by some other powerful legislator or by the governor,[77] as was long the practice in certain southern and border states. But, normally, the speaker is the dominant figure in the chamber and is a person of substantial authority in state politics generally—among the most powerful two or three people in state government. Indeed, the speaker of the California Assembly is generally recognized as a powerful actor in both California and national politics.[78] A speaker is normally chosen by the caucus of the majority party, all of whom vote for their candidate on the floor, but, in four southern states with very few Republican legislators, the actual choice is made on the floor. Unusual situations sometimes lead to the election of a speaker by a cross-party coalition of like-minded Democrats and Republicans, as occurred recently in Minnesota, New

★ ★ ★ ★

Jesse M. Unruh

There are two images of Mr. Unruh: the colorful "Big Daddy" as speaker of the [California] assembly (1961–1968) and the subdued post-1970 gubernatorial candidate and subsequent treasurer of the state after 1974. In his free-wheeling legislative days, Jesse was a physically imposing 300-pound cigar-chewing, scotch-drinking stereotype of the backroom politician. In 1970, he trimmed his weight, added a moustache, and shortened his name to Jess.

Jesse Unruh was born in Kansas in 1922. He grew up in poverty. He was a big child, bright, and spoke with a lisp that was ridiculed by his playmates. After a year of college in Texas, Jesse went to Santa Monica to work in the defense plants. A year later, Unruh went back to Texas, where he was married and enlisted in the Navy. At the end of World War II, the Unruhs settled in Southern California where Jesse enrolled at USC and became active in campus politics. In 1954 he was elected to the assembly, becoming chairman of the powerful Ways and Means Committee in 1959 and speaker in 1961. Now in his prime, he helped Governor Pat Brown steer some bills through the legislature while frustrating him on others. As Brown recalled his relationship with Speaker Unruh, "He never really understood affection; he was a suspicious person. There was no way you could ever get Jesse on your side except by firm and frank commitment; there was no mutual trust." On one occasion, Brown appealed to party loyalty to change Jesse's stand: "I literally begged him to work for the Democratic Party, which was an awful mistake. You know what he told me. He said, 'Fuck the Democratic Party' ". . . .

Republicans and Democrats alike felt the wrath of "Big Daddy" when they dared oppose him. When Brown called a special session of the legislature to pass the budget in 1963, Republicans refused to vote until they were assured how the money would be spent. Using an antiquated parliamentary maneuver, Unruh locked the doors to the assembly. After 24 hours, nine Republicans gave in and Jesse had the necessary two-thirds.

During his speakership, Unruh gained a national reputation for improving legislative facilities, legislative staff, and the level of compensation received by legislators. After initiating these reforms, Unruh lost his position to the Republican majority in the Assembly in 1968. He organized Senator Robert Kennedy's 1968 presidential campaign in the state and was standing next to Kennedy when he was assassinated at his primary victory celebration in Los Angeles. Shedding the "Big Daddy" image, Jesse won the Democratic gubernatorial primary in 1970, but lost to incumbent Ronald Reagan. In 1974 he was elected treasurer and was reelected in 1978.

Source: John H. Culver and John C. Syer, *Power and Politics in California* (New York: John Wiley, 1980), p. 98.

★ ★ ★ ★

Mexico, and Vermont.[79] Texas House Republicans purposely do not caucus (they are the minority), and some become committee chairpersons by supporting a conservative Democrat for speaker.[80]

There are exceptions, but in most states the speaker of the house has substantial powers within the legislative chamber, more internal chamber powers than the Speaker of the U.S. House of Representatives has. In many states, the speaker's powers are similar to those wielded by U.S. Representative Joseph Cannon, the powerful Speaker of the U.S. House of Representatives from 1903 to 1911. The state legislative speaker, sometimes with the advice of a committee, normally appoints all committee members and committee chairpersons, anew, every two years, shuffling legislators around among committees to achieve the balance the speaker wants. The various committees are often "stacked"—especially the financial committees and the committees to which the most important substantive legislation of the coming session will be referred—so as to predetermine committee action on many issues. In most states, the speaker assigns both majority- and minority-party legislators to committees. In some states, the speaker is expected to consult with the minority leader in deciding on minority-party committee assignments. In a few states, each party makes its own committee assignments.[81] Informal norms, of course, exist in these various legislative bodies, and speakers must observe those expectations. Normally, for example, first-year members are not appointed as committee chairpersons, and they are seldom appointed as members of the appropriations or taxation committees. As was true at the turn of the century in the U.S. House of Representatives, state legislative speakers and aspirants for the speakership use committee assignments and chair appointments as rewards to loyal supporters and as items of exchange in coalition building.

Other powers of a state house speaker are similar to those of the Speaker of the U.S. House of Representatives, except that, in many states, the speaker has even more discretion. In some states, for example, committee subject-matter jurisdiction is not well defined, and the speaker has some discretion in the choice of the committee to which to refer a particular bill. That choice can "grease the skids" and insure the prompt consideration and favorable reporting of the bill, or it can insure its being "pigeonholed" for the duration of the legislative session, thus effectively killing the bill. Once a bill is reported out of committee, the speaker can affect the chamber's decision by persuasion of the members; by the time set for consideration of the bill (When there is ample time? Just before a holiday? At the end of the session in the closing rush?); by recognition of members during debate and rulings on points of order; and, on many bills, by the choice of conference-committee members who must iron out differences with the state senate.

The importance of the presiding officer's discretion in parliamentary procedure becomes more clear when one considers specific examples. The New York Constitution requires the affirmative vote of a majority of the entire chamber membership to enact legislation, not just a majority of those present and voting. Thus, seventy-six assembly members must support a measure for it to clear the lower chamber. At the discretion of the speaker, there may be a "short roll call" (ostensibly to save precious legislative time), in which the clerk calls the member whose name is listed first, alphabetically, followed by the majority and minority leaders, and closes by calling on the member whose name is last in the alphabet. All members who were present when the chamber convened that day are listed as voting "aye," unless they raise their hands to be recorded as voting "nay." Absent members are thus recorded in favor of the measure, and their "votes" sometimes help the speaker pass favored legislation for which he does not have seventy-six votes in attendance. ("Taking a walk" to avoid voting on a bill, a common practice in some legislatures when the pressures are great, thus may not help an individual legislator in New York.) Or, if the opposition has the support to force a "slow roll call," in which each member must rise and cast a vote, the speaker can delay final announcement of the results for a quarter of an hour or more, while the sergeant at arms and the party staff round up the additional votes the speaker needs—from hallways, snack bars, legislative offices, rest rooms, or wherever they may be found. On occasion, when numerous members have been absent during a "slow roll call," the speaker has ruled that a favored measure received seventy-six "aye" votes, even though independent observers were confident that only seventy-four or seventy-five members in attendance had actually voted "aye." Reform groups managed to have electronic voting machines installed in both chambers of the New York legislature in 1967, but the presiding officers declined to use them very often, and the machines were removed in 1971. The old-fashioned voting procedures give presiding officers a greater ability to ensure the results they favor; electronic voting reduces that ability.[82] That, of course, is one reason why reform groups support the installation of electronic voting machines, which enable a vote to be taken and counted quickly, with each member's vote brightly displayed at the front of the chamber, and with the "yeas" and "nays" added up electronically.

Compared to other legislators, the speaker has substantial staff resources. In some states, control over the basic legislative staff is located in a committee composed of both representatives and senators (often called the legislative council), but the speaker is always one of the two leaders of that committee and normally appoints at least some of the representatives on it. Even in states with a legislative council, the speaker has greater staff resources than other representatives, and in many states, such as California, New York, and Michigan, the speaker's staff resources and discretionary budget add greatly to the power of the office.[83]

★ ★ ★ ★

Committee Assignments in a One-Party Dominant House

The task of making committee appointments is difficult and requires much deliberation by the speaker. . . . In order to aid the leader in his selection, committee preference forms are sent to each member. Each legislator fills out the questionnaire listing desired committees in order of preference. In practice the [speaker] attempt[s] to seat each member on a certain percentage of the committees he prefers. No single factor predetermines the selection of chairmen and vice chairmen; the presiding officer relies upon several determinants in aiding his selection. First, the type of committee is of primary importance. For the more important committees the [speaker] will appoint legislators who (a) have long years of legislative experience; (b) actively support the leadership's interest; (c) are of the same political party as the leadership; or (d) have a particular interest in serving on a committee which has a direct impact upon their home districts. Appointments to other, less important committees may be made on the basis of informational expertise, loyalty to the speaker, party affiliation, legislative experience, or district interest.

Source: Samuel A. Kirkpatrick, *The Legislative Process in Oklahoma* (Norman, Okla.: University of Oklahoma Press, 1978), p. 17.

★ ★ ★ ★

The speaker also controls various perquisites, such as office assignments and parking spaces for legislators, some of which are obviously more desirable than others. In legislatures which do not meet year-round, assignment to an interim committee (perhaps as chairperson) to study a problem of interest to the legislator or the legislator's constituents may be much sought after by a particular member, especially since for some, it may mean a chance every month or so to get away from the humdrum of making a living and enjoy the pleasures of the state capitol, expenses paid. But if the interim committee is formed to recommend action on a hot "no win" issue (such as abortion policy) the speaker may find most legislators reluctant to serve.

Like the Speaker of the U.S. House of Representatives, the speaker of a state lower chamber is at the center of the chamber's communications network, and, as such, is in a position to help, or not help, other members. Sometimes, the speaker may simply suggest a seemingly innocuous change in the wording of a bill, and this can mean the difference between a member's getting a pet piece of legislation passed or having it defeated. Members naturally like to insure that the speaker will keep them informed when their interests require it, and they usually behave accordingly. Further, as the highest ranking member of the chamber, the state speaker—like the U.S. House Speaker—is in a position to reward members psychologically by a warm smile or nod of the head, perhaps a hearty handshake or hug or to punish them by ignoring them or giving them the chilliest of greetings. Such psychological preference is effective by itself, but it can also affect a member's standing in the eyes of colleagues (and even constituents), and members know it.

The power of the house speaker in some states is augmented by the practice of interest-group contributions to general campaign accounts that are controlled by the speaker, who can then channel substantial campaign contributions to present and potential members of the house. Such contributions help insure that the speaker's party will remain the majority and that the speaker will remain the leader of the party in the chamber.[84] They also help the contributing organizations and individuals feel confident of access and a friendly hearing from the speaker when they need help.

Floor Leaders The floor leaders of the lower chambers of the state legislatures perform much the same duties as the floor leaders in the U.S. House of Representatives, although normally neither they nor the speaker have any of the assurances of lengthy tenure that leaders in the U.S. House have, and the state majority leader often fails to move up to speaker. Sometimes, too, when the majority party in the chamber has intense factions within it, the leader of the less-powerful faction will be elected majority leader as a way of maintaining party unity.

The majority leader normally is the speaker's lieutenant, although, by the nature of the legislative system, he or she has some independent authority also. The majority leader's main responsibility is to look out for the party's interests and to mobilize legislative support for the party's positions. When a member of the governor's party, the majority leader often speaks for the governor in the chamber. In consultation with the speaker and other leaders in the chamber, he or she plans legislative strategy and is normally in charge of floor tactics, and also may play a major role in the scheduling of legislation for floor debate.

The house minority leader is the leader of the minority party in the lower chamber. He or she looks out for the minority party's interests in the chamber, leads the minority party in floor debate and the planning of legislative tactics, and normally seeks to defeat or delay the majority party's legislative program. In many states, the minority leader also works at building a party record for use at election time and attempts to enact minority-party legislation. In some states, the minority leader serves on a house committee which makes all committee assignments. In most states, however, the most the minority leader can hope for is to persuade the speaker of the wisdom of the minority leader's committee recommendations. In many states the minority leader has a seat on the committee which conducts much of the legislature's housekeeping business, often including the supervision of the permanent legislative professional staff. When a member of the governor's party, the minority leader normally speaks for the governor on the house floor and often represents the governor in negotiations concerning legislation. Assisted by the governor's authority, the minority leader is in a much stronger position than when the governor is a member of the majority party in the chamber. That is especially so if the minority party has enough votes to uphold its governor's vetoes.

Party Whips Party whips, or assistant floor Leaders, as they are known in some states, are not recognized offices in every state legislature. Some states have both assistant floor leaders and whips. Where there are whips, some states fill the office by election in the party caucus, while others have allowed the speaker or floor leader to appoint the whip. The whips generally assist the floor leader in communicating with party members and in keeping track of which members support various pieces of legislation, which members might be persuaded, and which are opposed.

Tenure and Turnover of State House Speakers Because of the high rate of turnover in the membership of the state house of representatives, one would expect to find a higher rate of turnover in the chamber leadership offices than in Congress, and that is just what occurs. But the rate of turnover in leadership posts cannot be entirely explained by the shorter average tenure of the members, when compared to Congress. In four states, there appears to be a strong norm against serving more than one term as speaker, and in twelve more states, the speaker serves only one or two terms. In an equal number of states, however, there is fairly stable house leadership; three or more terms is not uncommon. And six of those states have permitted the same person to serve as speaker for twelve or more years, including a North Carolina speaker who served for twenty-four years and a Mississippi speaker who lasted twenty years (see Table 8.2).[85]

The variety in the length of time one person is permitted to serve as speaker appears to be the result of at least three factors, one of which is the rate of partisan change in the lower chamber. Another is the length of the governor's term in office, which appears to affect the length of the speaker's tenure, both directly and indirectly. The direct impact has been seen in those states, mostly in the South, where the governor has served one or two two-year terms (that is now changing to four-year terms), and has had a major voice in determining who would be speaker. A new speaker would be indebted to the new Governor. The indirect impact has been seen in a Speaker's ambitions. Speakers often seek election as governor, attorney general, and the like, abandoning the house seat in the process. Longer tenure in statewide executive offices thus forces longer tenure as speaker, if the speaker is to use the office (and its various powers and staff) as a resource in the statewide campaign.[86]

A third factor affecting the turnover rate of speakers, closely related to the second, is the size of the political opportunity structure in the state. The office of speaker is powerful and desirable. Where there are relatively few alternative offices available in a state, such as U.S. representative or U.S. senator, to which a state legislator has a reasonable chance of election, Schlesinger found state constitutional restrictions on succeeding oneself in state elective executive office, along with correspond-

TABLE 8.2

Patterns of Tenure for Speakers of State Lower Chambers, 1947–1980

New Speakers Every Term	Speakers Serve 1 or 2 Terms	1 or 2 Terms was the Norm; 3rd Term Speaker Now in Office	Most Serve 1 or 2 Terms; One Serves 3, 4, or 5	More Than One Speaker Serves 3 or More Terms	One Speaker Serves 6 or More Terms; Norm is More Than 2
No. Dakota	Alaska	Alabama	Arizona	California	Georgia
Utah	Connecticut	Indiana	Colorado	Hawaii	Mississippi
Wyoming	Iowa	Kentucky	Delaware	Maryland	So. Carolina
Arkansas	Kansas	Louisiana	Idaho	Massachusetts	Virginia
	Montana	Maine	Illinois	Michigan	Rhode Island[b]
	Nevada	Ohio	Pennsylvania	Minnesota	New York[b]
	Oregon	Tennessee	New Hampshire	Missouri	
	So. Dakota	Texas	Washington	New Mexico	
	Wisconsin	Vermont		Oklahoma	
	Florida[a]			West Virginia	
	New Jersey[a]				
	No. Carolina[a]				

A "term" is two years, even though in four states the state representatives are elected to four-year terms of office.

a. Speakers served only one term for 30 years or more; Speaker serving second term for first time in 1980.

b. Speakers are no longer serving six terms or more.

Source: Malcolm E. Jewell, "Survey on Selection of State Legislative Leaders," *Comparative State Politics Newsletter* 1 (May 1980): 8, 9.

ingly high rates of turnover in those offices.[87] While there are exceptions (and the pattern evident in Table 8.2 is weaker than that found by Schlesinger for state executive offices), the pattern suggests the existence of a dynamic in which legislators in states with limited opportunity structures insist on keeping each speaker's tenure short so as to give more members a chance of serving in that office.

It seems reasonable to expect the more professionalized (and institutionalized) state legislatures, such as those in California, New York, and other industrialized states, to follow the Congressional pattern more closely than the amateur legislatures. That is, those state legislatures with well-paid members and long annual sessions would seem likely to develop the institutional intensity and commitment which leads to orderly ladders of promotion (as has occurred in Congress) and to stable leadership. With some exceptions, that appears to be the case, although, even in the best-paid and most-professionalized state legislature, the speaker often wants and seeks a state executive office or a seat in Congress rather than reelection to the state legislature and the speaker's office. Some even leave the lower-chamber speakership for election to the state senate. Speakers may seek alternative offices out of the realization that they will, like their predecessors, be limited to only two or three terms and had best try to move up while they have the power and prestige of the speakership to help them. It is likely, however, that the lure of a seat in Congress or of state executive office is simply too great to ignore. And by moving on to Congress, governor, a judgeship, or attorney general, a speaker gives impetus to his or her successor in turn to move on to higher office.

The State Senates

Leadership structures in the forty-nine state senates and in the unicameral Nebraska legislature fall into two basic patterns, depending on whether or not the state constitution decrees (as 60 percent do) that the lieutenant governor is to be presiding officer (president) of the state senate.[88] Where the lieutenant governor is chosen by the voters rather than by the senators, he or she has few powers within the senate as presiding officer. Even parliamentary decisions are more under the control of the majority party's leader (the majority leader or the president pro tem, depending on the traditions of a particular state). That is because, in New York and many other states, "parliamentary decisions by the Lieutenant Governor as president of the Senate are subject to appeal, and such appeals are decided by majority votes. The President Pro Tempore . . . usually can control the votes of the majority."[89]

Where the senators elect one of their own to be president of the senate (or, in Tennessee, speaker of the senate), the internal organization is then more like that of the state lower chambers; the presiding officer has substantial powers within the chamber. But even in those states, the business of the senate is more likely than in the lower chamber to be guided by collegial leadership than by the sole authority of the president of the senate.[90] In some of the states which do not elect a lieutenant governor, the senator elected by his or her colleagues to be the president of the senate is also first in line of succession to the governorship.

The Lieutenant Governor as President of the Senate Where the lieutenant governor is president of the senate, his or her powers are normally limited to those set forth in the state constitution. The senate rules usually retain all authority possible for the president pro tem, the majority and minority leaders, and certain leadership committees, such as the Committee on Committees and the Rules Committee. Power in such state senates is much more diffuse than in the lower chambers of those states.

Just over half the thirty states which make the lieutenant governor the president of the senate empower him or her to assign bills to committees, although in many of those senates, committee jurisdiction is sufficiently clear that little discretion (and, thus, little effective power) is attached to that function. All but Georgia and Nevada permit the lieutenant governor, as president of the senate, to break a tie vote on senate roll calls, although four more states deny the lieutenant governor such authority when a bill is being voted on final passage. Barely half allow the lieutenant governor to cast a tie-breaking vote to determine which party will organize the senate (and thus control many senate decisions).[91]

Only seven of the thirty states give the lieutenant governor, as president of the senate, control over preparation of the senate calendar, and only nine give him or her any "housekeeping" authority. Of those nine, the Alabama lieutenant governor assigns senate offices, the Virginia lieutenant governor assigns senators' parking spaces, four lieutenant governors authorize certain types of expenditures, and three have some authority over hiring of senate staff.[92]

Six states give the lieutenant governor, as president of the senate, authority to appoint members to some or all of the standing committees of the senate, and five of those six permit him or her to name the committee chairpersons. Two more have the lieutenant governor as a member of the Committee on Committees, which makes such appointments. Four states give the lieutenant governor authority, as president of the senate, to appoint senators to conference committees (to iron out legislative differences with the house) or to joint or interim committees.[93] Such authority as is not given to the lieutenant governor, as president of the senate, is awarded to the president pro tem, the floor leaders (especially the majority leader), or to a senate leadership committee, usually called either the Committee on Rules or the Committee on Committees.

The Elected President of the Senate   In the twenty states where the lieutenant governor is not president of the senate, that office is officially filled by vote of all the senators, but unofficially it is the majority caucus which elects the president in a manner similar to the election of a speaker of the house. As is true of lower chambers, a state senate occasionally is organized by a cross-party coalition as was the 1981 Hawaii Senate.[94] Elected presiding officers normally have authority within the senate similar to that of the speaker of a lower chamber. Fourteen of the twenty elected senate presidents appoint members and chairpersons of standing committees, as well as members of joint, interim, and conference committees. Such appointive powers, of course, contribute to the bargaining which takes place between various contenders for president of the senate and particular senators. In four states, committee assignments are made by the Committee on Committees, of which the senate president is a key member. Committee assignments are made in Hawaii in party caucus, and Colorado gives that authority to the party floor leaders.[95]

The President Pro Tempore of the Senate   The office of president pro tempore of the state senate is unlikely to be as powerless as that of president pro tempore of the United States Senate, although some states invest the office with much less authority than others. The president pro tem is likely to have greatest power in those states where the lieutenant governor is president of the senate, although in some of those states, the office is ancillary to that of the majority leader. In the twenty state senates which elect their own president, the office of president pro tem is a much less important one and in half of them does not even exist (although four senates substitute an office, titled senate vice-president).[96]

In those states where the president pro tem is the real leader of the senate's majority party, his or her functions are much like those of the majority floor leader, described later, but the majority floor leader would then be the party's number-two leader, rather than number-one. Such problems are avoided in the New York Senate by having one senator hold both majority-party leadership posts.[97] In states where the majority floor leader is the party's number-one leader, the president pro tem is part of the chamber leadership and, thus, is normally a member of such key committees as the Rules Committee or the Committee on Committees (or both) and works with other party leaders to plan the party's legislative policy and tactics.

Floor Leaders   In state senates which elect their own president, the majority and minority floor leaders assume roles much like those of their counterparts in the lower chamber, with the exception that, in most states, the senators expect a more collegial leadership rather than strong, one-person leadership. This is probably because of the senate's smaller size in each state, because in many states it is a place for a party's elder leaders, (whereas the house is often seen as more of a proving ground for ambitious younger people), and because many state senators consciously seek to emulate the practices of the U.S. Senate.

In state senates presided over by a lieutenant governor, the majority leader is either the majority party's top leader in the senate or is second in command to the president pro tem. The minority leader is the minority party's top leader. As in other legislative chambers discussed earlier, the state senate floor leader's duties are to lead the party on the floor of the senate and to plan legislative policy, strategy, and tactics (usually in consultation with other party leaders in the senate).

Furthermore, the majority leader usually works with the president of the senate (and sometimes the president pro tem) in scheduling the business of the senate. Both floor leaders (as well as the elected senate president and president pro tem) usually have seats on the joint legislative committees and interim committees which govern the housekeeping functions of the legislature and which supervise the permanent professional legislative staff. In senates where committee assignments are made by a senate committee on committees, these leaders often all serve on the committee on committees, dominating its decisions. Like the other leaders discussed earlier, they are also central figures in the communications networks of their chambers.

Party Whips   Like the whips in Congress and the state lower chamber, whips in the state senates assist their party leaders in communicating with the party's senators and in keeping track of how various senators plan to vote on measures of importance to the party leadership. Because the state senates have relatively few members (the

TABLE 8.3

Patterns of Tenure for *Elected* Leaders of State Senates, 1947–1980 (NOT the Lieutenant Governor)

New Leader Every Term	Leaders Serve 1 or 2 Terms	1 or 2 Terms was the Norm; 3rd Term Leader Now in Office	Most Serve 1 or 2 Terms; One serves 3, 4, or 5.	More Than One Leader Serves 3 or More Terms	One Leader Serves 6 or More Terms; More Than 2 is the Norm
States with Elected Presidents (Not Lieutenant Governor)					
Florida	Alaska	Louisiana	Hawaii	Illinois	Kansas
	Colorado	Maine	Utah	Massachusetts	Arizona[b]
	New Hampshire	Minnesota		Tennessee	Maryland[b]
	New Jersey	Oregon		West Virginia	
	Wyoming				
	Montana[a]				
States Where Lieutenant Governor is Presiding Officer (Table concerns tenure of president pro tem)					
Arkansas	Alabama	Oklahoma	Connecticut	Indiana	California
Nebraska	Delaware		Georgia	New Mexico	Pennsylvania
No. Dakota	Iowa		Idaho	New York	So. Carolina
So. Dakota	Michigan		Mississippi	Ohio	Wisconsin
Texas	Missouri		Nevada	Virginia	Rhode Island[b]
	No. Carolina[a]		Vermont	Kentucky	
			Washington		

A "term" is two years.

a. Highest elected senate officer (president or president pro tem) served only one term for 30 years or more; 1980 incumbent is the first to serve a second term.

b. Highest elected senate officer (president or president pro tem) is no longer serving six terms or more.

Source: Malcolm E. Jewell, "Survey on Selection of State Legislative Leaders," *Comparative State Politics Newsletter* 1 (May 1980): 8–11.

209

smallest has twenty members; the largest sixty-seven), party leaders have a fairly easy time of communicating with fellow senators and have less need for whip systems than do leaders of the state lower chambers or of either chamber of Congress. Some state senates, thus, do not even have an office of party whip.

Tenure and Turnover of State Senate Leaders   The tenure of the president of the senate in thirty states is determined by the state's constitutional provision in regard to the lieutenant governor's term of office and ability to serve successive terms. But the tenure and turnover of the senate-elected president of the senate in twenty states is, like that of the speaker of the state house of representatives, determined by chamber politics and by both written and unwritten senate rules. So is the length of service and rate of turnover of the top senate-elected leader in those thirty states where the lieutenant governor is president of the senate.

Regardless of the role of the lieutenant governor in the state senate, a third of the states permit the highest elected senate leader only one or two terms as leader (see Table 8.3).[98] Interestingly enough, about a third of the states also restrict the house speaker to such limited service, but only ten states restrict the leaders of *both* legislative chambers to brief service.[99]

About a third of each kind of state senate (lieutenant governor presiding or not) opts for relative leadership stability, with six or more years of the same leader not unusual. Again, that percentage is the same as among lower chambers and, again, about half the states with "stable" state senate leadership also have stable house leadership, and vice versa.

SUMMARY

Leaders of American legislatures are chosen by their legislator colleagues, primarily on a partisan basis. Legislative leaders have various strands of authority which they must weave together to gain power over their respective legislative chambers. Some are more interested in, and skillful at, nurturing power than others. Thus, the degree of centralized authority within Congress and within each of the nation's state legislative chambers varies over time. A legislative leader normally cannot recruit new members of the institution (legislators) nor dismiss present members, and cannot financially reward them differentially by raising or lowering their pay. The nature of legislative leadership thus differs substantially from leadership in hierarchical organizations. Further, American legislative leaders must compete with executive leaders, nonlegislative leaders in the political party, interest-group lobbyists, public-opinion polls and media figures, and committee leaders in a contest over the control of legislative decision-making and public policy.

Each lower chamber is headed by a speaker, whose formal legislative authority exceeds that of any other member of the lower chamber and, in Congress and thirty states, any single member of the upper chamber. In some of the twenty states which permit the state senate to elect its own president from among the senators, the president of the senate is a figure to rival the Speaker of the House of Representatives in power. Each legislative chamber also has floor leaders. The minority leader of any chamber is normally his or her party's legislative leader. The majority leader in the House of Representatives is normally the Speaker's lieutenant. The majority leader in the U.S. Senate is his or her party's top leader, although committee chairpersons often go their own way. In the state senates, the majority leader may be his or her party's top leader in those states where the lieutenant governor presides over the senate, but may be second in authority to the president pro tempore of the state senate. Where the state senate elects its own presiding officer, the majority leader is normally a lieutenant of the president of the senate.

Congress has a stable leadership structure in both parties in both chambers, although House Republicans have both a more open recruitment process to positions of leadership than the other Congressional parties and more leadership turnover. House Democrats tend (with a recent exception) to promote the whip to majority leader and the majority leader to Speaker. Senate Democrats, over the past thirty years, have promoted the Democratic whip to Democratic floor leader (normally majority leader). More often than not, Senate Republicans also promote their whip to floor leader, but not always.

Congressional leaders are in their leadership posts much longer than most state legislative leaders, partly because of a norm in some state legislatures to rotate the leadership offices and partly because many state legislative leaders use the office as a stepping-stone to a more desirable position. Also, the shorter tenure of state legislative leaders reflects the shorter average length of service of state legislators, when compared to members of Congress, and the less-institutionalized nature of most state legislatures.

Notes

1. Joseph Cooper, "Congress in Organizational Perspective" in *Congress Reconsidered,* ed. Lawrence C. Dodd and Bruce I. Oppenheimer (New York: Praeger, 1977), p. 147.

2. Lest the reader think this point obvious, it should be noted that in some countries the party leader in one chamber of the national legislature may be chosen by, and subservient to, the party leader in the other chamber. In Venezuela, for example, the party *jefe* in the Chamber of Deputies determines the leader of the party in the Senate.

3. Kenneth Bradshaw and David Pring, *Parliament and Congress* (Austin, Texas: University of Texas Press, 1972), pp. 49–54.

4. Ibid., p. 55; and George B. Galloway, *History of the House of Representatives* (New York: Thomas Y. Crowell, 1961), Chapter 2.

5. Randall B. Ripley, *Party Leaders in the House of Representatives* (Washington, D.C.: Brookings Institution, 1967), p. 12.

6. Quoted by Ralph K. Huitt, "Congress: Retrospect and Prospect," *Journal of Politics* 38 (August 1976): 214. For a discussion of Speaker Cannon's exercise of power, see Charles O. Jones, "Joseph G. Cannon and Howard W. Smith: An Essay on the Limits of Leadership in the House of Representatives," *Journal of Politics* 30 (August 1968): 617–46.

7. Ripley, *Party Leaders in the House of Representatives,* p. 13.

8. Ibid., p. 18. Today the Speaker no longer has such authority, although speakers of many state lower chambers do.

9. Ibid., p. 19.

10. Barbara Hinckley, *Stability and Change in Congress,* 2nd ed. (New York: Harper and Row, 1978), p. 113.

11. Walter J. Oleszek, *Congressional Procedures and the Policy Process* (Washington, D.C.: Congressional Quarterly Press, 1978), p. 84.

12. Hinckley, *Stability and Change in Congress,* p. 114.

13. Ripley, *Party Leaders in the House of Representatives,* p. 23.

14. Ibid., p. 22; Richard F. Fenno, Jr., *Congressmen in Committees* (Boston: Little, Brown, 1973), pp. 19–21; and David B. Truman, *The Congressional Party* (New York: John Wiley, 1959), Chapter 6.

15. Lawrence C. Dodd and Bruce I. Oppenheimer, "The House in Transition", in *Congress Reconsidered,* ed. Lawrence C. Dodd and Bruce I. Oppenheimer (New York: Praeger, 1977), pp. 45–46.

16. Ibid., p. 46; Roger H. Davidson and Walter J. Oleszek, "Adaptation and Consolidation: Structural Innovation in the U.S. House of Representatives," *Legislative Studies Quarterly* 1 (February 1976); and Burdett A. Loomis, "Freshman Democrats in the 94th Congress: Actions in and Reactions to a Changing House" (Paper delivered at the 1977 Annual Meeting of the Midwest Political Science Association, Chicago, Ill.).

17. Dodd and Oppenheimer, "The House in Transition," pp. 46–48.

18. See *Congressional Quarterly Weekly Report,* September 13, 1980, pp. 2695–2700; and the papers presented at the Conference on Congressional Leadership, July 10 and 11, 1980, sponsored by the Everett McKinley Dirksen Congressional Leadership Research Center, Broadway and Fourth, Pekin, Ill., 61554.

19. Ripley, *Party Leaders in the House of Representatives,* p. 24. Tariff legislation, of course, is no longer of major impact, but other tax policy controlled by the Ways and Means Committee is of great importance.

20. Ibid.; and George B. Galloway, *History of the House of Representatives* (New York: Thomas Y. Crowell, 1961), p. 211.

21. Truman, *The Congressional Party,* pp. 202–27.

22. Bruce I. Oppenheimer and Robert L. Peabody, "How the Race for House Majority Leader Was Won—By One Vote," *Washington Monthly,* November 1977, p. 47.

23. Ripley, *Party Leaders in the House of Representatives,* p. 33.

24. See Jack Anderson, "O'Neill-Rhodes Feud Jars House Tradition," *Albuquerque Journal,* May 19, 1976.

25. Ripley, *Party Leaders in the House of Representatives,* pp. 29–30.

26. Hinckley, *Stability and Change in Congress,* pp. 124–25.

27. *Congressional Quarterly Weekly Report,* August 2, 1980, p. 2190.

28. *Congressional Quarterly Weekly Report,* December 20, 1980, p. 3600.

29. Introduction to Randall B. Ripley, "The Party Whip Organizations in the United States House of Representatives," in *Congressional Behavior,* ed. Nelson W. Polsby (New York: Random House, 1971), p. 225; reprinted from *American Political Science Review* 57 (September 1964): 197–225.

30. "House Democratic Whips: Massing Support," in *Inside Congress,* 2nd ed. (Washington, D.C.: Congressional Quarterly, 1979), p. 30.

31. Ripley, *Party Leaders in the House of Representatives,* p. 33.

32. An analysis of leadership efforts to affect members' voting decisions in the House, Ninety-third Congress, concluded that the party leadership generally and the whip system in particular are quite effective. Lawrence C. Dodd and Terry Sullivan, "Partisan Vote Gathering in the U.S. House of Representatives" (Paper delivered at the 1979 Annual Meeting of the American Political Science Association, Washington, D.C.).

33. Garrison Nelson, "Partisan Patterns of Leadership Change, 1789–1977," *American Political Science Review* 71 (September 1977): 921.

34. Ibid., p. 921.

35. Randall B. Ripley, *Congress: Process and Policy* (New York: W. W. Norton, 1975), pp. 130–31. The House Republican leadership is larger by yet one more position than the Democratic leadership. The Democrats have their Speaker/minority leader as chair of their Steering and Policy Committee. The analogous Republican Policy Committee chair has been separate from the floor leader since 1959 and is an independent leadership post. John Rhodes moved from that position to minority leader, after Gerald Ford was elevated to the vice-presidency in 1973. See Robert L. Peabody, *Leadership in Congress,* (Boston: Little, Brown, 1976), pp. 281–82.

36. Peabody, *Leadership in Congress,* p. 278.

37. Ibid., p. 279.

38. Oppenheimer and Peabody, "How The Race for House Majority Leader Was Won," pp. 47, 53. This was the first time since McCormack's election as majority leader that the Democrats had not elevated the party whip to the majority leader post. The whip sought the promotion in 1976 but came in last in a field of four, in part because of reportedly having received money from Korean lobbyist Tongsun Park.

39. Peabody, *Leadership in Congress,* p. 281.

40. Raymond E. Wolfinger, "Filibusters: Majority Rule, Presidential Leadership, and Senate Norms," in Polsby, *Congressional Behavior,* pp. 115–16; reprinted from Raymond E. Wolfinger, *Readings on Congress* (Englewood Cliffs, N.J.: Prentice-Hall, 1970).

41. David M. Olson, *The Legislative Process: A Comparative Approach* (New York: Harper and Row, 1980) p. 381.

42. Peabody, *Leadership in Congress,* p. 326

43. Randall B. Ripley, *Power in the Senate* (New York: St. Martin's Press, 1969), p. 26. See also Donald A. Gross, "Changing Patterns of Voting Agreement Among Senatorial Leadership, 1947–76" (Paper delivered at the Conference on Congressional Leadership, July 10 and 11, 1980, Everett McKinley Dirksen Congressional Leadership Center, Pekin. Ill).

44. Ralph K. Huitt, "Democratic Party Leadership in the Senate," in *Congress: Two Decades of Analysis,* ed. Ralph K. Huitt and Robert L. Peabody (New York: Harper and Row, 1969), pp. 146–47; reprinted from *American Political Science Review* 55 (June 1961): 331–44.

45. John G. Stewart, "Two Strategies of Leadership: Johnson and Mansfield," in Polsby, *Congressional Behavior,* pp. 61–92. See also Robert L. Peabody, "Senate Party Leadership: From the 1950's to the 1980's," and Garrison Nelson, "Senate Leadership Changes: A Theory of Institutional Interaction" (Papers delivered at the Conference on Congressional Leadership, July 10 and 11, 1980, Everett McKinley Dirksen Congressional Leadership Center, Pekin, Ill.).

46. Ralph K. Huitt, "The Internal Distribution of Influence: The Senate" in Huitt and Peabody, *Congress: Two Decades of Analysis,* pp. 181–90 provides an insightful discussion of the Senate floor leaders' relationships to other power centers.

47. Ripley, *Power in the Senate,* pp. 104–6.

48. Peabody, *Leadership in Congress,* p. 331.

49. Ibid.

50. Samuel Kernell, "Ambition and Politics: An Exploratory Study of the Political Careers of 19th Century Congressmen" (Paper delivered at the 1976 Annual Meeting of the American Political Science Association, Chicago, Ill.); Morris P. Fiorina, David W. Rohde, and Peter Wissel, "Historical Change in House Turnover," in *Congress in Change,* ed. Norman J. Ornstein (New York: Praeger, 1975), pp. 27–34.

51. Nelson W. Polsby, "The Institutionalization of the U.S. House of Representatives," *American Political Science Review* 62 (March 1968): 148. Clay had served in the Kentucky House of Representatives and two short nonconsecutive terms as U.S. senator from Kentucky (chosen by the Kentucky legislature) before his election to the U.S. House. After his third period of service in the U.S. House (and his third period of service as Speaker of that chamber), he was secretary of state and then served most of the rest of his life in the U.S. Senate. He sought the presidency three times.

52. Ibid., p. 149. Speakers Albert and O'Neill each had twenty-four years of continuous House service when promoted from majority leader to Speaker.

53. Fiorina, Rohde, and Wissel, "Historical Change in House Turnover," pp. 29–31; Polsby, "Institutionalization of the U.S. House of Representatives," pp. 146–49; and H. Douglas Price, "Congress and the Evolution of Legislative 'Professionalism'," in Ornstein, *Congress in Change,* p. 9.

54. Robert L. Peabody, "Party Leadership Change in the House of Representatives," *American Political Science Review* 61 (September 1967): 675–93.

55. Hinckley, *Stability and Change in Congress,* p. 122.

56. For accounts of such conflicts see Nelson W. Polsby, "Two Strategies of Influence: Choosing a Majority Leader, 1962," in Peabody, *Leadership in Congress,* pp. 66–99; Chapters 5 through

8 of Peabody, *Leadership in Congress;* and Larry L. King, "The Road to Power in Congress" in *Education of a Congressman,* ed. Robert L. Peabody (Indianapolis: Bobbs-Merrill, 1962), pp. 291–328.

57. Hinckley, *Stability and Change in Congress,* p. 125.

58. Wright had also served as chairman of the Speaker's Committee for the Democratic National Congressional Campaign Committee, a position which helped him meet many newly elected Democratic members. See Oppenheimer and Peabody, "How the Race for House Majority Leader Was Won," p. 50. As Peabody notes, Thomas P. "Tip" O'Neill had served as chairman of the Democratic Congressional Campaign Committee before and during service as majority whip. Peabody, *Leadership in Congress,* p. 273.

59. Nelson, "Partisan Patterns of Leadership Change," p. 924.

60. *Congressional Quarterly Weekly Report,* August 2, 1980, p. 2190; and December 20, 1980, p. 3600.

61. Peabody, *Leadership in Congress,* p. 13. Martin became Republican Leader in 1939; Halleck in 1959; Ford in 1965; and Rhodes in 1973.

62. Hinckley, *Stability and Change in Congress,* pp. 125–26; Peabody, "Party Leadership Change," pp. 686–88.

63. Nelson, "Partisan Patterns of Leadership Change," p. 939. Peabody makes a similar point in his "Party Leadership Change," pp. 686–88.

64. Peabody, "Party Leadership Change," pp. 687–89. In a more speculative vein, the more rigidly defined route to the top House Democratic office reminds us of Joseph A. Schlesinger's observation that, among political offices generally, ". . . the higher the office, the more evidence there is of orderly advancement" to it. *Ambition and Politics: Political Careers in the United States* (Chicago: Rand McNally, 1966), p. 97. One wonders if it is just a coincidence that, in an era when the Democrats have controlled the speakership for most of half a century, the route to the top on the Democratic side of the aisle has become more orderly than the route to the less important top office on the Republican side of the aisle.

65. Peabody, *Leadership in Congress,* p. 331.

66. *Congressional Quarterly Weekly Report,* December 11, 1976, pp. 3293–95; and January 8, 1977, pp. 18–19.

67. Hinckley, *Stability and Change in Congress,* p. 125.

68. Ideological extremity, personal abrasiveness, or not being thought of as a "responsible" member, however, can prevent a member from being appointed to the most important committees, especially in the House. Charles L. Clapp, *The Congressman: His Work as He Sees It* (New York: Doubleday, 1963), pp. 226–27; Fenno, *Congressmen in Committees,* pp. 20–21; and Nicholas A. Masters, "Committee Assignments in the House of Representatives," *American Political Science Review* 55 (June 1961): 345–57.

69. Oppenheimer and Peabody, "How the Race for House Majority Leader Was Won," p. 52.

70. Truman, *The Congressional Party,* p. 106.

71. Ibid., pp. 106–117, 205–9.

72. Barbara Hinckley, "Congressional Leadership Selection and Support: A Comparative Analysis," *Journal of Politics* 32 (May 1970): 268–87; William E. Sullivan, "Criteria for Selecting Party Leadership in Congress: An Empirical Test," *American Politics Quarterly* 3 (January 1975): 25–44.

73. Hinckley, *Stability and Change in Congress,* pp. 130–31; Gary Orfield, *Congressional Power: Congress and Social Change* (San Francisco: Harcourt Brace Jovanovich, 1975), pp. 7–8.

74. Hinckley, "Congressional Leadership Selection and Support," pp. 268–87. The exception is the House Republican chamber leaders who, like most of their House Republican colleagues, were policy conservatives.

75. Barbara Hinckley, *The Seniority System in Congress* (Bloomington: Indiana University Press, 1971), pp. 94–100.

76. Hinckley, *Stability and Change in Congress,* p. 128.

77. While the governor's preferences are still a factor to be given significant consideration, especially in Alabama, Kentucky, and Maryland, the ability of the governor to determine the outcome of the state leadership contest "is declining in most of the states where it used to be

strong—primarily in southern and border states." Malcolm E. Jewell, "Survey on Selection of State Legislative Leaders," *Comparative State Politics Newsletter* 1 (May 1980): 15. See also V. O. Key, Jr., *Southern Politics* (New York: Alfred A. Knopf, 1949); and Malcolm E. Jewell, *The State Legislature: Politics and Practice* (New York: Random House, 1962), Chapters 4 and 5.

78. Joel M. Fisher, Charles M. Price, and Charles G. Bell, *The Legislative Process in California* (Washington, D.C.: American Political Science Association, 1973), pp. 114–17. As is true of most social phenomena, however, the authority of the California speaker fluctuates and may be declining. See Vic Pollard, "Will the Imperial Speakership Survive the Assault on Government?" *California Journal* 11 (May 1980).

79. Paul L. Hain, Cal Clark, and Janet Clark, "The Legislature," in *New Mexico Government,* in rev. ed., ed. F. Chris Garcia and Paul L. Hain (Albuquerque: University of New Mexico Press, 1981); Jewell, "Survey on Selection of State Legislative Leaders," pp. 12–15. Jewell observes that even in states with normally strong legislative parties, the majority party in the chamber can be so divided that the minority party can either decide between contending majority-party factions and their leaders or can lure enough majority-party votes to elect a minority-party member as speaker. Such developments occurred in New York in 1965; in New Jersey in 1972; and in Illinois in 1959, 1961, and 1975. The threat of a cross-party coalition in the Wisconsin Assembly in 1981 resulted in substantial restrictions on the speaker's authority, at least until 1983. See Clarke Hagensick and John Bibby, "Curbing the Speaker's Power in Wisconsin," *Comparative State Politics Newsletter* 2 (August 1981): 9–10.

80. Jewell, "Survey on Selection of State Legislative Leaders," p. 12.

81. *American State Legislatures: Their Structures and Procedures,* rev. ed. (Lexington, Ky.: Council of State Governments, 1977), Table 4.6, p. 67. The Citizens Conference on State Legislatures strongly recommends giving the minority party in each state lower-chamber control of its own committee assignments. Such a reform, of course, would substantially limit the speaker's ability to "stack" committees. *State Legislatures: An Evaluation of Their Effectiveness* (New York: Praeger, 1971).

82. This discription of the New York Assembly speaker's powers is based on Alan G. Hevesi, *Legislative Politics in New York State* (New York: Praeger, 1975), pp. 7–11. A political scientist, Hevesi has been a staff member, and then an assemblyman, in the New York legislature.

83. Michael J. Bevicr, *Politics Backstage: Inside the California Legislature* (Philadelphia: Temple University Press, 1979), especially pp. 228–29; Gerald H. Stollman, *Michigan: State Legislators and Their Work* (Washington, D.C.: University Press of America, 1979), p. 74; Hevesi, *Legislative Politics in New York State,* p. 7.

84. William Endicott, "California: a New Law," in *Campaign Money: Reform and Reality in the States,* ed. Herbert E. Alexander (New York: Free Press, 1976).

85. Jewell, "Survey on Selection of State Legislative Leaders," p. 8.

86. Ibid., pp. 9–12.

87. Schlesinger, *Ambition and Politics,* Chapter 3.

88. *American State Legislatures,* Table 2.5, pp. 24–25.

89. Hevesi, *Legislative Politics in New York State,* p. 8.

90. A Michigan legislator summed it up succinctly for the *Detroit Free Press.* "The 38-member senate has 38 prima donnas," he said, "while the 110-member house has 109 sheep." Quoted in Charles Press and Kenneth Verburg, *State and Community Governments in the Federal System* (New York: John Wiley, 1979), p. 263.

91. *American State Legislatures,* Table 2.6, p. 26. In the U.S. Senate, the vice-president can break the tie on the vote to organize the Senate as well as break tie votes on legislation.

92. Ibid.

93. Ibid., Tables 2.6 and 4.6, pp. 26, 67.

94. Richard Kosaki, "Report on the Hawaii State Legislature, 1981," *Comparative State Politics Newsletter* 2 (August 1981): 13.

95. *American State Legislatures,* Table 4.6, p. 67.

96. Ibid., Table 2.5, p. 24–25.

97. Hevesi, *Legislative Politics in New York State,* p. 7.

98. Jewell, "Survey on Selection of State Legislative Leaders," pp. 8–12.

99. The House and Senate are in the same state political milieu, obviously, and the impact of the degree of legislative professionalism, length of the governor's term, and the size of the state political-opportunity structure might be expected to result in similar levels of leadership turnover in the two legislative chambers. Although one can compare Tables 8.2, p. 206, and 8.3, p. 209, in various ways, it seems fair to say that, in about half the states, similar patterns of leadership turnover occur in both legislative chambers. But the two legislative chambers are independent institutions, usually have different terms of office, and, about half the time, differ in leadership-turnover rates. Some differ dramatically. The Kansas and Wisconsin Senates, for instance, have long leadership tenure, while their respective lower chambers permit each speaker to serve only one or two terms, never more.

chapter 9

Political Parties and Other Organizations in Legislative Bodies

Preview

With the exception of Nebraska's legislature, American legislative bodies are organized by political party membership. The legislative parties are ideologically heterogeneous, consisting of all members elected under the party banner, regardless of political philosophy. Since state and national legislative nominations are dominated by primary elections, the party leaders in the legislative chambers must simply accept the electoral victors. Often, the party leaders find that the followers are not following. Compared to the levels of strict party voting in the British House of Commons, the rates of strict party voting in American legislatures are low. American legislative behavior consistently disappoints adherents of the British party model of legislative behavior. Such disappointment is inevitable, however, because the assumptions underlying the British party model are not present in the American political structure. Still, political party organization constitutes the most important single organization within the legislative bodies. Each legislative party organizes itself as it pleases; within the Congressional parties, significant changes have occurred in the past decade. Because the party and committee structure of Congress does not permit all members to express their concerns fully, nonparty organizations have proliferated in recent years. Superficially, most state legislative party organizations are similar to the Congressional party organizations, but these superficial similarities overlay important differences among the various state legislatures.

The Republican and Democratic parties have dominated Congress for over a century. The same has also been true in the state legislatures, except for periods in a few states when the legislatures were nonpartisan. But even then the two major political parties had impact on the legislative process. Today, only the unicameral Nebraska legislature is nonpartisan. Thus, most legislators take their seats after having first been nominated as either Democrats or Republicans and after having been elected as the nominees of one of those parties. An occasional Independent or minor-party nominee may be elected to a legislative body, but this has not happened often enough to change the domination of the legislatures by the two major parties.

POLITICAL PARTIES

What is a political party? The answer to this question is not as simple as it seems, especially when addressing the two major American political parties. American minor parties, only nominally electoral, are more easily defined. They are much like interest groups. While elections provide a focus for their existence and activity, they remain organizations which seek to influence, rather than control, public opinion and government policy.

What is meant by the "Republican party" or the "Democratic party?" One definition of a major political party in the United States is "any group, however loosely organized, seeking to elect governmental office-holders under a given label."[1] This definition emphasizes the *electoral activity* of the political party and the importance of the party *label*. While an interest group may seek to elect the candidates it supports, this is usually not its primary function. In any event, candidates supported by interest groups are not listed on election ballots under the label of the interest group.

American Political Party Characteristics

No simple definition and no differentiation of political parties from interest groups serves to explain fully what the two major American political parties are. They are certainly different from the European concept—or even the commonly held American concept—of political parties.[2] America's major political parties are different in four ways. First, they are *fragmented.* This fragmentation parallels the system of federalism—with federal, state, and local party organizations and processes. And, within the federal and state levels, the fragmentation parallels the separation of powers—with the party organizations and processes being divided into legislative and executive wings. Second, *membership by self-identification* characterizes the major American political parties. A person may change party affiliation without approval of any party organization. Third, American elections are generally characterized by *uncontrolled party nominations*—that is, the nominations are usually not decided within the party organizations, but, instead, are decided by the party electorate in direct primaries. Fourth, because of the other three factors, major American political parties are characterized by a *lack of party discipline.* Party organizations have little power to cause officials elected under the party label to follow the party line in their actions and votes.

Because of the special characteristics of the major political parties in the United States, one authority has determined that the only way to understand them is to consider them under three separate categories: the "party-in-the-electorate" are those who call themselves "Democrats" or "Republicans"; the "party organization" or the formal party machinery and party officials, such as the Republican State Central Committee or the Democratic National Committee; and the "party-in-government" or those elected to public office under a party label.[3] The "party-in-government" must be broken down further into an "executive party" and a "legislative party."

Legislators and the Party Organization

Elected legislators may or may not be good party loyalists. Most feel, as discussed earlier, that, on some issues at least, they must represent the greater community, not just their own constituency or their own party. Further, having been elected by vote of a large portion of the populace at a general election, members of the legislative party feel that their mandate is every bit as legitimate, if not more so, as that of leaders of the party organization. The top party-organization leaders, after all, tend to be chosen by a relatively small set of party elites. Thus, in the United States, a natural tension exists between party leaders outside the legislature, who enact party platforms and pass party resolutions calling for action by the legislature, and party members in the legislature. Members of the legislative party see it as *their* function, not that of outside party-organization leaders, to determine basic public policy, and they are likely to be subject to a set of influences from which the party-organization leaders not in the legislature are immune.[4] Often, in recent years, a former or incumbent member of the Congressional party has been elected chairperson of the Democratic or Republican National Committee, partly in an effort to bridge the gap between the party organization and the legislative party.

The British Party Model

The performance of the American legislative party and its relationship to the political-party organization outside the legislature is difficult to discuss without reference to what has become known as the "responsible party model" or the "British party model." This model, explicitly or implicitly, serves as the basis for the way many commentators think legislative parties "ought" to function.

The responsible party model evolved from observation of the British Parliament and British political parties during periods in which the members of each parliamentary party almost always voted together. The majority party in Parliament, by voting cohesively to enact the party's program, was seen as linking majority public opinion to legislative action. The fact that the election of British members of Parliament (MPs) from single-member districts under plurality-vote rules helped create comfortable *parliamentary* majorities for the strongest party in some elections in which no party received a majority of the popular vote nationwide was little commented on, in part because the strongest party usually came within a couple of percentage points of 50 percent.[5]

Students of British politics have differed over the amount of influence the extralegislative political-party organization has had and should have over the members of the parliamentary party (the MPs elected under the party label) and over whether policy initiatives ought to originate primarily with the leaders of the extralegislative party organization or with the leaders of the party in Parliament. But their descriptions of the functioning of the legislative party (or the "parliamentary party") have been in substantial agreement.[6]

The basic features of the British/responsible party model are predicated on the assumption that the political party which wins a majority of seats in the House of Commons would elect its leader in Parliament to be prime minister and would appoint other ministers to head the departments of government, assisted by junior ministers and civil servants. "The government," then, consists of the prime minister and the cabinet, who are, in turn, the leaders of the majority parliamentary party (or, failing that, of the governing coalition of parties) in the House of Commons. The majority party in Parliament has the legislative strength to enact legislation in keeping with the party's program and is expected to do so.

Once elected, a Parliament may last for five years, unless the government requests the Sovereign to dissolve Parliament and call earlier elections. Such dissolutions are often called when the prime minister and his or her advisors feel the majority party will have the best chance of winning, even if a substantial portion of the five-year term still remains. A major aspect of the responsible party model has been that, if the government, consisting of the leaders of the majority parliamentary party, loses a vote on a major policy issue (especially a declared vote of confidence or a vote on finance bills), then it is expected to request dissolution of Parliament and new elections, whether or not the time is propitious for facing the electorate. Such a defeat, of course, requires defection among some MPs of the majority party or the governing coalition. This possibility of causing the government to fall makes majority-party parliamentary members less likely to go their own way very often.[7]

The responsible party model seemed to reflect reality in the British Parliament until a decade or so ago. "Back-bench" MPs of the majority legislative party could routinely be persuaded to support government bills. After 1972, however, a combination of factors led to a number of defeats for the governing party, which, under normal expectations of the responsible party model, would have led the government to request dissolution of Parliament and new elections. But the government did not do this. Thus, the majority party's backbenchers perceived that a change had occurred in the unstated but fundamental rules of the parliamentary system, and they felt freer on most issues to oppose their own leaders without having to fret about dissolution of the government. As a consequence, their behavior became much more similar to that of members of the U.S. Congress.[8]

Evaluations of *American* legislative parties should not be based uncritically on assumptions of how legislators "ought" to behave under the British/responsible party model. That model assumes greater party discipline than in fact often exists in Britain. More importantly, American federalism and separation of powers have led to far more fragmentation of political power and authority in the United States than in Great Britain. To the extent a British party's continued control over the government depends on its members of Parliament voting to support the leaders in Parliament, then the MP is under greater pressure to vote with the party than an American legislator is.[9] In the United States, the separation of powers and the independent election of legislators and executives to fixed terms frees them from such pressure to support the legislative party leadership in order to insure continued party control of the government. Nor do American voters elect their legislators primarily on the basis of wanting the legislative party to control the executive departments of the government. Voters are free to vote Democratic, say, for the legislature and Republican for the executive, or vice versa, and they often do so.

Parties as Centralizing Forces

American legislators' loyalties lie primarily with the constituency, not the state or national party-organization leadership or the legislative-party leadership, and that is especially true for members of Congress. Top American party leaders, after all, seldom are in a position to deny a legislator reelection or to insure his or her continuation in office. Neither do a party's executive officers determine a legislator's electoral fate. Yet, despite the numerous reasons for weak party loyalty among legislators, the legislative parties-in-government remain the major centralizing forces, attempting to bring order to a decentralized and often chaotic legislative process.

In part, of course, legislative-party voting reflects the ideological differentiation between the two major parties, which is more distinct among party leaders (including legislators) than among the members of the "party in the electorate."[10] Increased legislative-party voting also results when most of the legislators in each party represent similar kinds of districts socioeconomically, but districts which are distinct from those the other party's legislators represent. In addition, legislators are likely to support their leaders when they can because it is from them that they receive desired committee assignments, assistance in navigating pet bills through the legislative mine field, and other considerations.

Congressional Parties

Among American voters, the Great Depression election of 1932, when Franklin D. Roosevelt was first elected President, marked a fundamental shift toward Democratic party identification. Thereafter, except for two brief periods (1947–48 and 1953–54), the Democrats held majorities in both houses of the U.S. Congress until the 1980 election. When the U.S. Senate convened in January of 1981, the Republicans in that body were in the majority, their candidates having won twenty-two of the 1980 Senate contests, the Democrats only twelve. House Republicans made a net gain of thirty-three seats in the 1980 elections, although this did not give them a majority. The 1981 Congress, then, was composed of a Senate with a Republican majority and a House with a Democratic majority, the first time there had been such split party control since 1931–33. That split control continued in 1983.

Because each chamber of the U.S. Congress is independent of the other in the exercise of power and in organizational matters, there are actually two Republican parties in Congress (House Republicans and Senate Republicans) and two Democratic party organizations, as well (House Democrats and Senate Democrats). Each of these *four* Congressional parties is largely independent of the others and of the party organizations outside the Congress. Each of the four Congressional parties elects its own leaders, writes its own rules of procedure, and makes its own separate decisions on various matters. Outsiders may lobby members to vote a particular way, but only Republican U.S. senators, for example, may vote on decisions of the Senate Republican conference, and only Democratic U.S. representatives are permitted to vote in the House Democratic caucus.[11]

U.S. HOUSE OF REPRESENTATIVES

The U.S. House of Representatives is organized by the Democratic and Republican parties in that chamber. The partisan affiliations of individual members influence greatly the opportunities available to them. For most of the past half century, only a Democrat (the majority party most of the time) could be Speaker of the House or chair a committee of the House.[12] Even the cloakrooms just off the House floor, where members mingle informally, are segregated by party affiliation, as is seating on the floor of the House and in committees. The impact on members of partisan seating and separate, partisan cloakrooms cannot be ignored since much of their time for informal conversation is thus restricted to their own party colleagues. Too much should not be made of that fact, of course, since substantial interaction with the other party's members does take place, especially among members of different parties who have similar political philosophies. Still, institutionally skewing the informal interactions of members toward their own fellow partisans affects the development of each member's network of informants and cue givers, especially for new members, and encourages voting cohesiveness among fellow partisans.

As discussed in Chapter 8, the leaders of the U.S. House of Representatives are basically party leaders, and they derive their authority from the legislative party. Even the Speaker is elected and conducts the office in a partisan manner, although he is expected to rise above partisan considerations in performing many of his duties. The majority and minority leaders of the House, of course, are elected by the Democratic caucus and the Republican conference. Committee leaders, too, ultimately draw their authority from their respective legislative parties, whose committees control assignments to committee vacancies and (theoretically at least) rank on committees.

221

The Party Caucus

The House Democratic caucus and the House Republican conference each consists of all members of the House who were elected to Congress under the respective party's label. All representatives elected as Republicans are automatically welcome as members of the House Republican conference; all members elected as Democrats are welcomed into the House Democratic caucus. No questions are asked about campaign promises, issue positions, interest-group support, or ideology. No oath or affirmation of support for basic party principles is required. Nor is a member likely to be evicted from the legislative party for voting against the party majority or party leadership in the chamber, or for voting against the party's presidential program. The punishments meted out by the House Democratic caucus in recent years for flagrant opposition to the party's presidential candidate have extended only to reduction in rank on committee, not to reassignment to lesser committees or expulsion from the caucus.

The House Democratic Caucus Those House members who want Congress to remedy the injustices in society and to be a dynamic institution for resolving social problems and improving the quality of American life have long been frustrated by the status quo orientation of the House. Many of the liberal Democratic representatives (mostly then of low seniority) banded together in the late 1950s to form the Democratic Study Group (DSG), discussed later, to press for changes in House procedures. With help from many Republicans and "good government" interest groups, DSG members succeeded in pushing through the 1970 Legislative Reorganization Act, which "liberalized and formalized parliamentary procedure in committees and on the floor of the House."[13] These changes in the House rules did not "alter the distribution of power positions, since those positions derive from the majority party."[14]

Large numbers of new Democrats began entering the House during each Congress in the late 1960s. They often replaced members who had first been elected three decades earlier. DSG members began to realize that they had the votes to make some changes in Democratic caucus rules and, possibly, to use the then-dormant Democratic caucus to offset the power of more-senior, conservative Democrats (especially committee chairpersons) whose authority was theoretically derived from the Democratic caucus, yet whose independent power was enhanced by the regular and unquestioning caucus ratification of seniority-based committee positions and rankings.[15] The importance of large numbers of new members with little attachment to the old ways must be stressed. At the caucus meetings at the opening of the Ninety-fourth Congress (January 1975), for example, a caucus in which three committee chairpersons were removed from their positions and major changes in the rules were adopted, 75 of the 291 members of the Democratic caucus were newly elected representatives, and fifty-two other Democratic members had four years or less of House service.

A key success for the liberals which opened the way to substantial revamping of the rules of the House Democratic caucus occurred in 1968 when "DSG Chairman James O'Hara of Michigan negotiated an agreement with Speaker McCormack requiring the Democratic Caucus to have regular monthly meetings."[16] Until 1968, the caucus had met at the beginning of each Congress to reelect leaders and to ratify the slate of committee assignments and chairs but, after that, met solely at the Speaker's discretion to discuss only issues the Speaker chose. He seldom convened the caucus. McCormack's eventual successor as Speaker, Carl Albert of Oklahoma, had helped the DSG persuade Speaker McCormack to accept a party rule stating "that a caucus meeting could be held each month if fifty members demanded the meeting in writing; the petition to the chair of the caucus would outline the proposed agenda."[17] Several such caucus meetings were held during the Ninety-first Congress (1969–70) to discuss reform and other issues. Some caucuses failed to achieve a quorum. The caucus approved appointment of a committee to study reform—the Hansen Committee named after its chairperson, Julia Butler Hansen. At the beginning of the Ninety-second Congress, the caucus approved many of the recommendations of that committee.[18] The new Speaker, Carl Albert, was much more receptive to such changes than had been Speaker McCormack.

During the 1970s, the House Democratic caucus made numerous changes in its procedures and rules, changes which clearly gave it the potential of becoming a major instrument for making policy (as was demonstrated when the Democratic caucus was used to force a floor vote on ending the oil-depletion allowance).[19] Today, nominations of Democrats for openings on House committees and as committee chairs (except for the Rules Committee) are determined by the Democratic Steering and Policy Committee, which is chaired by the Speaker and includes the majority leader, the whip and deputy whips, the caucus chairperson, several members appointed by the Speaker, and others elected by Democratic members by region.

The party leadership has much greater authority over members' committee assignments than before, although once on a committee, the norms of the House protect a member from removal from that committee. The Speaker alone nominates all Democratic members and the chairperson of the House Rules Committee. Despite the new rules, however, leaders in the U.S. House have much less authority over members' committee assignments than do leaders in the state legislatures.

Democratic caucus procedures now provide for individual secret-ballot approval or rejection of each of the nominations by the Steering and Policy Committee for chairpersons of committees and Appropriations Committee subcommittees.[20] These procedures were used in the Ninety-fifth Congress (1977–78) to remove Representative Robert Sikes (D., Florida) as the chair of the Military Construction Subcommittee of the Appropriations Committee after questions had been raised concerning his conflicts of interest from business activities. Earlier, the procedures had also been used to remove three chairpersons of standing committees at the beginning of the Ninety-fourth Congress (1975–76). In 1983, the Democrats declined to reappoint Phil Gramm of Texas to the House Budget Committee. Representative Gramm, who had been instrumental in passing President Reagan's budget in the prior Congress, resigned and sought reelection as a Republican.

In effect, it is still seniority which mostly determines who will chair a House committee, but that is true only as long as the senior member remains at least minimally acceptable to the party caucus. Party seniority on a full committee still determines the order in which Democratic committee members may "bid" (seek approval of a majority of committee Democrats) to chair a subcommittee. Other Democratic rules changes limit Democratic committee chairpersons in various ways that make arbitrary committee governance much less likely. Committees and committee chairpersons retain a great deal of independent authority, but, as one distinguished Congressional observer has put it: "Committees and their chairmen [are] now more firmly harnessed to the party system and the leadership than at any time since the latter part of the Woodrow Wilson administration."[21]

Democrats in the House continue to debate the extent to which the Democratic caucus should attempt to influence member voting on legislative issues, either in committee or on the floor of the House. In March 1978, for example, by an almost 2-to-1 vote, the caucus "urged" the House Ways and Means Committee to report a bill to roll back proposed Social Security tax increases. This was not a binding resolution, but it caused the committee to work actively on the question, at one point narrowly voting such a reduction and, a week later, reversing itself.[22] More-junior Democrats have pressed for caucus instruction on legislative issues to give themselves broader policy influence, as opposed to the rather narrow policy influence they obtain through their committee work. House leaders and committee and subcommittee chairpersons, on the other hand, tend to reject the idea of the caucus instructing Democratic committee members on legislation. The more-senior members argue that expertise should not be ignored and that caucus instruction raises a basic philosophical question concerning a member's responsibilities for voting as instructed or as he or she thinks best. Many Democrats appear to want to leave the question of the proper role of the caucus unresolved, as a "gun behind the door." Even some of those who backed the Social Security resolution in 1978 feel that "votes within the caucus should still be rare and should be limited to issues such as Social Security, where a committee was clearly frustrating the desires of many members."[23] Fear of the return of the overly powerful caucus of the past appears to limit the uses for which the Democratic caucus is being seriously considered.

The House Republican Conference   Developments during the past decade have been less dramatic within the House Republican conference, as the organization of House Republicans is called, than those in the Democratic caucus, and they require less discussion. Many of the changes in the Democratic caucus rules were made because, since the Democrats were the majority party in the House, changes in their party rules would enable the party's dominant faction to assert power in the House at large. Such motivations were missing in the House Republican conference and, in addition, the present rules of the conference seem to suit the policy goals of most Republican members. Republican representatives criticize the Democratic caucus for attempting to make decisions in caucus for the entire House, thus excluding the Republicans from effective participation in those decisions.

The excitement in the Democratic caucuses in recent years has been over changes in rules and challenges to committee chairpersons. Similar excitement in the Republican conference at the beginning of each Congress has often been missing; but, as discussed in the previous chapter, House Republicans *have* been willing to replace their floor leader. The House Republican conference meets frequently during each session for briefings and discussion of issues but seldom takes a vote on major legislative proposals.

Ranking minority members of committees are not in a position to exert the influence on legislation which committee chairpersons can exert, but they are important in a committee's deliberations. Further, the procedures used to select the minority party's ranking minority members also determine the way the party will select committee chairpersons when in the majority. House Republicans have, like the Democrats, formally modified the seniority rules by permitting, since 1971, all members of the House Republican conference to vote by secret ballot on each nomination for ranking minority member made by the Republican Committee on Committees.[24] The House Republican conference has not, however, overthrown any ranking minority members.

Party Committees

Both House parties, through the Democratic caucus and the Republican conference, create party committees with specific functions. House Republicans have a Republican Policy Committee, which advises the party conference on proposed policies and on tactics, as well as a Republican Research Committee. These committees primarily promote discussion of issues within the legislative party.[25] House Democrats combine this somewhat ignored function with the scheduling of legislation in their Steering and Policy Committee, a leadership committee (discussed earlier) which also serves as the Democratic committee on committees.

The House Republican Committee on Committees is chaired by the minority leader and includes a member from every state which has a Republican U.S. representative. Each member is elected by the Republicans in that state's delegation. Not all committee-on-committees members are equal, however. Each committee member has as many votes in committee decisions as there are Republican representatives from his or her state. House Republican committee-assignment decisions are therefore dominated by the large-delegation states, and the structure of the executive committee of this Republican Committee on Committees is even more skewed toward domination by the large states.

Of increasing importance, lately, are the Democratic Congressional Campaign Committee (an arm of the House Democratic caucus) and the National Republican Congressional Committee (an arm of the House Republican conference). These party committees, which are composed of U.S. representatives who belong to the relevant party, have small staffs and have as their one responsibility the election and reelection of the parties' candidates to the U.S. House of Representatives.

> They assist incumbent . . . representatives by providing speech-preparation services, television and radio tapes and scripts, press releases, legislative histories and roll-call research, photographic services, and campaign literature. For nonincumbent candidates—especially those in closely competitive districts—they provide campaign assistance that ranges from money and research on the record of the opponent to organizational help in the district and advice on the skillful use of press, radio, and television. Whereas the [party] national committee deals with the party's national [e.g. presidential and vice-presidential] candidates, national image, and national issues, the Hill committees minimize national issues and candidates if it is prudent to do so in the essentially local elections with which they are concerned. They are thus one more force for decentralization in national party politics.[26]

The mere existence of Congressional campaign committees is evidence of the schism between the national party committees, which tend to be dominated by those factions of the party most interested in controlling the presidency and willing to spend money on presidential elections but not on Congressional campaigns, and the Congressional parties. The Congressional campaign committees provide interest groups with a central location for making their campaign contributions. Interest groups hope these contributions will give them access to and influence with the party leaders in Congress. About 60 percent of each Congressional campaign committee's expenditures go to incumbent representatives seeking reelection. In 1980, the Republican committee spent over five times as much money as the Democratic committee. But even the Republican committee (averaging some $5,000 per campaign in 1980) is not the major source of funds for Congressional campaigns.[27] Still, although decisions on allocations of campaign funds can alienate colleagues who get less than they want from the committee, occupying the chair of a campaign committee, or its Speaker's subcommittee, has become a position of value to members with aspirations to legislative party leadership. Such a position permits the chairperson both to gain influence with colleagues, especially new members, and to demonstrate leadership abilities.

Other Groups in the House

The Democratic and Republican parties are the principal, but not the only, centers in the House. There are both formal and informal groups, including many which are officially organized legislative service agencies and thus are eligible to receive contributions from members' official clerk-hire allowances, to have offices in House buildings, and to have a House telephone number.[28] The conservative coalition, observable in the roll-call voting records but not in an organizational entity, will be discussed later, along with party cohesion.

Informal groups help members focus on an issue and gather and disseminate information about it when the formal structure of Congress is unwieldy. Such a situation arises, for instance, when the issue of concern cuts across the jurisdictions of several committees but is not a major concern of any of them. Representatives who wish to respond to constituent concerns about a particular problem often find it helpful to join the appropriate group.

> A representative or senator interested in demonstrating an affinity with constituents favoring equal rights for women, with those espousing increased military spending, and with unemployed coal miners might not find the party or committee system equal to that task. Memberships in the Coalition for Peace through Strength, the Congressional Clearinghouse on Women's Rights and the Congressional (or Senate) Coal Caucus would afford a member the opportunity to symbolize his or her positions.[29]

Members of Congress find it helpful to belong to various informal groups. In the Ninety-sixth Congress, all but one representative belonged to at least one such informal group.[30]

The Democratic Study Group   The most formally organized House group outside the two parties is the Democratic Study Group. The DSG, as it often is called, was organized by liberal House Democrats in 1959 to support passage of civil-rights legislation and to counteract the dominance of the House Democratic Party by southern conservatives. The founding of the DSG started what eventually became a movement toward the formation of extraparty organizations in Congress. DSG is a voluntary group of House Democrats with a membership roster, elected leaders, permanent staff, and a set of regularized procedures for meeting and arriving at various decisions.[31] Some 200 Democratic members now belong to the DSG, but some apparently belong for the primary purpose of obtaining the staff-information sheets rather than out of a sense of ideological identification with the majority of DSG members.[32] The organization takes issue positions, provides members with information, and has its own whip system to encourage communications among liberal Democrats and to increase the number of liberals in attendance on the floor to vote on important issues.

So that the original DSG founders would not be considered "subversive" of the institutionalized Democratic caucus (which controlled the House machinery, including committee assignments), they discussed their plans with the Speaker when DSG was originally formed and obtained "limited blessing." They chose the group's name carefully to "allay the fears of the Democratic party leadership that it was an attempt to set up a rival organization."[33] Because DSG members basically support the national party platform and most domestic programs of Democratic Presidents, the DSG and the elected leaders get along reasonably well.

> The DSG is made up of men loyal to the programs supported by the leaders and the administration. DSG members vote with the party and the leaders consider them a positive influence. . . . Typically, DSG leaders approach the central leaders to discuss a problem (either legislative or organizational) before taking any public position. Negotiation that takes place in these meetings has been so successful that there have been no major splits between the leadership and the DSG. . . . The implicit threat of DSG defection if the leaders thwart them on a major issue insures the leaders' willingness to compromise. At the same time the DSG leaders realize that open opposition to the Speaker would soon backfire: non-DSG members would frown on such disloyalty; many big city DSG members would, in a showdown, support the Speaker; and the Speaker could use his many powers to make life unpleasant for the leaders of an open rebellion.[34]

State Delegations   State party delegations are one of the first groups to which a new member turns. The incumbent state-delegation members of the relevant House party advise a new representative-elect of his or her chances for winning a seat on particular House committees, and they may urge their new colleague to seek appointment to the committee they think will be of greatest benefit to the home state. They then attempt to procure the preferred committee assignment for their junior colleague. In the case of members from metropolitan areas with strong outside party organizations, a representative's political future may depend on working with the other members of the home delegation of that party. Similar but less intense pressures encourage members from any state to work closely with their state delegations on a variety of issues of direct state interest. These issues include military bases and contracts, rules governing various kinds of intergovernmental transfers of money like revenue-sharing and welfare programs, and other matters of regional importance. The representative whose vote is contrary to that of all other members from his or her state or region must explain that vote, even on a minor measure. On the other hand, a vote cast in harmony with the delegation does not receive similar back-home attention.

State delegations that meet frequently can be sources of valuable information and can save each member's time in seeking out the facts on a bill. State party delegations that get along well internally are valuable sources of information and power. A state delegation's members on different committees can keep their home-state colleagues (and their staff members) advised concerning matters within their respective fields of expertise. Delegation leaders can often swap the delegation's support on one issue for House leadership support, or support from other state delegations, on issues of concern to the state.[35]

The Congressional Black Caucus   The Congressional Black Caucus was organized in 1969 to focus the attention of the American people, the Congress, and the executive branch on the needs of black Americans. The existence of the caucus also reminds black Americans from any Congressional district in the country that there are members of Congress who understand and speak for blacks and for disadvantaged Americans generally.[36] In the Ninety-seventh Congress (1981–82), all black members belonged to the Congressional Black Caucus; all were House members and Democrats.

The Congressional Black Caucus is a legislative support agency supported in part through contributions from members' clerk-hire allowances. It also receives support from sources outside Congress, as do numerous other legislative support agencies. Those funds support a paid staff of some seven persons to perform research and to provide information and coordination to members.[37]

Opinion differs concerning the success of the Congressional Black Caucus, in part because much of the CBC's efforts have been devoted to symbolic activities. But much of their activity has also been devoted to getting the concerns of blacks onto the official agenda of the national government and to getting those concerns talked about as well in public debate across the nation.[38] Their success in agenda setting and in persuading constituents that they truly are looking out for their constituents' interests has had much to do with the proliferation of informal groups in Congress over the past decade.

The Women's Caucus Most women U.S. representatives belong to the Women's Caucus, formally organized in 1977. The Caucus is bipartisan. It seeks to operate as a consensus group and to proceed only on those issues all members agree on. It has backed the Equal Rights Amendment and a federal study of women's pay scales, and the caucus conducted its own study of the conditions of retired women.[39] Women legislators, like their male counterparts, are affected by personal backgrounds, race, district characteristics, region of the nation represented, and political-party affiliation. Still, overall, since 1961, women in Congress have become more cohesive in their voting.[40]

Other Caucuses Partly because of the example of the Congressional Black Caucus and partly because forming such organizations proved to be good politics for representatives back home, House caucuses now include, for example, a Rural Caucus, a Metropolitan-Area Caucus, and a Suburban Caucus. These groups basically concern themselves with the appropriate way to package aid to various types of communities, each seeking to gain advantage for itself.

To counter the growth of the Sunbelt and to offset the clout of the larger state delegations in the House, New England members formed the New England Caucus in 1973. A Northeast-Midwest Economic Advancement Coalition was formed in 1976, the same year the lower chamber's handful of Hispanics formed the Hispanic caucus. An even more narrowly focused economic caucus is the Port Caucus, with 124 members and a full-time staff of four. The Port Caucus "has devoted most of its energies to promoting the interests of the merchant fleet and the shipping industry."[41] Equally narrow in its focus is the Steel Caucus, with some 170 members from Northeast and Midwest steel-producing districts.

As their names imply, nonparty caucuses in Congress are organized around a variety of concerns. Some are based on individual-member characteristics, others around a set of issues, and yet others around a point of view.[42] Although the full impact of their presence is only beginning to be examined, the perspectives and behavior of many members would appear to be affected by these organizations if for no other reason than that they provide reliable and relevant information in a timely manner.

U.S. SENATE

The U.S. Senate is organized by the Democratic and Republican parties, with each electing a floor leader, a whip, and a conference secretary. Both Senate parties call themselves "conferences." The majority party selects the president pro tempore and the committee chairpersons. As in the House, Senate seating on the floor is by party, as is seating on committees. Senate cloakrooms, informal meeting places just off the floor of the Senate, are also divided by party. As in the House, the physical separation of the members of the Senate parties has an impact on the development of close friendships and cue networks, although the smaller Senate membership ameliorates that impact.

Power in the U.S. Senate basically derives from political party, as do committee assignments, and chair and leadership positions. That committee assignments are *party* assignments was made painfully clear in the Senate debate over the committee assignments of the late Senator Wayne Morse of Oregon in 1953. That year, Morse was an Independent, having resigned from the Republican party and the Senate Republican conference and having declined to affiliate with the Democratic conference. When the 1953 session began, Morse, then an Independent from Oregon, was given no committee assignment by the Republican conference, and he received no committee assignment from the Democratic conference either. Morse argued that his prior committee assignments (to Armed Services and Labor and Public Welfare) were his as a Senator, not just as a *Republican* Senator, and that he had a right to remain on those committees as an Independent. The narrow Republican majority and Morse's opposition to President Eisenhower's right-to-work position, however, made his remaining on the Labor and Public Welfare Committee unacceptable to Republican leaders. After extensive partisan wrangling, Morse wound up assigned to the much less desirable Public Works Committee and District of Columbia Committee.[43] Committee assignments and one's rank on Senate committees within one's party is a matter for the party conference to decide.

In general, the Democratic and Republican conferences in the U.S. Senate are quite similar. Each elects a floor leader, a whip, and a conference secretary. Each has a committee on committees, called that by the Republicans, but called the Steering Committee by the Democrats. Each conference also has a Policy Committee and a Senatorial Campaign Committee, much like the House Campaign Committees.

Membership in the Senate Republican conference or in the Senate Democratic conference is, of course, available to any senator who is elected or appointed to the Senate under the appropriate party label. (In the event of a Senate vacancy, the governor of the relevant state appoints a Senator to serve until the next election.) But either conference will welcome senators elected as Independents or those elected under the banner of a minor party. Thus, when Senator Harry F. Byrd, Jr., of Virginia, formerly a Democrat, objected to signing a "loyalty oath" to support the Democratic presidential candidate in 1972 and successfully sought reelection to the Senate in 1970 as an Independent, he was welcomed back into the Democratic conference as an affiliated Independent.[44] Senator Byrd, not to be confused with Senate Democratic Floor Leader Robert C. Byrd of West Virginia, voted with the Democrats to organize the Senate, and drew his committee assignments from the Democratic conference. His change to Independent (or Independent-Democrat) status did not injure his committee rank, even though he defeated the Virginia Democratic party candidate in the 1970 general election.

A similar case occurred among Senate Republicans. In 1970, Republican Senator Charles Goodell of New York, an appointee, faced both a Democratic party candidate and a Conservative party candidate. Senator Goodell was nominated by the Liberal party as well as by the Republican Party. Conservative party candidate James L. Buckley, brother of the noted writer and commentator, won the general election with help from then Vice-President Spiro Agnew. Senator Buckley was welcomed into the Senate Republican conference as a Conservative-Republican, even though he had defeated the incumbent Republican—his party's choice for reelection—in the general election.[45]

The Senate party conferences are independent of the Democratic and Republican national parties even though the individual senators are leaders in their respective state parties. The Senate party conferences make their own decisions about whom, among the senators, to admit to membership. The rule of each conference appears to be to admit all who knock.

Senate history includes no era in which the majority-party conference was the dominant force in the chamber's legislative process in any degree approaching the centralized power, through the party caucus, which was held by House Speakers at the turn of the century. Randall Ripley has noted, however, that power in the Senate varies in the degree to which it is centralized and that 1885–1905, 1911–17, and 1933–37 were periods of relative centralization in the Senate.[46] Despite Senate Majority Leader Lyndon Johnson's reputation for forceful dominance of the Senate, Ripley argues:

> Johnson's skill came in making [each Senator's] personal maximization [of influence] consistent with party success. Although the period of his leadership has some attributes of centralization, Johnson's long-term impact was to help the Senate move from decentralization to individualism.[47]

Senate party conferences often provide a forum for the discussion of issues, but are not used as vehicles for the "instruction" of Senators. Neither party conference in the Senate has been the site of the type of reform drama which has occurred in the House Democratic caucus over the past decade, although some changes have occurred in the Senate.

Senate Democrats

Former Senator Mike Mansfield (D., Montana) retired in 1976, after sixteen years as Senate majority leader. His tenure in that position demonstrated the potential for longevity in the office. That sixteen-year period also saw a loosening of the grip of southern Democrats on the Senate Democratic conference and the Senate committee chairs. The lessening of southern influence in the Democratic conference took place in part as a result of attrition in the ranks of senior southern Democrats (mainly through death and retirement), but the process was speeded by Senator Mansfield's appointment of liberal and younger members to the Democratic Steering Committee, which makes Senate committee assignments for Democratic senators under the guidance of the floor leader. Further, Senator Mansfield was generally willing to let the Democratic conference, or the Senate, work its problems out, rather than attempt to dominate the body in the manner of his predecessor.[48] Senator Robert Byrd was elevated to the Democratic floor leader (majority leader) post from the position of whip when Senator Mansfield retired. Senator Byrd became minority leader when, in 1981, Republicans gained a majority in the Senate. He has accommodated individual senators and has generally functioned as a legislative technician rather than a policy initiator; he has not tried to dominate the Democratic conference or the Senate.

The Senate Democratic conference elects its floor leader to chair the conference and to chair both the Democratic Policy Committee and the Democratic Steering Committee. The leader does not head the Democratic Senatorial Campaign Committee, however. Members of the Policy Committee and the Steering Committee are appointed by the Democratic floor leader and remain on those committees as long as they remain in the Senate. Primarily because of continued service, both party committees were dominated by conservative Democrats until well into the 1960s, although both were largely (but not always) dominated by Lyndon Johnson when he was majority leader and chairperson of those committees. After Johnson's election as vice-president, both committees changed, becoming more independent and, by deliberate action of the new majority leader, more representative of the Democratic conference membership.

> Under Mansfield the Democratic Policy Committee underwent expansion in size and assumed a broader role in adopting positions on policy issues. It came to include the four formal leaders (the majority leader, majority whip, the President pro tempore of the Senate, and the secretary of the Democratic Conference), six members at large, and the four members of the Legislative Review Committee. In addition to giving Mansfield advice about legislation and floor scheduling, the Democratic Policy Committee met twice a month to debate policy and issue statements on matters ranging from tax reform to the withdrawal of forces from Vietnam. The group's activities took on a new emphasis since 1969, after the Nixon Administration came to power. As Mansfield commented, "When the Democrats were in charge, we bowed to the President. Under Nixon, we function primarily as a policy determining committee."[49]

The reforms enacted in the House Democratic caucus over the past decade or so have been echoed only faintly in the Senate Democratic conference. There was less pressure for change among Senate Democrats. Senators can hold more committee assignments at any one time than representatives. All Democratic senators are assigned, under the "Johnson Rule," to at least one of the Senate's major committees, regardless of seniority. Almost every senator serves as either chair or ranking minority member of a subcommittee depending on party—whether majority or minority.[50] There is a less skewed distribution of seniority among Senate Democrats than before. Although southern Democrats still have more than their "fair" share of positions of power, the distribution of seniority in the Senate today favors one region or ideology much less than it did twenty years ago.[51] Senate Democrats have, however, followed the lead of their party colleagues in the House in one respect: in 1975, they decided to select committee chairpersons by secret ballot upon the request of one fifth of the Democratic senators.[52] No incumbent Senate chairpersons have been turned out, but the change has made them somewhat more sensitive to the views of their junior colleagues and has reduced their ability to exercise their powers of office as arbitrarily as was the case a decade ago.

Senate Republicans

The Senate Republican conference, like its Democratic counterpart, contains members with a variety of ideological perspectives. One way in which Senate Republicans cope with that array of viewpoints is by dividing their party leadership functions among various senators. Unlike the situation among the Democrats, no one Republican senator holds more than one major leadership post. The Republican floor leader (majority leader as of 1981) is the chief party leader among Republican senators, but does *not* chair the Republican conference, the Republican Committee on Committees, the Republican Senatorial Campaign Committee, or the Republican Policy Committee. And the Republican floor leader and whip often are not even members of the Republican Committee on Committees.[53] No one Republican senator, then, holds as many formal strands of power within the Senate Republican party as the Democratic leader has within the Senate Democratic party.

231

Such institutional arrangements make strong and centralized Republican leadership more dependent on the abilities of the leader. But these arrangements do not render such strong leadership impossible, as the late Senator Everett Dirksen (R., Illinois) demonstrated from 1959 until his death in 1969.

> Dirksen had learned . . . that an inflexible negotiator got all or nothing—and in the politics of the Senate minority party that usually meant nothing.
> Dirksen was especially adept at uniting the bulk of his Republican colleagues so as to provide the balance of power on most of the far-reaching legislation passed during the 1960's. . . . How did Dirksen achieve his legislative success? From his perspective, it was merely a matter of providing lubrication for the legislative machinery, a little here, some there. For Dirksen, "the oil can was mightier than the sword."[54]

Senator Dirksen was typical of Senate Republican leaders in his conservative political philosophy. "By tradition, the G.O.P. almost uniformly has selected a senior conservative as its floor leader. . . . Moderates and liberals, always a minority within Republican ranks, have had to settle for lesser party positions, such as the party whip."[55] The contest to replace Senator Dirksen as minority leader in 1969 pitted Minority Whip Hugh Scott, a moderate-liberal from Pennsylvania, against arch-conservative Nebraska Senator Roman Hruska and moderate-conservative Howard Baker of Tennessee, who was also Senator Dirksen's son-in-law. Eight months earlier, Scott had narrowly defeated Hruska for the whip position. Hruska eventually withdrew in favor of Baker, who nevertheless lost the secret-ballot tally, in part because he was said to be too young, at forty-three, and too junior with three years of Senate service.[56] Baker had the necessary seniority when the office next came open, with Senator Scott's retirement at the end of the Ninety-fourth Congress, although he had sought the position again in 1971 and had, again, lost to Scott. Still, Baker's election over the more liberal minority whip, Robert P. Griffin of Michigan, was close.

> Many political commentators had considered Robert Griffin the front runner in the race. Griffin had the position of Minority Whip and seemed a cinch to move from there to the top position. Several political writers suggested that Jimmy Carter's victory changed the vote of a number of Republicans from Griffin to Baker. These Republicans would have supported Griffin if Ford had won the election because of Griffin's abilities as a legislative leader and his close relationship with Ford. With Carter's election, they decided to support Baker since he would be a better national spokesman for the Republican Party. According to this view, the Republicans needed an individual who could articulately put forth Republican alternatives rather than someone who could function well as a legislative technician.[57]

With Baker's election as Senate minority leader, Senate Republicans returned to their normal posture of being led by a conservative, although in Baker they had a moderate-conservative who could appeal to a broad spectrum of both the Senate party and the party in the national electorate. When his party gained a Senate majority in 1981, Senator Baker became majority leader (and all Senate committees were chaired by Republicans).

Senate Republicans are the most closely tied to seniority of the four Congressional parties. Except for the use of a modified version of the Democrats' "Johnson Rule" (which insures each Senator one major committee assignment, regardless of seniori-

NOTE TO:

Joyce

Dental

-Student Life Activities & Programs-

ty), the Senate Republican Committee on Committees determines committee assignments on the basis of seniority in the Senate Republican conference. If two Republican senators request assignment to the same committee vacancy, the choice is determined on the basis of seniority.

PARTISAN VOTING IN CONGRESS

In the earlier discussion of the responsible party model of legislatures it was noted that American legislatures exist in a separation-of-powers system of government rather than in a parliamentary system. Therefore, the pressure that majority-party legislators in Great Britain feel to support the party and maintain control of the government does not exist in the United States. Nor can American party leaders argue that a legislator was voted into office solely as a cog in a system intended to install the party's leader as prime minister. This difference, along with the size and diversity of the United States and the federal nature of our political system, pretty much insures that voting in Congress will not reach the levels of partisanship normally found in the British Parliament, or of most other major parliaments where parties dominate either.

Early studies of party voting in two-party legislatures defined a "party vote" as one in which 90 percent of the legislators of one of the two parties were opposed to 90 percent of the other party's legislators. That is a very restrictive view of a "party vote," so restrictive that only some 17 percent of the roll calls in the U.S. House of Representatives between 1921 and 1948 met the standard.[58] Only 5 to 8 percent of the roll-call votes in various Congresses between 1951 and 1967 met that restrictive 90 percent opposition test.[59]

A less restrictive criterion for a "party vote" is to consider any roll-call vote a party vote if a majority of one party voted "yes" while a majority of the other party voted "no." By that much looser standard, well over a third of the votes in the U.S. Congress each session are "party votes." But, by that standard, too, the percentage of roll-call votes on which the parties oppose one another has declined substantially this century,[60] as is evident from Table 9.1. Still, party affiliation remains the single best predictor of voting in Congress.

Does the low level of partisan votes in Congress mean that political parties are meaningless in our national legislative process? Not at all. Many votes are on relatively noncontroversial legislation, and most members of both parties vote the same way because almost all members of Congress vote "aye" on those measures. On other measures, partisan differences may have been settled ahead of time because of the majority's fear that the minority would be able to stall or defeat the measure unless concessions were made. Even with relatively low levels of partisan voting, political parties are important; they affect the outcome of major policy decisions.

Both Congressional parties are comprised of individuals with a wide range of policy views and the electoral independence to vote according to their own views of the public good. Despite that fundamental fact, however, there are clear and consistent differences between the Congressional parties on policy matters of great importance. For example, most Democrats are more likely than most Republicans in Congress to support social-welfare programs, including tax breaks and other assistance for low-income families; to support government intervention in the economy to achieve a variety of goals—environmental, job security, and worker health; and to support various kinds of assistance to agriculture. A study of Congressional voting from the Eighty-third Congress (1953–54) through the Eighty-eighth Congress

233

TABLE 9.1

Party Cohesion in Congress for 1963–1978: Percentage of Roll Calls with Majority vs. Majority

Year	Both houses	Senate	House
1963	48%	47%	49%
1964	41	36	55
1965	46	42	52
1966	46	50	41
1967	35	35	36
1968	33	32	35
1969	34	36	31
1970	32	35	27
1971	40	42	38
1972	33	36	27
1973	41	40	42
1974	37	44	29
1975	48	48	48
1976	37	37	36
1977	42	42	42
1978	38	45	33

Source: Frank J. Sorauf, *Party Politics in America,* 4th ed. (Boston: Little, Brown, 1980), p. 341. Data from *Congressional Quarterly Almanacs* for each year.

(1963–64), which was also confirmed by patterns observed in the Ninety-first Congress (1969–70), for example, found that in both House and Senate

> *party is a consistently strong predictor* on three [policy] dimensions, social welfare, agricultural assistance, and government management. . . . On the average, party is a weak predictor [of voting] on the international involvement and civil liberties dimensions. . . .[61] (Italics in original.)

A study designed to give the reader a "feel" for the differences between the parties in Congress, as well as the disparity within each Congressional party, is reflected in Figure 9.1. In this diagram, each party in the U.S. Senate is divided by region, on the (correct) assumption that region is related to a senator's voting and that basic social and political philosophies are closely related to the region of the country which a senator represents.[62]

For this analysis, Senate Democrats are divided between southern and nonsouthern ("northern") states while the Senate Republicans are divided into categories of eastern, southern and "noneastern" (other). The voting record of each party regional group of senators is then evaluated according to the percentage of times those senators voted in agreement with the positions of the Chamber of Commerce of the United States. Agreement with the Chamber of Commerce is considered a "probusiness" vote. As is clear from Figure 9.1, substantial differences exist within each party. Over 60 percent of southern Republican senators voted probusiness 76 percent or more of the time, while a similar percentage of Eastern Republicans voted probusiness less than a fourth of the time. No southern Republican senator voted less than 50 percent probusiness. The nonsouthern, noneastern Republicans fell in between their party colleagues in degree of business support. Similarly, southern Democrats were much more probusiness than their nonsouthern ("northern") party colleagues, although it is clear from the diagram that not all southern Democrats in the Senate today are automatically probusiness.

234

FIGURE 9.1

Support for Probusiness Positions by Party Groups, U.S. Senate, Ninety-fourth Congress, Second Session, 1976

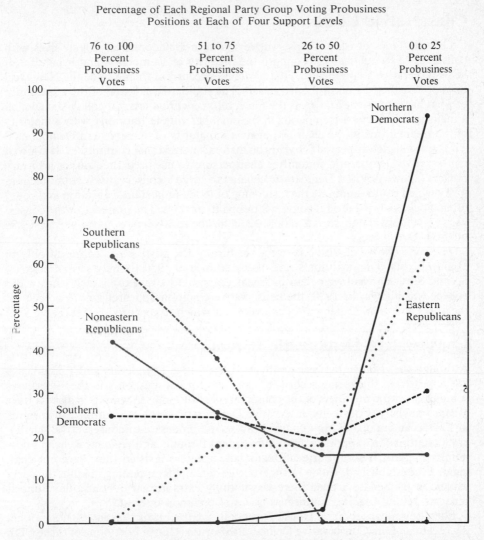

Percentage of Each Regional Party Group Voting Probusiness
Positions at Each of Four Support Levels

Each senator is ranked in terms of the percentage of votes which he cast in agreement with the positions of the Chamber of Commerce of the United States. "Noneastern" Republicans are all northern members except those from the eastern states.

Sources: William J. Keefe, *Congress and the American People* (Englewood Cliffs, N.J.: Prentice-Hall, 1980), p. 92. Data from *Congressional Quarterly Weekly Report,* February 5, 1977, p. 222.

A companion analysis of prolabor votes produced a mirror image of the pattern reflected in Figure 9.1. The analysis makes it clear that there are decided "wings" within each of the Senate parties, but there are also clear differences between the two parties in the Senate.

Conservative Coalition

On certain types of issues, conservative southern Democrats ally themselves with conservative Republicans, to oppose the majority of Democrats and a handful of less conservative Republicans. That has been a recurrent theme since the New Deal days of President Franklin D. Roosevelt. The standard definition of the appearance of what has come to be known as the *conservative coalition* is a roll-call vote on which a majority of southern Democrats in the chamber vote in harmony with a majority of the Republicans in the chamber, against a majority of nonsouthern Democrats.[63] The same alliance appeared for years on many Congressional committees. It allowed conservative Democratic committee chairpersons to use their then rather arbitrary powers (allowed by the Democratic caucus) to forge a conservative committee majority which could dominate the fashioning of much important legislation and could often block the legislation it could not design to its taste. The presence of the conservative coalition, of course, is a major reason for the relatively low party-voting scores in the U.S. Congress.

The conservative coalition is not a creature of the misty past of interest only to archaeologists. The coalition's rate of appearance in 1980 (Ninety-sixth Congress, Second Session) was lower than in recent years, but its rate of victory when it did appear was higher. In 1980, the conservative coalition appeared on 18 percent of the votes and won 72 percent of the votes on which it appeared.[64] (See Table 9.2.)

Conservative Democratic Forum

Although the alliance between southern conservative Democrats and Republicans has appeared in the voting records of Congress for decades, only in the 1980s have some Democratic members of the conservative coalition been willing to discuss their alliance publicly. Fourteen conservative Democratic senators identified themselves in 1981 as an organized but unnamed caucus of "moderate-to-conservative" Democrats interested in supporting (and influencing) Republican President Reagan's economic program. Those fourteen Democratic senators insisted they were not challenging the established Senate Democratic leadership. Responding in kind, the party leaders in the Senate argued there was nothing extraordinary about a few Sunbelt senators getting together to discuss issues of common interest.[65]

Forty-seven conservative House Democrats went a bit further in 1981, announcing creation of the Conservative Democratic Forum (CDF). Forty-one of those CDF members were from the eleven states of the old Confederacy.[66] The CDF took on great importance in 1981 because, in a chamber with 242 Democrats and 190 Republicans, forty-seven Democratic votes were of great importance to the passage of the Republican administration's budget cuts. The CDF's support for the President's budget cuts—which hurt midwest and northeast states more than southern states—resulted in the formation of a Gypsy Moth Caucus of some two dozen moderate Republicans from the Midwest and Northeast.[67] The Gypsy Moths' objective, of course, was to protect programs benefiting their constituents and to press for making more of the budget cuts, if they were to be made, in programs mainly to the advantage of the Sunbelt.

TABLE 9.2
Conservative Coalition Appearances and Victories, 1961–1980

	Coalition Appearances	Coalition Victories		
Year	Total*	Total**	Senate	House
1961	28%	55%	48%	74%
1962	14	62	71	44
1963	17	50	44	67
1964	15	51	47	67
1965	24	33	39	25
1966	25	45	51	32
1967	20	63	54	73
1968	24	73	80	63
1969	27	68	67	71
1970	22	66	64	70
1971	30	83	86	79
1972	27	69	63	79
1973	23	61	54	67
1974	24	59	54	67
1975	28	50	48	52
1976	24	58	58	59
1977	26	68	74	60
1978	21	52	46	57
1979	20	70	65	73
1980	18	72	75	67

*The percentage of the recorded votes for both houses of Congress on which the coalition appeared.

**Because the number of roll-call votes in the two chambers differ greatly, the total percentage is not necessarily midway between the percentages in the respective chambers.

Source: *Congressional Quarterly Weekly Report,* January 10, 1981, p. 85.

THE STATE LEGISLATURES

The importance of the legislative party in American state legislatures varies greatly between states and, in any given state, may vary substantially between different eras. In their classic study of four state legislatures in 1957, Wahlke, Eulau, Buchanan, and Ferguson found the legislative party to be extremely important in New Jersey, somewhat important in Ohio, and relatively unimportant in California and Tennessee.[68] As in other one-party dominant states, factions were important in Tennessee. California's weak legislative parties were partly the result of weak outside electoral parties and the practice of "crossfiling," an arrangement whereby the same individual might win the nomination of both political parties.[69] As a result of crossfiling, "a kind of modified, Republican nonpartisan spirit prevailed in the legislature."[70] An end to crossfiling in 1957, stronger Democratic precinct organizations in the state in the 1960s, and a surge of legislative newcomers (mostly Democrats) following a series of state house and state senate reapportionments (stemming from federal-court reapportionment decisions) resulted in fairly strong partisan organization of both chambers of the California legislature by the early 1970s.[71] In contrast, the legislative parties in New Jersey today are less powerful than they were in 1957. While still important, the majority-party caucus no longer dominates the New Jersey legislative process the way it used to.[72] The moderate importance of the legislative parties in Ohio appeared little changed a dozen years later.[73]

As noted earlier in the book, forty-nine of the fifty state legislatures are formally organized by the Democratic and Republican parties. Some of those partisan legislatures are virtually one-party bodies. In states such as Alabama, where all state legislators are Democrats, and in Arkansas, Georgia, Louisiana, Mississippi, Nevada, North Carolina, Rhode Island, South Carolina, Texas, and West Virginia, where in 1977 one or both chambers were 90 percent or more Democratic,[74] party affiliation has little to do with legislative behavior. In legislatures where everybody, or almost everybody, shares the Democratic party identity, party does not become the basis of divisions on legislative votes. Instead, factions organize around strong personalities or on the basis of interest-group association or regional division (urban-rural, metropolitan versus outstate). Stable coalitions may not develop.[75] Unfortunately, the voters are seldom able to decipher the rules of the game in such factionalized one-party legislative chambers and therefore are unable to hold legislators accountable.[76] A similar situation prevails in the nonpartisan Nebraska legislature. Following their examination of voting behavior in that institution, Welch and Carlson concluded "that party is the most important reference group in structuring legislative behavior . . . [and] in the absence of party no other kind of reference group serves a similar purpose."[77]

A tradition of strong legislative parties usually is found in states with strong outside electoral party competition. Most of the deviation from party voting in the state legislatures results from constituency pressures, regional interests, or ideological commitments which cause a legislator to vote against his or her party's issue positions. Thus, legislative parties seem to be strongest, and legislative party voting more frequent, in the states where most Democrats represent low-income areas, mainly in the urban centers, while Republicans tend to represent suburban and rural areas.[78] As many as 80 percent of the Massachusetts House of Representatives roll calls were partisan for several decades, for example, and levels of party voting are still frequently high in the Connecticut, Massachusetts, and New York legislatures.[79]

State Legislative Parties

The state legislative parties vary in the details of their organization, but most are similar in broad outline. In no state are the legislative parties as institutionalized as Congressional parties. Complex state legislative party structures and paid legislative party staff are the exception, not the rule.

In the forty-nine states with partisan legislatures, the party in each legislative chamber is organized independently of the party in the other legislative chamber. Today, the norm is for the legislative caucus to make its own decisions, rather than merely to affirm decisions made by the governor or the outside state party organization's chairperson, as happened in some states in the past.

In Congress, committee assignments are a responsibility of each chamber's party organizations, although discretion is limited by the norm that returning members have a right to continue on the same committee as in the previous Congress if they wish. That authority is held by the legislative party in only a handful of state legislatures. In forty of the state lower chambers, the speaker makes all committee assignments; the minority leader at best can only recommend them. In the lower chambers of Colorado, Hawaii, Illinois, Nevada, and Wisconsin, however, the minority leader or minority caucus makes minority-party assignments, while the majority leader or caucus or speaker assigns majority-party legislators to committees. The other lower chambers utilize *chamber* committees on committees (as contrasted to party committees on committees) or chamber or caucus elections to determine committee assignments. Even these mechanisms tend to give dominance of the process to majority-party leaders, however. Where the speaker appoints members of committees, he or she also appoints committee chairpersons. Where each legislative party makes its own committee appointments, the majority party determines the committee chairperson. Exceptions are North Dakota, where the speaker appoints the committees, but the majority caucus determines chairpersons, and South Carolina, where the speaker appoints the committees, but the committee chairpersons are elected.[80]

────────────── ★ ★ ★ ★ ──────────────

State Legislative Majorities Can Be Unstable

Although the Democrats lost the State House, they emerged from the 1980 elections with 25-24 control of the Washington State Senate. Suddenly at the end of the fifth week of the legislative session, Democratic Senator Peter Von Reichbauer, long a maverick and independent, switched parties and gave Republicans a 25-24 majority. Senate activities were shut down for a week while the Republican caucus changed all chairmanships and party ratios on committees. Many legislators were forced to change offices and some 25 Democratic staffers were ordered dismissed. . . .

The defecting senator gave as his reasons that the Democrats wanted to raise taxes and his disaffection with the leadership even though it had given him a chairmanship which he retained with the advent of Republican control. But his personal friendship with Republican Governor Spellman and protection in redistricting also appear to have entered into his decision. . . . Leaders in the defecting senator's district started a recall drive. . . .

With the new Republican control of the legislature as well as the governorship, party leaders quickly abandoned their long-time support for a redistricting commission and adopted their own plan. . . . [A] congressional plan was accepted which brought forth universal condemnation of extreme gerrymandering from the press, the Democrats and some local Republican leaders. . . .

Republicans began the session as moderate conservatives but, taking heart from the Reagan Administration and unexpected Senate control, they became more ideological. By the end of the session the welfare programs, the schools, and the environmentalists received set backs. Student tuitions were radically increased. With the removal of the 12 per cent interest rate the bankers were big winners as were the developers. . . .

Despite Republican pledges of "no new taxes," substantial increases were made in cigarette, liquor and gasoline taxes as well as users fees. These items will now be among the highest if not the highest in the nation.

Source: Hugh A. Bone, "Legislative Party Upheaval in Washington," *Comparative State Politics Newsletter* 2 (May 1981): 8–9.

────────────── ★ ★ ★ ★ ──────────────

The majority party leadership in the Massachusetts House of Representatives is unusually powerful. That legislative party is organized in clear gradations based on party loyalty on floor votes. Those closest to the speaker are the most loyal. The party is

> a status hierarchy rather than a peer group. Members of the majority are orga-
> nized around the speaker as a function of their willingness and ability to meet
> his expectations. . . . [P]ositions of power and authority within the House are
> distributed by the speaker using loyalty as the main criterion. . . . Within the
> majority, membership in each higher stratum is associated with an increase in
> voting support for the positions endorsed by the leadership.[81]

The state senates are more varied in the location of the authority to appoint committees and name committee chairpersons, but only half a dozen state senates give each party in the chamber committee assignment authority over its own caucus members. Only four states permit the lieutenant governor, as president of the senate, to appoint senators to committees, but eighteen state senates permit the top officer elected by vote of the chamber (president or president pro tem) to appoint all senators to committees. Seventeen utilize a senate committee, usually including some minority-party representation, to make committee assignments. Election to committees or appointment of all senators by the majority leader are used by a few states.[82]

Partisan Differences in the State Legislatures

Studies of party voting in the state legislatures face the difficulty of determining just what a roll-call vote in a given state legislature really means. The various state legislative chambers have different rules concerning recorded votes. Some have electronic voting systems, where each member casts a "yes" or "no" vote on every issue. A few have electronic voting systems, but often ignore them when they vote, because using the electronic system reduces the discretion of the legislative leaders.[83] Some state legislative bodies record all members as voting "aye" except those who specifically request that they be recorded as voting "nay." Thus, even members in the snack bar or restroom when the vote is taken are likely, in some states, to be recorded as voting "aye," especially if that is the desire of the presiding officer.

A further difficulty in determining the importance of the legislative party in the various states from roll-call-vote analysis is that in many states half or more of the recorded votes concern insignificant bills. In the 1967 California legislature, for example, "there were at least three bills introduced (and passed) because separate school districts wanted to take students on field trips to areas which had not been authorized in the Education Code."[84]

Comparisons of the importance of the legislative parties in the various states rely on analysis of roll calls on which a minimum percentage of the members (often 10 percent) votes "no." Such comparisons find that some states have much higher incidences of partisan voting in the legislature than others. In some New England states, for example, over 80 percent of the roll calls in a session have pitted a majority of one legislative party against the majority of the other. In some other two-party states, however, less than a third of the contested roll-call votes pit a majority of one party against a majority of the other.[85]

State legislative parties within the various states frequently take divergent stands on issues of importance to large sectors of the state's population. As one would expect, such policy differences normally are based on the socioeconomic characteristics of each party's support groups in the population and on issues of importance to the regions of each state which provide the bulk of each party's legislative strength.

240

Studies in the late 1960s revealed that the greatest partisan differences in the state legislatures existed on questions concerning appropriations and taxation, election laws (including primary elections and party nominating conventions), apportionment, labor legislation, and the administration of state government. In most states, strong partisan differences also existed over social-welfare programs.[86] Education policy and proposed constitutional amendments also resulted in strong partisan conflict in some states. See Figure 9.2 for an example of partisan differences on such questions in the Indiana legislature. These areas of partisan legislative conflict were quite similar to the ones found by Jewell a decade earlier.[87]

A comparison of partisan state legislative issues in 1963 and 1974 found substantial stability, both in the major issues facing the state legislators and in the issues which divided the various legislatures along partisan lines.[88] Most of the partisan issues found in both those years had also been found by Jewell. Both the 1963 and 1974 studies were based on surveys of incumbent state legislators, who were asked to list the most important policy questions which came before their respective state legislatures and, among other questions, the extent of partisan clash on the various issues. The authors found that, in both 1963 and 1974, the policy areas of "apportionment, taxation, labor, election-primaries-conventions, and administration divided along party lines in many states," whereas, again in both decades, conflict over "health, education, gambling, and courts-penal-crime issues did not" tend to be primarily along partisan lines.[89] Social-welfare policy was a highly partisan issue in the states in 1963, but much less so in 1974. The decline of partisanship in the state legislatures over social-welfare policy may reflect the increased federal role in this policy area and the concomitant reduction in state latitude, increased Republican acceptance of the government's role in meeting various needs of the disadvantaged, and Democratic disenchantment with welfare as a viable political issue. The two most important state legislative policy issues which emerged during the eleven years between the two studies were questions concerning natural resources and energy. In 1974, legislative divisions concerning these two policy areas were based more on regional interests and/or interest-group activities than on partisan differences.[90]

Partisan Leaders in the State Legislatures

A major responsibility of the political parties in the legislature is to organize the legislature and select legislative leaders. Normally, the majority-party caucus in the lower chamber decides who will be speaker and enforces party discipline on the floor to elect the speaker. A similar practice in the various state senates means that the majority-party caucus determines who will hold the highest elective office in the senate. In many formerly one-party legislatures, however, the practice of fighting it out for speaker on the house floor continues, so the few Republican representatives in Arkansas, Louisiana, Mississippi, and Texas, for example, are able to participate in the factional politics of selecting a speaker.[91]

In recent years, the automatic elevation of the majority party's choice for speaker has been disrupted in some states by dissident members of the majority party in collaboration with minority-party members. In the 1965 New York assembly, for example, Republican members resolved a bitter Democratic caucus disagreement by supporting one Democratic faction's candidate for speaker. More dramatically, a Republican was elected speaker of the New Jersey assembly in 1972 by secret ballot, even though Democrats held a one-vote majority in the chamber. Similarly, the loser for the speakership nomination in the Illinois House Democratic caucus obtained enough Republican support to be elected speaker in 1959 and managed to retain the office in 1961, even though by then Republicans held a majority of House seats.

241

FIGURE 9.2

Differences in the Political Attitudes of Republicans and Democrats

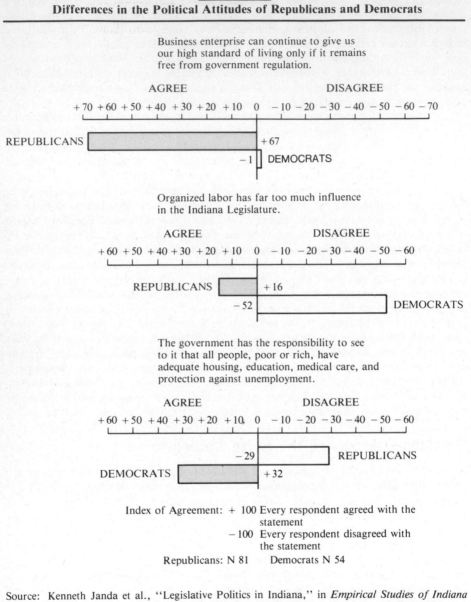

Business enterprise can continue to give us our high standard of living only if it remains free from government regulation.

Organized labor has far too much influence in the Indiana Legislature.

The government has the responsibility to see to it that all people, poor or rich, have adequate housing, education, medical care, and protection against unemployment.

Index of Agreement: + 100 Every respondent agreed with the statement
− 100 Every respondent disagreed with the statement

Republicans: N 81   Democrats N 54

Source: Kenneth Janda et al., "Legislative Politics in Indiana," in *Empirical Studies of Indiana Politics*, ed. James B. Kessler (Bloomington: Indiana University Press, 1970), p. 32.

The Democratic speaker of the Vermont House of Representatives was retained in that leadership post in 1979, despite a modest Republican majority in the chamber.[92] Oregon often has elected its house speakers and senate presidents by cross-party coalitions. In 1977, the Oregon House speaker, a liberal Democrat, was stripped of many of his functions in the House by a coalition of conservative Democrats and Republicans.[93]

Selection of the speaker by a cross-party coalition does not mean there is not structure to the choice. To the contrary, a study of such an election of the speaker of
the New Mexico House of Representatives in 1979 demonstrated that the voting
division in the contest for speaker fitted almost perfectly with voting blocs in the
previous session. Three dominant voting blocs emerged from a factor analysis of
roll-call votes in the previous session. When each representative's percentage of
times voting with the House majority on contested issues was compared to the prior
session's percentage of being on the winning side, the liberal Democrats (whose
speaker was ousted) were found to be 11.5 percentage points less successful in 1979
than in the prior session. House Republicans (almost all of whom had supported
the conservative Democrat for speaker) were 11.7 percentage points more successful
than in the prior session. Conservative Democrats, who had allied themselves with
Republicans to elect one of their own as speaker, were 6.3 percentage points more
successful.[94]

It seldom happens, but a legislative chamber can have exactly the same number
of Democrats and Republicans. Such a split in the membership makes the election
of a speaker very difficult, if even modest levels of party loyalty are customary in
the chamber. That situation developed in the lower chambers of both Washington
and Minnesota in 1979. The Washington house elected both a Republican and a
Democrat to every chamber office, meaning there was a Republican speaker and
a Democratic speaker. These officials issued joint rulings but alternated daily in presiding. Despite numerous (and expected) difficulties, the House did enact legislation.[95] The 1979 Minnesota House of Representatives resolved the same problem
differently. A negotiated agreement gave the speakership to a Republican and divided the committee chairs between the parties. Late in the session, the house, on
a party-line 67-66 vote, expelled a Republican because his campaign literature had
violated the state ethics law. A Democrat was elected to fill the resulting vacancy,
but the Democratic caucus was so bitterly divided that the Republicans were able
to choose which Democratic contender they wanted for speaker in the 1980 session.[96]

The importance of the political party in the state legislature, then, varies greatly.
When Democratic and Republican state legislators represent basically different
types of constituencies, substantial party differences will appear in the voting records
of the chambers. The majority party in a state legislature occasionally reaches a level
of authority rivaling that of the Congressional party in the days of King Caucus
at the turn of the century. Most often, however, the state legislative party is organized in less detail than the Congressional party and has less authority over the legislative careers of its members. This is especially so for the minority party. The weakness of the state legislative parties is especially evident in the frequency (and relative
ease) of the creation of cross-party coalitions in the state legislatures. In part, however, the relative ease with which cross-party legislative coalitions are formed at the
state level also reflects the generally less-institutionalized nature of the state legislatures and the smaller investments most individual legislators have made in their state
legislative careers, when compared to Congress.

Other Groups in the State Legislatures

Like their cousins in Congress, the state legislative parties often find they must compete with other groups or organizations, formal and informal, for the loyalty of legislators and for control over the agenda and policy decisions of the legislative chamber.
Such groups include the delegations from the most populous counties or cities in
the various states; legislators tied to particular interests in the state, such as agriculture, banking, organized labor, liquor, or education; and, in a few states, a Black

243

Caucus or a women's group. Rarely, an especially able lobbyist may have more power over legislative behavior than legislative leaders do. Liquor lobbyist Artie Samish was reputed to be that powerful in the California legislature in the 1940s.[97]

Regional divisions rival partisan divisions in many state legislatures. The split between northern California and southern California is well known and permeates the state's institutions, including the legislature.[98] Similarly, "big-city" versus "outstate" dissension erupts on numerous issues—especially state-spending formulas—in many states. In Illinois, Cook County (Chicago) legislators often find themselves fighting the "outstate" representatives. New York City, Salt Lake City, Boston, Atlanta, Detroit, St. Louis, and other cities, which are the largest population centers of their respective states, often find themselves perceived as wanting to dominate state government or needing special supervision by state government.[99] Indeed, one study of issues in the various state legislatures in 1973–74 found "a substantial amount of regional conflict" was reported more frequently than "heated partisan fights."[100] Some of the regional conflict, of course, is between a metropolitan area's inner city and its suburbs, rather than the urban-rural splits which were more important in the era of malapportionment that preceded the *Baker* v. *Carr* and subsequent "one-man, one-vote" federal-court decrees.

The legislators from the state's largest population centers often are acquainted with each other, even before their legislative service begins. They have some common interest in the state's formulas for allocating state funds for education, highways, health, and other programs and in the state's revenue system. Furthermore, "local legislation" of importance to their county or city requires a degree of cooperation if it is to succeed. Thus, unity often emerges among the members of a populous county's legislative delegation. Partisan differences often cut through that delegation unity, but the delegation's common interests sometimes override party cues. Election of legislators county wide appears to increase a delegation's unity, while election of those legislators by single-member districts decreases voting cohesion among the members of a county's state legislative delegation.[101]

As observed in Chapter 4, the number of minority and female state legislators has increased substantially since 1960 and in a few states, formal and informal groups of minorities or women have formed to discuss issues of special concern to these legislators. In the state legislatures, however, these special caucuses do not seem to have developed the capabilities or the impact of similar special caucuses in Congress.[102]

SUMMARY

Many people believe that the legislators of the two political parties ought to line up in opposing camps on almost every vote, with the majority party being held accountable at the next election for the legislation enacted, as well as for programs not pursued or passed. Some votes in American legislatures are indeed party votes, with most Democrats, say, voting "yes" and most Republicans voting "no." It is the exception, rather than the rule, however, for an American legislature to decide most questions by party-line votes. The structure of the American political system, the large size of the nation, and the diversity of opinion, even within some of the states, coupled with the use of primary elections to nominate legislators, militate against the evolution of legislative parties which are internally in agreement on all or most of the issues. Given the large number of effective pressures to which American legislators are subject and the relatively few powers of the legislative party leaders to enforce party discipline, the wonder may be that the political party label remains the most important single variable in determining the voting behavior of American legislators.

Congress and forty-nine of the state legislatures are organized by party and have legislative party caucuses and legislative party leaders in each chamber. The legislative party in each chamber is independent of that in the other chamber. Membership in the same legislative party does not necessarily mean agreement on a general social view or a philosophy of government. Thus, constituency influence, regional interests, lobbyist efforts, and a diversity of philosophy among the members of each legislative party can lead to relatively low party-unity scores in floor voting. Indeed, in the U.S. Congress, conservative southern Democrats sometimes have voted with the majority of Republicans more often than they have voted with the majority of Democrats.

Each legislative political party in Congress determines the committee assignments of its members, although by tradition members are assigned to the same committee each session unless they request a change. In most of the state legislatures, the minority party has no such control over these assignments. The majority party's leaders determine the committee assignments of all members and are free to shuffle the legislators among the various committees at the beginning of each session or every two years. The authority of the legislative-party caucus and legislative-party leaders varies greatly from state to state and, in any one legislative chamber, over time. Usually acting through the chamber's party caucus, the legislative party in some states attempts to assert a degree of authority over members' legislative behavior which is unheard of in other states or in other eras. In the U.S. Congress, the legislative party most inclined to use the caucus to determine policy outcomes is the House Democratic party. Within the House Democratic party, the Democratic Study Group has been a force for change in the House and for liberal policy positions on the issues.

Members of Congress derive much of their relatively autonomous authority within the chamber from their political parties and have substantial personal investments in maintaining party rule in Congress. State legislators, by and large, have less invested in a state legislative career and do not derive much power from legislative-party seniority on a committee. Thus, many state legislators find their less institutionalized habitats conducive to entering cross-party coalitions to seize control of the legislative chamber.

Notes

1. Leon Epstein, *Political Parties in Western Democracies* (New York: Praeger, 1967), p. 9.

2. For a discussion of the differences between European and American political parties, see Fred R. Harris, *America's Democracy: The Ideal and the Reality* (Glenview, Ill.: Scott, Foresman, 1980), pp. 248, 249.

3. Frank J. Sorauf, *Party Politics in America,* 4th ed. (Boston: Little, Brown, 1980), Chapter 1.

4. More extensive discussion of these tensions appears in Austin Ranney, *Pathways to Parliament* (Madison: University of Wisconsin Press, 1965); and in Samuel H. Beer, *British Politics in the Collectivist Age* (New York: Random House, 1965).

5. This discussion of the importance of the British party model to American analysis of parties and government generally draws in part on Leon D. Epstein's presidential address to the 1979 Annual Meeting of the American Political Science Association. "What Happened to the British Party Model?" *American Political Science Review* 74 (March 1980): 9–22. See also Evron M. Kirkpatrick, "Toward a More Responsible Two-Party System: Political Science, Policy Science, or Pseudo-Science?" *American Political Science Review* 65 (1971): 965–90; and Austin Ranney, *The Doctrine of Responsible Party Government* (Urbana, Ill.: University of Illinois Press, 1962). An excellent discussion of four popular models of how Congress (and Congressional parties) ought to work is in David J. Volger, *The Politics of Congress,* 3rd ed. (Boston: Allyn and Bacon, 1980), pp. 103–30.

6. Epstein, "What Happened to the British Party Model?"

7. Beer, *British Politics in the Collectivist Age;* and Robert McKenzie, *British Political Parties* (London: William Heinemann, 1955).

8. Philip Norton, "The Changing Face of the British House of Commons in the 1970s," *Legislative Studies Quarterly* 5 (August 1980): 333–57; John E. Schwarz, "Exploring a New Role in Policy-Making: The British House of Commons in the 1970s," *American Political Science Review* 74 (March 1980): 23–37; and Edward W. Crowe, "Cross-Voting in the British House of Commons: 1945–1974," *Journal of Politics* 42 (May 1980): 487–510.

9. Kenneth Bradshaw and David Pring, *Parliament and Congress* (Austin: University of Texas Press, 1972), pp. 80–82.

10. Herbert McClosky, Paul J. Hoffman, and Rosemary O'Hara, "Issue Conflict and Consensus Among Party Leaders and Followers," *American Political Science Review* 54 (June 1960): 406–27.

11. If the independence of one chamber's party members from influence or instructions of party members in the other chamber seems only reasonable, note that the party leader of the Venezuelan Chamber of Deputies appoints the party leader of the Venezuelan Senate. See R. Lynn Kelley, *The Venezuelan Senate: A Legislative Body in the Context of Development* (Ph.D. diss., University of New Mexico, 1973).

12. For an examination of factors which determine the role of the minority party in Congress, see Charles O. Jones, *The Minority Party in Congress* (Boston: Little, Brown, 1970).

13. Lawrence C. Dodd and Bruce I. Oppenheimer, "The House in Transition," in *Congress Reconsidered,* ed. Lawrence C. Dodd and Bruce I. Oppenheimer (New York: Praeger, 1977), p. 27.

14. Ibid.

15. "From 1951 to 1965, in fact, the Caucus had not bothered to meet in order to ratify the assignments recommended by its Committee on Committees." Roger H. Davidson and Walter J. Oleszek, *Congress Against Itself* (Bloomington: Indiana University Press, 1977), p. 44.

16. Richard Bolling, *Power in the House: A History of the Leadership of the House of Representatives* (New York: Putnam's, 1974), p. 253.

17. Dodd and Oppenheimer, "The House in Transition," p. 28.

18. Ibid.

19. The discussion which follows draws primarily from Dodd and Oppenheimer, "The House in Transition"; *Inside Congress,* 2nd ed. (Washington, D.C.: Congressional Quarterly, 1979), especially pp. 3–38; Davidson and Oleszek, *Congress Against Itself,* especially pp. 44–50 and 262–74; and Michael J. Malbin, "House Democrats Oust Senior Members from Power," *National Journal* 7 (January 25, 1975): 129–34.

20. An effort to subject chairpersons of subcommittees of the House Ways and Means Committee to individual caucus approval or rejection was defeated by the caucus at the beginning of the Ninety-fifth Congress. *Inside Congress,* 2nd ed., p. 9.

21. William J. Keefe, *Congress and the American People* (Englewood Cliffs, N.J.: Prentice-Hall, 1980), pp. 81–82.

22. *Inside Congress,* 2nd ed., p. 34.

23. Abner J. Mikva, (D., Illinois), as quoted in *Inside Congress,* p. 35.

24. David J. Vogler, *The Politics of Congress,* 2nd ed. (Boston: Allyn and Bacon, 1977), p. 232.

25. A somewhat dated but valuable study is Charles O. Jones, *Party and Policy-Making: The House Republican Policy Committee* (New Brunswick, N.J.: Rutgers University Press, 1964).

26. Sorauf, *Party Politics in America,* 4th ed., pp. 124–25.

27. Larry Light, "Republican Groups Dominate in Party Campaign Spending," *Congressional Quarterly Weekly Report,* November 1, 1980, pp. 3234–39.

28. *Congressional Quarterly Weekly Report,* September 27, 1980, p. 2854.

29. Arthur G. Stevens, Jr., Daniel P. Mulhollan, and Paul S. Rundquist, "U.S. Congressional Structure and Representation: The Role of Informal Groups," *Legislative Studies Quarterly* 6 (August 1981): 416–17.

30. Ibid., p. 419.

31. Arthur G. Stevens, Jr., Arthur H. Miller, and Thomas E. Mann, "Mobilization of Liberal Strength in the House, 1955–1970: The Democratic Study Group," *American Political Science Review* 68 (June 1974): 667; Mark F. Ferber, "The Formation of the Democratic Study Group," in *Congressional Behavior,* ed. Nelson W. Polsby (New York: Random House, 1971), p. 253.

32. *Congressional Quarterly Weekly Report,* February 3, 1981, p. 381.

33. Joseph P. Harris, *Congress and the Legislative Process* (New York: McGraw-Hill, 1967), p. 54.

34. Randall B. Ripley, *Party Leaders in the House of Representatives* (Washington, D.C.: Brookings Institution, 1967), p. 177.

35. On state delegations, see Barbara Deckard, "State Party Delegations in the U.S. House of Representatives: A Comparative Study of Group Cohesion," *Journal of Politics* 34 (February 1972): 199–222; Richard Born, "Cue-Taking Within State Party Delegations in the U.S. House of Representatives," *Journal of Politics* 38 (February 1976); and John H. Kessel, "The Washington Congressional Delegation," *Midwest Journal of Political Science* 8 (February 1964): 1–21.

36. Arthur B. Levy and Susan Stoudinger, "The Black Caucus in the 92nd Congress: Gauging Its Success," *Phylon* 39 (December 1978): 322–32.

37. Burdett A. Loomis, "Congressional Caucuses and the Politics of Representation," in *Congress Reconsidered,* 2nd ed., ed. Lawrence C. Dodd and Bruce I. Oppenheimer (Washington, D.C.: Congressional Quarterly, 1981), p. 208.

38. Daniel P. Mulhollan, Susan Webb Hammond, and Arthur G. Stevens, Jr., "Informal Groups and Agenda Setting in Congress" (Paper delivered at the 1981 Annual Meeting of the Midwest Political Science Association, Cincinnati, Ohio).

39. Sarah E. Warren, "The New Look of the Congressional Caucuses," *National Journal* 10 (April 1978): 678–79.

40. Kathleen A. Frankovic, "Sex and Voting in the U.S. House of Representatives: 1961–1975," *American Politics Quarterly* 5 (July 1977): 315–30.

41. Warren, "The New Look of the Congressional Caucuses," p. 678. Much of the discussion in this section on other caucuses is drawn from Warren.

42. Loomis, "Congressional Caucuses and the Politics of Representation," pp. 207–10.

43. Ralph K. Huitt, "The Morse Committee Assignment Controversy: A Study in Senate Norms," *American Political Science Review* 51 (June 1957): 313–29; reprinted in Ralph K. Huitt and Robert L. Peabody, *Congress: Two Decades of Analysis* (New York: Harper and Row, 1969), pp. 113–35. The Senate in the Eighty-third Congress included forty-eight Republicans, forty-seven Democrats, and one Independent (Morse). In 1955, Senator Morse joined the Senate Democratic conference (and the Democratic party) and received more prestigious committee assignments than he had held as a Republican.

44. *Politics in America,* 4th ed. (Washington, D.C.: Congressional Quarterly, 1971), p. 52.

45. Ibid. The Conservative party and the Liberal party are well-established minor parties in New York.

46. Randall B. Ripley, *Power in the Senate* (New York: St. Martin's Press, 1969), p. 15.

47. Ibid., p. 31.

48. John G. Stewart, "Two Strategies of Leadership: Johnson and Mansfield," in Polsby, *Congressional Behavior,* pp. 61–92.

49. Robert L. Peabody, *Leadership in Congress: Stability, Succession and Change* (Boston: Little, Brown, 1976), p. 338.

50. Largely as a result of the reforms voted through the House Democratic caucus, some second-term representatives chaired lesser House subcommittees in the Ninety-fifth Congress and a freshman chaired a minor subcommittee of the District of Columbia Committee in the Ninety-fourth Congress. Burdett A. Loomis, "The Congressional Office as a Small (?) Business: New Members Set up Shop," *Publius* 9 (Summer 1979): 40.

51. For an insightful analysis of the changing nature of the Senate, see Norman J. Ornstein, Robert L. Peabody, and David W. Rohde, "The Changing Senate: From the 1950s to the 1970s," in Dodd and Oppenheimer, *Congress Reconsidered,* pp. 3–20.

52. *Inside Congress,* 2nd ed., p. 6.

53. Peabody, *Leadership in Congress,* pp. 332–35, 350–51.

54. Ibid., pp. 423–24.

55. Ibid., p. 427.

56. Ibid., pp. 424–32.

57. Larry M. Schwab, *Changing Patterns of Congressional Politics* (New York: D. Van Nostrand, 1980), p. 99.

58. A. Lawrence Lowell, "The Influence of Party upon Legislation," *Annual Report of the American Historical Association* 1 (1901); Julius Turner, *Party and Constituency: Pressures on Congress* (Baltimore: Johns Hopkins Press, 1951), pp. 23–24.

59. Julius Turner, *Party and Constituency: Pressures on Congress,* rev. ed., ed. Edward V. Schneier (Baltimore: Johns Hopkins Press, 1970), pp. 17–18.

60. Jerome M. Clubb and Santa A. Traugott, "Partisan Cleavage and Cohesion in the House of Representatives, 1861–1974," *Journal of Interdisciplinary History* 7 (Winter 1977), cited in William J. Keefe, *Congress and the American People* (Englewood Cliffs, N.J.: Prentice-Hall, 1980), p. 90.

61. Aage R. Clausen, *How Congressmen Decide: A Policy Focus* (New York: St. Martin's Press, 1973), p. 94.

62. Region and ideology do not correlate perfectly, of course, but, for purposes of illustration, they go together well enough. The ability of region to split both Congressional parties on roll-call voting on environmental, consumer, and energy policy is noted by Barbara Sinclair, "House Voting Alignments in the 1970s—The Effects of New Issues and New Members" (Paper delivered at the 1980 Annual Meeting of the Midwest Political Science Association, Chicago, Ill.). The impact of ideology on Congressional voting in the early 1970s is stressed by Jerrold E. Schneider, *Ideological Coalitions in Congress* (Westport, Conn: Greenwood Press, 1979). Schneider argues that his data cast doubt on the conventional view of multidimensional Congressional voting; he finds that members of Congress can profitably be viewed as being arrayed on a single underlying liberal-conservative dimension. Some support for that position is also provided by William R. Shaffer, "Dimensions of Ideology in the U.S. Senate" (Paper delivered at the 1979 Annual Meeting of the Southern Political Science Association, Gatlinburg, Tenn.). See also John F. Hoadley, "The Dimensions of Congressional Voting, 1971–78: Some Preliminary Considerations" (Paper delivered at the 1980 Annual Meeting of the Midwest Political Science Association, Chicago, Ill.).

63. That there was, and is, a conscious conservative coalition has been clearly demonstrated by John F. Manley. For an insightful and entertaining analysis, see his "The Conservative Coalition in Congress," in Robert L. Peabody and Nelson W. Polsby, eds., *New Perspectives on the House of Representatives,* 3rd ed. (Chicago: Rand McNally, 1977), pp. 97–117. See also Mark C. Shelly, II, "The Conservative Coalition and the President, 1953–1978" (Paper delivered at the 1979 Annual Meeting of the Southern Political Science Association, Gatlinburg, Tenn.).

64. *Congressional Quarterly Weekly Report,* January 10, 1981, p. 85.

65. *Congressional Quarterly Weekly Report,* June 13, 1981, p. 1026.

66. Ibid.

67. Dennis Farney, "Gypsy Moths Feel Reagan Is Up a Tree Without Their Votes," *Wall Street Journal,* October 1, 1981, p. 1. The group named itself after the pest so prevalent in the Northeast.

68. John C. Wahlke, Heinz Eulau, William Buchanan, and LeRoy C. Ferguson, *The Legislative System: Explorations in Legislative Behavior* (New York: John Wiley, 1962), Chapter 15.

69. William Buchanan, *Legislative Partisanship: The Deviant Case of California* (Berkeley: University of California Press, 1963).

70. Charles M. Price, "The California Legislature: A Description and an Analysis," in *Consensus and Cleavage: Issues in California Politics,* ed. Charles M. Price and Earl R. Kruschke (San Francisco: Chandler, 1967), p. 273.

71. Bruce W. Robeck, *Legislators and Party Loyalty: The Impact of Reapportionment in California* (Washington, D.C.: University Press of America, 1978), p. 80; Alvin D. Sokolow and Richard W. Brandsma, "Partisanship and Seniority in Legislative Committee Assignments: California After Reapportionment," *Western Political Quarterly* 24 (December 1971): 740–60.

See also Henry A. Turner and John A. Vieg, *The Government and Politics of California* (New York: Thomas Y. Crowell, 1969).

72. Alan Rosenthal, *Legislative Performance in the States* (New York: Free Press, 1974), p. 57.

73. Thomas A. Flinn, "The Ohio General Assembly: A Developmental Analysis," in *State Legislative Innovation,* ed. James A. Robinson (New York: Praeger, 1973), pp. 267–75.

74. *American State Legislatures: Their Structures and Procedures,* rev. ed. (Lexington, Ky.: Council of State Governments, 1977), p. 20. Data are as of January 1977. No state legislative chamber was one-party Republican, although the Idaho and South Dakota lower chambers and the South Dakota and Vermont Senate were 2-to-1 Republican or more.

75. Samuel Patterson, "Dimensions of Voting Behavior in a One-Party State Legislature," *Public Opinion Quarterly* 26 (Summer 1962); 185–200. The situation in a one-party dominant legislature is different. In these legislatures, where the second party consistently wins some seats, the impact of party appears primarily on issues on which the governor has taken a stand. "Both . . . parties exhibited greater cohesion when the governor became a factor in voting", regardless of whether the governor's party was the dominant party in the legislature or the persistent minority. E. Lee Bernick, "The Impact of U. S. Governors on Party Voting in One-Party Dominated Legislatures," *Legislative Studies Quarterly* 3 (August 1978): 431–44.

76. V. O. Key, Jr., *Southern Politics* (New York: Vintage Books, Caravelle Edition, 1949), pp. 302–10.

77. Susan Welch and Eric H. Carlson, "The Impact of Party on Voting Behavior in a Nonpartisan Legislature," *American Political Science Review* 67 (September 1973): 865.

78. Wilder Crane, Jr., and Meredith W. Watts, Jr., *State Legislative Systems* (Englewood Cliffs, N.J.: Prentice-Hall, 1968), p. 92; David R. Derge, "Metropolitan and Outstate Alignments in Illinois and Missouri Legislative Delegations," *American Political Science Review* 52 (December 1958): 1051–65; Glen T. Broach, "A Comparative Dimensional Analysis of Partisan and Urban-Rural Voting in State Legislatures," *Journal of Politics* 34 (August 1972): pp. 905–21; and Malcolm E. Jewell, *The State Legislature: Politics and Practice* (New York: Random House, 1962), p. 53.

79. Samuel C. Patterson, "American State Legislatures and Public Policy," in *Politics in the American States,* ed. Herbert Jacob and Kenneth N. Vines (Boston: Little, Brown, 1976), p. 179.

80. *American State Legislatures: Their Structures and Procedures,* p. 67.

81. John J. Carroll and Arthur English, "Governing the House: Leadership of the State Legislative Party" (Paper delivered at the 1981 Annual Meeting of the Midwest Political Science Association, Cincinnati, Ohio).

82. *American State Legislatures: Their Structures and Procedures,* p. 67.

83. See Alan G. Hevesi, *Legislative Politics in New York State* (New York: Praeger, 1975), p. 9. The New York legislature removed the electronic voting machines a few years after installing them.

84. Robeck, *Legislators and Party Loyalty,* p. 82.

85. Malcolm E. Jewell, "The Political Setting," *State Legislatures in American Politics,* ed. Alexander Heard (Englewood Cliffs, N.J.: Prentice Hall, 1966), p. 90.

86. Wayne L. Francis, *Legislative Issues in the Fifty States* (Chicago: Rand McNally, 1967); Hugh L. LeBlanc, "Voting in State Senates: Party and Constituency Influences," *Midwest Journal of Political Science* 13 (February 1969): 33–57; Charles W. Wiggins, "Party Politics in the Iowa Legislature," *Midwest Journal of Political Science* 11 (February 1967): 87–94.

87. Malcolm E. Jewell, "Party Voting in American State Legislatures," *American Political Science Review* 49 (September 1955): 773–91.

88. Wayne L. Francis and Ronald E. Weber, "Legislative Issues in the 50 States: Managing Complexity Through Classification," *Legislative Studies Quarterly* 5 (August 1980): 407–21. This article is the basis for the remainder of this paragraph.

89. Ibid., p. 414. There are exceptions, of course. The state judiciary was the focus of strong partisan divisions in the 1970 Oklahoma legislature, for example. That judicial controversy saw one state supreme court justice impeached and two resign. Samuel A. Kirkpatrick, *The Legislative Process in Oklahoma* (Norman, Okla.: University of Oklahoma Press, 1978), pp. 147–49.

90. Francis and Weber, "Legislative Issues in the 50 States," pp. 417–18.

91. "Partisanship and Bipartisan Coalitions," *Comparative State Politics Newsletter* 1 (May 1980): 11.

92. "Partisanship and Bipartisan Coalitions," pp. 11–15. The Vermont speaker originally had been elected in 1975, with unanimous Democratic support and some Republican votes as well.

93. Ibid., p. 14.

94. Janet Clark and Cal Clark, "Policy Effects of a Bipartisan Legislative Coup" (Paper delivered at the 1980 Annual Meeting of the American Political Science Association, Washington, D.C.).

95. A major factor allowing the two-speaker system to work was that the Republican speaker and the Democratic speaker were personal friends. Hugh A. Bone, "Washington: A Tie in the House," *Comparative State Politics Newsletter* 1 (October 1979): 15–16; William F. Mullen and K. G. Wolsborn, "The Effects of the Tie in the Washington State Legislature in 1979" (Paper delivered at the 1980 Annual Meeting of the Western Social Science Association, San Francisco, Calif.).

96. Craig H. Grau, "Minnesota: An Evenly Divided House," *Comparative State Politics Newsletter* 1 (October 1979): 16; and *Comparative State Politics Newsletter* 1 (May 1980): 15.

97. John H. Culver and John C. Syer, *Power and Politics in California* (New York: John Wiley, 1980), p. 63.

98. Price, "The California Legislature," pp. 280–81.

99. See, for example, David R. Derge, "Metropolitan and Outstate Alignments in Illinois and Missouri Legislative Delegations," pp. 1051–65; Robert C. Benedict, "Making Haste Slowly: Republican Majorities in the Land of Zion" (Paper delivered at the 1980 Annual Meeting of the Western Social Science Association, Albuquerque, N.M.).

100. Francis and Weber, "Legislative Issues in the 50 States," p. 412.

101. Keith E. Hamm, Robert Harmel, and Robert J. Thompson, "The Impact of Districting on County Delegation Cohesion in Southern State Legislatures: A Comparative Analysis of Texas and South Carolina" (Paper delivered at the 1979 Annual Meeting of the Southern Political Science Association, Gatlinburg Tenn.).

102. William Boone and Nathaniel Jackson, "The New South and Black Legislators: An Analysis of Black Georgia State Legislators" (Paper delivered at the 1979 Annual Meeting of the Southern Political Science Association, Gatlinburg, Tenn.); Charles W. Dunn, "Black Caucuses and Political Machines in Legislative Bodies," *American Journal of Political Science* 17 (February 1973); Roger Handberg and Wanda Lowery, "Women State Legislators and Support for the Equal Rights Amendment," *Social Science Journal* 17 (January 1980); and Janice C. May, "The Texas Legislature: Regular and Special Sessions," *Comparative State Politics Newsletter* 2 (October 1981): 8.

chapter *10*

Legislative Committees

Preview

This chapter considers the role of committees in the American legislative process. Hardly any measure is voted on unless it has first been considered by a legislative committee. Standing or permanent committees are responsible for legislation drafting and reporting. There are also joint, select or special, and conference committees. The powers and prestige of standing committees differ greatly, with intense competition among legislators for the most coveted committee assignments. Committees have several general functions. Standing committees act as filters, screening the great numbers of legislative measures that are introduced. They serve as panels of experts as well as communications links with society and other branches of government. Committees also assist legislatures in their watchdog oversight of the executive department. Legislative norms, or informal rules of behavior, have important effects on the functioning of committees—especially the norms of apprenticeship, legislative work, specialization, and reciprocity. State legislatures have the same general types of committees as the U.S. Congress, but some use joint committees much more. Some state legislatures also use interim committees to work on legislative problems between sessions. Congressional committees are more stable in membership than state legislative committees. This is largely due to the seniority system which gives members the right to be assigned repeatedly to the same committees and provides for the elevation of the senior majority member of a Congressional committee to committee chair, while assignment to state legislative committees is usually made anew each two years.

The use of legislative committees in Western legislatures dates back to the earliest days of the British Parliament. In periods when the monarch's spies reported for persecution those who opposed the monarch's wishes, committees were used to allow secret and informal debate among members at meeting times and places told only to trusted legislators, well away from the king's agents.[1] Similar mechanisms were used in some of the early American colonial legislatures to allow legislators to avoid scrutiny of their work by the governor.[2] Called Grand Committees, these private meetings of the members were the precursors of today's Committee of the Whole House. In today's legislatures, the Committee of the Whole House (usually called the Committee of the Whole) is used as a device to permit all the members of the legislative chamber to meet as if they were in a committee, with less formal rules, to expedite business. As in the Grand Committees of old, a temporary chairperson presides rather than the permanent Speaker or presiding officer.

COMMITTEES IN THE U.S. CONGRESS

At first, the U.S. Congress was reluctant to establish standing, or permanent, committees. The only standing committee established by the House in the first three Congresses, for example, was the Committee on Elections, created in the First Congress.[3] Federalists feared that standing committees would rival the authority of the executive department heads. Others believed the entire membership of each Congressional chamber should be involved in the details of each piece of legislation.[4] The normal procedure in the early Congresses was to debate an issue in the Committee of the Whole; appoint a select committee to write the legislation, if a majority favored passage of legislation on the topic; and then have the Committee of the Whole consider the select committee's report. The Committee of the Whole's consideration of an issue prior to the appointment of a select committee left the broad outline of the chamber's wishes clear enough. The select committee merely filled in details; and no member who opposed the sense of the Committee of the Whole was appointed to the select committee.[5] The select committees of the early Congresses were subservient to the wishes of the entire chamber membership.

In the first two Congresses, the Committee of the Whole turned, in the absence of any institutionalized internal expertise, to the appropriate executive department for guidance concerning legislative proposals. However, when the Federalists lost control of the House in the Third Congress, such formal referrals of legislation to the executive ceased. By the end of the first decade of its existence, the U.S. Congress had begun to move into extensive use of standing committees but, even so, the entire membership of each chamber was involved in each bill at a level of detail which would astonish the Congressional observer of the 1980s.[6] Today, the U.S. Congress and the state legislatures refer almost all legislation to committees before discussing the topic on the floor of the chamber, and few observers can even imagine the modern American legislature operating without its committees.

Types of Congressional Committees

There are four types of Congressional committees: standing committees; select or special committees (the terms are interchangeable); joint committees; and conference committees. All committees of Congress (as opposed to committees of a Congressional party) include both Democrats and Republicans. Each is chaired by a member of the majority party, and so are the subcommittees.[7]

Standing Committees The standing committees are permanent, created by the rules of each chamber. These committees and their subcommittees do most of the work of the Congress, considering and reporting out almost all the legislation which is finally considered on the floor. The policy jurisdictions of these committees are set forth in the rules, and each committee jealously guards its jurisdiction because that defines its power.

The standing committees are the ones which have made the Congressional seniority system famous, for it is seniority on these permanent *legislative* committees (committees with the authority to report legislation to the floor for a vote) which gives individual members of Congress fairly autonomous authority. The other types of committees of Congress seldom are granted legislative authority. The House has twenty-two standing committees, the Senate fifteen. (See Table 10.1.)

The standing committees of Congress can be divided into three basic types: housekeeping, authorization, and money committees. *Housekeeping* committees are mainly concerned with the operations of the legislative chamber. The Senate Rules and Administration Committee is such a committee, although it has some modest additional authority concerning presidential succession. The House Administration Committee is similarly concerned primarily with internal matters. The House Rules Committee can also be considered a Housekeeping Committee in that its concern is the orderly flow of legislation to the floor of the House. But the House Rules Committee (unlike the Senate Rules Committee) has a substantial impact on the decisions of the House and, under the present "reformed" rules, is very much an arm of the chamber leadership, performing its housekeeping functions in harmony with the policy preferences of the Speaker.

The *money* committees of Congress are concerned with taxation, appropriations, and the budget. Tax policy, tariffs, and trade and revenue measures are the major

TABLE 10.1
Congressional Committees, Ninety-seventh Congress, 1981–1982

	House	Senate
Standing Committees	Agriculture	Agriculture, Nutrition,
	Appropriations	and Forestry
	Armed Services	Appropriations
	Banking, Finance, and	Armed Services
	Urban Affairs	Banking, Housing, and
	Budget	Urban Affairs
	District of Columbia	Budget
	Education and Labor	Commerce, Science, and
	Energy and Commerce	Transportation
	Foreign Affairs	Energy and Natural
	Government Operations	Resources
	House Administration	Environment and
	Interior and Insular Affairs	Public Works
	Judiciary	Finance
	Merchant Marine and Fisheries	Foreign Relations
	Post Office and Civil Service	Governmental Affairs
	Public Works and Transportation	Judiciary
	Rules	Labor and Human Resources
	Science and Technology	Rule and Administration
	Small Business	Veterans' Affairs
	Standards of Official Conduct	
	Veterans' Affairs	
	Ways and Means	
Select Committees	Aging	Aging
	Intelligence	Ethics
	Narcotics Abuse and Control	Indian Affairs
		Intelligence
		Small Business

Source: *Congressional Quarterly, Special Report,* March 28, 1981.

focus of the House Ways and Means Committee and the Senate Finance Committee, although both also function as authorization committees in their jurisdiction over Social Security, health insurance, welfare, and foreign trade. Because tax breaks and tax levels are so important to so many Americans, members of these two committees are given great respect in Congress.

The House Appropriations Committee and the Senate Appropriations Committee focus on government expenditures. No money can be spent by the government unless it has first been appropriated by Congress (although some kinds of "back-door" spending do exist, as with authorizations for Social Security and welfare).[8] Because they stand astride the flow of federal expenditures, the House and Senate Appropriations Committees and their members are very powerful actors in Congress.

The House and Senate Budget Committees differ from each other, as will be noted later, but both are concerned with the overall federal budget, balancing income against expenditures, and attempting to force the two chambers of Congress to develop the federal budget in a deliberate and informed fashion, rather than largely by noncoordinated decisions. Partly because they have been in existence only since 1975, and partly because of the structure of the budget process, these committees have been less powerful, overall, than the appropriations and taxation committees of each chamber.[9]

The *authorization* committees consider bills that authorize the existence of various government agencies and programs and set a recommended funding level for those agencies. That authorized funding level is a ceiling, above which the appropriations committees cannot go. But the appropriations committees are not required to appropriate as much money as has been authorized for a particular program or agency. Because there are usually more demands for money than money available for expenditure, it is not unusual for an agency's actual appropriation to be substantially less than its authorization. All standing committees of Congress except the appropriations, budget, and housekeeping committees are authorization committees.

Select Committees Select committees of Congress are established by one or another chamber for the duration of the Congress which creates them. They are sometimes called special committees. Although they are often reconstituted in several successive Congresses, these committees, unlike standing committees, must win a new vote of approval every two years, or they pass out of existence. See Table 10.1 for a list of the select committees of the Ninety-seventh Congress. Select committees are established to examine particular problems or situations, to placate an interest group, or to circumvent a standing committee with jurisdiction over (but little interest in) a particular policy area. Select committees are formally expected to report their findings and cease operations within two years. The Senate Select Committee on Ethics and the Senate Select Committee on Small Business, however, are two select committees which seem unlikely to be shut down soon; they may manage to convert to permanent committee status. Select committees seldom are granted legislative authority, but their recommendations are sometimes the basis of legislation that is subsequently, and separately, considered by a standing committee and enacted by Congress. Select committees often are effective in calling the attention of Congress and of the public to a particular problem and in legitimizing various claims or demands.[10]

Joint Committees Joint committees of Congress include both representatives and senators as members. Established by law, they are permanent committees, like the standing committees, but are rarely centers of power. They almost never have the power to consider and report legislation. An exception was the old Joint Committee on Atomic Energy, which did have legislative powers and—partly because of the exotic nature of its jurisdiction—had substantial authority over the development of the nation's nuclear policies.[11]

Joint committees are mainly expected to study problems and make recommendations to the two chambers of Congress or to the relevant standing committees of the two chambers. They are created primarily as instruments of coordination. The Ninety-sixth Congress (1979–80) had four joint committees. The Joint Economic Committee is charged with studying the President's annual Economic Report to Congress and making recommendations to both chambers. The Joint Taxation Committee makes recommendations concerning tax policies to the House Ways and Means Committee and the Senate Finance Committee. The Joint Committee on the Library (Library of Congress) and the Joint Committee on Printing are, as their names imply, housekeeping committees, intended to coordinate internal administrative matters of concern to both chambers.

Conference Committees   Conference committees are of a different species entirely from the committees already discussed. For a legislative proposal to become law, it must pass both chambers in identical form. Even if one word is changed (*the* is substituted for *a*) somewhere in the text of the bill, the bill cannot go forward toward enactment until the two chambers agree on which version to accept. The House and Senate often pass different versions of a piece of legislation and are unable to agree readily on a single version of the legislation that will be acceptable to a majority in both bodies. In such a situation, each chamber's presiding officer appoints members to a conference committee, which then tries to reconcile differences between the House and Senate versions of the bill and report back to the floor of each chamber a version of the bill which will be acceptable to both bodies. (No floor amendments are permitted to a bill reported back by a conference committee; the chamber vote is strictly "yes" or "no.") Once the conference committee's specific task is completed, the committee goes out of existence. Some last a few hours; others last for weeks or in rare cases for months.

Committees of the U.S. House of Representatives

The various committees of the House and Senate sometimes have different names and different jurisdictions. House committees are considered separately from Senate committees here. Committee assignments in both bodies are also treated separately.

Standing Committees of the House   The twenty-two standing committees of the U.S. House of Representatives are not of equal importance, do not all perform the same functions, and are treated somewhat differently within the House. The House Budget Committee, for example, is the only standing committee of Congress to which members are assigned on a temporary rather than on a permanent basis. Members of standing committees, other than the Budget Committee and the Rules Committee, have a recognized right to be reappointed to the committees they were on during the previous Congress.

The House Budget Committee was created by the Budget and Impoundment Control Act of 1974, as part of a series of institutional changes intended to bring greater order to the preparation of the federal budget and to offset the executive branch's dominance of the budgetary process. Assignment to the House Budget Committee is for a maximum of six years out of any ten, and half the Budget Committee members each Congress must be new members. Five of the Budget

Committee's twenty-five members must be from the Appropriations Committee, five must be from the Ways and Means Committee, and two others must be from among the Democratic and Republican party leaders. Appropriations Committee members approved of the creation of the Budget Committee as a means to prevent the other standing committees of Congress from using various "back-door" spending tactics to circumvent the normal appropriations process. But members of the Appropriations Committee and the Ways and Means Committee wanted to insure that the new Budget Committee would not dominate them. The Budget Committee membership restrictions seem to have accomplished that goal.[12]

Democrats on the House Rules Committee are also in an odd situation concerning appointments to standing committees. Members of all other standing committees (except the Budget Committee) have a right to be reappointed to the committee in successive Congresses, if they so choose. The party committee on committees merely fills vacancies on most committees. Democratic appointments to the House Rules Committee, however, are made by the Speaker, when the Democrats are the majority, and are made anew every Congress. Democratic members of the Rules Committee, therefore, must satisfy the Speaker or risk losing their Rules Committee assignments.[13] Neither the Speaker nor the Democratic Committee on Committees has such power over members of the other House committees.

Perhaps a useful way to categorize House standing committees is by the scope of the issues they handle. Some committees are concerned with national issues, while others primarily focus on the relatively narrow needs of committee-related clientele. Others are primarily housekeeping committees. (See Table 10.2.)

While the national-issue committees are exciting, not all members find them attractive.[14] Members' goals differ, as do their abilities. Most committees, even the least important ones, are attractive to some members, but a few, such as the Committee on Standards of Official Conduct, are so unattractive that members have to be assigned to them against their wishes.[15]

There is a status hierarchy, or pecking order, among House committees. Some are more important and desirable than others. One guide to their relative importance is the body of rules governing how chairpersons are chosen. The House Democratic caucus requires a caucus vote to approve or disapprove the nominee of the Democratic committee on committees for chairperson of each standing committee. But for most committees the rules allow the Democrats on that committee to determine who will be the chairpersons of subcommittees. Because of the power of the subcommittees of the House Appropriations Committee, however, the caucus also requires full caucus approval of the chairpersons of the Appropriations Committee's subcommittees.

Another convenient way to determine the relative attractiveness of House committees—and indirectly their prestige—is to examine the flow of members from one committee to another. When a representative leaves one committee to join another, he or she loses the years of seniority on the first committee and must begin anew as a junior member on the second committee. That is a substantial disincentive for changing committees, and members do so only if they find the alternative committee much more attractive than the one on which they had been serving.

Studies of transfers from each standing committee of the House to the others for the period 1963 through 1972 show that the three most desired committee assignments in the U.S. House were to Appropriations, Rules, and Ways and Means. Close behind were the Armed Services Committee, and Foreign Affairs Committee.[16] Members were willing to sacrifice even a decade of seniority on another committee to transfer to these more prestigious committees, and that was especially true of

TABLE 10.2
Committees Classified According to the Scope
of the Issues Handled

Senate Committees	House Committees
National Issue Committees	
Aeronautical & Space Sciences (Dis.)*	Science & Astronautics (Dis.)
Appropriations (Dis.)	Appropriations (Dis.)
Armed Services (Dis.)	Armed Services (Dis.)
Finance (Redis.)	Ways and Means (Redis.)
Foreign Relations	Foreign Affairs
Judiciary (Redis.)	Judiciary (Redis.)
	Rules
	Un-American Activities
Clientele-oriented Committees	
Agriculture & Forestry (Dis.)	Agriculture (Dis.)
Banking & Currency (Reg., Redis.)	Banking & Currency (Reg., Redis.)
Commerce (Reg.)	Interstate & Foreign Commerce (Reg.)
Interior & Insular Affairs (Dis.)	Interior & Insular Affairs (Dis.)
Labor & Public Welfare (Reg., Redis.)	Education & Labor (Reg., Redis.)
Public Works (Dis.)	Merchant Marine & Fisheries (Dis.)
	Public Works (Dis.)
	Veterans' Affairs (Dis.)
Housekeeping Committees	
District of Columbia	District of Columbia
Government Operations	Government Operations
Post Office & Civil Service (Dis.)	Post Office & Civil Service (Dis.)
Rules & Administration	House Administration
	Standards of Official Conduct

*The abbreviations in parentheses after the committee titles designate which of the categories the committees involved with such policies tend to fall into: distributive (involving government subsidy, with decisions reached relatively easily since no one group stands to lose much), regulatory (involving government regulation, with hard-fought decisions since some groups do stand to lose), and redistributive (involving government manipulation with class overtones and resulting in especially hard-fought decisions).

Source: George Goodwin, Jr., *The Little Legislatures: Committees of Congress* (Amherst: University of Massachusetts Press, 1970), pp. 102–3.

Ways and Means and Appropriations. (See Figure 10.1.) All five of the more prestigious committees consider issues of national scope. In addition, each of the first three committees is capable of being involved in virtually any issue of importance which is considered by Congress, if the committee chooses to be involved. Most issues of any importance are in some way related to taxation and revenue (Ways and Means Committee), even if merely to provide tax incentives for particular activities. Most require funding (Appropriations), and most require a "rule" (from the Rules Committee) prior to floor consideration by the entire chamber.

This analysis concerning the attractiveness of committees in the House was made before the recent wave of committee reforms. Those reforms have probably reduced somewhat the attractiveness of the Ways and Means Committee by taking away from that committee's Democratic members their control over Democratic commit-

FIGURE 10.1

Pattern of Movements Among U.S. House Committees, Eighty-eighth through Ninety-second Congresses

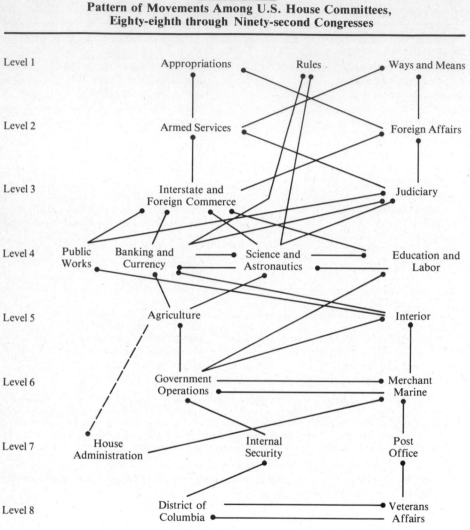

Note: With the exception of one member moving from Agriculture to House Administration (dashed line), all committee transfers in the decade charted were *upward* movements (such as from Foreign Affairs to Appropriations) or lateral movements (as from Banking and Currency to Science and Astronautics or vice versa). *No* member of a Level 1 committee transferred.

Source: Malcolm E. Jewell and Chu Chi-hung, "Membership Movement and Committee Attractiveness in the U.S. House of Representatives, 1963-1971," *American Journal of Political Science* 18 (May 1974): 437.

tee assignments (discussed later). The attractiveness of the Rules Committee as an independent center of power has also been diminished somewhat by the Speaker's special new power over appointments to that committee. But the list of the top five committees of the House has probably not changed, although many members also now seek appointment to a temporary term on the House Budget Committee. (Budget Committee members retain their rank on their "home" committees.)

Members are attracted to the top committees of the House because of the scope of authority of the committees and the intrinsically interesting nature of their subject matter, but many members are also attracted to them because being a member of such a committee brings power or status, or both. Appropriations, Ways and Means, and Rules are generally perceived as "power" committees.[17] When Richard Fenno, Jr., asked the members of the House Appropriations Committee and the House Ways and Means Committee why they had sought membership on those committees, an overwhelming majority replied that they sought "power," "prestige," or "importance." "[T]he members of the two committees possess special capacities to affect the political fortunes of their House colleagues and, . . . consequently, assignment to the two committees is highly prized by House members."[18] Involved in the power, prestige, or importance of a committee to which a member may be assigned is the matter of whether membership on the committee will be helpful to the member's reelection. In recent years, House members have found the Judiciary Committee less attractive because such membership does not aid reelection, partly because of the rise of single-issue groups, the low public interest in such subjects as judicial reform, and the inability of the committee to distribute funds to members' districts.[19]

Members are attracted to other committees as well for a variety of motives. Some are more concerned about insuring good decisions in a particular field of policy than about obtaining power within the chamber, although, frequently a member's desire for "good policy" is tinged with ideological fervor.[20] Some members pick their committees primarily to help their constituents and to insure reelection.

> The close correspondence between the Interior Committee's jurisdiction and the most pressing constituency problems of Western congressmen make the committee uniquely attractive to them. A Westerner . . . may be hard put to think of reasons why he should *not* seek membership on [Interior], at least until his tenure is secure.[21]

A mixture of motives is not uncommon. Those who seek to make a career within the House seem most likely to request assignment to a "power" committee. Such an assignment carries with it a very heavy committee workload, leading most of its members to concentrate exclusively on that one committee, and this can, incidentally, interfere with a serious ambition to seek election to the Senate or a governorship. Members interested in a career beyond the House (big-city mayor, governor, or U.S. senator are the most common) tend to choose committees which they believe will help them in that effort. The Interior Committee is popular among Westerners for that reason, as is Foreign Affairs, especially for representatives with ambition to serve in the U.S. Senate.[22]

Subcommittees in the House Developments in the House over the past few Congresses have increased the independent role of the standing committees' subcommittees. These developments include Democratic caucus rules limiting the number of committee and subcommittee chairs each member can hold (thus expanding the number of Democrats who can chair a committee or subcommittee). They also include the requirement that most committees must create subcommittees and the expansion of subcommittee autonomy, resulting from a Democratic caucus decision to vest authority over subcommittees and their chairpersons in the Democratic members of each standing committee, rather than in the standing-committee chairperson. The Democratic caucus today grants each subcommittee chair some authority over subcommittee staff, independent of the authority of the chairperson of the standing committee.[23]

Partially as a result of these reforms, the jurisdiction of the various subcommittees has become clarified and more or less accepted. The subcommittees have begun to perform a larger share of the work of the House. The number of special subcommittees has plummeted, while the number of standing subcommittees has grown dramatically—creating a sense of permanence among subcommittees and an atmosphere of continued policy impact (and control) for them from one Congress to the next.

> A standing subcommittee has a greater assurance that it will continue to exist in the next session of Congress in the same form. This enables a subcommittee to undertake major investigations that might require more than one session of Congress to complete. In addition, a standing subcommittee often acquires jurisdiction over future amendments to legislation it has previously handled.[24]

It is even possible that "the committees' status in the House and their recruitment patterns may be altered because assignments to committees will increasingly be viewed primarily as pathways to subcommittees."[25] Many of our observations about the standing committees of the House apply now to the subcommittees of those standing committees, and others may well apply over the next few Congresses.

Select Committees of the House Select committees, as noted earlier, serve a variety of purposes within the House, but most are in existence for a relatively short time. The House had three select committees during the Ninety-seventh Congress (1981–82), down from five such committees in the preceding Congress. The three were Aging, Intelligence, and Narcotics Abuse and Control, whose subjects of special interest are evident from their titles. The Select Committee on Intelligence is repeatedly established during each succeeding Congress, with members who also, for the most part, serve on related standing committees.

The appointment of a select committee to enable the House to circumvent a jurisdictional tangle is well illustrated by the 1977 appointment of a House Ad Hoc Select Committee on Energy. In part, that committee was appointed because of the large number of House committees and subcommittees which claimed a piece of energy-program jurisdiction and the resulting difficulty of obtaining coherent legislation. In part, it was appointed to enable the Speaker and his lieutenants to keep track of the development of the energy package and to get as much of the President's energy program through the House as possible. Because of objections from the chairs of the standing committees and subcommittees to the creation of this select committee, the Ad Hoc Select Committee on Energy was given "secondary jurisdiction over all the pieces of the energy package once the standing committees and subcommittees had an opportunity to work on them."[26]

> This achieved several important goals. First, it gave the process a sense of legitimacy in that the committee system would not be subverted and the relevant committee chairs could be placated. Second, it provided a mechanism for bringing the pieces of the program back together so it could be sent to the floor as a package. Third and most important, it allowed the ad hoc committee to serve as a safety valve. It could settle any remaining jurisdictional disputes, and it could protect the Carter energy program from the parochialism of the various committees.[27]

A rather complex set of rules allowed the Speaker to establish a deadline by which date the standing committees had to report their pieces of the energy legislation, but the Ad Hoc Select Committee on Energy was denied the authority to change, or "mark up" such legislation in committee. Instead, the select committee was required to propose any changes in the standing committee versions as floor amendments to be voted on by the entire chamber membership.[28] The select committee's authority was thus undermined significantly. Still, its appointment did allow the leadership of the House to keep better track of the vital energy legislation and to pull its disparate pieces together.

Committee Assignments in the House Except for members of the Budget Committee and Democrats on the Rules Committee, representatives who are reelected have a right to automatic reappointment to the standing committees on which they had served in the immediately prior Congress, unless a member's political party has lost so many seats in the House that the party is forced to reduce its membership on a particular committee. Even Democrats on the Rules Committee are unlikely to be removed from that committee, except for continued lack of cooperation with the Speaker.

A member's right to automatic reappointment to committees, of course, is the basis of the seniority system discussed at length later in this chapter. Once on a committee, a member's rank on the committee and within the party on the committee is determined primarily by continued service or seniority on the committee. A member who changes committee assignments begins as a junior member of the new committee, starting all over to accrue seniority as a member of the party on the *new* committee.[29] Despite changes in the rules, discussed later, the most senior majority-party committee member normally becomes chairperson of the committee, and the most senior minority-party committee member becomes "ranking minority member" of the committee. The emphasis on seniority in selection of committee chairpersons brings predictability to a career within Congress and makes unbroken service and continued automatic reappointment to the same standing committees very important to the members.[30]

The committee assignments made at the beginning of each Congress (every two years), then, are assignments to vacancies on committees. If they request reassignments, members returning to Congress may change committees. New members must all, of course, be given initial committee assignments. We will first discuss the mechanics of how committee assignments are made and then consider the factors which decide who gets what appointment.[31]

The fundamental fact of the committee-assignment process is that each political party in the U.S. House of Representatives is in control of the committee assignments of its own members. Thus, Democratic representatives must seek their committee assignments from the Democratic party committee on committees, called the Steering and Policy Committee, and Republican representatives must similarly seek their committee assignments from the Republican party Committee on Committees. Decisions of the party committees on committees are subject to approval of the party caucus and can be appealed to the caucus.

The parties negotiate between them the ratio of Democratic and Republican seats on the various committees of the House, with the ratio on each committee roughly proportional to each party's share of the total seats in the House. When the House is closely divided, however, the majority party normally receives extra seats on the Appropriations Committee, Rules Committee, and Ways and Means Committee. Such an extra margin of seats on these key committees is considered important to the majority party's ability to dominate the major policy decisions of the Congress. When a change occurs in the ratio of Democrats and Republicans in the House, the ratio of seats on the committees and the majority party's extra representation on the most important committees becomes a subject of controversy. This was the case following the 1980 elections, when the Republicans gained thirty-three seats in the House, but the Democrats preferred not to alter the distribution of seats on committees.

In any event, once each party knows the number of seats it will have on each committee, the party decides which party members to appoint to vacancies. Republican committee assignments are made by the House Republican party's Committee on Committees, which is unabashedly structured to insure that the Republican representatives from the six or eight states with the largest Republican delegations in the House control the committee-assignment process. Each state with any Republican representatives is entitled to a seat on the Committee on Committees, elected by that state's Republican members. But voting on the committee is weighted. Each members casts as many votes as there are Republican members from his or her state. The subcommittee which actually makes the decisions—later ratified by the full Committee on Committees and then by the House Republican conference—is even more decidedly weighted toward the large state delegations. And on the subcommittee too, each representative casts as many votes as his or her state has Republican representatives.

The Democratic committee on committees is the twenty-four-member House Democratic Steering and Policy Committee, chaired by the Speaker (or, if the party is in the minority, by the minority leader).[32] The Speaker, the majority leader, and the chair of the Democratic caucus serve ex officio on the Steering and Policy Committee. Nine members are appointed by the Speaker to insure representation of women, black members, and junior members. The whip and various deputy whips are also among the appointed members. Half the members of the committee are elected by members from various geographic regions of the country. Each member has one vote, but normally the Speaker's opinions carry the greatest weight. As mentioned earlier, the Speaker alone appoints Democratic members to the House Rules Committee.

The committee assignment process in the House is complex. An understanding of its importance begins with the realization that House members normally serve on only one or two House committees, although there are increasing examples of members being appointed to a third committee, sometimes on a temporary basis. As discussed earlier, individual members have diverse motivations which lead them to seek assignment to particular committees. These motivations may include constituency interests, individual backgrounds, policy concerns and opportunity, as well as each member's personal career objectives. No matter how much a member may desire a seat on a particular committee, however, it is unlikely that the wish will be fulfilled if a colleague from the same state and party is already serving on the committee, especially if the state is not large and the committee is fairly prestigious. But, if one of the vacancies on the committee was caused by the departure of a party colleague from the member's home state, then the member's chances of winning the committee assignment are enhanced. Indeed, the largest state delegations seem to "own" seats on the key committees of the House. Regional considerations are similarly weighted to serve members from smaller states.[33]

The party committees on committees consider a number of factors in making committee assignments. The committee's evaluation of the member plays an important part. "Responsible" members, who play by the rules—formal and informal—and who can be counted on to keep their word, exercise discretion on sensitive matters, support the party position when possible, and work hard at committee responsibilities, are more likely to win the assignments of their choice than are less well-reputed members. Indeed, some relatively junior members occasionally are sought out by the leadership and invited to request assignment to desirable committees. The practice of the committee on committees to assign only "responsible" members to the more important committees is one reason that few first-year representatives receive such prestige assignments. Such members normally will not yet have persuaded the party leadership that they are responsible members.

A very important factor in the decisions of each party's committee on committees is the fact that each party wants to be the majority party. One of the best ways for them to accomplish this goal is to give members committee assignments that will help them get reelected, thus retaining seats for that party. Members who can make a case that a particular committee assignment is important to their reelection chances are more likely to win the assignment than members who cannot make such a case. On the other hand, being from a relatively safe district—and thus being free of excessive outside pressure and of excessive need to woo the constituency—can mean that a member will have the time to devote to the demands of major committee membership, and this can sometimes help a member get a seat on a prestige committee.

A member's positions on issues can also help or hinder his or her quest for a particular committee assignment. During the Eisenhower years, for example, conservative Republicans controlled the Republican Committee on Committees. Regardless of other considerations, "they would not permit any Republican member to be appointed to the powerful Ways and Means Committee unless he *opposed* Eisenhower's liberal position on reciprocal trade. On the other hand, while Sam Rayburn held sway as Speaker, no Democrat was chosen to this committee unless he agreed to *support* the reciprocal trade program.[34]

Major interest groups have a stake in the decisions of the party committee on committees. Agricultural-interest groups, for example, frequently are consulted about assignments to the Agriculture Committee. "Democrats attempt to placate organized labor by placing pro-labor representatives on the Education and Labor Committee, while Republicans attempt to satisfy the National Association of Manufacturers by appointing pro-business members to the same committee. The most widely publicized groups connected with assignments to the Ways and Means Committee (which writes tax legislation) are spokesmen for the oil interests."[35]

Committees of the U.S. Senate

The Senate has fewer members than the House; therefore, it must divide its work among fewer committees than the House does. Further, senators receive more committee assignments than representatives do. Therefore, senators are able to pursue more simultaneous routes to committee power in Congress than are Representatives, and they are generally not the narrow policy-field specialists that the committee system in the House produces. In addition, because committees are smaller, a senator can reach a position of some influence on his or her committee more quickly than a representative can. It is not uncommon, for example, for a new majority-party senator to be chairperson of a minor Senate subcommittee. Similar status in the House usually requires at least two terms of House service. It is unusual, even in the Senate, for a very junior member to become chairperson of a standing committee, but, when the Republican party took control of the Ninety-seventh Congress Senate in 1981, the Veterans' Affairs Committee was chaired by a senator with only two years of service, and the Labor and Human Resources Committee by a senator with only four years of service. That was in dramatic contrast to the Ninety-sixth Congress, in which all but one of the Democratic chairpersons of the standing committees were in at least their third terms.[36]

Senate Standing Committees   There are fifteen standing committees in the Senate, as well as several select and special committees (see Table 10.1). In 1977, the number of Senate committees was reduced and committee jurisdictions and memberships rearranged. That major restructuring of Senate committees was the first since the Reorganization Act of 1946. This latest reorganization permits more rational consideration of today's issues, many of which were not thought important in 1946. For example, jurisdiction over energy questions was not a major focus of concern in 1946, but in 1977, the Senate wanted to reduce the numbers of committees that shared jurisdiction over energy legislation. So it enlarged the old Interior Committee's jurisdiction and gave it a new name: the Energy and Natural Resources Committee. Realignment of jurisdiction over transportation policy, on the other hand, was limited by senators (especially committee chairpersons) who did not want to lose influence over various aspects of transportation policy. The 1977 reorganization also reduced scheduling conflicts between each senator's various committee and subcommittee meetings.[37]

As in the House, some Senate committees are mainly national-issue committees, others are oriented primarily toward serving the needs of relatively narrow clientele groups, and yet others function mainly in a housekeeping capacity. Some committees were subtly transformed by the 1977 Senate committee reorganization. The old Interior and Insular Affairs committee, for example, had primarily been a clientele-oriented committee. With its added responsibilities, the new Energy and Natural Resources Committee is now as much a national-issue committee as it is a clientele-oriented one, although it could fall into old habits and transform the nation's energy program into a set of policies narrowly designed to satisfy powerful interest groups with special access to the committee and its staff.[38]

Also as in the House, the importance of the different Senate committees varies. To some degree, variations in importance and status are recognized by the new Senate rules, which classify thirteen of the fifteen Senate committees as "major" committees. The Senate's select and special committees are "minor" committee assignments, as are two standing committees—the Rules and Administration Committee and the Veterans' Affairs Committee.

Although the 1977 reorganization of the Senate committee structure makes earlier studies of the relative prestige of Senate committees seem dated, there are still clear categories of Senate committees beyond the *official* "major" and "minor" categories. The various studies of the subject over the past twenty years agree with Matthews that the Senate committees on Foreign Relations, Appropriations, and Finance are the most prestigious committees in the Senate, although the relative position of these top three committees may be a subject of debate.[39] Indeed, it may well be that the relative attractiveness of the three committees varies somewhat from session to session, although they all remain more attractive to senators overall than the remaining committees of the Senate. Because of the broad-ranging authority it possesses over the budget and because, unlike its House counterpart, the Senate Budget Committee is a permanent committee assignment, that committee is likely to be a much-sought, semi-prestige committee, as are Armed Services and Judiciary.[40] The Senate Foreign Relations Committee has greater prestige than its House counterpart, in large part because of the Senate committee's role in confirmation of ambassadorial and high State Department appointments and because of its role in ratification of treaties. The Senate Judiciary Committee must

264

clear all nominees for the federal bench, a responsibility not shared with the House Judiciary Committee.

Select Committees of the Senate   The select and special committees of the U. S. Senate serve the same basic functions as in the House. The Senate does not give its Ethics Committee and Small Business Committee permanent (standing) committee status—choosing instead to renew them each Congress as select committees. The House, as earlier noted, has standing committees of the same name, with similar jurisdictions. Like the House, the Senate has a Select Committee on Intelligence. It also has a Special Committee on Aging, to recognize the special problems of the rapidly growing number of elderly Americans, many of whose problems cut across the jurisdictions of various standing committees. The Senate also has a Select Committee on Indian Affairs, although it is not at all certain that the separate existence of this committee will continue to be renewed.

Committee Assignments in the Senate   As in the House, assignments to the committees of the U. S. Senate are a responsibility of the political parties in the Senate, and each member is entitled to continue serving on his or her committees from the previous Congress. The majority and minority parties work out each party's ratio of seats on the various committees, and then each party assigns its own members. The whole Senate ratifies the party lists. Independent or minor-party members who did not join a major-party caucus would get the least significant committees of the Senate, from which vantage points they would have little influence.

The rules of the Senate limit the number of committee and subcommittee assignments that each senator may hold and insure each senator at least one major committee assignment. Most senators hold seats on two or three major committees, plus one or two minor, select, or joint committees. But, in the Ninety-sixth Congress, two Democratic senators (Howard Metzenbaum of Ohio and Donald Riegle of Michigan) each held seats on four major committees; while both were members of the Budget Committee, and Metzenbaum was a member of the Judiciary Committee, their remaining committee assignments were of middling importance. Even members and chairpersons of the most prestigious Senate committees normally hold seats on two other standing committees, enabling them to participate in the legislative details of a much broader range of legislation than is permitted in the House (where membership on more than two committees is the exception, and members of prestige committees normally devote their entire attention to that one committee assignment). The greater specialization in the House, though, means that representatives tend to become greater subject-matter experts than senators, whose efforts are so widely spread that they are more dependent on staff members to work out legislative details.

The chairperson of the Senate Republican conference appoints the Republican Committee on Committees, which makes Republican committee assignments. Much depends on the personal style of the party floor leader, but the leader can have substantial impact on the committee-assignment process. The Republicans attempt to base their committee assignments on seniority but:

> In 1965, the Republican Conference made a formal change. Except for members already sitting, no Republican can now hold seats on more than one of the four most important committees: Foreign Relations, Appropriations, Finance and Armed Services. A Republican now serving on one of these cannot fill a vacancy on another one unless no other Republican wants it.[41]

Republican leaders still have some leverage, however, especially when two senators of comparable seniority covet an assignment. Sometimes, too, a senior member requests a committee transfer, with the intent of blocking a disliked junior Republican from an important committee. Thus, in 1973, Senator Robert Griffin (R., Michigan) reportedly moved from the Finance Committee to Foreign Relations, in large part to block Senator Edward Brooke (R., Massachusetts) from using a seat on Foreign Relations to espouse his dovish views on Vietnam.[42] Occasionally, such a blocking request is made in response to prodding by the party leadership.

Senate Democrats make committee assignments through their Steering Committee, chaired by the Democratic floor leader. When Lyndon Johnson was majority leader, he introduced the "Johnson Rule" in 1953 to improve the chances that each junior Democrat would receive at least one desirable committee assignment, and that policy has generally been followed since. The Johnson Rule gave Johnson greater flexibility in the assignment of senators to committee vacancies and enhanced his authority as majority leader. Seniority counts in Democratic committee assignments, as do region, political philosophies and issue positions, and the general reputations of those seeking assignments. Some observers are persuaded that chairpersons of important committees have in the past blocked the assignment of unwanted senators to the chairpersons' committees.[43]

> Undoubtedly . . . one of the major considerations in receiving a favorable [committee assignment] is whether the member . . . has by hard work mastered the specialized committee work he has been given, shown a willingness to compromise on his objectives based on an understanding of the problems of other senators, demonstrated loyalty to the Senate as an institution, and been cooperative with party leaders.[44]

While senators normally have to give up an existing committee assignment to receive a new one, that is not always the case. Sometimes the majority leader may ask a senator to accept an additional assignment to a relatively unimportant committee to retain majority-party control of the committee. The senator who seeks a more desirable committee assignment usually has to abandon one committee, but need not relinquish all of them. Because each senator serves on several committees, he or she can retain committee assignment and seniority on certain committees, while "trading" the other assignment for a bottom of the ladder seat on a more desirable committee. Overall then, the costs involved in climbing the committee ladder in the Senate are smaller—especially for a member of moderate seniority—than is the case in the House.

The number of seats on each committee in the Congress is not immutable. Rather, the number depends on the will of the chamber and changes can be, and are, made. Majority Leader Lyndon Johnson, for instance, with the agreement of Minority Leader Everett M. Dirksen (D., Illinois), obtained an increase in the size of the more sought-after Senate committees and a decrease in the size of the less desirable committees. Then, in order to be able to reward his own supporters more freely, Johnson for a time kept secret the increased number of seats on desirable committees, so that less-favored senators would not request assignment to them.[45] Expansions of committee size can, of course, change the ideological complexion of a committee, as was the case in regard to the House Rules Committee in the Eighty-eighth Congress. That committee was enlarged explicitly to bring its views more in line with the policies of the new Kennedy administration.[46]

Senators seek assignment to the various committees of the Senate for about the same range of reasons representatives seek committee assignments in the House.

———————————————★ ☆ ★ ★————————————————

Getting a Preferred Committee Assignment

After his election in 1964 to the remaining two years of a U.S. Senate term, Fred Harris went immediately to Washington, D.C. to be sworn in (and begin accumulating seniority). He was met at the Washington airport by an aide to his predecessor.

> He advised me to try to get on one of the "water" committees—the Interior and Insular Affairs Committee or the Public Works Committee. . . . He said that I should talk personally about obtaining this assignment with Senator Carl Hayden of Arizona, who was the dean of the Senate and an influential member of the [Democratic] Senate Steering Committee, which made committee assignments. . . .
>
> I . . . [went] to see Senator Hayden about committee assignments. . . . Senator Hayden had been a member of Congress since the first day of Arizona's statehood. Before that, he'd been a county sheriff, and he'd campaigned for Congress at stagecoach stations. . . . I took a seat in front of his desk and launched into my pitch about wanting to be on one of the "water" committees. As I talked, Senator Hayden's eyelids closed, and his face relaxed into an expressionless repose. My Lord, he's gone to sleep on me! I thought, and I cut my presentation short. But the moment I stopped talking, his eyes opened again. He sat up in his chair and said in a surprisingly firm voice, "All right, son, I'll help you get on either the Public Works Committee or the Interior Committee, and once you're on one or the other, I want you to vote for my Central Arizona Water Project." He hadn't been asleep at all.

Source: Fred R. Harris, *Potomac Fever* (New York: W.W. Norton, 1977), pp. 50, 53, 54.

———————————————★ ★ ★ ★————————————————

Some assignments bring the ability to help the home state or important interest groups within the state. Indeed, members occasionally report being under great pressure by a certain interest group to seek assignment to a particular committee so that the senator can be of greater service to the interest group.[47] Other committees give a senator a voice in determining national policies which are of interest to him or her. Yet others enable a member to achieve greater status within the Senate. Appropriations and Finance are committees that bring power, prestige, and the ability to affect policy decisions across a broad spectrum. These committee assignments also enable a member to assist many interest groups back home.

Committee Leaders in Congress

As has long been recognized, there are two kinds of leaders in Congress, the elected party and chamber leaders and the seniority-based committee leaders. Recent changes in the rules of the two chambers have resulted in enhanced authority for the Speaker of the House and the other elected leaders of that chamber and also in a degree of accountability to the party caucus for the committee chairpersons of both chambers. House committee chairpersons or ranking minority members are now subject to ratification by secret ballot in the caucuses of both parties.[48] In 1975, that procedure led to the removal of three chairpersons of standing committees in the House, although the basic seniority system was utilized to select the successors to those who were deposed. The House Democratic caucus also votes on the subcommittee chairpersons of the House Appropriations Committee, and in 1977, voted out the chairperson of one such subcommittee for conflicts of interest. No such expulsions have occurred in the Senate.

Committee Chairpersons The authority of committee chairs in both chambers has been restricted, so that they do not have the scope of authority over committee affairs or over subcommittees that they had a decade ago. More clearcut jurisdictions for subcommittees and their greater independence have enhanced the authority of the subcommittees and their chairpersons and have reduced somewhat the status and power of the chairpersons of the full committees. However, committee chairs still have substantial status and independent authority. They still hire and fire the majority-party committee staff, for example, thus predetermining the philosophies of the people who do the detailed research and draft much of the legislation for committee approval. Because the chairpersons of Congressional committees remain major independent actors in the legislative process and determine the course of most legislation, an examination of the route followed to become the chair of a committee is appropriate.

The essentials of the seniority system in the two chambers of Congress are the same. For purposes of becoming a committee chairperson, what counts is seniority on the committee in the majority party. A member who is defeated for reelection and later returns to Congress must start over again at the bottom of the seniority ladder of any committees to which he or she is assigned, even if they are the same committees on which the member had previously served. Such returning members, though, do outrank first-time members with no prior service. Often, by way of compensation, returning members are assigned to somewhat better committees than they had served on earlier.

When members are assigned to a committee, their seniority among fellow partisans is established in a clear fashion right then. Such clarity at the outset avoids difficulties ten or twenty years later.

> If two or more members go on a committee at the same time, note is taken of previous political experience. If previous political experience is equal, procedure is determined by lot, by alphabetical arrangement of names, or by the date when the incumbent's state came into the Union, (depending on the party and the chamber of interest). Once established, the seniority order is not disturbed.[49]

Only if a member declares as an Independent, openly and vigorously supports the other party's candidate for President, or otherwise commits a serious breach of party etiquette would the member risk loss of a committee assignment or of seniority in the party on the committee. Although this seldom occurs, such offenses *have* resulted in the loss of seniority on committee, as happened to two House Democrats who openly supported Republican Barry Goldwater for President in 1964. Thus, although rank on Congressional committees theoretically is a perquisite handed out by the party organization in Congress, in fact, committee rank is almost always awarded on the basis of one's length of service in the party on the committee.[50]

Use of committee seniority among majority-party members to determine who will chair a committee provides the institution with the stability of an automatic decision rule and clarifies the expectations of members. But the rule is not neutral, and it is criticized severely by some members. Congressional districts and states that reelect the same person to Congress repeatedly gain substantial independent power that is subject only to indirect party-caucus control or weak negotiation by elected party leaders in the chambers. States or districts which are politically competitive, and do not return the same members repeatedly, get smaller shares of that power.

Further, for years after the steady decline in the percentage of southern Democrats in Congress, the seniority of the remaining southern Democrats continued to entitle them to a disproportionately large share of committee chairs, even though they were mostly out of step philosophically with a majority of their Democratic Congressional colleagues. Conservative members of Congress successfully blocked changing the seniority system until the 1970s. Part of their willingness to submit to the recent rules changes, which have the potential at least of upsetting the established seniority system, may result from projections that the operation of the seniority system in the not too distant future will disproportionately reward nonsouthern and liberal Democrats.[51]

The seniority rule's defenders argue that it insures subject-matter competence, but then, so would a rule which called for a minimum number of years of service on a committee as a requirement to become eligible to chair it, followed by selection on the basis of ability. Further, strict adherence to years of committee service as a criterion by which to measure subject-matter competence would require that returning members with prior service on a committee be returned to that committee if they so desired, with their prior seniority recognized, but such is not the case.[52]

The "roll-of-the-dice" nature of the seniority system is well illustrated by the selection, in January 1981, of two junior Republicans to be chairpersons of standing committees of the Senate. Senator Orrin G. Hatch of Utah became chairperson of the Senate Labor and Human Resources Committee after only four years in the Senate, and after having ranked fourth of six minority members of the committee in the previous Congress. A "major" committee of the Senate, Labor and Human Resources is important to certain interest groups, but it is not among the more sought-after committee assignments. Still, its chair is in a position of substantial power. The committee's ranking Republican in the Ninety-sixth Congress (Schweiker of Pennsylvania) did not seek reelection. The second-ranking Republican (Javits of New York) was defeated. The remaining Republican ahead of Senator Hatch on the committee (Stafford of Vermont) chose instead to chair the Environment and Public Works Committee, of which he was ranking minority member in the Ninety-sixth Congress. Similarly, Senator Alan K. Simpson (R., Wyoming), with only two years' Senate service, vaulted from third ranking (of four) Republican on the Senate Veterans' Affairs Committee to chairperson of that committee. This is a "minor" committee, but it is a standing committee, and it reports legislation of great importance to a selective constituency. Senator Simpson became chairperson when the two Republicans senior to him on the committee chose to chair other committees on which they were the most senior members. Other Republican senators, senior to Senators Hatch and Simpson, chair important subcommittees of major Senate committees, but do not have the status of chairing their own standing committees. The seniority system can place a premium on chance.

Subcommittee Chairpersons So far, this discussion has focused on chairpersons of the standing committees of Congress, the only committees routinely granted the authority to write legislation and report it to the floor. The chairpersons of the subcommittees of these standing committees have recently gained greater independence in both chambers, including greater control over subcommittee staff and the power of having more clearly defined subject-matter jurisdiction. The chairperson of a standing committee no longer can arbitrarily decide which subcommittee will consider a particular piece of legislation or who will be the subcommittee chairpersons. Indeed, the selection of subcommittee chairs is more democratic and less seniority-encrusted than is the selection of the chairs of the standing committees. Further, restrictions on the number of subcommittees each member can chair has meant that relatively junior members now chair some of the subcommittees, giving a share of the power to areas of the country which do not have senior representatives or senators. The other side of the coin, however, is that authority is now so widely scattered as to make the development of coherent policy difficult when a broad piece of legislation, such as energy legislation, is being considered.[53]

In the House of Representatives, Democrats are limited by their party rules to membership on no more than five subcommittees.[54] Further, among the Democrats on each House committee, each member must be allowed to select one subcommittee membership before any member gets to select his or her second subcommittee assignment. This makes it easier for junior committee members to serve on the more important subcommittees of each standing committee.

Democratic party rules in the House create a Democratic caucus on each committee, comprised of all Democratic members of the committee. Except for subcommittees of the House Appropriations Committee—whose chairpersons are nominated by the Democratic Steering and Policy Committee and confirmed by vote of the House Democratic caucus—the Democratic caucus on each committee selects the chairpersons of the subcommittees by secret ballot. The committee caucus makes many other administrative decisions as well, although the chairperson of the committee is the leading figure in such deliberations.

The Democratic members of each committee "bid" for the position of subcommittee chair in their order of seniority. The most senior member of each subcommittee bids for the subcommittee chair and traditionally is confirmed as the chairperson of that subcommittee. To elect someone other than the most senior member as the chairperson, the Democrats on the subcommittee must first vote not to grant the chair to that senior member. Then, other members interested in chairing the subcommittee may bid for the post, again in order of seniority. In the Ninety-fourth Congress, under the new rules, two full committee chairpersons were voted out of subcommittee chairs they also held on the same committee. And, in 1979, the Democratic members of the House Commerce Committee and the Government Operations Committee elected three relatively junior Democrats as subcommittee chairpersons over other members with committee seniority greater than theirs. The choices apparently were dictated more by policy differences on issues before the committee than by any other factor.[55]

The Senate adopted new rules, effective in 1979, which restrict any one senator to chairing a total of three committees and subcommittees. However, no senator can chair more than one full committee, and a chairperson of a *major* committee may chair only one subcommittee of a major committee. That means, of course, that junior senators now chair some subcommittees and gain control of staff, agenda setting, holding hearings, and drafting and reporting legislation. Even new senators begin to feel that they belong and have a voice in Senate affairs when they find themselves the chairperson or ranking minority member of a Senate subcommittee, even if a relatively unimportant one. While the new Senate rules have provided even the most junior members of the majority party with an opportunity to chair a subcommittee, the senior senators still chair the most important subcommittees and committees, and no contests, similar to the seniority upsets in the House, have occurred in the Senate.

COMMITTEES IN THE STATE LEGISLATURES

As in Congress, the bulk of most state legislatures' work is accomplished in the standing committees of each chamber, although some use joint standing committees to a greater or lesser degree. Most of our discussion here applies to the workhorse joint legislative committees of state legislatures that use them, as well as to standing committees.

Legislative committees exist in all the states, and they perform about the same functions in the state legislatures as they do in the Congress. But the process of assigning members to the committees of the state legislatures and of selecting chairpersons of those committees is much more turbulent and obviously political than is the process in Congress. Further, the state legislatures have some types of committees, particularly interim committees, that do not exist in Congress.

The number of committees in the various state legislatures and the number of members of each committee vary widely among the states. Most lower chambers have between ten and twenty standing committees. Only fifteen states had twenty-one or more standing committees in 1978. The maximum number of committees (among states which did not make extensive use of joint legislative committees) was forty-five in North Carolina, and the minimum was six in Maryland. State senates normally have fewer committees than the lower chambers, which follows from their smaller chamber membership in each state. Only four state senates had over twenty-one standing committees; most had between nine and eighteen. Maryland had only five. The two chambers have equal numbers of committees in ten states, which makes creation of parallel legislative jurisdiction easier. And, in three states (Mississippi, Montana, and South Carolina), the smaller state senate actually has more committees than the lower chamber.[56]

Joint Legislative Committees

Fifteen states have one or more permanent *joint* standing legislative committees, which regularly consider legislation during the legislative session. With the demise of the Joint Committee on Atomic Energy, the U.S. Congress has no such joint legislative committee, nor do thirty-five of the states. In most of the fifteen states with joint legislative committees, the bulk of the legislative work is still done by the separate standing committees in each chamber. Massachusetts, however, has only four separate standing committees in each chamber, compared to twenty-one joint standing committees; Connecticut and Maine each have twenty-two joint standing committees and *no* separate standing committees of either chamber.[57] Most of the work of those state legislatures is done in joint committees on which both representatives and senators sit together, hold one hearing instead of two, and recommend legislation to the floors of the two chambers of the legislature. The bicameral nature of the legislature is preserved in the separate votes required on the floors of the two legislative chambers. Both Connecticut and Maine have over four times as many representatives as senators, which means that each senator has many committee assignments.[58]

Interim Committees

Many state legislatures also have *interim* committees, committees which meet during the interim between legislative sessions. Committee membership includes both representatives and senators. These committees are especially important in states that limit legislative sessions to ninety days or less per year. The U.S. Congress, on the other hand, meets as long as it needs to, and thus has no necessity for interim committees (and strong institutional jealousies between the two houses might not allow them to function well). Interim committees serve the state legislatures well, in permitting year-round participation in policymaking and oversight of the other branches of state government and in helping to develop subject-matter expertise among the legislators and the legislative staff. Subjects which require lengthy and careful consideration beyond what can reasonably be done in the state legislative sessions are often assigned to an interim committee, with a report expected at the next legislative session. The existence of interim committees also allows state legislative leaders to reward individual legislators by having topics important to them assigned to an interim committee and by permitting them to serve on, or chair, such a committee. This can assist favored legislators in their reelection attempts and thus help bind the legislators to the legislative leadership. Some interim committees employ temporary staff personnel from among key legislators' supporters in the constituency.

Interim committees are seldom granted legislative authority—the authority to release a bill directly to the floor of either chamber for a vote. Rather, an interim committee either issues a report and a set of recommendations for consideration by the legislature and its standing committees during the next session or it drafts legislation which members of the interim committee introduce during the legislative session (often with the interim committee's endorsement). Such legislation is then referred to a standing committee of the legislature, the same as with other legislation. The work of an interim committee has weight in the legislative session, however, because most members of an interim committee are members (sometimes chairpersons) of the related standing committees of the legislature.

While some interim committees are created by the legislative leadership more to reward supporters among their fellow legislators than to forward the public interest and the institutional interests of the legislature, many interim committees are created for a mixture of these motives. Occasionally, a state may have a controversial problem which suggests the need for investigation by an interim committee of the legislature, but few legislators (at least few the leaders trust) are willing even to serve on the committee, much less chair it, because the potential political costs may be much greater than the likely rewards. These problems may relate to such subjects as liquor law or license reform, sex education in the public schools, or the death penalty.[59]

Committee Assignments in State Legislatures

While the details vary from state to state, different committees of state legislatures have different levels of prestige. Some are very powerful and prestigious committees on which first-year members almost never serve. Others are sometimes suspected of being created just so the legislative leaders can assign certain out-of-favor colleagues to nonfunctioning (and thus powerless) committees, while meeting the rule that each legislator must be assigned to a certain number of committees. Normally, the taxation and appropriations committees of each legislative chamber are "prestige" committees. Where jurisdiction over taxation and spending is concentrated in a single committee (as it is in some state senates), that committee is doubly powerful and elite. Just being a member of such a committee often brings with it a degree of prestige in the legislature. Most members of such committees are dependable supporters of the top leadership in the chamber.

As in Congress, not all legislators have the same list of committee preferences. Legislators who also work for a local public-school system may want to be members of the Education Committee. Farmers and ranchers place a high priority on the chamber's Agriculture Committee. Attorneys like to serve on the Judiciary Committee and often try to keep nonattorneys *off* that committee. Executives of regulated industries, such as banking, insurance, trucking, and utilities may want to be on the relevant legislative committee, by whatever name. Similarly, legislators with strong labor support may want to be on either the labor or business committee of the chamber. The taxation committee, of course, affects most business people and professionals, so it wins high marks on that ground as well.

While state legislatures do not ignore the prior service, personal experience, and legislative expertise of individual members, the seniority system found in Congress is *not* duplicated in the state legislatures.[60] In part, that is probably the result of the fact that few state legislatures are as institutionalized on any dimension of organization as is Congress. After all, not many meet as long as Congress does, the best-paid state legislators earn much less than a member of Congress, and few serve in the state legislature as long as members of Congress do. In short, the state legislature is much less of a career focus than Congress and thus is less important and all-encompassing in the eyes of the members. The rules on committee assignments reflect that state of affairs.

Lower Chamber Committee Assignments The *Book of the States* lists only one lower chamber (Texas) as having even a "modified seniority system," although Rosenthal reports seniority systems functioning in the Arkansas and Virginia lower chambers in the early 1970s.[61] In the remainder, seniority is only one of many factors considered in the appointment of members to committees. Others are political philosophy, individual subject-matter expertise, region of the state represented, as well as the urban or rural nature of the legislator's constituency, and party affiliation. Usually, they also include faction within the party, the extent to which a legislator is considered "responsible" in the institutional context, and the legislator's relationship with the legislative party leadership.

The normal pattern in the lower chambers of the state legislatures is for the speaker of the house to appoint all members and chairpersons of all committees and to have an entirely free hand in doing so. Such powers are constrained of course by the speaker's need to create a coalition within his or her own party (and sometimes with members of the other party) to win election to the office of speaker, but no formal rule restricts the speaker's authority to determine committee assignments and committee chairs. Strong seniority norms of course would limit that discretion. In three lower chambers the speaker has authority only over the committee assignments of members of the speaker's own party, while the minority leader decides which members of his or her party will serve on which legislative committees. In Nevada, the appointing authority is granted to the majority and minority leaders respectively, rather than to the speaker. Three states use a variant of the committee on committees to make committee assignments, with the majority party's committee determining who will be committee chairs. Hawaii decides on committee assignments by vote of the party caucus, with the majority caucus choosing the committee chairpersons. But even in those states where the speaker's formal authority is limited, he or she in fact has a prominent voice in decisions concerning committee assignments, especially of majority-party members.

Some of the states which restrict the speaker's authority in appointing members to committees allow the speaker to decide which member will chair each committee, although in Kentucky chairpersons are elected and in Alaska they are nominated by the committee on committees and are confirmed by vote. Wyoming confirms the Speaker's appointment of chairpersons by vote of the majority caucus, while Hawaii and North Dakota elect their committee chairs in the majority caucus. The speaker thus determines committee chairs in forty-three of the lower chambers and has a strong voice in the selection of committee chairpersons in the remaining lower chambers.[62] The governor occasionally has a voice—sometimes the dominant one—in deciding committee assignments and chairs, but that is a phenomenon which appears to be disappearing as the various state legislatures become more institutionalized and independent of the executive.[63]

One of the consequences of centralized authority to make new committee assignments every two years is that, in most state lower chambers, there is lowered committee stability, although the more important committees of each chamber tend to have more senior legislators and thus to have a lower rate of turnover than lesser committees.[64] Substantial variation in committee membership stability occurs among states. In the 1977–78 Illinois House, for example, in only five of twenty-three committees did over 75 percent of reelected members return to the committee, while that return rate was less than 50 percent for eleven committees. In the Virginia House of 1976–77, by contrast, "the return rate never dropped below 80 percent for any committee."[65]

In the Kansas House of Representatives, there were fifty-nine instances of committee-chair turnover from 1961 through 1977. Over 40 percent of the committee chairs were new each legislature. Fifteen of those fifty-nine were the result of a change in party control, while eleven were caused by electoral defeat of a chairperson. Twenty-six (almost half) instances of chair turnover resulted from a committee chairperson's voluntarily leaving the house, including five who went to a nonlegislative office. Two cases resulted from a chairperson's assuming a position of legislative chamber leadership. Five resulted from a chairperson's moving from the chair of one committee to the chair of another.[66]

State legislative committee membership is even less stable than the committee-chair positions, despite what might be assumed to be the importance of retaining a few key members on each committee long enough to develop expertise within the legislative membership.[67] It may be that rotating legislative committee memberships weakens the legislature as an institution in its relationships with the other agencies of state government, but that may be less important than the ability of the legislature—through the legislative parties and the elected leaders—to be responsible to the electorate.

The contrast between the state lower chambers and the U.S. House of Representatives is great. In the national body, the Speaker has the dominant voice in the committee assignments of majority-party members only and then only to vacancies on committees. Stability of Congressional committee membership is high; responsiveness is low. The workings of the Congressional seniority system require that committee members be reappointed to "their" committees, Congress after Congress, and that the most senior member of the majority party—in terms of committee service—be appointed, normally, to chair each standing committee of the House. The authority of the Speaker of the U.S. House of Representatives over the membership of House committees is weak compared to the authority enjoyed by most state lower-chamber Speakers. Even the weakest of the state speakers has committee assignment powers which compare favorably with those of the Speaker of the U.S. House. The U.S. House Speaker has virtually no authority over who will chair the standing committees of the House, unless the Speaker wishes to wage a debilitating battle in the caucus against a specific chairperson. And even if the Speaker wins such a contest, the next senior member becomes the chairperson.

In contrast to the Speaker of the national lower chamber, the speakers of the state lower chambers have the authority to restructure the standing committees anew every two years. (In most states during the two-year period, the committee members and the chairpersons can be removed only by extraordinary vote of the chamber once they have been appointed.) The state legislative speaker normally has a pretty good idea about what issues will be on the legislative agenda during the ensuing two years and thus can use the office's power to appoint members and chairpersons of the standing committees as a way of structuring the legislature's decisions in advance. The speaker may "stack" the membership of the committees. This can predetermine the outcome of many issues since amending bills on the floor of the chamber may be a difficult process. Further, even though the members realize that the speaker has stacked certain committees with legislators who share the speaker's general philosophy, many legislators are so committed to "the process" and to the committee system that they are loath to vote against the policy positions taken by the committees that report the legislation to the floor of the chamber. Thus, control of committee philosophies in most cases amounts to control of the legislature's philosophy.

State Senate Committee Assignments   The locus of authority for committee assignments in the state senates is less concentrated than that of the state lower chambers, mainly because in many states the presiding officer of the state senate is the lieutenant governor.[68] Since, in those states, the presiding officer has not emerged from among the senators as their own freely elected leader (rather, he or she has been imposed on the senate, often with no senate experience), the senate's rules often give the lieutenant governor/president of the senate little authority within that body. He or she has only the authority granted by the state constitution, which is little enough in most cases.

Of the thirty states that make the lieutenant governor the president of the senate, only six give him or her authority to appoint members to some or all of the standing committees of the Senate. Five of those six permit the lieutenant governor, as president of the senate, to name committee chairpersons. In two more senates, the lieutenant governor is a member of the committee on committees, which makes senate committee assignments. A few more grant the lieutenant governor limited authority to appoint committee members if he or she is a member of the majority party in the senate, or they grant the lieutenant governor (as president of the senate) the authority to appoint members to conference committees, joint committees, and/or interim committees. The variations and gradations of the lieutenant governor's authority over committee assignments in the state senates are great.

In the states where the lieutenant governor presides over the state senate but the senators restrict that officer's authority over committee assignments, the power to appoint members to committees is lodged in a variety of sites. Most common is appointment by a committee on committees. Also popular is appointment by the president pro tem. Less common is appointment by the majority leader or by the majority and minority leaders, each responsible for his or her own party's appointments. The South Carolina and Virginia Senates elect members to committees.

Of the twenty state senates which elect their own presiding officer (president in nineteen states, speaker of the senate in Tennessee), fourteen grant that official the power to appoint members to committees. The Hawaii Senate makes such decisions in the party caucuses. Colorado gives that authority to the party floor leaders (majority leader and minority leader). Four states use a committee on committees, of which the president of the senate is a dominant member.

The freedom and flexibility of state senate leaders to assign senators to committees, as the leaders see fit every two years, is similar to the situation in the state lower chambers. Exceptions are Virginia, where the "senior member of the committee is automatically chairman,"[69] and New Mexico, where a written senate rule requires that the most senior member of the majority party in the chamber be given his or her pick of committees to chair, followed by the next most senior members of the majority party. New Mexico further requires the committee on committees to appoint members to committees according to their requests, with the most senior senators in both parties receiving their two preferred committee assignments each and the less senior members being assigned to less attractive committees. The New Mexico seniority rule applies chamberwide seniority, which results in committee chairpersons moving from less powerful committees to more powerful committees, even if they have not previously served on the more powerful committee they are appointed to chair. This seniority rule obviously makes committees of the New Mexico Senate fairly independent of the party leadership in the chamber in much the same way that committees of Congress are independent of the Congressional party leadership. The party leaders in the New Mexico Senate do not even have the authority to punish senators by refusing them transfers to more attractive committees.[70]

FUNCTIONS OF COMMITTEES

Congress and the American state legislatures have developed systems of legislative committees to help the legislatures get their work done and to help maintain the authority of the legislature as an institution. Committees filter and evaluate proposed legislation, develop expertise within the elected membership of the body, assist the legislature in communicating with various segments of society and with other components of the government, and enable the legislature to keep a watchful eye on the other branches of government.

Committees as Filters

One important function of legislative committees is to serve as filters. In the Ninety-fourth Congress (1975–76), for example, only 985 of the 16,982 bills introduced, less than 6 percent, were reported out of committee for floor consideration.[71] Thousands of proposals are introduced in each Congress and in each session of most state legislatures. Even the least active state legislature must consider hundreds of bills and resolutions each year, often in a legislative session limited to ninety days or less.[72] By referring the various proposals to committees for evaluation, the entire chamber membership is able to avoid wasting time on the less worthy measures and is aided by the committee's work when it does evaluate a measure.[73] If the committees did not divide the load and recommend to the entire body only the most worthwhile and important measures, the legislature would simply be unable to manage the load. Because committees are not exact replicas of chamberwide opinion, heavy reliance on them not only expedites the legislative process but also skews it toward the preferences of those serving on the relevant committees.

Why are legislative committees required today, when they were not required in earlier times? In part, the answer is that the large number of legislative proposals today reflects the size of the population and the population densities of many parts of the nation. In part, the large number of legislative proposals and their complexity is testimony to the government's growing role in an increasingly complex society. The large legislative workload is also the result of the increasing rate at which our society is changing. Technological and social change occurred relatively slowly two centuries ago. Major technological advances, however, have great impact upon society, and many of the resulting social consequences cry out for legislation to remedy inequities or to accommodate newly developed situations. Over the past quarter century, the development of household conveniences to reduce the burden of household chores, for example, coupled with effective means of family planning, helped more women to enter the work force. Social changes have come, many resulting in new legislative proposals at both the state and national level. Similarly, the development in new information-processing technology over the past couple of decades has led to various social dislocations, which, in turn, have resulted in legislation. A major part of the legislative response to the increased social and technological complexity of society—and to the resulting flood of legislative proposals—has been to assign such proposals to the legislative committees with appropriate jurisdiction before the entire chamber membership considers the measures. Then the entire chamber considers only those measures the committees consider worthy.

Committees as Experts

Today, the entire membership of a legislative chamber examines only those bills the committees report for passage. If committees are to consider legislation prior to extensive debate on the floor, a fairly automatic decision rule must exist to determine which committee will consider which bill. That problem is resolved by assigning each standing committee of the legislature jurisdiction, or authority, over certain types of bills. A bill concerning agriculture, for example, automatically goes to the Agriculture Committee.

Fixed jurisdiction of standing committees leads to subject-matter expertise among the members of a given committee, as does the tendency for many legislators to seek assignment to a committee whose work is already familiar to them. Farmers often seek seats on the agricultural committees of their legislatures, and bankers seek committee assignments which will allow them to use their expertise and, perhaps, to look out for their own interests and those of major groups of constituents.[74]

Although the personal preferences of members affect their perspectives, the expertise they represent on committees can help the legislature assess the merits of proposals without being overly dependent on interest-group representatives or the executive branch for information and for evaluation of various measures. These legislator-experts can correct errors in the first draft of a bill and can amend proposed legislation to eliminate some possible objections to it.

Expertise, of course, brings with it authority. As one observer has noted about Congressional committees:

> Committees which specialize and have exclusive jurisdiction over certain kinds of legislation become little legislatures themselves, with power largely independent of the elected leadership of the parent body. Centralized power and dispersed power are contradictions; to the degree that the latter exists the former is limited. It is necessary, therefore, to see the committees both as organs of investigation and deliberation, indispensable to Congress, and as subsystems of power, crucial both to the interests which seek access to government and to the work satisfactions and career aspirations of their members.[75]

Subcommittees are even more specialized than their parent committees and, especially under the present "reformed" rules of the U.S. House of Representatives, are themselves somewhat independent centers of authority over their relatively narrow areas of jurisdiction.

Committees as Communications Links

Legislative committees, by virtue of their expertise and relatively autonomous authority, are logical links in the process of communications between the relevant executive-department agencies with which each committee deals and the legislature as a whole. The legislative committee is also the logical decision-making site at which interest groups seek to change, promote, or halt proposed legislation of importance to them. After all, it is during the committee "mark-up" sessions (when the bill's final committee form is agreed to) that the most changes are made in a piece of legislation, and these changes are made with relatively little difficulty.

Public hearings are often held as part of a committee's process of information-gathering, decision-making, and communication. The public hearings provide committee members with information on important measures and also provide a forum for citizens and groups to air their views on the subject. Such an opportunity is important in leading the public to feel that the legislative process is fair and that it meets democratic expectations. Even if the final product does not satisfy some interested observers, the hearing is important because the disappointed contenders are likely to feel that the decision was arrived at "in the right way" and that "everyone had a chance to be heard."[76] Thus, diffuse systemic support is maintained. Public hearings also enable the legislature to educate the public on the merits of a particular controversy, if the news media cooperate, and to inform all interested parties of the reasons for the committee's (and, usually, the legislature's) decision.

The Oversight Function

As the legislature's experts on various fields of public policy, legislative committees and subcommittees are also the legislature's agents for insuring that the rest of the government and sometimes certain institutions in the private sector comply with the intent of the legislature. The legislative function of keeping an eye on the activities of the executive branch is called *legislative oversight*. This is an activity which is most visible when conducted as a committee hearing, but perhaps it is more effective when conducted quietly by telephone call, memo, and occasional private meetings between key bureaucrats and appointed executive officials and key committee leaders.[77] The official purpose of such oversight is to insure that legislative intent is honored in the executive branch's implementation of the legislation and in the judiciary's and bureaucracy's interpretation of it. The power to legislate, after all, means little if the legislation is not enforced. Other objectives of oversight activities include preserving the power of the legislature, as opposed to that of the executive; obtaining particular—sometimes detailed—decisions in specific cases from the agency being overseen; and gaining visibility or power for the chairperson of the legislative committee or subcommittee involved in oversight activity.[78]

LEGISLATIVE NORMS AND COMMITTEES

In legislatures—as in all societies and most small groups—there are norms, or informal rules of behavior, which are observed and enforced. These will be discussed in more detail in Chapter 13—their origin, how they are maintained, and their effects.

But certain norms have important effects on legislative committees, and these must be considered here.

The *courtesy norm* calls upon legislators to "disagree without being disagreeable," as it is sometimes put, and, as reinforced by the rules, to discuss and debate issues without making personal attacks on opponents. The *institutional patriotism norm* encourages a legislator to stand up for the legislature (and one's own chamber), as opposed to other branches of government. These two norms do not have as much impact on committees as four others—apprenticeship, legislative work, specialization, and reciprocity. These four are particularly important in the consideration of the functions of legislative committees.

The *apprenticeship norm* (of which the seniority system is the most obvious manifestation) once required a U. S. senator "to serve an unobtrusive apprenticeship . . . [and] to keep his mouth shut."[79] It was said that "the freshman who does not accept his lot as a temporary but very real second-class senator is met with thinly veiled hostility."[80] Donald R. Matthews noted back in 1959 that senators realized that "the practice of serving an apprenticeship is on the way out."[81] He was correct, although the seniority system remains. The probable reason most of the apprenticeship norm has mostly fallen by the wayside in the Senate (while the other five norms continue in force) is that:

> Unlike the other folkways, it is difficult to discern what benefits apprenticeship provided to the membership in general or collectively. . . . Today, not only do junior members not want or feel the need to serve an apprenticeship, but also the senior members do not expect them to do so. . . ."[82]

Clearly, seniority and experience in the Senate are still avenues to authority, but junior members now are generally accepted as active Senate participants. Changes in the formal Senate rules which have given first-term senators major committee assignments, subcommittee chairs, and additional staff are formal recognition of the changes in the norms of the Senate, and they contribute to the legitimation of the active newcomer. The *legislative work norm* requires that senators devote much of their time and energy to the "highly detailed, dull, and politically unrewarding" work of the Senate's committees.[83] This norm accounts for the seemingly odd disparity which at times exists between a well-known senator's support in the national party and the general public and his or her lack of authority within the Senate. As the late Senator Carl Hayden of Arizona reported being told when he arrived as one of Arizona's first two senators:

> There are two kinds of Congressmen—show horses and work horses. If you want to get your name in the paper, be a show horse. If you want to gain the respect of your colleagues, keep quiet and be a work horse.[84]

The *specialization norm* stipulates that:

> [A] senator should not try to know something about every bill that comes before the chamber or try to be active on a wide variety of measures. Rather, he ought to specialize, to focus his energies and attention on the relatively few matters that come before his committees or that directly and immediately affect his state. . . . In part, at least, senators *ought* to specialize because they *must.*[85]

The specialization norm also provides informal restraints in a chamber which has a formal rule of unlimited debate and "makes it possible for the Senate to stop talking and act."[86]

The *reciprocity norm* has both a personal and a committee aspect. Personally, reciprocity means that a senator's word ought to be good. As recent observers have

--- ★ ★ ★ ★ ---

Working Out Disagreement in Subcommittees: The Importance of Norms

Richard F. Fenno, Jr., stresses the importance that members of the House Appropriations Committee place on bringing a measure from the subcommittee to the full committee, or from the committee to the floor of the House, with members united behind the measure. While minority reports seldom emanate from this committee or its subcommittees, members are entitled to express "reservations" about a measure. They are then legitimately entitled to disagree openly at a later date. The importance of that informal norm in the dynamic of the intimate atmosphere of the powerful Appropriations Committee and its subcommittees is revealed in a quotation from a ranking minority subcommittee member:

> We had a gentleman's agreement in markup to make a $50 million cut—let them take it anywhere they want it. It was an across the board kind of cut. Well, I got to thinking about it afterward and got pretty unhappy. So I went to see the subcommittee chairman. I said, "That's not a big enough cut. I've got to reserve on that." He said, "Well, we've got to go in together on that; let's go down to my office and talk it over." So he got the Chairman of the Committee and a few others and we sat down and they said, "How much of a cut will you take?" I said, "$150 million." Well, we talked it back and forth. I argued that they wouldn't be hit by it, that $50 million was no better than nothing and that if we couldn't cut here we couldn't cut anywhere. I said they had more than they knew what to do with anyway and so on and so on. Finally, the subcommittee chairman said, "Will you take $100 million? I finally said, "All right. I'll take $100 million."

Source: Richard F. Fenno, Jr., *The Power of the Purse: Appropriations Politics in Congress* (Boston: Little, Brown, 1966), pp. 203–5.

--- ★ ★ ★ ★ ---

stressed: "Reciprocity, and particularly its aspect of individual integrity, continues to be important in an institution which operates informally and in which virtually all agreements are verbal."[87]

The personal aspect of reciprocity also holds that a senator ought to assist a colleague when he or she can and be repaid in kind[88] and ought to refrain from exercising his or her full powers under Senate rules and procedures, "[f]or if a Senator *does* push his formal powers to the limit, he has broken the implicit bargain and can expect, not cooperation from his colleagues, but only retaliation in kind."[89] The committee aspect of the reciprocity norm has to do with the weight that members of one committee give to the recommendations of another committee.

The U.S. House of Representatives also has informal rules of behavior. In outline, House norms are about the same as Senate norms, adjusted for the greater importance of a House member's (fewer) committee assignments, for the larger number of members, and for the importance of the state delegation for members from medium-sized and large states.[90] The apprenticeship norm in the House, like that in the Senate, has been weakened greatly in the past two decades, as have the formal rules reinforcing that norm. On balance, though, senior House members still have much more power than junior members (if nothing else, they know the rules better), and much of Clapp's early 1960s observations about House dynamics remains true today.

> Although junior members are being assimilated into the work of the House more easily and readily than formerly, the traditions and folklore of that body serve to impress on them the virtues of being patient and not being troublesome. . . . Thus advice such as "to get along, go along," and "a man is never defeated by the speech he didn't make" is passed along to the newcomer. . . .
> Apprenticeship may still precede full partnership, but the increased volume and complexity of the problems with which the Congress is compelled to cope dictate more efficient use of the membership. Freshmen are now advised to defer speaking only until the moment arrives when they have something significant to say . . . although they are cautioned to be sure they are well informed about their topic. They are also warned against speaking too often and on too many different subjects. . . . Freshmen who ignore this advice . . . irritate their peers and are often the subject of sanctions. . . . At times these men cannot understand why they are passed over for [committee] assignments for which they are intellectually prepared. The blunt truth is that colleagues do not wish to see them get ahead or to work with them, despite their qualifications.[91]

Because of the larger size of the House, informal norms alone do not suffice to restrain sufficiently the urge to speak out so that the lower chamber can conduct its business efficiently. Thus, the formal rules of the House are much more restrictive of an individual member's right to be heard on the floor of the chamber. In addition to routinely limiting the amount of debate to be allowed on each bill before it, the House also forbids nongermane amendments ("riders"), a device which senators find very useful. (To be germane, an amendment must be related to the subject of the bill.) Senators who try to attach riders to bills make no pretense that such amendments are germane.

The norms of apprenticeship (considerably weakened in recent times, although the seniority system is still strong), legislative work, specialization, and reciprocity make committees (and subcommittees) more important than they would otherwise be in the legislative process. As Barbara Hinckley has written about the norms of specialization and committee reciprocity:

> [They] strengthen the committee system, reinforce decentralized decision-making, and distribute influence widely through Senate and House. One looks to a few senators on corn, a few others on hogs, still others on housing. Such decentralization of policy-making limits the scope of congressional leadership . . . and contributes to a kind of "constituency representation" in which legislators whose constituencies are strongly interested in a certain area attempt to become specialists on the appropriate committee. At the same time these norms work against corporate decision-making: the Senate as a whole does not "deliberate" on agriculture policy. If the "corn" Senators are in agreement, one major part of the "deliberation" has occurred.[92]

It is interesting to note that the weakening of the apprenticeship norm and committee reciprocity in the U.S. House of Representatives in recent times has led to the appointment of special task forces by the Speaker—the energy organization bill in 1977, the tax bill in 1978, and the Chrysler-aid bill in 1979, for example—which cut across committee lines and create special opportunities for participation in legislative work by junior members.[93]

SUMMARY

Over a long period of time, committees of Congress and of many state legislatures have developed a substantial degree of organizational differentiation within the structure of the parent legislatures. Originally, the entire chamber membership discussed and debated each proposal and then with the broad outlines of the decision made, sent the proposal to an ad hoc committee composed entirely of members favorable to the proposal. That committee fleshed out the will of the chamber by considering details and then reported the product of its deliberations to the parent body. Today, in contrast, almost no measures come before the entire chamber membership for serious discussion without first having been examined and, normally, revised by a standing committee of the legislature.

The authority to draft and report legislation to the floor of the U.S. House and U.S. Senate is granted almost exclusively to the standing committees of each chamber (although, in the past, the Congressional Joint Committee on Atomic Energy had legislative authority). Occasionally, a select committee is given legislative authority in its narrow area of concern. The standing committees of Congress are the permanent committees of each chamber. Some are primarily concerned with authorizing legislation, others with appropriations or taxation, and yet others work mainly on housekeeping chores. The power and prestige of different committees vary greatly, resulting in intense competition for assignment to some and little interest shown in serving on others. Select and special committees are established anew each Congress, although many of them are renewed in numerous successive Congresses. Joint committees of Congress, with both representatives and senators as members, serve primarily a coordinating function, although some also serve as a source of information and expertise.

Committees have several important overall functions. They serve as filters to insure that only the most important and, from each committee's viewpoint, most responsible legislation is permitted to reach the floor of the chamber. In addition to filtering the numerous proposals introduced in each legislative chamber, so that only those thought to be the most worthy reach the entire membership, committees also provide the legislature with its own panel of experts among the elected legislators, avoiding undue dependence on either the legislative staff or the executive branch. Further, committees provide communications links with various sectors of society most concerned about each committee's area of jurisdiction and with the executive and judicial branches of government. A legislature's committees also enable it to maintain a watchful eye on the activities of the other branches of government to insure, through oversight, that the intent of the legislature is honored in the implementation of legislation.

State legislatures have the same array of committees—standing committees of each chamber, joint committees, and select, special or ad hoc committees—as Congress does. But some of the state legislatures use joint committees, as well as the standing committees of each chamber, to report legislation. Indeed, a few state legislatures depend exclusively on joint committees for the consideration and reporting of legislation. In addition, state legislatures use interim committees (which function during the interim between legislative sessions) to study special problems and report to the legislature.

Assignments to state legislative committees are made anew every two years. The individual or committee with committee-assignment responsibility can, in most state legislatures, change the members and chairpersons of the committees as they see fit. As a result of these committee-assignment rules and of relatively high turnover rates in state legislative membership, state legislative committees are much less stable than Congressional committees are.

Congressional committees are very stable since each member has a right to continue serving on his or her committee in each successive Congress. Assignments to committee vacancies are made by the party committee for committees for each Congressional party. The majority-party member with the longest continuous service on each committee virtually automatically becomes chairperson of that committee. This "seniority system" of choosing most committee and subcommittee leaders is part of a complex set of norms of legislative behavior. Other such informal rules call on members to be loyal to the legislature, to behave in certain ways toward other members, to find an area of specialization, and to work hard as a committee member. All legislative norms have important effects on the functioning of the legislature and of committees in particular.

Notes

1. Lauros G. McConachie, *Congressional Committees* (New York: Lenox Hill/Burt Franklin Reprints, 1973), pp. 7–11; originally published in 1898.

2. Ibid., p. 11.

3. George B. Galloway, *History of the House of Representatives* (New York: Thomas Y. Crowell, 1961), pp. 66–67.

4. George Goodwin, Jr., *The Little Legislatures: Committees of Congress* (Amherst: University of Massachusetts Press, 1970), p. 6.

5. Ibid., pp. 6–8; Kenneth A. Shepsle, *The Giant Jigsaw Puzzle: Democratic Committee Assignments in the Modern House* (Chicago: University of Chicago Press, 1978), pp. 10–12.

6. Goodwin, *The Little Legislatures,* pp. 7–9; Shepsle, *The Giant Jigsaw Puzzle,* pp. 12–13.

7. A thorough description of each type of committee is available in Walter J. Oleszek, "Overview of the Senate Committee System," Congressional Research Service for The Commission of the Operation of the Senate, April 23, 1976.

8. John W. Ellwood and James A. Thurber estimate that in 1974 only some 44 percent of the budget was directly controlled by the House and Senate Appropriations Committees. Authorizing committees sidestepped the appropriations committees "by granting agencies the authority to contract in advance of appropriations or to borrow from the public." In addition, some large programs, such as Social Security, provided for eligibility criteria and then stipulated that all who met those criteria were entitled to certain levels of benefits. This too meant that the Appropriations Committees had no real annual control over these types of expenditures. The budget committees were created, in large measure, to enable Congress to know what was being spent and to enable it to gain control of the budget again. See "The New Congressional Budget Process" in *Congress Reconsidered,* ed. Lawrence C. Dodd and Bruce I. Oppenheimer (New York: Praeger, 1977), pp. 163–92.

9. Ibid.; and James A. Thurber, "New Powers of the Purse: An Assessment of Congressional Budget Reform," in *Legislative Reform,* ed. Leroy N. Rieselbach (Lexington, Mass: Lexington Books, 1978). See also Lance T. LeLoup, Process Versus Policy: The U.S. House Budget Committee," *Legislative Studies Quarterly* 4 (May, 1979): 227–54.

10. V. Stanley Vardys, "Select Committees of the House of Representatives," *Midwest Journal of Political Science* 6 (August 1962): 247–65.

11. Harold P. Green and Alan Rosenthal, *Governing the Atom: The Integration of Powers* (New York: Atherton, 1963); Steven L. Del Sesto, "Nuclear Reactor Safety and the Rule of the Congressman: A Content Analysis of Congressional Hearings," *The Journal of Politics* 42 (February 1980): 227–41.

12. Thurber, "New Powers of the Purse."

13. Bruce I. Oppenheimer, "The Rules Committee: New Arm of Leadership in a Decentralized House," in Dodd and Oppenheimer, *Congress Reconsidered,* pp. 96–116. The Speaker has not, however, exercised his new power over the Rules Committee membership to remove a member.

14. Richard F. Fenno, Jr., *Congressmen in Committees* (Boston: Little, Brown, 1973), Chapter 1.

15. *Congressional Quarterly Weekly Report,* February 3, 1979, pp. 186–87.

16. Various analyses of House committees reveal similar patterns of prestige. Kenneth A. Shepsle, for example, analyzed both actual transfers and *requests for transfers* among Democratic representatives for a longer period—the Eighty-sixth through the Ninety-fourth Congresses—than Jewell and Chi-hung. The only disagreement between the Jewell/Chi-hung rankings and the Shepsle rankings is modest and affects the rankings of only some committees in Levels 5 through 7 of Figure 10.1. The overall rank of the various House committees is fairly clear, despite the fact that not all members want to serve on the most prestigious committees. See *The Giant Jigsaw Puzzle,* pp. 56–57.

17. David J. Vogler, *The Politics of Congress,* 2nd ed., (Boston: Allyn and Bacon, 1977), p. 162.

18. Fenno, *Congressmen in Committees,* p. 2.

19. Lynette P. Perkins, "Member Recruitment to a Mixed Goal Committee; the House Judiciary Committee," *Journal of Politics* 43 (May 1981): 348–64.

20. Ibid., pp. 9–11.

21. Ibid., p. 5. Some evidence, however, strongly suggests that committee assignments are not the "make or break" factors that some observers consider them to be. Other factors appear to be much more important in the individual member's reelection chances than whether or not he or she received a coveted committee assignment. Charles S. Bullock, "Freshman Committee Assignments and Re-Election in the United States House of Representatives," *American Political Science Review* 66 (September 1972): 1005; Linda L. Fowler, Scott R. Douglas, and Wesley D. Clark, Jr., "The Electoral Effects of House Committee Assignments," *Journal of Politics* 42 (February 1980): 307–19.

22. Fenno, *Congressmen in Committees,* pp. 8, 13. See also Charles S. Bullock, "Motivations for U.S. Congressional Committee Preferences," *Legislative Studies Quarterly* 1 (May 1976): 201–12.

23. This discussion is based on Steven H. Haeberle, "The Institutionalization of the Subcommittee in the United States House of Representatives," *Journal of Politics* 40 (November 1978): 1054–65); Norman J. Ornstein, "Causes and Consequences of Congressional Change: Subcommittee Reforms in the House of Representatives, 1970–73," in Norman J. Ornstein, ed., *Congress in Change: Evolution and Reform* (New York: Praeger, 1975), pp. 88–113.

24. Haeberle, "The Institutionalization of the Subcommittee," p. 1058.

25. Ibid., p. 1063.

26. Bruce I. Oppenheimer, "Policy Effects of U.S. House Reform: Decentralization and the Capacity to Resolve Energy Issues," *Legislative Studies Quarterly* 5 (February 1980): 11.

27. Ibid., p. 20.

28. David J. Vogler, "The Rise of Ad Hoc Committees in the House of Representatives" (Paper delivered at the 1978 Annual Meeting of the American Political Science Association, New York, N.Y.); cited in Oppenheimer, "Policy Effects of U.S. House Reform," p. 20.

29. Members also have seniority within the House of Representatives; this is important for such purposes as obtaining desirable office suites. It is also considered along with the other factors when more members want a particular committee assignment than there are vacant seats available on that committee. But it is seniority within the party on a committee which is the basis of the well-known and much-criticized "Congressional seniority system."

30. Nelson W. Polsby, Miriam Gallaher, and Barry S. Rundquist, "The Growth of the Seniority System in the U.S. House of Representatives," *American Political Science Review* 63 (September 1969): 787–807.

31. The following discussion draws from Roger H. Davidson and Walter J. Oleszek, *Congress Against Itself* (Bloomington: Indiana University Press, 1977); Irwin N. Gertzog, "The Routinization of Committee Assignments in the U.S. House of Representatives," *American Journal of Political Science* 20 (1976): 693–712; Goodwin, *The Little Legislatures;* Nicholas A. Masters, "Committee Assignments in the House of Representatives," *American Political Science Review* 55 (June 1961): 345–47; Herbert B. Asher, "The Changing Status of the Freshman Representative," in Ornstein, *Congress in Change,* pp. 216–39; and Shepsle, *The Giant Jigsaw Puzzle.*

32. From 1912 through 1974, the Democratic members of the House Ways and Means Committee functioned as the House Democratic committee on committees, a situation which arose through historical circumstance during the "revolt against the Speaker" of 1910, but which greatly restrained the effectiveness of moderate and liberal Democrats in the House. In 1975, as part of a wave of reform, the Democratic caucus removed committee-assignment authority from the Ways and Means members and invested this authority in the Steering and Policy Committee. For a discussion of Democratic committee assignments under the old regime, see Masters, "Committee Assignments in the House of Representatives," pp. 345–57; and David W. Rohde and Kenneth A. Shepsle, "Democratic Committee Assignments in the House of Representatives: Strategic Aspects of a Social Choice Process," *American Political Science Review* 67 (September 1973): 889–905.

33. "Naturally, if a freshman is to be successful in his quest (for a particular committee assignment) there must be a vacancy on the desired committee, and generally there must be no one with seniority from his own geographic zone and in his own political party who wants this particular assignment. Under the House rules, the country is divided geographically into zones, and usually no more than two members from the same zone can serve on any committee at a given time." Jim Wright, *You and Your Congressman* (New York: G.P. Putnam's, 1976), p. 138. See also Charles Bullock, "The Influence of State Party Delegations on House Committee Assignments," *Midwest Journal of Political Science* (April 1971): 525–46.

34. Wright, *You and Your Congressman,* p. 138.

35. Masters, "Committee Assignments in the House of Representatives," p. 354. Jon R. Bond, however, argues that an analysis of committee memberships of oil-state representatives does not support the argument that the oil-depletion allowance is the result of overrepresentation of oil-state members on the tax committees of Congress. "Oiling the Tax Committees in Congress, 1900–1974: Subgovernment Theory, the Overrepresentation Hypothesis, and the Oil Depletion Allowance," *American Journal of Political Science* 23 (November 1979): 651–64.

36. *Congressional Quarterly Weekly Report,* November 8, 1980, p. 3305.

37. Judith H. Parris, "The Senate Reorganizes Its Committees," *Political Science Quarterly* 94 (Summer 1979): 319–37; "Senate Committee Reform," in *Inside Congress,* 2nd ed. (Washington, D.C.: Congressional Quarterly, 1979).

38. Randall B. Ripley and Grace A. Franklin suggest that in its consideration of the President's energy legislation in 1977, the new Energy and Natural Resources Committee did indeed fall into old habits. *Congress, The Bureaucracy, and Public Policy,* rev. ed., (Homewood, Ill: Dorsey Press, 1980), pp. 141–44.

39. Donald R. Matthews, *U.S. Senators and Their World* (Chapel Hill, N.C.: University of North Carolina Press, 1960), Chapter 7.

40. Goodwin, *The Little Legislatures,* pp. 111–17; see also Stephen Horn, *Unused Power: The Work of the Senate Committee on Appropriations* (Washington, D.C.: Brookings Institution, 1970); and William L. Morrow, *Congressional Committees* (New York: Scribner's, 1969).

41. Randall B. Ripley, *Power in the Senate* (New York: St. Martin's, 1969), p. 137.

42. Carl P. Chelf, *Congress in the American System* (Chicago: Nelson-Hall, 1977), p. 96.

43. Ripley, *Power in the Senate,* pp. 132–36.

44. Goodwin, *The Little Legislatures,* p. 93. See also Matthews, *U.S. Senators and Their World,* Chapter 5. Richard F. Fenno, Jr., found similar considerations at work in the selection of new members of the Senate and House Appropriations Committees. *The Power of the Purse: Appropriations Politics in Congress* (Boston: Little, Brown, 1966), pp. 24–29, 521–29.

45. Goodwin, *The Little Legislatures,* p. 88. Louis P. Westefield found that "when deaths, retirements, and decisions at the polls do not produce a number of vacancies" on desired House committees, the leaders create additional seats on those committees to use as resources for gaining "leverage with the members." The technique also keeps the major House committees attuned to the party leaders, at least in the short run. Louis P. Westefield, "Majority Party Leadership and the Committee System in the House of Representatives," *American Political Science Review* 68 (December 1974): 1593–1604.

46. Milton C. Cummings, Jr., and Robert L. Peabody, "The Decision to Enlarge the Committee on Rules: An Analysis of the 1961 Vote," in *New Perspectives on the House of Representatives,* ed. Robert L. Peabody and Nelson W. Polsby (Chicago: Rand McNally, 1963), pp. 167–94.

47. Ripley, for example, quotes a senator as claiming to have been subjected to "terrific pressure from the oil industry to quit Appropriations and go on Finance." As Ripley notes, the Senate Finance Committee seat would have enabled the senator to help guard the oil industry's oil-depletion allowance in the tax code, a provision which since has been changed. *Power in the Senate,* p. 135. Southern members have sought to control the Senate Judiciary Committee out of a belief in states' rights and opposition to activist federal judges. See Barbara Hinckley, *Stability and Change in Congress,* 2nd ed. (New York: Harper and Row, 1978), p. 93.

48. Glenn R. Parker found Democratic representatives supported or opposed reappointment of U.S. House committee chairpersons on the basis of performance (procedural fairness; committee effectiveness) and personal criteria (party support, age, ideology). Most important was the respondent's evaluation of the committee leader's procedural and personal fairness. "The Selection of Committee Leaders in the House of Representatives," *American Politics Quarterly* 7 (January 1979): 71–93.

49. Goodwin, *The Little Legislatures,* p. 94.

50. For discussions of the seniority system and its impact, see Joseph S. Clark, *Congress: The Sapless Branch* (New York: Harper and Row, 1964), especially pp. 178–86; George Goodwin, Jr., "The Seniority System in Congress," *American Political Science Review* 57 (1959): 412–36; and Barbara Hinckley, *The Seniority System in Congress* (Bloomington: Indiana University Press, 1971).

51. Norman J. Ornstein and David W. Rohde, "Seniority and Future Power in Congress," in Ornstein, *Congress in Change,* pp. 72–87.

52. Goodwin, *The Little Legislatures,* p. 97.

53. An insightful discussion of the decentralization of power in the House is provided by Lawrence C. Dodd and Bruce I. Oppenheimer, "The House in Transition," in Dodd and Oppenheimer, *Congress Reconsidered,* especially pp. 32–40.

54. The following discussion draws on *Inside Congress,* 2nd ed.; *Congressional Quarterly Weekly Report,* February 3, 1979; John E. Stanga, Jr., and David N. Farnsworth, "Seniority and Democratic Reforms in the House of Representatives: Committees and Subcommittees," in *Rieselbach, Legislative Reform,* pp. 35–48; and Ornstein, Peabody, and Rohde, "The Changing Senate: From the 1950s to the 1970s."

55. *Congressional Quarterly Weekly Report,* February 3, 1979, pp. 183–84.

56. *Book of the States* (Lexington, Ky.: Council of State Governments, 1978), p. 40.

57. Ibid.

58. Citizens Conference on State Legislatures, *State Legislatures: An Evaluation of their Effectiveness* (New York: Praeger, 1971), pp. 129, 209.

59. Alan G. Hevesi, *Legislative Politics in New York State: A Comparative Analysis* (New York: Praeger, 1975), pp. 18–19.

60. Corey Rosen found that even though the legislatures of Alabama, California, Florida, Indiana, Montana, New York, Vermont, and Wisconsin reportedly did not have seniority systems, seniority still had some importance in the selection of committee chairpersons in those legislatures. Questionnaire responses from legislative committee chairpersons in those states indicated that the most important factor in their selection was subject-matter expertise, followed by ideological and political factors, with seniority third in importance. Objective analysis, however, revealed that "almost half the committee chairmen do rank first in committee seniority and another 31.5% rank second." Further, seniority was more important in the selection of chairpersons of "top" committees than of the chairpersons of less important committees. See "Seniority and the Selection of Committee Chairmen in American State Legislatures" (Paper delivered at the 1975 Annual Meeting of the Midwest Political Science Association, Chicago, Ill.).

61. *Book of the States,* 1978, p. 40; and Alan Rosenthal, *Legislative Performance in the States: Explorations of Committee Behavior* (New York: Free Press, 1974), p. 56.

62. This discussion is primarily from *Book of the States,* 1978, p. 40, and from *State Legislatures: An Evaluation of Their Effectiveness.*

63. On gubernatorial intervention in legislative committee assignments and selection of chairs, see Malcolm E. Jewell, *The State Legislature: Politics and Practice* (New York: Random House, 1962), Chapters 4 and 5; and V. O. Key, Jr., *Southern Politics* (New York: Alfred A. Knopf, 1949).

64. Hubert Harry Basehart, "The Effect of Membership Stability on Continuity and Experience in U.S. State Legislative Committees," *Legislative Studies Quarterly* 5 (February 1980): 55–68; James R. Oxendale, Jr., "The Impact of Membership Turnover on Internal Structures of State Legislative Lower Chambers" (Paper delivered at the 1979 Annual Meeting of the American Political Science Association, Washington, D.C.).

65. Keith E. Hamm, "Voting Patterns in State Legislative Committees" (Paper delivered at the 1980 Annual Meeting of the Southern Political Science Association, Atlanta, Ga.), p. 13.

66. Marvin A. Harder and Raymond G. Davis, *The Legislature as an Organization* (Lawrence, Kansas: Regents Press of Kansas, 1979), Table 3.3, p. 39.

67. Even the prestigious Taxation and Appropriations Committees have a fairly high rate of turnover among their chairpersons. See Harder and Davis, *The Legislature as an Organization;* and Rosenthal, *Legislative Performance in the States,* pp. 175–80.

68. The following discussion is based primarily on *American State Legislatures: Their Structures and Procedures,* Tables 2.6 and 4.6, pp. 26 and 67.

69. *Book of the States,* 1978, p. 40, footnote J.

70. Paul L. Hain, Cal Clark, and Janet Clark, "The Legislature," in *New Mexico Government,* rev. ed., ed. F. Chris Garcia and Paul L. Hain (Albuquerque: University of New Mexico Press, 1980).

71. William J. Keefe, *Congress and the American People* (Englewood Cliffs, N.J.: Prentice-Hall, 1980), p. 65.

72. In 1973, 14,781 bills and 184 resolutions were introduced in the New York legislature. In each of four other states, there were over 5000 bills introduced that year, and all but fifteen states saw 1000 or more bills introduced in their 1973 legislatures. *American State Legislatures: Their Structures and Procedures* (Lexington, Ky.: Council of State Governments, 1977), p. 77.

73. As Samuel A. Kirkpatrick points out, a "somewhat subtle function of the committee system involves killing legislation at the request of the author. At times during a legislator's career he may be asked to author a bill at the request of certain constituents. Often such legislation . . . does not benefit his entire constituency or the state. . . . [He] can rely upon the committee to kill the bill before it can be debated on the floor." *The Legislative Process in Oklahoma* (Norman: University of Oklahoma Press, 1978), p. 125. In some other state legislatures, the failure of a legislator to press for committee action or a public statement that a bill is being introduced "by request" are subtle signals to the committee to pigeonhole the bill.

74. Masters, "Committee Assignments in the House of Representatives," pp. 345–57; Rohde and Shepsle, "Democratic Committee Assignments in the House of Representatives," pp. 889–905; and Charles L. Clapp, *The Congressman: His Work as He Sees It,* (Garden City, N.Y.: Doubleday, Anchor, 1963), Chapter 5.

75. Ralph K. Huitt, "The Internal Distribution of Influence: The Senate," in *The Congress and America's Future,* ed. David B. Truman (Englewood Cliffs, N.J.: Prentice-Hall, 1965), p. 89.

76. David B. Truman, *The Governmental Process* (New York: Alfred A. Knopf, 1962), p. 375.

77. Excellent analyses of the intimate relationships which can develop among key members of legislative committees, senior committee staff personnel, top executive-branch personnel, and affected client industries are provided by Roger H. Davidson, "Breaking Up Those 'Cozy Triangles': An Impossible Dream?" in *Legislative Reform and Public Policy,* ed. Susan Welch and John G. Peters (New York: Praeger, 1977); and Ripley and Franklin, *Congress, The Bureaucracy, and Public Policy,* rev. ed.

78. Cornelius P. Cotter, "Legislative Oversight," in *Congress: The First Branch of Government,* ed. Alfred de Grazia (Garden City, N.Y.: Anchor Books, 1967); Lawrence C. Dodd and Richard L. Schott, *Congress and The Administrative State* (New York: John Wiley, 1979), Chapter 5; and Vogler, *The Politics of Congress,* 2nd ed., Chapter 4.

79. Donald R. Matthews, "The Folkways of the United States Senate: Conformity to Group Norms and Legislative Effectiveness," *American Political Science Review* 53 (December 1959): 1965. Another early student of the norms of Congress was Ralph K. Huitt, whose "The Morse Committee Assignment Controversy: A Study in Senate Norms," still enlightens us on the degree to which one must examine the *milieu* in which rules are interpreted if one is to understand legislative decisions. *American Political Science Review* 51 (June 1957): 313–29. See also Ralph K. Huitt, "The Outsider in the Senate: An Alternative Role," *American Political Science Review* 55 (September 1961): 566–75.

80. Matthews, "The Folkways of the United States Senate," p. 1066.

81. Ibid.

82. Norman J. Ornstein, Robert L. Peabody, and David W. Rohde, "The Changing Senate: From the 1950s to the 1970s," in Dodd and Oppenheimer, *Congress Reconsidered,* p. 8.

83. Matthews, "The Folkways of the United States Senate," p. 1067.

84. Ibid.

85. Ibid., pp. 1067–68.

86. Ibid., p. 1069.

87. Ornstein, Peabody, and Rohde, "The Changing Senate, p. 7.

88. Matthews, "The Folkways of the U.S. Senate," p. 1071.

89. Ibid., p. 1072. Leroy N. Rieselbach notes an occasion on which Senator Russell Long (D., Louisiana) moved consideration of a Social Security measure by number, rather than by name, and caught the measure's opponents napping. The majority leader then came to the floor to remark "What was done is fully within the rules and regulations of the Senate, but I think the way it was done raises a most serious question so far as the rights of any individual is concerned. There is such a thing as decorum and dignity in this body." He then obtained unanimous consent to have the measure voted on again. Rieselbach speculates that this event may have contributed to Senator Long's defeat for reelection to the assistant majority leader post. *Congressional Politics* (New York: McGraw-Hill, 1973), p. 144.

90. On House norms, see Herbert Asher, "The Learning of Legislative Norms," *American Political Science Review* 67 (June 1973): 499–513; Richard F. Fenno, Jr., "The Internal Distribution of Influence: The House," in *Congress and America's Future,* ed. David B. Truman (Englewood Cliffs, N.J.: Prentice-Hall, 1973), pp. 83–90; and Hinckley, *Stability and Change in Congress,* 2nd ed., pp. 59–85.

91. Clapp, *The Congressman: His Work as He Sees It*, pp. 12–13.

92. Hinckley, *Stability and Change in Congress,* p. 69. A similar point is made, more formally, by Barry R. Weingast, who notes that since "different institutions imply different outcomes, which affect member goals differentially, a rationale exists for establishing one set of norms over another." "A Rational Choice Perspective on Congressional Norms," *American Journal of Political Science* 23 (May 1979): 259.

93. Barbara Sinclair, "The Speaker's Task Force in the Post-Reform House of Representatives," *American Political Science Review* 75 (June 1981): 397.

chapter *11*

Legislative Committees in Action

Preview

Committees in action, or at work—in the U.S. Congress and in the state legislatures—are key decision-making sites. In the national Congress, committees are generally more important and have greater authority over legislation—with better-defined jurisdictions, better-established relationships with the executive departments and lobbyists, more emphasis on seniority and continuing committee membership—than is true in the state legislatures. In the Congress, although committee chairs are powerful, their power has been reduced somewhat, while subcommittee power has increased. Some committees have more authority over legislation than others. Committees are important in the legislative process for several reasons, including subject-matter expertise. Committee hearings serve a number of purposes, including oversight, public information, and as a safety valve for public expression, as well as the end of political advancement of committee members. Legislative committees have greater power in the U.S. Congress than in some other countries, notably Canada and Great Britain, and they also generally have greater independent power than similar committees do in state legislatures.

Chapter 10 discussed the functions and types of Congressional and state legislative committees, the relative attractiveness of membership on the various committees and how assignments to them are made, and the role of committee leaders. This chapter explores the environment in which legislative committees work and the forces which keep them attuned to the will of the chamber they serve. While stressing the authority of committees, the discussion addresses the limits of that authority, the dynamics by which committees make decisions, and the way in which actors not on the committee affect those decisions. Also discussed are the factors which cause some committees to be successful in getting their legislation enacted and cause others to suffer a greater rate of failures on the floor of the chamber.

CONGRESSIONAL COMMITTEES

In the Congress, each committee protects its own jurisdiction over certain subject matter—the right of the Senate Finance Committee to have tax bills sent to it for consideration, for example, or the right of the House Interior and Insular Affairs Committee to handle the committee work on a bill dealing with the national parks. However, there is inevitable overlap on broad general subjects—there are eighteen House committees dealing with some aspects of education, for example.

Each committee also wants to maintain its authority over legislation within its formal jurisdiction—that is, it wants the legislation it reports to be adopted by the full chamber, in the form and with the amendments agreed upon in committee. The committee also wants to be able to kill a measure or refuse to take it up—another expression of its authority—without having this action overridden by the full chamber. Similarly, each subcommittee seeks to protect its jurisdiction and wants the support of its asserted authority from the parent committee and the legislative chamber. Although there are separate committees of similar jurisdiction in each of the two houses of Congress, and even though they are involved in the same web of access, interaction, and influence, they often disagree on general policy or the details of legislation.

Committee Jurisdiction

The jurisdiction of each committee of Congress is written in the rules of the chamber from which the committee derives its authority or, in the case of joint committees, in the statute or joint resolution creating the committee. Largely as a result of the reforms of the early 1970s, each subcommittee of each standing committee of Congress now has clearly defined jurisdiction over certain areas of the full committee's general jurisdiction. The written statements of jurisdiction are extensive. A written description of the subject jurisdictions of the Senate's committees prepared in 1976 by the Temporary Select Committee to Study the Senate Committee System required, for example, forty-two pages, and it avoided discussing subcommittees.[1]

Given the complexity of the federal government, jurisdictional overlaps and disputes occasionally occur, as, for example, between the Senate Agriculture Committee and the Senate Foreign Relations Committee. The Agriculture Committee views the agricultural program as a way to help American farmers, by disposing of surplus agricultural products and keeping domestic agricultural prices up. The Foreign Relations Committee, on the other hand, views the program as an adjunct to "foreign policy and humanitarian assistance."[2] Those two perspectives occasionally result in tension between the two committees, as when President Carter stopped shipments of grain to the Soviet Union to punish that nation for its invasion of Afghanistan. The Agriculture Committee tended to view that action as punishing the nation's farmers. Similarly, tensions increased greatly between the Senate Armed Services Committee and the Senate Foreign Relations Committee in the late 1960s, when the latter began criticizing American policies in Southeast Asia, while the former continued to support those activities.[3]

Disputes about which committee has jurisdiction over a piece of legislation often appear merely to be arguments over committee status and authority in the legislature ("empire building"), and that is partly the case, but such disputes frequently arise because of differences in legislator preferences about public policy. The decision about which committee has jurisdiction over a particular piece of legislation may determine the basic philosophy which shapes the legislation. And legislation is sometimes carefully drafted so that it will be referred to one committee (or subcommittee), rather than to another. The 1963 civil-rights legislation, for example, was drafted in House form in one way to insure its referral to the sympathetic House Judiciary Committee, but was drafted a bit differently for introduction in the Senate so it could avoid the hostile Senate Judiciary Committee and be considered instead by the friendly Senate Commerce Committee.[4] If special drafting is not feasible, obtaining a joint referral (to two committees in the chamber) may serve the same purpose, since the measure will get a floor vote even if only one committee reports it out to the floor.[5] Both of these special tactics, however, are the exception, not the rule.

Committee Authority

The rules of the House and the rules of the Senate require that legislation of a certain type be referred to a particular committee and, recently, sometimes to a particular subcommittee of that committee. But jurisdiction does not necessarily mean control over the final floor decision. In one fairly recent eight-year period, the percentage of committee bills that passed *unamended* on the floor of the U.S. Senate averaged 65 percent, but varied from 40 percent to 92 percent, depending upon the committee involved. In the House, the average was 70 percent, varying from 41 percent to 96 percent. Ripley notes that, in large measure, floor "amendments reflect a 'second-guessing' of the judgment reported by the committee majority."[6]

At least during the decade ending in 1968, much of the variation in overall committee success was the result of the differing ability of committees to get their bills brought up and considered on the House floor.[7] Whether that is still the case is an open question, since the House Rules Committee (which must issue a "rule" before most legislation can proceed to the House floor) is now clearly an arm of the House leadership, rather than the independent bastion of authority it once was. It may be that House committees will continue to have differential success in gaining chamber consideration of their legislative recommendations, but, if so, that will clearly be a decision made by the chamber leadership. Getting a bill considered on the House floor may be affected by committee cohesion—the degree to which members of the committee stick together. That is suggested by the fact that, from 1959 through 1968, the fragmented and controversy-wracked House Education and Labor Committee was the least successful House committee in getting its bills to the House floor.

The Senate majority leader often discourages committees from reporting bills which have not had their controversial points negotiated to the point of probable floor success (although the leader does not block legislation from floor consideration), but Senate committee prestige and committee cohesion in the floor vote remain very important to committee success on the floor of the Senate.[8] Committee prestige seems to be less important for committee success on the floor of the House (or perhaps to success in getting a bill to the floor), but committee cohesiveness in the floor vote is important.[9]

Committees of Congress vary in the extent to which they retain control over policy decisions which fall within their jurisdictions. Fenno argues:

> The members of each congressional committee have certain goals that they want to achieve through membership on a committee. If there is a high level of consensus on goals, they will organize their committee internally in ways that seem likely to aid them in achieving these individual goals. However, each committee operates within a distinctive set of environmental constraints—most particularly the expectations of influential external groups. Committee members will, there-

fore, also organize their committees internally in ways that seem likely to satisfy the expectations of these groups that make up their environment. The members of each committee will develop strategies for accommodating the achievement of their individual goals to the satisfaction of key environmental expectations.[10]

The member goals most relevant to individual and committee behavior are "re-election, influence within the House, and good public policy."[11] A fourth goal, a career beyond the House, has some impact.[12] The external groups making demands on committee members differ in nature from committee to committee, but generally can be classified as members of the legislative chamber who are not on the committee: executive-branch personnel, party leaders, and clientele groups such as postal workers or farmers. Committee members tend to be most responsive to those external actors whom they perceive as most legitimate or most able to assist or hinder the committee member in the accomplishment of his or her own goals. The executive branch appeared to take the lead in setting the agenda for the House Appropriations, Ways and Means, and Foreign Affairs Committees. The employees of the U.S. Postal Service and the large mailing groups (mail-order houses and magazine publishers, for example) were the most influential in determining the policy posture of the House Post Office and Civil Service Committee in the period 1955 to 1966. The House Interior and Insular Affairs Committee, on the other hand, faced complex and pluralistic sets of interest-group coalitions that wanted special projects of various kinds. The House Education and Labor Committee faced numerous demands from all four types of external groups and often made its decisions in an intensely partisan atmosphere.[13] The money committees of the House (Appropriations, and Ways and Means), however, are expected by their colleagues to "make independent policy judgments (particularly vis-à-vis the executive branch)" and to be "responsive" to the other members of the House (sensitive to the wishes and sentiments of the larger chamber membership).[14]

A study of factions in U.S. House committees a decade after Fenno's study revealed stronger ideological and partisan influences in all but one of eight committees studied, while administrative influence was on the wane.[15] The decline of executive influence doubtless was partly a result of the intense disagreements between Congress and the President in the 1973–76 period, on which the latter study was based. However, the administration's position was still of some importance and was very important in the deliberations of the House Foreign Affairs Committee (which divided along ideological lines more than partisan lines) and the House Post Office and Civil Service Committee (on which partisan and ideological influences were also very important but "impossible to disentangle" because of their high correlation).[16]

A study which took advantage of the new rules on open House committee hearings found substantial differences among committees in the way they function and also differences in the internal dynamics of each committee as it deals with various types of issues. While most of the House committees studied from the Ninety-second through the Ninety-fifth Congresses (1971 through 1978) had a degree of committee identity which led to cooperation and unity on at least some issues, most also demonstrated substantial degrees of controversy within the committee.[17] Differences among committees are the result of several factors: the differing abilities of chairpersons to lead their committees; the subject matter of the committee and whether or not the committee attracts ideologues and extreme partisans; the degree of membership stability on a committee; and the varying ability of chairpersons to control who is assigned to their committees. If the subject matter of concern is not too volatile politically, more stable committees are more likely to arrive at a sense of committee purpose which to a large extent overcomes partisan and ideological differences. Less-prestigious committees with higher turnover, however, tend to have greater levels of partisan and ideological strife. Indeed, fairly stable partisan and ideological divisions within committees were the most common divisions that dominated internal committee dynamics. The tax-writing Ways and Means Committee gave evidence of the presence of the conservative coalition in its votes on matters before the committee from 1971 through 1974, although a high degree of unity of purpose and bipartisanship within the committee was also evident. But then, the committee lost its strong chairperson, Wilbur Mills (D., Arkansas); was enlarged by half; and was forced to create subcommittees.

> These changes had a major impact. Unable to resolve many matters through generating consensus, roll call votes became the chief decision making mechanism. . . . On those ballots, bipartisanship and integration declined while party and ideologically divisive roll calls increased. The conservative coalition remained strong as well.[18]

The House Armed Services Committee "appeared to have developed and maintained a bipartisan consensus based on common ideological outlook in support of a powerful American military."[19] In contrast, the House Agriculture Committee and the Committee on Banking, Finance and Urban Affairs had "unstructured and chaotic" voting patterns which appeared "meaningless." "No clearcut pattern of factional cleavage seems to characterize the committee[s]."[20]

That external events can affect Congress and Congressional committees is dramatically demonstrated by the changes in the House Post Office and Civil Service Committee in the late 1960s and early 1970s.

> A single event—the 1966 pre-Christmas mail breakdown in Chicago—triggered a public concern over postal issues that eventually shattered the monolithic, clientele-dominated environment of the Committee. . . . The climactic environmental event was the ten-day postal strike in March 1970. The effect of all this activity was to increase the salience of postal issues nationally and to bring the executive branch to leadership of the policy coalition (favoring postal reform) confronting the Post Office Committee.

> The tight clientele-Committee alliance had relied heavily on the low salience of its subject matter; under inconspicuous circumstances the minority of Committee members devoted to the alliance could act in the name of the majority, whose only interest in the Committee was to leave it. But in a time of high salience and under pressure from an executive-led policy coalition, a Committee majority would be perfectly willing to relinquish the constituency-re-election benefits of Committee membership.[21]

The result of the turmoil was the creation of the U.S. Postal Service and the removal of postal-worker pay raises from the direct control of Congress and of the House Post Office and Civil Service Committee.

Subject-Matter Expertise   Chamber rules determine much of the authority of a committee—the degree to which its decision to "bottle up" or delay a bill, kill it, amend or rewrite it, or recommend enactment is upheld, or at least is not overridden, by the full chamber. Another factor involved in committee authority, as pointed out in Chapter 10, is that the members of a particular committee usually know more about the subject matter under their jurisdiction than other members of Congress do. One important way for a member to become respected by his or her fellow committee members or by other colleagues in the legislative chamber is for the member to develop an area of specialization in which he or she is truly able to make a contribution to the other members. Otherwise, the chamber membership may be overly dependent on legislative staff and on executive-department personnel for its information and analysis. Although committee staff have a major impact on legislation, at both the state and national level, it is important for legislators that some of their number have the knowledge to evaluate proposals on their own. This value is so strong for legislators, as noted in Chapter 10, that legislative work and specialization are two of the six major norms of behavior found by Matthews in his classic study of the U.S. Senate. Similar sets of norms have been found in other American legislative bodies.[22]

Within each committee, various members become experts on different topics, and other committee members frequently accept the word of those experts and depend on their interpretation of legislation and events, barring jarring external evidence to the contrary. Each member, of course, is concerned to retain his or her credibility (and power). Once gained, a reputation for expertise brings great authority within Congress. Depending on the nature of the subject matter, even members of varying philosophical stripes may ask for voting advice from a recognized legislator-expert. Doing one's homework and knowing one's subject matter is an important source of power within Congress which other members and lobbyists understand and respect, even though members of the public may often remain unaware of the member's status as an expert.

> [G]iven the large number of subcommittee assignments [each senator] receives, he is likely to find one or two . . . that handle matters in which he rapidly can become expert. Each individual senator is quickly thrust into a subcommittee position in which he becomes the leading expert for the entire Senate. Then he is in a position to exercise power alone—or with the aid of a few staff members and perhaps with the agreement of one senator from the other party. The decisions thus made are almost always accepted by the entire Senate.[23]

The importance of subject-matter expertise, however, varies with the political salience of the topic, the level of public partisan differences, and the year. Proposals concerning regulation of business, labor legislation, welfare, and the like are questions on which many members held strong feelings before their election to Congress. While subject-matter expertise is helpful in the legislative maneuvering on such issues, it brings with it only modest authority over the topic. Partisan factors and policy statements made during Congressional campaigns—and by each party's presidential candidate during the last election campaign—are likely to overwhelm expertise, at least on the broad sweep of the policies adopted. The experts often have to content themselves with marginal adjustments here and there. On topics which tend not to be of great interest to the public, however, or to be "grabbers" in an election campaign, the subject-matter experts usually get their way. A member who is the most knowledgeable person in the chamber on laser technology, general aviation, housing, or some such topic can gain great authority within the chamber, based primarily on expertise. Similarly, a committee has a fairly free hand when dealing with relatively esoteric subject matter, but must take careful account of the temper of the chamber when drafting legislation concerning the more salient partisan issues of the day.

Committee Prestige and Cohesion Committees which successfully gauge and respond to the prevailing sentiment of the chamber, examine each question thoroughly, and make independent judgments on the issues are likely to retain the confidence of their colleagues and see a larger proportion of their legislation enacted, with fewer floor amendments. The higher the prestige of a committee in the chamber and the more cohesive is opinion in the committee on a given bill, the greater the chances of the committee's floor success. Marked dissension within a committee, on the other hand, means mixed signals will be received by legislators who are not on the committee, and this leads to more frequent committee defeats on the floor and a higher rate of floor amendments.[24]

From 1963 through 1971, the most successful House committee, in terms of getting its legislation passed by the House without amendment, was the House Ways and Means Committee. Of ninety-nine bills reported to the House floor by the Ways and Means Committee during that period, 96 percent passed the House without amendment.[25] The major subject matter of the bills reported by that committee are taxation, tariffs and trade agreements, and Social Security. These subjects are important, politically charged, and potentially controversial. The committee tries hard to remain sensitive to the wishes of the House, but to make its own decisions independent of the executive department. That apparently is what the House members want it to do.[26] The chairperson of the committee during the period discussed, Wilbur Mills of Arkansas, wanted

> more than anything not to have a minority report. He wants at least twenty votes (of the committee's 25 members) and one way he does it is drop out anything controversial. I don't mean just major policy questions that may be controversial but anything. If they come across a provision and some member raises an objection, he'll drop it out. They go through it once, make tentative decisions, again, and drop out anything controversial.[27]

Mills clearly placed great emphasis on avoiding a defeat on the floor of the House. He thought the committee,

> in addition to reporting technically sound bills, should report bills that can pass the House, and the best means of ensuring passage in the House is through compromise in the committee. His reputation and his committee's are at stake every time a Ways and Means bill comes before the House. . . .[28]

Under House Democratic party rules of the era, Mills was also chairperson of the Democratic party's committee on committees and used that post to insure that only "responsible" Democrats who agreed with his approach were appointed to his committee. Liberal Democrats were generally unhappy with their party's membership on that committee.

The degree of conflict surrounding an issue and the level of salience members of Congress believe an issue has for the public affect a committee's approach toward legislation. High-salience, low-conflict issues, such as health research, lead to high levels of Congressional involvement. Low-salience, high-conflict issues, such as regulation of the electronic-communications industry, discourage committee members from taking the initiative. (The benefits of doing so are outweighed by the costs.) In high-conflict areas, a member of Congress is likely to discover that successful development of governmental policy requires cooperation with the executive branch[29] and thus the executive department's views are likely to be of greater significance in committee decisions on such issues.

House-Senate Differences in Committee Authority   The House and the Senate differ somewhat in the extent to which each standing committee has independent authority over legislation in its subject-matter fields of jurisdiction. In general, each committee of each chamber is the true decision site concerning that chamber's action on a particular piece of legislation or policy field. Because of the smaller size of the Senate, however, and that chamber's greater dependence on unanimous consent on the floor (see Chapter 13), Senate committees have a bit less complete control over legislative details than House committees do. The larger House has, of necessity, adopted rules which restrict the fullness and robustness of debate in that chamber. The Senate, by contrast, continues to operate on the principle of unlimited debate, unless 60 percent of the membership chooses to cut off debate (by invoking "cloture"). The more streamlined floor procedures of the House present fewer opportunities than is the case in the Senate for the amendment of legislation on the floor. Thus, House votes are more on the order of "approve-disapprove" than "approve if improved." House committees are therefore a bit more likely than Senate committees to get their legislation accepted by the entire chamber without change.

As indicated in Chapter 10, there is also a difference in the authority of the budget committees of the two chambers. The Senate Budget Committee is a standing committee to which senators receive permanent appointment, like any other major standing committee of the Senate. The members develop seniority on the committee and a feeling that they have an investment in the committee's authority. Service on the House Budget Committee, on the other hand, is limited. A representative cannot be a permanent member of that committee. Further, of the twenty-five members of the House Budget Committee, five must be members of the House Appropriations Committee and five must be members of the House Ways and Means Committee. Those two committees are natural antagonists of the House Budget Committee, yet their "loaned" members retain rank on (and presumably loyalty to) their "home" committees. Within the chamber, then, the Senate Budget Committee has substantially greater, separate authority over budget matters than the House Budget Committee does.[30]

A third difference in the degree to which House and Senate committees are autonomous policymakers within their respective chambers is almost as much a potential difference as an actual difference. The Senate party conferences have indicated no predisposition to "instruct" party members on a particular Senate committee concerning party policy on matters before the committee. In the House, however, there have been indications that some Democrats believe it a proper function of the Democratic caucus to instruct a committee's Democrats on issue positions. In early 1978, for example, the House Ways and Means Committee was standing firm with the Carter administration in opposition to rolling back Social Security taxes. But many House Democrats wanted such a bill reported to the House floor, an action the committee refused to take. In an almost unheard-of move, and over the opposition of the Speaker and the majority leader, the Democratic caucus voted in April 1978 (150 to 57) in favor of a nonbinding resolution "urging Ways and Means to act on rollback legislation.[31] The committee thereafter reversed itself and reported the bill by a one-vote margin.

Conference Committees

Conference committees of Congress are important decision sites in the legislative process, even though they are short-lived. As noted in Chapter 10, if the second chamber to consider a bill changes it in any way, the chamber in which the bill originated must concur in those changes before the bill can go to the President for signature. Usually, the two versions are reconciled in an informal manner, but about 10 percent of the legislation winds up going to a House-Senate conference committee appointed specially for that particular bill. The legislation which does go to conference tends to be important legislation.[32]

If the chamber of origination dislikes the other chamber's amendments, it can let the bill die, amend the bill further and send it to the other chamber again, or "pass an entirely new version of the bill and send it" to the other chamber.[33] In cases where serious disagreements exist, however, a conference committee is usually convened. The conference committee is charged with working out a version which will be acceptable to a majority of the members of each chamber of Congress. A *separate* majority of conferees from each chamber must approve the conference version of a bill that is reported back to the two chambers.

The power of the conference committee comes from its ability to revise the bill before reporting a compromise version back to the floors of the two chambers and the fact that the rules prohibit amendments to a measure on the floor after it is reported by a conference committee. Members must vote "yes" or "no." In the rare event that a conference report is rejected by either chamber, the bill may be allowed to die or conferees (usually the same ones) may be instructed to try again.

In each chamber, the Speaker of the House and the president pro tem of the Senate officially (and separately) appoint the conferees, which include proportionate numbers of members of each party. But actual selection of conferees is normally made by the chairperson (for majority-party members) and the ranking minority member (for minority-party members) of the chamber committee with jurisdiction over the bill. Formerly, conferees were usually the senior members of the relevant committee, but under revised rules junior members with special knowledge of the legislation are now often appointed. Both chambers tend to appoint as conferees members of the relevant *subcommittee* which considered the legislation, and some House committee rules *require* that the conferees on a bill be members of the subcommittee or subcommittees that originally considered the bill.

Conferees are expected to support their chamber's position on the bill, but that is a difficult norm to follow on complex legislation—and if followed to the extreme would of course mean that no compromise could ever be reached. Since 1975, new rules have made it difficult for conference committees to meet in secret. Before then, most conference committee meetings were closed to the public and the press.

Experienced members of Congress have a pretty good idea which measures are likely to go to conference, and they behave accordingly.

> [C]onferees know they will have to bargain and cannot expect to win all points in dispute. Sometimes, particularly in the Senate, committee leaders will accept amendments on the floor that they really do not favor so that later on, in conference, they will have trading chips that they can give away in order to save some provision they really care about.
>
> Conference committees usually have considerable leeway in reaching final agreement. On some occasions they may even insert new legislative language in the bill, provisions contained in neither the House nor the Senate bill. On a few bills, however, they will receive specific instructions from their parent chamber on provisions on which they must insist.[34]

The insertion of new provisions (not in the version of either house) in a bill in conference is a violation of Congressional rules, but this happens occasionally anyway. Such new provisions are subject to a point of order in either chamber but often are adopted without objection as the price of getting a bill passed.

Conferees are concerned about their personal reputations and about the prestige of their committees and their respective chambers. Thus, what may appear to be minor differences between the two sets of conferees sometimes become sticking points. Dollar amounts often are compromised, and logrolling sometimes comes into play—that is, House conferees may agree to a particular Senate provision in return for Senate conferees agreeing to an unrelated House provision. The President and his aides sometimes get involved too in conference decisions, insisting on certain provisions under the threat of a veto.

Committee Governance

The committees of Congress must conform to certain rules set down by their parent chambers, but in many ways they are free to structure themselves as they see fit. Some rules, such as those governing the manner in which individual committee members are assigned to subcommittees; the manner of selection of subcommittee chairs; the minority party's share of staff positions; subcommittee chairperson control over subcommittee staff; and the requirements governing open or closed committee meetings, are mandated by the parent body. But within those general rules lies much room for flexibility and maneuvering. Each committee's rules must not conflict with chamber rules governing committees, and each committee's rules must be written, but the detailed rules of the committee and changes in those rules are decided on by vote of the committee members. Each House committee with twenty or more members is required to establish at least five subcommittees and to grant each of them jurisdiction, in writing, over certain areas within the full committee's jurisdiction. But, it is otherwise up to the committee as to how many subcommittees to establish, how many members will be on each subcommittee, and what jurisdiction to grant to each subcommittee and how much to retain at the full committee level.[35] Except for the Senate Budget Committee, the Senate Rules and Administration Committee, and the Senate Veterans' Affairs Committee, every standing committee of the Senate has created standing (permanent) subcommittees. Of those without subcommittees, only the Budget Committee is a major committee.

Through the 1960s, the chairpersons of Congressional committees were chosen on the basis of seniority in their party on the committee and, with few exceptions, were in charge of their committees' operations. Writing in the early 1960s, Ralph K. Huitt noted that, although there are institutional and situational limits on a committee chairperson's authority,

> the chairman of a major standing committee in the Senate is . . . in virtual control of his committee. He calls committee meetings, decides what bills will be considered, appoints subcommittee chairmen, controls the selection of witnesses, and, excepting bills of overriding importance, determines which bills favorably reported by his committee really will be pressed for floor consideration. . . . In practice, he chooses committee members who will go to the conference with the House on committee bills. . . . The chairman decides whether the staff will be as large and expert as money will buy or funds will be returned to the Treasury; whether the staff will be encouraged to be aggressive or passive; and whether a real fight will be made to carry the bill through floor and conference as the committee wrote it or the effort will be half-hearted.[36]

A leading expert on the U.S. House, Richard F. Fenno, Jr., noted that the actual authority of each committee chairperson in the House in the 1960s varied with his or her abilities, but "each committee chairman does have a formidable set of prerogatives—over procedure, agenda, hearings, subcommittee creation, subcommittee membership, subcommittee jurisdiction, staff membership, staff functions."[37] Perhaps foreseeing the consequences of subtle trends at the time, Fenno noted that the skillful and knowledgeable chairperson "can dominate his committee or subcommittee. But . . . it is impossible for a chairperson to dictate committee decisions against the wishes of a cohesive and determined majority of its members—at least in the long run."[38] Further, a chairperson who failed to heed the desires of his or her committee members "may bring about a revolt inside the committee which permanently weakens the influence of its chairman."[39] Yet, "seniority only partially governs the selection of subcommittee leaders. . . . The chairman may control subcommittee leadership by his power to determine their jurisdiction and to create or abolish subcommittees."[40] Thus, patterns within House committees in the 1960's varied "from autocracy to democracy."[41]

But strong-willed chairpersons who could maintain the support of a majority of the committee (often by influencing appointments to vacancies on that committee) were in a position to thwart the wishes of the House majority, as well as to deny committee members with a different perspective on committee issues any voice in policymaking. Such members often left for a more congenial committee, further augmenting the power of the chairperson. Concerning a chairperson's power, Berman noted in the early 1960s:

> It is difficult to exaggerate the power of a committee chairman. Even on committees with comparatively democratic procedures, chairmen are generally able to exercise firm control, and what the committee does is seldom different from what the chairman wants it to do. . . . The most awesome power of a chairman is his ability to prevent his committee from acting and thus prevent Congress from acting. . . . [T]he chairman is ordinarily the absolute master of the [committee's] agenda and he may be able to keep a bill that he opposes from ever being brought up. Moreover, he has the unlimited power of recognition. This means that he is perfectly free to impose silence on unfriendly members, giving the floor [at committee meetings] only to his cronies.[42]

Fenno's vision of the future—about the inability of a committee chairperson to withstand a determined and cohesive committee majority—proved correct within the decade. The excesses of committee chairpersons, out of step with the views of their party colleagues (especially Democrats), led to changes in the rules of each chamber which greatly limit the authority of chairpersons of standing committees. Committee chairs are still figures of great authority in Congress, but their ability to exercise their powers in an arbitrary and autocratic fashion and to withstand majority opinion in the chamber—and especially on the committee—has been greatly restricted by reforms which were enacted in the 1970s. Those reforms were adopted when a large percentage of the members of each chamber were in their first two or four years of service and were out of patience with the ability of more senior members to thwart arbitrarily the wishes of junior members.

House of Representatives Rules Changes   In 1970, the House rules were changed to end a chairperson's ability to prevent legislative action simply by refusing to convene the committee. A majority of members of a standing committee can now force a committee meeting within a week, after a formal written demand for such a meeting by any three committee members.[43] In that same year, 1970, the House required that each committee adopt written rules. This further checked the ability of a chairperson to act arbitrarily.

Many of the changes ("reforms") in the House were directed toward restricting the power of the chairpersons of standing committees. Overall, the reforms accomplished that goal, while strengthening the role of Speaker of the House in some respects and diffusing power to the subcommittee chairs. Much of the impetus for changes in House rules came from junior Democratic representatives, who found that they did not have the votes to force through rules changes on the floor of the whole House. Thus, largely as a result of leadership from the liberal Democratic Study Group, the reform-oriented Democrats decided to change the rules of the Democratic caucus, where they *did* have the necessary votes. Because Democrats were the majority party, a change in Democratic party rules concerning committee and subcommittee chairs effectively changed the House policies governing such matters.

Among the other changes in the rules of the House and of the House Democratic caucus was the requirement that chairpersons of standing committees and of subcommittees of the Appropriations Committee be approved individually by secret ballot in the Democratic caucus at the beginning of each Congress. Such a rule implied that the chairpersons should be more responsive to other members of Congress and should not necessarily be selected on the basis of seniority alone. Even the less-responsive committee chairpersons doubtless understood the implications of the new rules after the Democratic caucus, in 1975, deposed three chairs of standing committees. Lest the caucus be accused of radicalism, however, it should be noted that the vacant chairs were then filled by application of the seniority rule among the remaining members of the affected committees[44] and that no other chairpersons have been removed since 1975.

The authority of committee chairpersons to determine what subcommittees would exist, what the respective jurisdictions of the subcommittees would be, and who would chair them was also ended by Democratic caucus rules changes. The new rules required that such decisions be made by vote of all Democrats on each committee. This Democratic caucus in each committee also determines each subcommittee's share of the committee budget. Chairpersons of standing committees no longer can emasculate a subcommittee by cutting its budget. Further, the chairperson of a standing committee is now required to refer bills to the relevant subcommittee with jurisdiction within two weeks, rather than being able to kill a bill by refusing to so refer it.

House Republicans changed their official policy concerning the seniority norm before House Democrats did. In 1971, House Republicans decided that the "ranking member" of each committee was to be determined by secret ballot within the House Republican conference. No senior GOP members have been ousted under the new rule, however. The ranking minority member is the leading minority-party member of a committee and would normally become committee chairperson if the minority party became the majority party in the House. He or she is given control over minority funds and staff positions on the committee.

Other chamberwide changes made in House committee procedures in recent years include limitations on the use of proxy votes in committees; limitations on the use of closed meetings for committee business; provisions in the rules governing subcommittee assignments that help junior committee members get better subcommittee assignments; and rules in each party which restrict members to only one chair or ranking minority-member position—whether of a full committee, a subcommittee, or a select committee.

Senate Rules Changes   The Senate was a few years behind the House in making major changes in its rules concerning committees and the seniority system. That was partly because the Senate already had acted to insure junior members greater participation in the life of the chamber by adopting rules (such as the Democratic

"Johnson Rule") which insured each first-year senator at least one reasonably good committee assignment and allowed a few to have seats on some of the most desired committees in the Senate. The effect of recent Senate changes has also been to reduce somewhat the authority of Senate committee chairpersons.

In 1973, Senate Republicans (then the minority party) adopted a rule which gave the authority to determine each committee's ranking minority member to the Republicans on that committee, subject to ratification by the Senate Republican conference. Senate Democrats (then the majority party) followed suit in 1975 by adopting a rule that, beginning in 1977, a secret Democratic caucus ballot on any nominee for committee chairperson be required if one fifth of Senate Democrats requested such a vote. No chairperson or ranking minority member in the Senate has been deposed under the new rules, but those holding such positions are aware of their implications. New Senate rules also limit any senator to chairing only two subcommittees, in addition to chairing a standing committee. Such a rule, of course, means that junior majority-party members get to chair some of the less-important subcommittees—an experience which allows them to be accepted as legitimate actors within the Senate, rather than continuing to be the "apprentices" they were formerly expected to be.[45]

The Senate, like the House, has also adopted a rule requiring committees to open all committee sessions to the public and the press. The half dozen exceptions permitted require the committee to close a session by a majority vote taken in open session. Both the Senate and the House have also agreed to open conference committee sessions to the public and the press, rather than routinely convening them in private. This has increased the ability of junior senators to challenge the policy preferences of senior senators. So did the adoption of a rule, in 1975, which allows each senator to hire up to three extra staff members to work on a senator's committees, making more staff expertise available to them so that they no longer have to accept the statements of senior members as correct.

Committees in both chambers of Congress are now governed more democratically than they were a decade or so ago. Junior members have greater resources and support in the rules for challenging the policy preferences and the procedural decisions of senior members and chairpersons. Minority-party members have greater resources for developing alternatives to the majority party's positions. And subcommittees and their chairpersons are more independent of full committees and their chairpersons.

Committee chairs are still the most important members of their respective committees, unless they are unusually incompetent. Occasionally, another senior member of a committee is so effective that he or she becomes the dominant figure on the committee, but that also happened before the recent rules changes.[46] Chairpersons have sufficient powers and prerogatives, even after the rules changes of the 1970s, to be able to lead their committees in the direction the chairpersons want them to go, if the chairpersons are reasonably competent. Unless other members wish to challenge the chair, the chairperson controls the committee's agenda, the committee's funds, and the committee staff. The chair takes the lead in majority-party committee-member discussion of various committee-management issues. Committee members prefer harmonious relationships, and they realize that they must expect to work together over the years, so only major disagreements are normally likely to precipitate challenges to the chair's decisions. The normal approach is for a committee member to seek modification of the chair's plans by persuasion and dialogue. Members of committees do though have a greater voice in committee affairs than they did previously, and they have the resources to do battle with the

──────────────── ★ ★ ★ ★ ────────────────

Members of Congress Describe Committee Dynamics

The toughest kind of a majority to put together is one to reform a committee in the face of opposition from the chairman. As you get closer to the top of the hierarchy, the pressures on people who normally would be counted on to aid reformers are enormous and . . . [they] tend to chicken out.—Quoted in Charles L. Clapp, *The Congressman: His Work as He Sees It* (Washington, D.C.: Brookings Institution, 1963), p. 252.

There is great reluctance to challenge committee chairmen even though you don't agree with them. Everyone seems fearful; all members have pet projects and legislation they want passed. No one wants to tangle too much because they realize what the results would be.—Quoted in ibid.

────── is one of the most charming and delightful chairmen in the House, and highly skillful. He doesn't sidetrack us by ever refusing anything. He just schedules a workload in other areas which make it impossible for us to get our legislation heard.—Quoted in ibid., p. 256.

We have a rule in the [Senate] Labor Committee that says a majority of the Committee's members can take action if the chairman refuses. . . . He knows that we will invoke Committee rules if he holds up the legislation.—Quoted in Richard F. Fenno, Jr., *Congressmen in Committees* (Boston: Little, Brown, 1973), p. 177.

I'm as much a stranger in another subcommittee [of House Appropriations] as I would be in the legislative committee on Post Office and Civil Service. Each one does its work apart from all others.—Quoted in ibid., p. 95.

──────────────── ★ ★ ★ ★ ────────────────

chairperson, if necessary. A chairperson, however, is still in a position to be particularly effective in killing or saving bills concerning which the committee has no strong opinion but the chairperson does; in shaping the details of the numerous noncontroversial, fairly routine bills which come before the committee; and in structuring the alternatives on the few major, and often controversial, bills which come before the committee during each Congress.

Committee Hearings

Congressional committees have numerous sources of information on which to base their decisions. Committee staff members collect much information for the committees, for example, in both formal and informal communications (in person and by letter) with executive-branch personnel, interest-group representatives, corporations, unions, professional associations, ordinary citizens, and state and local officials. Still, when considering legislation, committees of Congress usually hold hearings—as the Constitution Subcommittee of the Senate Judiciary Committee did in

302

early 1982, for example, when it had the extension of the Voting Rights Act of 1965 under consideration.

Committee hearings serve a number of purposes, besides just providing committee members and Congress with information, although that is a very important function of committee hearings. And attendance at committee and subcommittee hearings helps committee members maintain their subject-matter expertise. They learn more on each subject than their colleagues who are not on the committee (and thus do not have to sit through what are often very boring proceedings). But the testimony before the committee may be deliberately "stacked" by the chairperson—as feminists charged was the case in a 1981 Senate subcommittee hearing on abortion. Committee members, themselves, are not necessarily unbiased either. Rather, as Huitt notes, "committee members themselves are participants in the struggle of contending groups, one phase of which is the public hearing."[47] Further, after observing hearings on inflation and price controls by the Senate Committee on Banking and Currency (in 1946), Huitt reported

> there emerged, not one picture of the factual situation, but two. The senators who supported OPA accepted one, those who opposed OPA the other. . . . Each group seemed to come into the hearings with a ready-made frame of reference. Facts which were compatible were fitted into it; facts which were not compatible, even when elaborately documented, were discounted, not perceived, or ignored.[48]

Even on the narrow topic involved, the committee had not "ever formulated a set of questions to which the hearings should supply answers."[49] Many members had entered with their minds made up and obviously had other purposes in mind than just obtaining information.

Congress also holds committee hearings "to oversee the administration of programs, to inform the public, and to protect its (Congress') integrity, dignity, reputation, and privileges."[50] In addition to the above functions, Congressional committee hearings perform a "safety-valve" function of airing grievances and "adjusting group conflicts."[51] Hearings are also helpful, especially for the chairperson of the committee or subcommittee, in advancing individual political careers. Occasionally, too, the committee record of a hearing provides the judiciary with a basis for determining legislative intent. A given hearing or set of hearings, of course, can perform several of the above functions at the same time.

Legislative Oversight Members and committees of Congress attempt to keep executive department personnel responsive to Congressional intent through a number of mechanisms, generally lumped together under the rubric "legislative oversight." Individual committee or subcommittee members correspond and talk with individuals in the executive branch—from civil servants to cabinet officers, and even the President. The "watchdog" agency of the Congress, the General Accounting Office (GAO), conducts audits of various kinds. Committee and subcommittee chairs communicate with executive-branch officials whose duties are related to the committee's jurisdiction. And lobbyists concerned about a particular field of policy are in frequent contact with the appropriate bureaucrats and Congressional actors in each policy-specific "subsystem" of policymaking (lobbyists, high-ranking bureaucrats, and relevant members of Congress).

A key Congressional weapon in the oversight of the executive branch is the holding of a formal hearing (or the threat of one), during which the non-Congressional actors in the subsystem are subject to interrogation by members of Congress. Such hearings can sometimes be unpleasant, and many members of Congress see them as necessary only when the normal, informal methods of oversight have broken down.[52] For example, in connection with their 1982 oversight hearings on the policies of President Reagan's Secretary of the Interior, James G. Watt, three separate House subcommittees (the Subcommittee on Public Lands and National Parks and the Subcommittee on Oversight and Investigations, both of the House Energy Committee, and the Subcommittee on Environment of the House Government Operations Committee) threatened to have the secretary cited for contempt of Congress for failure to furnish information they wanted.[53] Perhaps more important, a hearing can raise the visibility of the issues being discussed and may invite "outsiders" into the fray, thus permanently changing the dynamics of subsystem decision-making—in a manner possibly not to the liking of the relevant interest groups, government agencies, or members of Congress.[54]

Congressional committees vary greatly in the number of oversight hearings they conduct. Some "committees in both houses tend to give more attention to investigations of broad policy questions than to inquiries into agency implementation of programs."[55] While "congressional attention to bureaucratic agencies is haphazard,"[56] Senate committees are a bit more oriented toward oversight hearings than are their House counterparts.

Not all "oversight" is alike. The kind of oversight a committee is responsible for depends on the nature of the committee:

> The *appropriations committees* have responsibility for "fiscal" oversight: the duty to ensure that agencies spend funds in efficient and appropriate ways. The *authorization committees* have responsibility for "legislative" oversight of agencies within their jurisdiction. Their task is to determine whether particular programs work and to propose remedies to problems they uncover. The *government operations* committees have a responsibility for "investigative" oversight: a mandate for wide-ranging inquiry into government economy, efficiency, and effectiveness that may follow policies and programs across many agency lines.[57]

Congress and the American state legislatures expect their standing committees (and their subcommittees) to conduct oversight of the executive as an incidental adjunct to their main function of policy formulation, which involves the drafting of legislation for floor consideration. Only rarely is a special Congressional committee appointed with the sole purpose of investigation or oversight. But some other national legislatures do separate these functions. Indeed, in the British House of Commons, the most autonomous and authoritative committees—the only ones in which the position of committee chair seems to be a source of independent authority and a likely stepping-stone to a cabinet post—are the specialized committees, established specifically to oversee the bureaucracy, rather than to formulate policy. These include the Public Accounts Committee, traditionally chaired by a member of the opposition and armed with some subpoena powers, which "reviews expenditures to assure that money has been spent as the Commons intended it to be spent";[58] the Expenditures Committee, which keeps an eye out for waste in government spending; and the Select Committee on Nationalized Industries, which examines "general policy such as capital investment, wages and working conditions, and uneconomic services and prices," rather than day-to-day management questions.[59] Limited resources and a strong nonpartisan norm, however, limit the activities of these "supervisory" or oversight committees of the Commons.

Inform the Public Congressional hearings are sometimes held mostly for the purpose of educating or informing the public, although the *official* rationale given for the hearings may be that of gathering information needed in connection with legislation. This was the case when the Senate Governmental Affairs Committee held hearings in early 1982 on President Reagan's "New Federalism" proposals to transfer welfare, food stamps, and some forty other federal programs to the states.[60] The choice of witnesses, the conduct of the committee or subcommittee members and chairperson, the hearing atmosphere, and the amount of effort expended to insure proper coverage by the news media often attest that a hearing has been called for the purpose of informing or educating the general public. Opponents of the policy positions being advanced by the hearing may refer to it as "propaganda forum." An example of the use of committee hearings to inform or educate the public were the 1960s and 1970s Vietnam War hearings, held by the Senate Foreign Relations Committee, whose chairperson opposed American policy there and used the hearings to give a platform to those of like beliefs. Similarly, hearings on compulsory health insurance were first held in 1945–46, not because the committee thought the bill would pass, but to "educate the public" and get a larger portion of the populace to consider the idea.[61]

Committee hearings intended to influence public opinion do not always receive the media attention necessary to bring about immediate changes in either public opinion or elite opinion. Still, many such relatively obscure hearings result in large quantities of material on the subject being pulled together in one fairly accessible place. The House Education and Labor Committee, for example, held seventy-five days of hearings on one bill a few years ago. The committee heard 275 expert witnesses and evaluated "thirty-one different formulae for allocating federal school aid funds."[62] Such massive quantities of information do not interest the public directly, but they frequently become the basis for important subsequent analysis, leading various opinion molders (editors, journalists, scholars, public officials) to develop their own opinions and, in turn, to persuade the general public.

Safety Valve   There is ample indirect, though little direct, evidence, including statements by both legislators and lobbyists, that committee hearings are sometimes used as a kind of "safety valve," allowing people to air their grievances.[63] As a result of hearings, even those persons most intensely opposed to the proposed legislation may tend to feel that they have had a chance to "get it off their chest" and that the "rules of the game" have been honored. "[T]he public hearing may facilitate acceptance of almost any legislative product because it has been arrived at 'in the right way,' because 'everyone' had a chance to be heard."[64]

The importance legislators place on giving ordinary people a chance to let off steam is probably part of the reason numerous committees and subcommittees now hold hearings at various sites around the country, rather than only in Washington. The Democrats in control of the House Agriculture Committee announced 1982 field hearings in farm country to consider the financial problems of farmers.[65] Such a practice also enables the committee members who attend (often just one or two members of Congress are present) to get a better feel for how grassroots people are affected by various policies, programs, or agencies. At the same time, senators or representatives from states or districts where the hearings are held get a chance for local visibility.

Committee Investigations

The line between ordinary committee *hearings* and committee *investigations* is not necessarily clear. In investigations, a staff member is more likely to ask the questions of witnesses, whereas committee members do much of the questioning at hearings; an investigation is "usually concerned with the consideration of a special problem rather than a special legislative proposal; and the procedures of an investigating committee are likely to be more courtlike."[66] Further, at regular legislative hearings, numerous witnesses appear at their own request, while in investigations most witnesses are invited or subpoenaed to appear.

The power to investigate is an *implied power* of Congress, not a power explicitly spelled out in the U.S. Constitution. This power, which has been upheld by the U.S. Supreme Court,[67] extends to duly-constituted committees of Congress. The subpoena power, necessary to enforce the attendance of witnesses at the hearings, originally was granted only to select or special committees of either chamber, and a standing committee was first granted such powers only in 1827. The Legislative Reorganization Act of 1946 granted "permanent subpoena power to all standing committees of the Senate."[68] Until 1974, House leaders rejected giving such blanket subpoena power to all standing committees of the lower chamber, permitting only the Un-American Activities Committee, the Government Operations Committee, and the Appropriations Committee to issue subpoenas without first obtaining special authority from the full House. But House committees and subcommittees were finally granted general subpoena power in 1974, as part of a change in the House rules concerning committee jurisdiction.[69]

The first Congressional investigation was an inquiry in 1792 into the unsuccessful campaign of General St. Clair against the Indians.[70] That investigation gave rise to the establishment, by President George Washington, of the tradition that the chief executive could refuse to hand over to Congress papers "the disclosure of which would injure the public."[71] Although there wasn't any such executive refusal to the first Congressional investigation, the groundwork for the claim of "executive privilege" was laid on that occasion. (The federal courts recognize some executive claim to some implied right of executive privilege, as will be discussed in Chapter 15.)

Since 1792, Congress and its committees have investigated a diverse set of matters and questions—as Congressional opinion (or sometimes public opinion) has dictated. Investigations have, for example, focused on John Brown's raid at Harper's Ferry prior to the Civil War; charges at various times of influence peddling and corruption of public officials, including the Teapot Dome Scandal; purported subversion and disloyalty of citizens; and numerous examinations of what went wrong with a variety of government programs and policies. In early 1982, for example, Chairman Orvin G. Hatch (R., Utah) used the investigative powers of the Senate Labor and Human Resources Committee to spotlight abuses in employee-pension systems.[72]

But there are some limits on the investigatory power of Congress. Although the federal courts consistently interpret these investigatory powers broadly, there is no "general power to inquire into private affairs and compel disclosures; and a witness 'rightfully' might refuse to answer where the bounds of congressional power were exceeded or 'the questions are not pertinent to the matter under inquiry.' "[73] Further, persons being investigated and witnesses who are called to testify are still protected by the Bill of Rights, upon which Congress cannot "unjustifiably encroach."[74] "Witnesses cannot be compelled to give evidence against themselves. They cannot be subjected to unreasonable search and seizure. Nor can the First Amendment freedoms of speech, press, religion, or political belief and association be abridged."[75] An 1881 decision held that Congress is not constitutionally empowered to conduct "fruitless" investigations, that is, those which "could result in no valid legislation on the subject to which the inquiry referred,"[76] but later decisions have held that "a 'potential' for legislation is sufficient. It is enough that the subject is one on which Congress can legislate and 'would be materially aided by the information which the investigation was calculated to elicit.' "[77] Under pressure from public charges by various members of Congress in the late 1950s that the Court was impeding the fight against Communism, the U.S. Supreme Court held in *Barenblatt* v. *United States*[78] that First Amendment rights had to be balanced against competing public interests, and that the courts could *not* examine the motives of congressional inquisitors. Two 1961 decisions, *Wilkinson* v. *United States* and *Braden* v. *United States*, went further in upholding harassing techniques.

It thus appeared that the Court had recognized a practically unlimited power of congressional inquiry, but, in fact, due partly to changes in the Court's membership, *Braden* and *Wilkinson* marked the end of an era, and the Court began to reverse almost every contempt conviction that came before it. These reversals were accomplished for the most part without challenging the scope of investigatory power or querying the motives of the investigators. They were achieved primarily by strict judicial enforcement of the rules on pertinency, authorization, and procedure, plus strict observance of the constitutional standards governing criminal prosecutions.[79]

Thus, even though the Supreme Court at times is ready to insist on procedural restraints which protect individuals from the unreasonable exercise of Congressional power, it is clear that the power of Congress to investigate is very broad and that the Court is reluctant to encroach on the investigative powers of the legislative branch (although no committee may exceed the authority granted to it by the parent body[80]).

★ ★ ★ ★

Irresponsible Use of the Power of Investigation

The power of investigation is sometimes abused for political purposes. The House Committee on Un-American Activities, especially active during the 1950s and 1960s, was artful at abusing witnesses, as were Senator Joseph McCarthy (R., Wisconsin) and the Senate Government Operations Committee subcommittee which he chaired.

The Un-American Activities Committee . . . [was] empowered, among other things, to investigate the "objects of un-American propaganda activities in the United States," as well as "propaganda that . . . attacks the principle of the form of government as guaranteed by our Constitution. . . ." This authorizing resolution was derided by the Supreme Court in 1957, when for the first time it reversed the contempt conviction of a witness who had declined to answer questions of the committee. In a scathing opinion by Chief Justice Earl Warren, the Court referred deprecatingly to the authorizing resolution: "Who can define the meaning of 'un-American'?" it asked. "What is that single solitary 'principle of the form of government as guaranteed by our Constitution'?" . . .

The Committee on Un-American Activities holds the undisputed record for the number of contempt citations it has generated. Any of the witnesses who have gone to jail for defying the Committee could have avoided prosecution by the simple expedient of invoking the Fifth Amendment to the Constitution. The idea behind this Amendment, which forbids forcing a man to testify against himself, was to make it hard for officials to pursue inquiries into religious heresy or political heterodoxy. Anyone who seeks the protection of the Amendment, however, risks being humiliated and degraded by the congressional committee before which he is appearing. Some committee members and their staffs, prevented by the letter of the Fifth Amendment from compelling a witness to help send himself to jail, persistently violate the spirit of the Amendment by holding up such a person to ridicule. . . .

Senator McCarthy [who popularized the term "Fifth Amendment Communist" to describe a witness who exercised his or her constitutional right to remain silent] . . . did not himself hesitate to use another constitutional protection that is available to congressmen: the right to make defamatory statements without worrying about being sued for libel. The Constitution provides that "for any Speech or Debate in either house, [representatives and senators] shall not be questioned in any other Place. This privilege against suits for defamation was designed to prevent the Executive Branch from harassing its critics in Congress by means of legal action.

It serves a quite different purpose for a demagogue. For McCarthy it converted the Senate chamber into a sanctuary from which he was able to make unsubstantiated charges of subversion, espionage, and even treason, while remaining secure in the knowledge that he could not be brought to book for his slanders. Not only what he said on the floor but also the words he uttered in committee and the charges he made in official congressional reports were beyond the reach of the law. . . .

The news media helped him. Under ordinary circumstances, a publication that reports a defamatory statement is just as guilty of libel as the person who made the statement in the first place. This does not apply, however, to reports of congressional deliberations. A newspaper being sued for reporting a defamatory charge by McCarthy had to prove in its defense only that the senator had actually made the statement in an official proceeding, not that the statement was true. No serious consideration has ever been given to the possibility of revoking by statute the right of the press to disseminate congressional slanders.

Note: Senator McCarthy eventually was censured by the Senate for his excesses and ostracized by his colleagues. Members of the House Committee on Un-American Activities were never called to account, although their committee was later renamed the House Internal Security Committee to escape the infamy of the earlier name and eventually was disbanded by the House.

Source: Daniel M. Berman, *In Congress Assembled* (New York: Macmillan, 1964), pp. 180–86.

------------------------------ ★ ★ ★ ★ ------------------------------

COMMITTEES IN OTHER
NATIONAL LEGISLATURES

The focus in this book is on America's legislatures—the U.S. Congress and the state legislatures. But a look now and then at legislatures in other nations, in this instance at how their committees function, can help us understand our own better. No other national legislature gives its committees the central place in the legislative process which the committees of Congress enjoy. Indeed, after an examination of the committees of eight strong national legislatures, one authority concluded "the committee system in the American Congress is not only the strongest system in the present study, it is *by far* the strongest."[81] The strong committee system in Congress is partly a result of our separation-of-powers system which leads Congress to want to make an independent assessment even of legislation which has the strong backing of the President. In part, it results from the fragmentation of American political parties, which in turn is partially a consequence of the federal structure of American government and also partially a consequence of the separation-of-powers system that permits voters to "split a ticket" and vote Democratic, say, for Congress, while voting Republican for President.

In the British parliamentary system, the leaders of the majority party in the House of Commons are the cabinet, in charge of the government. There, the general thrust of legislation is developed under the cabinet's auspices. Bills are then discussed on the floor of the Commons. The role of committees is comparatively minor, so that

> the committee has *no* jurisdiction over the major principles involved. It is limited to discussing matters such as exemptions, implementation, adjustment, and wording. . . . They [committees] do not carry out investigations and have no power to summon witnesses or papers. . . . The committees are not specialized. The assignment of bills works by rotation. A committee may receive a bill on transportation one week and on social policy the following week. . . . [But it should be noted that] alongside the standing general committees in the Commons there are also some specialist [oversight] committees [which have greater autonomy and authority].[82]

Like their British cousins, committees in the Canadian House of Commons also have little autonomy and do not even consider some government bills. (Those bills not first examined by standing committees go directly to the Committee of the Whole.) In the past two decades, however, the Canadian House of Commons has undertaken "a deliberate and conscious effort to reform the committee system and make it an integral part of the parliamentary process."[83] Most legislation is now referred to committee. Still, a combination of strong, cohesive parties within the parent body and a focus on the Canadian prime minister and the cabinet, rather than on the majority in Commons, combine to leave the committees much less important in the legislative process than U.S. Congressional committees and also, as we will see, less important than committees in the Italian Parliament or the West German Bundestag.

The West German Bundestag is organized in a manner part way between the American Congress and the British Parliament. Although the Bundestag is organizationally separate from the government executive, it still depends on the executive for the initiation of most legislation. Drafts of legislation are first sent to the Bundesrat (composed of ministers from the governments of ten Länder—states), "so that when initially considered by the Bundestag the observations of the Bundesrat are available."[84] (The Bundesrat represents the Länder—states—in the national legislative process and has the authority to reject legislation which affects the power of the Länder governments.)

Standing committees of the Bundestag have jurisdiction over the principles—not just the details—of a bill, can initiate bills of their own and "are normally concerned with a particular aspect of public action across the board, . . . and in all cases permanent committees have a primary responsibility for legislative scrutiny. . . . Generally there is one ministry, one committee, though . . . many items have to be referred to two or more committees."[85] Further, "unlike the Congress, the chairmen of these

309

committees are selected roughly proportionally in regard to the parliamentary membership of each of the Bundestag parties. Thus the opposition parties will have a share of the committee chairmanships."[86]

The Bundestag also has special committees, which "are set up to deal with a specific problem and expire when their job is done,"[87] and investigatory committees, whose job is "to enquire into and establish the facts relating to questions referred to it. The underlying idea of an investigatory committee is that of a judicial inquiry into the conduct of individuals or the character of particular public transactions."[88] Of the standing committees of the Bundestag, only the Defense Committee has the power to conduct investigations in the manner of an investigatory committee.[89]

Another interesting departure from American practice in the German Bundestag is that appointment to the Joint Mediation Committee (which performs the functions of U.S. Congressional conference committees) is a permanent committee assignment. The membership of the Joint Mediation Committee does not change with each bill. The same members reconcile all bills on which the two chambers differ.

One authority has concluded that the Italian committee system lies somewhere between the American and West German committee systems in its importance within the national legislature, while the committee systems in all three of those nations are substantially more important than the committee systems of the Canadian and British Parliaments.[90] To a large degree, the importance of committees within the Italian legislative process comes from constitutional provisions which do "not allow Parliament to work without committees in lawmaking and in the investigative process."[91] One constitutional provision requires "that every bill must be examined by a committee before the House debates it."[92] Committee chairpersons are members of the majority coalition and are chosen by that coalition. But "by contrast with the United States Congress, chairpersons do not play a major role in the parliamentary process."[93] Nor is the position of chairperson of an Italian parliamentary committee a career post.

> No general rule can be given for the criteria underlying the selection of particular members to be committee chairmen. Many members become chairmen who have not had prior ministerial responsibilities and who have no hope of ever obtaining a government post. In other cases members are able to exploit their committee chairmanships as a stepping-stone to higher office.[94]

Committees of Congress then are not "typical" of the committees of other national legislatures, although some features of the committee systems of other nations are similar to features of Congressional committees. Among these are the tendency to divide committee jurisdiction along subject-matter lines that accord with the organization of the government and the inclination of members of the West German Bundestag to seek "better" committee assignments as they accrue experience in that legislative body.

Parliamentary government, coupled with strong electoral and parliamentary parties, reduces the independent importance of committees in the legislative process. The division of authority between the American Congress and an independently elected President, coupled with stable, but relatively weak and noncohesive political party organizations, allows the committees of the U.S. Congress to achieve a place of autonomous importance within the legislative process which is generally not found in the national legislatures of other nations.

STATE LEGISLATIVE COMMITTEES

The committees of the American state legislatures are very much like the committees of Congress, in terms of informal norms, committee dynamics, and the basic functions and purposes of committees. Some important differences exist, however, between the state legislative committees and their Congressional counterparts, as well as among the various state legislatures.

As indicated in Chapter 10, most state legislative committees have less stable membership than committees of Congress, and they have less independence from the policy preferences of the majority-party leadership of the chamber (especially in those bodies which elect their own speaker or president). Also, they usually have less clearly defined areas of jurisdiction than Congressional committees. Further, most state legislative committees have fewer members than most committees of Congress, a fact which makes the committee decision-making process of the state legislatures take on more of the dynamics of a small group.

Research on state legislatures is increasing, but many gaps remain in our knowledge, and some of what we think we know about state legislative committees is based on studies of only a few states.[95]

Committee Jurisdiction

State legislative committees differ in the extent to which their jurisdictions are clearly spelled out and in the extent to which committees dominate policy decisions within their jurisdictions, but few have the degree of jurisdictional definiteness which the committees of Congress have. Indeed, a study of all fifty state legislatures conducted in 1969 and 1970 made the following recommendation for thirty of the fifty state legislatures:

> A description of the jurisdiction of committees should be contained in the rules of both houses and assignment of bills should be made in accord with the jurisdiction of committees as described in the rules.[96]

Another criticism of two thirds of the state legislative committee systems made in that report was that there were too many committees in the various state legislatures and that each legislator was assigned to too many committees.

> In order to make it possible for members to concentrate their attention and contribute effectively, there should be no more than three committee assignments for each member of the lower house or four committee assignments for each member of the Senate. The multiplicity of assignments introduces problems of scheduling, strains the focus of attention of members, and creates an inordinately heavy workload for members if committees are as active as they should be.[97]

The authors of that report argue that ten to fifteen committees in each legislative chamber would be about right and that the committees of the two chambers in each state should be parallel in their subject-matter jurisdiction, so as to reduce the complexity of the legislative process. Restructuring the committee systems to provide for effective committee participation would probably also increase member satisfaction with the office of state legislator.[98]

Committee Authority

State legislative committees are important decision sites—their authority is upheld in the legislative process of many states. An analysis of bills introduced into the legislatures of California, Texas, and Wisconsin, for example, found that over 40 percent of the bills in each state died in committee.[99] Those bills that got out of the committee to the floor were likely to pass. Bills with strong, extralegislative opposition were likely to be kept bottled up in committee, at least in Texas and Wisconsin.[100] Yet, committees are relatively unimportant in some states. "Our committee system is, by and large, a joke,"[101] reported a former New Jersey legislator. The Citizens' Conference on State Legislatures has agreed, noting that "standing committees of the legislature seem to exist mostly on paper in New Jersey," and that

> it is the majority conference [caucus] which either kills the bill or recommends it for passage. For controversial, hard-to-handle issues, the legislature creates a commission often made up of only a few legislators and a majority of public members.[102]

Illinois legislative committees were also quite weak in the 1960s.

> If committees report a high percentage of bills favorably, the likelihood is that they are not really in control of the screening of legislation. Illustrative of an extremely permissive system are the committees of the Illinois House. . . . Committees simply do not want to assume responsibility for killing a bill. When a bill does die in committee, it is usually . . . because a sponsor does not wish to bring his measure to the floor. During the period from 1961 through 1965 only about 4 percent of all bills introduced in the [Illinois] House were defeated as a result of unfavorable committee action. Few other legislative committee systems are quite so permissive.[103]

Illinois legislative committees are now somewhat more rigorous in screening legislation, but are still quite weak when compared to Congressional committees.[104]

Variations clearly exist in the degree to which state legislative committees function as filters for the legislature. In Oregon and Washington, the house and senate committees reported favorably less than half the bills referred to them.[105] The committees of the Ohio House were a bit more restrictive and of the Ohio Senate a bit less so, in the 1971–72 session. In Ohio,

> the tendency is for bills to be more carefully screened in their house of origin and, having passed one house, to receive more cursory and favorable attention in the other. In the chamber that acted first in Ohio, for instance, three out of ten bills were reported favorably; in the chamber that acted second, eight out of ten were reported favorably.[106]

Based on his detailed analysis of committee systems in six states, Alan Rosenthal noted that "generally, House committees receive more bills and take negative action on a higher percentage than do their counterparts in the Senate. This is largely because the House is likelier to act first on legislation than is the Senate."[107] The difference may also be a result of the size of the two chambers; it may be more difficult for a committee to reject a colleague's bill in the more intimate atmosphere of the smaller senates. Overall, however, it appears that variations between chambers in the autonomous role of committees in the policymaking process are smaller than variations between state legislatures.[108]

Especially revealing of practices in some state legislatures was one report's recommendation for a balanced committee system:

> Committees, in their composition, should reflect as accurately as possible the makeup of the entire house of which they are a part. There should be no "killer," "graveyard," or "cinch" committees.[109]

"Killer" and "graveyard" committees are those used by the legislative leadership to kill bills. In the absence of rules setting forth committee jurisdictions, the leadership may refer bills they want killed to such committees, appointed with care to be responsive to the wishes of the leadership. Appointed with equal care are the "cinch" committees, which are used, again in the absence of chamber committee jurisdiction rules, to move favored bills through the legislative process more readily.

Without written jurisdiction rules, of course, one committee can serve as both the "graveyard" and the "cinch" committee.

The authority of the committees of some state legislatures is undermined somewhat by rules which prevent committees from killing legislation by refusing to report a bill for floor action. Congressional committees have such authority, although cumbersome and seldom-used "discharge" rules do exist for taking a bill away from a Congressional committee. Many state legislatures either require each committee to report out all bills—favorably, unfavorably, or without recommendation—to the floor or make it easy for the entire chamber to discharge a committee of responsibility for a bill. Either rule lessens a committee's ability to kill legislation it dislikes—or to bargain—and lessens the authority of committees within that legislature.

Some factors which affect the degree of independent authority held by legislative committees in the various states are fairly clear. While there are exceptions, the following general rules seem to summarize the matter well:[110]

1. Committees exercise less independent influence over legislation in two-party states where party discipline is high.
2. Committees exercise less influence in states where the governor is strong and the legislature is of the same party as the governor, but exercise more influence under divided government.
3. In states where the governor, the party, or a faction exercises strong influence over the legislature (for example, by appointing committee chairpersons), committees are not likely to play an independent role.
4. In contrast, committees are more likely to be influential in one-party states where the governor does not exert strong leadership.
5. Committees are more effective when they are fewer in number and characterized by a more rational division of labor.
6. Committees are more influential in more "professional" legislative settings.

Conference Committees

As is the case in Congress, the forty-nine bicameral state legislatures can enact legislation only when the final version passed by both legislative chambers is the same. Reconciliation of differing views of the two chambers is required. Some legislation fails, not because the two chambers disagree on broad philosophy, but because they are unable to agree on details.

In some circumstances (especially as the legislative session draws to a close), conferees—and legislative chamber leaders—have tremendous power within the legislative process, especially when the general appropriations act is in conference mere hours before the end of the legislative session.

State legislative rules governing conference committees vary widely. Some states provide for two types of conference committees, recognizing a reality which Congress officially ignores but tacitly accepts. In these states, a conference committee, when first meeting, may consider *only* those aspects of the legislation on which the two chambers differ. If the conferees are unable to reach agreement on a version of the legislation by considering only those disputed portions of the bill, they may then return to their respective chambers, either to have new conferees appointed or to have a "free" conference committee appointed (often with the same conferees from each chamber). A "free" conference committee is authorized to negotiate both those sections of the bill on which the chambers disagree *and* those which read alike.[111] Often, being able to change key wording in the sections that passed both

———————————— ★ ★ ★ ★ ————————————

Classification of Performance of State Legislature Committee Systems

. . . [C]ombining both senate and house committees, it is possible to roughly classify, according to their relative performance, committee systems of the fifty states.

The "better-performing" committees are referred bills, make choices, amend or substitute, prevail on the floor during sessions, and continue working with some results during the interim. Systems in fourteen states are in this category: Arizona, California, Florida, Hawaii, Iowa, Kentucky, Minnesota, Nevada, North Dakota, Ohio, Oklahoma, Washington, West Virginia, and Wisconsin. The "poorer-performing" committees do not make choices; they amend or substitute infrequently or see their recommendations disregarded on the floor; and they either do not continue or produce little between sessions. Systems in the following twenty states are in this category: Alabama, Arkansas, Connecticut, Delaware, Georgia, Illinois, Indiana, Massachusetts, Michigan, Missouri, Montana, New Hampshire, New Jersey, New York, Pennsylvania, Rhode Island, Texas, Utah, Vermont, and Wyoming. An intermediate category of "medium-performing" committees includes those that fail to meet an important criterion during the session or do not continue or continue with little production during the interim. Systems in the following sixteen states are in this category: Alaska, Colorado, Idaho, Kansas, Louisiana, Maine, Maryland, Mississippi, Nebraska, New Mexico, North Carolina, Oregon, South Dakota, Tennessee, and Virginia. There are naturally variations within each class. There may also be a few cases in the sixteen-state intermediate grouping that, on the basis of other information, could be placed in one of the other groupings. But there are sharp differences between the fourteen cases in the "better-performing" and the twenty in the "poorer-performing" categories.

Note: Information is based on interviews with a legislator from each state, plus published material available.
Source: Alan Rosenthal, *Legislative Performance in the States: Explorations of Committee Behavior* (New York: Free Press, 1974), pp. 42–43.

———————————— ★ ★ ★ ★ ————————————

chambers in the same form enables the conferees to reach agreement on the portions of the legislation which are in dispute. (Congressional conferees, as has been noted, also change undisputed portions of legislation in conference, but there is no special provision in the Congressional rules concerning the exercise of this power.)

Committee Hearings

Like Congressional committees, state legislative committees normally hold hearings on legislation assigned to them, though such hearings may sometimes be perfunctory and often without benefit of a transcript or even a formal record. In some state legislatures, however, hearings are occasionally omitted, even on major bills, especially toward the end of a legislative session. Thus, one study criticized a fifth of the nation's state legislatures, including some of the better-paid, more "professional" ones for their occasional failure to hold public hearings:

> There is no justification for permitting any major piece of legislation to become law without having been subjected to extensive, thorough, well-planned, and well-prepared public hearings, in which representatives of the public, civic organizations, and interest groups are not only invited but encouraged to participate.[112]

Public hearings in the state legislatures are often more "down to earth" than Congressional hearings, and they more often seem devoted to catharsis—giving citizens a chance to let off steam. Ordinary citizens who want to speak out on a subject are more common as witnesses in state-level public hearings, although Congressional hearings held "out in the field" come closer to state legislative hearings in this respect. Professional lobbyists testify in state legislative hearings (as in Congress), but state-level lobbyists often prefer to give only perfunctory testimony in the official hearings, because they have talked ahead of time to those committee members not considered hostile to their client or clients.

Despite their relatively weak position in the legislative process, when compared to Congressional committees, state legislative committees still have enough authority that "the committee hearing is generally the most important source of information for legislators, and lobbyists tend to flock to the committee rooms as the focal point of their contact with legislators."[113] In addition, it is easier in most states than in Congress for the committees to hold "executive session" meetings, where members can exchange views frankly and negotiate compromises out of public view. Increasing adoption of "sunshine rules," however, are opening more state legislative committee activities to the public.

In addition to committee hearings that are primarily intended to shed light on a specific legislative proposal and, perhaps, to help the committee improve the proposal, state legislative committees also hold exploratory hearings on general problem areas to determine what types of legislation might be needed; conduct investigations of various kinds, some of which are intended primarily to inform or alert the public or to further a legislator's career, or both; and hold oversight hearings. In states that restrict the length of legislative sessions, the standing committees of the legislature often find that they do not have adequate time to examine thoroughly a problem area not precisely defined in advance, to conduct thorough investigations, or to deal effectively with errant executive agencies. If the committee has sufficient authority to be effective in such activities, it may be too pressed by narrow legislative demands during the legislative session to have time for much activity not directly related to bills already introduced. In such states, the legislature often entrusts investigations, information-gathering hearings, and oversight activity to *interim committees.* These committees conduct hearings periodically during the interim between legislative sessions, fleshing out their efforts by using full-time legislative staff to pursue leads developed and to pull information together for the committee. Since interim committees normally reflect the desires of the relevant standing committees of the legislature or of the legislative leadership, or both, they frequently are quite effective in their chosen activities.

State legislative committees, like Congressional committees, sometimes hold oversight hearings to insure that the intent of the legislature is being honored in the implementation of legislation. The degree to which state-level legislative oversight is accomplished by legislative committees is in part obviously dependent on the strength of the committee system within any given state legislature. Some oversight activity at the state level results from constituency and partisan pressure, while some (especially in those state legislatures without well-institutionalized procedures for such review activity) results from the concerns and feelings of individual legislators about the appropriateness of such activity.[114] As in Congress, much of a legislature's activity aimed at keeping state agencies attuned to legislative preferences is informal. Some, too, is initiated by bureaucrats, who are sensitive to especially powerful legislators and who either contact those legislators for their opinions or anticipate their reactions and behave accordingly.

In some states, especially those without full-time or almost full-time legislatures, the legislators

> do not have the time, interest, or inclination to develop the kind of uninterrupted day-to-day relationships with the administrative side [of the "cozy triangle" of lobbyists, legislators and bureaucrats] that has so long prevailed in the Congress. The turnover rate is high, meaning that many men who have acquired some measure of specialized expertise leave the legislature before they can establish themselves as strong men vis-a-vis the corresponding executive agency. . . . There are, of course, exceptions . . . [but] there is very little systematic oversight of the general operation of agencies. The basic assumption of legislators, leaders included, appears to be that the agencies are doing what they are supposed to do. If trouble occurs or a scandal breaks, then the legislature may get involved.[115]

Committee Dynamics in State Legislatures

Most of the observations made about the internal dynamics of Congressional committees also hold for state legislative committees. But the shorter tenure of state legislators, in the legislature and especially on any given committee, should be strongly noted. Also, the combination of briefer legislative sessions, high committee-membership turnover (compared to Congress), and relatively fluid committee jurisdictions for most state legislatures means that, compared to Congress, state legislative committees are less likely to develop subject-matter expertise, stable patterns of interaction among the members of the committee, or a "committee spirit." Thus, the committees are less likely to be autonomous policy actors and are more likely to be influenced by interest-group lobbying and by partisan considerations (such as the preferences of party leaders within the chamber). Further, although committee chairpersons in state legislatures often wield substantial authority and normally are the actual leaders of their committees, they usually are much less independent of the chamber leadership (especially in the lower chambers) than are committee chairpersons in Congress.

Substantial variation occurs in the extent to which state legislative committees maintain a united front on the floor of the legislative chamber. As in Congress, the money committees of the legislature sometimes adopt a united position in support of the committee bill and vote together against all attempts to amend the bill on the floor. Such a strategy increases a committee's authority within the legislature (and that of each of its individual members), and this is often seen as "responsible" behavior in the sense that money requests almost always exceed the funds available; somebody must determine which projects are funded and who will pay the taxes to provide the wherewithall for such funding.

The degree of committee cohesion in floor voting, however, involves more than just the subject matter of a bill. Different "environmental" factors in the various states also affect cohesion. Based on analysis of one session for each of three state lower chambers in the 1976–78 era, Hamm concludes:

> [T]he institutional environment does appear to affect the level of committee consensus, being the highest in the state legislature [Virginia House] with the greatest committee membership stability and with the greatest degree of importance placed on decisions made in committees; the lowest consensus scores are registered in the state legislature [Illinois House] with the greatest instability in committee membership and the lowest importance attached to committee decisions; Maryland falls, as expected, somewhere between the two. . . . The extent to which the most frequent dissenters [from the majority committee position] are likely to be minority party members is directly related, in most cases, to the strength of the opposition party. In basically one-party dominant states, the minority party members do not . . . differentiate themselves from the majority party in terms of their propensity to dissent.[116]

Votes within committees tend to be more consensual—and also tend to be more unanimous—on bills reported out of the committee with a favorable recommendation than committee votes on bills which are either killed in committee or are reported to the floor unfavorably (a procedure which is required in some state legislatures but is unheard of in Congress).[117]

SUMMARY

Committees of American legislatures are key decision-making sites in the legislative process. The committee systems of the state legislatures, however, are usually pale reflections of the committee system in Congress. The Congressional committees have well-defined jurisdiction; written rules of procedure; stable and experienced committee membership; and, for the most part, well-defined interaction patterns among members of each committee. The Congressional committees also have well-established relationships with executive-branch personnel and lobbyists, which permits much decision-making by consensus of those interested members of the "cozy triangle." The still-strong Congressional seniority system, which includes each member's recognized right to be reappointed continually to the same committees he or she sat on in the previous Congress and the presumption that each committee's most senior majority party member should chair the committee, give committees of the U.S. Congress a degree of autonomy and legislative authority found in no other national legislature and in none of the state legislatures. Recent rules changes have weakened Congressional committee chairpersons somewhat and have dispersed authority to standing subcommittees of the standing committees of Congress—especially in the House—but committee chairpersons still have great independent authority in Congress.

Committees vary in prestige and in their ability to retain authority over their areas of subject-matter jurisdiction. Both the state legislative and the Congressional committees that are cohesive on the floor of the chamber—presenting a united front to their colleagues—are more likely to have their bills passed by the entire chamber, and to have them passed without amendment, than are committees on which there is a high rate of dissent. Committees with jurisdiction over taxation and appropriations are generally high-status committees in any legislature. Other subject-matter committees are of intermediate importance or are considered unattractive by most members of the legislature, although those who can serve a particular constituency interest by membership on a committee sometimes find even the least-prestigious committee assignment a worthwhile investment of energy.

Legislative committees are powerful for a number of reasons, including subject-matter expertise among the elected members of the legislature. Legislator-experts maintain the legislature's ability to deal with executive-branch personnel and serve as information sources for colleagues who eventually have to cast votes on each committee's bills that come to the floor.

Committee hearings serve a variety of functions. They provide committee members and others with information concerning particular legislation; assist the legislature in retaining its authority within the overall structure of government, by the exercise of oversight and the conduct of investigations; and they perform a cathartic, or safety-valve function, by letting people vent their anger and frustrations concerning a particular topic. Hearings are also frequently used to inform or educate the public on a particular topic, as well as to advance the political careers or political points of view of certain legislators.

Both Congress and the state legislatures have standing committees—to consider legislation before it is debated and voted on by the entire chamber. This differs from the practice in national legislatures in some countries, where a bill is discussed and a general chamber position is taken before the bill is sent to committee. American state legislative committees normally have less control over their jurisdictions than Congressional committees do, and this is especially so in states that require committees to report out all legislation which is assigned to them. As a result of differing environmental factors (including partisan composition, institutional tradition, authority of the governor, and the number and size of legislative committees), state legislatures vary widely in the authority of their committees in the legislative process. Committees in some states make virtually no decisions; in other states, they kill over half the bills introduced and extensively rewrite many of the bills which they do report out to the floor. In none of the states, however, do the legislative committees even approach the authority of the committees of Congress.

Notes

1. "The Senate Committee System: Jurisdictions, Referrals, Numbers and Sizes, and Limitations on Membership," First Staff Report to the Temporary Select Committee to Study the Senate Committee System (Washington, D.C.: U.S. Government Printing Office, July, 1976).

2. Ibid., p. 53. The reorganization of some House committees' jurisdiction in the 1970s led to an increased level of intercommittee competition for jurisdiction and to drafting of legislation "in such a way as to maximize the jurisdictional claims of each committee." Richard F. Bensel, "The Influence of Committee Jurisdictions on Legislative Behavior," (Paper delivered at the 1979 Annual Meeting of the Southern Political Science Association, Gatlinburg, Tennessee).

3. Leroy N. Rieselbach, *Congressional Politics* (New York: McGraw-Hill, 1973), p. 80.

4. Walter J. Oleszek, *Congressional Procedures and the Policy Process* (Washington, D.C.: Congressional Quarterly Press, 1978), p. 55.

5. T. R. Reid, *Congressional Odyssey: The Saga of a Senate Bill* (San Francisco: W. J. Freeman, 1980), pp. 16–21. *Joint* referral sends a bill to two or more committees at the same time. *Sequential* referral means it goes first to one committee and then another, which may bode ill for the bill since it can be bottled up in either of the successive committees. *Split* referral means part of the bill goes to one committee at the same time another part of the bill is sent to a different committee. Oleszek, *Congressional Procedures and the Policy Process,* p. 57.

6. Randall B. Ripley, *Congress: Process and Policy* (New York: W. W. Norton, 1975), p. 117.

7. Anne L. Lewis, "Floor Success as a Measure of Committee Performance in the House," *The Journal of Politics* 40 (May 1978): 460–67.

8. Randall B. Ripley, *Power in the Senate* (New York: St. Martin's Press, 1969), pp. 149–52; Donald R. Matthews, *U.S. Senators and Their World* (Chapel Hill, N.C.: University of North Carolina Press, 1960), p. 169.

9. James Dyson and John Soule, "Congressional Committee Behavior on Roll Call Votes: The U.S. House of Representatives, 1955–64," *Midwest Journal of Political Science* 14 (November 1970): 626–47.

10. Richard F. Fenno, Jr., *Congressmen in Committees* (Boston: Little, Brown, 1973), pp. xiv–xv. Much of the following discussion draws on Fenno.

11. *Ibid.,* p. 1.

12. Lynette P. Perkins found that only a minority of the members of the House Judiciary Committee of the early 1970s were primarily on the committee because of policy goals, and those were the committee members who dominated the committee. The large number of Judiciary Committee members whose primary goal was reelection, and the lesser number seeking a higher office, had low levels of interest and participation in committee activities. "Influences of Members' Goals on Their Committee Behavior: The U.S. House Judiciary Committee," *Legislative Studies Quarterly* 5 (August 1980): 373–92.

13. Fenno, *Congressmen in Committees,* pp. 15, 22, 23, 27, 31, 36, 65.

14. Ibid., p. 78.

15. Glenn R. Parker and Suzanne L. Parker, "Factions in Committees: The U.S. House of Representatives," *American Political Science Review* 73 (March 1979): 85–102.

16. Ibid., pp. 94, 95, 97. Deering reports that the House Foreign Affairs Committee and the Senate Foreign Relations Committee continue to allow the executive branch great flexibility, but the House committee remains more disposed to support the President, while the Senate committee continues its "love/hate relationship with the Executive—often critical but generally supportive." Both committees are also more decentralized and more active in areas such as international trade which are not "intimately linked to questions of high level diplomacy and national security." See Christopher J. Deering, "Adaptation and Consolidation in Congress's Foreign Policy Committees: Evolution in the Seventies" (Paper delivered at the 1980 Annual Meeting of the Midwest Political Science Association, Chicago, Ill.), p. 30.

17. Joseph K. Unekis and Leroy N. Rieselbach, "The Structure of Congressional Committee Decision Making" (Paper delivered at the 1979 Annual Meeting of the American Political Science Association, Washington, D.C.). For a detailed analysis of committee decision-making within one House committee, see James T. Murphy, "Political Parties and the Porkbarrel: Party Conflict and Cooperation in House Public Works Committee Decision Making," *American Political Science Review* 68 (March 1974): 169–85.

18. Unekis and Rieselbach, "The Structure of Congressional Decision Making," p. 24.

19. Ibid., p. 11.

20. Ibid., pp. 8 and 12.

21. Fenno, *Congressmen in Committees,* pp. 281–83.

22. Donald R. Matthews, "The Folkways of the United States Senate: Conformity to Group Norms and Legislative Effectiveness, *American Political Science Review* 53 (December 1959): 1064–89. Similar norms were found in the state legislatures of California, New Jersey, Ohio, and Tennessee. See John C. Wahlke, Heinz Eulau, William Buchanan, and LeRoy C. Ferguson, *The Legislative System: Explorations in Legislative Behavior* (New York: John Wiley, 1962), Chapter 17.

23. Ripley, *Power in the Senate,* pp. 152–53.

24. Thomas W. Casstevens, "The Committee Function: An Influence Equation," *American Political Science Review* 66 (March 1972): 160–62. James W. Dyson and John W. Soule demur. See their "Congressional Committee Behavior on Roll Call Votes: The U.S. House of Representatives 1955–64," pp. 626–47.

25. Ripley, *Congress: Process and Policy,* p. 117.

26. Fenno, *Congressmen in Committees,* pp. 18–21.

27. Quoted in John F. Manley, *The Politics of Finance: The House Committee on Ways and Means* (Boston: Little, Brown, 1970), p. 113.

28. Ibid., p. 111.

29. David E. Price, "Policy-Making in Congressional Committees: The Impact of 'Environmental' Factors," *American Political Science Review* 72 (June 1978): 548–74.

30. John W. Ellwood and James A. Thurber, "The New Congressional Budget Process: The Hows

and Whys of House-Senate Differences," in *Congress Reconsidered,* ed. Lawrence C. Dodd and Bruce I. Oppenheimer (New York: Praeger, 1977), pp. 163–92.

31. "Party Caucus Role on Legislative Issues," in *Inside Congress,* 2nd ed. (Washington, D.C.: Congressional Quarterly, 1979), p. 34.

32. Oleszek, *Congressional Procedures and the Policy Process,* p. 181. Additional information on Congressional conference committees is also found in Manley, *The Politics of Finance,* Chapter 12; David J. Vogler, *The Third House* (Evanston, Ill.: Northwestern University Press, 1971); and Gerald S. Strom and Barry S. Rundquist, "A Revised Theory of Winning in House and Senate Conferences," *American Political Science Review* 71 (June 1977): 448–53.

33. Oleszek, *Congressional Procedures and the Policy Process,* p. 185.

34. Ripley, *Congress: Process and Policy,* pp. 113–14.

35. On subcommittees and other House committee reform, see Catherine E. Rudder, "Committee Reform and the Revenue Process," in Dodd and Oppenheimer, *Congress Reconsidered,* pp. 117–39. See also *Inside Congress,* 2nd ed.

36. Ralph K. Huitt, "The Internal Distribution of Influence: The Senate," in *The Congress and America's Future,* ed. David B. Truman (Englewood Cliffs, N.J.: Prentice-Hall, 1965), p. 89.

37. Richard F. Fenno, Jr., "The Internal Distribution of Influence: The House," in Truman, *The Congress and America's Future,* p. 55.

38. Ibid., p. 56.

39. Ibid.

40. Ibid., p. 57.

41. Ibid., p. 56.

42. Daniel M. Berman, *In Congress Assembled: The Legislative Process in Government* (New York: Macmillan, 1964), pp. 121–22.

43. The discussion of changes in House and Senate rules draws primarily on Lawrence C. Dodd and Bruce I. Oppenheimer, "The House in Transition," and Norman J. Ornstein, Robert L. Peabody, and David W. Rohde, "The Changing Senate: From the 1950's to the 1970's," both in Dodd and Oppenheimer, *Congress Reconsidered,* pp. 3–53.; *Inside Congress,* 2nd ed.; and Oleszek, *Congressional Procedures and the Policy Process,* pp. 61–70.

44. For an analysis of the modest immediate impact on policy of the replacement of the three deposed chairpersons, see John Berg, "The Effects of Seniority Reform on Three House Committees in the 94th Congress," in *Legislative Reform,* ed. Leroy N. Rieselbach (Lexington, Mass: D. C. Heath, 1978), pp. 49–59.

45. Matthews, *U.S. Senators and Their World,* pp. 84–92.

46. George Goodwin, Jr., *The Little Legislatures: Committees of Congress* (Amherst: University of Massachusetts Press, 1970), pp. 138–39.

47. Ralph K. Huitt, "The Congressional Committee: A Case Study," *American Political Science Review* 48 (June 1954); reprinted in Ralph K. Huitt and Robert L. Peabody, *Congress: Two Decades of Analysis* (New York: Harper and Row, 1969), pp. 110–11.

48. Ibid., p. 96.

49. Ibid.

50. Louis Fisher, *The Constitution Between Friends* (New York: St. Martin's Press, 1978), p. 140.

51. David B. Truman, *The Governmental Process* (New York: Alfred A. Knopf, 1962), p. 372. See also Robert Luce, *Legislative Assemblies* (Boston: Houghton Mifflin, 1924), pp. 142–48.

52. Morris S. Ogul, "Congressional Oversight: Structures and Incentives," in Dodd and Oppenheimer, *Congress Reconsidered,* pp. 207–21.

53. *New York Times,* February 23, 1982, p. 8.

54. For a well-written, theoretical explication of subgovernments and the dynamics of Congressional oversight, see Randall B. Ripley and Grace A. Franklin, *Congress, The Bureaucracy, and Public Policy,* rev. ed. (Homewood, Ill.: Dorsey Press, 1980).

55. Lawrence C. Dodd and Richard L. Schott, *Congress and the Administrative State* (New York: John Wiley, 1979), p. 170. See also Lawrence C. Dodd, George Shipley, and Philip Diehl, "Patterns of Congressional Committee Surveillance" (Paper delivered at the 1978 Annual

Meeting of the Midwest Political Science Association, Chicago, Ill.); cited in Dodd and Schott, p. 71.

56. Dodd and Schott, *Congress and the Administrative State,* p. 170.

57. Ibid., p. 157.

58. John E. Schwartz and L. Earl Shaw, *The United States Congress in Comparative Perspective* (Hinsdale, Ill.: Dryden Press, 1976), p. 75. The British also provide for a degree of oversight from the floor of Parliament through the device of questioning of ministers during the first hour of each day's meeting.

59. Ibid., p. 280.

60. *Washington Post,* February 5, 1982, p. A3.

61. Truman, *The Governmental Process,* pp. 375–77.

62. Carl B. Chelf, *Congress in the American System* (Chicago: Nelson-Hall, 1977), p. 92.

63. Truman, *The Governmental Process,* pp. 375–77.

64. Ibid., p. 375.

65. *Congressional Quarterly Weekly Report,* January 16, 1982, pp. 73–104.

66. Goodwin, *The Little Legislatures,* p. 165.

67. *McGrain* v. *Daugherty,* 273 U.S. 135, 175 (1927). For a discussion, see C. Herman Pritchett, *The Federal System in Constitutional Law* (Englewood Cliffs, N.J.: Prentice-Hall, 1978), pp. 253–58.

68. *Powers of Congress* (Washington, D.C.: Congressional Quarterly, 1976), p. 164.

69. Ibid., p. 165.

70. Fisher, *The Constitution Between Friends,* p. 140.

71. Ibid., p. 141.

72. *New York Times*, February 23, 1982, p. 8.

73. Pritchett, *The Federal System in Constitutional Law,* p. 254. The phrases quoted by Pritchett are from the Supreme Court, from *McGrain* v. *Daugherty,* 273 U.S. 135 (1927).

74. *Watkins* v. *United States,* 354 U.S. 178, 198 (1957); cited in Fisher, *The Constitution Between Friends,* p. 145.

75. Ibid.

76. *Kilbourn* v. *Thompson,* 103 U.S. 168, 194–95 (1881); cited in Fisher, *The Constitution Between Friends,* p. 145.

77. Fisher, *The Constitution Between Friends,* p. 145; *McGrain* v. *Daugherty,* 273 U.S. 135, 177 (1927).

78. *Barenblatt* v. *United States,* 360 U.S. 109 (1959).

79. Pritchett, *The Federal System in Constitutional Law,* pp. 254–55.

80. *United States* v. *Rumely,* 345 U.S. 41 (1953).

81. The national legislatures included in the study were those of Canada, Great Britain, India, Italy, Japan, the Philippines, West Germany, and the United States. See Malcolm Shaw, "Conclusion," in *Committees in Legislatures: A Comparative Analysis,* ed. John D. Lees and Malcolm Shaw (Durham, N.C.: Duke University Press, 1979), p. 387.

82. Schwartz and Shaw, *The United States Congress in Comparative Perspective*, p. 75. See also S. A. Walkland, "Committees in the British House of Commons," in Lees and Shaw, *Committees in Legislatures,* pp. 242–87.

83. Michael Rush, "Committees in the Canadian House of Commons," in Lees and Shaw, *Committees in Legislatures,* p. 191.

84. Nevil Johnson, "Committees in the West German Bundestag," in Lees and Shaw, *Committees in Legislatures,* p. 104.

85. Ibid., p. 112.

86. Schwartz and Shaw, *The United States Congress in Comparative Perspective,* p. 78. See also Gerhard Lowenberg and Samuel C. Patterson, *Comparing Legislatures* (Boston: Little, Brown, 1979), pp. 205, 206.

87. Johnson, "Committees in the West German Bundestag," p. 113.

88. Ibid., p. 114.

89. Ibid. There are also two joint Bundestag-Bundesrat committees, the more important of which—the Mediation Committee—works out differences between the two chambers. In addition, the Bundestag has a number of special-purpose committees, of which the most important (the Council of Elders) is a chamber-management committee, headed by the President of the Bundestag. Ibid., pp. 114–16.

90. Shaw, "Conclusion," p. 384.

91. Francesco D'Onofrio, "Committees in the Italian Parliament," in Lees and Shaw, *Committees in Legislatures,* p. 75.

92. Ibid., p. 75. The provision is Article 72 of the Italian Constitution.

93. Ibid., p. 81.

94. Ibid., p. 82.

95. Legislative research generally has been aided greatly by the *Comparative Legislative Studies Newsletter,* ed. Michael L. Mezey, and by the founding of the *Legislative Studies Quarterly,* ed. Malcolm E. Jewell, Gerhard Loewenberg, and Samuel C. Patterson, in which the *Newsletter* is now published along with original legislative research. Also of great importance to the study of state legislatures is Jewell's *Comparative State Politics Newsletter* (University of Kentucky), which contains current reports on the legislatures of the various states.

96. The Citizens Conference on State Legislatures, *State Legislatures: An Evaluation of Their Effectiveness* (New York: Praeger, 1971), p. 98. The recommendation applied to only one chamber in two of those thirty states; the other chamber already had written jurisdictional rules.

97. Ibid. Some state legislatures have reduced their number of committees since that report was issued.

98. James David Barber, *The Lawmakers* (New Haven, Conn.: Yale University Press, 1965), pp. 178–81.

99. Keith E. Hamm, "The Effects of Demand Patterns on Committee Decision-Making in State Legislatures: A Comparative Analysis" (Paper delivered at the 1978 Annual Meeting of the Midwest Political Science Association, Chicago, Ill.).

100. Keith E. Hamm, "U.S. State Legislative Committee Decisions: Similar Results in Different Settings," *Legislative Studies Quarterly* 5 (February 1980): 31–54.

101. Quoted in Alan Rosenthal, *Legislative Performance in the States: Explorations of Committee Behavior* (New York: Free Press, 1974), p. 37.

102. The Citizens Conference on State Legislatures, *State Legislatures: An Evaluation of Their Effectiveness,* p. 250.

103. Rosenthal, *Legislative Performance in the States,* pp. 21–22; Samuel K. Gove and Richard J. Carlson, *An Introduction to the Illinois General Assembly* (Urbana, Ill.: Institute of Government and Public Affairs, University of Illinois, 1968), p. 36; cited in Rosenthal, *Legislative Performance in the States,* p. 22.

104. Samuel K. Gove, Richard W. Carlson, and Richard J. Carlson, *The Illinois Legislature* (Urbana, Ill.: The University of Illinois Press, 1976), pp. 101–3.

105. Rosenthal, *Legislative Performance in the States,* p. 22.

106. Ibid., p. 22; and Alan Rosenthal, *Staffing the Ohio Legislature* (New Brunswick, N.J.: Center for State Legislative Research and Service, Eagleton Institute of Politics, 1972), p. 6; cited in Rosenthal, *Legislative Performance in the States,* p. 22.

107. Rosenthal, *Legislative Performance in the States,* p. 24. Indirect support for Rosenthal's argument is found in the analysis of "winning" in House-Senate conferences in Congress. "The reason Senate conferees win more often in conference is that the Senate more often acts second to the House on legislation. . . . [T]he House wins about as many conferences when the Senate initiates legislative action as the Senate wins when the House initiates legislative action. . . . The Senate wins because it acts second. . . ." Gerald S. Strom and Barry S. Rundquist, "A Revised Theory of Winning in House-Senate Conferences," *American Political Science Review* 71 (June 1977): 448–53.

108. Eugene Declercq, "Inter-House Differences in American State Legislatures," *Journal of Politics* 39 (August 1977): 780–81.

109. The Citizens Conference on State Legislatures, *State Legislatures: An Evaluation of Their Effectiveness,* p. 123.

110. Thomas R. Dye, *Politics in States and Communities,* 4th ed. (Englewood Cliffs, N.J.: Prentice-Hall, 1981), pp. 138–39. Summary is drawn from Alan Rosenthal, "Legislative Committee Systems: An Exploratory Analysis," *Western Political Quarterly* 26 (June 1973): 252–62.

111. The procedures governing state legislative conference committees are sketched in *Legislative Openness* (Kansas City, Mo.: Citizens' Conference on State Legislatures, 1974).

112. The Citizens Conference on State Legislatures, *State Legislatures: An Evaluation of Their Effectiveness,* p. 146.

113. Harmon Zeigler and Michael Baer, *Lobbying: Interaction and Influence in American State Legislatures* (Belmont, Calif.: Wadsworth, 1969), p. 126.

114. William Lyons and Larry W. Thomas, "Oversight in State Legislatures: Structural-Attitudinal Interaction" (Paper delivered at the 1979 Annual Meeting of the Southern Political Science Association, Gatlinburg, Tenn.).

115. Alan G. Hevesi, *Legislative Politics in New York State* (New York: Praeger, 1975), pp. 190–91.

116. Keith E. Hamm, "Voting Patterns in State Legislative Committees" (Paper delivered at the 1980 Annual Meeting of the Southern Political Science Association, Atlanta, Ga.), pp. 22 and 24.

117. Ibid., p. 30.

chapter 12

Legislative Staff

Preview

Staff assistance to the modern legislature greatly increases the capacity of the legislature as an institution and its independence from the executive branch and interest groups. The U.S. Congress is the best-staffed legislature in the world. Congress has large policy-neutral research staffs, such as the Congressional Research Service and the Library of Congress, which are centrally directed. But more than most legislatures, Congress places extensive staff resources under the control of committee chairs and ranking minority members and under the control of individual legislators as well. These committee and personal staffs contribute to decentralized authority patterns in Congress. Most state and other national legislatures place the bulk of their staff resources under the authority of the legislative chamber leaders, who then enhance their authority within the legislature by judicious allocation of staff assistance to the various legislative committees and individual legislators. Some state legislatures—like some European legislative bodies—provide staff resources through the legislative party, enhancing the authority of the party caucuses and their leaders at the expense of committee leaders. The extent of staff resources available to a legislature, including data-processing capability, affects its ability to compete with other political institutions for authority. The manner in which legislative staff resources are internally organized and controlled affects the relative importance of different legislative members.

Staff assistance is necessary for modern legislatures to function effectively. *Staff* is an all-encompassing term which can include the people who maintain the building in which the legislature convenes; file clerks, typists, telephone operators, and secretaries; and professional aides, such as attorneys, economists, political scientists, computer specialists, scientific and technical personnel, as well as personnel recruited from the ranks of senior executive-department bureaucrats, who bring with them an insider's understanding of the operations of a particular agency. Some staff members are employees of the entire legislature or of one of its agencies, such as the Library of Congress. Some are employees of the House or the Senate. Some work for a particular committee or subcommittee of the legislature, including joint committees. Some members of a legislative staff are expected to perform in a nonpartisan manner; others are clearly "majority" or "minority" staff personnel. Some staff members are employed by individual legislators, to assist in legislative work or to help the legislator with constituents, or both.

Events in the past half century have resulted in an ever-increasing volume of demands on state and national legislatures. In addition, the subjects considered by legislatures have grown increasingly complex and technical. As a result, legislatures have had to develop an improved institutional and organizational capacity to process and analyze new and increased volumes of complex information. That means legislatures have had to hire help—staff employees.

One student of the subject summarizes the case for legislative staffing as follows:

> Legislatures have created staff research agencies, then, to provide them with two essential ingredients of good policy decisions: (1) accurate, thorough, relevant information, carefully analyzed from the legislative perspective; and (2) the necessary time for the legislators to apply this information and analysis accurately in evaluating available policy alternatives. In a real sense, the staff acts as gatekeepers, as an intervening bureaucracy in a two-step flow of demands, requests, information, and so on between the members of the legislature and the network of advocates seeking legislative action. They filter the competing demands for legislative attention and help decide who and what is to be granted access. They specialize in interpreting technical aspects in terms comprehensible to the legislator. Thus, by supplying the first ingredient, the research staff helps to make the second possible.[1]

Control over legislative staff personnel and information-processing capability is equated with power in the legislature. The manner in which a legislature organizes such resources affects the distribution of authority within that legislature. For example, Chapters 10 and 11 observed that the subcommittees of Congress were gaining independent authority over staffing, a change which reduces the power of the full standing committees and their chairpersons and enhances the power of subcommittees and their chairs. Similarly, the allocation to the minority party of control over a fixed share of staff positions increases the effectiveness and sense of job satisfaction of minority-party legislators.

In contrast to the substantial staff resources under the control of members of Congress as individuals (personal staff) and as committee members and chairs (committee staff), most state legislatures centralize control of chamber staff and information-processing capabilities under the authority of the leadership. That situation both reflects and reinforces the greater authority within the chamber of the leaders of American state legislatures, when compared to Congress. Staff centralization also weakens the ability of individual legislators to take issue effectively with the executive department or with lobbyists.

Most informed observers do not quarrel with the argument that the modern legislature must have a staff of its own to cope with the increased volume and complexity of demands imposed upon it. There is, however, debate about the optimal size of legislative staff. Inadequate staff support, like excessively short legislative sessions, means that legislators must depend on executive bureaucrats and interest-group representatives for the information legislators need. But that is not to say that an infinite supply of staff support is necessarily beneficial. Indeed, there is some present debate about whether Congress has gone above the optimal level of staff assistance.

STAFF IN THE U.S. CONGRESS

The early U.S. Congresses had minimal staff assistance. After some fifty years, Congressional committees began to hire their own clerical help. During the last two decades of the nineteenth century, limited clerical assistance for individual members of Congress was approved.[2] Probably not coincidentally, the provision of limited staff assistance to individual members occurred about the same time that Ripley (using different indicators) concludes that the "modern" Congress emerged.[3]

The size of the Congressional staff grew slowly until the 1940s and accelerated with the passage of the Legislative Reorganization Act of 1946. The numbers of congressional staff have grown dramatically in the past twenty-five years, from 5,203 employees in 1955 to close to 18,000 employees in 1979, not counting the 6,400 employees who work for the four major Congressional research offices.[4] (See Figure 12.1.)

When the Republicans gained a majority in the 1981 U.S. Senate, the leadership promised to reduce the size of Senate committee staffs by 10 percent, and the Democratic leadership, not to be outdone, promised to reduce the number of Democratic committee staff members by 15 percent.[5] At least a modest reduction in overall Senate committee staff personnel seemed likely after funding for Senate committees in 1981 was reduced by 10 percent from that authorized in 1980, even though the new level of funding ($41.7 million) was only 0.7 percent less than what the committees· actually spent in 1981.[6]

Congressional Committee Staff

Although limited clerical staff assistance had been provided for the committees of Congress from the earliest Congresses, it was 1924 before Congress authorized committees regularly to employ "professional staff, in contrast to clerical staff."[7] At the time of the passage of the Legislative Reorganization Act of 1946, Congressional committee staff numbered less than 200 employees in the Senate and only some 114 in the House. Very few of these staff employees could claim to be experts or "professional" staff members.[8] The 1946 act authorized each committee of Congress to hire four professional staff members and six clerks, with extra assistance over and above that made available to the appropriations committees of each chamber.[9]

The decision to create professional staffs for Congressional committees was a recognition of the increased workload of Congress and the increasing complexity of the matters before it. Members felt the need to have their own resources—to permit them to be less dependent on frequently biased information furnished by the executive branch and by interest groups.

Today, the committees of Congress have sufficient staffs of professional and clerical employees to enable them to be independent if they wish. Control over committee staff personnel is primarily vested in the chairperson and ranking minority member of the committee (and, for subcommittee staff personnel, the chairperson and ranking minority member of the subcommittee). The chairperson hires and fires the majority staff, while the ranking minority member hires and fires the minority staff. Since staff personnel are clearly subject to the members who hire them—and have little or no job security—they are mainly responsive to the *committee* (or subcommittee) leaders who hire and can fire them, rather than to the party leaders in the *chamber.* Whether a member feels he or she can rely on a committee staffer's work without having it checked by a personal staff aide often depends on how close the member is to the chairperson's position on the issue under consideration. Furthermore, the quantity of committee staff resources and the manner in which the staff is recruited and controlled enable the committees of Congress, and especially their chairpersons, to be independent of the central chamber leadership, as well as independent of the executive branch of government and of interest groups.

In 1947, the standing committees of the House employed 167 staff people; now,

FIGURE 12.1
Where Hill Staffers Work

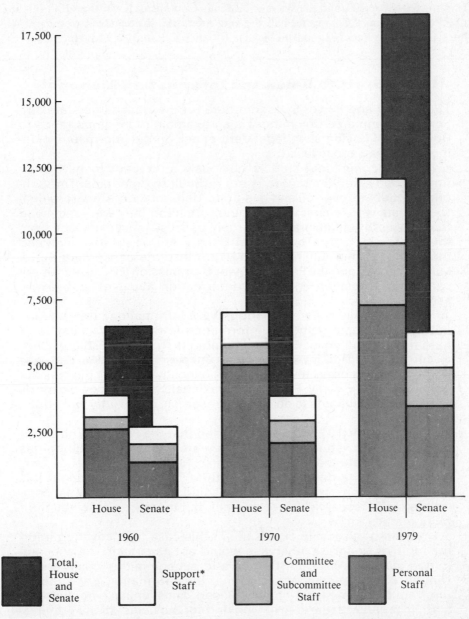

*Includes employees in offices such as the House Clerk, Capitol architect and sergeants-at-arms.

Sources: *Congressional Quarterly Weekly Report*, November 24, 1979, p. 2636. Data from House Appropriations Committee, Senate Disbursing Office.

they employ almost 2,000. Similarly, Senate committee staff numbers have grown from 232 to a little over 1,000, from 1947 to the present.[10] Committees vary in the number of staff personnel they employ. In the House, the Administration Committee employed over 200 people at the beginning of the 1981 session, the Appropriations Committee about 100, and the Ways and Means Committee fewer than 100. In 1981 the Senate Judiciary Committee had 172 staff members, the Senate Government Affairs Committee had 162, and the Senate Finance Committee had 41.[11]

──────────────── ★ ★ ★ ★ ────────────────

Using Staff to Break the Information Monopoly

The Energy and Power Subcommittee [of the House Interstate and Foreign Commerce Committee] is an example of the importance to Congress of having an independent check on the information coming from the Executive. . . .

The [subcommittee] staff is obviously structured to be a fact-finding body, and the reason is not difficult to determine. Throughout the debate over oil-and-gas-price deregulation, Congressional Democrats were suspicious of the information they were receiving from the Ford Administration—largely because most of it came from the energy industry. The Federal Energy Administration accepted the figures of the American Petroleum Institute concerning petroleum reserves, and the Federal Power Commission (FPC) used American Gas Association figures for information about natural-gas reserves.

To counter this apparent monopoly [of information], the subcommittee went about gathering information in three ways. First . . . it held hearings to collect data and opinions from interested parties. Second, it used its investigators to uncover information that was known to the energy industry and the executive branch, but was not coming out voluntarily. Finally, it occasionally asked its own experts or outside consultants to do original research, or to verify work done by others.

. . . In October 1975, the staff learned that the FPC had known for four years that natural-gas suppliers were deliberately holding gas off the interstate market and failing to fill their contracts, as they waited for future deregulation. But the FPC did nothing about this situation until pressured by Congress and the courts. . . . Most committee staff "research" is not original, but merely an assembling of facts already known. . . .

How did partisanship contribute in this case to uncovering information that Congress otherwise would not have had? The subcommittee staff was loyal to [Democratic subcommittee chairperson] Dingell, and shared his suspicion that the information it was receiving from the Administration was biased. Thus, unlike a nonpartisan staff, it began with the idea of "looking for the holes" in the Administration's position. It did not have to start from scratch in its analysis or give equal weight to opposing claims. Such a procedure may not be scholarly, but it does save time—a precious commodity.

Source: Michael J. Malbin, "Congressional Committee Staffs: Who's in Charge Here?" *The Public Interest* 47 (Spring 1977): 27–28.

──────────────── ★ ★ ★ ★ ────────────────

Policy-Neutral Professionals vs. Policy Entrepreneurs   Even among observers and participants who agree that legislatures and their committees require staff assistance, some disagreement exists on the proper *role* of staff personnel. For years, the dominant view was that professional staff should behave in what David Price calls a "professional" manner:

> What is preferable, according to this [traditional] view, is a competent, "professional" staff for each committee—a staff well versed in the subject matter at hand, accessible to, and capable of, augmenting the capacity of each member to make rational policy choices. . . . Moreover, "professionalism" has been generally used to indicate not merely competence but "neutral competence" as well.
> . . .[12]

The staff of the Joint Committee on Internal Revenue Taxation (JCIRT) is generally considered as approaching the neutral competence norm rather closely.[13] But even that committee staff has not been considered completely neutral by all, although neutrality is the professed rule by which the staff functions. The norm of "neutrality on public policy has, some policymakers feel, at times been broken by the JCIRT staff, especially while Colin F. Stam was chief of staff."[14]

> Stam's activity as Chief of Staff has been severely criticized by liberal Senators. . . . For these Senators not only was Stam of little help but his expertise was sullied because it buttressed, in the main, the views of their antagonists. . . .
> [T]he impact of the staff's work leaned toward the conservative side under Stam's leadership, norms of neutrality and objectivity notwithstanding . . .
> "Colin Stam's personal philosophy," said a Senator in praise of the staff chief, "was that the tax law should be used for raising revenue and not for social reform. If that makes him a conservative then I suppose he's a conservative."[15]

The norm of neutrality, and liberal complaints that Stam and his staff violated those norms, led Stam's successor as chief of staff, Laurence N. Woodworth, to shift the fifty-member staff's behavior so that it was perceived as more impartial and of assistance to all members of the House and Senate tax-writing committees.[16] It is very difficult, of course, for a staff to maintain a posture which will lead all legislators to agree that the staff is being truly neutral.

In his examination of the functioning of Congressional committees and their staffs, Price found many staff members functioning in about the way traditional norms dictated, but he observed that some staff aides rejected the traditionally defined, policy-neutral "professional" role:

> For the "professional," expertise was the *summum bonum,* neutrality a basic norm, and the analysis of proposals coming from elsewhere his primary legislative task. . . . The "policy entrepreneur," however, saw his job in a different light. He was committed to a continual "search" for policy gaps and opportunities. He was more willing to use his position to implement his own policy preferences and to let political considerations influence the role he assumed. He recognized the need to inform himself in the committee's policy areas and to hold his own preferences in abeyance in order to assist certain members, but in the end he valued creativity more than expertness and did not hesitate to establish a particular identification with the interests and ambitions of the chairman or (sometimes) other members.
> While the "policy entrepreneur," then, was not a purely political aide or an old-style patronage appointee, he did differ from the "professional" in his activist notion of his job and in his partisanship. . . .
> . . . [T]he same situations that present legislators with considerable "slack" in terms of their own roles and responsibilities generally give staff members a comparable freedom to spur and shape their mentors' initiatives.[17]

329

Even the "policy-entrepreneur" staff member, of course, must remember that he or she works for a committee of legislators. Thus, there is a limit on the degree of independent action. And few staffers would appear to be "pure" entrepreneurs.[18] Within those limits, though, much can be done by a staff member to initiate ideas and policies. When asked how he responded to accusations that he and his associates were "playing senator" or "manipulating" the committee, the head of a particularly entrepreneurial committee staff recognized the limits on staff members, while at the same time defending the entrepreneurial style:

> [W]e certainly don't think of our staff like you would some reference book, to be taken down off the shelf and used occasionally. We see it as part of our job to present alternatives to the senator, to lay out things before him that he might want to do. That doesn't mean that we're telling him every damn move he makes.[19]

The policy-neutral professional style is summed up by a staff member of a different Senate committee:

> It's not part of our job to sit around dreaming up bills and then go to the senator and tell him, "Here's something you ought to introduce." Sometimes we may find a *problem* in a bill, and then we might say, "You have a problem here and here is how you might take care of it," but whether the senator does it or not is up to him. Sometimes too we'll take an idea which a senator has barely developed and help him make something out of it. . . . But the idea always comes from the senator. Don't put us down as one of those staffs that manipulate their senators like a bunch of marionettes. We don't act; we react. . . .[20]

A case can be made for both views of the "proper" role of Congressional staff. The policy-neutral professional role should enhance the capacities of all committee members equally, since all members theoretically should then be able to place faith in the information provided by the staff. In almost every field of expertise, however, there are traditionalists and innovators, and there are at least two perspectives on "truth" or "reality." As different members succeed to the committee and subcommittee chairs, the authority to hire and fire staff employees might shift from a legislator with one point of view to one with a different point of view. Likewise, the hiring authority's opinion might shift on what constitutes "neutral" policy advice and what constitutes staff "politicking" or entrepreneurial behavior. The traditional policy-neutral prescription implies that staff members should be available to consult on ideas and proposals from the bureaucracy and interest groups or from committee members, but that they should be very cautious in advancing ideas of their own. Such a perspective, of course, means that staff members may deny the committee (and the public) some of the most important benefits of staff expertise—innovative ideas. That perspective also tilts the committee dynamic in favor of the status quo—that is, the staff should do nothing to change current policy unless nudged by outside forces or by committee members with specific instructions or questions.

Policy-entrepreneur staff members give the committee (and the public) the benefit of their ideas and do not necessarily accept the status quo. But they run the risk that some committee members and other legislators may be unable or unwilling automatically to accept committee staff recommendations and that some committee members may not feel free to work in confidence with committee staff. Price's research into the enactment of various consumer laws, however, suggests that at least some of the time policy-entrepreneur staff members may well come closer than their policy-neutral colleagues to helping a legislative committee discover the "public interest." More important than the ability of policy-entrepreneur staff members to discuss matters knowledgeably and neutrally with all committee members, Price argues, is their ability "to seek information on their own terms and to use it critically."[21] Such an ability implies an effort to ferret out information that interest groups and executive agencies may, for reasons of their own, prefer to keep buried.

The rise of the policy-entrepreneur role among Congressional committee staff has prompted the criticism that legislation is being written by the staff rather than by members of Congress; inspired suggestions for trimming the staff budget; and encouraged members of Congress to hire *personal* staff legislative assistants to help them keep track of proposals developed by committee staff members.

Opponents of the entrepreneurial style can take some comfort in the knowledge that "neutral professional" Congressional committee staff members remain on the Congressional payroll longer than the entrepreneurs and presumably develop long-term influence. Entrepreneurs have a higher turnover rate apparently because "for staff members with deeply felt policy agendas, the Hill experience is both frustrating and consuming, and such people are said to burn out rather quickly."[22]

Partisan vs. Nonpartisan Committee Staff   The reformers who pushed through the Legislative Reorganization Act of 1946 seem to have assumed that

> the appointment of "professional" staff to assist the committees of Congress meant two things. First, it meant that appointment would be based on substantive or technical merit, not political or partisan considerations. Second, . . . firing could be only for technical cause, not political considerations. . . . Associated with, and sometimes seemingly derived from, expertise is the notion of *consensus,* if not on final proposals then at least on forms of evidence and argument. . . . [I]n the ideal case technical experts, proceeding from the same theoretical framework and contemplating the same set of data, should reach agreement.[23]

Congressional committee staff were originally hired on a political patronage basis. The 1946 act supposedly eliminated partisan politics from the hiring process, stressing instead professional and neutral competence.[24] But, soon after the passage of that act, committees began to increase the size of their staffs through the subterfuge of hiring investigative staff and others for special positions. Many committees then began distinguishing between the permanent nonpartisan professional staff and the other, partisan, professional staff. Recognition of the policy influence of staff eventually led to most committee staff posts being considered partisan, as is evident from the "housecleaning" of Senate committee staffs in 1981, following the Republican takeover of that chamber. The minority party now receives a third or so of the staff positions on each committee. But the job performance of a long-time partisan committee employee who has a policy-neutral professional job orientation can save that person's job when the partisan composition of the chamber and the committee shifts. As one senior Senate committee staff member observed,

> there is some difference between hiring and retaining. . . . [F]olks are retained on quite a professional basis, although they might not be hired anew that way.[25]

As one senator explained, there are advantages for members of Congress in having some partisan staff members:

> On Appropriations, for instance, there is a question of who we can talk to in a sensitive area. We have a problem on the extent to which we can sit down and discuss a political problem with a professional staff member. . . . We need someone on the committee [staff] that we can talk to about issues involving our state that are also political. We need to know how far we can go within the framework of the committee. We have no other means of doing so other than seeking out this man who is both a professional and a partisan.[26]

331

But, just as there are differences between the political parties, so there are factions within each party. And to the extent the committee or subcommittee chairperson or ranking minority member controls the hiring of partisan committee staff, his or her fellow partisans may find that their ability to work with their own party's staff members on a committee or subcommittee depends in large measure on how closely they are aligned philosophically with that hiring authority.

> While majority staff members [of the Senate Labor and Public Welfare Committee] were appointed at the subcommittee level and served a variety of masters in a variety of ways, minority staff hiring was centralized and the ties of allegiance were mainly to Javits, who had become ranking Republican after Barry Goldwater left the Senate in 1964. That shift produced what one of Javits's more conservative colleagues termed a "housecleaning": "They fired them all. By 'they' I mean Javits. He has complete control over the staff. . . . If they weren't fired, it was made so uncomfortable for them that they had to go. . . ." That Javits's men were less accessible than a "neutral" staff might have been was evident; "I can't get the time of day from the staff," complained one conservative member.[27]

While partisanship in committee staff tends to undermine the "neutral-professional" role of committee staff personnel, it does so in a manner different from that of entrepreneurial behavior, as Price makes clear:

> Some activist senators, while desiring anything but "neutrality" in their [committee] staffs, did not encourage much in the way of "policy entrepreneurship" either. Yarborough, for example, tended to immerse himself in the details of legislation and to use his aides for following up rather than generating additional ideas. . . . That staff men like Lee and Kurzman stimulated their mentors and made their own distinctive contributions to the Committee's legislative undertakings was not to be doubted, but their influence was best explained not so much by their own strategies and the "slack" they were given as by the way their goals coincided with those of their mentors and their orientations proved serviceable in the realization of those goals.[28]

On many occasions, as noted earlier, a partisan professional committee staff member is of much greater assistance in helping a member achieve his or her goals than a strictly policy-neutral professional staff member would be.

The committee staffs of Congress are not composed completely of either stridently partisan or active entrepreneurial staff personnel, and many committee staff members are reticent about making strong policy recommendations.[29] Some committees, such as the House Appropriations Committee and the Joint Committee on Internal Revenue Taxation are generally recognized as having policy-neutral professional staffs, which try not to operate in a partisan mode or as entrepreneurs.[30] And as noted earlier, the less intensely partisan and less ideological staffers tend to stay on the job longer. Although one should expect continued efforts to "improve" the quality of staff assistance available to members of Congress, some mix of policy-neutral professionals, mildly and fervently partisan professionals, and entrepreneurial activists on the staff may serve Congress (and the public) well.

Personal Staffs

Like committee staffs, the personal staffs of members of Congress have expanded significantly since the turn of the century. Personal staff members work directly for individual representatives or senators and are paid by government funds allocated to each member for that purpose.

Back in 1947, the 435 members of the U.S. House of Representatives employed 1,440 personal staff people to run their offices and take care of home-state political matters. By 1981, this figure had risen to 7,000. Similarly, the 100 members of the U.S. Senate each employed only about 7 personal staff members in 1947, but each employs an average of 36 today.[31] Population growth in the United States is one reason why the numbers of personal staff members of U.S. representatives and senators have grown; there are still only 100 Senators and 435 Representatives, but the number of people each serves has increased considerably since 1947. Personal staffs have also grown because members need more help to keep track of the large number of more complex proposals before Congress. Because committee staffs of Congress may have their own views about what is proper policy in their respective spheres of authority and because members of Congress do not all have equal access to the various committee staffs, representatives and senators find it important to have at least some competent and trustworthy personal assistance to evaluate the numerous recommendations of interest groups, executive agencies, and Congressional committees and their staffs. In addition, the constituency-oriented members of a personal staff can do much of the work required for reelection, allowing even junior senators and representatives to concentrate on being active participants in the legislative process. "A member can act as a full-time legislator during the week, while his 'presence' in the district is maintained by offices, staff, publicity, and personal weekend appearances."[32] Indeed, a perennial complaint of candidates running against incumbent members of Congress is the campaign assistance that paid personal staff gives to the incumbent. The importance of such help goes beyond just the reelection campaign though. Having the staff to perform the "errand-boy" functions discussed in Chapters 5 and 6 throughout one's term appears to be important to incumbent survival.[33]

In 1979, U.S. representatives were permitted up to twenty-two personal staff members, the "clerk-hire allowance" in dollars for staff salaries being $288,156 per representative.[34] Senators are provided funds to hire three legislative assistants each to assist the senator in his or her legislative duties. Every senator also receives an additional "clerk-hire" allowance based upon the population of the senator's state. Senators from states with over 21 million residents receive twice the "clerk-hire" allowance of those from states with less than 2 million residents; others range in between. The 1980 "clerk-hire" allowance for senators ranged from $508,221 per senator to $1,021,167.[35] Senators and representatives have considerable leeway in how they use their clerk-hire. They may decide to have a greater number of lower-paid staff members, or a lower number of higher-paid staff members. Each of the two U.S. senators from New Mexico, for example, receive the minimum clerk-hire allowance, in addition to funds for three legislative assistants, but, in 1980, one had a personal staff of thirty-five, while the other had forty-nine staff employees.[36] In 1977, the size of a senator's staff ranged from a low of fifteen personnel to a high of seventy-five.[37] The allocation of personal staff slots between constituency offices and the Washington office varies between members too. So does the allocation of staff between constituency service and work on legislative issues.

The larger Senate personal staffs tend to be more formally organized than the House staffs. Some are so large that senators have hired management consultants to help organize them! As one Senate staffer said, there is a hierarchy in the Senate:

> You have a system of layers here—the Senators only talk to Senators, the administrative assistants to administrative assistants, the legislative assistants to legislative assistants, etc.[38]

──────────────────── ★ ★ ★ ★ ────────────────────

Personal Staff and Electoral Security

The following discussion concerns a Democratic U.S. representative who defeated an incumbent Republican in 1964 and has held the seat since.

> The Democratic incumbent maintains three well-staffed offices in the district. These offices process a steady flow of constituency requests for aid in dealing with government agencies. Social security and veterans' matters are the most common kind of work handled. In this respect we find a difference between the Democratic incumbent and his principal Republican predecessor. The latter remarked:

> When I was in office I had four staff members. Now they have a regiment. That's just not necessary. It's a waste of the taxpayer's money, a frivolous expense.

> The matter of the congressional staff is worthy of special notice. The retired Republican congressman . . . spontaneously brought it up. In discussing examples of the "hypocrisy" of modern congressmen, the retiree pointed to the 1967 expansion of the congressional staff, a particularly heinous example in his view. He stated flatly:

> No congressman could possibly use sixteen staff members.

> Necessity aside, the Democratic congressman . . . is using them (ten in his district), and they don't appear to be hurting him any. In fact, a principal campaign theme of this congressman has been . . .

> Send me to Washington. I will protect the little guy from the government.

> No doubt he needs lots of staff to help him in his efforts.

Source: Morris P. Fiorina, *Congress: Keystone of the Washington Establishment* (New Haven: Yale University Press, 1977), p. 35.

──────────────────── ★ ★ ★ ★ ────────────────────

In the House, on the other hand, there is usually less rank consciousness, although there, too, it is generally recognized that a member's administrative assistant (AA) is the top staff person. Congressional AAs perform a variety of functions. Some are in complete charge of the representative's or senator's staff; others are more limited in their duties, and the Congressional member takes a larger role in the management of the office. But, within each House or Senate member's office, the AA is still "more important" than any other staff member.

Legislative assistants (LAs) are staff members whose primary responsibility is to assist the member in his or her legislative work, although members vary in the extent to which they rely on their LAs for this kind of assistance. A study done in 1969, for example, found that many representatives had no legislative assistant on their personal staff, and that those who did often did not rely on them much in making up their minds about how to vote.[39] Other evidence suggests that senators are more dependent on their top staff assistants for voting cues than are representatives, because each senator serves on more committees, has more constituency demands, and normally has less time to do his or her "homework."[40]

There is no job security for those who serve on the personal staff of a U.S. senator or a U.S. representative. These personal staff members serve at the pleasure of the member of Congress who hired them, and the personal staff members have no right to stay on with the member's successor. Moreover, it is difficult for a personal staff member to bring a successful complaint concerning job discrimination on the basis of sex or race. The job bias laws that apply to executive agencies do not apply to the Congress. The House adopted a rule in 1965 to bar job discrimination, but enforcement through the Committee on Standards of Official Conduct is such that it discourages complaints. The Senate adopted a job discrimination rule in 1977, but no machinery has been set up to enforce it. The Supreme Court ruled in June 1979 that a female staff member could sue a member of Congress in the courts for job discrimination. But the Court did not decide on the merits of that case. Nor did it decide whether or not the "Speech or Debate" clause of the Constitution protects members from suits by their employees.[41]

Congressional Research Agencies

In addition to personal staff and committee staff employees, the research agencies of Congress help members to independently develop policy initiatives and evaluate policy proposals emanating from elsewhere. These agencies are the Congressional Budget Office, the Congressional Research Service of the Library of Congress, the General Accounting Office, and the Office of Technology Assessment. These agencies are fairly independent entities and are expected to perform research for all members and all committees of Congress in the traditional policy-neutral professional manner. While the Congressional Budget Office and the General Accounting Office are criticized by some members for what they see as falling short of the traditional posture, in general the research agencies of Congress are given high marks for maintaining a sufficiently neutral professional role that they are available to and useful to virtually all members of Congress and to all committees of Congress. They perform both major studies (with priority given to committee requests, over individual member requests) and quick-reference services.[42] Some duplication and overlap exists in the functions of these agencies, but there has been greater coordination among them in recent years.[43] Despite the available staff assistance, many members inevitably feel that they do not receive adequate information on the nation's needs and the impact of various proposed bills on those needs. They are, however, able to learn what each bill does and who supports and opposes it, and usually why.[44]

Congressional Budget Office   In 1974 Congress reorganized its budget process. That reorganization was partly the result of a battle with President Nixon over control of the federal budget. It was also the result of a longer-run contest with the executive branch. Many members of Congress had long felt that Congress was too dependent on executive agencies, especially the Office of Management and Budget. In their view, this dependency resulted from the uncoordinated procedures Congress had been using when considering proposals for authorizations, appropriations, and taxes. Before 1974, the taxation and appropriations committees often had not coordinated their actions. Furthermore, the various authorizing committees had developed techniques which permitted them to provide funding for many of their pet projects or agencies without the approval of the appropriations committees.[45] Many members felt Congress no longer exercised meaningful control of the federal purse strings.

335

The outcome of the reorganization in 1974 was the creation of a budget committee, with staff, in each chamber of Congress and the establishment of the Congressional Budget Office (CBO). The CBO is made up of a staff of over 200 employees, headed by a director. The CBO staff works closely with the two budget committees of Congress. CBO's director is appointed to a four-year term by the Speaker of the House and the president pro tem of the Senate, in consultation with the chairpersons of the House and Senate Budget Committees. CBO is intended to be a source of analysis and information concerning the budget, and it was created so that members of Congress would not have to depend on the executive department's Office of Management and Budget (OMB). OMB is responsible for assisting the President in the development of the executive budget, and it has often not been responsive to the needs of members of Congress. Because CBO is structured differently from OMB, CBO provides members with different information than is available from OMB.[46]

In a review of the first few years of CBO operation, Thurber noted that the agency fulfills four general responsibilities:

1. Monitoring the economy and estimating its impact on government actions.
2. Writing policy analyses of existing and recommended programs.
3. Improving the flow and quality of budgetary information to members and committees.
4. Analyzing the costs and effects of alternative budgetary choices.

> CBO meets these responsibilities first by providing information and analysis to the two budget committees (80 percent of the time); second it provides support to Appropriations, Ways and Means, and Finance (10 percent of CBO's time), in limited degree to other committees (5 percent of its time), and to individual members (5 percent).[47]

It would probably be impossible for the staffs of the tax-writing, appropriations, and budget committees of Congress to avoid being criticized by liberals for being too fiscally conservative or by conservatives for being too free with federal money, and that is also true concerning the staff of the Congressional Budget Office. Even though the director and staff argue that they attempt to be as objective as possible, CBO is criticized by some observers as being oriented toward an activist federal government role. Critics believe "that CBO analyses assume the government should help shape the economy through spending programs, tax cuts and monetary controls."[48] CBO Director Rivlin argues that the agency's critics are actually mounting "an attack on mainstream economics,"[49] and notes that the agency has used standard commercial economic models to develop its projections. The staff director of the Senate Budget Committee, who defends CBO's record of objectivity, notes that, since CBO is criticized by both the left and the right, it is probably fairly objective.[50]

Congressional Research Service The Congressional Research Service (CRS) of the Library of Congress has about 850 employees and is "the most often used of the [four] support agencies."[51] One of its major services is the preparation of law indices and digests. Another is "providing research services and preparing analyses, gathering data, and preparing legislative materials."[52] Since 1970, CRS has also provided policy research and analysis assistance to the members and committees of Congress.[53] The numerous requests for specific facts (population statistics, provisions of a particular law, and the like) are handled by the Quick Reference Division.[54] CRS also prepares speech drafts, analyses of various issues, and briefing papers on issues. It conducts seminars and briefings on current legislative issues for

336

members and their staffs. It assists committees by suggesting possible witnesses for committee hearings. CRS also provides research reports for Congress on internal procedural and organizational questions, such as committee jurisdictions and the rules of each chamber.[55]

CRS works diligently to maintain its nonpartisan image.

> Materials prepared by CRS are supposed to be non-partisan, and every piece of work prepared by the CRS staff is screened at three different levels to ensure its objectivity, accuracy and professionalism. If a member insists that a study support a particular point of view, CRS indelibly marks it with the words "Directed Writing."[56]

General Accounting Office   The General Accounting Office (GAO) employs over 5,000 people, almost half of whom work in regional offices around the nation or in overseas offices. GAO is a quasi-independent oversight agency of Congress, headed by the comptroller general. The comptroller general is appointed by the President, subject to Senate confirmation, for a single fifteen-year term and cannot be reappointed.

About a third of the agency's work each year is in response to specific Congressional requests, but much of the agency's activities are undertaken on its own initiative, as Congress intended.

> As Congress' watchdog over executive branch spending, the GAO conducts independent reviews, audits and investigations of federal activities; develops standards for the government's accounting systems; provides legal opinions on government fiscal practices and settles claims for and against the government.[57]

About half the employees of GAO are engaged in the agency's auditing function. These audits are not narrow accounting expeditions; they are dominated by a Congressional "oversight" perspective and are broadly defined. They include

> not only examining accounting records and financial transactions and reports, but also checking for compliance with applicable laws and regulations; examining the efficiency and economy of operations; and reviewing the results of operations to evaluate whether the desired results, including legislative prescribed objectives, have been effectively achieved.[58]

As two informed observers conclude:

> Clearly, the auditing activity of the GAO can uncover administrative problems of which Congress was simply unaware; it also provides an information base for Congress that is critical to its conduct of oversight.[59]

GAO is intended to be nonpartisan and—as the lengthy term of the comptroller general testifies—free from direct partisan control. The agency is criticized from time to time by the targets of its investigations and by their friends in Congress for being "politically motivated." Generally, however, GAO is thought to do its job well and without overt partisanship. It may sometimes be so careful in some of its investigations that the timeliness of the result is sacrificed. Some observers also criticize the GAO for providing the audited agencies with a draft copy of the GAO report for comment, prior to the writing of the final report, and for being overly concerned about anticipating the reactions of powerful members of Congress.[60]

Office of Technology Assessment   As its name implies, the Office of Technology Assessment, which was created in 1972, assists Congress in understanding the impact of scientific and technological developments on society and government and provides answers to questions posed by committees and members. Like the other staff research agencies of Congress, it helps Congress remain capable of independent

337

analysis of information and controversies. As a result, Congress does not need to rely upon special-interest or point-of-view assessments from large chemical, computer, drug, or nuclear companies, or on similar reports provided by government agencies.

Many of the issues referred to the Office of Technology Assessment (OTA) are very complex, and they are susceptible to answers only on a probabilistic or "best-guess" basis by informed experts. OTA has a staff of over 130 employees and is authorized to use consultants and to contract with others for much of its research. It is authorized to undertake projects on its own, but it has been "overwhelmed with requests, receiving three to four times as many as it has the capacity to handle."[61]

One informed analysis of OTA and its relationships with Congress is pessimistic about the ability of the agency to perform its assigned mission in a continued policy-neutral professional manner, which can be very important to the public.

> [T]he strong political interests of congressional committees—who are the "clients" of OTA—render OTA reports, which strive for objectivity, vulnerable to political attacks if their findings or implications conflict with deeply entrenched political currents in the Congress. The ability of OTA to survive in such a situation is not at all certain.[62]

STAFF SUPPORT IN OTHER NATIONAL LEGISLATURES

It is probably no accident that the national legislature generally regarded as the most important in terms of impact on national policymaking, independent of the executive, is also the national legislature with the most ample support services and staff. That legislature is the U.S. Congress. No other national legislature even comes close to having access to the resources that are available to Congress and its members, although most have a legislative library of sorts and at least a modest research capacity. It should also be kept in mind that some legislators of other nations have their official staff resources supplemented by the interest groups or political party with which they are affiliated. Even counting such assistance, however, other nations' legislators do not have the resources available to members of Congress.

As in most American state legislatures, other national legislative bodies concentrate staff resources under the direct or indirect control of legislative leaders and provide individual members and committees with only minimal staff assistance under their own control. That is pretty much the case with the British House of Commons, the Canadian House of Commons, and the Italian Parliament, although the latter two provide each committee with one civil-service type "clerk," and the Public Accounts Committee and the Committee on External Affairs and National Defense of the Canadian Commons each have additional staff on a permanent basis.[63] The "clerks" are required to perform various mundane tasks, but are more analogous to the "professional" staff of Congress in terms of education and ability.

No other national legislature has the level of committee staff resources so generously granted the committees of the American Congress. The resources available to the committees of Congress, of course, both reflect and reinforce the strength of committees in that body. The Japanese Diet does provide each committee with a research staff of six to nine researchers, but such committee staff personnel are centrally hired and fired; the committee does not make the decision on what staff members are retained or released. In addition, many Diet staff personnel are on temporary loan from various ministries of government and owe their principal loyalty to the ministry, not to the Diet or its committee.[64]

The Canadian House of Commons and the West German Bundestag control staff assistance through the legislative parties. In Canada, research staffs are provided for "any party with more than twelve members in the House of Commons."[65] Little of those resources are made available to individual MPs. Rather, the party focuses its staff resource on the committee work of the House of Commons or, in the case of the majority party, on the work of the cabinet committees. The West German legislative parties receive allowances for their staffs. "At the end of the fifth Bundestag, the SPD employed thirty-three academically qualified assistants and sixty-seven other staff,"[66] while other legislative parties employed as few as twenty-four staff members in total. Most of the legislative party staff personnel in the Bundestag are assigned to party working groups, each of which develops party-policy positions on various issues.

Most national legislatures provide minimal personal staff, at best, for individual legislators who do not hold leadership posts. None provide the ample staffs that most U.S. representatives and senators consider barely adequate. (Again, such U.S. legislative staff resources presumably have to do with the independent power position of the U.S. Congress in the American political system.) West German Bundestag members are provided individual offices and some funds for staff.[67] By contrast, British MPs

> have no research staffs of their own. Several together have an office room and may employ a secretary (each member is given a very limited amount of funds to do this). Members are also entitled to use the research staff of the House of Commons Library, but the staff at the library comprises so few professional persons that there is a ratio of MP's (excluding ministers) to staff of over forty to one.[68]

As for the resources available to American state legislators, it is worth keeping in mind that some of them have staff and information-processing capabilities that exceed those available to most national legislatures.[69] This observation must be tempered, of course, by the realization that some of the American states have populations and economies that are also much larger than those of many foreign nations.

STATE LEGISLATIVE STAFF

By the very nature of the subject, generalizations about staff support in the American state legislatures are hazardous. It has been noted repeatedly that each state legislature is unique. Still, we offer tentative generalizations and numerous specific examples of what appear to be "representative" cases among the state legislatures. In general, however, it should be noted that those state legislatures which are more professionalized in terms of legislative pay and length of sessions and more institutionalized in terms of the development of detailed organizational norms and rules are more likely than the amateur or citizen legislatures to have substantial staff resources available to them.[70] With some exceptions, that means that the states with the most ample staff available to assist state legislators are the more populous, industrialized states. Even the most well-staffed American state legislature, however, falls far short of having the level of staff resources found in the U.S. Congress. Indeed, some of the *committees* of Congress have more staff assistance than many entire state legislatures. Still, it is hard to argue that either the California legislature, with over 700 professional and over 1,100 clerical staff employees in 1974, or the New York legislature, with over 1,400 employees in 1974,[71] are hampered by lack of staff in the performance of their duties.

339

Types of State Legislative Staffs

A major difference between the state legislatures and Congress in terms of staff is that the percentage of centrally controlled legislative staff resources is much greater in the various states than it is in Congress. Committee chairpersons and individual legislators in the states have much less control over staff resources and, thus, less independent ability to contest issues than do their counterparts in Congress. Interestingly, some Tennessee *local* governments have provided funds for staff assistance to their own state legislators, presumably to improve the effectiveness of the legislators.[72]

Despite their poor comparison with Congress, state legislative staffs have grown substantially over the past twenty years.

> The early 1970s appears to be a period for the diffusion of the innovations of the 1960s in staff services to a larger number of States and for the expansion of existing staffs.[73]

Why the growth of state legislative staff? The reasons are mainly the same as for the growth of Congressional staff. Professional staff helps state legislators cope with an increasing quantity and complexity of legislation. As with Congress, the assistance of legislative staff more nearly enables a state legislature to be an independent, coequal branch of government. As a person with experience as a senior legislative staff professional in Florida and Louisiana observed concerning the benefits of adequate legislative staff:

> In the past we often found the Florida Legislature and the other Legislatures making 10 and 20 percent across-the-board cuts because they knew there was padding or excesses in state government. This is no longer the case. The Legislature is now able to critically review what is happening. If there is padding, cuts can be made without simultaneously destroying the other operations of state government.[74]

Most legislators agree with outside observers on the need for professional staff in the state legislatures. For example, a survey of legislators in Arkansas, Connecticut, Florida, Maryland, Mississippi, New Jersey and Wisconsin from 1967 to 1971 revealed

> that the single improvement most frequently mentioned as necessary by members of state legislatures is more professional staff. Generally, members agree on the overriding need for more staff to support standing committees.[75]

There are limits, however, to the value of advice from centralized nonpartisan, professional staffs with strong policy-neutral rules and norms. In large part, that is why legislators continue to depend on committee hearings, personal advisors, and lobbyists. For example, among Nevada legislators, whose staff assistance comes from the centralized, nonpartisan Legislative Counsel Bureau,

> [c]ommittee hearings are favored as sources that are useful in identifying alternatives, identifying costs and benefits, and pointing toward future trends and problems, and that are accessible and convenient to use. Yet only a few members see hearings as thorough information sources or as sources of concise, reliable, or factual information. The Legislative Counsel Bureau, on the other hand, rates highly on just such points. It is generally thought to be weak only in identifying future trends, in revealing the indirect effects of legislation, and in its value as a politically sensitive source. Members generally recognize that the nonpartisan agency makes every attempt to stand outside the political currents swirling around pieces of legislation.[76]

Nonpartisan staff assistance is particularly valuable in helping legislators reach decisions on detailed matters like scientific or technical questions that cannot be resolved on the basis of partisan, basic philosophical, or ideological responses. A nonpartisan staff can also be valuable in collecting certain types of information. Nonpartisan staff is less valuable to a member who is trying to assess the *political* consequences of supporting or opposing a particular measure. A member of the Michigan Legislative Reference Service observed:

> We can't give them what they often want to know—whether something is good or bad, right or wrong for them. What we can give are facts and figures—but that's not all that's needed.[77]

The California assembly's experience in consciously making the staff more "politically" sensitive suggests that the political limitations inherent in staff assistance can be overcome.[78] One approach to the problem, which has as a by-product the strengthening of the party caucuses within the legislative process, is to follow Wisconsin's successful venture in providing professional staff assistance to the party caucuses in each legislative chamber.[79]

Like members of Congress, many state legislators feel the need for *personal* staff assistance to help evaluate the merits (from partisan and constituency perspectives, as well as from the perspective of the individual legislator's possible ambitions for alternative offices) of the many legislative proposals on which they must vote each session. Some personal staff assistance is now provided to all legislators in about half of the states. Some states provide personal staff only to senators. Almost half of the state legislatures that provide personal staff assistance only do so during the legislative session.[80] As might be expected, the states which provide personal staff assistance to legislators tend to be those which provide legislative offices and fairly good legislative salaries. California is, year after year, at or near the top in both legislator compensation and staff support.

Despite the differences among the various states, the staffs of most state legislatures are much more centralized than those of Congress. As the staffs have grown in recent years, however, a degree of staff decentralization has taken place in many state legislatures. (California has one of the most extensive and least centralized state legislative staffs.) Among state legislative committees, the appropriations and taxation committees typically have the most assistance and the most control over their own staffs, although they, too, are often dependent on centralized legislative staff agencies, such as the budget analyst and the legislative auditor. The trend toward less centralized state legislative staff, as noted earlier, can mean a degree of decentralization of authority within the state legislatures. But, even with what appears to be decentralization of staff in some state legislatures, there still seems to be a much greater degree of central control in those legislatures than is presently held in Congress by the Speaker and other chamber leaders. For example, a summary of staffing available to state legislative committees in the various states shows that New York provides professional and secretarial or clerical assistance to all state legislative committees.[81] That summary does not, however, tell us the degree of control the committees each have over their staffs:

> In New York, the distribution of legislative staffs depends overwhelmingly on the will of the Assembly Speaker and the Senate Majority Leader, although certain traditional staff allotments to important committees and senior members do have the effect of limiting leadership choices to some extent.[82]

> Staff grants are distributed by the leaders in widely differing amounts to senior legislators. These are often political rewards. A committee chairman's request for additional funds may be satisfied if he proves a need and notably if he has been

341

loyal. Joint Legislative Committee [interim committee] funds vary from committee to committee and the determination of who gets what rests with the leaders.[83]

The Impact of State Legislative Staffing

Does the availability of state legislative staff make a difference? Most observers believe it must, although the details of just how such resources make their impact felt are still being debated.[84] Still, as one of the most knowledgeable observers of state legislatures observed:

★ ★ ★ ★
The Staff of the California Legislature

Widespread use of support staff is definitely one of the most noteworthy aspects of the California Legislature. All members . . . are entitled to employ aides and assign them either to their office in the capitol building or to field offices in their home district. On top of assistance for individual members, staff consultants are hired to support the work of the committees. The more important the committee, for instance the appropriations committees in either house, the larger the staff attached to it. Another type of nonelected legislative employee is . . . staff . . . hired to assist the leadership in either house . . . as well as people employed by the senate and assembly offices of research. . . . The research offices prepare analyses of pending bills and collect information on issues likely to be discussed in the legislature.

Beyond individual, committee, and chamber staff, there is joint staff whose function is to serve the entire legislature. There are three major components of this staff. First, the legislative counsel (together with 150 support personnel of whom nearly sixty are lawyers) drafts the actual bills introduced in the senate and the assembly after consultation with their sponsors. This office is an impartial one that is not to be used to support or oppose pending legislation. . . . Second, the legislative analyst (together with a staff of approximately eighty people) prepares a document assessing the annual budget submitted to the Legislature by the governor. Note that this unit provides an independent source of budgetary information to legislators, thereby hopefully reducing reliance on the executive branch expertise in fiscal matters. . . .

. . . Given the increased reliance on the advice of staff by members of the legislature, lobbyists and liaison officials from state executive departments now direct much of their attention to legislative aides. . . . When briefed by staff today, legislators may not be as clear as they once were about the original source of the information they are receiving. Legislative staff also contributes to incumbent advantage during reelection campaigns. . . . To compensate for this disadvantage, challengers must raise a great deal of campaign money from interest groups. Increased staffing originally was intended to liberate legislators from these very interests, not to encourage candidates to accept large contributions. . . .

Source: John C. Culver and John C. Syer, *Power and Politics in California* (New York: John Wiley, 1980), pp. 104–6.

★ ★ ★ ★

> There is general consensus, with which we agree, that staffing commit-
> tees—providing them with an important resource—had positive effect on their
> capacity. The question is whether this change in committee capacity resulted
> in a change of committee performance.[85]

After careful examination of the performance of the committees in the New Jersey
assembly, after they were provided with staff assistance as part of a conscious effort
to improve the chamber's use of committees, Rosenthal found only slight change
in most indicators of performance, but a substantial increase in the rate at which
committees with staff resources amended the bills referred to them. "Resources, as
denoted by staff support, definitely matter," he concluded.[86] Further, "of all the resources standing committees can draw on for their tasks of formulating and controlling state policies and programs, staff is probably the most important one."[87]

Provision of adequate staff was one of the most important factors considered by
the Citizens Conference on State Legislatures (CCSL) in their ranking of the fifty
American state legislatures according to institutional capability.[88] Using CCSL ranking of the various state legislatures as the basis for evaluating the fifty state legislatures' impact on fifteen different policies, LeLoup found strong evidence for the argument that "increased institutional capability facilitate[s] the translation of public
needs and demands into more responsive policy."[89] The provision of adequate legislative staff, despite the problems of how best to utilize them, can indeed make a difference.

LEGISLATIVE INFORMATION-PROCESSING CAPACITY

The ability of a legislature to make intelligent use of modern information-processing
capabilities—computers and their allied equipment—adds to the legislature's ability
to remain informed and to maintain its independence from outside forces, especially
interest groups and executive agencies of government. As is the case with most other
areas of American life, from retail grocery stores to insurance companies, American
legislatures have adopted some of the technology of the computer age.[90]

Computers in the legislature are used both for internal legislative scheduling and
as an aid in the analysis of legislative proposals. Internal-scheduling matters may
include current committee-meeting schedules, topics, and meeting-room locations,
available by inquiry through a computer terminal in a central location or in members' offices. Computers also aid in determining the status of a particular bill—where
it is in the legislative process, what and when the next hurdle is, and what amendments have been made to it. "Statutory retrieval"—finding out what laws on a subject are already on the books and how a particular legislative proposal will affect
those laws—is another function for computers.

Most legislators are not adept at the use of computers, nor do most of them have
the time to do their own programming, even if they could. Further, questions of
confidentiality of certain types of information and the need for intimate acquaintance
with the data systems used by various agencies (to insure comparability of data from
the various agencies and to insure that the information developed really means what
it appears to mean) almost mandate that the legislature's computerized information-processing system be operated by staff employees. The person who controls information has power. Because much information is available quickly through the
computer system, the process by which computer services are made available to legislators is important to the power relationships within the legislature.

It is clear that legislatures, as institutions, have little choice but to develop their

343

own computer capability, if they wish to retain the ability to meet executive agencies and interest groups on terms of equality. It seems reasonable to expect the legislative leaders to try to structure the provision of legislative computer assistance in such a way as to enhance the leaders' authority. One should also expect other legislators to attempt to use the institution's computers to enhance their own power, not that of the leaders.

Congress and most of the state legislatures already have developed substantial computer capacity, both in legislative "housekeeping" functions (payroll, keeping track of bills wending their way through the legislative process, and maintaining or creating the schedule of committee meetings) and for some policy-related functions. As in staffing patterns, Congress has led most of the state legislatures in the use of computers to aid members in constituency-related tasks, as well as in the staffs' policy-analysis tasks.[91] The use of the new electronic technologies in Congress has been slowed both by members' awareness of the power potential inherent in the technology and by their dislike of the "coldness" of computers. While there are rules governing the use of Congressional computers, they are circumvented fairly easily and fairly frequently.[92] Even if all the rules were observed carefully, the assistance of a computer to give prompt service to constituents benefits each member at election time. Further, computerized automatic typewriters can "mix paragraphs to respond in specific and shaded manners to particular inquiries."[93] Perhaps because they know that they are less likely to be defeated for reelections, the more senior members of the House appear to use available computer assistance less extensively than do newcomers. In July 1976, 167 representativeswere taking advantage of the rule prmitting them "to use part of their clerk-hire funds for computer services (38% of the entire House)".[94]Three fourths of the first-term members were among those using available computer services. The junior members most likely to use compyters extensively seemed to be those "from marginal district[s] who came to Congress with little previous experience in elective office.[95]

State legislatures find computers helpful in budget and fiscal matters, particularly education funding, and in keeping current on various federal-aid programs and controls.[96] Individual state legislators, like members of Congress, find computers helpful in constituency relationships, but, in most states, the level of resources readily avail-

---
★ ★ ★ ★

Targeting the Mail: Just Press a Button

The re-election plan that Derry Daly worked out in 1972 for Michigan Republican Senator Robert P. Griffin was a model of vote gathering techniques that politicians have since said they felt were essential for any candidate in a close race.

Daly was a direct mail expert with the J. Walter Thompson Co. advertising firm; in addition, he understood computers and their wonderful capacity to sort out useful groups of voters from much larger lists of citizens. His plan, essentially, called for using the Senate computer, sophisticated direct mail techniques and taxpayer funds to convince Michigan residents to vote for Griffin.

A key issue in that election was school busing, which Griffin opposed. His opponent, State Attorney General Frank J. Kelley, had been wavering on the issue.

Daly proposed mass mailings to blue-collar households in three key counties which had voted Democratic in the last three congressional elections. In these counties, Daly reasoned, busing was likely to be an emotional issue.

In a memorandum entitled a "plan for making optimum use of direct mail as a medium of personal persuasion in Senator Griffin's 1972 re-election campaign," Daly told Griffin he should try to "capitalize on the unrest of this group, attempting to switch them to the Republican camp and thus gain more votes in these counties."

Griffin could accomplish this, Daly said, by blanketing these counties with a special computerized letter outlining his opposition to busing.

Another target for the anti-busing letter, Daly said, should be "higher-income car[-owning] households in non-black tracts" in a fourth Michigan county.

As laid out in Daly's memo, Griffin was to obtain the names and addresses of such households by entering into the Senate computer the "Polk 01 list: Non-duplicating residential car households," a commercially available electronic mailing list. Then, using a second electronic list compiled from census data, all addresses on the Polk 01 list located in black census tracts were to be eliminated with a simple computer command. The computer could then electronically address the envelopes so that they would go only to the targeted households.

Other proposed mailings included 142,000 copies of Griffin's "special newsletter on pensions" to blue-collar households in 11 counties; 200,000 pieces of mail on Griffin's support for lower property taxes to "higher-income households" throughout the entire state; and letters "stressing the senator's stance on farm issues" to every farmer on the mailing list of the state department of agriculture.

To comply with Senate restrictions on the use of the free congressional mailing privilege, known as the frank, Daly specified in his memo that letters designed to get out the vote or to raise funds were to be printed, stuffed into envelopes and mailed with campaign funds.

Letters dealing solely with legislation or national issues, on the other hand, could be printed, stuffed and mailed at taxpayer expense, Daly said.

For the letters sent out at taxpayer expense, the sole cost to the senator's campaign committee would be the price of renting electronic mailing lists—in the form of reels of computer tape—from commercial marketing firms, the memo said. On Nov. 7, Griffin rode the busing issue to a second term in the Senate, winning a narrow victory over Democrat Kelley. Following his re-election, Griffin wrote Daly a thank-you note.

Source: "Targeting the Mail: Just Press a Button," *Inside Congress,* 2nd ed. (Washington, D.C.: Congressional Quarterly, 1979), p. 143.

★ ★ ★ ★

able to a legislator is not up to Congressional standards. At both the state and national level, continued growth of the role of computers and associated automated data-processing equipment in the legislature seems almost certain.

SUMMARY

Staff assistance to legislative bodies greatly increases their capacity as legislatures and their independence from outside actors, such as executive agencies and interest groups. The staff assistance provided to modern legislatures includes legislative research agencies (most of which strive for policy-neutral, fact-finding roles); legislative and chamber centralized staff, who keep the legislative procedure coordinated; leadership aides (partisan actors, loyal to the leader); committee staff (some of whom prefer policy-neutral roles, some policy-entrepreneur roles, and some partisan roles, often depending on the environment of the committee and the desires of its chairperson); and personal staff (most of whom are responsive to the desires and policy preferences of the legislator who employs them).

In virtually all aspects of legislative staff resources, the U.S. Congress is the most amply staffed legislature in the world. The American state legislatures are far behind Congress in the provision of research agencies, committee staffs, and especially personal staff. Substantial variations exist in the staffing patterns of the different states, but, in general, they tend toward more centralized staffs than are found in Congress. The states also vary a great deal in the size of their staffs. The legislatures of the most populous states tend to have the largest staffs, although the relationship is not perfect. The legislatures of the largest states, indeed, have staff resources fully equal to that available to most national legislatures, and superior to many.

Some European legislatures and some state legislatures provide most staff resources through the legislative party, enhancing the authority of the party caucus at the expense of other actors in the legislative process. The practice in the U.S. Congress of allocating substantial staff resources to its committees, and of giving control over those staffs to the chairpersons and ranking minority members of the committees and subcommittees, enhances the independent authority of Congressional committees and their chairpersons and ranking minority members. Practice in the state legislatures tends toward keeping such staff resources under the ultimate authority of the central chamber leadership and assigning them—often conditionally—to the various committees. Such a practice, of course, maintains the overall authority of the central chamber leadership.

The use of electronic processing equipment—computers—in legislatures is growing. The adoption of computer support has been forced upon the modern legislature largely by the increasing use of such facilities by interest groups and executive agencies, although the adoption of such resources substantially increases the legislature's capacity. Control over, and access to, the legislature's computer resources can substantially affect the power relationships within the legislature. Members who control such resources gain power.

Staff support for American legislatures has increased dramatically over the past few decades. Adequate staff greatly enhances the capacity of the legislature, but also has the potential of affecting its policy choices. Indeed, it is clear that policy-entrepreneurial staff members can, within the loose limits established by their legislator-bosses, substantially affect policy decisions. Legislative staff thus deserves continued attention by students of legislatures and the legislative process.

Notes

1. Alan P. Balutis, "Legislative Staffing: A Review of Current Trends," in *Legislative Staffing: A Comparative Perspective,* ed. James J. Heaphey and Alan P. Balutis (New York: John Wiley, 1975), p. 27. For a general discussion of the importance of adequate Congressional staff, see James A. Robinson, "Decision-Making in Congress," in *Congress: The First Branch of Government,* ed. Alfred de Grazia (Garden City, N.Y.: Doubleday, Anchor Books, 1967), pp. 244–80.

2. Samuel C. Patterson, "The Professional Staffs of Congressional Committees," *Administrative Science Quarterly* 15 (March 1970): 23; Lauros G. McConachie, *Congressional Committees* (1898; reprint ed., New York: Burt Franklin 1973), especially pp. 64–67.

3. Randall B. Ripley, *Congress: Process and Policy* (New York: W.W. Norton, 1975), pp. 33–41.

4. *Congressional Quarterly Weekly Report,* November 24, 1979, pp. 2638, 2650. Included in the above figures but not discussed further because of their limited impact on policy are the 1,900 or so employees of the Architect of the Capitol and the 50-odd workers in the Botanic Garden. *Not* included in the above figures are the 7,600 or so employees of the Government Printing Office, which is an arm of Congress but does most of its work for the executive branch. Further information on these and other Congressional employees is available from Harrison W. Fox, Jr., and Susan Webb Hammond, *Congressional Staffs: The Invisible Force in American Lawmaking* (New York: Free Press, 1977).

5. *Washington Post,* January 14, 1981, pp. B-1, B-4.

6. *Congressional Quarterly Weekly Report,* March 7, 1981, p. 430.

7. Patterson, "The Professional Staffs of Congressional Committees," p. 23.

8. Fox and Hammond, *Congressional Staffs,* pp. 18–21.

9. Patterson, "The Professional Staffs of Congressional Committees," p. 23.

10. *Washington Post,* January 14, 1981, pp. B-1, B-4.

11. Ibid.

12. David E. Price, "Professionals and 'Entrepreneurs': Staff Orientations and Policy Making on Three Senate Committees," *Journal of Politics* 33 (May 1971): 316, 317.

13. In addition to Price, two others who agree with the description of the JCIRT staff as neutrally competent professionals are Michael J. Malbin, "Congressional Committee Staffs: Who's in Charge Here?" *The Public Interest* 47 (Spring 1977): 20–22; and John F. Manley, "Congressional Staff and Public Policy-Making: The Joint Committee on Internal Revenue Taxation," *Journal of Politics* 30 (November 1968): 1046–67; reprinted in Nelson Polsby, ed., *Congressional Behavior* (New York: Random House, 1971), pp. 42–60.

14. Manley, "Congressional Staff and Public Policy-Making," p. 46.

15. Ibid., p. 47.

16. Ibid., p. 48.

17. David E. Price, *Who Makes the Laws? Creativity and Power in Senate Committees* (Cambridge, Mass.: Schenkman, 1972), pp. 329–31.

18. Thomas C. Stenger, "Congressional Committee Staffers' Policy Orientations in the Hearing Process" (Paper delivered at the 1978 Annual Meeting of the Midwest Political Science Association, Chicago, Ill.).

19. Price, "Professionals and 'Entrepreneurs,' " p. 324.

20. Price, *Who Makes the Laws?* p. 196.

21. Price, "Professionals and 'Entrepreneurs,' " p. 324.

22. Robert H. Salisbury and Kenneth A. Shepsle, "Congressional Staff Turnover: Its Causes and Consequences" (Paper delivered at the 1979 Annual Meeting of the Southern Political Science Association, Gatlinburg, Tenn.), p. 60.

23. Ibid., pp. 9, 10.

24. James D. Cochrane, "Partisan Aspects of Congressional Committee Staffing," *Western Political Quarterly* 17 (June 1964): 339.

25. Quoted in Randall B. Ripley, *Power in the Senate* (New York: St. Martin's Press, 1969), p. 200.

26. Ibid., p. 201.

27. Price, "Professionals and 'Entrepreneurs,' " pp. 332–33.

28. Ibid., p. 334.

29. Robert Zwier, "The Role of Congressional Staff in the Information Network of the House" (Paper delivered at the 1978 Annual Meeting of the Midwest Political Science Association, Chicago, Ill.).

30. Cochrane, "Partisan Aspects of Congressional Committee Staffing," p. 340; Malbin, "Congressional Committee Staffs: Who's In Charge Here?", pp. 20–22; and Manley, "Congressional Staff and Public Policy-Making," pp. 1046–67.

31. *Washington Post,* January 24, 1981, pp. B-1, B-4.

32. Burdett A. Loomis, "The Congressional Office as a Small (?) Business: New Members Set Up Shop," *Publius* 9 (Summer 1979): 37.

33. Morris P. Fiorina, *Congress—Keystone of the Washington Establishment* (New Haven, Conn.: Yale University Press, 1977); and Morris P. Fiorina, "The Case of the Vanishing Marginals: The Bureaucracy Did It," *American Political Science Review* 71 (March 1977): 177–81.

34. *Congressional Quarterly Weekly Report,* July 28, 1979, p. 1521. Each member is actually limited to eighteen employees, but (if it can be done without exceeding the $288,156 annual allowance) may add four extra staffers for selected narrow categories of work. The staff working conditions vary widely. See David W. Brady, "Personnel Policies in the U.S. House of Representatives" (Paper delivered at the 1979 Annual Meeting of the American Political Science Association, Washington, D.C.).

35. *Congressional Quarterly Weekly Report,* November 24, 1979, p. 2643.

36. *Albuquerque Journal,* June 6, 1979, p. B-1.

37. Susan Webb Hammond, "Congressional Change and Reform: Staffing the Congress," in Leroy N. Rieselbach, *Legislative Reform* (Lexington, Mass.: D.C. Heath, 1978), p. 184.

38. Harrison W. Fox, Jr., and Susan Webb Hammond, "The Growth of Congressional Staffs," in *Congress Against the President* (Academy of Political Science Proceedings, vol. 32, 1975), p. 122.

39. Donald R. Matthews and James A. Stimson, *Yeas and Nays: Normal Decision-Making in the U.S. House of Representatives* (New York: John Wiley, 1975), pp. 23–24.

40. Ripley, *Congress: Process and Policy,* pp. 150–58.

41. *Congressional Quarterly Weekly Report,* June 9, 1979, pp. 1103, 1104.

42. Fox and Hammond, *Congressional Staffs,* p. 130.

43. *Congressional Quarterly Weekly Report,* November 24, 1979, p. 2650.

44. Louis Sandy Maisel, "Information and Decision-Making in House Offices" (Paper delivered at the 1979 Annual Meeting of the American Political Science Association, Washington, D.C.).

45. John W. Ellwood and James A. Thurber, "The New Congressional Budget Process: The Hows and Whys of House-Senate Differences," in *Congress Reconsidered,* ed. Lawrence C. Dodd and Bruce I. Oppenheimer (New York: Praeger, 1977), pp. 163–92; and William G. Munselle, "Presidential Impoundment and Congressional Reform," in Rieselbach, *Legislative Reform,* pp. 173–81.

46. Douglas H. Shumavon, "OMB, CBO, and Information Presented to Congress" (Paper delivered at the 1980 Annual Meeting of the Midwest Political Science Association, Chicago, Ill.). See also Edward I. Sidlow and Douglas H. Shumavon, "Congressional Budget Committee Staffs and the Uses of Information" (Paper delivered at the 1981 Annual Meeting of the Midwest Political Science Association, Cincinnati, Ohio).

47. James A. Thurber, "New Powers of the Purse: An Assessment of Congressional Budget Reform," in Rieselbach, *Legislative Reform,* p. 163.

48. *Congressional Quarterly Weekly Report,* November 24, 1979, p. 2653.

49. Ibid.

50. Ibid., p. 2654.

51. Fox and Hammond, *Congressional Staffs,* p. 131.

52. Ibid.

53. Ibid.

54. Ibid., p. 132.

55. Ibid., pp. 116, 132.

56. *Congressional Quarterly Weekly Report,* November 24, 1979, p. 2651.

57. Ibid., p. 2650.

58. Joseph Pois, "The General Accounting Office as a Congressional Resource," in *Congressional Support Agencies, Papers Prepared for the Commission on the Operation of the Senate* (Washington, D.C., 1976), p. 32; quoted in Lawrence C. Dodd and Richard L. Schott, *Congress and the Administrative State* (New York: John Wiley, 1979), p. 252.

59. Dodd and Schott, *Congress and the Administrative State,* p. 252.

60. *Congressional Quarterly Weekly Report,* November 24, 1979, p. 2649.

61. Dodd and Schott, *Congress and the Administrative State,* p. 257.

62. E. B. Skomlikoff, "The Office of Technology Assessment," in *Congressional Support Agencies, Papers Prepared for the Commission of the Operation of the Senate,* p. 61; quoted in Dodd and Schott, p. 258.

63. See S. A. Walkland, "Committees in the British House of Commons," pp. 248, 263, 268; Michael Rush, "Committees in the Canadian House of Commons," pp. 222, 224; and Francesco D'Onofrio, "Committees in the Italian Parliament," pp. 96, 97, all in *Committees in Legislatures: A Comparative Analysis,* ed. John D. Lees and Malcolm Shaw (Durham, N.C.: Duke University Press, 1979).

64. Hans H. Baerwald, "Committees in the Japanese Diet," in Lees and Shaw, *Committees in Legislatures,* pp. 349–50.

65. Rush, "Committees in the Canadian House of Commons," p. 224.

66. Nevil Johnson, "Committees in the West German Bundestag," in Lees and Shaw, *Committees in Legislatures,* p. 108.

67. Ibid., p. 109.

68. John E. Schwartz and L. Earl Shaw, *The United States Congress in Comparative Perspective* (Hinsdale, Ill.: Dryden Press, 1976), p. 75.

69. Samuel C. Patterson, "American State Legislatures and Public Policy," in *Politics in the American States,* 3rd ed., ed. Herbert Jacob and Kenneth N. Vines (Boston: Little, Brown, 1976), pp. 146–47.

70. To those familiar with the literature on legislatures, this statement may sound like a tautology, since some measures of "legislative professionalism" include staff resources in ranking the legislatures. Such is the case, for example, in work done by John G. Grumm, "The Effects of Legislative Structure on Legislative Performance," in *State and Urban Politics: Readings in Comparative Public Policy,* ed. Richard I. Hofferbert and Ira Sharkansky (Boston: Little, Brown, 1971); and by Ira Sharkansky and Richard Hofferbert, "Dimensions of State Politics, Economics and Public Policy," *American Political Science Review* 62 (September 1969). The newcomer to the field, however, can return to earlier chapters and save lengthy repetition here.

71. Patterson, "American State Legislatures and Public Policy," p. 146.

72. *The Book of the States, 1976–77* (Lexington, Ky.: Council of State Governments, 1976), p. 40; cited in Charles Press and Kenneth VerBerg, *State and Community Governments in the Federal System* (New York: John Wiley, 1979), p. 247.

73. Karl T. Kurtz, "The State Legislatures," *The Book of the States, 1974–75* (Lexington, Ky.: Council of State Governments, 1974), p. 60.

74. Quoted in Alan P. Balutis and Daron K. Butler, "Legislative Staffing: Perceptions in Seven States," in *State Government,* (Winter 1977), p. 45.

75. Alan Rosenthal, *Legislative Performance in the States* (New York: Free Press, 1974), p. 147.

76. Robert B. Bradley, "Motivations in Legislative Information Use," *Legislative Studies Quarterly* 5 (August 1980): 397.

77. H. Owen Porter, "Legislative Information Needs and Staff Resources in the American States," in Heaphey and Balutis, *Legislative Staffing: A Comparative Perspective,* p. 49.

78. When led by the avowedly "political" speaker, Jesse Unruh, the California assembly's response to the need for political appraisals as well as for expertise was to shift "the legislature's staffing pattern from the technical experts to the political experts. . . . These new staff were specialists, but their orientation was more than just to internal areas of expertise. Committee consultants were a liaison with the legislature's environment." Raymond Davis, "The Evolution of California Legislative Staff," in Heaphey and Balutis, *Legislative Staffing,* p. 202.

79. Alan Rosenthal, "An Analysis of Institutional Effects: Staffing Legislative Parties in Wisconsin," *Journal of Politics* 32 (August 1970): 531–62.

80. *American State Legislatures: Their Structures and Procedures* (Lexington, Ky.: Council of State Governments, 1977), p. 43.

81. Ibid., p. 42.

82. Alan G. Hevesi, *Legislative Politics in New York State* (New York: Praeger, 1975), p. 61.

83. Ibid., p. 20.

84. Samuel C. Patterson, for example, reminds us that "reforms" are not necessarily "changes for the better," in "Conclusions: On The Study of Legislative Reform" in *Legislative Reform and Public Policy,* ed. Susan Welch and John G. Peters (New York: Praeger, 1977), p. 216. Patricia K. Freeman and Ronald D. Hedlund similarly note that—in the Iowa and Wisconsin legislatures, at least—increased computer capacity influenced the expeditiousness with which bills were enacted (time lapsed from introduction to final reading) but that "increasing the policy trained staff reduces expeditiousness." See "The Policy Impact of State Legislative Science and Technology Capacity," a paper presented at the 1979 Annual Meeting of the Southern Political Science Association, Gatlinburg, Tenn.). While the rapidity with which legislation is enacted should not necessarily be considered a positive measure of improved legislatures, the differing impact of different types of resources on the legislative process is nothing to ignore.

85. Rosenthal, *Legislative Performance in the States,* p. 125.

86. Ibid., p. 138.

87. Ibid., p. 138.

88. In their 1971 report on the fifty state legislatures, the Citizens Conference on State Legislatures noted that only ten of the states had adequate staff assistance. See *The Sometimes Governments* (New York: Bantam Books, 1971). Partly as a result of that report, numerous states have since increased their staff resources. The Citizens Conference report also concluded that those states with the most extensive staff resources were the most effective. The report is discussed in Rosenthal, *Legislative Performance in the States,* pp. 148–51.

89. The report used by LeLoup is the Citizens Conference on State Legislatures, *State Legislatures: An Evaluation of their Effectiveness* (New York: Praeger, 1971). See Lance T. LeLoup, "Reassessing the Mediating Impact of Legislative Capability," in *American Political Science Review* 72 (June 1978): 616–21.

90. For a survey of the use of computers in legislatures, see John A. Worthley, "Legislative Information Systems: A Review and Analysis of Recent Experience," *Western Political Quarterly* 30 (September 1977): 418–30. More extended discussion is available in John A. Worthley, ed., *Comparative Legislative Information Systems: The Use of Computer Technology in the Public Policy Process* (Washington, D.C.: National Science Foundation, 1976); and in Kenneth Janda, "Information Systems for Congress," in de Grazia, *Congress: The First Branch of Government,* pp. 403–43.

91. *Inside Congress,* 2nd ed. (Washington, D.C.: Congressional Quarterly, 1979), pp. 141–46; Robert L. Chartrand, "Legislative Information Services for the Congress: Present and Potential," in Worthley, *Comparative Legislative Information Systems,* pp. 32–44.

92. *Inside Congress,* 2nd ed., pp. 142–44.

93. Burdett A. Loomis, "The Congressional Office as a Small (?) Business," p. 53.

94. Ibid.

95. Stephen F. Frantzich, "Technology Innovation Among Members of the House of Representatives," *Polity* 12 (Winter 1979): 348.

96. Worthley, "Legislative Information Systems," p. 421.

chapter 13

Floor Procedures and Decision-Making in Legislatures

Preview

Debate and voting on the floor of a legislative chamber take place under rather elaborate rules, both formal and informal. These rules limit the possibilities inherent in each legislative situation in much the same manner that the banks on the sides of a river are limits on the maneuvering of a riverboat. There's room for maneuvering—as there is sometimes for creative interpretation of legislative rules—but there are limits too.

Informal and formal legislative rules sometimes do not matter much, but at other times they are crucial. A clear, strong, and persistent legislative majority can generally get its way, regardless of the rules, but that majority usually has to be very large and very intent on its purposes if it is to overcome intense opposition. Rules can often permit a minority to delay legislative action, to obtain amendments as the price of ending obstruction, and, near the end of a legislative session, to win some victories. The rules of some legislatures are more tolerant of obstructionist minorities, while the rules in other legislatures are less so.

How do new legislators learn the norms of the body to which they have been elected—the informal "rules of the game," what is expected of them? How are these informal rules, or norms, established and maintained? What rules govern the scheduling of legislation for debate, and what procedures govern decision-making on the floor? How do legislators decide how to vote on the numerous issues which come before them? These are some of the questions which will be considered in this chapter, first as they relate to the U.S. Congress and then to the state legislatures.

CONGRESSIONAL NORMS

Legislative rules—formal and informal—seem much more important to the members of a legislative body than to those who are outside observers. But an understanding of the more exciting, dynamic aspects of the legislative process depends upon a basic understanding of the legislative rules and their applications. This is certainly true in regard to observers of the U.S. Congress, and the rules which an observer needs to understand include the "unwritten but generally accepted and informally enforced norms of conduct in the chamber."[1]

Norms of behavior are enforced in all societies and in most small groups. It is not surprising then, as observed in Chapter 10, that legislators have found certain types of behavior help them all to survive in the legislative fishbowl and that following the generally accepted norms helps members to become accepted by their colleagues. Such informal rules of behavior have been charted extensively in Congress.

> [N]ormative rules of conduct—called here folkways— . . . perform important functions. They provide motivation for the performance of legislative duties that, perhaps, would not otherwise be performed. They discourage long-windedness in a chamber of one hundred highly verbal men, dependent upon publicity, and unrestrained by any formal limitations on debate. They encourage the development of expertise and division of labor and discourage those who would challenge it. They soften the inevitable personal conflict of a legislative body so that adversaries and competitors can meet (at the very least) in an atmosphere of antagonistic cooperation or (at best) in an atmosphere of friendship and mutual respect. They encourage senators to become "compromisers" and "bargainers" and to use their substantial powers with caution and restraint. Without these folkways the Senate could hardly operate in anything like its present form.[2]

Donald R. Matthews found six basic norms of behavior in the U.S. Senate of the late 1950s. Although most senators observed those norms, some refused to do so and others had difficulty doing so. Violators of the norms tended to be former governors, presidential aspirants, political newcomers, committed liberals (seeking changes in the status quo), and senators from large competitive two-party states.[3] The six norms Matthews labeled are: apprenticeship, legislative work, reciprocity, specialization, courtesy, and institutional patriotism. Similar norms are also recognized in the U.S. House of Representatives. The application of the first four norms to committee activity was discussed extensively in Chapter 10, but they will be touched on again here as they apply to decision-making on the floor of the Senate and the House.

As noted in Chapter 10, the *apprenticeship* norm has been greatly weakened over the past quarter century, but substantial differences in Congressional status still attend a member of above average ability who has ten or more years of seniority compared to a first- or second-term member of comparable natural ability. A senior member often can garner votes from his colleagues which a junior member simply could not collect. In part that is because, even in today's Congress, junior members hesitate to make such a request of senior members. Also, senior members (especially committee or subcommittee chairs of the more important committees) are the very people with whom other members want to be on good terms. It takes time for a member to build a reputation in the chamber which he or she can use in persuading colleagues to help out on a controversial floor vote. Still, in both chambers of Congress, junior members now participate much more actively than they did in the 1950s. For example, a freshman member of the House Education and Labor Committee in the early 1970s remarked:

> I never dreamed the older members would have allowed us freshmen to contribute so much and participate. . . . On my subcommittees I participate, get amendments passed, and open doors I never thought I could.[4]

The *legislative work* norm calls upon a member to perform his or her committee work responsibly, while the *specialization* norm presses members to devote their energies primarily to matters which are within the authority of their committees or which directly affect their respective states. As noted in Chapter 10, these norms are important buttresses to the Congressional committee system. But they also affect floor behavior. For one thing, they tend to influence members to defer to the committee which reports a bill. For another, they mean that members known for not doing their homework are given little credence in floor debate and seldom are turned to by colleagues for cues on how to vote. On the other hand, members generally recognized as true specialists on a given topic are carefully listened to and have great influence on how their colleagues vote. In the Senate, with its rule of unlimited debate, the specialization norm is especially important for it discourages senators from discussing a subject unless they are substantially better informed than the other senators. Thus, the specialization norm "makes it possible for the Senate to stop talking and act."[5]

The *reciprocity* norm recognizes that

> every senator, at one time or another, is in a position to help out a colleague. The folkways of the Senate hold that a senator ought to provide this assistance—and that he be repaid in kind.[6]

There are, however, "some things a senator just can't do in return for help."[7] That is, a senator can expect assistance on minor matters but cannot expect his or her colleagues to go against their basic policy beliefs. In the Senate, the norm of reciprocity is especially important since a single senator's objection to the routine request for "unanimous consent" to waive the rules can slow the legislative process to a crawl. The senator who repeatedly objects to unanimous consent will soon discover other senators using their power to block his or her bills.[8] The difficulty with the norm of reciprocity is that if members are not careful, they may carry too far the accommodating aspects of reciprocity expectations. The result constitutes "log rolling," a situation common with public-works bills. Within limits, everybody's project passes as long as it does not directly clash with anyone else's. The result may mean much credit back home for the members for "bringing home the pork," but it may well not be in the overall public interest.

The *courtesy* norm calls upon members not to let political disagreements become personal ones. It is buttressed on the chamber floor by numerous formal rules, such as the requirement that all floor remarks technically be made to the presiding officer and that a member may not criticize another state or call into question the motives of a fellow member.

> Personal attacks, unnecessary unpleasantness, pursuing a line of thought or action that might embarrass a colleague needlessly, are all thought to be self-defeating—"after all, your enemies on one issue may be your friends on the next."[9]

Those who follow the norm find that it makes it possible for them to continue to work with each other over the years, calling upon one another for personal favors and support, with as little acrimony or awkwardness as possible.

The *institutional patriotism* norm is probably a bit stronger in the U.S. Senate than in the U.S. House of Representatives or the various state legislative chambers. But in all such bodies, the members value a commitment to protecting the legislature (and one's own legislative chamber) as an institution and to "avoiding behavior that would bring it or its members into disrepute."[10] U.S. senators

> are expected to *believe* that they belong to the greatest legislative and deliberative body in the world. They are expected to be a bit suspicious of the President and the bureaucrats and just a little disdainful of the House.[11]

U.S. representatives frequently become annoyed by what they consider to be the Senate's affectations, and they like to refer to the Senate, not as the "upper" chamber but as the "other body."[12] But like their colleagues in "the other body," representatives are also quick to defend the authority and privileges of Congress against executive or judicial interference.

Maintenance and Change of Norms

Legislative norms can undermine the formal rules. Conversely, members who are dissatisfied with the workings of the legislature under the terms of the accepted norms sometimes resort to changes in the formal rules in an effort to change the way the legislature functions. In considering the dynamics of maintenance and change in legislative norms, it should be noted that both center around the new member.

The regular election of new legislators, who may or may not accept the norms of the body, is one factor leading to change in legislative norms. But legislative newcomers are not a random assortment of citizens. They have already been "screened" by the recruitment process; for the most part, they accept the dominant values of the social system (especially in single-member, plurality-election districts) and are skilled in the art of compromise. There are differences in values and attitudes among legislators but not the full range one would find in a random sample of the citizenry.

As newcomers begin to function in a legislature, however, they are likely to notice that the norms of behavior to which they are being introduced are *not* neutral. That is, the norms advantage certain types of members and disadvantage others—often the newcomers. Such realization is likely to lead the newcomers to question the norms. Indeed, a major reason for the recent changes in the rules of the two houses of Congress and for the diminishing impact of the apprenticeship norm in both chambers was that the members from the more competitive districts and states realized that this particular norm was strengthening the position of conservative members (mostly southern Democrats) from one-party areas of the nation.[13]

Like newcomers to most social groups, new members of Congress are socialized into their roles as representatives and senators. Seminars for new members are held before a new Congress begins. These seminars teach the new members the formal rules of how the chamber operates and what fields of policy their particular committees are responsible for. But the seminars also help the new member to understand many of the less formal rules of Congress. It is common, for example, for the party leaders and committee chairpersons to pass on words of wisdom and suggestions for behavior. Occasionally, such advice is rejected, as it was in 1974, when most first-year Democrats voted in caucus to oust three committee chairpersons. But, for the most part, the advice is effective. Probably more effective are the numerous instances of advice given in quiet, one-on-one sessions. To avoid unpleasantness with an erring junior colleague, such advice occasionally is transmitted through a legislative aide to the new member's aide.[14] Most of the discussion of rules and norms appears to occur with a new member's own party colleagues, fellow state delegation members, and fellow committee members. The organization of Congress is such that, except for interactions at committee meetings, new members have few opportunities to get acquainted with members from the other party.[15]

Much of the continuity in American legislative norms can be explained by the recruitment process. The process filters out those who do not accept the dominant American values, including the generalized political norms of compromise and maintaining civil relationships with political opponents. The legislative recruitment process probably tends toward the election of those persons who are either already supportive of most of the legislative norms or are likely to accept them, once they become legislators. Asher, for example, notes that in the Ninety-first Congress, "freshmen largely knew the general House norms prior to entering Congress, . . . the amount of norm learning was surprisingly low," and during their first five months in office, "the extent of attitude change toward the norms was minimal."[16]

Interaction of Norms and Written Rules

Many of the written rules of procedure of the U.S. Congress have, in fact, been superseded by "practice" and tradition. Other rules have been substantially modified by the generally accepted norms of behavior. Indeed, as noted earlier, the unwritten rules of a legislative body can become so strong that members who dislike their effects may have to resort to enactment of formal rules in an effort to change the way the legislative body makes decisions. In essence, that is what happened in Congress when formal rules were adopted which subjected the chairpersons of standing committees to individual caucus votes. These rules explicitly stated that the norm of awarding the chair of a committee to that committee's most senior majority-party member need no longer be honored. From the evidence, it appears that changing the formal rules is not always sufficient to change legislator behavior. Even when three U.S. House committee chairpersons were deposed, their successors were those next eligible under the workings of the seniority norm. The seniority norm has also been modified in the U.S. House under the Democratic party's new system of electing subcommittee chairpersons by vote of all Democrats on the parent committee.[17]

SCHEDULING LEGISLATION IN CONGRESS

Once a bill has been acted upon favorably by a committee of Congress, it must win a vote on the chamber floor before it can be sent to the other chamber or to the President for signature. Not all bills are equally important, so not all are treated the same way once they are reported out of committee. But all bills must be scheduled for floor action if they are to be voted on. (See Figure 13.1.) The decision of the chamber leaders concerning which bills to consider first on the floor and which bills to delay becomes especially important as a session approaches an end. Numerous bills which would receive a majority approval if voted on are allowed to die because of the press of time and the leaders' priorities. During the session, the leaders may move quickly to schedule a vote while they can win, or they may delay a vote while building a majority. Control over the legislative agenda is a very important part of the majority-party leaders' control over policy decisions. Even a seemingly mundane question, such as whether to have a vote in the U.S. House on Monday or Wednesday, can determine the outcome on many bills. The reason is that many U.S. representatives go home on Thursday evenings, not to be seen in the Capitol again until Tuesday morning. The members of this "Tuesday-to-Thursday Club" are mainly from the Northeast, and more of them are "liberals" than "conservatives." Votes taken in the middle of the week on most pieces of domestic legislation, therefore, have a more liberal flavor than votes taken Friday through Monday.[18]

Scheduling Legislation in the U.S. House of Representatives

The procedure for scheduling bills for floor consideration in the House is complex and depends on the nature of the bill and its importance.[19] A bill granting citizenship to a particular individual or settling an individual claim against the government,

FIGURE 13.1

A Bill Becomes Law

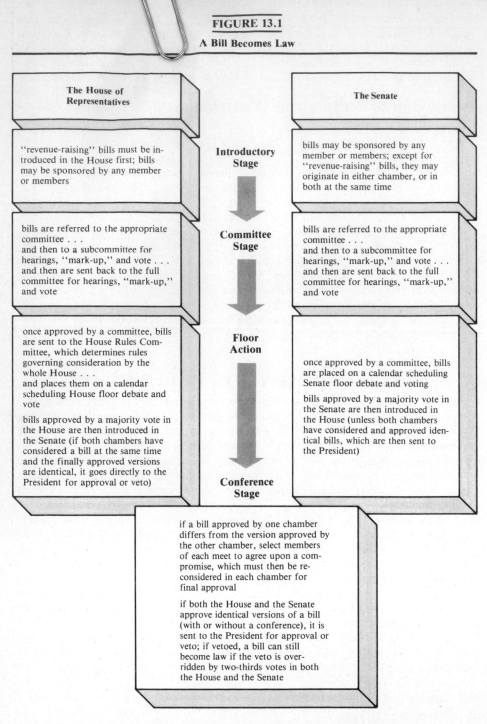

The House of Representatives

The Senate

Introductory Stage

"revenue-raising" bills must be introduced in the House first; bills may be sponsored by any member or members

bills may be sponsored by any member or members; except for "revenue-raising" bills, they may originate in either chamber, or in both at the same time

Committee Stage

bills are referred to the appropriate committee . . .
and then to a subcommittee for hearings, "mark-up," and vote . . .
and then are sent back to the full committee for hearings, "mark-up," and vote

bills are referred to the appropriate committee . . .
and then to a subcommittee for hearings, "mark-up," and vote . . .
and then are sent back to the full committee for hearings, "mark-up," and vote

Floor Action

once approved by a committee, bills are sent to the House Rules Committee, which determines rules governing consideration by the whole House . . .
and places them on a calendar scheduling House floor debate and vote

bills approved by a majority vote in the House are then introduced in the Senate (if both chambers have considered a bill at the same time and the finally approved versions are identical, it goes directly to the President for approval or veto)

once approved by a committee, bills are placed on a calendar scheduling Senate floor debate and voting

bills approved by a majority vote in the Senate are then introduced in the House (unless both chambers have considered and approved identical bills, which are then sent to the President)

Conference Stage

if a bill approved by one chamber differs from the version approved by the other chamber, select members of each meet to agree upon a compromise, which must then be reconsidered in each chamber for final approval

if both the House and the Senate approve identical versions of a bill (with or without a conference), it is sent to the President for approval or veto; if vetoed, a bill can still become law if the veto is overridden by two-thirds votes in both the House and the Senate

Source: Fred Harris, *America's Democracy* (Glenview, Ill.: Scott, Foresman, 1980), p. 368.

for example, goes on the *Private Calendar.* A "calendar" is a schedule of House business. Different calendars list different kinds of bills and are considered at different times. Bills on the Private Calendar, for example, are considered on the first Tuesday of each month and, at the Speaker's discretion, may also be considered on the third Tuesday of the month.

Bills which raise or lower revenue (taxation measures) must be passed first in the House rather than in the Senate (Article I, Section 7, U.S. Constitution), and they are placed on the *Union Calendar* in the House, as are all bills that involve the expenditure of money. Other important bills are placed on the *House Calendar.* District of Columbia legislation is considered on special days each month.

Less important and noncontroversial legislation which normally would be considered on one of the above calendars may be expedited through the House on the *Consent Calendar* at the request of the sponsor (the member who introduced the legislation). Consent Calendar bills go through with minimal debate, but must be on the calendar for three days before being voted on. If one member objects to passage, the bill must be delayed and considered again the next time Consent Calendar business is taken up. If there are three or more objections at the second occasion, the bill is removed from the Consent Calendar. This may kill the bill because it may not be important enough to merit priority on one of the major calendars of the House.

Each party appoints three official "objectors" to screen legislation on the Consent Calendar. Bill sponsors are well advised to contact the objectors a day or two before their measure comes before the House, lest an unanswered question cause an objection to be raised. A different set of objectors is appointed by party leaders to screen private bills, which must be on the Private Calendar seven days before consideration on the floor. Two or more objections are sufficient to send a Private Calendar bill back to committee. Such bills normally then reappear in an "omnibus bill" with other private legislation, and the package is then voted on like other legislation.[20]

Legislation may also be expedited through the House on specified days by "suspension of the rules," a motion which may be made by any member. The motion requires a two-thirds vote for passage. The Speaker has control over measures to be considered under suspension of the rules because of his absolute right to recognize or refuse to recognize members on the floor. Until recognized (called on) by the Speaker, members cannot move suspension of the rules. Thus, any such effort to expedite passage of a bill must be made with the blessing of the Speaker. Debate on such measures is limited, and amendments are forbidden. The suspension-of-the-rules device originally was used to expedite relatively noncontroversial measures, and suspension motions normally passed without difficulty. In the Ninety-fifth Congress, however, some members began voting "no" out of annoyance at what they perceived to be abuse of the procedure, and suspension motions began to fail. Since then, the Democratic caucus has set guidelines for Democratic Speakers to follow concerning the suspension-of-the-rules procedure—another case of formal rules being established when members perceived a norm was being violated.[21]

The House Rules Committee   Most measures placed on the calendars of the House must receive a "rule" from the House Rules Committee before they may be considered on the floor of the House. Exceptions are the Appropriations Committee's general appropriations measures, the Budget Committee's budget resolutions, various housekeeping measures from the House Administration Committee, revenue-raising bills from the House Ways and Means Committee, and resolutions from the Committee on Standards of Official Conduct (Ethics), recommending action against a House member or employee. These exceptions to the Rules Committee's authority are referred to as "privileged" measures. Often, however, a committee *prefers* to seek a rule—usually a closed rule—to insure that the committee's version of a bill will not be amended on the floor. The Ways and Means Committee, for example, prefers closed rules on tax bills. Such an approach obviously enhances the committee's power over tax legislation.

The Rules Committee performs a "traffic cop" function of structuring the flow of legislation. After a measure has been granted a rule, the decision about when to bring it to the floor is still up to the majority-party leadership. In practice, of course, the Rules Committee is not a neutral traffic cop, since political philosophy enters into its decisions. The Rules Committee may negotiate substantive changes in the legislation as it is reported from the various committees of the House in exchange for a rule permitting the bill to go forward to the floor of the chamber. A bill may be blocked by the Rules Committee's refusal to schedule a hearing on a committee's request for a rule, or by the Rules Committee's refusal to grant a rule after a hearing is held. Before the reforms of the 1970s made the Rules Committee responsive to the wishes of the Speaker, the committee was a major hurdle—often a fatal one—for liberal legislation, especially civil-rights legislation.[22] It is still an important step in the process of legislative consideration because the Speaker does not have the time to supervise the committee's every action. Each rule must itself receive a majority vote of the chamber membership, but only very rarely is a proposed rule rejected on the floor.

In addition to permitting a bill to proceed to the floor of the House, the rule granted each measure also stipulates the terms under which a bill or resolution will be considered on the floor. The rule sets the amount of time provided for debate on the measure and which members will be in charge of alloting time in support or opposition; whether or not the measure may be amended on the floor (or, perhaps, what *parts* of the measure are subject to amendment); and whether certain "points of order" (parliamentary objections) against the measure will be waived. An "open rule" permits extensive but germane amendment on the floor of the House. A "closed rule" may forbid all amendments. A "modified closed rule" permits only amendments that are accepted by the committee which considered the legislation. Under a closed rule, House members not on the original committee must accept the committee version of a bill as it stands or reject it entirely. One study found that, from 1939 to 1960, closed rules were granted less than 8 percent of the time, and then only on bills that were unusually complex, especially subject to log rolling on the floor, or on taxation and appropriation measures.[23] Clearly, however, the Rules Committee's power to control the flow of bills to the floor of the House and to establish the terms of consideration of legislation by the entire chamber is a substantial grant of authority, and one which is not paralleled in the U.S. Senate.

In addition to dominating the flow of legislation from House committees to the House floor, the Rules Committee sometimes helps House members avoid voting on "no-win" measures. It can do this by denying a rule and taking the heat itself, thus preventing the measure from reaching the floor. Such situations tend to arise when members perceive that whichever way they vote on a measure, an intense and powerful constituency group will be made angry.[24] The fact that those sitting on the Rules Committee tend to be members from safe constituencies buffers them from the so-called "hot" issues.

The Democratic caucus of the House of Representatives changed its rules in 1973 to give the caucus authority to intervene, on request of fifty Democratic representatives, if a committee asks for a closed rule or a modified closed rule. By majority vote, the caucus can instruct the Democratic members of the Rules Committee to issue a rule permitting particular amendments to be introduced during floor debate on the bill. As long as Democrats are in the majority in the House, of course, they will hold a majority on the Rules Committee.

The new Democratic caucus rule, while directed at the Rules Committee, is especially useful in restricting the authority of the House Ways and Means Committee over taxation legislation. That committee had been able to obtain a closed rule almost routinely to avoid floor amendments to tax legislation. Many liberals felt that business and conservative interests dominated the Ways and Means Committee and that being able to amend tax legislation on the House floor would have an important balancing effect. An early indicator of the importance of the new rule was its use, over Ways and Means Committee objections, to amend the Tax Reduction Act of 1975 on the floor of the House to repeal the oil-depletion allowance from the federal tax code.[25]

Forcing a Bill from Committee   The strength of the committee system in the U.S. House of Representatives is buttressed by the rules of the House which make it very difficult to force a committee to release a bill against the committee's will. One way around a committee is to suspend the rules (as discussed earlier) by a two-thirds vote. For minor legislation which may be stalled in committee because of more pressing concerns, such an approach might work, if the Speaker supported the action.

The better-known procedure for discharging a committee of its responsibility for considering a measure is the use of a discharge petition, which requires the signatures of half the House membership. A discharge petition can be used to wrest a bill from any committee of the House, including the Rules Committee, but it seldom actually does more than focus attention on the issue in question. As House Majority Leader Jim Wright colorfully explains it:

> As a practical matter, however, successful discharge petitions are almost as rare as whooping cranes. During seventeen years in the House, I've seen only two bills brought to the House floor and passed as a direct result of a discharge petition, and one of these later was killed in the Senate. But sometimes the threat of a successful petition will cause an unfavorable committee reluctantly to schedule hearings and bring a bill to the membership when it becomes apparent that most of their colleagues want the chance to vote on it.[26]

One reason discharge petitions are not more successful is that the discharge-petition process violates the House norm of giving proper consideration to the wishes of the experts on the relevant committee (especially for complex or highly technical legislation) and appears to be an attack on the committee system itself. If one committee's authority can be undermined, then so can the committee on which each member serves. And if a member's committee has little authority, then the member has little authority in the 435-member House. Despite the rarity of outright success on discharge petitions, the availability of the process as a mechanism for wresting a bill from a committee does provide the House with the assurance that it need not be helpless if the membership as a whole wants to act and the particular committee with legislative jurisdiction disagrees.

A House committee which wishes to get its nonprivileged legislation to the floor of the House, over the objections of the Rules Committee, can attempt to do so by means of the seldom-used *Calendar Wednesday* mechanism. The House rules provide that, unless the House decides otherwise by unanimous consent (as it usually does) or by a two-thirds vote, the Speaker, each Wednesday, must call on the standing committees of the House in alphabetical order to permit them to bring to the floor measures on the House Calendar or Union Calendar that have not received a rule from the Rules Committee. Limitations on the time permitted for each measure and the opportunities available for opponents to prevent action usually make Calendar Wednesday impractical as a mechanism for bypassing the Rules Committee. Nor are committees that are low in the alphabet likely to get much benefit from the procedure. Calendar Wednesday procedure has been used successfully only twice, the last time in 1960.

Scheduling Legislation in the U.S. Senate

The Senate is a much smaller body than the House and the number of members affects the manner in which legislative business is scheduled. Representatives have busy schedules, but a senator's days are even more crowded, both because most senators have larger and more diverse constituencies than representatives and because senators serve on more committees and subcommittees than representatives do. Because of the many demands on senators, it is the practice of the Senate to be flexible in scheduling legislation for the floor. Within limits, senators can normally obtain changes in the Senate schedule to accommodate their personal schedules. The Senate schedule tends to be flexible, personal, and, in practice, less rigidly in line with the formal rules than is the case in the House.

The Senate seldom resorts to the formal use of its complex rules for bringing bills to the floor. Instead, what most frequently occurs is that legislation and resolutions are considered under "unanimous consent" agreements (unanimous consent of all senators on the floor to set aside the rules) ordinarily obtained before legislation is brought to the floor.

Despite the informal nature of Senate scheduling, there are two formal calendars of business. The *Executive Calendar* is for all Senate activity concerning executive appointments of various kinds and treaties (Article II, Section 2, U.S. Constitution). All other business goes on the *Calendar of General Orders.* The Senate has no roadblock, between Senate committee action and the Senate floor, analogous to the House requirement of obtaining a rule from the House Rules Committee. With the unanimous consent of those present, and with careful consultation between the majority leader and the minority leader, the Senate can shift with ease from the Executive Calendar to the Calendar of General Orders. Unlike the House, the Senate can be brought to a standstill by the determined opposition of a few members. But the Senate and its leaders are also less constrained by formal chamber-scheduling rules.

The scheduling of floor action by the leaders of the Senate is a complex—though informal—process, which requires the leadership to be sensitive to the wishes of the Senate as a whole, as well as to the desires of individual senators. Leaders must keep senators and their staffs well advised of impending action. How does a senator obtain the agreement of opposition senators to permit a vote on a bill? He or she seldom needs to resort to threats, but

> a senator may offer a blocked measure as a nongermane amendment on the floor
> to almost any measure. [Or] a senator can resort to the threat of a filibuster or
> of objection to all unanimous consent requests until the measure is scheduled
> for floor action.[27]

──────────★ ★ ★ ★──────────

Scheduling Business in the Senate

Complex agreements usually set the guidelines for consideration of specific major legislation [by the Senate]. They are proposed orally, usually by the leadership, and are recorded in writing after protracted negotiation among party leaders and key senators. They may establish the sequential order in which measures will be taken up, pinpoint the time period when measures are to reach the floor, and set rules for debate, including a frequent requirement that all amendments must be germane to the bill under consideration. Prior to 1975, most unanimous consent agreements were worked out during floor debate on a measure. They were offered to extricate the Senate from a difficult parliamentary situation. Now such agreements are regularly worked out in advance of floor debate, approved by the Senate, and then transmitted in written form to all senators. . . .

Another device used to move legislation to the floor is of relatively recent origin. The track system was instituted in the early 1970s by Majority Leader Mike Mansfield, with the concurrence of the minority leadership and other senators. It permits the Senate to work on several pieces of legislation simultaneously, by designating specific time periods during the day when each proposal will be considered. The system is particularly beneficial when there are numerous important bills awaiting floor action, or when there is protracted floor conflict over one bill.

Prior to the initiation of the track system, legislative business came to an abrupt halt during filibusters. The "two track system enables the Senate to circumvent that barrier," commented Majority Whip Alan Cranston, D-Calif. The Senate "can now continue to work on all other legislation on one 'track' while a filibuster against a particular piece of legislation is . . . in progress on the other 'track.'"

Source: Walter J. Oleszek, *Congressional Procedures and the Policy Process* (Washington, D.C.: Congressional Quarterly Press, 1978), pp. 138–39, 140.

──────────★ ★ ★ ★──────────

FLOOR PROCEDURES IN CONGRESS

The conduct of business on the floors of the House and Senate is carried out under a complex set of rules that are overlaid with two centuries of tradition and interpretation. Before discussing decision-making, which is affected by many variables, an examination of the rules governing procedures on the floors of Congress is in order.

House Floor Procedures

Many activities take up the mornings of U.S. representatives, including committee meetings, doing "homework" on the issues coming up before a member's committees or the entire House, and dealing with various constituent matters. The House normally convenes at noon, but sometimes restructures its schedule for the convenience of the members and committees. The daily session begins with an opening prayer, receipt of messages from the President or the Senate, and one-minute speeches which are given by members at the beginning of each day's session on whatever topic a member chooses. Some days there are many such brief speeches, other days not.

In the Ninety-sixth Congress (1979–80), the use of the short opening speeches—mainly by Republicans critical of the Democratic majority and the Democratic President—became a controversial issue. The extent of the controversy reflects the importance that a relatively minor rules change can have. Such speeches had caused no equivalent level of partisan controversy in the thirty odd years during which House rules had permitted them, but that was before the House began televising its proceedings in March 1979. An estimated five million Americans watch those TV broadcasts, excerpts of which may also be shown on other news programs.

Because of the individual and partisan benefits of making such speeches in front of the chamber's newly authorized television cameras, the time devoted to the brief commentaries had begun to consume an hour or more of each session, rather than the five-to-ten minutes which had been the norm. The Democratic leadership at one point considered not beginning each day's televised proceedings until after the "special orders" speeches, but withdrew the proposal in the face of strong bipartisan opposition. The majority leader then announced, while presiding, that such speeches could only be given at the *end* of each day's session, rather than at the beginning. The ensuing protests led the Democratic leaders to agree to set aside brief periods, often twenty minutes, for such short speeches at the beginning of each day's session.[28]

Once its opening ceremonies are completed, the House proceeds with the business of the day. Consideration of a bill scheduled for debate begins by House acceptance of the rule for that bill unless the measure under consideration is "privileged." The rule is very seldom defeated by floor vote and, in fact, floor efforts to defeat a rule are efforts to defeat the measure in question because

> the resolution of the Rules Committee [the rule] is not subject to amendment and its outright rejection would almost surely mean that the bill would never come before the House.[29]

That is, the House may not revise the rule; it must accept it or risk not being allowed to debate and vote on the measure in question at all. (Democratic representatives, remember, can use their caucus to influence the type of rule issued on the most important measures.)

The Committee of the Whole House   Next, the House almost always resolves itself into the Committee of the Whole to debate each measure and propose amendments to it (if amendments are permitted under that particular rule). All items on the Union Calendar (money bills and revenue bills) are privileged items but, under House rules, must be taken up in the Committee of the Whole before being voted on formally by the House. At the request of the Appropriations Committee or the Ways and Means Committee, their bills may also be considered under a closed rule or a modified closed rule.

The Committee of the Whole consists of all members of the House. It functions under less formal rules of procedure than the House of Representatives. Until the Legislative Reorganization Act of 1970, votes in the Committee of the Whole were not recorded.[30] Votes taken were either voice votes, with the presiding member determining which side won; or a "division," in which first the members supporting a measure and then the members opposing the measure stand and are counted; or a "teller vote," where members file past appointed tellers who count them as they divide to one side for "yes" and to the other side for "no." Until 1970, any of these types of vote left no record of which way individual members had voted. This enabled members to leave outsiders in the dark about their true sentiments concerning legislation. Some members reportedly voted with special interests in the unrecorded Committee of the Whole, then, for the public record took the opposite position. Such action was occasionally reported by news correspondents, and it lessened the people's faith in the legislative process and in government generally. This kind of behavior now occurs less often because of new rules.

The 1970 changes provided for *recorded* teller votes by requiring members to sign their voting cards and deposit them in ballot boxes. Alternatively, the chamber's relatively new electronic voting machine may be used for a record roll-call vote or to demonstrate the presence of a quorum. The introduction of electronic voting has reduced the time required to conduct a roll-call vote from over half an hour to about a quarter of an hour. This change, of course, gives the floor managers and party leaders less time than before to "arm twist" while the vote is in progress. Members can also enter through a side door, vote at one of the forty-odd voting stations on the floor, and leave before the House leaders or their agents can catch them to try to change their votes. These new leadership disadvantages are partially offset by the immediate information that is provided to the managers of a bill on how each member voted. To obtain a record vote in the Committee of the Whole now requires a demand by 20 members. In contrast, any one member can demand a record vote when the House is sitting as the House of Representatives, although a fifth of those present must sustain the demand if it is challenged.

Proposed legislation can be amended in the Committee of the Whole (unless the legislation is being considered under a closed rule), but can be enacted (passed) only by the House convened as the House of Representatives. The Committee of the Whole cannot enact a bill. Less time is provided for debate on each matter in the Committee of the Whole than in the House, which helps expedite the conduct of business. When the House sits as the Committee of the Whole, the mace, the symbol of authority, is removed from the front of the chamber, to be returned when the Committee of the Whole "rises" and the House of Representatives reconvenes.

The Speaker steps down as presiding officer when the House sits as the Committee of the Whole, appointing another member to serve in that capacity. The quorum necessary for conducting business in the Committee of the Whole is only 100 members, compared to 218 for the House of Representatives. Once a quorum is established, it is assumed to be in existence unless a member obtains recognition from the presiding officer and calls attention to the lack of a quorum. Decisions of the Committee of the Whole can be—and occasionally are—made by vote of only 51 members (less than 12 percent of the total House membership). These decisions frequently turn out to be decisions of the House. After the House reconvenes, amendments rejected in the Committee of the Whole cannot be proposed again on the floor. Amendments which succeed in the Committee of the Whole, however, can be brought up for reconsideration in the House prior to final passage. This rule, of course, increases the likelihood that each bill—even those considered under "open" rules—will be enacted in the form preferred by the standing committee of jurisdiction. That strengthens the standing committee's authority, since members who are most likely to attend a Committee of the Whole are those who sit on the standing committee of jurisdiction and others with an interest in the legislation. Surprises occasionally occur, however, when opponents organize quietly and get an amendment adopted in the Committee of the Whole. But to be able to appeal such amendments to the House is important to the authority of the standing committees, since a strong norm among otherwise disinterested members is to support the committee system and their "experts."

Recent changes in the rules have made voting in the Committee of the Whole more visible. This visibility greatly increases the number of members who come to the Committee of the Whole, thus generally providing a less biased set of decision-makers than formerly was the case. The distortions caused by the committee's modest quorum requirement are thus reduced. The impact of the rules changes in regard to the Committee of the Whole is substantial and complex.

> The provisions of the 1970 [Legislative Reorganization] Act would seem to be advancing the representational and the lawmaking functions of Congress equally. But in reality the victory goes to representation over lawmaking. The great increase in roll-call votes made possible by the new system has led to a situation in which representatives are continually being called out of committee and subcommittee meetings (where the real fashioning of legislation takes place) to take part in roll-call votes on the floor. The dramatic changes produced by the Legislative Reorganization Act of 1970 have served to highlight the underlying conflict between maximizing representation and maximizing lawmaking. Reforms that make it easier to call for recorded votes and that reduce the amount of time needed for such votes inevitably lead to an increase in floor votes, that, under the old system, would have been resolved in committee. Perhaps most important, the floor votes are constantly calling members out of hearings or committee markup sessions to perform their representational commitments on the floor. There is an obvious overlap between the two spheres of action (committees and House floor) and the two functions (representation and lawmaking) but the tension between the two remains.[31]

Despite the reduced bias resulting from the increased number of members voting in the Committee of the Whole, House procedures still permit "irrational" decisions to be made. For example, a measure or section of a bill which might not pass if voted on separately sometimes passes because of the manner in which the voting is conducted in the House or the Committee of the Whole. If a proposed amendment to a section of a bill is defeated, no vote on the original version is ever taken, so it is not certain that the membership would approve that section.[32] Such a rule—again—bolsters the authority of the standing committee in the House, because it gives the benefit of the doubt to the version which came out of committee.

Amendments   Members may have different motivations in regard to amendments to bills. If the bill appears likely to be lost altogether unless there is agreement to an amendment that will make it acceptable to a particular group, some members who really prefer the "pure" bill as reported from committee, may nevertheless vote for the amendment because they prefer "half a loaf to none." But other members may vote against the amendment because they prefer no bill at all to "a fraud on the people." Conversely, opponents of a bill may support a "killer amendment," intended to make the bill so offensive as to ruin its chances for final passage. But members with little interest in the subject may vote one way or another on "saving" or "killing" amendments simply on the basis of their first-order preference—whether they prefer the unamended bill to the amended bill—without consideration of whether they prefer the amended bill (or the unamended bill) to *no* bill at all. That can be rational behavior because of the difficulties involved in predicting subsequent amendments, final passage, action by the other chamber, and conference committee decisions. Legislative leaders and sophisticated legislative strategists, managing a given bill, must weigh the opinions and intensity of interest of the various members (and their advisors) and "play" the chambers accordingly.[33]

One of the skills important to success as a legislator is the ability to draft a bill or an amendment to get what one wants, while maintaining sufficient support to win. Often, that includes folding in items the managers do not really want (or necessarily approve of)—sometimes with the hope of bargaining it away in conference, or sometimes with the expectation that the other chamber will amend the provision out. The dynamics of legislating are complex and hard to control. Effective legislators and legislative leaders must be attuned to subtle indicators and must be able to tolerate decision-making in the face of great uncertainty and in a dynamic, changing environment. It is difficult for descriptions of the process—even post hoc case studies—to convey the uncertainties, excitement, tension, and frustrations often involved in working in such an environment, especially when legislators must keep track of so many bills as to have little time to work through the possibilities inherent in each, yet must be ready to explain—weeks later, if necessary—exactly why they voted the way they did on a particular amendment. And the questioner, back home, often does not have the remotest notion of the complexity of the decision-making environment of the legislators and may be very suspicious of their motives as "politicians."

The general rule in the House is that amendments must be germane. That is, they must be related to the subject of the measure under consideration. Nongermane amendments may be permitted if the rule under which the measure is considered has waived (prevented) points of order against them, or if there is a consensus in favor of a particular amendment.

Certain kinds of amendments are technically germane, but substantially affect government policy beyond the narrow intent of the proposed legislation involved. Aggressively conservative members of the House have managed to use such amendments very effectively in recent Congresses, especially the "limitation rider" on appropriations bills. Such riders have

> "forced the full House to vote on politically sensitive issues. . . . Riders clog the appropriations process. They lead to hours and days of debate on non-fiscal matters that make it virtually impossible for Congress to complete action on money bills before the beginning of the government's fiscal year. . . . Abortion riders have been the most troublesome. The so-called Hyde amendment kept the funds bill for the Departments of Labor and Health, Education and Welfare tied up for two months into the new fiscal year in 1977 and prevented enactment of that bill in 1979. . . . Of the two days of House debate devoted this year [1980] to the Treasury and Postal Service appropriations bill . . . scarcely an hour was given to discussion of money matters. The rest revolved around a string of controversial riders that did such things as prohibit the government purchase of typewriters from communist countries, restrain the IRS from taking tax-exempt status from private "white flight" schools and stop consideration of a withholding tax on interest income. Of the 19 amendments adopted, only one altered the funds appropriated in the bill.[34]

The increased use of controversial limitation riders has led to consideration of ways to restrict their introduction, but such efforts are stymied by the realization that restricting the use of limitation riders will also limit somewhat the ability of Congress—and individual members—to control the various agencies of government.

Debate on a particular measure is strictly limited in the House, as it must be if that large body is to process any legislative business at all. But House debate can make a difference. While observers and members often argue that most members either make up their minds ahead of time or decide on the floor after a quick check with a few knowledgeable members whom they trust, others note that a few words

———————————————— ★ ★ ★ ★ ————————————————

House Appropriations Bill Riders Increasing

The term *rider* generally refers to a provision tacked onto a bill that is not germane, or pertinent, to the bill's purpose. . . .

They are commonly used in the Senate, where non-germane amendments are considered fair play. House rules prohibit non-germane amendments on most bills, but avenues around those rules are well-traveled.

Riders often have been used to slip legislation past a hostile president by hitching it to a more favored bill. . . . Riders are sometimes offered on the Senate or House floor in order to bypass unsympathetic committees. That was the technique used by Senate Majority Leader Lyndon B. Johnson in 1960 to call up his civil rights bill. Johnson offered the bill as an amendment to an obscure piece of legislation aiding a federally impacted school district in Missouri. . . .

House members can waive their rule against non-germane provisions and as a result have, like the Senate, often created some strange legislative bedfellows. A bill passed by the House this year under suspension of the rules . . . simultaneously set new nutritional requirements for infant formulas and increased federal penalties for marijuana trafficking. . . .

Riders on appropriations bills are a special breed.

Limitation riders, which merely restrict the use of funds appropriated by the bill, are technically considered germane and therefore are permissible in both the House and Senate. These riders do not actually change existing law, but they often have the effect of legislation.

Legislative riders, which change existing law or put new duties on government agencies, are for the most part not allowed on money bills under the rules of either chamber. The rules, however, may be waived with unanimous consent or a two-thirds vote of the members.

. . . House members have offered a record high number of riders to appropriations bills this year [67 through September 26, 1980], and 75 percent of those offered were adopted.

The floor amendments dealt with a wide variety of social issues and regulatory practices. They [proposed prohibiting] abortion and busing, [exempting] the hostages in Iran from income taxes, [calling] a halt to the decennial reapportionment of House seats, [prohibiting] a withholding tax on interest and dividend income, and much more. [From 1963 through 1976, no more than 33 such limitation riders had been offered in a calendar year and no more than 15 had been adopted.]

Source: *Congressional Quarterly Weekly Report,* November 1, 1980, pp. 3252, 3253.

———————————————— ★ ★ ★ ★ ————————————————

by a recognized expert or a strong endorsement by a respected leader can frequently sway votes—and that may be sufficient on a close vote. An impassioned plea by a member who "talks at the drop of a hat," however, is unlikely even to be listened to by undecided members who are busy getting an opinion from someone they trust. Members seek little explanation of an amendment by a recognized "far out" liberal or conservative.

For each measure before the House, a "floor manager" is appointed, most often the chairperson or ranking minority member of the standing committee or subcommittee that reported the measure. The increased practice of appointing the chairperson or ranking member of a *sub*committee as floor manager in recent years—rather than the automatic appointment of the chairperson or ranking member of the *full* committee—is another recognition of the growing decentralization of authority in the House. The floor manager for a bill, or for opposition to a bill, is responsible for legislative strategy; for advising other members on the merits or flaws of the measure; for accepting "friendly amendments" (in the case of the supporting floor manager) or resisting (or proposing, for the opposition floor manager) unfriendly amendments. They work with their respective House party leaders and allocate their side's debate time among members with whom they agree about the measure. Skillful floor managers often determine the outcome on a measure, and the development of a reputation as a skillful parliamentarian greatly enhances a legislator's reputation in the chamber. Such a reputation is usually important if the legislator has any aspirations to a chamber leadership post.

Despite House rules intended to expedite business, opponents of a measure can obstruct and delay:

> Members may raise numerous points of order, make scores of parliamentary inquiries, or offer trivial amendments. They may demand record votes on every amendment, ask unanimous consent to speak additional minutes on each amendment, make certain that all time for general debate is used, or, if the chair declares amendments nongermane, appeal the ruling and demand record votes on each appeal.[35]

Proponents of a measure may delay action while finding the additional votes needed to win (cooperation of the majority leader and Speaker is especially helpful when this is done). Opponents may seek to delay a bill long enough so that supporters will give up. Obstructionism can be especially effective if a measure has a narrow majority and many of its supporters are not intense in their support. It is even more effective as the end of a Congress approaches.

Senate Floor Procedures

Many of the differences between the rules of procedure on the floor of the House and those in the Senate result largely from the fact that there are only 100 senators, compared to 435 representatives.[36] Thus, the Senate can have a rule like "unlimited debate," subject to the invocation of "cloture," a motion to shut off debate. Such an unlimited debate rule would paralyze the House—both because there are more House members, each of whom wants to speak, and because it would be much easier to find a hard-core group of ten or twenty members to mount a lengthy filibuster (extended debate).

As in the House, legislative strategists use the rules as best they can to win, and the rules are not neutral.

> [T]he rules clearly affect the distribution of power. . . . Senate procedures build the fragmentation which characterizes the chamber permanently into the system. The rules protect the power base of the committees and they enhance the position of the minorities (on any given question). The advantage lies with those who are opposed to change; victory at any of the multiple veto points kills a bill. To pass, legislation must move over all the hurdles successfully, and proponents must mobilize their strength at each stage of the process if they are to prevail.[37]

The Senate normally convenes at noon. Sometimes to accommodate the membership or the workload, a unanimous consent request of the leadership requires an earlier or later hour to convene. First comes a prayer, followed by the reading of the previous day's *Journal.* The reading of the *Journal* normally is waived by unanimous consent, unless senators who seek to delay action on some matter insist that it be read.[38] The numerous opportunities for delay presented by the beginning of a new legislative day are so great that when a determined minority is conducting a filibuster, the proponents of the bill under attack attempt to recess each night rather than adjourn. Adjournment is mandatory if a quorum is not present, but recessing at the end of each day means that, even though calendar days pass, the Senate remains in the same "legislative day" until it adjourns. After that, the legislative day and the calendar day again become the same. When the Senate returns after recessing, it resumes consideration of the unfinished business without going through the opening stages, and can thereby avoid new opportunities for the minority to obstruct.

Following the prayer and the (usually waived) reading of the *Journal,* the Senate normally enters the "morning hour" (which usually exceeds an hour in length), during which messages from the House and the executive branch are received, measures are introduced and referred to committee, and committee reports are presented. Senators are then permitted to make brief speeches (or insert them in the *Congressional Record*) on whatever topics they wish, following which the Senate takes up unfinished legislative business from the previous day or begins new business.

Many bills are taken up under unanimous consent agreements (discussed earlier), but senators who are opposed to a particular bill may object to its being brought up and may engage in extended debate to prevent the bill's consideration. Such procedural obstruction can continue at great length throughout the Senate's consideration of the bill. Sometimes the senators obstructing a bill really hope to kill it; on other occasions, they may be seeking certain concessions; and sometimes they may just be seeking to make a point, call public attention to a problem, or gain favorable publicity back home. In these instances, extended debate may just last long enough to claim the desired media attention. Serious opponents of a measure conscientiously keep track of the presence or absence of a quorum on the floor (fifty-one senators) and call the lack of a quorum to the attention of the Senate. Such a tactic requires senators supporting the measure to remain near the floor—an annoying and often disrupting situation—and it can consume the Senate's time through numerous quorum calls. Senators opposing a measure sometimes do not answer the quorum call, in hopes of forcing an adjournment for lack of a quorum, leaving them the opportunity for further delay at the beginning of the next legislative day.

Senate quorum calls and roll-call votes are *not* conducted by teller voting or electronic devices. Rather, senators call out their "yes" or "no" votes when their names are called. The Senate sometimes uses voice votes and division, which are similar to the House procedures. But any eleven senators can force a roll-call vote.

Most measures are considered under unanimous consent agreements and most go through rather quickly after they reach the floor. Often, business is conducted with much less than a quorum actually in attendance on the floor, although senators come quickly to the floor to vote when the final vote warning is sounded.

As in the House, each measure has a floor manager whose duties are similar to the House counterpart, including insuring that the measure's supporters are there to vote. Unlike the House, however, the Senate, by unanimous consent, ordinarily permits the floor manager to be accompanied on the floor of the Senate by staff assistants. As in the House, the skill of the floor manager in parliamentary tactics, in sensing the mood of the chamber, in working out compromises that will finesse serious opposition, and in knowing when compromise is *not* necessary has much to do with a measure's success or failure on the floor.

A bill which has serious opposition in the Senate will not receive unanimous consent for its consideration. Rather, Senate opponents will take advantage of every delaying tactic the rules permit, and, in the Senate, the rules permit quite a few. A filibuster can occur on the motion to consider a bill, as well as on a vote on the measure itself or on an amendment to it. For years, the filibuster was synonymous with southern objection to federal civil-rights legislation. But filibusters have also been conducted in the last decade against campaign-finance legislation, various military bills, natural-gas price deregulation, and two Supreme Court nominations. The objective of a filibuster may be to wring concessions from the majority or to force the legislative matter in question to be withdrawn. Filibusters are most effective when a session of Congress is approaching an end, but they can be effective at other times as well. Even the implicit threat of a filibuster can often result in significant concessions from a measure's supporters.

The principle of unlimited debate has existed in the U.S. Senate from the earliest days of that body. Because of the filibuster, the Senate has been defended as the bastion of protection for the minority. But, of course, the filibuster protects only those beleagured interests which happen to find sufficient numbers of champions in the U.S. Senate, and it works primarily in defense of the status quo. A filibuster can be curtailed by the invocation of cloture, a resolution to bring an end to debate on a measure. Until 1975, a two-thirds vote of those present and voting in the Senate was required to invoke cloture. That year, the rules of the Senate were changed to permit cloture to be imposed if 60 percent (three fifths) of *all* senators so voted. The effort to make that rule change had itself to overcome a filibuster under the old rules, but today:

> Two days after a cloture petition is filed, the vote is held on ending the filibuster. If a minimum of 60% vote is attained, the time of each senator is limited for further debate to one hour. But upon the failure of a cloture vote, the majority leaders in the 1960s and 1970s have promptly filed a second petition, and even a third. If on the third try, they still cannot get a 60% vote, then the bill at issue is withdrawn and the Senate goes on to other bills. . . .
>
> [From] 1917–1960, 23 cloture petitions were filed to stop filibusters, of which only four (or 17%) were successful. In the 1961–75 period the use of cloture petitions, and their success, increased markedly: 80 petitions were filed, of which 20 (25%) were successful. . . . In the period beginning with 1975, the number of cloture petitions and their success rate greatly increased.[39]

Of the twenty-four attempts to invoke cloture in 1975 and 1976, for example, fourteen (58.3 percent!) were successful.[40] The power of the filibuster was substantially reduced by a seemingly modest change—reducing the requirement for cloture from two thirds of those present and voting to three fifths of all senators. After cloture is voted, Senate rules call for a vote on the measure after no more than 100 hours of additional debate.

The institution of a "two-track system" in the early 1970s by former Majority Leader Mike Mansfield (D., Montana) reduced the overall impact on the Senate of a filibuster. Under this practice, rather than bring all its business to a halt, the Senate can continue to work on other business during those hours not devoted to the track on which the filibuster is taking place. To that extent, of course, the pressure on the rest of the Senate to yield to the minority conducting the filibuster is not as great. Here again, a relatively minor change in the rules—in the name of "efficiency"—has had a substantial effect on the distribution of power in the Senate. Still, the ability to delay a bill almost indefinitely and to consume the Senate's time and energies places an intense minority of the Senate in a strong bargaining position. Oddly enough, actually conducting a filibuster sometimes appears to be less effective than just threatening one, in a circumstance where the threat is credible. This appears to have been the case, for example, in the maneuvering over the provisions of the Civil Rights Act of 1957.[41]

VOTING DECISIONS IN CONGRESS

Members of Congress cast hundreds of record votes on the floor each year, even more unrecorded votes, and numerous more votes in committee. Members cannot personally examine each issue in advance and develop the level of expertise to make a truly independent, intelligent decision, except possibly for issues coming before their own committees or involving their own constituencies. Thus, senators and representatives must choose which votes merit their careful consideration and which will receive cursory attention—with voting decisions on the latter guided mainly by advice from others.

The Influence Dynamic

Actors seeking to influence a legislator's voting decisions can be generally classified as constituents, other members, executive-branch personnel, legislative staff employees, party leaders (especially legislative chamber leaders), and interest groups— although not all of these attempt to influence every voting decision. One would not expect each legislator to be attuned to the same source or sources of information and advice on every vote. The available evidence is that indeed different types of votes attune the legislator differently to the array of actors seeking to influence his or her vote. Thus, when voting on farm legislation, urban Representative Smith may depend greatly on advice from his legislative assistant and from a home-state colleague who is a member of the Agriculture Committee. But on defense issues he may be most attuned to an assistant secretary of defense who is a good friend and, on certain votes, to key constituents in the defense-contracting business. On issues concerning the elderly, on the other hand, he does his own research both because of his committee assignments and because of his personal interest and knowledge.[42]

The influence dynamic is complex and not easily sorted out. For example, a member's vote may be the object of an intense but indirect lobbying campaign, yet the member may honestly report to a researcher that he or she was "not lobbied at all" on a particular vote. As Donald R. Matthews explains:

> If the lobbyist and senator are in general agreement, the senator is unlikely to think of him as a lobbyist or to feel his efforts at influence as "pressure." But when a lobbyist tries to persuade or coerce a senator toward action that the senator does not relish, the psychological atmosphere is very different—the senator is likely to feel "lobbied" or "pressured."[43]

The political party affiliation of U.S. representatives and senators statistically "predicts" most voting on some dimensions of policy (such as government management of the economy, agricultural assistance, and social welfare), while being much less closely related to voting on other issue dimensions (such as international involvement and civil liberties.) The relationship is not simple and is not necessarily causal.[44] Certainly, a high degree of party-label relationship to voting patterns on particular issues is not by itself evidence that the party leaders in the legislative chamber "controlled" a member's vote. The same result, for example, might well come about if each member's *constituency* demands dominated his or her voting decisions. Yet, a member's party affiliation and the party's philosophical or ideological stance on a general issue field, as well as the legislative party's position on a particular bill or amendment, clearly is an important and powerful influence on a member's voting decisions.

Not to be ignored, either, is the large degree of independence members have on most votes. Members usually seek office, after all, because they feel strongly about certain issues. Their issue positions and party affiliation are correlated, of course—with most members of the two legislative parties aligning on opposite sides of certain issues—but that is not evidence of a lack of "free will" among legislators. Indeed, as one astute student of the factors affecting the way members of Congress decide to vote observes:

> Most congressmen occupy seats that are virtually sinecures. . . . Their political organizations are personal pieces of political property on which reliance may be placed in repeated elections. These organizations will certainly involve interest groups on whom the congressman is at least partially dependent and with whom he is probably in sympathy, such as a labor union in an industrial district. Other interest groups must *go to* the congressman and win his favor to the point of getting a hearing. As his incumbency becomes well-established, however, the congressman becomes more independent of even his most consistent backers, for they need him as much as, or more than, he needs them. On the other hand, the congressman is probably sufficiently sympathetic to the views of those groups who most consistently support him that his own policy preferences will seldom be the cause of a falling-out.[45]

Further, as discussed in Chapter 6, if an observer wishes to determine the extent of constituency influence over a legislator's voting decisions, the observer must remember Fenno's conclusion that a constituency is not a homogeneous entity and Dexter's conclusion that, within rather broad limits, a legislator has substantial freedom to vote as he or she pleases.[46] Legislators create their own coalitions within their districts and, as a result, they have their own perspectives of that constituency. An observer must be careful to view a particular constituency in the same way the legislator views it, in order to determine the extent to which "the constituency" affects a voting decision. Also, a representative may sometimes vote to protect the interests of his or her state or region rather than just the interests of the district.

Voting Cues

Because a legislator cannot know ahead of time how various votes will be reported in the press, whether a vote will be by roll call or by voice, or just how the vote on a particular issue will be structured, the legislator normally does relatively little advance preparation or research, unless the issue concerns his or her own committees or constituency. In fact, some votes come with virtually no advance notice, as amendments are voted on, although there are now procedures that encourage members to publish their proposed amendments a day in advance.

When a vote is imminent, a member of Congress seeks information on which to base a decision and relies heavily on voting cues from colleagues. Reliance on others is most extensive when the member's own committee did not consider the bill, and it is not of special concern to his or her constituency, state, or region. The information the member needs for a decision on how to vote

> must be digested . . . compressed to the point that it can be managed within the time and cognitive capabilities of the congressman. . . . Second, their information should be politically relevant. A congressman needs to know, not only what the policy consequences of given votes will be, but also what the political consequences will be, either in terms of effects in his constituency or in terms of the reward structure within the House. . . . Third, useful information is explicitly evaluative . . . because evaluative information is of necessity directly focused on the issue at hand, and is thus largely devoid of irrelevant arguments and facts.

> These kinds of requirements for useful information help to explain why certain sources are relied upon as extensively as they are. In particular, fellow congressmen tend to meet these criteria admirably. Sensitive to their colleagues' information needs, they do digest information well, take political consequences into account, and explicitly evaluate or urge their positions on others.[47]

Many members of Congress argue that no particular vote is likely to make much difference in their careers. They are aware that, except for salient, emotionally charged issues, such as busing or prayers in the schools, few constituents are aware of how members voted on any specific issue. Many members, though, do believe that their constituents "have a fairly accurate composite image" of their voting records.

> I think perhaps instead of getting called on one particular vote you establish a reputation or maybe an image based on your attitude toward a number of votes.[48]

It *is* important, however, to have a fairly high percentage of answering roll calls.

> An articulate congressman can usually explain his position on an issue to the satisfaction of most constituents, but the charge of missing an important vote (and thereby failing to represent his district) is embarrassing and dangerous. Random or irrational voting may be politically safer than missing votes.[49]

Members who have been reelected a number of times reasonably conclude that their constituents approve of their voting record or "composite image," and they are cautious when it comes to changing their position on a particular issue or set of issues. Further, their past decisions on various issues tend to lead them back to the same sources of information, reinforcing previous behavior. Given the limited time for reflection or research on a large number of voting decisions, a member may quite rationally vote in accordance with past positions on issues.[50]

The stability of a member's voting positions seems to satisfy the *attentive* constituents. Too, there is roll-call evidence from voting patterns in the late 1960s and early 1970s that suggests that, given sufficient public arousal, "members of Congress do respond to societal demands."[51] Members are cautious about making basic changes in their voting decisions on major issues, and "the change that does occur tends to be gradual rather than dramatic."[52]

Many legislators feel that while their staff members are valuable assistants, they may not be as politically sensitive as other members of Congress. Therefore, with large numbers of votes to be cast on complicated legislation involving complex issues, and with limited time to do the research personally, a legislator may look for guidance from his or her colleagues. The fact that all members must face the electorate gives them an experience in common and a psychological sense of group identity. A legislator learns fairly quickly which members share his or her philosophy.

> Referring to the judgement of their cue-givers, members repeatedly asserted that, "I know them well enough that I would probably come out at about the same point they do." . . . When issues are too difficult and numerous for independent evaluation, cues from sources of known performance are likely to carry great weight.
>
> Members, unlike outside cue sources, are usually present at the time of voting decision on the floor. . . . Briefings on the Floor, behind the Rail, and in the Cloakrooms may figure more proximately in many decisions than weeks of committee hearings and hours of debate.
>
> Finally, the member is part of an ongoing social subsystem, one that will continue after the issue of the day is forgotten. The member who wishes to remain in good standing in that subsystem is accountable for his advice. Few issues are important enough to risk practicing deception on colleagues, and the potential cue-taker is secure in that knowledge when he selects another member as his source of evaluation.[53]

This discussion is not arguing that party leadership, interest-group activity, administrative desires, staff advice, or personal reading and research by each member have no impact on voting decisions. In fact, they matter a great deal. But there is little time for personal research, and the impact of the other sources of influence usually is indirect. When a carefully selected sample of U.S. representatives was asked about the factors which had influenced their voting decisions on various issues (soon after the votes were taken) and how much influence each factor had over the member's decision about how to vote,

> the two actors most in the minds of congressmen as they decide are fellow congressmen and constituencies, with interest groups and administration coming next.[54]

Constituency and fellow members of Congress were mentioned most often spontaneously in interviews with the members and were credited with influence by most other members when they were asked about them (see Table 13.1).[55]

Table 13.1
Importance of Various Information Sources to Congresspersons

Importance	Constit-uency	Fellow Congressmen	Party Leadership	Interest Groups	Adminis-tration	Staff	Reading
Determinative	7%	5%	0%	1%	4%	1%	0%
Major Importance	31	42	5	25	14	8	17
Minor Importance	51	28	32	40	21	26	32
Not Important	12	25	63	35	61	66	52
Total %	101%	100%	100%	101%	100%	101%	101%
Total n	222	221	222	222	222	221	221

Source: John W. Kingdon, *Congressmen's Voting Decisions* (New York: Harper and Row, 1973), p. 19.

The impact of information from outside sources (other than other members) often is filtered through the "experts" within the chamber. On each legislative proposal brought before Congress, relevant information and arguments are provided by interest groups, committee staff, and executive-agency personnel. Those arguments focus primarily on the members of the subcommittee that considers the legislation and on the full committee members, as well as on the party leaders in the chamber if the issue is a major one. At other times, the chamber party leaders simply accept the information provided by the committee leaders (or top executive-agency personnel) without further research on their own. Members of the relevant subcommittee or committee transmit outside information, usually in abbreviated form, both to fellow members directly and to intermediaries such as the Democratic Study Group or party leaders. These intermediate cue-givers also provide cues to fellow members. Obviously, this description of cue-giving is incomplete, focusing on main pathways. Some members of Congress who are not on the relevant committee or subcommittee are likely to be closely associated with interest groups or constituents with strong feelings about many measures coming before the chamber. These members not only receive information directly from the interest group or other outside sources but are also likely to function as cue-givers, at least for a few fellow members. But the main path of influence from the outside does seem to be through the recognized experts within the chamber.[56] Obviously, a member who is a cue-giver on one vote is likely to be a cue-taker on the next vote, on which he or she is less well informed. Cues are important on issues on which a member is not well versed, primarily because those issues are not of great concern to the constituents and are not within the jurisdiction of the member's committee.

Not all members of Congress go to the same cue-giver. The "experts" on the relevant committee often disagree on what constitutes preferred policy, because of disagreement either on ends or on the impact or effectiveness of various alternative means. Thus, a member might well be persuaded to vote "yes" if he or she chooses to seek advice from one colleague, but might wind up voting "no," if he or she first consults with another colleague of a different mind. The choice of whom to consult is based on a number of factors, including personal friendship, state represented, party affiliation of the cue-seeker and possible cue-givers, and the reputations of possible cue-givers as conservative or liberal on the issues involved in the upcoming vote.[57] That the expert is from the legislator's own state or region can add confidence to a member's belief that he or she would be likely to arrive at the same policy position as the cue-giver were the member to assess all the facts from the perspective of his or her own constituency.

Figure 13.2 is a model approximating the series of decisions each member makes on each vote in the House. Most votes are readily resolved at Step A or Step B. They are either noncontroversial or all of the member's cue-givers agree, so the member goes along with the committee, state delegation, and party ("the environment") and votes accordingly, with minimal effort to gain information. If the various cue-givers upon which the member depends disagree (Step B), then the member must give the matter a bit more consideration. If the vote is important to the member's goals—either personal ideological goals or constituency related legislative goals— then the member must decide what cues to follow (Steps C-1 through C-6). The member's choice of cue-givers depends on the salience of the issue and the actions of others. If the vote is not especially important to the member's own goals, he or she normally votes according to the cues provided by like-minded colleagues who are thought to be experts on the subject, or by party leaders.[58]

FIGURE 13.2

An Integrative Model of Legislative Voting Decisions

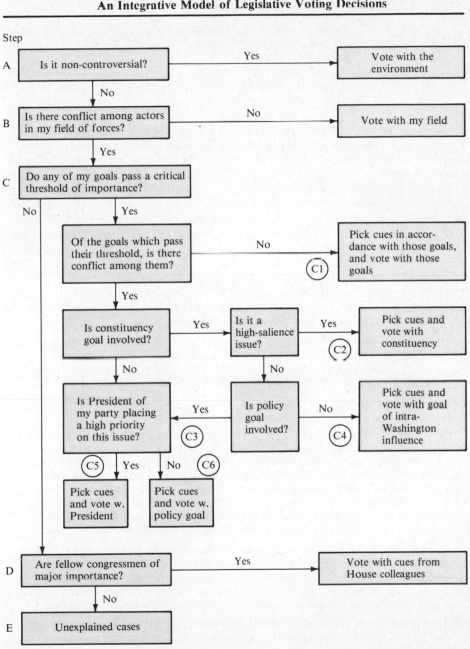

Source: John W. Kingdon, "Models of Legislative Voting," *Journal of Politics* 39 (August 1977): 575.

STATE LEGISLATURES

State Legislative Norms

In many respects, the norms operating in American state legislatures are similar to those in Congress. A major study of four state legislatures conducted in the late 1950s, for example, found that almost all of the 500 state legislators interviewed were able to respond quickly and insightfully when asked about norms in the state legislature. "Of all respondents, only two perceived no rules of the game; over half readily named at least four rules (the median number of rules named being 3.14)."[59]

The most frequently mentioned norm in three of the four states (it was third most frequent in Tennessee) was "a rule requiring from all members *performance of obligations* which they may specifically take on, for whatever reasons, in the course of their legislative activities."[60] This rule was not on a check list, remember. The importance of a legislator keeping his or her word was mentioned by legislators in response to an open-ended question. The emphasis placed on different norms in the four state legislatures varied somewhat, but there was substantial agreement on the importance of norms which sound remarkably like those Matthews found in the U.S. Senate. This is the case, as well, in Oklahoma (1973), Texas (1981), and Wisconsin (1960).[61]

Similar norms are found in other state legislatures, although there is substantial variation in the degree to which a set of such informal rules of conduct is shared or enforced. Generally, the more time members spend in session each year, the more extensive the shared set of norms seems to be. The importance of norms in the New York State Senate, for example, is revealed in the behavior of Republican Walter Mahoney, majority leader and president pro tempore from 1954 to 1964:

> On [one] occasion Mahoney promised a Democratic lawmaker his help in getting a certain bill passed. Weeks later the bill came up for debate on the floor of the Senate, but Mahoney was out of the chamber, making a phone call. In near panic, the Democrat ran out, searching for Mahoney. He reminded Mahoney of his pledge of support. By then . . . the roll call was almost over, with the nays in the majority. Mahoney rushed back into the chamber and asked that his name be called immediately on the basis of his right to "explain his vote." Under the rules, after debate is closed, members are permitted to speak for two minutes during the roll call. Mahoney rose and said, "Gentlemen, several weeks ago I promised to help get this particular bill passed. I gave my word, but I forgot about the whole thing. I always keep my word; it is the only way to operate. But now I'm in a position in which only you can help me to keep my promise by voting for this bill." Thereupon, most Republicans who had already voted nay rose to change their votes (the count becomes official only after the roll call is completed and the secretary has announced its outcome) and the bill passed.
>
> Mahoney took great pains to develop in the members the feeling that the [New York] Senate was one of the world's greatest deliberative bodies. He made the members believe, as he did, that no one had the right to challenge any of its prerogatives. He was very successful in developing [institutional] patriotism, which proved particularly effective in cases where he chose to challenge the governor.[62]

Perhaps the greatest difference between the norms of state legislatures and Congress is that, in the states, there is less emphasis on *specialization.* The four-state study mentioned earlier, for example, found relatively little deference to the committee system, compared to Congress.[63] The lesser state legislative attention to specialization seems to be related to high rates of state legislator turnover and the instability of committee membership, although some exceptions to that pattern exist.[64]

New members seldom understand a legislature's rules when they arrive, whether formal or informal. If a new member is to learn the norms and conduct himself or

376

herself accordingly, he or she must have at least a minimal degree of commitment to membership in the legislature and a sufficiently long and intense interaction with established members to learn the rules of the game. That duration and intensity is sometimes lacking in the "amateur" state legislatures, which meet each year for only a few months or less. Those legislators perceive their role as a sideline, rather than as their major occupation. This reduces the intensity with which they focus their concern on acquiring legislative effectiveness, although impressionistic evidence suggests that the most effective state legislators are those who understand and work within the chamber's set of norms. High turnover of members also affects the extent to which behavioral norms are transmitted to new members. Thus, state legislatures vary in the extent to which members share an understanding of, and a commitment to, a set of legislative norms. But, as noted earlier, state legislators do subscribe (with varying degrees of intensity) to norms of legislator behavior, and newcomers are socialized into accepting those sets of informal rules. With their higher rates of newcomers, state legislatures are more rapidly affected than Congress by changes in the degree to which new members accept or reject the dominant norms of the body, although, for the most part, newcomers accept the existing norms.

Almost all state legislatures recognize the importance of helping newcomers learn the rules of the game. Formal orientation sessions are held for freshmen—some before the legislative session convenes, some soon after. Some such orientation meetings are sponsored by the legislative parties; others are sponsored by the legislature and its central staff. In addition to informing new members about staff resources available, the formal rules, and the "nuts and bolts" of getting legislation drafted, introduced and perhaps enacted, the leaders of the legislature also brief the newcomers on appropriate behavior.[65]

As in Congress, much of the transmission of legislative norms to new state legislators is informal. Sometimes, the novice can be embarrassed on the floor, as was the new Massachusetts state senator who inquired whether

> he could later move to take the bill off the table if he voted to table in the first instance. He was told [by the President of the Senate] that he could but, after the vote was cast, an oldtimer leaned over and told him that not for two hundred years had anybody been so presumptuous as to move to take from the table what another Massachusetts senator had put there. The new member did not break decorum and went along with tradition.[66]

★ ★ ★ ★

Texas Legislative Norms

[Freshman Representative Martin is] pathetically ignorant of politics and the legislative process. His first act in Austin was to "fire" the staff of the committee chairman he defeated last November, not realizing that chairmanships do not pass by inheritance. . . . [He] tangled with Representative Washington in committee over welfare spending; afterward told a hometown reporter that Craig had threatened to get him beat in the next election. Oops—all committee meetings are recorded, and the tape revealed no such threat. Washington said, "There are two cardinal rules in the Legislature—you don't lie *on* a member and you don't lie *to* a member—and he broke both."

House members found a remedy for Martin's shenanigans; they shunned him as they would a leper.

Source: "The Ten Best and the Ten Worst Legislators," *Texas Monthly*, July 1981, p. 111.

★ ★ ★ ★

Bill Flow in State Legislatures

The general outline of a bill's progress, through the legislative system of hurdles to enactment as law, is the same in the state legislatures as in Congress. The bill must be introduced by a member in either chamber for "first reading"; is referred to a committee or committees; must be reported out of the committee to the floor; must be "read" (announced) once or twice more;[67] must be scheduled for a vote and win, amended or not; and then is sent to the other chamber (except in the unicameral Nebraska legislature). There, again, the bill must go to committee, then to the floor, and then win. If amended in the second chamber, the two versions must be reconciled, normally by the use of a conference committee appointed for that purpose. It then goes to the governor for approval or veto (except in North Carolina, where the governor has no veto). The legislature can then override the governor's veto, if supporters have the votes. The requirements for overriding the veto vary among the states from a simple majority of each chamber to a three-fourths majority.

In general, control over the flow of legislation in American state legislatures is more concentrated than is the case in Congress. In many state legislatures, especially the ones with short sessions, strategic considerations result in a crush of legislation coming to the floor for decision in the last few days and hours of a legislative session. Some of the end-of-session crush may result from bills being held by the money committees until after the bill-submission deadline so as to be able to estimate total demand for spending before passing any bills. Some results from the strategy of various committees—or each chamber—of holding certain bills hostage to insure enough votes to pass a particularly important bill. Sometimes the crush is a deliberate leadership tactic. A last-minute crush of legislation gives the leaders of the legislative chambers great power over which bills become law, since the leaders decide which bills get voted on in those closing hours and which are abandoned because of lack of time. Legislators know they will need the leaders' help at the end of the session and thus hesitate to anger them. Thus, too, efforts to reduce the last-minute crush of legislation are not equally supported by all actors. Still, to insure that legislators at least have a chance to acquaint themselves with most measures, over forty of the state legislatures have established deadlines beyond which special permission must be obtained (usually by extraordinary vote of the chamber) to introduce legislation. Most states also permit bills to be submitted for introduction ("prefiled") before the legislature convenes, so as to give members time to consider the large number of bills they will face. Other states utilize "split sessions" for the same reason.[68]

From Committee to the Floor   As the discussion in Chapters 10 and 11 made clear, the committee systems of the various state legislatures vary markedly in the extent to which they authoritatively filter legislation for the parent chamber, rejecting measures the committee majority opposes and forwarding only approved measures to the floor. Most state legislatures are similar to Congress in their requirement that all measures be considered by committees before coming to the floor of the chamber. However, some permit various exceptions normally for "emergencies." If the tradition of using committees as a screening device does not exist, the committee stage may be avoided on leadership measures or administration bills. The New Jersey assembly has recently improved somewhat the place of its committees within the legislative process, but, of 112 bills proposed in 1970–71 by Republican Governor Cahill, 30 entirely circumvented the assembly's committees.[69]

Some two thirds of the state legislatures authorize their committees to kill bills in committee by inaction, although some of those bodies also make it fairly easy to force a committee to relinquish a bill to the chamber floor. A minority of states

378

reduce the authority of committees further by requiring them to report *all* measures to the floor, even if some are reported with an adverse recommendation. Other states permit a committee, at its discretion, to release a bill to the floor with a negative recommendation, rather than continue to hold it. A favorable recommendation places the sponsor in a better position to have the bill enacted, because even the least institutionalized state legislature is more likely to enact legislation that has been approved by the relevant committee than legislation which the relevant committee opposes. But requiring all legislation to be reported does give the bill's supporters a chance to have the committee position overturned by vote of the chamber, and to make the effort without the ill will of a cumbersome "discharge" process. The rules of some state legislatures require committees to report all bills, but still rig the dynamic in favor of committee authority. In Florida, for example, "bills reported unfavorably by standing committees are automatically tabled and can be taken up and placed on the calendar only by a two-thirds vote."[70]

Scheduling Legislation on the Floor   Although details vary from state to state, overall the formal and informal rules in the various state legislatures give the leaders of each chamber's majority party (and Nebraska's nonpartisan leaders) substantial discretion in the scheduling of legislation for floor consideration and voting.

> Assignment of bills on the calendars is performed in a variety of ways, but the agency actually making the decisions which fix the calendar will almost always include the most significant and powerful members of the body. In some houses there is a committee called "Calendar Committee," "Steering Committee," or some similar name, composed in some instances of committee chairmen, in others of the top legislative leadership. In other houses, the calendar is determined by the majority party caucus and some other party agency.

> The agenda for floor action is generally much more simple in state legislatures than in the U.S. House of Representatives. In place of a number of different kinds of calendars . . . there is frequently little more than a listing of bills one day for action the next.[71]

The states vary in their use of the device of the Committee of the Whole for debate and amendment of legislation on the floor of the chamber to expedite business. Some use that mechanism regularly; others very seldom. Those states that use the Committee of the Whole mechanism debate and amend in the Committee of the Whole, and a measure can be defeated there, but the Committee of the Whole can only *recommend* passage. Final passage must be accomplished under the more formal rules of the parent chamber, after the Committee of the Whole "rises" and the House or Senate reconvenes.

The rules of procedure on the floors of the state legislative chambers permit little opportunity for the kind of excessive delay permitted in Congress. Some state legislative bodies forbid a member to speak more than once on the same issue. Nor do the legislative *norms* in the various state bodies support delaying activity. Legislative leaders normally either bottle up the measures they oppose in committee or round up the votes to defeat them on the floor.

Over three-fourths of the state legislatures require roll-call votes on final passage of legislation (often the result of state constitutional requirements), and the remaining states permit a handful of members to require it.[72] The great majority of lower chambers have available an electronic voting device. Almost half of the upper chambers also have such devices, but some prefer the traditional roll call. On votes where passage is sure, many presiding officers merely ask for a show of hands by those members who wish to be recorded in opposition.

In Congress, unless the absence of a quorum is noted, a majority of those present and voting can decide on adoption or rejection of a measure. In the Committee of the Whole House of Representatives, as previously noted, that means decisions can be made by a vote that is substantially less than half the chamber membership. In contrast, 60 percent of the states require a majority of the entire chamber membership to vote in favor of a measure for it to be agreed to.[73]

In many state legislatures, the sponsoring member of a measure retains substantial authority over it during its legislative travels. The sponsor is responsible, in most states, for insuring that the committee considers and reports the bill and for defending the bill on the floor of the chamber. The floor-manager role, thus, is likely to be assigned to the bill's sponsor, rather than to the chairperson of the committee that reported the bill to the floor. In some chambers, the sponsor is granted the right to open or close debate on the bill, or both.

The use of Consent Calendars for expediting the passage of noncontroversial legislation is found in one or both chambers of over two thirds of the state legislatures, a substantial increase over the number of a decade ago. The procedure is similar to that used in Congress, although details vary. A single objection suffices to remove a bill from the Consent Calendar in some states.[74]

Legislation which applies only to a particular area of the state—especially to a particular local government—is generally referred to as "local legislation" or a "local bill." The formal rules of the various state legislatures usually make no distinction between "local legislation" and "general legislation" and, indeed, some legislatures must resort to detailed "general" classification to circumvent state constitutional restrictions on overly specific legislation of this type. The norms in some states, however, may dictate special consideration of local bills. An example of such legislation might be a measure

> regulating the hunting season in a specifically named county. By invariably observed informal rules in many legislatures such local bills are decided entirely by the legislator or legislators from the affected district.
>
> In such cases the legislative vote "passing" the measure is wholly fictional in that no one but the interested member is even present in the hall when the matter is brought up, although if legally required the record may later report a vote that was never taken. . . . Where this kind of delegated authority on local matters prevails, however, there is usually found another strong informal rule of procedure. When members of a delegation do not agree unanimously on a local matter, the measure will not pass. It is also quite common to find that informal rules require that the measure bear the approval of a local unit of government (e.g. city council) before the legislator is allowed the privilege of this autonomous local-bill procedure.[75]

Some legislatures also have further informal limitations on the ability of a legislator to enact local bills with such autonomy, such as, for example, a requirement that the legislator not have been too difficult for the legislative leadership to deal with. Otherwise, the required accommodation of the legislator's local bill may never occur.[76]

Voting Decisions of State Legislators

The forces surrounding the voting decisions of state legislators have not been examined as closely as those bearing on the decisions of members of Congress. But the general configuration appears to be similar to that found in the national legislature, except that the role of committees is a bit muted. The relative strength of the various

──────────── ★ ★ ★ ★ ────────────

The Rules Committee Rules

The Calendar was limited . . . because the session was nearing its end and the Rules Committee (of the West Virginia House of Delegates) was in control. You see, during the last two weeks of a legislative session, when the volume of business is largest, the decision to defeat a bill is made, not by the 100 elected delegates in the House, but by the handful of delegates who make up the House Rules Committee. . . .

When a bill is reported to the floor from committee, it is put on the "calendar" so the House may vote on it. However, legislators tend to behave a bit like students with homework: they postpone major assignments. As a result, the "calendar" of bills gets unwieldy during the last two weeks of the session.

The Rules Committee was invented, in theory, as a "traffic cop" to go into action late in the sessions and "schedule" the consideration of bills, thus avoiding a logjam of last-minute legislation. The Committee is made up of the floor leaders, committee chairmen, and a few extras, usually people who worked their way into the inner circle by carrying water for the leadership or by voting right in the election for Speaker.

Under a resolution routinely approved early in the session by a coalition of leadership folks and naive freshmen, the Rules Committee is granted authority to put bills on a "special calendar" that takes precedence over the "regular calendar" of the House. In theory, the Committee only schedules bills to ensure an "orderly" flow of business. In practice, the Committee has assumed the power to judge bills on the basis of substance and policy.

In practice, also, if your bill is not chosen for the "special calendar" chances are it will never make it to the floor for a vote. As soon as the special calendar has been completed each day, the House automatically adjourns. And just try getting the two-thirds vote necessary to suspend the rules and get your bill to the floor. (I tried once, and got six votes, plus a lot of scorn for my outlandish violation of the "rules of the game.") So year after year, the session ends without the "regular calendar" ever being voted on, and the bills left there die a quiet *de facto* death.

In effect, the Rules Committees have become mini-legislatures. It takes seven legislators to control the House Committee and six to control the Senate Committee. The intelligent lobbyist concentrates on them. After all, a cynic might ask, why buy a majority of the entire Legislature when you need only to pay for 13 members.

Source: Larry Sonis, "OK, Everybody, Vote Yes: A Day in the Life of a State Legislator," *Washington Monthly,* June 1979, pp. 26–27.

──────────── ★ ★ ★ ★ ────────────

types of actors, of course, varies greatly from state to state, and it differs from Congress also. In some states, for example, the legislator (and the legislature as an institution) may be ill-prepared to resist pressure from the governor, especially if his or her colleagues in the political party support the governor's demands and the governor's party controls the legislature. At other times in various states, the speaker of the house and other legislative leaders are capable of marshaling the resources necessary to force their preference—in opposition to the governor's—on individual legislators. When the governor and the top legislative leaders are working in close collaboration, however, it is very difficult for the average legislator to resist them. The cooperation of the leaders and the governor, after all, is required for the passage of each legislator's pet or local legislation.

In a diminishing number of states, the legislature's resources and independent information-gathering and research capability are insufficient to maintain true legislative independence from the major economic interest groups in the state and from the state's executive agencies.[77] Montana, in the late 1950s, is perhaps an extreme case, but worth noting:

> Long known for the excellence of its lobbying activities, Anaconda's attorneys follow with keen scrutiny the course of every measure under consideration by the legislature. Its strength rests not only in its wealth and resources, but also in its elaborate network of relationships with key citizens, banks, legal firms and business organizations throughout the state. Rare is that unit of local government—county, city, or school district—that does not have among its official family an associate, in some capacity, of the Anaconda Company. . . . It should be emphasized that Anaconda has used its great power largely in a negative fashion—to prevent government actions which it opposed. . . .[78]

With occasional exceptions, the state legislatures are more independent of economic interests than they were at the turn of the century, when they were sometimes simply bought wholesale. However, the popular stereotype of the legislator or legislature for sale lingers. The occasional prosecution for bribery—of state legislators or members of Congress—reinforces that stereotype, which is unfair to the overwhelming majority of American legislators.

Despite the large number of inattentive constituents, and perhaps because of them, state legislators are sensitive to opinion among the attentive public within their districts. While it is difficult to untangle the various forces pressing on legislators, especially when demographic factors in their districts correlate highly with their partisan affiliations, it is clear that constituency influence cannot be ignored and frequently determines legislator votes.[79] Most state legislatures require record votes on numerous matters which would be decided by nonrecord votes in Congress, thus enhancing the potential for constituents to hold a legislator responsible for his or her vote.

Cue-taking also occurs within the state legislatures just as in Congress, although the extent of internal legislative authority on various issues seems to vary greatly among the state legislatures. Much depends on the status of the committee system and the overall institutionalization of the legislature. With variance based upon the type of policy under consideration and the strength of the legislative party system, cue-giving and cue-taking of a form similar to that which occurs in Congress take place in many state legislatures, and probably in all of them. The four-state study of California, New Jersey, Ohio, and Tennessee in 1957, for example, found both subject-matter experts and friendship networks which appeared to have an impact on voting. Although their questionnaire was not designed specifically to test cue-giving and cue-taking, the authors of that study found indirect evidence that it was occurring.[80] Acceptance of voting cues from colleagues "whose judgements

382

they respect and whose interests they share" is common in the Kansas legislature.[81] Evidence that legislators recognize the importance of cue-giving and cue-taking among members is also found in Michigan, where one analyst concluded that the experts within the chamber were major sources of information for less well-informed colleagues.[82]

SUMMARY

Congress and the American state legislatures consider proposals under a complex set of formal and informal rules of procedure and behavior which make a difference as to which actors are advantaged and which disadvantaged. The rules may not have been designed with such impact in mind, but legislative rules of procedure are no exception to the general proposition that rules seldom are truly neutral. Thus, for example, legislative rules favor those who, in any given legislative battle, oppose a bill. Overall, the procedures of American legislative bodies bias the decision-making process toward incremental decision-making, rather than toward bold new policy departures.[83] But without rules, orderly consideration of the public's needs could not take place. And without an understanding of the formal rules of a legislative body and of the manner in which those formal rules are tempered by informal norms of behavior, the observer has little chance of understanding what is happening in a legislative body.

Generally, there is great similarity between the two chambers of Congress and between Congress and the state legislatures. All consider only measures introduced by members; all provide staff assistance in the drafting of legislation; all have committee systems for the consideration of legislation and resolutions; all provide for legislative leaders to schedule the flow of legislation to the floor; all provide mechanisms for the control of deliberations on the floor of the chamber; and all provide decision-rules by which all citizens know when a particular proposal has been enacted into the statutes (which we must all obey) and when a measure has been defeated. Also, the various legislative bodies have developed sets of informal norms of behavior which vary somewhat according to the size of the membership, the degree of institutionalization of the legislature, and the nature of the political environment in which the legislature functions. To greater or lesser degrees, for example, the various American legislatures recognize norms that press members to learn the ropes and appreciate the insights of more experienced members; to perform the tedious but necessary work of the chamber; to specialize; to protect the legislature as an institution; and to work out modes of behavior which smooth the rough edges of political controversy and permit members to continue working civilly with (or against) colleagues with distasteful political philosophies.

The most complex system of scheduling legislation from committees to the floor of the chamber is found in the U.S. House of Representatives, which requires that legislation be scheduled for floor consideration on one of five calendars, and then permits such floor consideration only with the acquiescence of the Rules Committee, under the conditions laid down by that committee. By contrast, some state legislative bodies function with only a list of measures that are to be considered during the next day or two.

Voting procedures, on the other hand, are more rigidly detailed in many state legislatures than in Congress. The national legislature passes many measures by voice vote or by other nonrecorded votes. Many state legislatures, on the other hand, require record votes on every measure that the legislature enacts, and some state legislatures also routinely record votes on amendments. The most distinctive feature

383

of the rules of procedure in the U.S. Senate is the need for cooperation and mutual understanding if the normal procedure of considering measures under unanimous agreement is to be used. The Senate, however, is much more flexible than the larger House and can permit the luxury of "unlimited debate," while the House has severely restricted a member's ability to speak on the floor. The U.S. Senate traditionally has permitted intense opponents of a particular bill to engage in extended debate (a filibuster) unless, under current rules, 60 percent of all senators invoke cloture by voting to shut off debate. The various state legislative bodies tend toward numerous restrictions on a member's ability to speak on the floor, even though most are smaller than the U.S. Senate.

Legislators obtain advice from lobbyists, executive officials, staff members, and party leaders before casting their votes, but the voting cues they pay most attention to are those from fellow legislators and from their constituents. The constituents, after all, have the ultimate sanction—the ending of the legislator's public life. Fellow legislators (selected by the member seeking advice) are usually trustworthy and convenient sources of politically relevant, condensed information (voting cues) on the multitude of votes about which each member must decide. Outside actors have influence, of course, but much of that influence is indirect—filtered through legislative "experts" on the subject.

Notes

1. Donald R. Matthews, "The Folkways of the United States Senate: Conformity to Group Norms and Legislative Effectiveness," *American Political Science Review* 53 (December 1959): 1064. Another early student of the norms of Congress was Ralph K. Huitt, whose "The Morse Committee Assignment Controversy: A Study in Senate Norms," still enlightens us on the degree to which one must examine the *milieu* in which rules are interpreted if one is to understand legislative decisions. *American Political Science Review* 51 (June 1957): 313–29.

2. Matthews, "The Folkways of the United States Senate," p. 1074.

3. Ibid., pp. 1074–86.

4. Richard F. Fenno, Jr., *Congressmen in Committees* (Boston: Little, Brown, 1973), p. 101.

5. Matthews, "The Folkways of the United States Senate," p. 1069.

6. Ibid., p. 1071.

7. Ibid., p. 1073.

8. Ibid., p. 1072. But see Ralph K. Huitt, "The Outsider in the Senate: An Alternative Role," *American Political Science Review* 55 (September 1961): 566–75.

9. Matthews, "The Folkways of the United States Senate," p. 1070.

10. Norman J. Ornstein, Robert L. Peabody, and David W. Rohde, "The Changing Senate: From the 1950's to the 1970s," in *Congress Reconsidered,* ed. Lawrence C. Dodd and Bruce J. Oppenheimer (New York: Praeger, 1977), p. 6.

11. Matthews, "The Folkways of the United States Senate," p. 1073.

12. Charles L. Clapp, *The Congressman: His Work as He Sees It* (Garden City, N.Y.: Doubleday, Anchor, 1963), pp. 38–40.

13. For the Senate, see Ornstein, Peabody, and Rohde, "The Changing Senate," p. 8. In the Ninety-first Congress (1969), Herbert Asher found that 58 percent of the House first-termers agreed that they should serve an apprenticeship when asked that question in their first two months as members. Support for the other major norms varied from 68 percent to 100 percent of the first-term members. Three months later, only 42 percent of them supported the apprenticeship norm. Support for the other norms also varied somewhat, but none dropped below 68 percent. Among more senior members, 80 percent or more supported the other norms, but only 38 percent agreed first-term members should serve apprenticeships. "The Learning of Legislative Norms," *American Political Science Review* 67 (June 1973): 499–513. The apprenticeship norm weakened even further over the next three Congresses. By the

Ninety-fourth Congress, only 19 percent of newcomers thought the apprenticeship norm was "Very Important," compared to 25 percent who thought it "Not Very Important." Further, the participation of newcomers on the House floor and on conference committees had grown substantially since the Ninety-first Congress. See Burdett A. Loomis, "Freshman Democrats in the 94th Congress: Actions in and Reactions to a Changing House" (Paper delivered at the 1977 Annual Meeting of the Midwest Political Science Association, Chicago, Illinois).

14. Ralph K. Huitt, "The Outsider in the Senate: An Alternative Role," *American Political Science Review* 55 (1961): 566–75.

15. Clapp, *The Congressman: His Work as He Sees It,* pp. 12–22.

16. Herbert Asher, "The Learning of Legislative Norms," (Abstract).

17. *Congressional Quarterly Weekly Report,* February 3, 1979, p. 183.

18. Alan Fiellin notes that members of the "Tuesday-To-Thursday Club" may be improving their chances for reelection or promotion to an alternative elective office by spending half or more of their time back home, but such frequent absences "from 'the Hill' earns the member a reputation as a parttime congressman. For many House colleagues, particularly those that count, this is a violation of the norm requiring that each member carry his share of the work load and spend nearly full-time in Washington while the House is in Session. . . . For most members . . . the deviation results in some reduction in prestige and influence with House colleagues." See "The Functions of Informal Groups: A State Delegation," *Journal of Politics* 24 (February 1962); quoted in Robert L. Peabody and Nelson W. Polsby, eds., *New Perspectives on the House of Representatives,* 2nd ed. (Chicago: Rand McNally, 1969), pp. 121–22.

19. Well-written, extensive discussions of the rules and tactics for getting a bill to the floor of the House or Senate and for winning on the floor are available. See especially Walter J. Oleszek, *Congressional Procedures and the Policy Process* (Washington, D.C.: Congressional Quarterly, 1978), Chapters 4 through 8; T. R. Reid, *Congressional Odyssey: The Saga of a Senate Bill* (San Francisco: W. H. Freeman, 1980); Robert L. Peabody, Jeffrey M. Berry, William G. Frasure, and Jerry Goldman, *To Enact a Law* (New York: Praeger, 1972); and Erwin L. Levine and Elizabeth M. Wexler, *PL 94–112: An Act of Congress* (New York: Macmillan, 1981). The following discussion draws on all of the above.

20. This discussion draws on Oleszek, *Congressional Procedures and the Policy Process,* pp. 80–87; and David J. Vogler, *The Politics of Congress,* 2nd edition (Boston: Allyn and Bacon, 1977), pp. 213–19.

21. "House Use of Suspensions Grows Drastically," *Inside Congress,* 2nd ed. (Washington, D.C.: Congressional Quarterly Press, 1979), pp. 17–19.

22. A good current description of the Rules Committee's role in the House is Bruce I. Oppenheimer, "The Rules Committee: New Arm of Leadership in a Decentralized House," in Dodd and Oppenheimer, *Congress Reconsidered.* Accounts of the prereform Rules Committee abound. Noteworthy are Daniel M. Berman, *A Bill Becomes A Law* (New York: Macmillan, 1962), especially pp. 19–25 and 74–76; and James A. Robinson, *The House Rules Committee* (Indianapolis: Bobbs-Merrill, 1963).

23. Robinson, *The House Rules Committee,* p. 44.

24. Milton C. Cummings, Jr., and Robert L. Peabody, "The Decision to Enlarge the Committee on Rules: An Analysis of the 1961 Vote," in Peabody and Polsby, *New Perspectives on the House of Representatives,* pp. 253–80.

25. Oleszek, *Congressional Procedures and the Policy Process,* p. 92.

26. Jim Wright, *You and Your Congressman* (New York: G.P. Putnam's, 1976), p. 142.

27. Oleszek, *Congressional Procedures and the Policy Process,* pp. 146–47.

28. Irwin B. Arieff, "One Minute Speeches Retained: Move Fails to put a Damper on Congress' 'Happy Hour,' " *Congressional Quarterly Weekly Report,* August 2, 1980, p. 2191.

29. Daniel M. Berman, *In Congress Assembled* (New York: Macmillan, 1964), p. 251.

30. The discussion which follows draws in part on "1970 Legislative Reorganization Act: First Year's Record," in *Congress in Change,* ed. Norman J. Ornstein (New York: Praeger, 1975), excerpted from *Congressional Quarterly Weekly Report,* March 4, 1972, pp. 485–91; and on Vogler, *The Politics of Congress,* pp. 18–20.

31. Vogler, *The Politics of Congress,* p. 20.

32. William H. Riker, "The Paradox of Voting and Congressional Rules for the Voting on Amendments," *American Political Science Review* 52 (June 1958): 349–66.

33. Formal analyses of these types of decisions are found in James M. Enelow and David H. Hoehler, "The Amendment in Legislative Strategy: Sophisticated Voting in the U.S. Congress," *Journal of Politics* 42 (May 1980): 396–413; Robin Farquharson, *Theory of Voting* (New Haven: Yale University Press, 1969); and William H. Riker and Steven J. Brams, "The Paradox of Vote Trading: Effects of Decision Rules and Voting Strategies on Externalities," *American Political Science Review* 69 (September 1975): pp. 929–42.

34. Alan Murray, "House Funding Bill Riders Become Potent Policy Force," *Congressional Quarterly Weekly Report,* November 1, 1980, p. 3251.

35. Oleszek, *Congressional Procedures and the Policy Process,* p. 113.

36. Much of the following discussion draws on Oleszek, *Congressional Procedures and the Policy Process,* pp. 151–79; Harold G. Ast, "Procedural Flow of Bills, Resolutions, Nominations, and Treaties," Office of the Secretary of the Senate, October 31, 1977; Stanley Bach, "Congressional Reform—Senate (95th Congress): Issue Brief Number IB77004," Library of Congress, Congressional Research Service, August 17, 1977; Lewis A. Froman, Jr., *The Congressional Process: Strategies, Rules and Procedures* (Boston: Little, Brown, 1967); and Vogler, *The Politics of Congress.*

37. Leroy N. Rieselbach, *Congressional Politics* (New York: McGraw-Hill, 1973), pp. 127–28.

38. For years, representatives were able to delay the business of the House in this way too, but a rules change in 1971 eliminated that procedural delaying tactic.

39. David M. Olson, *The Legislative Process: A Comparative Approach* (New York: Harper and Row, 1980), p. 380.

40. Ibid.

41. Lewis Froman, *The Congressional Process,* pp. 121–22.

42. David C. Kozak, "Decision Settings in Congress," (Paper delivered at the Legislative Studies Groups at the 1980 Annual Meeting of the American Political Science Association, Washington, D.C.).

43. Matthews, *U.S. Senators and Their World* (New York: Random House, 1960), p. 178. See also Lester W. Milbrath, *The Washington Lobbyists* (Chicago: Rand McNally, 1963), Chapter 12.

44. Aage R. Clausen, *How Congressmen Decide: A Policy Focus* (New York: St. Martin's Press, 1973), pp. 91–99.

45. Ibid., p. 153.

46. Richard F. Fenno, Jr., *Home Style: House Members in their Districts* (Boston: Little, Brown, 1978), especially Chapter 1; and Lewis Anthony Dexter, *The Sociology and Politics of Congress* (Chicago: Rand McNally, 1969), pp. 77–79.

47. John W. Kingdon, *Congressmen's Voting Decisions* (New York: Harper and Row, 1973), pp. 219–20.

48. Donald R. Matthews and James A. Stimson, *Yeas and Nays: Normal Decision-Making in the U.S. House of Representatives* (New York: John Wiley, 1975), p. 47.

49. Ibid., p. 40. Some observers suggest that the new electronic vote system in the House has led some members to call for roll-call votes on relatively noncontroversial issues just to raise their attendance records on roll-call votes.

50. Herbert D. Asher and Herbert P. Weisberg, "Voting Change in Congress: Some Dynamic Perspectives on an Evolutionary Process," *American Journal of Political Science* 22 (May 1978): 391–425; and Kingdon, *Congressmen's Voting Decisions,* pp. 254–57.

51. Aage P. Clausen and Carl L. Van Horn, "The Congressional Response to a Decade of Change: 1963–1972," *Journal of Politics* 39 (August 1977): 624–66.

52. Asher and Weisberg, "Voting Change in Congress," p. 391.

53. Matthews and Stimson, *Yeas and Nays,* p. 51.

54. John W. Kingdon, *Congressmen's Voting Decisions,* p. 17.

55. Ibid., p. 18.

56. Matthews and Stimson, *Yeas and Nays,* pp. 81–85.

57. Kingdon, *Congressmen's Voting Decisions,* Chapter 5; and Richard Born, "Cue-Taking within State Party Delegations in the U.S. House of Representatives," *Journal of Politics* 38 (February 1976): 71–94.

58. William H. Panning reminds us that cues are more important on more evenly divided roll-call votes and that members sometimes use cues negatively, voting against a bill because a particular group or member is supporting it. "Bandwagon Effects on Congressional Voting," (Paper delivered at the 1978 Annual Meeting of the Midwest Political Science Association, Chicago, Illinois).

59. The question asked was, "We've been told that every legislature has its *unofficial* rules of the game—certain things members must do and things they must not do if they want the respect and cooperation of fellow-members. What are some of these things—these "rules of the game"—that a member must observe to hold the respect and cooperation of his fellow members? . . . How do the other members make things difficult for . . . people when they don't follow the rules of the game?" John C. Wahlke, Heinz Eulau, William Buchanan, and LeRoy C. Ferguson, *The Legislative System: Explorations in Legislative Behavior* (New York: John Wiley, 1962), p. 143.

60. Ibid., p. 144. This rule was strongly echoed by new California representatives nine years later. See Charles G. Bell and Charles M. Price, *The First Term: A Study of Legislative Socialization* (Beverly Hills, Calif.: Sage, 1975), Chapter 4.

61. Samuel A. Kirkpatrick, *The Legislative Process in Oklahoma* (Norman, Okla.: University of Oklahoma Press, 1978), Chapter 5; Samuel C. Patterson, "The Role of the Deviant in the State Legislative System: The Wisconsin Assembly," *Western Political Quarterly* 14 (June 1961): pp. 460–72; Lelan E. McLemore, "The Structuring of Legislative Behavior: Norm Patterns in a State Legislature" (Ph.D. diss., University of Oklahoma, 1973): cited in Kirkpatrick; and "The Ten Best and The Ten Worst Legislators," *Texas Monthly,* July 1981, pp. 100–113.

62. Alan G. Hevesi, *Legislative Politics in New York State* (New York: Praeger, 1975), pp. 35–36.

63. Wahlke, Eulau, Buchanan, and Ferguson, *The Legislative System,* p. 147.

64. Alan Rosenthal, *Legislative Performance in the States* (New York: Free Press, 1974), Chapter 8.

65. *American State Legislatures: Their Structures and Procedures* (Lexington, Ky.: Council of State Governments, 1971), p. 2. Kansas has a "rather cursory" orientation session for new members which is "designed primarily to acquaint new members with available staff services," but which includes a "small-scale mock legislative session." Marvin A. Harder and Raymond G. Davis, *The Legislature as an Organization: A Study of the Kansas Legislature* (Lawrence, Kansas: Regents Press of Kansas, 1979), p. 129. New California legislators also receive a "series of formal orientation meetings . . . [dealing] with the nuts and bolts aspects of being a legislator." Bell and Price, *The First Term: A Study of Legislative Socialization,* p. 48.

66. Duane Lockard, "The State Legislator," in *State Legislatures in American Politics,* ed. Alexander Heard (Englewood Cliffs, N.J.: Prentice-Hall, 1966), p. 108.

67. The "readings"—announcement of bills by title and possibly by summary of what they do—help all members remain apprised of what is being introduced or proposed for passage. Normally, three "readings" are required, although an actual reading of a bill is unusual. "This terminology derives from the British Parliament, where, before literacy was common, a clerk read a bill three separate times, so that it would be understood. Even now, when literacy is common and printing presses are available to provide all members with copies of bills, it is customary to discuss legislative process in terms of 'readings,' although the reading usually consists of having a clerk read the number and title [of the bill]." Wilder Crane, Jr., and Meredith W. Watts, Jr., *State Legislative Systems* (Englewood Cliffs, N.J.: Prentice-Hall, 1968), p. 81.

68. *American State Legislatures: Their Structures and Procedures* (Lexington, Ky.: Council of State Governments, 1977), pp. 6–7, 63–65. In many states with filing deadlines, the leaders file "dummy" bills by vague title (e.g., "a bill to protect the public health and welfare") but with the rest of the bill blank. Such a dummy bill can be used, if necessary, late in the session to circumvent the requirement for obtaining special permission of the members.

69. Rosenthal, *Legislative Performance in the States,* p. 128.

70. Ibid., p. 21.

71. John C. Wahlke, "Organization and Procedure," in *State Legislatures in American Politics,* ed. Alexander Heard (Englewood Cliffs, N.J.: Prentice-Hall, 1966), p. 147.

72. *American State Legislatures,* 1977, p. 73.

73. Ibid.

74. Ibid. In this context, "Consent Calendar means any special calendar for consideration of routine or noncontroversial bills, usually by a shortened debating or parliamentary procedure." Some chambers have one vote on all items on the Consent Calendar but have the "journal reflect that the roll call was taken on each bill listed." *American State Legislatures,* 1971, p. 13.

75. Wahlke, "Organization and Procedure," p. 149.

76. Thomas A. Henderson and Glen Abney note, based on conversations with legislators in three states, that a legislator's career ambition has a major impact on his or her attitude toward local legislation. "For the man who has aspirations to state-wide office, local legislation is a high source of risk. These legislators perceive local legislation as a difficult thicket to negotiate, as they can never be sure whose interests are being promoted and at whose expense." The legislator who serves to advertise his or her private career, whose ambition is to remain in the legislature, or who has "little ambition within or without the legislature" all are more positive toward local legislation. "The State Legislator and Intergovernmental Relations," *Publius* 7 (Spring 1977): 85–100 (quotation on p. 90). The leverage that leaders gain over legislators through control over local legislation apparently varies in similar manner.

77. Citizens' Conference on State Legislatures, *State Legislatures: An Evaluation of Their Effectiveness* (New York: Praeger, 1971), pp. 19–23.

78. Thomas Payne, "Under the Copper Dome: Politics in Montana," in *Western Politics,* ed. Frank H. Joneas (Salt Lake City: University of Utah Press, 1961), pp. 197–99.

79. Wilder W. Crane, Jr., "Do Representatives Represent?" *Journal of Politics* 22 (May 1960): 295–99; Thomas R. Dye, "A Comparison of Constituency Influences in the Upper and Lower Chambers of a State Legislature," *Western Political Quarterly* 14 (June 1961): 473–80; Robert J. Huckshorn, "Decision-Making Stimuli in the State Legislative Process," *Western Political Quarterly* 18 (March 1965): 164–85; and Hugh L. LeBlanc, "Voting in State Senates: Party and Constituency Influences," *Midwest Journal of Political Science* 13 (February 1969): 33–57.

80. Wahlke, Eulau, Buchanan, and Ferguson, *The Legislative System,* Chapters 9 and 10.

81. Marvin A. Harder and Raymond G. Davis, *The Legislature as an Organization: A Study of the Kansas Legislature,* p. 55.

82. H. Owen Porter, "Legislative Experts and Outsiders: The Two-Step Flow of Communication," *Journal of Politics* 36 (August 1974); 703–31.

83. Burdett A. Loomis argues that recent "reforms" in Congress may, in fact, have strengthened the incremental tendencies in Congress. "[D]ecentralization, additional member resources, and the new budget process probably serve to dampen, rather than encourage, the possibilities for major [policy] change." See "Policy Speculation and the Congress: An Issues-Based Approach" (Paper delivered at the 1980 Annual Meeting of the American Political Science Association, Washington, D.C.).

PART IV

JUSTICE·UNDER·L

Legislatures in the Governmental System

chapter *14*

The Legislature and the Executive

Preview

The American structure of government requires that the legislature and the executive work together to accomplish most of the policy goals each prefers and gives each branch the ability to influence the other. The President and most of the governors have the veto power, a degree of control over the bureaucracy and its expertise, substantial authority over the budget, day-to-day command of the government, and—through these various grants of authority—the ability to reward and punish individual legislators. In addition, the President has extensive powers over the military and over the conduct of foreign affairs. Congress and the state legislatures have the basic legislative authority, including control over appropriations of money and changes in the tax code. They also can override the executive veto if enough legislators feel strongly about the vetoed legislation, have a "legislative veto" over certain proposed executive actions, and can impeach and remove executive officials from office. While the two branches of government understand the need for cooperation in the conduct of the public business, there are built-in tensions between them that arise from their differing perspectives. For example, each legislator's constituency is much smaller than that of the chief executive, leading many legislators to have relatively parochial perspectives. Partisan factors sometimes intrude. Further, the time perspective of legislators differs from that of elected executives because their terms of office differ; legislators are more likely to continue for many terms. Tension also arises from different internal organizational structures and differences in the backgrounds and experience of the people in the two branches.

It is common for those who write about the office of the chief executive in the American political system to refer to the various "roles" of the President or of state governors and to note that one of the roles of an American chief executive is to be "chief legislator."[1] At the national level that designation results from the President's constitutional authority to veto legislation enacted by Congress, subject to that veto's being overridden by a two-thirds vote in each chamber. But the emphasis on the President's legislative leadership comes also from the recognition that, in reality, the President devotes much of the resources of the office to working with Congress, attempting to get executive-sponsored programs enacted or preventing unwanted legislation from passing.

This chapter will discuss the interactions of Congress with the President as well as the White House staff and the other top executive personnel in their capacities as *administrative* spokespersons rather than as agency or *department* spokespersons. It will also discuss the interactions of the state legislatures with the governor and the governor's aides and will assess state legislative relationships with statewide elected executive officers other than the governor, including the state attorney general and the state treasurer. The relationship between Congress and the bureaucracy and between state legislatures and various state bureaucracies will be considered in the next chapter.

A COMPARATIVE PERSPECTIVE ON EXECUTIVE-LEGISLATIVE RELATIONS

The interaction between legislators and executives is affected not only by their differing perspectives but by the formal constitutional relationships of the two offices. A brief comparison of the British and West German political structures with the American may provide a broader view of the subject and an understanding that some characteristics of American executive-legislative relations flow mainly from differing responsibilities and perspectives and some flow primarily from the constitutional structure of government that both joins and separates the two branches.

American legislators are elected independently of the chief executive, although a modest "coattail" effect sometimes links legislative and executive electoral fortunes. In contrast, the majority party or majority coalition in the British House of Commons selects the prime minister. Voting against a member of Parliament is the only avenue open for most citizens to express disapproval of the prime minister. Therefore, an unpopular prime minister is likely to cause the defeat of certain members of Parliament. The same is true in West Germany where the national parties and the national legislature determine who will be the chancellor. In both British and West German systems the chief executives select cabinet members from among the ranks of the national legislators, often using these posts as a reward for their supporters.

In both Great Britain and West Germany, the national legislatures have the power to remove the chief executive by majority vote. The American Congress theoretically has a similar power—that is, impeachment by majority vote of the U.S. House and conviction by a two-thirds vote in the U.S. Senate. But the American President is elected for a fixed, four-year term, and it is almost impossible to dislodge the President by impeachment before that period expires.

The prime minister of Great Britain and the chancellor of West Germany have the authority to dissolve the national legislature and require new elections before elections would otherwise be regularly held (although, in West Germany, this is more difficult to do and is uncommon). By contrast, the American President has no such authority. Congressional elections occur every two years (for all of the members of the House and one third of the members of the Senate), and the President has no mechanism of any sort for hastening the demise of a Congress which the President dislikes.

In Great Britain, the prime minister is the leader of the majority party in Parliament. Other majority-party leaders in Parliament head the major agencies of government, and securing a cabinet portfolio (position as head of an agency of government) is a reasonable career goal for a member of Parliament. With very rare exceptions, cabinet members arrive at that rank only after some fourteen years of service in the House of Commons (many of those years spent in subcabinet, apprenticeship posts,

391

while holding a seat in Parliament). British prime ministers during this century have averaged over twenty years in the House of Commons before reaching the top office.[2]

The West German system lies somewhere between the British and the American systems. The national parties have a large voice in the decision about the election of the chancellor.[3] A career in the national legislature is not the only route to a cabinet position or to becoming chancellor. But most Germans who attain such positions without a seat in the national legislature stand for election for such a seat at the first opportunity, and "over 90% of the members of German cabinets in the history of the Federal Republic have simultaneously held seats in the Bundestag."[4] The West German chancellor may come from outside the Bundestag (the lower chamber of the national legislature), not having been leader of the majority party there. Both former chancellors Willy Brandt and Kurt Kiesinger rose to that position without being members of the Bundestag at the time, although Brandt had formerly served in that body. Both, however, ran for and were elected to seats in the Bundestag soon after assuming the chancellorship.

Despite some differences between the two systems, both encourage the overlap of personnel between the legislative and executive branches of the government—and this is a significant difference from the American structure of government. Both state and national constitutions in the United States forbid legislators from serving as executive-department officers without first resigning from the legislature. In addition to depriving legislative leaders of the insights and knowledge obtainable only through service in a national-government executive capacity, these constitutional provisions also deny the executive branch the talents of many American legislators who are unwilling to give up their independence and, in Congress, their seniority, for a (probably short) term in a cabinet or subcabinet office.

As two astute observers of national legislatures observe:

> The top political executives in Germany are with few exceptions also members of parliament, and this overlap creates a day-to-day closeness between the two institutions that resembles the British system. But cabinet ministers in Germany, like their American counterparts, in many instances achieve their offices as a result of non-legislative experience; therefore they do not share the common background with members of parliament which their British colleagues have.[5]

American constitutional provisions that require the separation of *personnel* between the legislative and executive branches of government and deny each branch control over the election or tenure of the other create a greater distance between the two branches than exists in parliamentary systems, and thus have a substantial impact on the relationships between the legislature and the executive. The separation of *personnel,* however, does not totally separate the *functions* of the two branches of government. Indeed, much of the discussion of American legislatures revolves around the *degree* to which the legislature should accept policy initiatives and leadership from the executive, and the extent to which the legislature should develop its own independent capability to function as a fully equal branch of the government.

While American constitutions demand a separation of personnel between the legislature and the executive, then,

> the lawmaking function cannot be neatly separated from the function of executing the laws. Those who carry out the laws have always and everywhere had a strong influence over the formulation of the laws and over their actual meaning in practice. This duality has never been more obvious than it is today, when executives, including the American president, play a large role in proposing laws and a larger role in determining their effectiveness through their influence over the administrative apparatus of the modern state. Concurrently, legislatures probably have greater influence than ever over the administration of public policy.[6]

With this comparative discussion in mind, the relationship between Congress and the President can be explored.[7]

THE U.S. CONGRESS AND THE PRESIDENT

In order to govern, the U.S. Congress and the President must arrive at some accommodation with each other. Members of Congress are unlikely to get their bills passed over the opposition of a determined President who is armed with the veto. Presidents must have appropriations to run the administration—money which can come only from Congress—and they must have a degree of Congressional cooperation to get their policy proposals enacted, even though most such proposals are modified extensively by Congress.

The relationship between Congress and the President is largely structured by the formal powers granted each actor by the Constitution (see Chapter 3), as well as by statutory delegations of authority made to the President or statutory restrictions on presidential prerogatives. The relationship is colored, as well, by the different constituencies and terms of office, by the personalities involved, by partisanship, by the issues that may become important at any given time, and by whether the focus of concern at any moment is on domestic or international questions.

Invitation to Conflict

Various observers of Congressional-presidential interactions have noted that the structure of American government was designed to *promote* conflict between the two branches of government.[8] Though the branches are independent of each other in selection and tenure of personnel, they share responsibilities. That alone is likely to create tension. Careful examination reveals that American legislative-executive conflict generally stems from five major differences between the two branches.

The first major difference is that of *constituency*. Only the President is elected by the entire nation, and only the President has had to build a coalition sufficient to win a national election. Although Congress collectively represents the entire nation, no individual member of Congress has a national constituency.[9]

Members of Congress, as discussed in Chapter 2, are divided between their duties as members of the *national* legislature and their duties as delegates from their *local* constituencies. One way to resolve the resulting tension is to see no conflict between local interests and national interests and, when the President's view of the national interest threatens the local interest, to argue that the President is wrong. Legislator responses to administration proposals concerning various Department of Agriculture programs, for example, may be largely determined by the type of agricultural product produced in a member's state or district.[10] Similarly, water projects often are approved by Congressional logrolling even though many of the projects are not economically feasible, despite efforts to juggle calculations to make them look legitimate. Indeed, one of the ironies of the Tellico Dam controversy (over whether the possible extinction of the snail darter and, to a lesser degree, whether the flooding of an ancient Indian burial ground should be allowed to halt construction of the project) was that few news personnel or members of Congress bothered to note that the entire project was financially irrational anyhow.[11]

The *party system* provides a second basis for conflict, especially when Congress is controlled by one party and the White House by the other. With only a third of the Senate elected at the same time as the President, and with House election outcomes increasingly independent of the outcome of the presidential election, some executive-legislative disagreement is to be expected on the basis of party label and constituency. That disagreement is aggravated by the electoral college which is biased toward the populous industrial states. Since each state awards its electoral college votes to the plurality winner statewide, the presidency is usually skewed toward a big-city, big-state constituency. In contrast, the U.S. Senate overrepresents the small states, while many U.S. representatives with authority in Congress represent districts in which the largest city has 100,000 or fewer residents. While the disproportionate seniority of these small-town members is offset by the general growth in Congressional reelectability, there are clear-cut presidential and Congressional "wings" of both major parties. It is no accident that the more conservative wing is the "Congressional wing" of the national party, while the party stalwarts centered in the metropolitan areas of the nation are generally referred to as members of the "presidential wing" of the party.[12]

The third major source of friction between members of Congress and the President is their *differing tenures.* A President can serve for only two, four-year terms, and many are permitted only one term by the voters.[13] Most members of Congress, however, can look forward to extended service. An active President must move with haste. But the structure and procedures of Congress are designed to insure thorough deliberation of each measure. Further, members of Congress have incentives to move incrementally rather than innovatively on policy decisions, since doing otherwise might cost them their seats.[14] Even when the leaders of Congress agree with the President on the urgency of a particular measure, the decentralization of authority in Congress still makes it difficult to obtain fast action, as President Carter discovered in 1977 when he asked for enactment of his energy program on an emergency basis. And even if Congress moves reasonably fast, the diffusion of authority to committees and subcommittees, which are dominated by perspectives different from the President's, is likely to result in legislation which is substantially different from that proposed by the President and the executive department.[15]

Organizational differences between Congress and the executive branch constitute a fourth contribution to tension and conflict between them. Despite the frequent presidential complaint that the President must negotiate with subordinates and has a hard time staying in control of the executive branch,[16] power in the American executive is much more firmly centralized than it is in Congress. As Keefe observes:

> Power in Congress is lodged in nooks and crannies, making decentralization the most important characteristic of the institution. The customs, rules, and practices of Congress support the member inclined to resist the president's legislative proposals. . . . The terms of legislation are set largely in committee. . . . Many of the classic disputes of American politics have occurred between a "liberal" president, impatient to see one of his major legislative proposals adopted, and a "conservative" chairman, bent on delaying, revising, or defeating it. Seniority, the independent status of committees, the power of committee and subcommittee chairmen, and the rules that may be invoked to delay action . . . usually serve to diminish the influence of the chief executive on the legislature.[17]

A fifth source of conflict between Congress and the President is their differing *access to experts and information.* Many members of Congress are knowledgeable in their own right on matters that their committees consider, but the types of experts available in the executive branch are different. Most members of Congress start out as generalists and tend to distrust pure specialists who do not see the "big picture." They especially distrust experts from the executive agencies, and thus often hire their own experts. But the demands of Congress insure that the Congressional experts have a different perspective from those of the executive, again usually in terms of a broader view. Some kinds of expertise get out of date quickly when one leaves active involvement in research activities or leaves one's network of information. Other kinds of experts are simply hard to find.

> [A]n element of expertise almost invariably lacking on Capitol Hill, even in experienced and permanent staff, is the comprehension of administrative necessities that can only come from responsibility for program operation. Even when the congressional majority and the president are political allies, the separation of administrative from legislative responsibility reduces the degree of attention given in the legislative process to questions of administrative feasibility. . . .[18]

> Congress is especially at a disadvantage in matters concerning foreign policy and national security policy, matters in which the president relies on classified information that is generally unavailable to Congress.[19]

Of course, to the extent the President has information Congress does not have, and to the extent that each relies on information and advice from different kinds of experts, they are likely to have different perspectives on the important issues of the day. That inevitably leads to further friction.

The Balance of Presidential-Congressional Power

Members of Congress and the President recognize the factors which cause friction between them, and both understand the necessity for at least a degree of cooperation between the two branches of government. The President and members of Congress, however, feel differently about the prerogatives of their own branch of government, and different individuals feel differently about the need to seek accommodation with the other branch. Clashes based on different perceptions of institutional authority clearly occur, and will continue to occur, but the intensity of those clashes varies, depending on the personalities involved. Each actor in the relationship has resources for bargaining with the other, although well-informed observers differ in their assessment of the degree to which each actor is the relatively helpless victim of the other.

Congress has authority over the annual appropriations acts, without which the executive branch must close up shop. And, of course, Congress can refuse to enact legislation that the President wants or refuse to fund certain programs at levels high enough to make the President happy. The Senate has the power to confirm or reject presidential appointees and the authority to ratify or reject treaties that the President enters into with other nations. Ultimately, Congress also has the impeachment power.

The President has substantial independent authority as well, including the power to veto legislation. His is the dominant voice in foreign affairs, through the right to receive foreign ambassadors (and thus to recognize their governments), the power to negotiate treaties with other nations (subject to ratification by the Senate), and the authority to enter into "executive agreements" with other nations. The President's power as commander in chief of the nation's armed forces underscores his authority in foreign affairs, although that power is also helpful in domestic politics. The President's domestic powers are much less overwhelming, leading some observers to note that there are "two presidencies: one for domestic policy and the other for defense and foreign policy."[20] An examination of executive and legislative influence over foreign policymaking compared to domestic policymaking in the U.S., Great Britain, France, and West Germany found greater executive dominance of foreign policymaking in all four nations. That suggests the executive dominance in foreign policymaking is more a function of the nature of the policy area than of the structure of government.[21]

395

Foreign Affairs   In foreign affairs and defense matters, Congress must contend with a situation in which the executive has access to information that is denied most legislators and in which the information "fed" to legislators sometimes is carefully selected. Further, both the Constitution and public opinion place most faith in the executive in the matter of foreign affairs, and members of Congress generally have had little direct personal experience in that area. The constitutional authority of Congress over foreign affairs involves the confirmation of appointments and promotions to key positions in the diplomatic corps and the military; to the ratification or amendment of treaties (a power which presidents now often can elude through the use of executive agreements, which need not receive Senate ratification); the power to declare war; legislation over tariffs and trade matters; and ordinarily, the most important foreign affairs weapon of Congress—control over appropriations.

While not dominant, Congress is not entirely powerless in foreign affairs and defense policy. Indeed, Congressional influence varies with the type of decision. By their very nature, crisis situations minimize Congressional influence and maximize executive authority. But noncrisis strategic policymaking involves substantial Congressional involvement. Furthermore, certain types of defense and foreign policy decisions (primarily implementation decisions) permit extensive exercise of Congressional authority. Indeed, decisions concerning procurement of military weapons systems are notorious for Congressional intervention on behalf of home-state contractors. And such programs as Food for Peace are subject to extensive manipulation by key members of Congress from various agricultural states.[22]

Although Congress is reluctant to undermine the executive's ability to represent the nation lest the U.S. become ineffectual in the conduct of foreign relations, Congress does have the ability to affect most decisions in this policy area since most require funding for implementation. Thus even most executive agreements are indirectly subject to Congressional action. Executive recalcitrance and refusal to be forthcoming and cooperative in working with Congress to give it a meaningful role in foreign-policy formulation during the late 1960s and the early 1970s led Congress to enact legislation which somewhat improved its chances of influencing American foreign policy. These statutes include the Case Act of 1972, the War Powers Resolution of 1973, the Hughes-Ryan Amendment (1974) to the Foreign Assistance Act, the National Emergencies Act (1976), and the Budget and Impoundment Control Act of 1974. Executive circumvention or violations of these statutes has occurred, but the statutes have helped Congress some.[23]

The Case Act requires the secretary of state "to transmit to Congress within sixty days the text of 'any international agreement, other than a treaty,' to which the United States is a party."[24] Notification after the fact, of course, is less satisfactory to members of Congress than participation in the making of policy. That dissatisfaction, coupled with flagrant Nixon and Ford administration violations of the Case Act, has led some members of Congress to seek enactment of legislation to require a waiting period before executive agreements could go into effect—to permit Congress to review or modify them, or both.[25]

The National Emergencies Act was adopted in response to the discovery by a Senate special committee in 1973 that there were "some 470 provisions of federal law that could be triggered during a "time of war" or a "national emergency" declared by Congress or the president."[26] Many of those 470 provisions broadened the President's domestic authority; others bolstered his already formidable authority in the conduct of foreign affairs. The committee noted that presidents had allowed "national emergencies" to continue long past the event, permitting the President

396

★ ★ ★ ★

Presidential Nominations Are Usually Confirmed

Sen. Joseph Biden: Can you tell me who is the Prime Minister of South Africa?
William P. Clark: No, sir, I cannot.
Biden: Can you tell me who the Prime Minister of Zimbabwe is?
Clark: It would be a guess.
Biden: What are the countries in Europe, in NATO, that are most reluctant to go along with theater nuclear-force modernization?
Clark: I am not in a position . . . to categorize them.
Biden: Can you tell us, just from the accounts in the newspapers, what is happening to the British Labor Party these days?
Clark: I don't think I can tell with specificity what is happening in the British Labor Party today.

So it went as William P. Clark, 49, a genial judge apparently innocent of any knowledge of foreign affairs, flunked question after question from the Senate Foreign Relations Committee last week. But with a wince at his F-minus testimony, the panel voted (10 to 4, with three members unhappily "present") to confirm Clark as Deputy Secretary of State. The appointment left foreign capitals gaping. "Nitwit," snapped the daily De Volkskrant in Amsterdam. The London Daily Mirror complained: "America's allies in Europe— Europe, Mr. Clark, you must have heard of it—will hope he is never in charge in a time of crisis."

Clark's only credentials for the job were a flair for administration and the confidence of Ronald Reagan. In the 1950s he flunked out of Loyola Law School. Reading law on his own, he passed the California Bar exam on his second try. In the 1960s Clark worked on Reagan's first gubernatorial campaign, ultimately becoming his chief of staff, scaling back the state's balky superagencies and reducing complex issues to one-page memos for the governor. In 1973 Reagan named Clark to the California Supreme Court, where he earned a reputation for workmanlike opinions and a competent staff.

Clark's critics argued that he might conceivably qualify as Under Secretary for Administration, but said he was a terrible choice for the department's sensitive No. 2 position (he succeeds Warren Christopher, whose last assignment was to negotiate the release of the U.S. hostages in Iran). Clark's backers said his friendship with Reagan would offset his loose grip on foreign affairs. One of his missions may be to keep an eye on Secretary of State Alexander Haig, a politically ambitious operator. In private, Haig was said to be pleased by the contrast between Clark's dim-bulb hearings and his own four-star performance last month. If Clark hopes to keep up with the boss, he will have to do a good deal more homework than he has done so far.

★ ★ ★ ★

to retain emergency powers. The National Emergencies Act ended existing "emergencies," gave Congress the power to terminate future "emergencies" declared by presidents, and provided that future "emergencies" would automatically terminate after one year "unless the president informs Congress within ninety days before the end of the year that the emergency is to continue. . . . [The] effect may be important politically. A president who does not end an emergency, or who continues it, is subject to questions. Not the least of which is why an emergency still exists a year after his administration has been working on it."[27]

The War Powers Resolution of 1973 (enacted over President Nixon's veto) seeks to involve the judgment of Congress in decisions that are likely to require committing American armed forces to hostilities. This resolution was enacted shortly after "the unprecedented cutoff of funding for the aerial war over Cambodia."[28] The War Powers Resolution

> requires the president "in every possible instance" to "consult with Congress" before he introduces armed forces into hostilities or into situations leading to hostilities. He must also consult regularly with Congress until the forces have been withdrawn. . . .[29]

The War Powers Resolution requires the President to notify Congress in writing (within forty–eight hours) of his committing U.S. armed forces to combat or the likelihood of combat and, thereafter, to withdraw such forces within sixty days unless both houses of Congress (by law or by declaration of war) approve the presidential action. (There is an allowance of an additional thirty days for withdrawal of forces, if presidentially certified "unavoidable" difficulties prevent earlier withdrawal.) But the Resolution, especially in regard to "consultation," does not limit the President as much as Congress might have expected. In several activities with great potential for hostilities that were undertaken in Southeast Asia in April 1975, President Ford chose not to "consult" with leaders of Congress, but he did honor the War Powers Resolution clause that requires the President to "report" to Congress within forty-eight hours on activities that might lead to hostilities.[30] In the *Mayaguez* incident of May 1975 (an American merchant ship seized by Cambodia was rescued by U.S. Navy and Marine forces), the military rescue operation was under way (although shots had not yet been fired) before leaders of Congress were "consulted" by President Ford.[31]

President Carter also ignored the consultation requirement of the War Powers Resolution, extending the string of precedents which greatly undermine the effectiveness of that measure. President Carter's unsuccessful April 1980 helicopter mission to rescue fifty-two American hostages held in Iran was carried out with no advance consultation with Congressional leaders. The Senate majority leader had been told the day before that a rescue mission might be attempted, but was given no details. Although the chairperson of the Senate Foreign Relations Committee protested this lack of advance consultation, most members of Congress acquiesced, and many members stated their agreement with President Carter's explanation that the need for absolute secrecy overrode his obligation to discuss the mission with Congressional leaders ahead of time. Other members of Congress agreed with the U.S. attorney general that the War Powers Resolution did not apply because "this was viewed as a rescue operation, not a military operation."[32]

During the Carter administration, the intensity of Congressional feelings about control of the executive in foreign affairs waned a bit as a Democratic Congress worked with a Democratic President, as the Vietnam imbroglio faded into the past, as frustration over the Iranian crisis grew, and as new members of Congress—without the residue of bitter feelings from the Congressional confrontations with President Nixon—gained an increasing percentage of seats. Various restrictions were eased somewhat, including the Hughes-Ryan Amendment's requirement that prior notice of CIA covert operations be given to eight Congressional committees. The law now requires the President to notify the Intelligence Committee of each chamber of covert operations, except when "vital interests" of the United States are involved.[33]

Domestic Policymaking   The President is much less powerful in the development of domestic policy than in the setting of foreign and defense policy. In the domestic field, the President must exercise leadership by using the office's media dominance to set the public agenda, by cajoling and persuading key members of Congress of the correctness of presidential positions, and by selective use of the office's limited quantities of patronage and favors.

Presidential dominance of the public agenda is aided by the constitutional requirement that the President report to Congress each year on the state of the union, and by statutory requirements for presidential budget messages. The State of the Union address, given in January of each year, is an especially favorable opportunity for the President to spell out for the public as well as members of Congress the President's views on what Congress ought to do during the following year. The budget message allows the President to provide the details of how presidential goals ought to be accomplished.

Presidents do not always have to depend on Congressional action in domestic policymaking. In certain situations, the President can issue an executive order, rather than merely fret about lack of Congressional action. Many executive orders lack specific statutory authority and must be justified on constitutional rather than legislative grounds. For example, during the long period when conservative coalition obstructionism in Congress blocked civil-rights legislation, Presidents Roosevelt, Truman, and Kennedy each issued executive orders implementing certain civil-rights policies, asserting a sometimes-challenged constitutional authority to do so.[34]

An important factor that affects a President's relationship with Congress is presidential popularity. As noted in Chapter 5, presidential popularity affects Congressional elections. The way this happens is rather complicated, but there does appear to be some direct link between a President's election performance in a Congressional district and the district representative's support in Congress for the President's programs.[35]

Presidential popularity between elections also affects a President's success in both chambers of Congress. Although presidential support, as reflected in national public-opinion polls, has only a weak correlation with presidential success in Congress overall, members are sensitive to the President's standing among their own partisans in the electorate, and they respond to the President's legislative proposals accordingly. Further, the correlation between presidential prestige, as reflected in national public-opinion polls, and presidential support on roll-call votes in Congress is stronger on foreign-policy issues than on domestic-policy issues. The analysis of the public-opinion roll-call relationship is complicated by an absence of polls on presidential popularity in each Congressional district and by the fact that members of Congress appear to be more responsive to their perception of their key constituents' opinions about the President than they are to the results of a national public-opinion poll. Still, it is clear that the President's standing in the public eye is an important factor in his ability to get presidential programs through Congress.[36] A good example is President Reagan's ability to get most of his economic program

———————————— ★ ★ ★ ★ ————————————

"Open" and "Closed"
Presidential Leadership of Congress

The President advances his program in Congress by means which C.P. Snow . . . terms "open politics" and "closed politics," one visible and the other covert. In open politics the President sets forth his proposals for legislation, sends appointments and treaties to the Senate, brings Congress into extra session and puts an agenda before it, and makes public statements explaining and defending his legislative actions. His chief weapon in open politics is his messages—his State of the Union message rendered each January. . . .

Congress, too, invites messages, and therefore leadership, from the President. The Budget and Accounting Act of 1921 bids the President to submit an executive budget each January. This ponderous tome . . . with its accompanying message is a detailed statement of policy objectives with means of achieving them for Congress's guidance. The Employment Act of 1946 calls for an Economic Report from the President that permits him to lay out policies fostering free competitive enterprise and maintaining employment, production, and purchasing power at maximum levels.

Theodore Roosevelt began the practice of supplementing his messages with actual drafts of bills. . . .

The Constitution endows the President with the veto, a most powerful weapon in the game of open politics. The veto's grave defect is that it is total and not partial. The President must accept or reject a bill as a whole; he cannot veto particular items and approve the rest. . . .

The President plying the strong approach may, as another tactic of open politics, take his legislative program to the people. His unrivaled power to command the nation's attention and its disposition to side with him against all foes endows him with a capacity no legislator enjoys. . . .

The President in his relations with Congress also engages in the process of closed politics. Relatively unpublicized, unseen, and unofficial, closed politics employs the personal contact, the patronage lever, the choice viands of the pork barrel, and sundry other exertions of power and influence. The negotiation in the White House office or Congressional cloakroom, the Presidential phone calls to the legislator deciding how to vote, the accommodations and compromise necessary to patch together a legislative majority for an administration bill, are the warp and woof of closed politics. The resort to closed politics is a constant reminder of the weakness of open politics. . . .

The President personally is, or should be, at the center of closed politics. There is no substitute for the force of his word or gesture. . . . His dealings and exertions cover the entire range from soft to hard sell. Kennedy . . . met weekly with the legislative leaders of his party and breakfasted or lunched with the Speaker of the House and the majority and assistant leader of the Senate. He also conferred systematically and individually with the chairmen of each of the standing committees. . . .

Kennedy's attentions embraced Republicans as well as Democrats. Everett Dirksen was the object of various blandishments, including privileged rides in the President's helicopter. . . .

Lyndon Johnson . . . was master of two indispensable competences in closed politics. He was ingenious at discovering politically feasible compromises, and he commanded a relentless, overpowering persuasiveness at bringing those he confronted around to supporting them. . . .

In dealing and bargaining with legislators, the President operates from an array of vantage points. He can dole out various degrees of help in the next Congressional elections. He manipulates the several executive beneficiences like pork barrel and defense contracts. The Kennedy administration, laboring mightily to induce Southern Democrats to vote for its measures, generated good feeling by increasing price supports for Southern cotton and awarding Southern plants big defense contracts. . . .

Despite the weakness of his individual weapons, if the President chooses to direct his available means of both closed and open politics upon a selected objective, he can gather an imposing arsenal.

Source: Louis W. Koenig, *The Chief Executive*, rev. ed (New York: Harcourt Brace and World, 1968), pp. 136–39.

──────────────── ★ ★ ★ ★ ────────────────

through Congress in 1981. Many Democratic representatives supported the presidential program because they thought their constituents wanted them to.[37]

Maintaining good relationships with Congress is important enough to presidents that a White House Office of Congressional Relations has evolved. The status of the office varies with the President, as does the office's basic set of legislative strategies, but normally it has a dozen or so "professional" staff members, in addition to secretarial assistance. The Congressional relations staff is headed by an assistant to the President. This assistant sometimes is a member of the President's inner circle and at other times is not. The Office of Congressional Relations gathers intelligence on Capitol Hill, advises the President and his top lieutenants concerning the status of various programs and proposals in Congress, coordinates—or at least attempts to coordinate—the liaison activities of the various executive departments and agencies on Capitol Hill, attempts to represent Congressional perspectives within the White House, and lobbies Congress to enact the President's programs.[38] Although the Congressional relations staff ultimately is dependent on the President's supporting activities (such as telephone calls, goodwill functions at the White House, and Congressional leadership breakfasts), staff experience on Capitol Hill and staff sensitivity to the way things are done in Congress make quite a bit of difference in the success of the President's programs. One major reason frequently given for President Carter's difficulties with Congress, for example, was that his top Congressional liaison assistant was no more experienced at working with Congress than the President was prior to inauguration.[39]

Despite the Presidents' difficulties with Congress, the resources normally available to a President and to presidential advisors seem truly formidable to individual members of Congress. These resources constitute a substantial arsenal, and, during the presidencies of Lyndon B. Johnson and Richard M. Nixon, there was much concern (since substantially abated) about whether the office had become an "imperial presidency."[40] A President does not deal with just one member of Congress, however, but with Congress as an institution, an institution in which well-insulated key members often can deny the President legislation that he wants, or else they can demand such a price for passage of the legislation that the President must ask whether it is worth the price.

President Kennedy had served in both chambers of Congress for a total of fourteen years before his election as President. As a representative and as a senator, he had perceived the presidency as an extremely powerful office, relative to the Congress. Later, however, as President, he observed:

> It is very easy to defeat a bill in the Congress. It is much more difficult to pass one. To go through a subcommittee . . . and get a majority vote, the full committee and get a majority vote, go to the Rules Committee and get a rule, go to the Floor of the House and get a majority, start over again in the Senate, subcommittee and full committee, and in the Senate there is unlimited debate, so you can never bring a matter to a vote if there is enough determination on the part of the opponents, even if they are a minority, to go through the Senate with the bill. And then unanimously get a conference between the House and Senate to adjust the bill . . . and have this done on a controversial piece of legislation where powerful groups are opposing it, that is an extremely difficult task.[41]

Presidential and Legislative Vetoes

Refusal to enact a presidential program is not the only means of obstruction available to Congress. Increasingly, Congress has created and used the *legislative veto*. And presidents can obstruct the will of Congress through the exercise of a presidential veto over legislation.

Presidential Vetoes The President is given the power of the veto by the U.S. Constitution (Article I, Section 7). Vetoed legislation becomes law only if two thirds of the members in each chamber thereafter vote to override the veto. It is very difficult to get two thirds of the members in both chambers of Congress to agree

---

★ ★ ★ ★

White House Lobbying Staff Chosen

The White House legislative liaison staff is headed by Max L. Friedersdorf, who describes himself as "the ham in the sandwich" between Capitol Hill and President Reagan.

Friedersdorf, 51, is said to know just about every member of Congress personally and to understand their needs. He has hired an experienced staff with many Hill contacts and a sure knowledge of how to "tell a member what he needs to know in a minute," as one congressional aide remarked.

Most recently chairman of the Federal Election Commission, Friedersdorf became chief lobbyist for President Ford after working as a White House liaison for President Nixon. A former journalist, he came to Washington in 1961 as administrative assistant to former Rep. Richard L. Roudebush, R-Ind. (1961–71).

Hired as chief Senate lobbyist was Powell Moore, who came to Washington in 1964 as an aide to former Sen. Richard B. Russell, D-Ga. (1933–71). He worked in the Nixon administration as deputy director of public information at the Department of Justice and as a White House lobbyist from 1973–75.

Moore's staff will be made up of:

Pamela J. Turner, 36, who spent the last five years as top aide to Sen. John Tower, R-Texas. Previously she spent eight years in a similar post with former Sen. Edward J. Gurney, R-Fla. (House 1963–69; Senate 1969–74).

David Swanson, 38, a Senate Energy Committee staff member since 1978. In 1974–77 he was an aide to former Rep. John B. Anderson, R-Ill. (1961–81).

William J. Gribbin, 37, an analyst since 1977 for the Senate Republican Policy Committee where he specialized in health, welfare and Social Security. He also was an aide to former Sen. James L. Buckley, C-N.Y. (1971–77).

Named chief House lobbyist was Kenneth M. Duberstein, 36, former director of business-government relations for the Committee for Economic Development, a Washington-based think tank. Duberstein also worked for former Sen. Jacob K. Javits, R-N.Y. (House, 1947–54; Senate, 1957–81), and as director of congressional relations for the General Services Administration and the Department of Labor under Nixon and Ford.

His staff will consist of:

Nancy Risque, 34, a former lobbyist for Standard Oil of Ohio.

David Wright, 31, administrative assistant since 1977 to Rep. William C. Wampler, R-Va., and previously an aide at the House Agriculture Committee.

John Dressendorfer, 40, chief lobbyist since 1974 for the Uniformed Services University of the Health Sciences in Bethesda, Md., with prior experience in lobbying for the Navy and for the deputy secretary of defense.

M. B. Oglesby, 38, since 1979 a staff member of the House Commerce Committee specializing in transportation. From 1977 to 1979, he was deputy and acting director of the Washington office of the state of Illinois.

Serving as the lobbying office's "inside man," tracking White House developments, will be Paul Russo, 37. Russo directed congressional relations for the Reagan for President Committee and was special assistant to Gov. Reagan in 1973–75. Russo also has worked for Rep. Thomas B. Evans Jr., R-Del., for the Republican National Committee and for the Ford campaign.

Two staff members who came with Friedersdorf from the Federal Election Commission are legislative counsel Sherrie Cooksey, 27, former minority counsel for the Senate Rules Committee, and administrative assistant Nancy Kennedy, 41.

Source: *Congressional Quarterly Weekly Report*, January 24, 1981, p. 174.

★ ★ ★ ★

on anything, much less on support for a controversial, vetoed bill. So, the presidential veto power is a substantial constitutional grant of authority to the President over the legislative process. A presidential veto rejects the entire bill, however; it is not an "item veto," such as most American governors have on appropriations bills. The President must accept the entire bill or reject the entire bill. Members of Congress have become skilled at putting together bills that contain provisions the President wants, along with items that members of Congress want and that the President opposes. They do this in the hope that the "sweeteners" will make the disliked provisions sufficiently palatable to the President that there will be no veto of the whole bill. (A "rider" to an appropriations act is a favorite method for getting minor items past a possible veto.)

Presidents sometimes use their veto power in a more positive fashion, although the tactic does not always succeed. By threatening to veto a measure unless certain conditions are met, presidents can often persuade Congress to make changes in legislation while the measure is being considered by the legislature.

The presidential veto is also used as a means of keeping legislators aware of the President's authority and of their own dependence on the President to get their pet legislation passed. President Franklin D. Roosevelt "was known to say to his aides 'Give me a bill that I can veto' to remind legislators that they had the President to reckon with."[42]

The President's *pocket veto* can be even more effective than the regular veto, because it gives Congress no opportunity to override the veto. The pocket veto comes about from the constitutional provision that says that if a President neither signs nor vetoes a bill within ten days (Sundays excepted) after its receipt from Congress, it becomes law—*if* Congress is still in session. If Congress has adjourned during that ten-day period, however, and the President neither signs nor vetoes the bill, he cannot return the legislation to the house of origin with a veto message, and it dies in the President's pocket. President Nixon insisted that the pocket veto applied to measures sent to him while Congress was in *temporary* recess—not adjourned *sine die* (permanently). President Ford originally agreed with that argument. But in 1974, the U.S. Court of Appeals for the District of Columbia ruled that such an expansion of the idea of the pocket veto violated the intent of the Constitution and the authority of Congress as an institution.[43]

The Legislative Veto Over the years, Congress has regularly enacted legislation that sets forth general policies, but leaves substantial discretion to the executive department to fill in the details and to apply the law to specific cases. Until the days of the New Deal and its accompanying vast expansion of national government responsibilities and bureaucracy, the federal courts were prone to hold that delegation of authority from Congress to an executive agency must be clear and precise. The delegation of authority was likely to be rejected by the court unless the statute involved was fairly narrow, or "if the executive's only functions were to act on a specific contingency, or if the executive were to 'fill up the details' of a general congressional scheme."[44] As one observer summarized the matter:

> Substantive due process in the area of economic regulation was all but formally interred during the New Deal by several Supreme Court decisions. Similarly, power to legislate under the commerce clause received sweeping judicial approval. . . . [T]he delegation of immense authority (to the executive by Congress), authority not restrained by narrow and precise standards, could not have been achieved without the acquiescence of the legislative branch. More ambitious attempts of the executive to act without congressional support have been uniformly

and emphatically rejected by the Supreme Court. . . . Yet now, ironically, sentiment in favor of widespread use of the legislative veto is most strongly concentrated in Congress, and its most articulate spokesmen stress that one of their primary intentions in supporting the [legislative] veto is precisely to restrain overly exuberant administrative agencies.[45]

In recent years, the legislative veto has become an important weapon in the Congressional battle to regain some control over an executive branch that many legislators believe has become too powerful.

Understanding the operation of the legislative veto requires that one understand the President's veto authority with respect to various kinds of measures passed by Congress. The President can veto proposed statutes (laws) after they have passed both chambers. He also can veto *joint resolutions* (passed by both the House and the Senate) if they have the force of law and "are legislative in character and effect."[46] But the President can *not* veto a *concurrent resolution,* which is a measure passed by both chambers but which is not legislative in character and effect. Reasonable observers sometimes disagree about what constitutes legislative character and effect, but the theoretical point is that Congress should not legislate by a mechanism which avoids the possibility of a presidential veto. Also, the President can *not* veto a single-chamber resolution (which has passed either the House or the Senate and is not submitted to the other chamber). Single-chamber resolutions are also called "simple resolutions." A simple resolution, obviously, is not a substitute for legislation because it has passed only one chamber of Congress. The importance of the distinction among various kinds of resolutions is pointed up by President Roosevelt's suggestion, in 1937, that Congress permit him to reorganize the executive branch, subject to Congressional rejection by *joint* resolution. Such a law would have given the President authority to reorganize unless two thirds of the members of each chamber of Congress objected, because the joint resolution would be subject to a presidential veto. Eventually Congress granted President Roosevelt the authority to reorganize the executive branch, subject to a *concurrent* resolution. A question was raised at the time as to whether such a concurrent resolution would be "legislative" and thus subject to presidential veto. The consensus seemed to be that it would not be, since the President would be deemed to have accepted the condition by not vetoing the basic legislation containing the provision. That argument is still unresolved, but subsequent reorganization measures have provided for disapproval of executive reorganization plans by simple resolution of *either* chamber of Congress.[47]

Although writing Congressional vetoes into legislation dates from the middle of the nineteenth century, the great bulk of such laws has been enacted since 1968, as Congress has shown increasing frustration about the "legislative" and policymaking activities of the expanding bureaucracy.

> By 1976 the [legislative veto] device had become so common that extensive hearings were held in both houses on legislation to extend the principle of the legislative veto to actions of the executive branch generally. The House of Representatives voted 265 to 135 in favor of the measure, which lost nevertheless because the vote happened to have been taken under suspension of the rules requiring a two-thirds majority.[48]

Some recent legislation provides for basically negative legislative vetoes in which both chambers, one chamber, or a committee of one or both chambers can prevent executive action by the timely passage of a resolution of disapproval. Other recent statutes provide that executive action can proceed past a certain stage only by obtaining *positive* approval from Congress or from a committee or committees of Congress.

For example, the Post Office Appropriations Act of 1971 provided that the U.S. Post Office had to obtain advance approval of sites for new postal facilities from the House and Senate public works committees before spending money for design and construction.[49]

The constitutionality of the legislative veto is still basically unresolved. All presidents since Herbert Hoover have objected to this Congressional device especially in the laws permitting reorganization of the executive branch subject to Congressional veto.[50] However, Ronald Reagan supported the legislative veto during his 1980 presidential campaign.[51]

★ ★ ★ ★

Senate Supports Reagan on AWACS Sale

President Reagan narrowly won the first major test of his authority in foreign policy Oct. 28 [1981] when the Senate, in a dramatic 48-52 vote, rejected a resolution to disapprove the sale to Saudi Arabia of five AWACS radar planes and other arms.

Fifty senators had cosponsored a version of the resolution. But the president's appeals for loyalty led eight first-term senators among the cosponsors—seven of them Republicans—to switch at the last minute and vote against the resolution. . . .

A majority of each house would have had to pass the veto resolution (H Con Res 194) for it to take effect under a 1976 law that gave Congress the right to veto major arms sales. Congress had 30 days after receiving formal notice of the $8.5 billion sale on Oct. 1 to do so; the House had voted 301-111 against the sale Oct. 14. . . .

The Senate vote to allow the sale preserved Congress' record of never having used its arms sale veto power, though the threat of a veto has forced previous administrations to alter the terms of other weapons deals.

It also gave Reagan a momentous victory in a contest that had pitted his presidency against another of Washington's most potent lobbies—the American Jewish community, which fought the deal because of Israel's strong opposition to it.

The debate, which began in earnest in the spring, had centered on fears that Saudi Arabia might use the AWACS (Airborne Warning and Control System) planes against Israel in concert with other Arab nations or might fail to guard the AWACS's secrets from falling into unfriendly hands. . . .

Cranston said Edward Zorinsky of Nebraska, the only Democrat to cosponsor the resolution but vote against it, had acknowledged that a visit with Reagan on the day of the vote had changed his mind as well.

"Ed Zorinsky said the president told him, 'How can I meet with a foreign leader and have him believe I'm in charge of the government if I can't sell five airplanes?'" Cranston said, repeating Zorinsky's explanation for switching.

Source: Richard Whittle, *Congressional Quarterly Weekly Report,* October 31, 1981, pp. 2095–97.

★ ★ ★ ★

Presidential objections to various forms of the Congressional veto have led presidents to veto some legislation containing a legislative veto provision, but some bills have been signed because the substance of the legislation was badly desired by the President. Occasionally, presidential signatures of bills containing a provision for a Congressional veto have been accompanied by presidential statements that the legislative veto provisions were unconstitutional, or would be ignored by the President, or both.[52] In addition to arguments that *any* legislative veto contravenes the separation of powers between the legislative and executive branches, especially vigorous and separate arguments have been made against lodging the legislative veto in just one chamber of Congress or in particular committees of Congress, because it is said that doing so voids the constitutional requirement for the two chambers to agree on policy decisions. Scholars also point out that the legislative veto over administrative agency rule-making authority results in bargaining between the agencies and the relevant Congressional committees and chairpersons, giving affected interest groups enhanced resources for negating policy initiatives by administrative agencies.[53]

In December 1980, the Ninth Circuit Court of Appeals ruled that a legislative provision permitting a single chamber of Congress to overturn decisions of the Immigration and Naturalization Service violated the separation-of-powers doctrine. The court stressed that action by two chambers (not just one) is required to exercise legislative authority.[54] The case was a narrowly defined one which may not be a harbinger of a Supreme Court ruling that legislative vetoes are generally unconstitutional. Many specialists, however, expect the court eventually to rule unconstitutional some existing statutory provisions providing for legislative vetoes by one chamber or by Congressional committee.

EXECUTIVE-LEGISLATIVE RELATIONS IN THE STATES

Most of the observations about relations between Congress and the President apply also to relations between the various state governors and their state legislatures. Of course, the "two-presidencies" discussion (in regard to foreign affairs and domestic issues) does not apply, because the governors have no responsibilities analogous to the President's responsibilities in foreign affairs.

The relationship between the governor and the legislature is also a bit different from that between the President and Congress. In addition to the governor, most states have several other independently elected executives, with their own independent, constitutional authority, and the lesser state executives have their own ambitions, constituency bases, and policy goals. These factors may not be in harmony with those of the governor, but the lesser state executives are not under the governor's authority.

Sources of State Legislative-Executive Tension

There are fundamental tensions in the governor's relationship with the legislature that parallel those at the national level—tensions that are inherent in the structure of government in the various states and in the differing responsibilities and perspectives of state legislators and executives. Popular governors sometimes have electoral coattails, but their coattails can also be surprisingly short.[55] The terms of office of governor and of state legislators are fixed. The governor cannot dissolve the legislature and call for new elections. And the legislature cannot remove executive officers except by impeachment.

The governor is likely to have assisted some legislators in their political careers—helping to recruit some to run for office and campaigning for others—and certain legislators are important factors in the plans of any statewide candidate. But the state chief executive and the legislature are formally independent of each other in recruitment and tenure in office, and they are fairly independent of each other in practice too.

As at the national level, the governor represents the entire state population, while each legislator represents only about 5 percent or less of that population (and in most states, 1 to 3 percent of the population). Governors especially and, to a lesser extent, other elected state executives can claim authority from their statewide constituencies. The legislature as a whole represents the entire state population, but individual legislators, like their national counterparts, cannot claim to represent all the citizens. State legislators, like members of Congress, also frequently find themselves torn between a persuasive case about the interest of the state as a whole and their awareness that a particular proposal may not be in the narrow interests of their key constituency supporters.

Although the election of a state governor is not complicated by a mechanism such as the electoral college, many state parties are nevertheless split into "wings," similar to those of the national parties. Republican legislators from metropolitan areas, for example, often see the state's problems differently from their small-town or rural party colleagues. Where an urban-based Republican governor faces a Republican legislature that is controlled by the rural wing of the party, the governor often feels as though the "other" party is in charge of the legislature. Yet, the average voter often does not understand why the governor cannot get along with the legislature when the governor's own party is in control. Occasionally, but not often, a governor faces a situation where some fellow party members in the legislature join a cross-party coalition to elect the speaker of the house from the other party.

A common occurrence in the states is the election of a governor of one party and a legislature in which one or both chambers is controlled by the other party. In 1981, that was the situation in twenty-six of the forty-nine states that elect partisan legislatures. The leaders of the opposition party sometimes have an interest in embarrassing the governor, if possible, and in making it appear that the governor is not in charge, is not competent, or is dishonest. Such a partisan division between the legislature and the governor inevitably leads to conflict between the two branches of government. Where the governor and the legislative majorities are of the same party, partisan considerations often help smooth over the other divisive features of separation-of-powers government. Not infrequently, of course, some of the independently elected state executives are not of the governor's party, and they may assist the governor's partisan opponents in the legislature in their efforts to embarrass the state's chief executive. Alternatively, the governor's office and the legislature may be controlled by the same party, while a lesser executive office is controlled by the opposition party. Then, the governor and legislature sometimes conspire to harass the hapless lesser state executive official.

The various terms of office of state officials are also important in state politics, although the dynamic is less easily described than that of the Congress. Governors and other executive officials who hope to accomplish much while in office (and especially those who aspire to higher office) must work diligently and rapidly, and even more so in states that limit the tenure in office of state executive officials. Although state legislative tenure is much shorter on the average than Congressional tenure,

408

legislators generally are able to return if they choose. Chamber and committee leaders are more likely than most of their colleagues to feel confident of reelection, and these leaders are the legislators with the greatest influence over the fate of executive proposals.

Legislator ambitions are more likely to interfere with orderly transactions of business between the legislature and the state's executive officers than is the case at the national level. The leaders of the state legislature, including the speaker of the house, are often ambitious for statewide office, including higher offices desired by incumbent state executives or the offices held by those executives. The ambitions of individual legislators frequently cause difficulties for incumbent state executive officials. They can be easy targets for the legislator planning to run against the incumbent or they can be prevented from having an impressive record on which to base a campaign for a yet higher office. When the ambitious legislator is speaker or majority leader, or holds some other key legislative post, the executive's difficulties are compounded. Because of the complexity of the legislative process, a clever state legislator in the right leadership post can delay and frustrate an executive proposal for selfish reasons, yet make it very difficult for political adversaries to demonstrate clearly to the press and the public where the responsibility for their frustration lies. That is especially the case when the ambitious legislator and the executive official are members of the same political party.

As at the national level, a governor generally has greater access to trusted experts and greater information-processing resources than state legislators do. The gap in available information and expertise between governor and legislator is often greater at the state than the national level, especially in states with amateur or citizen legislatures or in those states which do not provide substantial staff support to the state legislature.

State legislatures are organized in such a way that power within each chamber generally is more concentrated than is the case in Congress. This gives recalcitrant legislative leaders more authority in bargaining with the governor than they would have if legislative power were widely dispersed, as it is in Congress. However, the ability of state legislative leaders to commit the legislature at least to broad policy positions gives the governor somebody with whom to bargain, and this can substantially improve the level of communications and feelings of trust between the two branches of government.

Gubernatorial Resources in Legislative Leadership

Not all governors are equally equipped by their state constitutions with resources for persuading a recalcitrant legislature to do as the governor wishes. The governor of North Carolina, for example, does not have the power to veto legislation, and the vetoes of six other governors can be overridden by a *majority* of the elected members of each legislative chamber (not just a majority of those present and voting). The remaining states require that three fifths, or two thirds, or in Alaska, three fourths of the legislators in each chamber must support an attempt to override a veto, or the governor's veto stands.[56] Not surprisingly, the probability of a governor's veto being overridden varies with the state, although in no state can the veto be overridden routinely. The rate at which vetoes are overridden involves much more than just formal rules, however. Other factors include partisan or ideological differences, or both, between the governor and the legislature. California, for example, requires a two-thirds vote of the membership in both chambers (not just two thirds of those present and voting) to override a veto. Yet from 1933 through 1948, the California legislature overrode twenty-eight vetoes, while from 1950 through 1973, not a single

409

veto was overridden. Illinois allows 60 percent of the chamber membership (not just 60 percent of those present and voting) to override the governor's veto, but the legislature overrode only three vetoes from 1868 to 1968.[57]

Three-fourths of the American states give their governor the power to veto individual items in an appropriations bill (called the line-item veto) before signing the remainder of the measure into law.[58] The line-item veto authority discourages state legislators from adding "riders" to an appropriations bill, a Congressional practice against which presidents are protected only by their ability to veto the entire bill or to use other presidential powers.

Just over a fourth of the states grant the governor the pocket veto.[59] In those states, bills passed in the last few days of a legislative session—the closing rush—must receive the governor's signature or they fail to become law; the legislature has no opportunity to override a pocket veto. Because of the dynamics of legislative bargaining and the struggle for power which often breaks out in state legislatures, a disproportionate number of important bills, as well as many bills of interest to only one or a few legislators, are passed in the closing rush. Legislators who want to be sure their late-in-the-session legislation is not put in the governor's pocket and forgotten must maintain a good working relationship with the governor.

In addition to the power of the veto, governors normally have the right to deliver messages to the legislature (and in most states are mandated to give an annual state of the state message), to prepare the state budget, and to call special legislative sessions.[60]

When the governor calls the legislature into special session, he or she specifies the date to convene and the items to be considered. This power is more substantial

---

★ ★ ★ ★

Innovative Use of the Item Veto

Governor Patrick Lucey [Democrat of Wisconsin, 1971–77] . . . struck out the word "not" in the phrase "not less than 50 percent" in a bill having to do with funds to promote tourism. In doing so, he changed a 50 percent "floor" on state participation in cooperative advertising to a 50 percent "ceiling." On another occasion Governor Lucey crossed out the "2" from a $25 million highway bonding bill thus reducing the authorization to $5 million. But in this case the state attorney general later ruled this an improper use of the item veto [under the Wisconsin Constitution's provisions].

Governors of eight states (Alaska, California, Hawaii, Massachusetts, Missouri, New Jersey, Pennsylvania and Tennessee) have the authority to reduce appropriations. The power to reduce expenditure items, of course, may not be very helpful to a governor who thinks legislative appropriations are too low. But for a governor, such as Michael Dukakis [Massachusetts 1974–78] who thought welfare spending was too high, or Governor Jerry Brown [California, 1974–82] who thinks overall state spending is excessive, this power makes him the virtual gatekeeper of state funds.

Source: Charles Press and Kenneth VerBurg, *State and Community Governments in the Federal System* (New York: John Wiley, 1979), p. 312.

★ ★ ★ ★

---

in states with short legislative sessions, because it means that the legislators' ordinary lives will be disrupted for the special session, and thus they may be more willing to bargain with the governor during the regular legislative session, rather than risk an inconvenient special session. Full-time state legislatures can avoid letting the governor call a special session by recessing rather than adjourning.

A few states require that the recommended budget be prepared in cooperation with legislative officials, but in most states, the governor controls the preparation of the executive budget, which then becomes the basis of legislative discussion about state finances. In states where the governor is given constitutional authority over the preparation of the executive budget, however, there is a growing practice for a standing legislative committee, an interim legislative committee, or the legislative staff to perform an independent analysis of state financial needs and present to the legislature a set of budget estimates that are independent of the governor's figures. The executive budget often becomes the top of the "realistic" range likely to be appropriated (because of the governor's need for the loyalty of state executive-branch subordinates) and the legislative budget the bottom. Actual legislative appropriations then fall between the two figures.

One cannot look only at the governor's formal powers to gain an idea of the influence of that office on the legislature. The states that provide the greatest formal powers and greatest resources to the governor for leading the state also tend to have professional legislatures and ample legislative support services. Thus, in those states the legislature has the capability of developing an independent perspective on the state's needs and on possible solutions to its problems. Some governors with only modest formal powers deal with citizen legislatures that are restricted to short legislative sessions and do not have much in the way of staff assistance. These governors may well be able to dominate their legislatures to an extent not possible in states where both the governor and the legislature have greater resources. On the other hand, in those states where the governor's term is short and where he or she is denied much constitutional legislative authority, there may be substantial party organization in the legislature led by a dynamic speaker or majority leader, resulting in legislative dominance of the executive. For example, writing about South Carolina, back in the 1940s, V. O. Key, Jr., noted:

> South Carolina's chief executive has limited power. . . . He has power of appointment to state office except many of the really important state agencies. . . .
> The legislature has grasped firm control of the critical sectors of state administration. The chairman of the senate finance committee and the chairman of the house ways and means committee, with the governor as a minority of one, compose the state budget commission. The state highway commission . . . consists of fourteen members, one from each judicial circuit elected by the legislative delegation from the circuit. The public service commission, the utility regulatory agency, consists of seven members elected by the legislature. Not only does the legislature choose the chiefs of some of the more important state agencies; now and again individual legislators hold these posts by election of their colleagues.[61]

As elsewhere, of course, things change. In 1968–69, the South Carolina governor was ranked as one of the three weakest governors in the nation in terms of formal constitutional powers.[62] Still, the office was sufficiently attractive in 1974 that one candidate spent a quarter of a million dollars in a gubernatorial primary that left the Democratic party in disarray and allowed a Republican to capture the office of governor for the first time in almost 100 years.[63]

Even in states where the governor's formal powers are weak, he or she still has legislative influence. In addition to the veto, to information-processing capability, and—in most states—to a major voice in establishing the state's budget, the governor has*visibility.* This permits domination of the legislative agenda. Astute use of the ability to command the attention of the news media can enable the governor to determine both the issues to be considered by the legislature (the legislative agenda) and the context in which legislative decisions will be interpreted or understood by the public.

Like the national executive, the governor woos or punishes legislators by granting or withholding the opportunity to bring key constituents by on short notice for a "hello" and by careful use of invitations to breakfast, lunch, or social events at the governor's mansion. To the extent a governor is chief of the political party, he or she can assist or resist when a legislator seeks an alternative office. A governor is most powerful, of course, when a legislator desires a judgeship or some other post which is under the chief executive's appointment control. With the exception of five states that elect judges by legislative vote, the governor plays a key role in the appointment of state judges, if only to vacancies in the middle of a judicial term.[64] Consultation on gubernatorial appointment to other offices of concern to various legislators or their constituents may also hinge on the legislator's relationship with the governor. While the relevant offices vary with the state, they can include the state prosecutor assigned to a county, irrigation authority officials, airport commissioners, highway commissioners and highway department district officials, and a large variety of other state officials whose decisions are significant to a legislator and his or her most important constituents.

Legislative Resources

As at the national level, the state legislature is not helpless against executive demands. Even in states that give the chief executive extensive formal authority over the legislature, the governor still needs a majority vote in each chamber to enact his or her programs and appropriations. The governor cannot maintain such majorities for long without taking into consideration the opinions and philosophies prevalent in the legislature. Thus, bargaining and logrolling are integral components of the executive-legislative relationship, and many programs endorsed by the governor are changed by the legislature before passage.

──────────────────── ★ ★ ★ ★ ────────────────────

Senatorial Courtesy in Texas

McAllen, Texas' mayor, Othal Brand, "saw the handwriting on the wall." Senator Hector Uribe was going to invoke his senator's privilege of veto power over state appointees in his district to block Brand's nomination to the board of the state Department of Corrections. . . .

As Brand's hometown representative, Uribe had been urged by Mexican Americans to invoke senatorial courtesy to block the appointment. The Senate Nominations Subcommittee set a hearing for May 20, and Brand, not one to back off from a fight, flew to Austin with two planeloads of supporters to defend himself. . . .

In objecting to Brand's appointment, Uribe concluded "The crux of this is not what Mayor Brand knew (about police brutality) but what he should have known," and he prevailed upon the Senate to deny the appointment.

Source: Susan Duffy, *Texas Monthly,* July 1981, pp. 84, 88.

──────────────────── ★ ★ ★ ★ ────────────────────

Power in the state legislatures is usually more concentrated than in Congress, and the chamber leaders are more able to dominate the legislative process. That strengthens the hand of the legislature's leaders in negotiating with or doing battle against the executive. Also, the leaders of the legislature sometimes ally themselves with a lesser, independently elected state executive official. That is especially likely to happen when the legislative majority and the lesser executive officer are not members of the governor's political party.

As noted earlier, state legislatures vary greatly in the extent to which they have resources of their own that permit them to develop their own information, independent of the governor, the rest of the executive branch, or of interest groups. Those state legislatures with ample staff and information-processing capacity are in a position to be independent of the governor's leadership, if they choose. Those legislatures without such in-house support usually find themselves too dependent on executive-branch information to be truly independent.

Many state legislators, like many members of Congress, are increasingly concerned about executive domination of the policymaking process and are frustrated that their attempts to write their intent clearly into law does not always seem to be effective. Various state legislatures, like Congress, have responded to these feelings of frustration in a number of ways, but one response has been to incorporate into various statutes the right of a legislative veto. The state legislatures appear to be especially concerned with legislative veto power over rules issued by various state agencies ("bureaucratic legislating"). This will be discussed further in the next chapter which deals with legislative-bureaucratic relationships.

Working Relations Between Governors and Legislatures

Just as there are substantial differences in the formal powers granted governors by their state constitutions, great variety also exists in the skills of intrigue and political infighting of individual politicians. The two factors (formal powers and personal skill and dedication) intertwine with state traditions in determining a given governor's influence over the state's legislature. But in many states, at various times, the governor dominates the legislature to a degree unthinkable at the national level. The governor of New York is one who is constitutionally granted a great deal of authority, causing him to be ranked regularly as one of the most powerful of the fifty governors. Not all governors have the constitutional authority over the legislature that the New York governor has, and some who do are not personally equipped or philosophically inclined to use such powers to their ultimate capacity. In addition, much depends on the structure and condition of the governor's party organization outside the legislature and of the governor's standing in the state party. A governor who controls patronage to a legislator's area and has either the party clout or the constitutional authority to determine the fate of each legislator's desired local legislation has substantial power in the legislature.[65]

Governors have some influence over all legislators, but more over legislators of the governor's own party. Even within the governor's party, variation exists. A governor with a modest majority in a legislative chamber needs the support of most of his or her legislative party to enact a legislative program and normally will use the various carrots and sticks available to persuade legislators. On the other hand, a governor with an overwhelming majority in the legislature usually has no need to demand high rates of individual legislator support and sees no reason to expend the resources required to try to keep a high rate of support for his or her programs, even among fellow partisans. An overly large majority is also likely to break down into factionalism. As one keen observer has noted, from the governor's perspective

413

★ ★ ★ ★

The Powerful Governor of New York

The governor of New York has enormous resources that enable him to become the dominant force in the legislative process. The Constitution empowers him to recommend legislation, call special sessions, veto bills, employ the item veto on budget matters, issue messages of necessity to speed the passage of bills, and prepare and submit the state budget. He heads a large and well-organized professional staff. . . .

New York's governor . . . is the center of public demand and expectations regarding the legislative solution of major problems and is the focus of attention for the mass media.

As political leader, he is the chief dispenser of political reward and/or punishment. Job patronage is big business, and according to Governor Rockefeller himself, it encompasses between 10,000 and 15,000 jobs. The extent to which such job patronage is employed to effect legislative decisions varies with the personal taste and style of the chief executive.

The result is that the governor is authorized and required both by law and tradition to prepare a legislative program of his own conception and a budget which together delineate the agenda of important measures that the legislature has to deal with each year. Today legislators await the governor's program because they know that it is the basis of their own legislative work. They no longer resent the intrusion of his initiative on what was once their privilege. . . .

This means that today there is little argument about the established fact that the governor proposes. Conflict can arise only about the question of to what extent he should dispose over the final outcome of legislative proposals. The success of the governor in getting what he wants is subject to several variables, and some of these are beyond his immediate control.

The first, of course, is the status of the political environment. If the governor is of a different party than that of the majority in both or even in one house of the legislature, then he must expect difficulty. . . .

But party division is only part of the story. Ideological considerations, which often transcend party lines, can also be a major factor. . . . While political leaders, in dealing with one another, are quite capable of ignoring or transcending ideological divisions in the general interest, there are always limits beyond which a political leader cannot or will not go in sacrificing or disregarding his or his party's basic principles for the purpose of accommodating a fellow leader.

Another variable of a different sort is, of course, the personality of the individuals involved. . . . Where there is friendship and mutual respect, the chances for minimizing conflict are better. Where there is personal dislike, distrust and suspicion, hostility becomes more likely and grows easier and faster.

Source: Alan G. Hevesi, *Legislative Politics in New York State* (New York: Praeger, 1975), pp. 122–23.

★ ★ ★ ★

"the optimum legislative contingent, then, would appear to be a comfortable majority—say about 55 percent—in both houses of the legislature."[66]

The governor's support usually is higher among fellow partisans in the legislature than among opposition-party legislators, but sometimes, the legislature, not just the governor's party, rallies behind a governor to enact a particular bill.[67] A study of legislative roll-call votes—in two different sessions each of the legislatures of seven state senates with one-party dominated legislatures—found that when the governor's position on a measure was made clear and the governor became involved in legislative consideration of the measure, "there is a rather large shift toward more partisan voting among the senators."[68] Generally, the distinctions between the parties clarify somewhat on such votes, with most of the governor's partisans voting with the governor, and most of the opposition party voting to the contrary. Much less partisan voting patterns are found on issues with which the governor is not greatly involved.[69] Further, both when the governor's legislative partisans were in the majority and when they were in the minority, the minority party in the legislature showed greater cohesiveness on gubernatorial issues than did the majority party.[70]

A 1974 study based on questionnaire responses from 1,256 state legislators in all fifty states found that the governor was influential in the legislative process, but that his or her influence was surprisingly indirect. For example, in response to a question concerning cue-givers (on whom legislators relied in deciding how to vote), the legislators ranked sources within the legislature and interest-group sources well ahead of the governor—in first- and second-choice mentions as well as in number of total mentions.[71] As the authors of the study note, however, governors usually are not present just prior to a roll-call vote, and they often are hard to reach personally, thus failing the "availability" requirement to be an important cue-giver. Besides, the governor's party leader in the chamber usually constitutes a substitute cue-giver for the governor.

A question which has not been satisfactorily answered is the exact dynamic by which a governor is able to persuade fellow partisans in the legislature to go along with his or her legislative program, but the major factor in the relationship appears to be the governor's position in the electoral party. Aspirants for the gubernatorial nomination build coalitions within the party and the electorate. Legislators within the governor's coalition in the party are more closely tied to the governor and his or her program, and they vote with the governor at a higher rate than their fellow partisans in the legislature. Legislators in whose districts the governor does well electorally, especially in the gubernatorial primary, evince the highest levels of gubernatorial support. Morehouse found a higher correlation between a legislator's loyalty to the governor and the governor's subsequent primary-election percentage in the legislator's district than between loyalty and earlier gubernatorial performance in the district. She concludes:

> [T]he influence of the governor over his legislative party is based on his political leadership within the electoral party, the party outside the legislature. If the governor has been successful in building a coalition to support him in the primary and election, he is also successful in building a coalition within the legislature to pass his legislation. . . . The high correlation between outside party organization generates discipline within the legislative party. . . . Based on my findings, a model of gubernatorial influence would give the most weight to the ability of the governor to form winning coalitions both within and outside the legislature. There may not be a time lag here. The two processes probably occur simultaneously. Instead of the legislative party being an independent entity, it is subject to the direction and influence of the governor's coalition within the electoral or-

ganization. Although it is an advantage to a governor to have a majority in the legislature, this is not an automatic guarantee that his legislation will pass.[72]

The relationship is not unidirectional, of course. One reason a gubernatorial candidate does well in a legislative district is that the legislator and other party leaders in that district agree with the governor's position on most issues of the day or like the candidate personally, or both, and "work the district" accordingly. Of course, legislators who are originally tepid toward a particular gubernatorial candidate are likely to warm up to him or her if the legislative constituency strongly supports that particular gubernatorial candidate.

SUMMARY

American legislative-executive relationships are structured by constitutional provisions at both the national and state level. These provisions mandate a separation of personnel between the legislature and the executive and allocate certain powers to the executive and certain powers to the legislature, while providing for an overlap of functions. Unlike parliamentary governments, the election and tenure in office of each branch of government in the United States is formally independent of the other, although the two are weakly linked electorally through the political party. Both because of the executive's constitutional powers and because of the nature of the modern state, as well as because of the public's expectations, the American executive seeks to provide leadership to the American legislature. That the executive formulates policies and programs for legislative consideration and seeks to have them enacted does not differentiate American executive-legislative relations from parliamentary systems. American constitutional provisions, however, affect the degree to which the members of the executive and the legislative branches share common backgrounds and the means used by the executive to assert leadership of the legislature, as well as the propensity and methods of legislators to leave their own independent imprint on legislation.

The tensions between the American executive and the American legislature stem primarily from five factors. First is the differing constituencies of the elected executive and the legislators. The executive is elected by all the people, while each legislator represents only a fraction of the whole. Second, partisan differences frequently divide the chief executive from the majority in the legislature, a circumstance that is not a problem in parliamentary systems. A third source of tension is the differing tenures and terms of the chief executive and the legislator, especially at the national level. If the chief executive is to accomplish anything worthwhile, it must be done with dispatch. In contrast, many powerful legislators are under no such time constraints and indeed may have an interest in limiting action to incremental change, at most. Organizational differences between the two branches of government are a fourth source of friction. Not only is the legislative committee structure not always congruent with the administrative structure of the executive, but, by their very natures, legislative organizations are flat, with more dispersal of authority, rather than hierarchical as in the executive branch of government. The fifth major source of tension between the American legislature and the American executive is the executive's greater resource base and greater access to information and expertise. To the extent the legislature has information and expertise of its own available, the legislature's experts are likely to see matters differently from the executive's experts.

Despite the tensions between them, the two branches of government must develop a modus operandi if any of the actors are to gain satisfaction from their positions.

The legislature is armed with control over taxes and appropriations, basic legislative authority, and—ultimately—the power to impeach and remove the executive from office. The chief executive has the power to veto legislation (subject to its being over-ridden), substantial control over the development of the budget, some power to issue executive orders, media visibility which permits domination of discussion and of the agenda, and various kinds of patronage. The President is especially powerful in the roles of commander in chief and chief of foreign relations. Congress clearly plays a secondary role in the conduct of defense and foreign affairs, although since 1973, Congress has asserted authority in those spheres. Congress (and to a lesser extent, the various state legislatures) has made increasingly greater use of the "legislative veto" to retain control over certain types of actions by the President and various government agencies.

Governors sometimes are able to dominate their state legislatures to a degree which recent presidents have been unable to approach. This is because of their place in the state party organization and because of the closer relationship between state and local party organizations than between national and local party organizations. But state legislatures tend to have more centralized power than Congress, and when strong state legislative leaders choose to confront governors, the governors often discover that they have to negotiate to get what they want.

Notes

1. Clinton Rossiter, *The American Presidency,* rev. ed. (New York: Harcourt Brace Jovanovich, 1960). Louis W. Koenig's authoritative study of the presidency devotes an entire chapter (of sixteen) to legislative leadership. *The Chief Executive,* rev. ed. (New York: Harcourt Brace Jovanovich, 1968). The insightful analysis of the presidency by Robert J. Sickels includes two (of fourteen) chapters on presidential leadership of and interactions with Congress. *The Presidency: An Introduction* (Englewood Cliffs, N.J.: Prentice-Hall, 1980). See also Thad Beyle and J. Oliver Williams, *The American Governor in Behavioral Perspective* (New York: Harper and Row, 1972); and Sara McCally Morehouse, "The Governor as Political Leader" in *Politics in the American States,* 3rd ed., ed. Herbert Jacob and Kenneth N. Vines (Boston: Little, Brown, 1976).

2. Gerhard Loewenberg and Samuel C. Patterson, *Comparing Legislatures* (Boston: Little, Brown, 1979), p. 236; and Hugh Heclo, "Presidential and Prime Ministerial Selections," in D. R. Matthews, ed. *Perspectives on Presidential Selection* (Washington, D.C.: Brookings Institution, 1973), cited in Loewenberg and Patterson. As is so often the case, many variables affect these statistics. One may not simply say that the lengthy British service prior to attaining cabinet rank is "caused" by their parliamentary system without attention to numerous other factors as well. Although all cabinet members in Australia and Canada are selected from national parliaments, their national legislative service prior to cabinet appointment has been much briefer than in Britain. See Joseph A. Schlesinger, "Political Careers and Party Leadership," in *Political Leadership in Industrialized Societies,* ed. Lewis J. Edinger (New York: John Wiley, 1967), pp. 286–87.

3. This discussion is based upon Loewenberg and Patterson, *Comparing Legislatures,* pp. 237–41. Data are from Edzard Schmidt-Jortig, "Die Bundestagszugehörigkeit der Bonner Minister," *Zeitschrift fur Parlamentsfragen* 5 (October 1974): 312–16; cited in Loewenberg and Patterson.

4. Loewenberg and Patterson, p. 23.

5. Ibid., pp. 237–38.

6. Ibid., p. 232.

7. Although we cite specific sources throughout, the general discussion which follows is greatly influenced by George C. Edwards III, *Presidential Influence in Congress* (San Francisco: W.H. Freeman, 1980); Louis W. Koenig, *Congress and the President* (Chicago: Scott, Foresman, 1965); Loewenberg and Patterson, *Comparing Legislatures,* Chapter 7; Nelson W. Polsby, *Congress and the Presidency,* 3rd. ed. (Englewood Cliffs, N.J.: Prentice-Hall, 1976);

and John B. Schwartz and L. Earl Shaw, *The United States Congress in Comparative Perspective* (Hinsdale, Ill: Dryden Press, 1976), especially Chapters 6, 7, and 8.

8. See, for example, Edwards, *Presidential Influence in Congress,* Chapter 2; Dorothy Buckton James, *The Contemporary Presidency* (Indianapolis: Bobbs-Merrill, Pegasus, 1974), Chapter 7; and Koenig, *Congress and the President,* pp. 141–47.

9. Those members of Congress (usually senators) who aspire to the presidency seek to build a national coalition, but they may seek to build a winning coalition around different premises and constituency bases than the incumbent President.

10. On this dynamic, generally, see John A. Ferejohn, *Pork Barrel Politics* (Stanford, Calif.: Stanford University Press, 1974). See also Charles O. Jones, "Representation in Congress: The Case of the House Agricultural Committee," *American Political Science Review* 55 (June 1961): 358–67.

11. Only by assuming there would be no interest payment on the cost of the dam, by downplaying nonmonetary (e.g., environmental and social) costs, and by exaggerating economic benefits could local boosters and developers and the U.S. Corps of Engineers justify the costs of the Tellico Dam. *Congressional Quarterly Weekly Report,* January 27, 1979, p. 178.

12. For an insightful, if dated, discussion of the two wings of each major party, see James MacGregor Burns, *The Deadlock of Democracy* (Englewood Cliffs, N.J.: Prentice-Hall, 1963).

13. Persons who succeed to less than two years of a predecessor's presidency can serve two additional terms in their own right. Thus, the maximum tenure as President is ten years. (U.S. Constitution, Amendment XXII).

14. Burdett A. Loomis, "Policy Speculation and the Congress: An Issues Based Approach" (Paper delivered at the 1980 Annual Meeting of the American Political Science Association, Washington, D.C.).

15. *Congressional Quarterly Weekly Report,* October 14, 1978, p. 2925.

16. "He'll sit here," Truman would remark (tapping his desk for emphasis), "and he'll say 'Do this! Do that!' *And Nothing will happen.* Poor Ike—it won't be a bit like the Army. He'll find it very frustrating." Quoted in Richard E. Neustadt, *Presidential Power* (New York: John Wiley, 1962), p. 9.

17. William J. Keefe, *Congress and the American People* (Englewood Cliffs, N.J.: Prentice-Hall, 1980), p. 106.

18. James L. Sundquist, "Congress and the President: Enemies or Partners?" in *Congress Reconsidered,* ed. Lawrence C. Dodd and Bruce I. Oppenheimer (New York: Praeger, 1977), p. 235.

19. Edwards, *Presidential Influence in Congress,* p. 46. As Edwards also notes, the deference extended to the Presidents on the automatic assumption that he and his advisors know more than we do about foreign affairs has faded as a result of the discovery that many ordinary Americans had a better idea from the national news media of what was really occurring in Vietnam and Southeast Asia during the late 1960s and early 1970s than one would have had after reading all the secret intelligence reports available to the President (pp. 15–17). Still, only a rash member of Congress would challenge the President on sensitive international questions, if the President alluded to classified information.

20. Aaron Wildavsky, "The Two Presidencies," *Trans-Action* 4 (December 1966): 7–14. For a criticism of Wildavsky's position, see Lee Sigelman, "A Reassessment of the Two Presidencies Thesis," *Journal of Politics* 41 (November 1979): 1195–1205.

21. Schwartz and Shaw, *The United States Congress in Comparative Perspective,* especially pp. 234–44.

22. Randall B. Ripley and Grace A. Franklin, *Congress, the Bureaucracy, and Public Policy,* rev. ed. (Homewood, Ill.: Dorsey Press, 1980), pp. 184–97.

23. Harvey G. Zeidenstein, "The Reassertion of Congressional Power: New Curbs on the President," *Political Science Quarterly* 93 (Fall 1978): 393–409; and William J. Lanouette, "Who's Setting Foreign Policy—Carter or Congress?" *National Journal,* July 15, 1978, pp. 1116–23.

24. Louis Fisher, *The Constitution Between Friends: Congress, the President, and the Law* (New York: St. Martin's Press, 1978), p. 209.

25. Ibid., pp. 210–13.

26. Zeidenstein, "The Reassertion of Congressional Power, p. 394.

27. Ibid.

28. Thomas M. Franck, "After the Fall: The New Procedural Framework for Congressional Control Over the War Power," *American Journal of International Law* 71 (July-October, 1977): 605.

29. Zeidenstein, "The Reassertion of Congressional Power, p. 395.

30. Franck, "After the Fall," pp. 614–16.

31. Ibid., pp. 617–20.

32. *Congressional Quarterly Weekly Report,* April 26, 1980, pp. 1067–68; and May 3, 1980, pp. 1156, 1162–63.

33. *Congressional Quarterly Weekly Report,* September 20, 1980, p. 2796; and December 6, 1980, p. 3505. A summary of Congressional-CIA relations during the years the Hughes-Ryan Amendment was in force is available in Zeidenstein, "The Reassertion of Congressional Power, pp. 398–402.

34. Sickels, *The Presidency: An Introduction,* pp. 115–16.

35. Kathryn Newcomer Harmon and Marsha L. Brauen, "Joint Electoral Outcomes as Cues for Congressional Support of Presidents," (Paper delivered at the 1978 Annual Meeting of the Midwest Political Science Association, Chicago, Ill.); reported in Michael L. Mezey, ed., "Comparative Legislative Studies Newsletter," *Legislative Studies Quarterly* 3 (August 1978): 520.

36. Edwards, "Presidential Influence in the House, pp. 101–113. See also his article, "Presidential Influence in the Senate: Presidential Prestige as a Source of Presidential Power," *American Politics Quarterly* 5 (October 1977): 481–500. John R. Bond and Richard Fleisher controlled for ideology and found that increasing presidential popularity increased the support among the president's fellow partisans in Congress, but decreased support among opposition party members of Congress. The negative impact among opposition party members, however, was less dramatic than the positive impact among the President's fellow partisans. Still, the President who faces a Congress controlled by the other major party may be in the odd position of gaining in public opinion and—as a result—losing support in Congress. See "The Limits of Presidential Popularity As a Source of Influence in the U.S. House," *Legislative Studies Quarterly* 5 (February 1980): 69–78.

37. *Congressional Quarterly Weekly Report,* August 1, 1981, pp. 1371–80.

38. Joseph A. Pika, "White House Boundary Roles: Linking Advisory Systems and Presidential Publics" (Paper delivered at the 1979 Annual Meeting of the American Political Science Association, Washington, D.C.). See also Lawrence F. O'Brien, *No Final Victories* (Garden City, N.Y.: Doubleday, 1974).

39. Richard E. Cohen, "The Carter-Congress Rift—Who's Really to Blame?" *National Journal,* April 22, 1978, pp. 630–32; Eric L. Davis, "Legislative Liaison in the Carter Administration" (Paper delivered at the 1978 Annual Meeting of the Midwest Political Science Association, Chicago, Ill.).

40. This popular phrase came from the catchy title of Arthur M. Schlesinger's book, *The Imperial Presidency* (Boston: Houghton Mifflin, 1973).

41. December 17, 1962 television interview. Quoted in Thomas E. Cronin, *The State of the Presidency* (Boston: Little, Brown, 1975), p. 87.

42. Koenig, *The Chief Executive,* rev. ed., p. 137.

43. *Kennedy* v. *Sampson,* 364 F. Supp. 1075, 1087 (D.D.C. 1973). The case and the legal status of the pocket veto during various types of Congressional adjournments is discussed in Fisher, *The Constitution Between Friends.* A case might be made for a pocket veto if Congress had a lengthy intrasession adjournment and left no procedure for receipt of a presidential veto message, but that is a very unlikely eventuality.

44. John R. Bolton, *The Legislative Veto: Unseparating the Powers* (Washington, D.C.: American Enterprise Institute, 1977), p. 6.

45. Ibid., pp. 6, 8.

46. Fisher, *The Constitution Between Friends,* p. 99.

47. Ibid., pp. 100–103.

48. Sickels, *The Presidency: An Introduction,* p. 112.

49. Bolton, *The Legislative Veto,* p. 2.

50. Alan Murray, "Courts Veto Legislative Veto in Deportation Controversy," *Congressional Quarterly Weekly Report,* January 3, 1981, p. 36.

51. Ibid.

52. Bolton, *The Legislative Veto,* pp. 10–13.

53. Harold Bruff and Ernest Gellhorn, *Harvard Law Review* 90 (1977): 1396.

54. Murray, "Courts Veto Legislative Veto in Deportation Controversy," p. 35; James J. Kilpatrick, "The Legislative Veto, One More Time," syndicated column in the *Albuquerque Journal,* January 21, 1981, p. A-5.

55. Frank J. Sorauf, *Party Politics in America* (Boston: Little, Brown, 1980), pp. 228–31; and Malcolm E. Jewell and David M. Olson, *American State Political Parties and Elections* (Homewood, Ill.: Dorsey Press, 1980), pp. 253–62.

56. Some states have various minor unique provisions of their own. See *American State Legislatures: Their Structures and Procedures* (Lexington, Ky.: Council of State Governments, 1977), pp. 74–75.

57. Ibid., pp. 74–75; and Charles R. Adrian, *State and Local Governments* (New York: McGraw-Hill, 1976), p. 242.

58. *American State Legislatures: Their Structures and Procedures,* pp. 74–75.

59. Ibid.

60. Ibid., p. 617; and Joseph A. Schlesinger, "The Politics of the Executive," in *Politics in the American States,* 2nd ed., ed. Herbert Jacob and Kenneth N. Vines (Boston: Little, Brown, 1971), pp. 228–33.

61. V. O. Key, Jr., *Southern Politics* (New York: Vintage, Caravelle, 1949), pp. 150–51.

62. Schlesinger, "The Politics of the Executive," p. 232.

63. Morehouse, "The Governor as Political Leader," pp. 206–7.

64. Kenneth N. Vines and Herbert Jacob, "State Courts and Public Policy," in Jacob and Vines, *Politics in the American States,* 3rd ed., pp. 251–55.

65. Malcolm E. Jewell, *The State Legislature,* 2nd. ed. (New York: Random House, 1969), pp. 77–80.

66. Morehouse, "The Governor as Political Leader," p. 231.

67. Lee Bernick, "The Impact of U.S. Governors on Party Voting in One-Party Dominated Legislatures," *Legislative Studies Quarterly* 3 (August 1978): 439–41.

68. Ibid., p. 436, 438.

69. Ibid., pp. 439–40.

70. Ibid., pp. 439–41.

71. Eric M. Uslaner and Ronald F. Weber, *Patterns of Decision Making in State Legislatures* (New York: Praeger, 1977), pp. 33–41.

72. Morehouse, "The Governor as Political Leader," pp. 232–33. See also her "The Governor and His Legislative Party," *American Political Science Review* 60 (December 1966): 933–41.

chapter *15*

The Legislature and the Bureaucracy

Preview

Because of the differences in both their official positions and their backgrounds, legislators and bureaucrats often see public issues in disparate ways. Yet the bureaucracy depends on the legislature for its very existence, and the legislature depends on the bureaucracy for help in the development of legislation and for implementation of the programs enacted by the legislature. Legislative ability to control bureaucratic decisions appears consistent with democratic ideals, but most legislative intervention seems to be on behalf of narrow, organized interest groups rather than "the public interest." Shared concern among key bureaucrats, legislators and interest-group representatives over specific, narrow, policy areas results in intense communications among a small set of actors, a phenomenon referred to as *subgovernments* or *cozy triangles.* While members of such subgovernments normally compromise their differences, they seem to protect the fundamental interests of the private interest groups and bureaucracies involved. Legislative concern over the growth of government bureaucracy and its authority have led to the development of numerous techniques for restraining the bureaucrats. These include traditional legislative oversight activities, carried out largely by the committees and subcommittees of Congress; in recent years, sunset legislation which provides for periodic review of bureaucratic agencies resulting in either reauthorization or termination; and use of the legislative veto.

The legislature and the bureaucracy must deal with each other extensively. It is the legislature that creates new programs and agencies which the bureaucracy then staffs and operates. The legislature may expand old programs and agencies or terminate them. The legislature determines the appropriations which pay for the bureaucracy's salaries and provide funding for the programs it administers. Obviously, then, bureaucrats desire to retain the favor of the legislature. They do not wish to place their own futures or the futures of their agencies in jeopardy. Frequently, they desire to expand their budget and program. Promotions are much more readily obtained in a growing agency than in a stagnant or shrinking one. Further, the prestige of a growing agency tends to increase, while the prestige of an agency that is starved for funds inevitably declines.

Legislatures—and individual members within them—concern themselves with burgeoning government agencies and personnel. They try to make sure that the laws which have been passed are implemented as intended. Legislatures seek to ferret out waste, and they see no need to expand the budgets of agencies that are wasting money. What constitutes "waste," of course, is sometimes subject to debate. At the same time, legislatures receive a good deal of service from the bureaucracy. Even though legislative staffs are growing, legislators still depend on agency bureaucrats for information and ideas, including draft bills, and for success in much of the constituency-service work that makes a legislator look good back home.

But the fact that the legislature and the bureaucracy each feel they need to interact and coexist does not insure that the relationship between these two sets of government actors will be easy. While cooperation is preferred by both the bureaucracy and the legislature, the relationship between them is often in fact downright uncomfortable.

While it is necessary for the legislature to influence executive agencies and to insure that legislative mandates are not countermanded by the bureaucracy, the problems of democracy would not be solved if the legislature were to dominate the bureaucracy completely. The legislature is, of course, central to representative democracy. It is especially important in the development of solutions to societal problems, both because of its function in legitimizing government decisions and because the legislative process tends to lead to solutions that are widely acceptable, even when universal support is not possible. But many important policies set forth in legislation require that administrators be given independent discretion if the program is to be effective and if it is to be administered according to such "universalist" values as treating all citizens equally and fairly. There is substantial evidence that legislative intervention in daily administrative decisions may result in the unfair distortion of policy implementation. The ability of the legislature to intervene forcefully in the administration of the laws remains important to legislators' constituents, but norms of restraint among legislators also serve a valuable purpose.[1]

CONGRESS AND THE BUREAUCRACY

As noted in earlier chapters, American legislators tend to be generalists. After election to a legislature, they develop or enhance legislative expertise in the subjects which are of most concern to their constituents and in the policy and program areas that fall under the jurisdiction of their legislative committees. But legislative expertise is not the same as bureaucratic expertise. The bureaucrat is seldom required to look at the "big picture" or to take time to deal with questions outside the concern of one particular agency. Legislators, on the other hand, are distracted by a wide array of demands. In addition, the American legislator is generally not experienced in the administrative relationships that so frequently dominate the perspectives of bureaucrats.

The executive branch of American government, in which the vast bulk of government bureaucrats are employed, is organized the way it is mainly because of the demands of various interests in the society. It is no accident that we have a Department of Agriculture, a Department of Education, and a Department of Labor. The Department of Defense, for example, is the center of concern for such organizations and interests as defense contractors and associations of retired military officers. Bureaucrats, then, should be seen not just as neutral policy experts but, often, as advocates for a particular point of view, and, frequently, as spokespersons for a particular interest group or set of interest groups. Each government agency tends to look out for its clientele groups, and the clientele groups and organizations, in turn, defend the agency from its enemies in the general public, elsewhere in the executive branch, and in the legislature.

Frequently, there is a direct legislative-bureaucracy link. The same political forces that led to the creation of an executive department or agency in the first place are also likely to have persuaded the legislature of the importance of the concerns of that department or agency. Often, a legislative committee or subcommittee will have been established in Congress to deal primarily with the activities of a particular department or agency. If the agency or department grows in importance, the committee is likely to do so too. If the department or agency declines in importance, the committee is also likely to decline in importance. Legislative committees, then, are less than neutral agents in the legislative-bureaucracy linkage.[2]

Congress and Bureaucratic Initiatives

Members of Congress are greatly dependent on their staff aides to pull together relevant information for them. Members and their staffs are also dependent on the agencies of government, both for information and for estimates of what effect various legislative proposals might have.

★ ★ ★ ★

The Natural Ally

Suspicion of the bureaucracy is so deep-seated in the grass roots of the country that running against the bureaucracy is one of the traditional rites of electioneering. And Congress would seem to be almost the last bastion of defense the public has against the expanding size and power of the bureaucracy.

In fact, Congress is the natural ally of the bureaucracy in its expansionism and in its subterranean war with the President. For every bureaucracy there is either a congressional subcommittee to "oversee" it or one whose legislative work meshes with it. An almost complete coincidence of interests exists between these committees and the bureaucracies they monitor. The power structure of Congress is built on the committee system and the bureaucracies constitute the raison d'etre of the subcommittees. The loss of a bureaucracy's power or influence through a cutting of its budget or a threatened reorganization translates into a similar loss for the key members of the subcommittee. Throw in, too, the fact that each subcommittee has exactly the same constituency as its counterpart bureaucracy: the urban coalitions, for example, which have a mutually supportive liaison with HUD, maintain a similar relationship with the House Subcommittee on Housing and Community Development. So while candidates talk economy, incumbents know that the votes lie in spending. As the aide of one senator who has a record of unfailing backing for the programs of "his" bureaucracy told me, "My senator gets elected for what he supports on behalf of organized groups, not for what he dismantles on the public's behalf."

It's not that the organized groups control the voters—for the most part, they don't. But they do have the money to finance an opposing candidate, and a well-heeled opponent is what an incumbent fears the most.

Source: Leonard Reed, "The Bureaucracy: The Cleverest Lobby of them All," in *Inside the System*, 4th ed., ed. Charles Peters and Nicholas Lemann (New York: Holt, Rinehart, and Winston, 1979), p. 194.

★ ★ ★ ★

Congress originates a large number of bills each year—that is, the bills are actually drafted in Congress. But even these bills are often greatly affected by the views of bureaucrats. More frequently, legislation may have its origin in a government agency. This occurs in a number of ways. The government agency may draft a bill for a member of Congress or for a high-level executive official to resolve some problem that the legislator or the official perceives to be important. More common, the government agency itself perceives a problem and drafts a bill to meet it. Some of the bills that originate in a government agency may, in fact, have been suggested by an interest group with which the agency has a symbiotic relationship. Still other bills may stem from the agency's desire to clarify some problem in the law or to enhance the agency's importance.

Much proposed legislation that originates with bureaus of government goes through established channels, from lower-level bureaus to top-agency officials, and then to the President's immediate lieutenants for clearance, before being sent to the Congress. Some measures are merely allowed to be forwarded directly to Congress as agency bills. Others are incorporated into the President's program and, thus, are given more attention by the White House Office of Congressional Relations. The central executive-department screening of the thousands of legislative proposals that well up each year from the various agencies of the national government is performed within each major agency first, then by the Office of Management and Budget (OMB), with frequent detailed guidance from the White House.[3] OMB is concerned not only with the financial and fiscal impact of legislation, but also with program content.

It is not uncommon for a legislative proposal that has been rejected by top administration officials or by OMB to surface in Congress anyhow. This may occur—much to the irritation of top administration officials—when a lower-level bureau, which has a different view on an issue than the President or top presidential aides, circumvents the central clearance process and goes directly to a Congressional committee or subcommittee with which the bureau regularly deals.[4] Sometimes, no one knows what bureaucrat has disobeyed higher executive authority, and everyone involved denies knowing how it might have occurred. On other occasions, the identity of the

---

★ ★ ★ ★

The Role of Federal Agencies in Policy Development

[The figure opposite] is a simple model of the place of bureaucratic agencies in policy development and formulation. The solid lines in the figure represent the flow of legislative proposals and actual legislation; the dotted lines represent the transmission of advice and information related to the development of policy but not actually legislation per se. The bureau, as the model suggests, is often a rich source of legislative proposals both upwards into the political echelons of agency leadership and laterally into the Congress. Those forwarded upwards may actually come at the request of the agency leadership (possibly at presidential urging) or may be initiatives from the bureaucracy for new legislation or amendments to existing authority. They may be part of a developing presidential program or, as "agency bills," be the result of bureaucratic stimulus.

Agency bills or proposals which are initiated by the bureaus are usually reviewed by the agency leadership and if acceptable, are for-

FIGURE 15.1

The Role of Federal Agencies in Policy Development

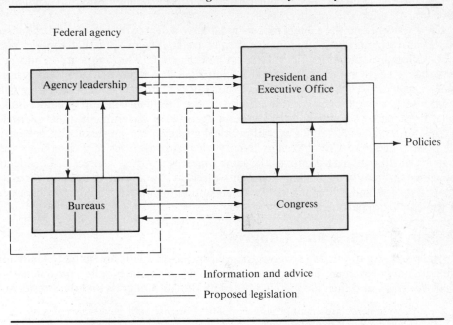

Information and advice

Proposed legislation

warded to the Office of Management and Budget in the Executive Office. The OMB examines the proposal, consults with other agencies affected, makes a determination whether the proposal is consistent with the president's programme, and either holds it back or consents to its being sent to the Hill. Agency legislative proposals that are produced at presidential request follow largely the same route as agency bills. . . .

As the line in the figure running from the bureaus to Congress indicates, legislative proposals can also flow laterally between the two institutions. Part of this flow may represent bureau proposals that are blocked at the agency or OMB review level. . . . These "end runs" are not looked on with favor . . . but especially in the subsystem arena there are few sanctions that can be brought to bear against an offending bureau.

. . . The president . . . may [also] request an agency or interagency task force to draft an executive order or presidential reorganization plan, and stamp what is produced by the agency with his imprimatur. Executive orders . . . do not pass through the congressional process. In the model they flow along the line from agency to presidency to policy.

Source: From *Congress and the Administrative State* by Lawrence C. Dodd and Richard L. Schott. Copyright © 1979 by John Wiley & Sons, Inc. Reprinted by permission.

★ ★ ★ ★

offending bureaucrat may be known, but no punishment within the administration may be forthcoming because the strength of the bureau's supporting clientele group or because the issue involved is not central to the President's program. Inflicting punishment, after all, entails costs.

The President and the cabinet officers must have a degree of support and cooperation from their nominal subordinates if they are to govern. But that support and cooperation are not automatic; they must be earned. Top level executives and bureaucrats "engage in mutually profitable exchanges."[5] A degree of autonomy is normally one of the demands of lower-level bureaucrats, in return for which they will usually seek to avoid open confrontation with the President and top appointed officials. Presidents may elect to attack certain agencies of government, their clientele groups, or both, as part of an overall political strategy, but presidents do not have the political resources to challenge directly *all* major agencies of government and their supporting interest groups at the same time, even if they wanted to. Presidents recognize this reality by picking their fights carefully, by seeking to develop "credit" where they can, and by making many cabinet appointments from among the clientele of the cabinet departments.[6]

Subgovernments and Congress

As the preceding discussion suggests, many routine decisions are actually made for the national government by *subgovernments,*—also sometimes called *subsystems* or *cozy triangles*—and then are merely ratified by the full Congress and the President.[7]

> Subgovernments are small groups of political actors, both governmental and nongovernmental, that specialize in specific issue areas. . . . They are . . . most prevalent and influential in the least visible policy areas. . . .
>
> A typical subgovernment is composed of members of the House and/or Senate, members of congressional staffs, a few bureaucrats, and representatives of private groups and organizations interested in the policy area. Usually the members of Congress and staff members are from the committees or subcommittees that have principal or perhaps exclusive jurisdiction over the policy area dominated by the subgovernment. The congressional members of the subgovernment are also usually the few most senior members of a relevant committee or subcommittee. The bureaucrats in a subgovernment are likely to be the chief of a bureau with jurisdiction paralleling that of the congressional committee or subcommittee and a few of his or her top assistants. The non-governmental members of a subgovernment are most likely to be a few lobbyists for interest groups with the heaviest stake in the nature of governmental policy in the area.
>
> Most of the policymaking in which the subgovernments engage consists of routine matters . . . policy that is not currently embroiled in a high degree of controversy. . . . Since most policymaking is routine most of the time, subgovernments can often function for long periods of time without much interference or control from individuals or institutions outside the subgovernment.[8]

Congressional decision-making concerning military veterans policy provides an example of such a subgovernment. Congressional decision-making on veterans' issues centers in the House and Senate Veterans' Affairs Committees, with intense involvement by top Veterans' Administration officials and by numerous veterans organizations' lobbyists.[9] While interest-group representatives and Veterans' Administration spokespersons are very influential in this subgovernment and gain informal access to legislative decision-making in its formative stages, one should not forget that the subgovernment also provides a mechanism for informed (if somewhat biased) *legisla-*

tive decision-making on proposed statutes as well as a mechanism for legislators to exercise informal oversight over the Veterans' Administration bureaucrats.

Types of Subgovernment Issue Areas   The nature of a policy field affects the patterns of interaction within the subsystem and between the members of the subsystem and other actors, as well as the extent to which decisions made within a subsystem are or are not automatically ratified on the floor of Congress. Borrowing from Lowi and others, for example, Ripley and Franklin distinguish four major categories of domestic public policy subgovernments.[10] *Distributive* policies and programs, for example, promote "private activities that are said to be desirable to society as a whole and . . . convey tangible governmental benefits to the individuals, groups, and corporations" involved in those activities.[11] Decisions concerning distributive policies (such as subsidized water projects and agricultural price supports) "are not considered in light of each other; rather they are disaggregated. Thus, there appear to be only winners and no losers."[12]*Redistributive* policies, in contrast, involve

> a conscious attempt to manipulate the allocation of wealth, property, rights, or some other value among broad classes or groups in society, (and thus) the actors perceive that there will be distinct winners and losers. The stakes are thought to be high and this fact means that the policymaking process will be marked by a high degree of visibility and conflict.[13]

Redistributive issues include the rate of progressivity of the personal income tax, affirmative action legislation, food stamps, and other types of assistance to lower-income people. The distinction in the dynamic of interactions is not whether some group or individual is receiving tangible benefits from the government; that is the case with both distributive and redistributive policy. The distinction is whether or not the way the decision-making process is structured causes people consciously to perceive "winners" and "losers" in a decision. The "losers" are likely to create a controversy over the decision. That is not the case in a distributive-issue dynamic (when public funds are used to benefit "society") even though a particular industry or corporation is the vehicle and beneficiary of the collective social benefit.

In addition to distributive and redistributive policy arenas, Ripley and Franklin note the presence of two types of regulatory policy decisions. *Competitive regulatory policy* decisions, such as those allocating television and radio broadcasting licenses, is similar to distributive policy, in that some interests are given massive tangible benefits without much generalized controversy. In such cases, subsystem decision-making is fairly stable and hidden.[14]

Protective regulatory policy, in contrast, is designed to protect the public from various harmful acts of private individuals or corporations. Thus, the government prohibits or regulates certain harmful activities such as air pollution or false advertising. Here, the issues confronting Congress shift frequently, and so do the relevant coalitions. This leads to a more visible, conflict-ridden, and less closed decision-making process for these types of policies.[15]

In *foreign policy* and *defense policy,* similarly, some types of decision-making are more subject to debate and divisiveness than others. The routine details of operating the defense establishment, for example, convey tangible benefits to select interests, but, as in the case of distributive policy, there is no clearly identified and massive class of "losers" to protest these decisions. Crisis decisions, of necessity, are made by a small set of officials. But strategic policy decisions result in conflict between different agencies of government, and they involve different philosophies of interna-

427

───────────── ★ ★ ★ ★ ─────────────

Subgovernment Relationships and Incrementalism

Within the executive branch two relationships are critical—that of the President with Executive Office personnel and presidential appointees throughout the government . . . and that of Executive Office personnel and presidential appointees with civil servants throughout the government. . . .

Three relationships are critical within Congress. Committee and subcommittee leaders play an intermediary role between party leaders and rank-and-file members, but party leaders also need and maintain direct ties to the rank and file; . . . The committee and subcommittee leaders are typically the most important individuals in deciding what emerges from Congress in substantive terms. The party leaders make the strategic and tactical decisions about how best to get the work of committees and subcommittees approved by the full House and Senate. . . .

There are also three critical relationships between the executive branch and Congress: those between the President and the party leaders (largely on strategic and tactical matters), between the Executive Office personnel and presidential appointees and committee and subcommittee leaders (on substantive matters), and between policy level actors in the civil and military service and committee and subcommittee leaders in Congress (on substantive matters).

To get very dramatic policy movement out of the government, the eight relationships portrayed in Figure [15.2 below] must all be marked by a high degree of mutual confidence and trust, and there must also be a high degree of agreement on the nature of the problems facing society and the nature of proper solutions to those problems. These conditions are absent more than they are present, which helps to explain the normal posture of the government as moving very slowly on only a few problems at a time.

FIGURE 15.2

Critical Relationships for Policymaking in the National Government

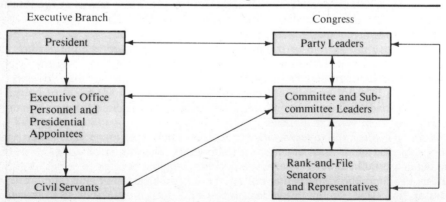

Source: Randall B. Ripley and Grace A. Franklin, *Congress, the Bureaucracy, and Public Policy,* rev. ed., (Homewood, Ill: Dorsey Press, 1980), pp. 5, 6.

───────────── ★ ★ ★ ★ ─────────────

tional relations and defense. Subgovernments of experts are very influential on strategic issues, but these issues are usually debated at length, with the periodic shifts in major strategic policy requiring Congressional approval following extensive Congressional debate.[16]

Subgovernment policy dominance is usually greatest in policy fields characterized by low conflict and complex, technical issues. Under such circumstances, members of Congress who are not on the relevant committee have little reason to challenge its recommendations; doing so would be a violation of generally understood norms, unless the challenger has a valid reason. Members who attack a subgovernment can also make enemies. A more promising approach, in terms of payoff for the individual member, often is to seek a particular decision within the existing framework of relationships rather than to challenge the subgovernment's dominance of the policy field. Unless the policy field becomes salient to a larger audience and somewhat controversial, the President and top presidential assistants are similarly disinclined to create enemies.

After saying all this, it should be noted that from the public's point of view conflict can provide the opportunity for outsiders to open up the decision-making process and force consideration of points of view and values normally disregarded by the subgovernment involved.

Subgovernments are long-lived, but they are not immutable. Circumstances sometimes change, creating challenges from without which cannot be coped with readily by the subgovernment, even through a strategy of cooptation and accommodation. The tobacco subgovernment, for example (the tobacco industry, the related bureaus of the Department of Agriculture, and the relevant Congressional subcommittees), has been unable to contain totally the health-related challenges to federal tobacco policy. To be sure, the tobacco subgovernment still dominates its policy field— tobacco farmers still receive government assistance, for example. But the decisions of the tobacco subgovernment are no longer *automatically* ratified, either by Congress, as a whole, or by top executive officials.[17] Most challenges to subgovernments fail. When they succeed, the victory is often only partial. The nuclear power industry is being challenged now, mostly by environmental groups, for influence in nuclear power policy. Although the clearly promotional policies of the 1950s and early 1960s have waned, the outcome of the struggle for nuclear policy dominance is not yet clear.[18]

Congressional Decentralization and Subgovernments The changes in the internal structure of Congress over the past decade (discussed in earlier chapters), and especially the growth of the independent authority of permanent subcommittees of the standing committees of Congress, have further decentralized subgovernments. While it is convenient to describe subgovernments as "triangles" of influence, composed of key members of Congress, executive agencies, and interest groups, it should be kept in mind that not all triangles are equilateral.[19] That is, in some subgovernments, the members of Congress dominate policymaking; in others, the greatest influence is held by executive-agency bureaucrats; and, in yet others, the representatives of private interests have the dominant voice. In addition, while the individual members of Congress with the greatest subgovernment authority often are the committee and subcommittee chairpersons, personal idiosyncrasy frequently determines which members will devote the greatest time and effort to the oversight of an agency, thus gaining subgovernment power.[20]

Further, significant changes in the resources of the various actors is likely to change power relationships within a given subgovernment. Whatever the other merits of the devolution of authority to Congressional subcommittees, some

429

observers of Congress fear that the increased number, authority, independence, and permanence of Congressional subcommittees will mean greater subgovernment influence for private interest groups or executive agencies, or both. Thus, paradoxically, Congress' structural reforms may result in lesser authority in decision-making for the Congressional members of the subgovernment. For example, Dodd and Schott argue that even though the enhanced role of subcommittees has increased the number of members of Congress actively involved in subgovernmental politics,

> [t]he power of Congress within a particular subsystem is very much a function of the authority of the individual members who head the congressional side of a subsystem triangle. The power of individual congressional actors is itself a product of numerous subsidiary resources . . . [which include] their strategic bargaining position vis-à-vis agencies and interest groups. This position depends on the number of agencies and programs falling within their general purview and the dependence of agencies on them for support.[21]

> The coming of subcommittees government has undermined the strategic bargaining position of Congress in regard to the agencies. By its very nature, subcommittee government involves carving up committee jurisdictions into a larger set of smaller jurisdictions.[22]

> If numerous interest groups fall within a committee's policy domain, the committee and its leaders often have the upper hand; each interest group knows that it needs the committee more than the committee needs it. . . . By contrast, if a committee or subcommittee deals with legislation affecting only a small range of interest groups, the members of the committee are limited in the number of groups they can help and from whom they can receive electoral support. If, simultaneously, the interest groups have numerous other subcommittees or committees to whom they can turn, any one subcommittee tends to become more dependent on one interest group than that group is on the committee or subcommittees.[23]

Within limits, most Americans would argue that access to government decision-makers is proper for those citizens most strongly affected by the decision. The difficulty arising from subgovernments, however, is that major interest groups appear to have such close relationships with Congressional and bureaucratic decision-makers that the views of interest groups are likely to take precedence over the more diffuse "public interest" that members of Congress and the senior bureaucrats of the subgovernment are supposed to represent. Also, the prevalence of subgovernments in the decision-making process contributes to the "incrementalist" bias of that process; major changes in policy are resisted by the subgovernments, because the interest groups with intimate access to key members of Congress and key bureaucrats usually are doing well under the existing arrangement. Congressional and bureaucratic members of a subgovernment also tend to oppose major policy changes, not only because they are sensitive to interest-group wishes, but also because major changes in policy or organizational structure might jeopardize their own authority over policy decisions and undercut their own authority as experts. In the case of members of Congress, this would likely reduce the electoral support they receive from the relevant interest groups and bureaucracies.

Congressional Oversight of Bureaucracies

Although members of Congress, interest-group representatives, and high-level bureaucrats work together as members of subgovernments to develop policy in many areas, members of Congress still tend to distrust the bureaucracy in general. Many would agree with U.S. Representative Jim Wright (D., Texas), now House Majority Leader, who observed: "There are a lot of people in the executive branch, under every administration, who would like to write the laws of the land without the inconvenience of running for Congress."[24]

As a result of generalized distrust of bureaucrats and of the feeling that the bureaucracy constitutes a very real challenge to the authority of Congress, most members of Congress place substantial emphasis on oversight of the bureaucracy, while conceding that such oversight is erratic, inadequate, and often ineffective.[25] Oversight includes concern for honesty and efficiency in the expenditure of public monies, but most members of Congress are even more concerned that the executive branch faithfully implement both the letter and the intent of Congress. A broad definition is provided by Ogul: "Legislative oversight is behavior by legislators and their staffs, individually or collectively, which results in an impact, intended or not, on bureaucratic behavior."[26] Other observers prefer to focus on intentional impact on specific agencies and departments of government.[27]

Delegation of Power?   In a system of government that stresses the separation of powers and checks and balances among the various branches of government, a question inevitably arises concerning how much delegation of authority from the legislature to the executive is permitted. How finely must the laws describe the various eventualities for which they are providing? The question has been debated from the earliest days of the Republic. Almost all Americans would object, for example, if Congress convened, authorized the President to levy taxes and spend money as he saw fit, granted the President the authority to rule by executive order, and then went home. Clearly, that would be excessive delegation of legislative authority. Few people, however, would agree with the purists that *no* delegation of authority is constitutionally permissible. Most observers agree that the needs of government in modern society require some ability of bureaucrats to fit existing law to a variety of cases and thus of executive agencies to promulgate rules and regulations for the conduct of their business. That is even more the case, of course, for regulatory agencies created by Congress. The question of subjecting such rules and regulations to subsequent negation by Congress is very much alive and has led to enactment of "legislative veto" provisions—discussed later—concerning certain acts of various agencies.

The practical answer to the question of how much delegation of legislative authority to the President and presidential subordinates is permissible has been that Congress could delegate as much of its powers as the federal judiciary would agree to. The judiciary has become involved in the question because those who oppose regulations promulgated by government agencies have used the legal defense that the particular agency has acted under a law which made an unconstitutional delegation of legislative authority to the executive branch.[28]

As one insightful authority has noted:

> In its decisions on the delegation of legislative powers to the President, the Court characteristically offers high-sounding tributes to the genius of the separation doctrine, and then proceeds to adopt a practical and workable definition of the concept. . . . The permissibility of delegation thus becomes a matter of definition, with strong pragmatic overtones. In reconciling the abstract merits of the separation doctrine with the practical needs of the government, the Supreme Court inspired one author to compose an ingenious syllogism, laying bare the rationale:

> MAJOR PREMISE: Legislative power cannot be constitutionally delegated by Congress.

431

MINOR PREMISE: It is essential that certain powers be delegated to administrative officers and regulatory commissions.

CONCLUSION: Therefore the powers thus delegated are not legislative powers.[29]

Vague vs. Specific Legislative Provisions   Many laws passed by Congress grant the executive branch, and various agencies within it, substantial authority to establish rules and regulations and to apply rather vague general principles, such as "the public interest," to specific situations. Since bureaucrats may have a different perspective on matters of policy than members of Congress, members of Congress are not always happy with the implementation of legislation. Yet, when Congress chooses to make a grant of authority, it is responsible for the consequences and cannot in good conscience ignore its responsibility to insure proper implementation of the Congressional mandate. In part, the difficulty is inevitable, given the impossibility of specifying in advance every possible administrative contingency and the preferences of Congress for each. In part, however, Congress has only itself to blame for enacting legislation in policy areas about which the members have not adequately informed themselves or for working out "compromise language" which gets the legislation passed at the expense of leaving bureaucrats, members of Congress, and private individuals with different impressions about exactly what the legislation mandates.

An example of the types of compromises worked out to resolve differences and to save face is found in the Emergency Employment Act of 1971.

> The [Nixon] Administration pressed for legislation closer to the Senate measure. The Senate had authorized a two-year "transitional" program, to be phased out when the jobless rate fell to 4.5 percent. The House supported a five-year, $5 billion program that could provide permanent jobs. Under the House plan, programs serving localities with high unemployment would continue even after the national figures fell.
>
> The compromise bill was designed to meet the President's basic concerns, with at least reassuring language, while preserving some of the important House innovations. The conference committee and the Administration agreed on a two-year, $2.25 billion program with language describing the program as transitional. The House spokesmen, however, won the point of continuing programs in localities with more than 6-percent unemployed even after the national jobless level declined. The Administration wanted an explicit veterans' preference, but settled for "special consideration" for former servicemen.
>
> With the basic political arrangement made, there was no passionate interest in sorting out all the ambiguities contained in the bill.[30]

Why Oversight?   Some of the distrust Congress feels toward the bureaucracy arises from the vastly divergent loyalties and perspectives on national priorities of bureaucrats in a particular agency, on the one hand, and the average member of Congress on the other. Thus, an agency may interpret an act of Congress in a manner most satisfactory to the agency's point of view, regardless of the manifest intent of Congress. Sometimes, such an interpretation may involve astonishing feats of linguistic flexibility.

Members of Congress often focus on deliberate bureaucratic misinterpretation of Congressional intent, or on ineptness of bureaucrats, or both. But the felt need for Congressional oversight of the bureaucracy also stems from the large number of laws passed, the vagueness with which some are drafted, the different legitimate inter-

★ ★ ★ ★

Why Legislative Guidelines Sometimes Are Vague

Kenneth Culp Davis . . . offers several reasons why clear [statutory] guidelines are not always feasible or even desirable. First, legislators and their staff lack the time and the expertise to draft bills for highly specialized areas; that invites vague formulations of objectives. Second, even the experts find it difficult to develop standards that will be both specific and workable, and they prefer, for that reason, general formulations in order to give agency heads some flexibility in applying the statute to concrete problems. Third, if the statement of objectives becomes too specific the consensus needed for legislative and presidential support is likely to melt away. Previous supporters begin to say, "Oh, is *that* what you meant!" Furthermore, a too precise statement of objectives might make implementation troublesome:

> When the society is sharply divided, . . . a legislative body may wisely keep the policy objectives largely open. Vague or meaningless standards may then be preferable to precise and meaningful ones.

Source: Louis Fisher, *President and Congress: Power and Policy* (New York: Free Press, 1972), pp. 78–79; quoting Kenneth Culp Davis, *Discretionary Justice: A Preliminary Inquiry* (Baton Rouge, La.: Louisiana State University Press, 1969), p. 49.

★ ★ ★ ★

pretations of those statutes, as they apply to specific circumstances, and the importance to society of bureaucratic interpretation and application of the laws.

Like so many other Congressional activities, oversight of the bureaucracy is accomplished primarily, but not exclusively, through the standing committees and subcommittees of Congress. The leadership of the two chambers is seldom actively involved. The decisions concerning how much oversight activity to engage in and what components of the bureaucracy to oversee actively are made by the committee leaders. The Legislative Reorganization Act of 1946 required all committees of Congress to include oversight activities as one of their continual functions. The Government Operations Committees of the House and the Senate (now the Senate Governmental Affairs Committee) were especially mandated to oversee the performance of the various agencies of government and to look across the normal bureaucratic boundaries which tend to limit other committee reviews. Those charges were repeated in the Legislative Reorganization Act of 1970, which also mandated a biennial report from each committee on its oversight activities and granted the General Accounting Office oversight authority.

As part of the battle by Congress with the "imperial presidency," generally, and with President Nixon over impoundment of congressionally appropriated funds, in 1974 Congress strengthened its oversight capability even further, at least on paper. The Budget and Impoundment Control Act, passed that year, created Budget Committees in both chambers of Congress, a Congressional Budget Office, and a new budget procedure that provided for closer examination of the budget and a process for making choices between programs which previously had been considered indently of each other. The same year saw the passage of legislation that established .. Office of Program Review and Evaluation in the General Accounting Office and required both the Department of Treasury and the Office of Management and Budget to provide various arms of Congress information which previously had been difficult to obtain.

What does Congress hope to accomplish by oversight activities? A 1977 report from the Committee on Government Operations of the U.S. Senate lists five primary goals of oversight activity, all of which are related to the accountability of the bureaucracy to Congress:

1. Ensuring that the administrative branch implements the laws in accordance with Congressional intent.
2. Determining policy effectiveness by gauging the appropriateness of a policy and determining whether its impact is in line with Congressional standards.
3. Preventing waste and dishonesty by ensuring that agencies operate honestly and efficiently.
4. Preventing abuse in the administrative process by keeping tabs on agency use of discretionary authority.
5. Representing the public interest by monitoring and constraining agency-clientele group relations.[31]

Ironically, much Congressional oversight of the bureaucracy is conducted by *Congressional* bureaucrats (such as those in GAO) who report to Congress, rather than to the President, and much of the direct oversight activity conducted by members themselves also depends in large part on Congressional bureaucracy (that is, staff) support. Indeed, once the conditions arise that lead members of Congress to desire active oversight of an agency, an important factor in determining the extent and quality of that oversight activity is the availability of appropriate Congressional staff resources.

> Availability of staff and the willingness to use it are often important preconditions to substantial oversight. Oversight without effective staff work is normally impossible. But the amount of oversight performed does not depend mainly on the size of the staff available. Adequate staff is a necessary precondition to oversight but is not a sufficient one. Other factors such as member priorities seem to be more basic.[32]

Oversight Techniques Numerous factors can either prompt or retard active Congressional oversight of different government agencies, and there are various kinds of oversight activity. Despite the prevalence of subgovernments and the ample opportunities each subgovernment provides particular members of Congress to influence policy on a regular basis, the image which probably comes most quickly to mind when Congressional oversight of the bureaucracy is mentioned is a formal committee hearing in which members of the committee badger hapless administrators. And, indeed, such hearings (or the implicit or explicit threat of them) are very effective tools in the oversight process.

Formal committee oversight hearings are held for a number of reasons, including partisan advantage, electoral considerations, publicity for an ambitious chairperson, or antipathy for a particular program or administrator. But, for the most part, the members of each Congressional committee or subcommittee feel some proprietary interest in "their" agencies. Often, they are on the committee because they want to serve a particular constituency interest, and they are cautious about conducting formal oversight hearings for fear they will hurt federal programs serving that interest. Careful planning for hearings can sometimes avoid such injury and can actually help document the need for additional activities by the relevant government

434

agency, thus helping to build the case for larger appropriations. Occasionally, hearings are held so a committee can protect "its" agency.[33]

An intemperate oversight hearing, on the other hand, can hurt an agency and is usually an indicator that the other, less visible, mechanisms of Congressional oversight have failed. Sometimes, increased oversight activity is sought by bureaucrats whose policy views are not prevailing within the agency or by those bureaucrats who want to gain additional political resources with which to resist certain outside interests.[34]

Congress and Congressional committees guide the various agencies of government to some degree by enacting authorizing bills and amendments, as well as by the amounts of money provided in annual appropriations legislation. Guidance can take the form of specific directives in authorizing legislation or appropriations acts. Some guidance can come in the form of questions or comments by members at legislative mark-up meetings or from statements in the committee report, rather than in the law itself.

Agency appropriations acts must be passed every year to fund the agency's operations, giving the relevant appropriations subcommittees (where oversight activity

★ ★ ★ ★

Factors Contributing to Active Legislative Oversight of the Bureaucracy

There seems to be no single pattern which explains legislative oversight in all circumstances. There are only common factors which combine in different ways under specified sets of circumstances. . . .

Oversight is most likely to occur when the following are present: a legal basis for committee or individual activity and money available; adequate staff resources defined in terms of numbers, skills, and attitudes; subject matter that is not unusually technical or complex enough to require special expertise; activities involved that are centralized in one executive department; an issue with high visibility and large political payoffs; decentralized committee operations or a chairman of the full committee who is a strong advocate of oversight in a given area; a desire of important people, usually those with committee or subcommittee chairmanships, to oversee; unhappiness of key committee members with the conduct of executive personnel, a lack of confidence in top executive personnel, or personal antipathy toward them; control of the house of the Congress involved by one political party and of the presidency by the other; poor treatment of members of the Congress, especially those on relevant committees, by executive officials; a member's strong interest in the work of his committee and the particular subject matter at hand; and committee positions highly sought by persons with more than average competence. In general . . . reversing these factors [leads to less oversight activity rather than more].

Source: Morris S. Ogul, *Congress Oversees the Bureaucracy* (Pittsburgh: University of Pittsburgh Press, 1976), pp. 21–22.

★ ★ ★ ★

within the House and Senate appropriations committees takes place) ample opportunities to advise bureaucrats of subcommittee policy preferences.[35] If members of Congress are truly unhappy about a program, distrust its administrators, or strongly object to spending for a particular purpose, they can add restrictive language to the appropriations act, forbidding the use of any of the monies appropriated for the disliked purposes. One of the best known such restrictions was the "Hyde Amendment" to the appropriations act for the Department of Health, Education and Welfare (now the Department of Health and Welfare). This amendment forbids federal funds being used to pay for abortions for women who are welfare recipients, unless the life of the mother is endangered by the continuation of the pregnancy. Opponents of the amendment argue that it effectively denies poor women the same right to abortions that are available for most other American women. Members of Congress who objected to government funding of abortions supported this rider to force the federal agency to accept their policy preferences, something the executive agency would not have done if it had not been required to do so.

Similarly, the Legal Services Corporation has been subject to numerous appropriations act restrictions. Many conservative members of Congress objected to the LSC's active profile in seeking legal redress of grievances for poor people, so they introduced various amendments to the appropriations act each year to restrict LSC activities. For example, one such restriction, adopted in 1980, prohibited LSC attorneys from accepting abortion cases, unless the abortion was necessary to save the life of the mother or the pregnancy resulted from rape or incest.[36]

Agencies can also be instructed through authorizing legislation, although this approach is less convenient than appropriations acts, because most authorizations are for a number of years, rather than one, and some agency authorizations are permanent. But when an agency's authorization must be renewed, the reauthorization legislation offers opportunities for Congress to direct and restrict the agency in certain ways. That was the situation concerning the Federal Trade Commission in 1977. FTC's pro-consumer stance had angered numerous large corporations, who wanted FTC activities restricted when the agency's reauthorizing legislation was considered. As a result, FTC operated under a series of stop-gap authorization measures from 1977 to 1980, because its opponents did not want to kill it outright, and its supporters would not accept the proposed restrictions. FTC's reauthorization was eventually passed, but at the price of a provision for a Congressional veto of its regulations by majority vote of both chambers of Congress (through a concurrent resolution, not subject to presidential veto). The reauthorizing legislation also restricted FTC investigations of the insurance industry and prohibited the FTC "from petitioning the patents commissioner to cancel a company's trademark on the ground that it had become the common descriptive name of an item."[37] This latter prohibition resulted from FTC's earlier conclusion that many consumers who were asking for Formica products—and paying for the brand name—actually thought they were asking for a generic product and would have preferred some lower-priced plastic laminate. FTC was allowed to continue its rule-making procedure concerning television advertising aimed at children,

> but the FTC would have to consider whether the advertising was deceptive, not merely unfair. Unfairness as a standard for determining improper advertising would be suspended for three years.[38]

The legislative process favors an agency's critics, when they seek to restrict agency action through the annual appropriations act or through amendments to reauthorizing legislation. The agency, after all, must have the legislation, so the agency's supporters in Congress must compromise, as FTC's defenders discovered. An agency with permanent legislative authorization is less vulnerable to amendments to its authorizing legislation, because it generally suffers no damage if agency supporters block the legislation entirely. But permanent agency mandates are occasionally amended, usually following intensive lobbying by agency opponents. Thus, in 1965, the tobacco industry pushed through Congress a four-year moratorium on FTC regulations of cigarette advertising at a time when that agency was considering tobacco advertising restrictions because of health hazards.[39] After Congress mandates agency policies against the agency's will, the agency's opponents in Congress feel the necessity for frequent oversight activities to insure that the agency—however reluctantly—is honoring that Congressional mandate.

Because oversight activities have not succeeded in redirecting certain agencies' energies, and because some congresspersons feel the symbiotic committee-agency relationship prevents hard-nosed oversight, dissatisfied members of Congress support *sunset legislation.* Sunset laws establish a staggered set of dates on which various agencies—even those which now have permanent authorization—would have their

---

★ ★ ★ ★

Subgovernments and Congressional Oversight: A Pessimistic View

. . . [T]he reluctance of Congress to reform its oversight structure stems in large measure from the fear that such reform would weaken subcommittee government and thus the power positions it offers individual members. This reluctance appears reinforced by the play of special interests. Indeed, interest groups generally find subcommittee government to their advantage, and its rise over the past decades has strengthened subsystem politics and with it the access of lobbyists to the Congress.

The reforms of the 1970s, however, have done little to restrict the power of lobbies or to threaten their role in subsystem politics. The failure to strengthen the committees on government operations left responsibility for oversight in the hands of committees and subcommittees that are central actors in the various subsystems. The failure to pass stringent lobby laws, together with inadequate campaign finance and ethics legislation, have left the lobbies in a strong position. We doubt that Congress will be able to reform its oversight structure in a meaningful way until it places responsibility for oversight in a committee or set of committees that are independent of subsystem politics and the access to special interests it provides.

Thus in each of the three problem areas facing Congress as it attempts to conduct oversight—its position in relation to agencies and bureaus, its access to information, and the influence of special interests—Congress has failed to provide meaningful and effective solutions. Nor is effective oversight reform possible so long as the pull of subcommittee government is stronger than the desire to assure effective implementation of public policy.

Source: From *Congress and the Administrative State* by Lawrence C. Dodd and Richard L. Schott. Copyright © 1979 by John Wiley & Sons, Inc. Reprinted by permission.

★ ★ ★ ★

---

authorizations (their agency charters) terminated, unless Congress reauthorized the agencies prior to that date. Each agency's authorization legislation presumably would be the cause of committee hearings that would result in active oversight of the agency. For each agency, too, Congress presumably would ask itself if the agency really deserved reauthorization. The agency would have to defend its programs, and some which would have been allowed to continue unchallenged without sunset legislation might well fail to be renewed. The necessity of reauthorization would reverse the usual advantage of agency supporters, make the agency more vulnerable to attack by its opponents in Congress, and make redirection or restrictions by legislation easier to accomplish.[40] Because sunset legislation would interfere with the intimate relationships between the standing committees or subcommittees of Congress and their various executive agencies, many members (especially committee and subcommittee chairpersons) oppose it.

Up to now, the discussion has focused on the obvious, deliberate, or "manifest" oversight activities of Congress and the committees of Congress. As Ogul points out, however, much Congressional oversight of the bureaucracy is *latent*—"that accomplished in fact while another legislative activity is obstensibly being performed."[41] Latent oversight is unsystematic, but often effective. Exchange of views occurs in many Congressional-bureaucratic interactions, leading bureaucrats to take into account in decision-making what they *perceive* to be the policy preferences of the members of Congress most important to them and their agency. These interactions, which give guidance to bureaucrats, can take place in legislative meetings or hearings concerning the "marking up" of a bill (in contrast to formal oversight hearings in which the committee is consciously attempting to evaluate agency performance), or during the course of Congressional casework interaction with an agency (although casework requests can mislead bureaucrats, since many members support individual constituent requests that they would oppose as general agency policy.) Oversight by a narrow subset of members of Congress obviously occurs in the various subgovernment interactions of key members of Congress, bureaucrats, and lobbyists.

Oversight also occurs through deliberate individual-member activity, although such action is more effective when it comes from a member (or chair) of a Congressional committee closely related to the overseen agency. Members sufficiently stress the importance of oversight that over 300 Congressional aides were sent to a three-day workshop on oversight and investigations that was conducted by the Congressional Research Service (CRS) in December 1978. CRS subsequently published a workbook on oversight for members and their staffs.[42]

The Legislative Veto As discussed in Chapter 14, the legislative veto is a powerful weapon in the struggle for policy dominance between Congress and the President. It is also a mechanism by which Congress attempts to retain authority over the sprawling federal bureaucracy, especially the regulatory and rule-making bodies. Although the question of the constitutionality of the practice has not been clearly resolved, Congress has granted itself veto powers over numerous agency decisions by writing such provisions into authorizing legislation. Some acts provide that agency decisions are negated if *either* chamber of Congress passes a veto resolution. Other agencies face a legislative veto only if a concurrent resolution passes, which requires a majority vote of both chambers, but is not subject to presidential veto. A few agencies are subject to legislative veto by joint resolution, which requires action by both chambers of Congress and is subject to presidential veto. In the eighteen years from 1960 through mid-1978, one analysis found 21

★ ★ ★ ★

The Legislative Veto and Used Cars

The dangers of the so-called "legislative veto"—now under attack by the federal courts—are superbly illustrated by the fate of the used-car regulation proposed by the Federal Trade Commission.

The suggested FTC rule would force used-car dealers to inform buyers about their warranty rights as well as such defects as cracked engine heads, damaged ball-joint seals, bad suspension systems and leakage in the transmission, colling, brake and steering systems.

For the second year in a row, the proposed used-car regulation is being considered by Congress. It can be nullified by a simple majority vote in both houses—the "legislative veto." This, of course, gives special-interest groups like the used-car lobby a second chance to fight regulations that would protect the public from being cheated. . . .

There doesn't have to be an actual legislative veto to get the special interests what they want. Sometimes the mere possibility of such a veto is enough of a threat to cow the regulatory agency. In fact, that's exactly what FTC Commissioner Michael Pertschuk claims happened in the case of the used-car rule. It started off requiring used-car dealers to inspect their vehicles and tell customers about any defects they found. But the inspection requirement was gutted by the FTC.

"I tend to believe that the Commission would have been more hospitable to (such a) requirement in the Used Car Rule had not the threat of congressional veto been so imminent. . . . I believe that the present Used Car Rule . . . was fashioned consciously or unconsciously to provide the lowest profile target for dealer lobbying and congressional antipathy." The result ". . . was a rule that is so totally unobjectionable and modest that any member of Congress voting against it should blush with shame."

Source: From "The Legislative Veto and Used Cars" by Jack Anderson from *Alburquerque Journal*, Feburary 18, 1982. Copyright © 1982 United Feature Syndicate, Inc. Reprinted by permission.

Note: In May 1982 Congress vetoed the FTC rule on used cars. Consumer groups sued in federal court, challenging the constitutionality of Congress' action.

★ ★ ★ ★

single-chamber budget deferral resolutions had passed the Senate and 28 had passed the House. For other types of successful single-chamber legislative veto resolutions, the count was 10 in the Senate and 9 in the House, out of almost 300 such resolutions introduced. During that same period, 13 concurrent resolutions had passed (out of almost 300 introduced), while no joint resolutions of legislative veto (requiring presidential signature) had passed, although 12 had been introduced.[43] Data are not readily available on the number of times Congress has exercised a variation on the theme—a requirement that one or both chambers must *approve* an executive proposal before it can go into effect. Nor is information available on the impact on agency behavior of the unsuccessful legislative veto resolutions.

Even more controversial, constitutionally, are legislative provisions that require approval by Congressional *committees* before an agency can proceed with implementation of a program. The Post Office Department Appropriation Act of 1971, for example, provided that funds for design and construction of new facilities would be available only for locations approved by the Committee on Public Works in each chamber.[44]

Presidents are prone to veto authorizing legislation that contains provisions for a legislative veto, but some such legislation has been enacted over a President's veto, and some has reluctantly been accepted by a President, as the price of gaining any program at all. Not all members of Congress support the practice of creating legislative veto powers. Some oppose legislative veto legislation because of their concern for the separation of powers between the branches of government. Some wish to spare themselves the political difficulties of being petitioned to exercise the legislative veto when an agency offends a particularly powerful interest group. Others are strong agency supporters, and they recognize that the option of a legislative veto is likely to make the agency unduly cautious, or less vigorous in program implementation, or subject to interest-group pressure.

LEGISLATIVE-BUREAUCRATIC RELATIONSHIPS IN PARLIAMENTARY SYSTEMS

A simplistic view of most parliamentary systems is that because the leaders of the executive branch are the same people who are the leaders of the legislature, there are few sources of friction in legislative-bureaucratic relationships. Such a viewpoint, of course, ignores the policy distortions caused by subgovernments, the policy preferences of opposition members of the parliament, and the dissension of backbenchers. It also overlooks the difficulty a member of parliament may encounter in actually gaining control of agency affairs after his or her appointment as minister in charge of that agency.

Even the legislative veto is not unique to the United States nor to separation-of-powers systems. In Great Britain, the legislative veto

> has its counterpart in the procedures of the British Parliament by which a Joint Committee on Statutory Instruments must scrutinize every exercise of delegated lawmaking power by the cabinet and must, in some cases, obtain formal parliamentary approval before the executive action can take effect. It has its counterpart, too, in arrangements by which the German Bundestag can annul exercises of delegated legislation.[45]

Reorganization of the administrative agencies of the British government, however, is not subject to a legislative veto. The prime minister has the authority to reorganize and to determine which agencies of government will be headed by a cabinet member. Presumably because the prime minister is also the leader of the dominant parliamentary party, he or she is permitted great authority in these matters.

Formal oversight activity by select committees of the British House of Commons is conducted, but not in the same manner as in Congress. Instead of the sometimes heavy-handed attempts by Congressional committees to affect implementation of policy, the British committees "are obliged to remain cautiously on one side of that unclear line dividing the content of policy from its implementation."[46] Members can, of course, take advantage of the House of Commons question period—four hours each week—during which they may question cabinet ministers about various matters. Each question must be addressed to the appropriate Cabinet minister, and discussion follows response to *written* questions. Congress and the American state legislatures have no such periods set aside for interrogation of executive officers, but they often achieve about the same result through questions at committee hearings.

West German legislators have a question period each week, during which they may inquire of executive officials about matters of concern to legislators and their constitutents. In addition, the standing committees of the German Bundestag exercise an oversight power in a manner similar to Congressional committees. Attitudes of parliamentary members differ greatly between West Germany and Great Britain, too, and that affects the relationship between parliament and the executive.

> The German parliament can go beyond oversight to supervision and control over the implementation of policy because its members differentiate themselves from the government more clearly than British MPs do. Fewer German than British MPs hold executive office. Since the cabinet is composed of members of two parties, the parliamentary majority does not see in the cabinet only its own party leadership. The parliamentary caucuses, even those of the governing parties, have their own leadership, much like American caucuses; they do not automatically accept the leadership of their cabinet ministers. Specialized committees and an extensive staff raise the ability of the Bundestag to exercise an informed surveillance over the administration.[47]

STATE LEGISLATIVE-BUREAUCRATIC RELATIONSHIPS

The legislative-bureaucratic relationship in the American states is similar in most respects to that at the national level. The interactions between legislators and bureaucrats occur in a separation-of-powers structure of government in which legislators and bureaucrats tend to have differing personal experiences and points of view. But, in most states, the legislators have substantially less experience than the bureaucrats in dealing with the policy issues involved. Also, state legislatures have too few staff and information resources to draw on in their contest with the bureaucracy for policy supremacy. Indeed, one student of the subject feels that resource constraints on the abilities of state legislatures to conduct effective oversight are more important than any other constraints.[48] A few legislators—especially young attorneys—may be serving in the legislature with an eye toward developing a network of contacts among the permanent agency staff, rather than for the purpose of jousting with them over policies or program implementation. State legislatures are also less institutionalized and less decentralized than the chambers of Congress, and committee assignments are less permanent. Thus, the committee leaders normally have not developed the lengthy and intimate relationships with interest-group representatives and relevant bureaucrats that one finds in the national-level subgovernments. All these factors probably give the bureaucrats the advantage in establishing certain types of policy, when there is no dramatic philosophical disagreement between the administrative agencies and the legislature. But it should be noted that state legislators are generally less a part of the ongoing system than are members of Congress, and they frequently come to their jobs with an anti-bureaucracy perspective.

Like their national counterparts, state legislators often turn to state bureaucrats for assistance in devising and implementing policy positions. For this reason, state legislators and state bureaucrats usually work together relatively harmoniously. As in Congress, legislative guidance to bureaucrats may be given as a result of many legislative activities, such as enacting legislation or conducting budget hearings, in addition to formal oversight hearings. But, especially in states with amateur legislatures, or high legislator turnover, or both, the intimate web of personal relationships constituting a subgovernment either does not develop or is fragile. That means that few legislators in such states feel any sense of institutional or personal loyalty to a particular agency of government or any shared responsibility for its past sins of omission or commission. Many legislators tend to perceive themselves as outsiders, rather than as part of "the system," and, thus, they desire agency accountability and the tools for vigorous oversight in the often limited time available to them in their public roles. The key variables, obviously, have a substantial range among the states. The full-time, professional state legislator, for example, is likely to have a relationship with the bureaucracy much like that of a national legislator.

The extent to which angry legislators may frighten agency heads obviously depends on the overall relationship between the governor and the legislature. Where the governor dominates the legislature, legislative carping is simply absorbed, and it only affects bureaucratic behavior marginally. Where the governor is weak, bureaucrats are more likely to behave obsequiously toward key legislators. Overall, though, state legislators usually want to be able to find out what state agencies are doing (and why), as well as how well they are performing. And the legislators want to be able to take forceful action when they deem it necessary. When state legislators do intervene, the effect seems mainly to be prevention of agressive bureaucratic intervention in the private economic sector.[49]

Over the past quarter century, American state legislatures have, for the most part, developed the legal and institutional capacity to act vigorously when they want to. Although the governors of some states have successfully opposed the implementation of one or the other innovation, the legislative veto as well as program audit and evaluation capacity have spread steadily among the states. The extent of adoptions of sunset legislation by the states has been dramatic. The first sunset legislation was enacted in Colorado in 1976, at the urging of Common Cause, the citizens' lobby, in an effort to make the bureaucracy more accountable. The next five years saw the concept spread (in one form or another) to over two thirds of the states, a virtually unheard-of rate of adoption for a new idea, especially one which had the potential of making a substantial shift in the balance of political power within a state.[50] Much of the capacity of state legislatures to use these new approaches for oversight of the bureaucracy in an effective manner stems from the increased support services available to legislators. Ironically, then, as in Congress, the increased ability of the state legislatures to check the state bureaucracy stems in part from the growing bureaucratization of the state legislatures themselves.

Development of the institutional capacity for the effective exercise of legislative oversight and the "routinization" of such oversight activities appears to cause a change in the motivations prompting oversight activity. Where the capacity is substantial and the conduct of oversight is routine, oversight activity by legislators appears to be motivated by constituency and partisan factors. In legislatures with minimal structural capacity to conduct oversight activities, in contrast, such oversight activities as occur are the result mainly of individual legislator attitudes.[51]

Audit and Program Evaluation Capability

An important feature of a legislature's ability to oversee the various agencies of state government is the capability to determine whether appropriated monies have been spent as intended and whether the programs of the various state agencies are effective. Mere financial integrity alone is not sufficient reason for continued funding of a state agency. Some societal benefit from the agency's activities must also be evident. If possible, legislators try to gain some idea about which agencies are most effective in their use of appropriated funds, although such comparisons often wind up being very much like the comparison of apples to oranges.

Over the past decade or so, most states have shifted the "post audit" function to a separate official or agency controlled by the legislature, although some states with a legislative audit capability also have an executive auditor as well. Post audit analysis consists of examining the records of an agency, after the money has been spent, to determine if it has been spent according to law. Normally the pre-audit function (approving requests for purchase of new equipment, travel, or hiring new workers) is under the control of the governor. Some state legislatures have also given the office of legislative auditor the responsibility for *program evaluation,* which is an analysis of the operations and results of various state agencies and their programs. Most program evaluation staff members, however, are not accountants.

Some legislatures have created program evaluation staffs that are separate from the legislative auditor; some are attached to standing committees of the legislature or to interim committees. Much of the work of the legislative audit and pro-gram-evaluation agencies is self-directed; much is routine. At times, however, the legislature, or a committee, will direct the auditor or the program evaluators to focus on particular agencies for special audits or special evaluations.[52]

These legislative staff agencies are specifically designed for oversight of the state bureaucracy. To a degree, they perform functions similar to some of the functions of the General Accounting Office of the Congress, the Congressional Research Ser-

---

★ ★ ★ ★

Post Audit and Program Evaluation Capacity

Legislatures have most often sought to carry out oversight of the executive branch through the development of the post audit and program evaluation functions. The trend has been to place the state post auditor (who examines expenditures after the fact for their legality and propriety) within the legislative branch, rather than having this official independently elected or under the executive branch. At present there are 40 states where there is an auditor selected by the legislature. In states where the post auditor is not a legislative employee, some auditing may be done by fiscal or research staff.

Program and performance evaluation units have also been established in numerous states, either as part of the legislative post audit staff or as independent legislative staff offices. This is a reflection of the rapidly growing interest of legislatures in evaluating agency performance and program effectiveness as contrasted to simply auditing for fiscal or legal compliance. With the enactment of sunset laws . . . the task of evaluating agencies and programs subject to sunset has frequently been assigned to audit and performance evaluation committees.

Source: William Pound and Carl Tubbesing, "The State Legislatures," in *Book of the States: 1978–1979* (Lexington, Ky.: Council of State Governments, 1978), pp. 1–2.

★ ★ ★ ★

---

vice, and the Congressional Budget Office. Numbers of state program-evaluation agencies had been slowly increasing, but the "sunset" boom caused most state legislatures without program evaluation capability to develop that capacity, and the boom caused those with such a capacity to augment it substantially. After all, if a legislature wishes to evaluate an agency to determine whether to reauthorize it or let it die, where better to turn for information than to the legislature's own evaluation staff? The needed information is not obtained exclusively from legislative program-evaluation offices, however. Depending on the state, legislative staff reporting to particular committees may develop most of the information used by the legislature in deliberating about a sunset vote, or the executive agency's own self-evaluation may be the major source of information. But, for many state legislatures, the evolution of a legislative staff capability for evaluating state agency performance has made the transition to implementation of sunset legislation much less chaotic than it otherwise would have been.

Sunset Legislation

As just noted, some version of sunset legislation has been enacted by over two thirds of the fifty states. Sunset laws provide for

> a periodic review of agencies and their programs to determine: if they are performing according to legislative intent; if they are efficient or at least employing the most efficient means of accomplishing that mandate; and, ultimately, if the agency's services are required in the future; if not, the agency should be allowed to disappear—that is, go off "into the sunset." The clout of most Sunset laws is this termination emphasis. . . . [S]tate legislatures have always had this ability to terminate; Sunset legislation, however, provides a more formal, required, periodic, and possibly more systematic review of agency actions. . . . [But] the prime purpose of Sunset is evaluation, not termination, of the agency and its programs.[53]

There is general agreement that for a law to qualify as sunset legislation, it must include a specific date on which each agency concerned will cease to exist unless positive action is taken by the legislature to reauthorize the agency. Without affirmative legislative action, the agency dies.

A major distinction among the sunset laws of the various states is whether the legislation is selective or comprehensive. In states with comprehensive sunset legislation, every agency of state government is involved in the sunset process, before the cycle of reviews is completed. Cycles vary in length, with most mandating review of each agency every four, six, or eight years. Most states, however, exempt the major executive departments of state government from sunset provisions, since all participants realize that such agencies will not actually be terminated. Over three fourths of the states that have enacted sunset legislation have selective, rather than comprehensive, sunset laws. The focus of selective sunset laws usually is on regulatory agencies and occupational licensing boards.[54]

Enactment of sunset legislation changes the dynamic of the legislative process with respect to each affected agency, as noted earlier. Those legislators who wish to maintain the status quo concerning the agency no longer have the procedural advantage within the legislature. When not faced with a sunset law termination date, an agency's legislator friends can protect the agency from its enemies simply by killing any legislation that affects the agency adversely. When sunset applies to their pet agency, however, legislators must enact *new* legislation, perhaps making concessions in the process. They may be forced to accept changes in the status quo, since the agency's enemies now are in a position to change the status quo dramatically by killing the reauthorization bill, allowing the agency to die. Most legislators, however, merely want to alter a particular agency's orientation or procedural rules; few actually want to terminate the agency. The advantage of the reformers, then, in the face of logrolling among the legislative supporters of the various agencies facing sunset law deadlines ("I'll support reauthorization of the Board of Thanato Practice—undertakers—if you will support reauthorization of the Board of Licensure for Barbers") and of heavy lobbying by those interest groups with whom the agency has symbiotic relationships, is less overwhelming than it would be if the agency's enemies actually wanted to terminate it.

Sunset laws have been in existence for too short a period to enable observers to evaluate their overall impact on legislative-bureaucratic relationships or to determine if they are effective. There is some evidence, however, that few state agencies need fear actual termination. The Alabama sunset committee reviewed 209 agencies in the first year the sunset laws applied and abolished only one advisory body.[55] In Oklahoma, the sunset law scheduled 21 agencies for review in 1978. Twelve of those 21 agencies were allowed to die, but they were "very minor, very insignificant agencies," according to the director of the legislative staff.[56] Hawaii terminated two regulatory agencies in 1978, but both were mere "paper" organizations, not functioning entities. Similarly, "the 21 agencies terminated under the limited Sunset bill in Indiana in 1978 were . . . largely inactive advisory commissions."[57] Common Cause (the organization which has pressed for sunset legislation) reports that various state agencies have been eliminated under sunset laws because of duplication of services and because legislators concluded that such a function should not be performed by a state agency.[58] Some states have used sunset law leverage to modify state agencies, short of termination,[59] although some state agencies have been able to expand their mandates (and, of course, their budgets) as a result of sunset legislation.[60] These summary reports do not provide us with information on the degree to which state agencies have changed (if at all) in their attitudes toward and interactions with the public or the legislature. It may be that despite the lack of large numbers of agency terminations through sunset reviews, careful observation will demonstrate greater bureaucratic responsiveness to legislative intent or to the public's needs as a result of them.

Why did so many states adopt sunset legislation before it was proven to be effective in the first states that adopted it? In large part, the reason seems to be that "legislators vote for sunset laws to show they're doing *something* to curb Big Government."[61] Voting to terminate a specific agency in the face of strong lobbying on behalf of that agency is something else. Perhaps, too, legislators anticipated not only that they would reap the benefits of appearing to be on the side of "good government," but also that the type of dynamic which occurred in Texas would occur in their state.

> [I]n Texas during the 1978 elections, interest groups that desired to have certain state licensing boards continued, often increased their financial contributions to state legislative candidates dramatically. For example, realtors, whose board was to be reviewed in 1979, increased their contributions from $47,000 in 1976 to $77,000 in 1978, while the accountants (also scheduled for review) who gave only $1,100 in 1976 increased their help several times over to $14,700 in 1978. And the legislative candidate who received the largest total contribution just happened to be the chair of the Sunset review commission.[62]

445

———————————— ★ ★ ★ ★ ————————————

Sunset Laws: A Negative Appraisal

. . . A sunset law simply sets deadlines for agencies or programs to go out of business—unless legislators decide they're needed and vote to reestablish them. . . .

In the half-dozen states in which agencies were scheduled to die by the end of last year, the sunset mechanism has not been a potent agent for change at all. . . .

Colorado, the sunset pioneer, is a good example. . . . The first round of agency reviews can best be described as chaotic. Audits were completed late, and legislators largely ignored them. Hearings were sparsely attended by the public, but the agencies' staffs and supporters were out in force.

As in most states, Colorado's regulatory boards are dominated by the industries the boards are supposed to regulate. So naturally the regulated industries were strongly opposed to abolishing their boards, and turned out in large numbers to campaign against deregulation. Intense lobbying by local undertakers, for example, resulted in the passage of a last-minute bill saving their licensing board from extinction.

Ultimately, the legislature did abolish three small boards: The Athletic Commission, the Board of Professional Sanitarians, and the Board of Shorthand Reporters. Shorthand reporters were not deregulated, however; licensing authority merely was transferred to another agency. Two boards, licensing barbers and cosmetologists, were consolidated. But another two—one regulating collection agencies, the other overseeing the safety of ski lifts—were reestablished and given expanded authority.

. . . The combined annual budget of the three agencies abolished was $6,810. Sunset audits and hearings cost the state an estimated $212,300. . . .

. . . Alabama's [sunset law] applies to every state agency. It specifies that on the tenth day of each regular session, both houses of the legislature must begin considering and voting on agencies scheduled to die. Neither house may take up other business until both have completed action on sunset. Last year nearly 300 agencies were up for review.

Because there were so many, each agency was allotted just 15 minutes of committee hearings. When the time came to vote, the House of Representatives ran through the nearly 300 separate sunset resolutions in quick succession. . . . In the Senate, however, the sunset resolutions were held hostage [for days] as part of a filibuster over an unrelated issue. . . . Meanwhile, under the sunset law, the House couldn't take up any other business until the Senate had finished voting on all the sunset resolutions. . . .

In the end . . . [a] few agencies were axed, but all were "paper" boards that had ceased functioning long ago. Any active agency had "enough supporters lobbying to keep it from being terminated" explained Rep. James R. Solomon, Jr. . . .

446

The sunset provisions in Georgia were "torpedoed" by special interests, according to the *Atlanta Journal.* The legislature reestablished all ten licensing boards scheduled for termination in 1978, despite critical reports by the state auditor's office, which had spent about $90,000 reviewing the boards. "I think, for the most part, we've wasted our time," one auditor told reporters.

Finally, in Oregon . . . the costs are outweighing the supposed benefits. To evaluate the nine occupational licensing boards up for termination in 1980, for example, the legislature has hired five new full-time researchers and spent $200,000. Sunset hearings have been attended almost solely by board members and their licensees, who have used the occasion to introduce bills that would not only reestablish the boards, but would also expand their power to restrict business competition.

In sum, state sunset laws have not brought about the demise of one agency or program of any significant size. Only a few tiny, mostly moribund boards—some of which existed only on paper—have been abolished. Some agencies have been reestablished with expanded regulatory powers and enlarged budgets to match. . . .

The evidence suggests that legislators vote for sunset laws to show they're doing *something* to curb Big Government. But when the time comes for the sun to set, they reestablish agencies without much thought, or find a few tiny boards whose authority can be reassigned or abolished without arousing much opposition.

Source: Barry Mitzman, "Sunset Laws: Why They Aren't Working," *Washington Monthly,* June 1979, pp. 48–51.

------------------------------------ ★ ★ ★ ★ ------------------------------------

The Legislative Veto in the States

The legislative veto is alive and well in the states, especially with respect to the rules and regulations promulgated by various agencies of state government. Over three fourths of the states now have legislative committees to review administrative rules and regulations, although the details of the procedure vary widely. Some states provide only for making comments or "legislative observations," in the hope that such observations will suffice to bring about corrections; some provide for legislative negation of rules or regulations, but allow the governor a role in the process (sometimes the power to veto the negating resolution); and a minority of the states provide unfettered legislative authority—by concurrent resolution, single-chamber resolution, or action of a special legislative committee—to veto agency rules or regulations.[63] Where formal legislative review procedures have been established, they have been broad in scope rather than restricted to just a limited number of agencies. The actual review process, however, tends to focus on rules about which citizens or interest groups lodge complaints.[64]

The reasons for state legislator concern over the rules and regulations promulgated by state agencies are essentially the same as those that cause concern in Congress. In order to cope with various social maladies, the state legislatures have created agencies of state government with the authority to promulgate rules and

———————————— ★ ★ ★ ★ ————————————

Policy Consequences of Legislative Review of Agency Rules

. . . [T]he establishment of a joint legislative committee for review of agency rules is not neutral in terms of its policy consequences. The evidence suggests that the mechanism is most frequently used to block or moderate aggressive regulation. . . .

[In Michigan] the normal approach of the committee was to ask the agency personnel if all interested parties were satisfied with the proposed regulations. The legislators involved were primarily concerned with preventing displeasure on the part of any important constituents. . . . [T]hose persons and organizations opposing regulation were apparently better able to communicate their objections than other groups.

It is also fairly clear that the committee does not act to break up policy subsystems or to reassert the "public" interest where agencies have been captured by the groups they regulate. The . . . committee objections are rule-specific and not agency-specific, and the fact that restrictive rules are frequently disapproved indicates that the substantive impact of the mechanism is to moderate regulation. . . .

In 1979 [Tennessee's] Alcoholic Beverage Commission proposed rules which would have legalized advertisement of the retail prices of liquor. The agency rule-making hearing was well attended by consumer groups and others favoring such a change. The legislative committees (one in each House) empowered to review regulations both voted overwhelmingly to suspend the agency's rules. Interestingly, the liquor lobby did not participate in the agency hearings but waited until the matter was brought before the legislative committees before attempting to influence the policy.

Source: Marcus E. Ethridge, "Legislative Participation in Policy Implementation: An Analysis of the Michigan Experience" (Paper delivered at the 1981 Annual Meeting of the Midwest Political Science Association, Cincinnati, Ohio), pp. 19–21.

———————————— ★ ★ ★ ★ ————————————

regulations related to the agency's mission. Because state governments are expected to respond to many problems and citizen demands, many agencies with rule-making authority have been created. The result is that "in most states today the body of law created by the rule-making process matches or exceeds the statutory law of those states."[65]

Although figures from various states can be cited to demonstrate that the state bureaucracies "legislate" more than the state legislatures, most informed observers and participants would be reluctant to eliminate or even severely restrict the rule-making authority of the state agencies. Such restrictions are simply likely to lead to informal or hidden decision-rules within each agency. Formal rules are available to a wider set of interested parties and are subject to review by higher-level executive officials, both elected and appointed. Formal rules are also subject to examination by state legislators and, in most states, to either "legislative comment" or legislative negation. Legislative comment on, or negation of, bureaucratic rule-making accords with democratic philosophy by keeping the state's lawmaking authority ultimately in the hands of popularly elected lawmakers. But it may increase interest-group influence over agency actions, both by legislative negation of rules interest groups dislike and through affecting bureaucratic behavior by causing bureaucratic anticipation of legislative reaction. This can lead to a more legislative-sensitive (and, often, interest group-sensitive) perspective, when rules and regulations are developed. The legislative-review process can also add to the paperwork blizzard and incrementally contribute to the growth of the very bureaucracies the review process is designed to control.

One study of the states in which the legislature had some type of rule review authority found that although the legislature sometimes got off to a slow start in utilizing its newly obtained authority, legislative objections were raised to large numbers of administrative rules. About 20 percent of the rules submitted to the Michigan Joint Committee on Administrative Rules in 1975–78, for example, were either rejected or revised. The rejection rate in Montana in 1977–78 was 15.6 percent. And, in the first year of Florida's "legislative observations" system, over 95 percent of the rules reviewed contained some kind of error noted by the Florida Joint Administrative Procedures Committee, while some 8 percent of the rules reviewed were either without statutory foundation or exceeded the statutory authority of the agency promulgating the rule. The overall error rate in Florida has been reduced to about 33 percent. Many legislative objections to administrative rules are procedural (such as inadequate public notice), and others relate to minor difficulties, such as language the legislative staff or committee thinks was ambiguous or the failure to cite the agency's statutory authority to issue the rule. The substantive objection most often raised by legislative review—according to a survey of several states—was that "the rules exceeded [the agency's] statutory authority or [were] contrary to the general statutes."[66]

In the states in which the legislature has a clear-cut legislative veto, the state agencies have generally been responsive to legislative objections to portions of their rules and regulations. In the states where advisory "legislative observations" have been instituted, the agencies have been less responsive. The Florida legislature's unhappiness with agency footdragging led to authority for its advisory legislative review committee to "bring action in state court to obtain a judicial determination of the validity of a rule to which it objected, but which the agency refused to alter or withdraw."[67] Agency responsiveness improved dramatically.

Legislative Control of Federal Funds

The overall relationship between state legislatures and state administrative agencies is similar to that between Congress and agencies of the federal government. But the state legislatures must contend with a difficulty Congress does not have. A major source of a state legislature's authority over administrative agencies is the legislature's control of the purse strings. The proliferation of federal sources of funds for various activities, however, has sometimes made it possible for elected state executives and various state agencies to obtain funds for programs that they want to implement, even if the state legislature denies a request for state appropriations for the programs. In addition to the policy implications of such a situation, where executive agencies can get federal funds for programs to which the legislature objects, conservative state legislators often become especially distressed when a state agency obtains a federal grant that will, at the expiration of the federal funds, leave a substantial number of citizens without the service to which they will have been accustomed, leading to demands that the state legislature thereafter fund the program and continue it.

State legislators, naturally enough, feel that if they are unable to control federal grant money to state agencies, they will lose control over the basic policymaking function that the legislature is supposed to dominate.

> Because federal funds comprise an average of 25 percent of state budgets, legislatures have become increasingly concerned with how this money is received by state agencies, how it is spent, and how it is integrated with state funds appropriated to the same agencies.[68]

Over three fourths of the state legislatures now have some mechanism for reviewing the federal funds of various state agencies. The Oregon and Pennsylvania legislatures go so far as to require "that all federal funds going to state government must be appropriated in the normal manner by the legislature." "A challenge to a Pennsylvania law requiring legislative appropriation of all federal funds was dismissed in 1979 by the U.S. Supreme Court, thus upholding the Pennsylvania court ruling that such appropriation did not violate constitutional principles."[69] Other legislatures have provided for less rigorous review of federal funds, and some have taken the availability of federal monies into account when appropriating state funds.[70] Still, in many states, the various executive agencies are able, through federal funding, to circumvent the legislature's control over fundamental policymaking. In those states, the legislators occasionally resort to various kinds of vigorous oversight activities in an effort to retain control over agency programs and activities.

SUMMARY

If decisions made by legislatures are to be meaningful, those decisions must be implemented. For the most part, such implementation depends on governmental agencies and their employees—the bureaucracy. Because of differences in perspective between bureaucrats and legislators, it is inevitable that tensions will arise between the two sets of actors. Such tensions occur in parliamentary systems as well as in separation-of-powers systems. Bureaucrats are dependent on the legislature for funding and for authorization of programs. Legislators are dependent on bureaucrats for suggested solutions to social problems and for implementation. So legislators attempt to utilize their powers of funding and authorization to keep the bureaucracy attuned to legislative preferences. The outcome of the struggle for policy dominance has implications both for the immediate distribution of societal resources and for the relevance of representative democracy.

Legislators and bureaucrats do, of course, work together. Indeed, the same organized interest groups that work for or against the election or reelection of various legislators also probably helped create most of the agencies of government, and they interact regularly with the senior bureaucrats of such agencies. These "subgovernments" of legislators, bureaucrats, and interest groups tend to dominate policy development and implementation in narrow fields of policy—such as that relating to veterans or the television broadcasting industry, for example—although subgovernments vary in the relative authority possessed by sets of actors in each leg of the subgovernment "triangle." Still, the fundamental interests of an organized interest group that participates regularly in a subgovernment activity tend to be protected.

Paradoxically, Congressional "reform"—decentralization of power to large numbers of permanent standing subcommittees—may have increased the authority of subgovernments and of private interest groups in the legislative process by fragmenting Congressional authority.

Bills introduced in the legislature sometimes originate with an individual legislator or the legislator's staff assistants, but most bills are the product of the government's bureaucracy. Some measures originating from the bureaucracy arise from experience within the agency; others are requested from the White House and cabinet officers; still others are inspired by interest groups. Some agency proposals are agreed to by top executive officials. Others are rejected by top executive officials, but still find their way to friendly legislators; and some of these measures become law.

A major reason for active legislative oversight of the bureaucracy is that many responsibilities are delegated to the executive branch of government. Executive agencies, then, promulgate rules and regulations that have the force of law, and some of these rules and regulations may not be consistent with legislative preferences, or may be inconsistent with the preferences of at least those legislators who are actively involved in that particular field of policy. Because of the nature of the legislative process and the nature of some of the social controversies the legislature is expected to resolve, many laws that are enacted by legislatures include vague language that is subject to differing interpretations. Those differences of interpretation can have substantial consequences and, thus, become sources of controversy, inviting active legislative oversight over the bureaucracy.

Legislative attempts to influence bureaucratic behavior include numerous informal interactions, as well as unintended "oversight" activity as the legislators consider proposed legislation. Clear-cut instructions to an agency can be included in its annual appropriation, and the legislative changes made in its appropriations requests are in themselves implicit signals. Instructions can also be placed in an agency's basic authorizing legislation, although this is normally less readily accomplished than messages through appropriations legislation, because some agencies are permanently authorized and others have long-term authorizations. The passage of sunset legislation in the various states is an effort to change the authorizing legislation dynamic and force accountability of agencies to the legislature—with the ultimate threat of the agency's being allowed to die for lack of reauthorization. The overall effectiveness of sunset legislation is yet to be determined.

Another mechanism by which both Congress and the state legislatures have sought to control executive agency rules and regulations, especially major decisions, is the inclusion of various kinds of legislative-veto provisions in authorization legislation. Thus, some bureaucratic actions may be vetoed by vote of either chamber of a legislature, some by vote of both chambers, and a few by vote of a legislative committee. Some bureaucratic actions must be proposed by executive agencies and then must await approval by the legislature or a legislative committee. While legislative-executive relationships are less distant in parliamentary systems, the same basic legislative-bureaucratic relationships and differences of perspective still exist there, resulting in variants of the legislative veto.

Legislative-bureaucratic relationships obviously are affected by the nature of the legislature. States with full-time, paid, professional legislatures more nearly resemble Congress in the nature of the relationship between legislators and bureaucrats. States with amateur or citizen legislatures that meet only briefly each year tend to have less well-developed sets of relationships among legislators, lobbyists, and bureaucrats.

Many state legislatures are increasing their capacity for effective oversight of state agencies. One way of doing that is by providing for substantial legislative staff post-audit capability, as well as for sophisticated program-evaluation capability. Another is through sunset legislation. A third recent development is the extension of greater state legislative authority over federal funds available to the various agencies of state government. In general, state legislatures are increasing their effectiveness in the contest for control over state policymaking and implementation.

Notes

1. On these points, see Richard C. Elling, "State Legislative Impact on the State Administrative Process: Scope and Efficacy" (Paper delivered at the 1980 Annual Meeting of the Midwest Political Science Association, Chicgao, Ill.); and Richard Elmore, "Mapping Backward: Using Implementation Analysis to Structure Policy Decisions" (Paper delivered at the 1979 Annual Meeting of the American Political Science Association, Washington, D.C.).

2. Extensive discussions of this point are found in Lawrence C. Dodd and Richard L. Schott, *Congress and the Administrative State* (New York: John Wiley, 1979); and Randall B. Ripley and Grace A. Franklin, *Congress, the Bureaucracy, and Public Policy,* rev. ed. (Homewood, Ill: Dorsey Press, 1980). The overall consideration here of the subject of legislative-bureaucratic relationships has been greatly influenced by these two works.

3. Robert S. Gilmour, "Central Legislative Clearance: A Revised Perspective," *Public Administration Review,* March/April 1971; reprinted in Ronald C. Moe, ed. *Congress and the President* (Pacific Palisades, Calif.: Goodyear, 1971), pp. 109–20.

4. Dodd and Schott, *Congress and the Administrative State,* especially Chapter 7.

5. Robert J. Sickels, *Presidential Transactions* (Englewood Cliffs, N.J.: Prentice-Hall, 1974), p. 58.

6. Ibid., pp. 28–32.

7. In addition to Dodd and Schott, *Congress and the Administrative State,* and Ripley and Franklin, *Congress, the Bureaucracy, and Public Policy,* see also Roger H. Davidson, "Breaking Up These 'Cozy Triangles': An Impossible Dream?" in *Legislative Reform and Public Policy,* ed. Susan Welch and John G. Peters (New York: Praeger, 1977); J. Leiper Freeman, *The Political Process: Executive Bureau-Legislative Committee Relations,* rev. ed. (New York: Random House, 1965); and Douglass Cater, *Power in Washington* (New York: Random House, 1964). Ernest S. Griffith referred to the same phenomenon as "whirlpools of special social interest and problems." *The Impasse of Democracy* (New York: Harrison-Hilton Books, 1939), p. 182. The Griffith quotation is from Freeman, p. 6.

8. Ripley and Franklin, *Congress, the Bureaucracy and Public Policy,* pp. 7–9.

9. Ibid., pp. 107–8.

10. Ibid., pp. 20–28, 87–210. See also Theodore J. Lowi, "American Business, Public Policy, Case Studies, and Political Theory," *World Politics* 16 (July 1964): 677–715; and "Four Systems of Policy, Politics, and Choice," *Public Administration Review* 32 (July/August, 1972): 298–310, both cited in Ripley and Franklin. See also the following cited works: M. T. Hayes, "The Semi-Sovereign Pressure Groups: A Critique of Current Theory and an Alternative Typology," *Journal of Politics* 40 (February 1978): 134–61; L. A. Froman, Jr., "The Categorization of Policy Contents," in *Political Science and Public Policy,* ed. Austin Ranney (Chicago: Markham, 1968); and R. H. Salisbury, "The Analysis of Public Policy: A Search for Theories and Roles," in Ranney, *Political Science and Public Policy.* See also James Sundquist, *Politics and Policy* (Washington, D.C.: Brookings Institution, 1968).

11. Ripley and Franklin, *Congress, the Bureaucracy, and Public Policy,* p. 21.

12. Ibid.

13. Ibid., p. 25.

14. Ibid., p. 23–24.

15. Ibid., pp. 24, 121–53.

16. Ibid., pp. 26–28, 184–210.

17. Ibid., pp. 104–7. See also A. Lee Fritschler, *Smoking and Politics* (New York: Appleton-Century-Crofts, 1969); and Kenneth M. Friedman, *Public Policy and Smoking-Health Controversy* (Lexington, Mass.: Lexington Books, 1975).

18. One insightful study which anticipates the continued decline of nuclear power is Barry E. Weingast, "Congress, Regulation and the Decline of Nuclear Power," *Public Policy* 28 (Spring 1981): 231–55.

19. David Nachmias and David H. Rosenbloom, *Bureaucratic Government USA* (New York: St. Martin's Press, 1980), p. 54 and Chapter 5.

20. Loch Johnson, "The U.S. Congress and the CIA: Monitoring the Dark Side of Government," *Legislative Studies Quarterly* (November 1980): 477–500.

21. Dodd and Schott, *Congress and the Administrative State,* p. 174.

22. Ibid., p. 175.

23. Ibid., pp. 181–82.

24. Quoted by U.S. Representative John Brademas, "Oversight Rationality, Congressional Oversight, and Decentralization: An Exchange," *Publius: The Journal of Federalism* 8 (Spring 1978): 112.

25. Morris S. Ogul, *Congress Oversees the Bureaucracy* (Pittsburgh: University of Pittsburgh Press, 1976), especially Chapter 7; and Thomas A. Henderson, *Congressional Oversight of Executive Agencies: A Study of the House Committee on Government Operations* (Gainesville: University of Florida Press, 1970).

26. Ogul, *Congress Oversees the Bureaucracy,* p. 11.

27. See, for example, Joel D. Aberbach, "Changes in Congressional Oversight," *American Behavioral Scientist* 22 (May/June 1979): 493–515; and Joel D. Aberbach, "Bureaucrats and Clientele Groups: A View from Capital Hill," *American Journal of Political Science* (November 1978): 818–32.

28. John R. Bolton, *The Legislative Veto: Unseparating the Powers* (Washington, D.C.: American Enterprise Institute for Public Policy Research, 1977), pp. 5–8. Bolton notes that "the doctrine [that legislative powers could not be delegated to the executive] has fallen into such disrepute that a respected administrative-law commentator has warned attorneys not to raise it on behalf of their clients" (p. 7). K. C. Davis, *Administrative Law Treatise* (St. Paul, Minnesota: West, 1958), Section 2.01, is quoted by Bolton: "Lawyers who try to win cases by arguing that congressional delegations are unconstitutional almost invariably do more harm than good to their clients' interests. . . . The vaguest standards are held adequate, and various delegations without standards have been upheld" (p. 8). It is possible to discern a contrary trend in more recent judicial rulings, however. Bolton, for example, calls attention to *National Cable Television Association* v. *United States,* 415 U.S. 336 (1974).

29. Louis Fisher, *President and Congress: Power and Policy* (New York: Free Press, 1972), pp. 56–57. The original authorship of the syllogism is uncertain. See his Chapter 3 for an insightful and easily understood discussion of the dimensions of the problem.

30. Gary Orfield, *Congressional Power: Congress and Social Change* (New York: Harcourt Brace Jovanovich, 1975), p. 227.

31. U.S. Senate, Committee on Government Operations, *Congressional Oversight of Regulatory Agencies,* vol. 2, 95th Cong., 1st sess., February 1977, pp. 4–5; presented in Dodd and Schott, *Congress and the Administrative State,* p. 156.

32. Ogul, *Congress Oversees the Bureaucracy,* p. 13.

33. The Joint Committee on Atomic Energy took such steps when it was defending the Atomic Energy Commission, for instance. H. L. Nieburg, "The Eisenhower AEC and Congress: A Study in Executive-Legislative Relations," *Midwest Journal of Political Science* (May 1962). See also Seymour Scher, "Conditions for Legislative Control," *Journal of Politics* (August 1963).

34. John P. Bradley, "Shaping Administrative Policy with the Aid of Congressional Oversight: The Senate Finance Committee and Medicare," *Western Political Quarterly* 33 (December 1980): 492–501.

35. Alan Schick, "The Battle of the Budget," in *Congress Against the President,* ed. Harvey C. Mansfield, Sr. (New York: Praeger, 1975).

36. *Congressional Quarterly Weekly Report,* June 21, 1980, p. 1767.

37. *Congressional Quarterly Weekly Report,* May 24, 1980, pp. 1407–9.

38. Ibid., p. 1409.

39. Ripley and Franklin, *Congress, the Bureaucracy, and Public Policy,* rev. ed., pp. 104–7; and Friedman, *Public Policy and the Smoking-Health Controversy.*

40. Bruce Adams and Betsy Sherman, "Sunset Implementation: A Positive Partnership to Make Government Work," *Public Administration Review* 38 (January/February, 1978): 78–81.

41. Morris S. Ogul, "Congressional Oversight: Structures and Incentives," in Lawrence C. Dodd and Bruce I. Oppenheimer, *Congress Reconsidered* (New York: Praeger, 1977), p. 214; see also Ogul, *Congress Oversees the Bureaucracy,* Chapter 6.

42. Richard E. Cohen, "Will the 96th Become the 'Oversight Congress'?" *National Journal,* January 13, 1979, pp. 44–49.

43. Ibid., p. 48.

44. John R. Bolton, *The Legislative Veto,* p. 2, footnote 8.

45. Gerhard Loewenberg and Samuel C. Patterson, *Comparing Legislatures* (Boston: Little, Brown, 1979), p. 271.

46. Ibid., p. 274.

47. Ibid., pp. 275–76. See also John E. Schwartz and L. Earl Shaw, *The United States Congress in Comparative Perspective* (Hinsdale, Ill.: Dryden Press, 1976), especially Chapter 7.

48. Elling, "State Legislative Impact on the State Administrative Process: Scope and Efficacy".

49. Marcus E. Ethridge, "Legislative Participation in Policy Implementation: Analysis of the Michigan Experience" (Paper delivered at the 1981 Annual Meeting of the Midwest Political Science Association, Cincinnati, Ohio).

50. William Pound, "The State Legislatures," in *The Book of the States, 1980–81* (Lexington, Ky.: Council of State Governments, 1980), pp. 81–82.

51. William Lyons and Larry W. Thomas, "Oversight in State Legislatures: Structural-Attitudinal Interaction" (Paper delivered at the 1979 Annual Meeting of the Southern Political Science Association, Gatlinburg, Tenn.).

52. An excellent survey of the auditing and program-evaluation capabilities of state legislatures is available in Richard E. Brown, ed. *The Effectiveness of Legislative Program Review* (New Brunswick, N.J.: Transaction Books, 1979). A program-specific discussion of some of the problems is in Richard F. Elmore, *Complexity and Control: What Legislators and Administrators Can Do About Implementation* (Seattle, Wash.: University of Washington Institute of Government Research, 1979).

53. Keith E. Hamm and Roby D. Robertson, "New Methods of State Legislative Oversight: A Comparative Analysis of Adoption and Implementation" (Paper delivered at the 1979 Annual Meeting of the American Political Science Association, Washington, D.C.), p. 12.

54. Ibid., pp. 14–15; and Adams and Sherman, "Sunset Implementation," pp. 78–81.

55. "Hundreds of Agencies on 'Hit' Lists," *State Government News,* January 1978, p. 2.

56. Barry Mitzman, "Sunset Laws: Why They Aren't Working," *Washington Monthly,* June 1979, p. 51.

57. Hamm and Robertson, "New Methods of State Legislative Oversight," p. 49. See also Common Cause, *Making Government Work: A Common Cause Report on State Sunset Activity* (Washington, D.C.: Common Cause, 1978); cited in Hamm and Robertson.

58. Common Cause, *Making Government Work,* p. 69.

59. Pound, "The State Legislatures," p. 82.

60. Mitzman, "Sunset Laws: Why They Aren't Working," p. 51.

61. Ibid.

62. Hamm and Robertson, "New Methods of State Legislative Oversight," p. 51.

63. Ibid., pp. 5–10; and Pound, "The State Legislatures," p. 81.

64. Hamm and Robertson, "New Methods of State Legislative Oversight," p. 34. This section draws generally on Hamm and Robertson.

65. National Conference of State Legislatures, *Restoring the Balance: Legislative Review of Administrative Regulations* (Denver: National Conference of State Legislatures, 1978), p. 7; cited in Hamm and Robertson, "New Methods of State Legislative Oversight."

66. Hamm and Robertson, "New Methods of State Legislative Oversight," p. 38. The data in the above paragraph are from pages 35–38.

67. Ibid., p. 42.

68. William Pound and Carl Tubbesing, "The State Legislatures," in *The Book of the States, 1978–79* (Lexington, Ky.: Council of State Governments, 1978), p. 3.

69. Pound, "The State Legislatures," p. 82.

70. Larry Walker, "State Legislative Control of Federal Aid" (Paper delivered at the 1978 Annual Meeting of the American Political Science Association, New York, N.Y.).

chapter 16

The Legislature and the Judiciary

Preview

In the American separation-of-powers government, the judiciary has successfully asserted the right to have the final say concerning the constitutionality of laws passed by the legislature, and that is true at both the state and the national level. If the courts find a law unconstitutional, the legislature may propose a constitutional amendment or it may enact a law similar to the one declared unconstitutional but changed enough to get around the constitutional objection. The legislature is dependent on the judiciary to apply the laws to specific cases. If legislators dislike the judicial interpretation of a statute, they may revise the statute to insure it is interpreted as the legislature desires. In most states and at the national level, the powers of the legislature include the right to impeach judges and remove them from office, as well as authority over the courts' budgets and the judges' salaries. In a few states, the legislature chooses the judges; in some others it has a role in their selection. In most states the number of trial court judges (and, sometimes, appellate judges) is set by statute and can be changed by act of the legislature. Congress has the authority to change the number of federal judges and occasionally does so. The U.S. Senate must confirm all presidential nominees to the federal judiciary. The Senate has used that power, through a device called senatorial courtesy, to dominate the selection of U.S. district judges.

The United States government and all fifty state governments are separation-of-powers governments. That is, the executive branch, the legislature, and the judiciary are separate from each other. Members of one branch are forbidden to serve as members of any other branch of government. Legislators may not simultaneously serve as judges, just as they may not simultaneously be officers of the executive branch. This does not mean, however, that the legislature and the judiciary share no responsibilities or functions. Both branches, for example, make law. The accumulation of judicial precedents—past judicial decisions in similar situations—constitutes *case law.* The legislature can change case law (except that interpreting a constitutional provision) by enacting a statute on the subject, since *statutory law* supersedes case law. After the legislature has enacted a law, though, the judiciary must decide what the law means in each specific case that comes into court and must apply the law. The law, and much of the work of the legislature, would be meaningless without judicial application and judicial interpretation.

CONGRESS AND THE JUDICIARY

The relationship between Congress and the federal judiciary is complex, but the actions of each affect the other. The U.S. Supreme Court was established by the U.S. Constitution, but the lower federal courts are created by act of Congress. The Congressional power to create courts comes mainly from Article III, Section 1 of the Constitution, which reads:

> The judicial Power of the United States, shall be vested in one supreme Court, and in such inferior Courts as the Congress may from time to time ordain and establish.

The authority of Congress to create courts also stems from the legislative article of the Constitution, Article I, Section 8, which grants Congress the power: "To constitute Tribunals inferior to the Supreme Court." Federal district courts and federal courts of appeal are *constitutional courts,* established under Article III of the U.S. Constitution, as are some of the other courts created by Congress. Courts created under the authority granted to Congress by Article I of the Constitution *(legislative courts)*—such as the Court of Military Justice—differ in various ways from constitutional courts, including term of office for the judges. Congress has some greater flexibility when creating courts under Article I than under Article III. But, regardless of the type of court, all federal courts other than the U.S. Supreme Court have been created by act of Congress (some were created by the First Congress), and they can be abolished by act of Congress.[1]

Federal judges and Supreme Court justices are nominated to office by the President, but they must be confirmed (approved) individually by the U.S. Senate. All such judges are subject to removal from the bench through the impeachment process. The *only* federal officials ever removed from office by impeachment and conviction have been four federal district judges.[2] The federal judiciary is also subject to the Congressional appropriations process, which determines the level of staff assistance for the federal courts and also sets judicial salaries. Congressional control over judicial salaries is limited by the constitutional provision (Article III, Section 1) that the salaries of federal judges "shall not be diminished during their Continuance in Office."[3]

The U.S. Constitution (Article III, Section 2) confers limited original jurisdiction upon the U.S. Supreme Court, but, other than that, "no federal court has any power to hear any case unless Congress has conferred it."[4] Federal court jurisdiction thus extends only as far as Congress chooses to permit. That fact was made clear in 1869. After the U.S. Supreme Court had heard a case challenging the constitutionality of one of the Reconstruction Acts, but before the Court had decided the case, "Congress passed a law that prevented the appeal of that type of case to the Supreme Court, which thereupon held that it had no power to decide the case."[5] In the 1960s, when the U.S. Supreme Court was making historic rulings concerning legislative apportionment, Congress seriously considered removing such matters from the Court's jurisdiction. Congressional supporters of the Court's actions, however, were able to prevent passage of limiting legislation.[6]

In addition to its control over court jurisdiction, Congress also controls the size of the federal judiciary and the U.S. Supreme Court. The number of justices on the U.S. Supreme Court is not stated in the Constitution; it is fixed by act of Congress.

That number has been set at six, seven, and ten, but has remained unchanged at nine since 1869.[7]

The size of the lesser federal judiciary has slowly expanded, along with the nation, although expansions of the judiciary have often occurred after a party long out of power has regained the reins of government.[8] The most recent expansion of the judiciary—and the largest ever—was the 1978 Democratic Congressional and presidential decision to create 117 additional federal district judgeships and 35 additional circuit court of appeals judgeships. Democratic President Jimmy Carter had the pleasure of making those new judicial appointments.

It is clear from this discussion that Congress has substantial authority with respect to the federal judiciary. The judiciary, however, is not bereft of power of its own. The U.S. judiciary, especially the Supreme Court, has become the ultimate arbiter of the Constitution. This will be discussed later in the chapter. The judiciary also interprets the meaning of the law in specific cases, "makes law" through many of its decisions, and sometimes settles disputes between Congress and the executive, or between one chamber of Congress and a member of Congress, as in the case of the attempted expulsion of Representative Adam Clayton Powell (D., New York) by the U.S. House of Representatives.[9]

Judicial Review

As noted in Chapter 4, the U.S. Supreme Court has interpreted the U.S. Constitution in such a way as to expand the powers of Congress (and of the national government) in its decisions concerning the meaning of the "necessary-and-proper" clause of the Constitution (Article I, Section 8) and concerning the investigative powers of Congress. The Constitution is silent when it comes to the question of precisely who should interpret the Constitution, but in 1803 the U.S. Supreme Court settled that question in the celebrated case of *Marbury* v. *Madison.* The general public now apparently accepts as only natural and right that it is the U.S. Supreme Court which—almost like the oracles of old—should interpret the U.S. Constitution and apply its ancient words to current situations.[10]

The *Marbury* v. *Madison* decision constrains the powers of Congress somewhat, because it establishes the authority of the federal judiciary (and especially the U.S. Supreme Court) to interpret the Constitution and to refuse to enforce legislation which, in the Court's view, is in conflict with the constitution. As Chief Justice John Marshall noted in the Court's decision:

> Between these alternatives there is no middle ground. The Constitution is either a superior paramount law, unchangeable by ordinary means, or it is on a level with ordinary legislative acts, and, like other acts, is alterable when the legislature shall please to alter it. . . .
>
> If an act of the legislature, repugnant to the Constitution, is void, does it, notwithstanding its invalidity, bind the courts, and oblige them to give it effect? Or, in other words, though it be not law, does it constitute a rule as operative as if it was a law? This would be to overthrow in fact what was established in theory.
>
> It is emphatically the province and duty of the judicial department to say what the law is. Those who apply the rule to particular cases, must of necessity expound and interpret that rule. If two laws conflict with each other, the courts must decide on the operation of each.
>
> So if the law be in opposition to the Constitution, if both the law and the Constitution apply to a particular case, so that the court must either decide that case

conformably to the law, disregarding the Constitution, or conformably to the Constitution, disregarding the law, the court must determine which of these conflicting rules governs the case. This is of the very essence of judicial duty.

The Constitution declares "that no bill of attainder or ex post facto law shall be passed."

If, however, such a bill should be passed, and a person should be prosecuted under it, must the court condemn to death those victims whom the Constitution endeavors to preserve? . . .

Why does a judge swear to discharge his duties agreeably to the Constitution of the United States, if that Constitution forms no rule for his government—if it is closed upon him and cannot be inspected by him? . . .

Thus, the particular phraseology of the Constitution of the United States confirms and strengthens the principle, supposed to be essential to all written constitutions, that a law repugnant to the Constitution is void; and that courts, as well as other departments, are bound by that instrument.[11]

In fact, judicial declarations that acts of Congress are unconstitutional are fairly rare. Since 1803, only 100 or so federal laws have been declared unconstitutional by the U.S. Supreme Court.[12] All but a handful of those cases have been decided since the 1860s. A ruling that an act of Congress is unconstitutional gains wide publicity and may become a major political issue as in 1935 when the high Court struck down the major components of the New Deal. Through 1937, most such decisions by the Supreme Court were in protection of property rights. Since 1937, such decisions have tended to protect individual liberties.

Responses to Judicial Rejection of Statutes When the Supreme Court does find a federal statute to be unconstitutional, the Court walks a fine line, in that "the securing of personal liberty in opposition to majority will inevitably generates some degree of public disfavor. . . . On the other hand, effective judicial defense of constitutional rights demands at least some degree of public acceptance."[13] Fortunately for the Supreme Court, both the elected officials and the general citizenry of the nation for the most part accept the Court's self-proclaimed role as the guardian of the Constitution. Indeed, the continued reluctance of Congress to exclude legislation of questionable constitutionality from judicial review (as Congress once did in 1868) amounts to acquiescence in the Supreme Court's exercise of judicial review. The authority of Congress to place certain types of legislation off limits to the Court's review, however, apparently is a sufficient "gun behind the door" to insure substantial judicial restraint and responsibility in the exercise of the power of judicial review.[14] Voiding an act of Congress as unconstitutional is a decision the Court does not take lightly. Some observers of the judicial-legislative dynamic have noted that numerous Court-curbing bills are introduced in Congress only when the Court is out of harmony with the policy preferences of the elected branches of government. Such bill introductions in large numbers not infrequently lead to modifications of the Court's position, even though the Court-curbing bills do not pass.[15]

A different response to repeated judicial rejection of important legislation is exemmlified by President Franklin D. Roosevelt's reaction, in 1937, to Supreme Court rulings striking down much New Deal legislation. Roosevelt asked Congress (and the public) to let him appoint a new Supreme Court justice for each sitting justice over age 70, to a maximum of fifteen members. Had Congress agreed, Roosevelt could have appointed enough new members to change the Court's repeated finding

★ ★ ★ ★

The Supreme Court and
Congressional-Presidential Disagreements

The Court . . . is the overseer of the no man's land of the Constitution; it is the arbiter of the "great silences" of that document which demark the boundaries which, at least in traditional theory, separate the component parts of government in the United States. In thus arbitrating between the Congress and the President, the Court in effect picks a side to support; and even on the same issue, sometimes the Court favors the President, and sometimes it is the Congress upon whom the Court smiles. It is rare that the odd branch—the one, that is, whose acts have been branded by the Court as unconstitutional—can hope to overcome successfully the combined political strength of the Supreme Court plus the other branch with which the Court has allied itself. Therefore, when there is genuine conflict between policy goals favored by the President and the Congress, the Supreme Court may well have an opportunity to have the determinative say by throwing its weight in support of either of the two contestants. This is a real power and it is important.

Source: Glendon A. Schubert, *Constitutional Politics* (New York: Holt, Rinehart, and Winston, 1960), p. 305.

★ ★ ★ ★

that New Deal legislation was unconstitutional.[16] Such a response to a negative Court decision has not been successful for over a century. In 1869 President Grant was able to reverse the Supreme Court's position on what constituted legal tender after Congress had expanded the size of the Court to nine—the last change in the size of the Supreme Court. The Court had been reduced in size three years earlier, over President Andrew Johnson's veto, by an act which required the President to leave the next three vacancies on the court unfilled. "The obvious reason for this was the distrust of Johnson by the Radical Republican majority of the Congress and the fear—doubtless well justified—that Johnson appointees would have voted against the constitutionality of the Reconstruction legislation."[17] Other baldly political changes in the size of the Supreme Court had been enacted earlier, in 1801, 1802, 1807, 1837 and 1863.[18] The defeat of FDR's Court-packing plan in 1937—and the intensity of the public outcry against that plan—has led most observers to conclude that the number of Supreme Court justices is unlikely to be changed, although that it remains constitutionally within the power of Congress to make such a change is not in dispute. Interestingly enough, the Court began accepting most of the revised New Deal laws soon after the Court-packing plan was announced.

Congress can respond to a Supreme Court decision that a particular statute is unconstitutional by rewriting the legislation, enacting the same fundamental principle but revising the details of the statute enough so that it will meet a Court test. An angry majority in Congress took that approach in the 1950's, for example, when the Supreme Court found various "internal-security" laws to be unconstitutional.[19]

460

★ ★ ★ ★

Members Move to Rein in Supreme Court

Angered by years of Supreme Court decisions they oppose, a group of senators and representatives is trying an old and controversial method of getting around Supreme Court rulings.

They have introduced bills that would take away the Supreme Court's authority to hear cases on the volatile issues of abortion, school desegregation and school prayer.

The effect of such measures, if enacted, would be to clear the way for 50 separate and potentially different state laws on these matters.

The legislative move is a new tack for opponents of court decisions in these areas, who have been unable for years to muster the votes for constitutional amendments or new laws to overturn the rulings.

Sponsors of the court-curbing bills . . . are frank to say that the theory behind their efforts is simple—if you don't like the way the court decides a case, tell the judges they can't decide it. . . .

The new court-curbing bills—23 in the House, four in the Senate—have prompted a serious debate on the role of the legislative and judicial branches of government and the meaning of the Constitution.

The Senate Judiciary Committee's Subcommittee on the Constitution, led by Sen. Orrin G. Hatch, R-Utah, an advocate of the court-curbing approach, held hearings on the jurisdictional issue May 20–21. . . .

[The] hearings are focusing on the issue of court jurisdiction, and not on any particular bill that deals with a specific subject such as abortion.

The heart of the controversy is whether Congress can strip the Supreme Court of its authority to hear certain cases.

A secondary question . . . is whether Congress has authority to take cases away from the federal district and appellate courts, leaving issues to be decided solely in the state courts.

The debate centers on interpretations of Article III of the Constitution, which establishes the federal judiciary and outlines its powers. . . .

Constitutional law specialists do not agree on the legality of the court-curbing bills. Some . . . believe Article III, Section Two allows Congress to strip the Supreme Court of authority to hear a category of cases.

But others . . . do not. They argue that such a bill would prevent the Supreme Court from exercising its constitutional role as the final arbiter of constitutional issues. . . .

There is less argument about congressional power to curb the jurisdiction of the lower federal courts, with many academic experts conceding that Congress could substantially reduce the authority of these courts or even abolish them altogether. . . .

The current jurisdiction bills were a long time in the making. The starting point was the Supreme Court's landmark decision in *Brown v. Board of Education,* the 1954 ruling that . . . said that school segregation deprived blacks of equal protection under the law. . . .

[Then] in 1973, . . . the court . . . struck down state anti-abortion laws in *Roe v. Wade.* . . .

The third controversial issue, school prayer, erupted in 1962 when the court ruled in *Engle v. Vitale* that the use of a non-denominational school prayer was "wholly inconsistent" with a clause in the First Amendment prohibiting the establishment of a religion. . . .

For years, members of Congress upset by these decisions have tried unsuccessfully to overturn the rulings through legislation or constitutional amendments. All attempts have failed. . . .

Only in the abortion area has Congress been able to narrow the effect of the Supreme Court decision. It has prohibited federal funding of abortions except in cases of rape, incest or when the mother's life is in danger. . . .

The Supreme Court has upheld the congressional funding restrictions as well as a state's decision not to spend state funds for abortion.

Source: Nadine Cohodas, "Members Move to Rein in Supreme Court," *Congressional Quarterly Weekly Report,* May 30, 1981, pp. 947–51.

──────────────────────── ★ ★ ★ ★ ────────────────────────

Another avenue open to Congress, when the Supreme Court holds a particular law to be unconstitutional, is to submit a constitutional amendment to the states for ratification, proposing a change in the Constitution to accommodate the will of Congress. That approach has been utilized successfully on four occasions,[20] the most well known being the Sixteenth Amendment, passed in 1913, to permit the federal income tax. The most recent use of this technique, and the only successful one since 1913, was the Twenty-sixth Amendment, which became the law of the land in 1971. That amendment was proposed by Congress after the Supreme Court had ruled that Congress lacked the authority to establish the voting age (at eighteen) for state and local elections. The constitutional amendment approach to overruling the Supreme Court has also been attempted—unsuccessfully—in response to Court decisions concerning prayer in the schools, school integration, busing of school children to achieve racial balance, and abortion. An undermining of some of those decisions *without* constitutional amendments has been achieved to some degree through restrictive federal legislation, especially restrictions on the use of federal funds for various purposes.

Statutory Interpretation   The judiciary must interpret the laws, if it is to enforce them. As discussed in earlier chapters, the exigencies of the legislative process often result in laws which are not entirely clear and sometimes result in statutes that have been left vague, deliberately. Most of the time, as in the case of bureaucratic interpretation of legislation, the judicial interpretation and application of the law determines the reality of what a given statute says or means in the society. Often, the judicial contest is over whether or not the bureaucratic interpretation is correct. Occasionally, Congress amends legislation to clarify its intent, thus repudiating the Court's interpretation of a statute, and, sometimes, Congress enacts an entirely new law to accomplish the same end. In 1961, for example, the Supreme Court held that

---
★ ★ ★ ★

Cycles of Judicial-Legislative Tension

[T]he courts, and particularly the Supreme Court at the pinnacle of the federal judiciary, act as policy makers in a way generally held to be reserved for the elected branches of government. The power of "judicial review", the authority to interpret the Constitution and statutes and to declare the latter "null and void" when inconsistent with the former, lies at the base of the court's policy-making position. The courts can thus, using the vehicle of specific cases, render decisions which impose limits on what Congress can do, or which enunciate substantive decisions of a sort that the legislature might otherwise be expected to enact. For instance, . . . the Court rather than Congress has been the chief architect of national policies requiring legislative reapportionment and forbidding prayer in the public schools.

Such policy decisions pose problems for Congress; the Court, having prevented the legislature from acting or having interpreted congressional action in a way inconsistent with legislative intent, in essence makes demands on Congress to accept its dictates. The senators and representatives must decide whether to permit the judicial determination to stand or whether to take steps, usually through passage of legislation, to reassert legislative policy priorities. Thus, constitutional amendments were introduced in the Senate to reverse Court holdings with regard to reapportionment and prayer in the public schools. . . . [T]he purpose of each was to reject the demands for such policies and to substitute the legislature's point of view for that of the judiciary.

The courts do not always make demands of this indirect sort; rather, history suggests that there are recurring periods in which the judiciary seems to render opinions that threaten congressional policy-making prerogatives with respect to major issues—e.g., civil rights—which concern major political interests in the nation. The legislature, for its part, is seldom willing to accept court-announced policy initiatives passively, especially when important political relationships are altered. Congress often takes, or seems ready to take, counteractions to reverse the courts; thus, there have been cycles of conflict between court and Congress, with the former making demands by acting as a policy maker in ways which threaten the latter. The legislature acts to reassert its preeminence, and the judiciary, recognizing its inability to compel a hostile Congress, tends to retreat, to mitigate its challenges, in such circumstances.

Source: Leroy N. Rieselbach, *Congressional Politics* (New York: McGraw-Hill, 1973), pp. 225–26.

★ ★ ★ ★

"Congress had not meant to prevent the Department of Justice from obtaining access to copies of confidential Census reports."[21] That interpretation was overturned by an act of Congress which explicitly prohibited such access. Twenty-one such "overrulings" of Supreme Court statutory interpretations occurred between 1945 and 1957.[22] Obviously, when the judiciary's role is merely that of determining Congressional intent, rather than determining the constitutionality of a given statute, Congress finds its task of "correcting" the Court much easier. Still, getting any bill through Congress can be difficult, and the interests served by the Court's opinion will seek to insure that the overruling legislation is stalled. As one respected observer notes:

> In legal theory, Congress can always overrule the Court's interpretation of federal statutes, at least prospectively. This is the official view frequently touted by the Court itself. Of course, it is utterly unrealistic. . . . We do not mean to suggest that Congress cannot, and does not, overrule the Court. But we do suggest that the blithe notion that Congress can readily change its mind, and disagree with the Court in cases that involve "merely" statutory interpretation, is politically naive. It is much more accurate to say that: (a) the Supreme Court's decisions interpreting federal statutes are, from a practical point of view, hardly less "final" than the Court's decisions interpreting the Constitution; and, conversely, (b) the Congress can, and does, overrule the Court on constitutional points only somewhat less frequently than on statutory points.[23]

Congressional Impact on the Selection of Judicial Personnel

Members of the federal judiciary are, by constitutional mandate, nominated to their judicial office by the President and confirmed by the U.S. Senate.[24] Except for some members of "legislative courts" (created under powers granted to Congress by Article I rather than Article III of the Constitution), federal judges then hold office for life, subject to the "good-behavior" requirement. The discussion here is limited to the nomination and confirmation of federal district judges, federal circuit court of appeals judges, and U.S. Supreme Court justices, the courts normally referred to as "the federal courts," or "the federal judiciary." All are constitutional courts ("Article III" courts).

Federal District Judges There are some signs that the Senate's role in the nomination of federal district judges may be changing, though such a change would require reversal of two centuries of tradition. The traditional roles of the Senate and the President in the selection of federal district judges have been almost the reverse of what the Constitution stipulates. United States senators have used their confirmation power to bolster their authority back home and to improve their chances for reelection. They have done so through a device normally referred to as "senatorial courtesy," which seeks to insure that a senator's political enemies back home do not receive federal appointments, especially appointments to long-term positions of power, such as a federal judgeship. (Each federal judicial district lies entirely within a state, comprising the entire state or a part of a state.) The essence of senatorial courtesy is that if the senior U.S. senator (of the President's party) from a state objects to the appointment of a particular individual to the federal bench in that senator's state, the entire Senate will refuse to confirm the nominee.

Senatorial courtesy is not absolute. It varies a bit. Its earliest manifestation seems to have come in 1789, during George Washington's first term as President. It developed from a dispute between the administration and Georgia's senators over who would be appointed naval officer of the port of Savannah. The Senate rejected the administration's nominee for the post because the Georgia senators objected.[25] Obviously, if the Senate collectively supports the senators from each state in matters of appointment to federal office within each state, regardless of the merits of each

★ ★ ★ ★

Senatorial Courtesy

An unwritten agreement among senators that requires the President to confer with the senator or senators of his party from a state before he makes a nomination to fill a federal office located in that state. The Senate will almost invariably reject a presidential nominee when the senator involved raises a personal objection. When neither senator of a state is of the President's party, the President is apt to consult state party leaders.

Significance: Senatorial courtesy has resulted in the transference of federal patronage within a state from the President to senators of his party. This means that such senators normally choose the appointees and give their names to the President so that he can make the formal appointments. Federal positions affected by senatorial courtesy include judges, district attorneys, customs officials, and field service officials of most important agencies. Presidents may reject senatorial recommendations, but this rarely occurs.

Source: Jack C. Plano and Milton Greenberg, *The American Political Dictionary*, 5th ed. (New York: Holt, Rinehart, and Winston, 1979), p. 189.

★ ★ ★ ★

case, then each state's senators can control federal appointments in their state. But the two senators from a state often represent either different political parties or different factions within the same political party. The former problem was resolved by the present Senate tradition of supporting senators' objections to home-state appointments *only* when the senator is a member of the President's party. The party-faction problem was resolved less explicitly, but the thrust was to support the senior senator of the President's party from each state. The junior senator seldom was left completely out of the picture, but neither did he or she have the chamber-wide support that the senior senator from the state could muster, so the junior senator was left to negotiate as good a deal as possible with the senior member for influence over home-state federal appointments. Complications also arise when a senator becomes President or vice-president, since even then he or she tends to resist giving up control over federal appointments in the home state. Vice-president Lyndon B. Johnson, for example, preferred not to yield his control over federal patronage in Texas to U.S. Senator Ralph Yarborough (D., Texas), with whom Johnson was often in political conflict. The two men finally worked out a system under which they alternated in deciding about appointees to federal posts in Texas.

The actual selection practice for nominating federal district judges varies with the idiosyncracies of each state's political system and the importance each senator places on the selection of federal judges for his or her state. An important factor, of course, is the senator's overall standing in the Senate. The dominant pattern, however, is for the state's senior senator of the President's party to decide whom to nominate for each vacant federal district judgeship and, then, send that name to the White House. Occasionally, more than one name is sent for a vacancy. Unless the White House objects to the nominee on political grounds, it forwards the name to the Justice Department for an evaluation of the prospective nominee's ability and a background check by the FBI. Depending on the President, the American Bar Association may also be asked to evaluate the prospective nominee's qualifications for the bench. If all goes well for the senator's nominee, he or she eventually becomes the President's nominee. The nomination is made formally by the President and is sent to the Senate for evaluation and confirmation. If the prospective judicial nominee is rejected by the administration, the senator normally makes a second choice. Sometimes, the President has a candidate for a vacant judgeship. In such a situation, a prudent President has presidential aides discuss the matter with the relevant Senator, to work out an accommodation and avoid a Senate rejection. Rarely, the Senate may confirm a judicial nominee over the objections of the relevant senator, but that is decidedly the exception.

The traditional pattern in senatorial decisions about whom to support for federal judgeships has been that partisan patronage considerations loom large in the choice, and this results in some federal judges of questionable competence. As part of a larger effort to improve the federal judiciary and to increase the number of racial minority and woman judges, the Carter administration pressed for "merit selection" of judges.[26] Probably in part because they sensed an opportunity to begin participating more effectively in the choice of federal district judges, members of the House of Representatives have also sought the creation of merit-selection commissions in each state to recommend people for vacant federal judgeships. When such commissions have been established, however, they have been created by the U.S. senators from each state, and the commissions vary substantially in composition in the twenty odd states which have them. Some senators have used the form of the merit-selection commission without changing the fact of political patronage. Others have created commissions to which the senators have appointed a majority of members, but have allowed other actors, such as U.S. representatives or the state bar association, to appoint some commission members.[27] The creation of the merit-selection commissions gave Republican U.S. senators greater influence over federal judgeship appointments in their states when a Democrat (Carter) was President than they could have asserted under traditional senatorial courtesy norms.

The importance of being a senator of the President's party was reduced somewhat—in terms of controlling judicial appointments back home—by the "blue-slip" method, developed by former Senator James Eastland (D., Mississippi), when he was chairperson of the Senate Judiciary Committee. (All nominations to the federal judiciary are referred to the Judiciary Committee, where they may be killed, delayed, or favorably reported to the floor of the Senate.) Under the blue-slip system, the Judiciary Committee sent a blue form to *both* senators from each state in which a federal judgeship nomination was made, regardless of the senators' partisan affiliations. A senator who opposed a particular candidate for a federal judgeship merely failed to return the blue slip to the Judiciary Committee, and the committee would, after waiting a reasonable length of time, kill the nomination. Normally, no discussion took place in the committee in such cases, and no action on the floor of the Senate was required.[28] The nomination merely died from lack of positive action. The cross-party conservative coalition nature of such a strategy is obvious: what the Republican senators could not obtain through the time-honored senatorial courtesy tradition, they obtained by the cooperation of a friendly conservative Democratic committee chairperson. Such a process almost certainly skewed the federal judiciary in a conservative direction, philosophically.

When liberal Democratic Senator Edward M. Kennedy (D., Massachusetts) became Judiciary Committee chairperson in January 1979, he announced that, although he would continue the practice of sending the blue slips to both senators from each state, he would not automatically kill a nomination for the lack of a blue slip, but that lack of senatorial response would be taken into consideration by the committee. The earlier importance of Senator Eastland's automatic blue-slip death of nominees that were opposed by Republican senators, serving in a Democratic Senate under a Democratic President, is reflected in the fact that all seven Republicans on the Senate Judiciary Committee protested Senator Kennedy's change of policy on the grounds that "a senator is best qualified to evaluate judicial candidates in his home state and should have a right to veto" such candidates.[29] The partisan impact of such "vetoes" by Republican senators is perhaps more obvious when one realizes that Presidents make over 90 percent of their judicial appointments from among the ranks of their own fellow partisans. Not surprisingly, when Republican Senator Strom Thurmond (D., North Carolina) became Judiciary Committee chairperson in January 1981, he announced that he would continue Senator Kennedy's nonbinding blue-slip policy, thus maintaining control of federal judgeship appointments in the hands of Republican senators and the Republican President.[30]

Federal Court of Appeals Judges   Presidents have a bit more freedom with respect to the appointment of federal court of appeals judges than with federal district judges, in part because the appellate courts are much more important than the district courts and, perhaps more importantly, because the federal courts of appeal circuits each include more than one state. Thus no single senator can alone claim to represent the citizenry over whom the court of appeals judge will wield authority. But traditions develop, and the various states in each court of appeals jurisdiction feel they have a "claim" on certain seats on that court. When a given state's seat on the court of appeals is vacated, that state's senators have the greatest voice in the selection of the new appellate judge and probably can block confirmation of the President's nominee, if the nomination is not cleared with them first. Depending on the overall political situation at the moment and the balance of obligations between a given senator and the White House, as well as the executive's own balance of obligations and set of priorities, the senator may actually make the selection, as is commonly done for federal district judgeships.

    As part of his effort to improve the federal judiciary and to reduce the cronyism involved in appointment to the federal bench, President Carter established commissions in each federal judicial circuit to help select candidates for appointment to the courts of appeals. Political factors continued to be important, but President Carter set new records in the percentage of his appellate appointees who were women or racial minorities. The large number of positions available to Carter helped him establish that record, of course, because he was able to open the recruitment net more widely while still appointing many senators' favorite candidates. The Reagan administration abolished the court of appeals candidate-selection commissions and placed the responsibility for developing lists of nominees back in the office of the attorney general.[31]

    The process of selecting court of appeals nominees varies with each President. But regardless of the details of the selection process, the White House finds life easier if the relevant senators are approached and given a voice in the selection process for "their" court of appeals judges.

U.S. Supreme Court Justices   The usual patronage considerations of U.S. senators no longer apply when appointments to the U.S. Supreme Court are involved. Like any nominee to high office who comes before the Senate for confirmation, of course,

———————————— ★ ★ ★ ★ ————————————

Nixon Supreme Court Appointments

For month after month, from August 1969 through April 1970, the attention of the country was focused on the sharpest conflict between Presidential and Congressional powers in the appointment of Justices since the Administration of President Ulysses S. Grant. In a nation where the Supreme Court had become the symbol of the government's movement toward racial justice, the struggle had elemental political importance.

Presidents had come to expect confirmation of Supreme Court nominees almost as a matter of course. While there had been a good deal of criticism of several nominees, the only twentieth-century defeat was suffered by President Hoover in 1930. On that occasion the President, weakened by the Depression disaster, had been unable to win confirmation for Judge John Parker, who was severely attacked for hostile attitudes by the labor movement and the NAACP. Since that time no Presidential choice was voted down, although a 1968 filibuster forced President Johnson to end his effort to elevate Justice Abe Fortas to Chief Justice.

President Nixon had experienced no difficulty in naming a new Chief Justice, and expected none in filling the seat vacated by the resignation of Justice Fortas. He had promised to name conservatives to the Court and confidently set about doing it. The new Chief Justice, Warren Burger, had been confirmed with virtually no opposition, in spite of his very conservative record on the Court of Appeals and his relatively undistinguished legal background. The Senate Judiciary Committee held a perfunctory hour-and-a-half hearing, largely devoted to favorable statements by Senators. The committee didn't even bother to issue a formal report before the Senate vote. After a three-hour discussion on the Senate floor, Burger was confirmed by a 74–3 vote. With this easy victory in selecting the nation's fifteenth Chief Justice, the President seemed in a very powerful position.

In filling his second vacancy, the President turned to an unknown federal appeals court judge from South Carolina, Clement F. Haynsworth, Jr. Although Judge Haynsworth was criticized by civil rights groups as a conservative member of a Southern court that had handled a great deal of civil rights litigation, no significant Senate fight was expected. Many liberals had strongly argued during the 1950s and 1960s against Southern opposition to nominees based on civil rights grounds, and ideological attacks were widely seen as illegitimate. The Senate's role in the confirmation process had atrophied, so much so that no one seriously thought a nomination of a President could be defeated. . . .

The Haynsworth nomination fight was a classic illustration of a seldom noticed variation of the filibuster approach to the legislative process. By greatly prolonging the highly publicized hearings, critics succeeded in focusing attention on the judge's record and creating a major new national issue. While the President clearly enjoys unequaled access to the news media at any given point in time, the sustained impact on public opinion of a long and well-orchestrated hearing can be vast.

Source: Gary Orfield, *Congressional Power: Congress and Social Change* (New York: Harcourt Brace Jovanovich, 1975), pp. 104–5.

--------------------------★ ★ ★ ★--------------------------

a Supreme Court nominee prefers to have the enthusiastic endorsement of home-state senators. U.S. Supreme Court appointments are as important as any a President makes. The screening and selection process for filling a vacancy on the high Court seldom involves the Senate, until the President submits the name of a nominee for the Court seat.

Because of the power of the Supreme Court and the life-term appointment to the office, many observers argue that the Senate, in its confirmation process, should consider not just the narrow legal competence and personal integrity of nominees, but also their basic political philosophy and their judicial philosophy. Presidents, understandably, tend to argue that unless some obvious flaw of character or ability is found—presumably a flaw not discovered by the administration during its own check of the prospective nominee—the Senate should honor the President's choice. But that argument carries more substantial weight when applied to presidential nominations to cabinet and subcabinet positions. The President, after all, is responsible for the actions of these officials and can fire them.

From 1789 through 1897, the Senate confirmed sixty-four of eighty-six (74.4 percent) of the Supreme Court nominations submitted by presidents. Over a fourth of the nominees were rejected. Some of these rejections were based primarily on the merits of individual nominees, but most rejections were political in nature. Lame-duck presidents fared poorly in winning confirmation for their nominees, as did presidents whose party or faction was the minority in the Senate.[32]

The twentieth-century record of Senate confirmations, through the late 1960s, led to speculation that the modern "imperial presidency" also got its way with Supreme Court nominations. The President and the Justice Department selected Supreme Court nominees, and the Senate, with one exception in 1930, confirmed them. Since 1968, however, three of eight nominations have been rejected. One of those three—the nomination of Associate Justice Fortas to be chief justice of the Court—was made by lame-duck President Johnson whose popularity had been greatly diminished by the Vietnam conflict. The other two recent rejections were of President Nixon's nominations of conservative southern judges to be associate justices. Federal Court of Appeals Judge Clement F. Haynsworth, Jr., was attacked as an opponent of civil rights and organized labor, but might well have been confirmed despite that, if it had not been for serious questions about his having decided cases in which he had a financial conflict of interest. Judge Haynsworth's nomination was rejected by the Senate, despite the President's intense arm-twisting campaign for him.[33]

President Nixon's response to the Senate's rejection of Judge Haynsworth for the high Court was to reassert that the judge was well qualified for the SupremeCourt and then to nominate an even less qualified southern federal judge, G. Harrold Carswell, "who had a record of opposition to civil rights and an unusual number of reversals of his decisions by higher courts. Whereas Haynsworth enjoyed the support of the bench and bar in the South, Carswell did not."[34] The Carswell nomination led former Senator Roman Hruska (R., Nebraska) to respond as follows (to his later regret) to complaints that Judge Carswell was of mediocre calibre:

> Even if he were mediocre, there are a lot of mediocre judges and people and lawyers. They are entitled to a little representation, aren't they, and a little chance? We can't have all Brandeises and Cardozos and Frankfurters and stuff like that there.[35]

Senator Hruska's colleagues disagreed, but only because the fairly small number of senators originally opposed to the nomination took full advantage of the chamber's rules to delay the nomination, while looking for additional support. The Haynsworth fight had been so exhausting that many senators simply had no stomach for another battle so soon. The Democratic majority leader scheduled the controversial Voting Rights Bill ahead of the Carswell nomination, a decision which postponed the Senate vote on the nomination by almost a month, but put pressure on conservative senators not to continue to delay a vote on the Voting Rights Bill lest they lose their Supreme Court nominee. The delay allowed various practicing attorneys, law-school professors, and judges time to examine Judge Carswell's record and protest the appointment to their respective senators. In the end, the Senate rejected the nomination, despite strong lobbying from the White House. An exhausted Senate then confirmed the President's third nominee for that Supreme Court vacancy, conservative federal Judge Harry Blackmun of Minnesota, by a 94–0 vote. The next year, the Senate confirmed a southern conservative, Lewis Powell, and an ideological conservative, William Rehnquist, for two other Court vacancies, although some observers wondered if the latter nomination would ever have been approved had there been no earlier Haynsworth and Carswell battle scars. Rhenquist's nomination was confirmed by a vote of 68 to 26.

Senators are reluctant to state openly that they are voting for or against a Supreme Court nominee on the basis of the nominee's ideology, although there appears to be no strong consensus against the propriety of considering ideological or philosophical predispositions, along with other factors. An analysis of the split votes on confirmation (or on cloture, in the cases of Fortas' nomination to be chief justice) of Fortas, Haynsworth, Carswell, and Rehnquist to the Supreme Court finds substantial evidence of ideological voting, but the nominee's ideological position alone has not been sufficient to cause senators to overcome what may be a presumption that the President's nominee ought to be confirmed. After all, the other Nixon appointees to the high Court had ideological positions similar to those of the three Nixon nominees who drew so much Senate opposition. If many Senators are to oppose a nominee for ideological reasons, then, they need an extra excuse. In the case of Fortas and Haynsworth, the stated reasons for opposition were reservations about the financial ethics of the nominees. "Yet only six senators voted against both. In general, those who opposed Fortas supported Haynsworth and vice versa."[36] That suggests that once an acceptable excuse exists for voting on the basis of the nominee's ideology, many senators will vote accordingly. The fact that strong cases were made that Carswell, Haynsworth, and Rehnquist were racists also provided "acceptable" reasons for opposition. Thus, "Although ideology alone is not sufficient to excite strong opposition to a [Supreme Court] nominee, it appears to play a significant role in determining which senators will and which will not oppose a nominee when other issues are raised. . . ."[37]

Despite the resurgence of Senate review of Supreme Court nominees and the apparent increased willingness of the Senate to reject unfit nominees (unfit ideologically or technically, depending on one's perspective), Glendon Schubert's observation of two decades ago still has the ring of truth:

> Most presidents have included their estimates of a [Supreme Court] candidate's acceptability to the Senate as a major factor to be weighed in making nominations. There are times. . . . when the President's own chances for reelection were dependent upon his success in avoiding an open rejection, by the Senate, of his leadership. . . . [M]ost presidents have felt that the wiser course lay in avoiding such risk-taking. The path of avoidance has lain in the selection of safe nominees, whose acceptability to the Senate was assured in advance. Senatorial confirmation has functioned, therefore, largely as a device to ensure that men whose views were considered to be deviant from those of the dominant political forces of the time would not receive serious consideration for appointment to the court.[38]

LEGISLATIVE-JUDICIAL RELATIONS IN OTHER NATIONS

The relationship between Congress and the federal judiciary is dominated by the separation of powers and the courts' power of judicial review. The relationship is also strongly affected by the political nature of the process used to select federal judges. Those relationships, collectively, are unique to the United States.

The British political system, for instance, differs fundamentally from the American. In Great Britain, the House of Lords (the upper chamber of Parliament, which includes many peers appointed for life by the government) constitutes the ultimate appellate court. Parliament is expected to legislate constitutionally and takes its responsibilities seriously. The absence of a single written constitution such as the American Constitution contributes to the viability of this approach.

The American practice of limiting the national legislature's authority in a written constitution and establishing an independent entity to enforce those constitutional limitations on the legislature is reflected in both France and West Germany. Neither, however, grants the judiciary in general the authority to rule legislation unconstitutional. Rather, each has created a special extralegislative body to serve as constitutional referee.

The French Fifth Republic has a Constitutional Council which decides whether laws are valid under the provisions of the Constitution. Members of the Constitutional Council ". . . are chosen equally by the President, the President of the Assembly, and the President of the Senate."[39] Although the Constitutional Council exercises its authority with great restraint, in 1981 it ruled that portions of the new socialist government's nationalization laws were unconstitutional.[40]

The West German Constitution provides for a Federal Constitutional Court, half of whose members are elected by the Bundestag (lower chamber) and half by the Bundesrat (upper chamber, responsible to the various länders or states). An examination of that Court's decisions through 1972 revealed an apparent consensus for giving substantial latitude to the legislature and the government. The attitude of the Federal Constitutional Court seems to be that "when it is possible for the Court to rule that a given statute (is) consonant with the constitution and could be interpreted in harmony with it, even in cases of substantial doubt, the presumption of constitutionality should prevail. . . . Only when the presumption could *not* be possibly sustained should a statute be designated as unconstitutional."[41]

In general, even where the constitution places limits on the powers of the national legislature, there seems a greater willingness elsewhere to give the legislature the benefit of the doubt concerning the constitutionality of its actions than is the case in the United States. Such an approach is as logical as the American tradition of judicial review. Justice Marshall's argument setting forth the logical basis for judicial review of the constitutionality of U.S. laws was, after all, based on the justices' oath to uphold the Constitution of the United States. Yet the members of Congress and the President take the same oath and presumably do not seek to violate that oath deliberately. America has opted to place greater reliance on the judiciary as protector of the Constitution than most other nations have. That gives us the benefit of a more considered approach by officials not directly subject to the popular mandate at the next election. Such an approach has worked well for the U.S., but placing a greater constitutional responsibility on the shoulders of elected legislators—the branch often thought most responsive to the people—also makes great sense.

A partial explanation for the American development of a more general power of judicial review than elsewhere may lie in the American judicial selection process, discussed earlier. United States federal judges are selected in a very political manner, with extensive legislative participation. That is much less the case in other Western nations. Most Western judicial systems recruit judges from a narrow spectrum of specially trained apprentices. Conscious efforts are made to minimize the encroachment of partisan politics on the judicial selection process.[42] While such an approach may do much to develop an impartial judiciary, it may well render that judiciary less suitable as a repository of constitutional authority than is the U.S. judiciary.

STATE LEGISLATURES AND THE JUDICIARY

The American federal judiciary exercises the power of judicial review over legislation adopted by state legislatures to insure conformity with federal statutes and the U.S. Constitution. It was in the exercise of this authority, for example, that the U.S. Supreme Court found unconstitutional the state laws that apportioned the various state legislatures unfairly and those state laws requiring racially segregated schools. The "Supremacy Clause" of the U.S. Constitution (Article VI) states:

> This Constitution, and the Laws of the United States which shall be made in Pursuance thereof; and all Treaties made, or which shall be made, under the Authority of the United States, shall be the supreme Law of the Land; and the Judges in every State shall be bound thereby, any Thing in the Constitution or Laws of any State to the Contrary notwithstanding.

The logic of the U.S. Supreme Court decision in *Marbury* v. *Madison* (discussed earlier) leads to the conclusion, from the Supremacy Clause, that neither state courts nor federal courts may enforce a state law that conflicts with the provisions of the U.S. Constitution or with the valid laws and treaties of the United States. This point of view was set forth very clearly by the U.S. Supreme Court in *McCulloch* v. *Maryland* in 1819.

Much of the history of the United States revolves around the proper scope of the national government's power and Supreme Court interpretations of the U.S. Constitution which, along with amendments to the Constitution, have expanded the scope of the national government's authority. It is sufficient here, though, to note that the national government's authority is extensive and that state legislation which conflicts with national statutory or constitutional law must yield.

One of the most insightful members of the U.S. Supreme Court felt that the power of the nation's highest Court to rule on the constitutionality of state laws was even more important than the Court's authority over federal legislation. Justice Holmes once observed:

> I do not think the United States would come to an end if we lost our power to declare an Act of Congress void. I do think the Union would be imperiled if we could not make that declaration as to the laws of the several states.[43]

The State Judiciary and Judicial Review

In addition to being in harmony with federal laws and the U.S. Constitution, a state law must not conflict with the state's constitution. Each of the fifty states has its own judiciary. Within each state's judicial structure is a court of "last resort," known by various names, but most frequently called the supreme court (which will be used generically here). Each state supreme court has successfully asserted its right authoritatively to interpret the state constitution, much as the U.S. Supreme Court has succeeded in staking out its claim as the authoritative interpreter of the U.S. Constitution. Thus, the state supreme courts are significant policymaking institutions. They decide the limits of the state regulatory body's authority over regulated utilities, resolve disagreements over the responsibilities of local governments, and interpret the executive and legislative provisions in the state constitution. One state supreme court may consistently interpret the state legislature's powers generously, while being very conservative in the interpretation of the governor's authority. A neighboring state's high court, with very similar constitutional language, may make the reverse choice and see the chief executive's authority as broad and sweeping, while viewing that of the legislature as narrow and limited. Such decisions by the state supreme court obviously have great impact on the state legislature's ability to dominate public policy in the state.

All fifty state supreme courts are similar, in that they have found authority for the state judiciary (and, ultimately, the state's highest court) to interpret the state constitution and to decide which acts of the state legislature are, or are not, in conflict with the state constitution. Indeed, when the U.S. Supreme Court decided *Marbury* v. *Madison* in 1803, over half of the states of the Union already clearly recognized a state principle of judicial review.[44] This authority involves very minor and technical issues more often than the grand, sweeping issues of the day, because most state constitutions are littered with detailed provisions that ought to be in the statutes, but which have been placed in the state constitution as added protection for some interest group.

Sometimes, a state statute violates both the state constitution and the U.S. Constitution. Sometimes, a statute may violate one, but not the other. The state judiciary is obligated to find a state law unconstitutional if it violates *either* the U.S. Constitution *or* the state constitution. A good example is the question of children's rights to equality of education. In many states, the laws governing public schools call for funding almost entirely from local property tax revenues, with no real state effort to equalize, from district to district, the amount of money spent on each child's education. As a result, children in poor areas (sometimes, just in the poor part of the same town) have out-of-date books, large numbers of children per teacher, no "frills," and dismal physical surroundings, all of which affect what a child is likely to learn. Children in wealthy areas, in contrast, may have new books, cheerful surroundings, small classes, and many educational "frills," including extensive art and music programs, fine physical education facilities, and modern science laboratories. Understandably, the children in the wealthy school districts on the average

----------------------★ ★ ★ ★----------------------

State Courts Interpret State Legislatures' Authority

On April 3, 1981, Justice Edward S. Conway of the New York State Supreme Court, a general trial court, issued a summary judgement in a declaratory judgement action that the executive branch can not spend federal funds without an appropriation by the Legislature. Specifically, Judge Conway ruled that "programs for which federal funds are received embrace matters traditionally of state concern. . . . Granting the executive sole control over the expenditures of these funds" violates separation of powers and normal legislative and executive roles.

The Appellate Division of the state Supreme Court on June 2 reversed the trial court by holding that the Legislature lacks the authority to appropriate federal funds. However, on July 6 the state Court of Appeals ruled that the legislature was entitled to exercise some control over federal funds. The Court stated that the state constitution "requires that there be a specific legislative appropriation each time the moneys in the State Treasury are spent." The decision was by a 4–3 margin.

Source: Joseph F. Zimmerman, "New York Legislature Given Role in Spending Federal Funds," *Comparative State Politics Newsletter* 2 (August 1981): 26.

----------------------★ ★ ★ ★----------------------

learn more and probably do better in life later on. There is no real argument about whether this state of affairs is fair or not. The argument is over whether poor children have a constitutional right to receive an education in the public schools comparable to what wealthy and middle-class children receive. Local school districts are local units of government, created under state law, and a method of financing them which results in great disparities in the quality of schools is also a result of state law.

Is substantial variation in per-pupil educational expenditures a violation of the equal protection clause of the Fourteenth Amendment to the U.S. Constitution or of the various bills of rights of the state constitutions? The first major case decided on the subject was *Serrano* v. *Priest*,[45] in which the California Supreme Court ruled that children have a state constitutional right to equality of education. But, in a similar case, *Rodriguez* v. *San Antonio Independent School Board*,[46] the U.S. Supreme Court found (in a 5-to-4 vote) no violation of the Equal Protection Clause of the Fourteenth Amendment to the U.S. Constitution. Nor has the Texas Supreme Court found a state constitutional right to equal educational opportunity, although numerous state supreme courts have found such a state constitutional right. Different state legislatures, then, find themselves mandated differently with respect to state aid to local school districts because of differences in state constitutions or in state supreme court interpretations, or both. The Texas legislature is not forbidden to enact legislation equalizing per-pupil educational expenditures, but neither is it required to do so. The California legislature is required to do so.

Like their federal court counterparts, state judges also interpret state statutes enacted by the legislature, applying them to specific cases, deciding whether a particular statute applies to a particular situation, and filling in the blanks. As the chief judge of New York state's highest court observed:

The court makes new law by every decision, and in many instances the legislature is asking us to fill in blanks. When antitrust laws are passed prohibiting "unreasonable restraints of trade", with no definition in the law regarding what is unreasonable, or when a Family Court is empowered to decide cases regarding families without a definition of a family, we must assume that it was intended that we fill in the blanks.[47]

State Legislative Authority over State Courts

In many ways, the authority of state legislatures over state courts is similar to that of the Congress with respect to federal courts, but there is a difference too. For the most part, the basic structure of the state judicial systems is set forth in each state's constitution.[48] Thus, whereas Congress has a free hand to structure the federal courts below the U.S. Supreme Court as the Congress sees fit, most state legislatures theoretically are less free to make fundamental restructuring of the state courts. But, since most states place the initiation of constitutional amendments in the hands of the state legislature, the legislature is in fact able to restructure the state judicial system, if it can persuade the voters of the wisdom of doing so. Such restructuring is not uncommon. Over the past decade, for example, several states that previously had no intermediate state appellate court (analogous to the U.S. Circuit Court of Appeals) have amended their constitutions to create such courts. The 1980 Idaho legislature created an appellate court by statute, a power granted that legislature by the Idaho Constitution.[49] Other states have made fundamental reorganizations of the structure of state courts to reduce jurisdictional overlap among the various types of courts, to make the judicial system appear less confusing, or to eliminate certain types of courts, such as the infamous justice of the peace courts in some states, or both. In each such "reform" of the judicial branch, the state legislature played a major role, even though for the most part, a blue-ribbon citizens commission, the state bar association, and the judiciary were also actively involved.

State Legislative Control over the Size and Salaries of the Judiciary Changing (usually expanding) the number of lower court state judgeships can normally be accomplished by statute rather than by constitutional amendment. Sometimes, the driving force behind the legislature's action is a less than lofty motive. The 1968 expansion of New York state's judiciary, for example, was a decision made for a mixture of reasons, as the following observation notes:

> Most local political organizations are, of course, very much interested in judgeships, viewing them as patronage assets. In 1968, the legislature created 125 additional judgeships. Before the bill was enacted, however, local political leaders in each county busily bargained among themselves about the division of the spoils. Of course, however, clearance by the legislative leaders was required not only concerning the bill itself but also concerning the division of 125 new positions.

> Consequently, the difficult question arose of how the parties could predetermine the division of the spoils in a situation where the law required that all judges be elected by the people. The solution was found in the application of the device of bipartisan or tripartisan endorsements.

> Queens County, for example, was allotted nine additional Supreme Court [trial court] judgeships, as well as other judicial positions. The local Democratic, Republican, and Liberal party officials thereupon agreed that the Democrats would get five; the Republicans, three; and the Liberals, one judgeship. Each party would then endorse all judicial candidates of the others. As a result, little option remained for the average voter. . . .[50]

The authority to establish judicial salaries is normally given to the legislature, as is control over the budgets of the various state court systems. Not infrequently, controversies arise between the legislature and the judges over how much money is needed for such expenses as those for psychiatrists, expert witnesses, jury fees, court maintenance, court administrative personnel, and the like. Although the state bar association often looks out for the interests of the judiciary in the legislature, the state judiciary in some states has hired a lobbyist to represent the interests of the courts before the legislature. Also fairly common is the creation, by statute, of a body like New York's Judicial Conference to perform certain tasks within the judicial system and make recommendations to the legislature for judicial system changes. The chairperson of the judiciary committee of each chamber of the New York legislature is "entitled by statute to attend meetings of the conference and to make recommendations to it."[51]

The judiciary committee in each chamber usually guides a legislature's decisions concerning the state courts. Normally, legislators consider that committee a desirable assignment, ranking just behind the appropriations and taxation committees. In addition to considering legislation affecting the structure of the state court system, the judiciary committees generally have jurisdiction over proposed changes to the state criminal code. In states in which the senate must confirm judicial appointments, the senate judiciary committee normally passes on the merits of each gubernatorial appointee, before the nomination goes to the senate floor. Attorneys in the legislature like to serve on their chamber's judiciary committee, because their expertise can be used there, because work on the committee is educational in a way directly useful to an attorney, and because judiciary committee membership enhances the member's status in professional legal circles. Lawyers are likely to argue that attorneys should be given preference for assignment to the judiciary committee (although they tend not to agree to apply the same argument to teacher legislators and the education committee), and some legislative chambers permit *only* attorneys to serve on the judiciary committee.[52]

State Legislative Power Over Judicial Personnel The most commonly found power that state legislators have over state judges across the United States is the power of impeachment by the lower chamber and trial by the upper chamber—with removal from the bench upon conviction by extraordinary vote of the upper chamber. Forty-five of the fifty states provide for the same impeachment process for judges that is provided for executive officers.[53] With minor variations, the state impeachment processes resemble the national government's impeachment process. In many states, an alternative mechanism not involving the legislature also exists for removing errant judges, and for disciplining judges short of removal. Such mechanisms are available in many of the forty-five impeachment states as well as in the five states that use judicial standards commissions (the names vary) to discipline judges in lieu of providing for impeachment by the legislature. Among the forty-five impeachment states, sixteen also provide for involvement of the legislature in the removal of judges by means other than impeachment. Several of the New England states, for example, have constitutional provisions like that of Maine, which provides that the governor may remove a judge "on the address of both branches of the legislature."[54] Utah permits removal of state judges by a two-thirds vote of the members of each legislative chamber, if the legislature prefers that method to impeachment. Washington has a similar clause, but requires a three-fourths vote in each chamber.[55]

State legislative involvement in the *selection* of judges varies greatly. At one extreme are the states of Connecticut, Rhode Island, South Carolina, and Virginia, where state judges are elected by the states legislature. (Rhode Island's General Assembly elects only supreme court justices). In Vermont, the more important state judges are appointed by the governor, but are retained in office by periodic vote of the General Assembly. Another half-dozen states require senate confirmation of the governor's appointees to the bench. The bulk of the states, however, give the legislature only such influence over the selection of judicial personnel as they can wield through informal means, such as through their local political leadership in the twenty-six states that elect their judges. Many attorneys seek election to the legislature partly because of the possibility of securing a judgeship later on, and many *are* subsequently elected to a judicial office or appointed to a judicial vacancy. The greatest movement from legislature to the bench occurs in those states where the state legislature elects the judges.[56]

SUMMARY

The relationship between the legislature and the judiciary in the United States is peculiar to our separation-of-powers government. A few states permit the legislature to select their judges. A few others follow the national model and require senate confirmation of executive-department nominees to judgeships. The U.S. Senate, through the device of senatorial courtesy during the confirmation process, has gained substantial control over appointments to U.S. district judgeships.

American legislators may not serve as judges. Yet, both institutions—courts and legislatures—"make law." The decisions of judges cumulatively add up to the case law. Statutes enacted by the legislature may replace case law, where applicable, but statutes tend to need clarifying by the judges who must implement them. Further, the American judiciary has been successful in asserting its authority to refuse to enforce statutes that conflict with the applicable constitutional law.

The judiciary has an advantage in the contest for supremacy by its power of judicial review of legislation, but it is hampered by its relatively passive role; courts and judges must await cases on a particular legal point before being in a position to affect the law. (Sometimes such cases are remarkably fast in coming.) The legislature, in contrast, is the organ of government intended to be *active,* to look for problems in society and propose statutory remedy. Further, the legislature has numerous strengths in the contest with the judicial branch for determination of public policy. Case law may be overridden by statute. Specific judicial decisions interpreting a statute can be reversed by revising (and clarifying) the statute after the judiciary has arrived at an interpretation out of harmony with legislative wishes. A law that has been declared unconstitutional can often be "repaired" to achieve the same general social objective without offending judicial sensibilities concerning constitutionality. Alternatively, the legislature can pursue its wishes by initiating the process of amending the constitution. Congress can restrict the jurisdiction of the federal courts, but rarely does so.

Almost unheard of today, but still available to Congress, is a "declaration of war" on the judiciary by expanding the highest Court so as to add members whose political philosophies will bring the Court into compliance with legislative thinking. To be effective, of course, such action requires that the executive act as the legislature's accomplice. Similarly, Congress and most state legislatures can remove offending judges through the impeachment process, allowing a cooperating executive to replace those impeached judges with jurists who agree with the legislature and the executive. Lesser sanctions, especially in an inflation-ridden economy, include legislative refusal to provide adequate funding for court activities or judicial pay raises. Such actions, however, are generally seen as petty and probably are ineffective, if not counterproductive.

On the whole, both legislators and jurists are aware of the limitations of their power, and they attempt to avoid open confrontations. At the national level, at least, there is evidence that both sets of actors are sensitive to public opinion and to the limits that exist on their ability to stretch their powers. Thus, there is a cycle of increasing and abating tension as the legislature and the courts seek to resolve the most salient political questions of each generation.

Notes

1. Jack W. Peltason, *Corwin & Peltason's Understanding the Constitution,* 8th ed. (New York: Holt, Rinehart and Winston, 1979), pp. 74, 103.

2. Raoul Berger, *Impeachment: The Constitutional Problem* (Cambridge, Mass.: Harvard University Press, 1974).

3. That constitutional clause is still important. To minimize constituent complaints about pay raises, Congress created a complex mechanism to raise the pay of top federal officials, including members of Congress, without a vote of Congress but subject to Congressional veto. Congress eventually vetoed the 1980 pay raise, but not until after it had gone into effect. Federal judges thus were able to keep their pay raise even though other federal officials lost theirs. Elder Witt, "Supreme Court," *Congressional Quarterly Weekly Report,* February 7, 1981, p. 282.

4. Peltason, *Corwin & Peltason's Understanding the Constitution,* p. 103.

5. Ibid. p. 109. The case was *Ex parte McCardle,* 74 U.S. 506 (1869).

6. Robert G. Dixon, Jr., *Democratic Representation: Reapportionment in Law and Politics* (New York: Oxford University Press, 1968), especially Chapters 15 and 16.

7. Glendon A. Schubert, *Judicial Policy-Making* (Chicago: Scott-Foresman, 1965), pp. 147–48.

8. Jack W. Peltason, *Federal Courts in the Political Process* (New York: Random House, 1955).

9. *Powell* v. *McCormack,* 395 U.S. 486 (1969). In 1967 Representative Powell had been excluded from the House at the beginning of the Congress based on charges of financial misconduct. He was not permitted to take the oath of office and be "seated." Although the vote to exclude requires only a majority, over two thirds of the members voted for exclusion. To the suprise of many observers, the Supreme Court overturned precedents and held that the House had no authority to go beyond the question of whether Mr. Powell met the formal requirements for membership, which he did. The right of each chamber to vote expulsion of a member who has been seated (by two-thirds vote) was not raised. Peltason, *Corwin & Peltason's Understanding the Constitution,* p. 50.

10. State courts had earlier claimed, successfully, the right to declare which state statutes were and were not constitutional. Alfred H. Kelly and Winfred Harbison, *The American Constitution* (New York: W.W. Norton, 1970), p. 229 and Chapter 9, generally.

11. From the Supreme Court's decision in *Marbury* v. *Madison,* 1 Cranch 137 (1803); reprinted in Peter Woll, ed., *American Government: Readings and Cases,* 7th ed. (Boston: Little, Brown, 1981), pp. 533–37. Justice Marshall's opinion has been the subject of much criticism over the succeeding generations, but he achieved his goal—the firm establishment of the U.S. Supreme Court's claim to the authority to interpret the Constitution and to determine what acts of the executive and the legislature were, or were not, constitutional. For a discussion of the legal arguments, see Chapter 1 of Alexander M. Bickel, *The Least Dangerous Branch: The Supreme Court at the Bar of Politics* (Indianapolis: Bobbs-Merrill, 1962); or Woll, *American Government,* Chapter 9.

12. Jack C. Plano and Milton Greenberg, *The American Political Dictionary,* 5th ed. (New York: Holt, Rinehart, and Winston, 1979), p. 259.

13. Jesse H. Choper, *Judicial Review and the National Political Process* (Chicago: University of Chicago Press, 1979), p. 128.

14. An insightful discussion of the matter is available in Chaper, *Judicial Review and the National Political Process,* Chapter 1, and in John R. Schmidhauser and Larry L. Berg, *The Supreme Court and Congress* (New York: Free Press, 1972).

15. Roger Handberg and Harold F. Hill, Jr., "Court Curbing, Court Reversals, and Judicial Review," *Law and Society Review* 14 (Winter 1980): 309–21. See also the entire issue of *Judicature* 65, no. 4 (October 1981).

16. Analyses of the dispute are abundant. See, for example, Robert Scigliano, *The Supreme Court and the Presidency* (New York: Free Press, 1971).

17. Glendon A. Schubert, *Constitutional Politics* (New York: Holt, Rinehart, and Winston, 1960), p. 267.

18. Ibid.

19. Leroy N. Rieselbach, *Congressional Politics* (New York: McGraw-Hill, 1973), pp. 224–29.

20. Choper, *Judicial Review and the National Political Process,* p. 49. The others are the Eleventh and the Fourteenth Amendments.

21. Daniel M. Berman, *In Congress Assembled* (New York: Macmillan, 1964), p. 385.

22. Rieselbach, *Congressional Politics,* p. 228.

23. Schubert, *Constitutional Politics,* pp. 257–58.

24. A good overall view of the U.S. judicial selection process is Harold W. Chase, *Federal Judges: The Appointing Process* (Minneapolis: University of Minnesota Press, 1972).

25. *Congressional Quarterly Weekly Report,* February 3, 1979, p. 192.

26. It is not at all clear that the states which shifted to merit-selection panels received either better qualified federal judges or more women and minority judges. See Charles W. Hucker, "Report Card on Judicial Merit Selection," *Congressional Quarterly Weekly Report,* February 3, 1979, pp. 189–90.

27. Ibid., pp. 189–94.

28. Ibid., p. 192; Nadine Cohodas, "How Reagan Will Pick Judges is Unclear, But Philosophy Will Play an Important Role," *Congressional Quarterly Weekly Report,* February 14, 1981, pp. 299–303.

29. Hucker, "Report Card on Judicial Merit Selection," p. 192.

30. Cohodas, "How Reagan Will Pick Judges is Unclear," p. 303.

31. *Congressional Quarterly Weekly Report,* December 26, 1981, p. 2559.

32. Schubert, *Judicial Policy-Making,* p. 44. See also Joseph P. Harris, *The Advice and Consent of the Senate: A Study of the Confirmation of Appointments by the United States Senate* (Berkeley: University of California Press, 1953).

33. This discussion draws in part on Gary Orfield, *Congressional Power: Congress and Social Change* (New York: Harcourt Brace Jovanovich, 1975), Chapter 6.

34. Robert J. Sickels, *The Presidency* (Englewood Cliffs, N.J.: Prentice-Hall, 1980), p. 250.

35. *Washington Post,* March 17, 1970; quoted in Orfield, *Congressional Power,* p. 113.

36. Wayne Sulfridge, "Ideology as a Factor in Senate Consideration of Supreme Court Nominations," *Journal of Politics* 42 (May 1980): 564.

37. Ibid., p. 567.

38. Schubert, *Judicial Policy-Making,* p. 44.

39. John E. Schwarz and L. Earl Shaw, *The United States Congress in Comparative Perspective* (Hinsdale, Ill.: Dryden Press, 1976), p. 61.

40. Richard Eder, "Mitterand's Modest Revolution," *New York Times Magazine,* February 7, 1982, p. 66.

41. Fritz Nova, "Political Innovation of the West German Constitutional Court: The State of Discussion on Judicial Review," *American Political Science Review* 70 (March 1976): 123.

42. Mogens N. Pedersen, "Lawyers in Politics: The Danish Folketing and U.S. Legislatures," in *Comparative Legislative Behavior,* ed. Samuel C. Patterson and John C. Wahlke (New York: John Wiley, 1972), Chapter 2.

43. Oliver Wendell Holmes, *Collected Legal Papers* (New York: Harcourt, Brace, and World, 1920), pp. 295–96; quoted in Peltason, *Corwin and Peltason's Understanding the Constitution,* p. 29.

479

44. Kelly and Harbison, *The American Constitution,* p. 229.

45. 938254, L.A., California Supreme Court, 29820 (1971).

46. 411 U.S. 1 (1973).

47. Alan G. Hevesi, *Legislative Politics in New York State* (New York: Praeger, 1975), p. 131.

48. For a discussion of state judicial systems, generally, see Kenneth N. Vines and Herbert Jacob, "State Courts and Public Policy," in Herbert Jacob and Kenneth N. Vines, *Politics in the American States,* 3rd ed. (Boston: Little, Brown, 1976); and Charles Press and Kenneth VerBerg, *State and Community Governments in the Federal System* (New York: John Wiley, 1979), Chapter 9.

49. Neil D. McFeeley, "Idaho Appellate Court Approved by Legislature," *Comparative State Politics Newsletter* 2 (October 1981): 20–21.

50. Hevesi, *Legislative Politics in New York State* p. 136.

51. Ibid., pp. 133–34.

52. Alan Rosenthal, *Legislative Life: People, Process and Performance in the States* (New York: Harper and Row, 1981), p. 185. This excellent overview of state legislatures in the United States became available only in the final stages of this work.

53. *The Book of the States, 1980–81* (Lexington, Ky.: Council of State Governments, 1980), pp. 158–63.

54. Ibid., p. 160.

55. Ibid.

56. Bradley Cannon, "The Impact of Formal Selection Processes on Characteristics of Judges—Reconsidered", *Law and Society Review* 13 (May 1972): 570–93.

Epilogue

Overview and Prospects

In August of 1982, a House-Senate conference committee of the U.S. Congress met and recommended one of the largest tax increases in U.S. history (with some tax reform, too, including a withholding tax on interest and dividends). Only a year earlier—pushed hard by President Ronald Reagan—the Congress had enacted a federal tax *reduction* of historic proportions. The 1982 tax increase, reported by the conference committee, zipped through both the U.S. House and Senate on the same day, despite its controversial and "politically difficult" nature.

President Reagan lobbied members of Congress long and hard—and effectively—for the tax-increase bill, even longer and harder than he had lobbied them the preceding year for tax reduction. The 1982 tax-increase bill was enacted as a result of the votes (in both houses) of a Republican-Democratic coalition—in this instance involving many of the liberals and moderates of both parties more than the strongest conservatives. In the House, the 1982 tax-increase bill had the vigorous backing of liberal Democratic Speaker Thomas P. "Tip" O'Neill (D., Massachusetts) and was adopted with more Democratic than Republican votes (123 to 103). In the Senate, liberal Democratic leaders, such as Alan Cranston (D., California) and Edward M. Kennedy (D., Massachusetts), worked for the bill's passage, and, with the defection from the President's position by eleven Republican senators, the bill could not have been passed without the votes of nine Democratic senators.[1]

Action on the 1982 tax-increase bill in the U.S. Congress illustrated a couple of important points about America's legislatures, points that we have made earlier in this book. First, the influence of party affiliation on legislator action is not as great as it once was (though still important, of course). Second, despite the decentralization of legislative power (especially in the U.S. Congress, through an increase in subcommittee power) and the decrease in the power of legislative party leaders (particularly in the state legislatures), America's legislative bodies can still move rapidly, especially when backed by fairly unified public opinion and pushed by a strong executive.

CONGRESS

There have been important changes in Congress in recent years.[2] The Congress has become more open—with more *recorded* votes in the House and more open committee sessions in both bodies. The workload of members has expanded; the number of committee meetings greatly increased, and the volume of mail tripled between 1972 and 1979. The importance of incumbency has grown, and the number of "safe" seats has increased. Still, despite adequate salaries and other benefits, there has been a large membership turnover because of a decline in "careerism" and a greater number of retirements—possibly tied to the heavier member workload and the lowered public esteem for Congress as an institution, among other factors.[3]

The power of subcommittees has increased, as the authority of committee chairs has decreased. In the House, this decentralization of power has been offset somewhat by the increased powers of the Democratic caucus and of the Democratic Speaker. There has been marked growth in the number of member, committee, subcommittee, and institutional staff—a growth in the "staff bureaucracy."

As an institution, Congress has become more assertive, more independent, in its relations with the President and the executive department. Still, when a President is backed by public opinion on an issue—as President Reagan was in the 1982 tax fight—Congress can be enormously influenced by a strong and persuasive chief executive. Within Congress, members have become more individualistic, more independent of their leaders and party ties and organizations. Party is still very important, but there is less partisan voting.

Congress has changed, evolved, and it will continue to evolve. But there has never been a "revolutionary" change in Congress, and none can be expected in the future. One authority, Samuel C. Patterson, has written that if America's great nineteenth-century Congressional politician, Henry Clay, were to visit that body today, it would still seem very familiar to him, adding, "Institutions simply do not change very much, which is why they are called institutions."[4] And that conclusion about recent changes in Congress points us toward what we might expect concerning the *future* of Congress as an institution. As Patterson put it, "So it surely will be true that the Congress of the 1980s will not be very different from the Congress of the 1970s—but, equally, it will not be the same."[5]

Congress has become more "democratic"—that is, individual members are now less subject on individual votes to the control of Congressional party organizations, committee chairs, or institutional leaders. It is not likely that this trend will be reversed soon. Members will not easily give up this independence. The weakening of party organizations back home (because of the party primary, the increased importance of television, and the greatly reduced ability of a party in government to dole out welfare, jobs, and contracts for the party faithful) helps to produce individualistic campaigns and individualistic members of Congress.

The decentralization of authority involved in the enhanced importance and power of subcommittees and their chairs serves the political, career, and ideology goals of individual members of Congress. So this trend is not likely to be reversed soon, either. But, as was seen in the case of the 1982 tax-increase bill, Congress can still move rapidly when public opinion and a strong and persuasive President demand it. Rapid action can also be facilitated—and probably will be in the future—by the referral of legislative measures, especially in the House, to ad hoc committees (as with energy issues during the Carter administration) or to joint or other multi-committee groupings. In both houses, the budget process will surely continue to be used to facilitate the making of policy by cutting across substantive, taxing, and spending committee jurisdictions.

STATE LEGISLATURES

As compared with the 1950s, the state legislatures of the 1960s and 1970s were, of course, more "formally" representative, as a result of reapportionment. They were also more "descriptively" representative, in that they contained more women and minority members, although these bodies continue to be dominated by white males.

State legislatures have become more "professional"—that is, they are generally better staffed and better paid and have interim committees operating between sessions. Yet, there is lower public interest in state legislative campaigns and state legislative activities than in the campaigns and activities of Congress. One consequence is high interest-group influence in state legislatures. Although decorum has improved, state legislatures still do not usually enjoy very good public opinion. Few people decide to make state legislative service a career, and there is high turnover in the membership of state legislatures.

Party control and the influence of party legislative leaders is weakening in most state legislatures.[6] In a number of state legislatures, there have been speaker elections by cross-party coalitions. These trends will probably continue in the future.

CONCLUSION

Legislative bodies make their decisions in public. The process is often time-consuming, the debate sometimes rancorous and confusing. The legislative body often bogs down in trivial—and even frivolous—matters and sometimes makes a spectacle of itself. (Bismarck is reputed to have said that those who would retain their respect for law and sausages should never see either being made.) But, as someone has observed, these are also criticisms that can be leveled against democracy itself. Legislatures can sometimes initiate new approaches to new problems. They can be mobilized for rapid action—especially by a strong and persuasive chief executive—when public opinion demands it. They function particularly impressively to monitor, veto, and oversee the activities of the executive department—both as institutions and in the "casework" efforts of individual members. They may sometimes look and act like "democracy in the raw," but they are and will remain an essential element of any democratic form of government.

Notes

1. David Broder, *Washington Post;* reprinted in *Albuquerque Journal,* August 26, 1982, p. 4.

2. See "Overview of Principal Legislative Developments of the 1970s," *Final Report of the Select Committee on Committees, U.S. House of Representatives, 1980,* House Report No. 96–866 (Washington, D.C.: U.S. Government Printing Office, 1980).

3. Roger H. Davidson, "The Two Congresses and How They Are Changing," in *Congress and Public Policy,* ed. David C. Kozak and John D. McCartney (Homewood, Ill.: Dorsey Press, 1982), pp. 464–75.

4. Samuel C. Patterson, "Congress the Peculiar Institution," in Kozak and McCartney, *Congress and Public Policy,* p. 460.

5. Ibid., p. 461.

6. David C. Saffell, *State and Local Government: Politics and Public Policies,* 2nd ed. (Reading, Mass.: Addison-Wesley, 1982), pp. 124, 125.

Acknowledgments

Literary Selections

Chapter 6
Congressional Quarterly Weekly Report: from "Sting Ploy May 'Chill' Hill-Public Dealings" by Irwin Arieff and David Tarr from *Congressional Quarterly Weekly Report,* February 9, 1980. Copyright © 1980 by Congressional Quarterly, Inc. Reprinted by permission.

Chapter 7
Congressional Quarterly, Inc.: from "The Broadcast Lobby: Resistant to Change" from *The Washington Lobby,* 3rd edition. Copyright © 1979 by Congressional Quarterly, Inc. Reprinted by permission. From "Congressional Quarterly Special Report: Washington Fund-Raisers" by Bill Keller and Irwin B. Arieff from *Congressional Quarterly Weekly Report,* May 17, 1980. Copyright © 1980 by Congressional Quarterly, Inc. Reprinted by permission.

Fred R. Harris: from Fred R. Harris, *America's Democracy: The Ideal and the Reality.* Scott, Foresman and Company, 1980, pp. 220–221.

Northeastern Political Science Association: from "Political Choice and Expenditure Change in New Hampshire and Vermont" by Richard Winters from *Polity,* Summer 1980. Reprinted by permission of the Northeastern Political Science Association.

Praeger Publishers: from Alan G. Hevesi, *Legislative Politics in New York State.* New York: Praeger Publishers, 1975, pp. 35–36, 189.

The Texas Observer: from interview by Ronnie Dugger with Texas State Senator Lloyd Doggett, from the *Texas Observer,* March 13, 1981. Copyright © 1981 by the *Texas Observer.* Reprinted by permission.

Chapter 8
American Political Science Association: from "Democratic Party Leadership in the Senate" by Ralph K. Huitt from *American Political Science Review* 55, June 1961. Reprinted by permission of the American Political Science Association.

H. Douglas Price: from "The Congressional Career Then and Now" by H. Douglas Price from *Congressional Behavior* edited by Nelson W. Polsby, 1971. Reprinted by permission of H. Douglas Price.

University of Oklahoma Press: from Samuel A. Kirkpatrick, *The Legislative Process in Oklahoma.* Norman, Oklahoma: University of Oklahoma Press, 1978, p. 17.

Chapter 9
Comparative State Politics Newsletter: from "Legislative Party Upheaval in Washington" by Hugh A. Bone from *Comparative State Politics Newsletter,* Vol. 2, #3, May 1981. Reprinted by permission.

Chapter 11
The Free Press: from Alan Rosenthal, *Legislative Performance in the States.* New York: The Free Press, 1974, pp. 21–22, 24, 42.

Little, Brown and Company: from Richard F. Fenno, Jr., *Congressmen in Committees.* Copyright © 1973 by Little, Brown and Company (Inc.). Reprinted by permission.

Prentice-Hall Inc.: from C. Herman Pritchett, *The Federal System in Constitutional Law.* Englewood Cliffs, N.J.: Prentice-Hall, Inc., 1978, pp. 254–255.

Chapter 12
Congressional Quarterly, Inc.: from "Targeting the Mail: Just Press a Button" from *Inside Congress,* 2nd edition. Copyright © 1979 by Congressional Quarterly, Inc. Reprinted by permission.

The Journal of Politics: from "Professionals and 'Entrepreneurs': Staff Orientations and Policy Making on Three Senate Committees" by David E. Price from *The Journal of Politics,* May 1971. Reprinted by permission.

The Public Interest: from "Congressional Committee Staffs: Who's in Charge Here?" by Michael J. Malbin from *The Public Interest,* Spring 1977. Copyright © 1977 by *The Public Interest.* Reprinted by permission.

Schenkman Publishing Company: from David E. Price, *Who Makes the Laws? Creativity and Power in Senate Committees.* Cambridge, Massachusetts: Schenkman Publishing Company, Inc., 1972, pp. 196, 329–331.

Yale University Press: from Morris P. Fiorina, *Congress: Keystone of the Washington Establishment.* New Haven, Connecticut: Yale University Press, 1977, p. 35.

Chapter 13

Allyn & Bacon: from David J. Vogler, *The Politics of Congress.* Boston: Allyn & Bacon, 1977, p. 20.

American Assembly: from "Organization and Procedure" by John C. Wahlke from *State Legislatures in American Politics* edited by Alexander Heard, 1966. Reprinted by permission of the American Assembly.

American Political Science Association: from "The Folkways of the United States Senate" by Donald R. Matthews from *American Political Science Review* 53, December 1959. Reprinted by permission of the American Political Science Association.

Congressional Quarterly, Inc.: from "House Funding Bill Riders Become Potent Policy Force" by Alan Murray from *Congressional Quarterly Weekly Report,* Nov. 1, 1980. Copyright © 1980 by Congressional Quarterly, Inc. Reprinted by permission.

Texas Monthly: from "The Ten Best and Ten Worst Legislators." Reprinted with permission from the July 1981 issue of *Texas Monthly.* Copyright © 1981 by *Texas Monthly.*

The Washington Monthly Co.: from "OK, Everybody, Vote Yes: A Day in the Life of a State Legislator" by Larry Sonis. Reprinted with permission from the June 1979 issue of *The Washington Monthly.* Copyright © 1979 by The Washington Monthly Co., 2712 Ontario Rd., N.W., Washington, D.C. 20009.

Chapter 14

Congressional Quarterly, Inc.: from "White House Lobbying Staff Chosen" from *Congressional Quarterly Weekly Report,* Jan. 24, 1981. Copyright © 1981 by Congressional Quarterly, Inc. Reprinted by permission. From "Senate Supports Reagan on AWACS Sale" by Richard Whittle from *Congressional Quarterly Weekly Report,* Oct. 31, 1981. Copyright © 1981 by Congressional Quarterly, Inc. Reprinted by permission.

Newsweek, Inc.: from "A Truly Open Mind" by Tom Mathews with Fred Coleman and Gerald C. Lubenow from *Newsweek,* February 16, 1981. Copyright © 1981, by Newsweek, Inc. All Rights Reserved. Reprinted by permission.

Texas Monthly: from "Reporter" section by Susan Duffy. Reprinted with permission from the July 1981 issue of *Texas Monthly.* Copyright © 1981 by *Texas Monthly.*

Chapter 15

The Council of State Governments: from "The State Legislatures" by William Pound and Carl Tubbesing from *The Book of the States:* 1978–79, pp. 1–3. Copyright © 1978 by The Council of State Governments, Lexington, Kentucky. Reprinted by permission.

The Dorsey Press: text and figure from *Congress, the Bureaucracy, and Public Policy,* Revised Edition by Randall B. Ripley and Grace A. Franklin. Copyright © 1980 by The Dorsey Press. Reprinted by permission.

Marcus E. Ethridge, III: from "Legislative Participation in Policy Implementation: An Analysis of the Michigan Experience" by Marcus E. Etheridge, III, presented at the 1981 Midwest Political Science Association meeting. Copyright © 1981 by Marcus E. Etheridge, III. Reprinted by permission.

Keith E. Hamm and Roby D. Robertson: from "Factors Influencing the Adoption of New Methods of Legislative Oversight in the U.S. States" by Keith E. Hamm and Roby D. Robertson from *Legislative Studies Quarterly* VI, February 1981. Reprinted by permission of the authors. From "New Methods of State Legislative Oversight: A Comparative Analysis of Adoption and Implementation" by Keith E. Hamm and Roby D. Robertson. Copyright © 1979 by Keith E. Hamm and Roby D. Robertson. Reprinted by permission.

The Washington Monthly Co.: from "Sunset Laws: Why They Aren't Working" by Barry Mitzman. Reprinted with permission from the June 1979 issue of *The Washington Monthly.* Copyright ©

1979 by The Washington Monthly Co., 2712 Ontario St., N.W., Washington, D.C. 20009. From "The Bureaucracy: The Cleverest Lobby of Them All" by Leonard Reed. Reprinted with permission from the April 1978 issue of *The Washington Monthly.* Copyright © 1978 by The Washington Monthly Co., 2712 Ontario Road, N.W., Washington, D.C. 20009.

Chapter 16

CBS College Publishing: from *The American Political Dictionary,* 6th Edition, by Jack C. Plano and Milton Greenberg. Copyright © 1982 by CBS College Publishing. Reprinted by permission of CBS College Publishing, a division of CBS, Inc.

Congressional Quarterly, Inc.: from "Members Move to Rein in Supreme Court" by Nadine Cohodas from *Congressional Quarterly Weekly Report,* May 30, 1981. Copyright © 1981 by Congressional Quarterly, Inc. Reprinted by permission.

Holt, Rinehart & Winston: from Glendon A. Schubert, *Constitutional Politics.* New York: Holt, Rinehart & Winston, 1960, pp. 257–258, 305.

Tables and Figures

Chapter 4

Table 4.1 from J. C. Wahlke, E. Eulau, W. Buchanan and L. C. Ferguson, *The Legislative System* (New York: John Wiley, 1962), p. 489; "Legislative Supplement," (Santa Fe: NM Rural Electrification Cooperative Association, 1981); and S. C. Patterson, R. D. Hedlund and G. R. Boynton, *Representatives and Represented* (New York: John Wiley, 1975), p. 28.

Table 4.2 from *State and Community Governments in the Federal System* (John Wiley, 1979) Reprinted from "Tenure and Turnover of Legislative Personnel" by Charles S. Hyneman in volume no. 195 of *The Annals* of The American Academy of Political and Social Science. Copyright © 1938 by the American Academy of Political and Social Science.

Table 4.4 from *The Chicano Political Experience: Three Perspectives* by F. Chris Garcia and Rudolph O. de la Garza. Copyright © 1977 by F. Chris Garcia; and "Chicano Politics" by Fernando V. Padilla and Antonio Sisneros. Copyright © 1980 by Fernando V. Padilla and Antonio Sisneros. Data from both sources reprinted by permission.

Figures 4.1 and 4.2 from S. S. Schramm, "Women and Representation: Self-Government and Role Change," *Western Political Quarterly* 34 (March, 1981), p. 52.

Chapter 5

Table 5.2 from J. Cooper and W. West, "The Congressional Career in the 1970's," in L. C. Dodd and B. I. Oppenheimer, editors, *Congress Reconsidered,* 2nd ed. (Washington D.C.: Congressional Quarterly Press, 1981), p. 99; original data are from *Congressional Quarterly Weekly Reports,* March 25, 1978, p. 755 and July 7, 1979, p. 1351. Copyright Congressional Quarterly Inc.

Table 5.3 from "Nader Study Links Spending and Success in Senate Campaigns" (Washington, D.C.: A Report Released by Congress Watch, November 16, 1978). The last 8 races in the Congress Watch list of bigger spending winners have been omitted here. Reprinted by permission.

Tables 5.4 and 5.5 from M. E. Jewell, "Survey on State Campaign Financing," *Comparative State Politics Newsletter,* Vol. 1, No. 2 (University of Kentucky, January, 1980), pp. 16–17.

Figure 5.1 from Rare Book Division, New York Public Library as it appeared in *The Encyclopedia of American Government* New & Updated, p. 117, Copyright © 1981 by DPG Reference Publishing, Inc., Guilford, Connecticut.

Figure 5.2 from *Congressional Quarterly Weekly Report,* January 10, 1982, p. 70. Copyright 1981 Congressional Quarterly Inc.

Chapter 6

Table 6.1 from G. R. Boynton, R. D. Hedlund, and S. C. Patterson, *Representatives and Represented: Bases of Public Support for the American Legislatures* (John Wiley & Sons, 1975), p. 117.

Figure 6.1 from E. C. Ladd, Jr., "What the Voters Really Want," *Fortune Magazine,* December 18, 1978, p. 48. *Fortune* Magazine Art Department/Chartmakers, Inc.

Chapter 7

Table 7.1 data for 1972 from R. A. Diamond, ed., *Dollar Politics: The Issue of Campaign Spending,* Vol. 2 (Washington, D.C.: Congressional Quarterly Press, 1973). Data for 1974 from Common Cause, *1974 Congressional Campaign Finances* (Washington, D.C.: *Common Cause,* 1976).

Table 7.2 from II. Zeigler and M. Baer, *Lobbying: Interaction and Influence in American State Legislatures* (Belmont, California: Wadsworth Publishing Company, 1969). Reprinted by permission of Brooks/Cole Publishing Company, Monterey, California.

Chapter 8

Table 8.1 from B. Hinckley, *The Seniority System in Congress* (Bloomington: Indiana University Press, 1971), p. 96.

Tables 8.2 and 8.3 from M. E. Jewell, "Survey on Selection of State Legislative Leaders," *Comparative State Newsletter* 1 (May, 1980), pp. 8–11.

Figure 8.1 © Robert L. Peabody, *Leadership in Congress: Stability, Succession, and Change,* 1976 Johns Hopkins University.

Figure 8.2 from B. Hinckley, drawing on articles by Nelson Polsby in the March 1968 *American Political Science Review,* pp. 147, 149, and in the September 1967 *American Political Science Review,* pp. 792, 793.

Chapter 9

Table 9.1 from *Congressional Quarterly Almanacs,* data compiled from 1963–1978. Copyright Congressional Quarterly Inc.

Table 9.2 from *Congressional Quarterly Weekly Report,* January 10, 1981, p. 85. Copyright 1981 Congressional Quarterly Inc.

Figure 9.1 from *Congressional Quarterly Weekly Report,* February 5, 1977, p. 222. Copyright 1977 Congressional Quarterly Inc.

Figure 9.2 from K. Janda et al., "Legislative Politics in Indiana," in J. B. Kessler's *Empirical Studies of Indiana Politics* (Bloomington: Indiana University Press, 1970), p. 32.

Chapter 10

Table 10.1 from *Congressional Quarterly Special Report,* March 28, 1981. Copyright 1981 Congressional Quarterly Inc.

Table 10.2 from G. Goodwin, Jr., *The Little Legislatures: Committees of Congress* (Amherst: University of Massachusetts Press, 1970), pp. 102–103.

Figure 10.1 from Malcolm E. Jewell and Chu Chi-hung, "Membership Movement and Committee Attractiveness in the U.S. House of Representatives, 1963–1971," published in the *American Journal of Political Science,* Vol. 18, No. 2, p. 437, May 1974, The University of Texas Press.

Chapter 12

Figure 12.1 from *Congressional Quarterly Weekly Report,* November 24, 1979, p. 2636. Copyright 1979 Congressional Quarterly Inc.

Chapter 13

Table 13.1 from *Congressmen's Voting Decisions,* Second Edition by John W. Kingdon. Copyright © 1981 by Harper & Row Publishers, Inc. Reprinted by permission of the publisher.

Figure 13.1 from F. Harris, *America's Democracy* (Glenview, Ill.: Scott, Foresman & Company, 1980), p. 367. Copyright © 1980.

Figure 13.2 from J. W. Kingdon, "Models of Legislative Voting," *Journal of Politics,* 39 (August, 1977), p. 575.

Picture Credits

Part Opener photos: 1, 1847 Senate—Library of Congress; 55, Scott, Foresman; 179, Scott, Foresman; 389, The New York Times.

Index